The Voucher Wor...

£1

May be redeemed in accordance with the condit...
establishments whose gazetteer entry sho...

The Voucher Worth

£1

May be redeemed in accordance with the conditions overleaf at any of the
establishments whose gazetteer entry shows the symbol ⓥ.

The Voucher Worth

£1

May be redeemed in accordance with the conditions overleaf at any of the
establishments whose gazetteer entry shows the symbol ⓥ.

The Voucher Worth

£1

May be redeemed in accordance with the conditions overleaf at any of the
establishments whose gazetteer entry shows the symbol ⓥ.

The Voucher Worth

£1

May be redeemed in accordance with the conditions overleaf at any of the
establishments whose gazetteer entry shows the symbol ⓥ.

The Voucher Worth

£1

May be redeemed in accordance with the conditions overleaf at any of the
establishments whose gazetteer entry shows the symbol ⓥ.

Conditions

A copy of AA Guesthouses, Farmhouses and Inns in Britain 1987 must be produced with this voucher.
Only one voucher per person or party accepted.
Not redeemable for cash. No change given.
The voucher will not be valid after 31st December, 1987.
Use of the voucher is restricted to when payment is made before leaving the premises.
The voucher will only be accepted against accommodation at full tariff rates.

Conditions

A copy of AA Guesthouses, Farmhouses and Inns in Britain 1987 must be produced with this voucher.
Only one voucher per person or party accepted.
Not redeemable for cash. No change given.
The voucher will not be valid after 31st December, 1987.
Use of the voucher is restricted to when payment is made before leaving the premises.
The voucher will only be accepted against accommodation at full tariff rates.

Conditions

A copy of AA Guesthouses, Farmhouses and Inns in Britain 1987 must be produced with this voucher.
Only one voucher per person or party accepted.
Not redeemable for cash. No change given.
The voucher will not be valid after 31st December, 1987.
Use of the voucher is restricted to when payment is made before leaving the premises.
The voucher will only be accepted against accommodation at full tariff rates.

Conditions

A copy of AA Guesthouses, Farmhouses and Inns in Britain 1987 must be produced with this voucher.
Only one voucher per person or party accepted.
Not redeemable for cash. No change given.
The voucher will not be valid after 31st December, 1987.
Use of the voucher is restricted to when payment is made before leaving the premises.
The voucher will only be accepted against accommodation at full tariff rates.

Conditions

A copy of AA Guesthouses, Farmhouses and Inns in Britain 1987 must be produced with this voucher.
Only one voucher per person or party accepted.
Not redeemable for cash. No change given.
The voucher will not be valid after 31st December, 1987.
Use of the voucher is restricted to when payment is made before leaving the premises.
The voucher will only be accepted against accommodation at full tariff rates.

Conditions

A copy of AA Guesthouses, Farmhouses and Inns in Britain 1987 must be produced with this voucher.
Only one voucher per person or party accepted.
Not redeemable for cash. No change given.
The voucher will not be valid after 31st December, 1987.
Use of the voucher is restricted to when payment is made before leaving the premises.
The voucher will only be accepted against accommodation at full tariff rates.

AA

GUESTHOUSES, FARMHOUSES AND INNS IN BRITAIN

Editor: Barbara Littlewood
Designer: Gerry McElroy
Colour illustrations on pp 7–16: Alan Roe
Farmhouse Food illustrations: Elizabeth Baldin

Gazetteer: Compiled by the Publications Research Unit, in co-operation with the Accommodation Inspectorate, of the Automobile Association.

Maps: prepared by the Cartographic Services Department of the Automobile Association

Cover shows Kents Farm, Cadnam, Hampshire. Photo by Wyn Voysey.

Head of Advertisement Sales: Christopher Heard, tel 0256 20123 (ext 2020)
Advertisement Production: Karen Weeks, tel 0256 20123 (ext 3525)
Advertisement Sales Representatives:
London, East Anglia, East Midlands, Central-Southern and South-East England: Edward May, tel 0256 20123 (ext 3524) or 0256 467568
South-West, West, West Midlands: Bryan Thompson, tel 0272 393296
Wales, North of England, Scotland: Arthur Williams, tel 0222 620267

Typeset by CCC, printed and bound in Great Britain by William Clowes Limited, Beccles and London

Colour produced by J B Shears & Sons Ltd, Basingstoke, Hampshire

Every effort is made to ensure accuracy, but the publishers do not hold themselves responsible for any consequences that may arise from errors or omissions. Whilst the contents are believed correct at the time of going to press, changes may have occurred since that time or will occur during the currency of this book. The up to date position may be checked through AA regional offices.

Published by the Automobile Association, Fanum House, Basingstoke, Hampshire RG21 2EA

ISBN 0 86145 381 6
AA Reference. 59543

Contents

AA GUESTHOUSE
OF THE YEAR

When we look for the AA Guesthouse of the Year Award Winners, the assessment starts, as it should, at reception. Guests must be personally welcomed, offered help with luggage, be shown to their rooms and asked if they have everything they need. Bedrooms should be attractively furnished, with comfortable beds, and a good supply of soap and towels. Bathrooms, if not en suite, should be pointed out, as should the whereabouts of the lounge and dining room. The lounge should be welcoming, and have enough armchairs and sofas to seat all the guests comfortably. Service in the dining room should be efficient and friendly, and the food well cooked and attractively served.

All these points are just what one might expect from any well-run establishment, but we are looking for something more: an attitude on the part of the owners that shows that they really do want their guests to enjoy their stay. This can express itself in a number of ways – little personal touches in the bedrooms, such as fresh flowers, a few books and magazines, or the offer of a cup of tea on arrival – regardless of whether kettles are provided in the rooms. Some friendly conversation before or after dinner often helps to put people at their ease, makes them feel that someone cares whether they are enjoying themselves, and ensures that they will want to come back again. All the guesthouses that we have selected as award winners for 1986–7 have this sometimes elusive quality that fixes them in one's memory as outstanding places to stay.

The Tanyard

BOUGHTON MONCHELSEA · KENT

The outright winner of our 1986–7 Guesthouse of the Year Award is The Tanyard, run by Mrs Jan Davies. You approach by a winding Wealden lane, and suddenly, there before you stands a perfect-looking medieval house in lovely gardens, waiting with its door open. It is a 14th-century timbered yeoman's house, later used as a tannery, that seems to have been plucked out of history and set down in the idyllic countryside of the Kentish Weald.

When you are welcomed inside by Mrs Davies or her assistant, you will see that the interior is as beautifully preserved as the outside, with exposed timbers and freshly painted walls respecting the original character of the house. When you are shown upstairs, you will find that the bedrooms are a delight; large and comfortable, with individual, carefully chosen furnishings (each room has its own colour scheme) in keeping with the atmosphere of the house. All rooms have private bathrooms, and have been neatly fitted out to blend with the style of the bedrooms, and are provided with good quality toiletries and towels. The top floor of the house has been converted into a luxurious family suite of three large rooms, plus bathroom. Downstairs, the lounge is charming, comfortably furnished, with a huge inglenook fireplace in which log fires blaze in cold weather. Drinks are served here, and there are plenty of magazines and books, and a few board games. When dinner is ready, you are led in to the small dining room and shown to

your table. Mrs Davies does a set menu, but if guests dislike any of the dishes, she will always offer an alternative. The food is excellent, and the final course, a selection of really good English farmhouse cheeses, is highly to be recommended.

Mrs Davies has been running the Tanyard as a guesthouse for about four years, although the family has lived there longer, and has put a great deal of thought and good taste into the very skilful conversion, so that guests will always feel comfortable. A former airline stewardess, she certainly has the knack of looking after people extremely well, and has managed to create an atmosphere that suggests more a private country-house-party than a commercial operation. Although it is never easy to choose the winner from among all the finalists, we felt that the Tanyard was outstanding: for the warmth of welcome, for the standard of the decor and furnishings and for the attention to the needs of the guests. Once you have stayed there, it is a place you will dream of coming back to.

Full details of facilities and prices will be found in the gazetteer entry under Boughton Monchelsea.

Chapel House

ATHERSTONE · WARWICKSHIRE

The highspot of Mr and Mrs Roberts' career in the hotel business was to be asked, in the summer of 1985, to entertain the Prince and Princess of Wales to a buffet luncheon after their visit to the 600th anniversary celebrations of Atherstone church. It is easy to see why they were chosen, as their guesthouse and restaurant have a very high reputation in the area, and Chapel House is a most attractive 18th-century building, in a quiet cul-de-sac off the market place, and surrounded by lovely walled gardens. The fact that these enclose a swimming pool was not relevant to the royal visit, but is certainly a bonus for guests in hot summer weather. Mrs Roberts offers a warm welcome to guests on arrival, offering a cup of tea after showing you to your room. All the rooms are individually furnished, with several well-chosen old pieces, and good, comfortable beds. Most rooms have a private bath or shower, well equipped with soap, towels and shampoo. There are no kettles in the rooms, but early-morning tea and a newspaper are offered. Guests can have before-dinner drinks in the comfortable lounge and meals are served round a splendid antique table in the centre of an elegant dining room. During the week there is only a set menu, but the dishes are very nicely

cooked and plentifully served. On Fridays and Saturdays, however, the à la carte restaurant, which caters for non-residents, comes into its own, and has become locally very popular indeed. Mrs Roberts has steadily built up this side of the business since she and her husband bought Chapel House about eight years ago.

Both have extensive experience in catering, and cooking could be said to be in Mrs Roberts' blood, as both her grandmothers were professional cooks. At Chapel House, guests can rely on being properly looked after, comfortably housed, well fed and generally made to feel at home, and this is proved by the high proportion of guests who return many times.

Full details of facilities and prices will be found in the gazetteer entry under Atherstone

Lasswade House

LLANWRTYD WELLS·POWYS

This handsome building, with a small swimming pool in the garden, stands on the edge of a Welsh country village that looks out on the hills of Mynydd Eppynt. It is fine walking country, and excellent for bird-watching, as the many books on the subject that Philip Ross has available for guests at Lasswade to borrow will testify. He will also organize horse-riding and fishing locally, so here is a paradise for those who love the country. It is also ideal for those who love comfort. Philip and Patricia Ross have made an excellent job of converting what was basically an Edwardian family house, built by a Scottish lady and named after her home-town of Lasswade near Edinburgh. They bought the house about eight years ago, and found themselves launched into the catering business, after careers in textile marketing, almost by accident.

However, there is no hint of amateurishness in their approach to the business, and both are blessed with a friendliness of manner that immediately puts guests at their ease. You will be greeted on arrival, helped with your luggage, and shown your room. All the bedrooms are well-proportioned, nicely furnished and generous in regard to space.

Fresh flowers, books and ornaments make it easy to settle in and the private bathrooms are really quite luxurious – one even has its own steambath. An alarm clock and a radio as well as the television are also thoughtful touches, but the atmosphere is so friendly that there is really no incentive to spend an evening watching television. Philip or Patricia will invite you to

come down to the lounge as soon as you are ready. This is a very elegant and comfortable room, with antique furniture and a lovely view over the countryside from the large windows. There is a hospitality bar, but they will usually be there to talk to all the guests and serve drinks. In a very unhurried but well-organized way, they will tell you what the menu selection is for dinner, and if you do not like the table d'hôte menu, you can turn to the à la carte menu for a very small extra charge. The food is very good, all home-made, and the portions more than ample, so that the four courses, ending with an excellent cheese-board, present quite a challenge. Coffee is served in the lounge and the Ross's usually find time to circulate among the guests, and make sure that everyone has an enjoyable evening. If, on the other hand, you want to be left to your own devices, you can be sure that no pressure will be put on you to make conversation.

In all, Lasswade House is a place that really understands how to cater for its guests. The Ross's really seem to enjoy what they are doing, and this creates the uniquely relaxing and sociable atmosphere. Certainly a place to remember and to recommend.

Full details of facilities and prices will be found in the gazetteer entry under Llanwrtyd Wells

West Layton Manor Hotel

WEST LAYTON · YORKSHIRE

The spacious elegance and luxury of country life in times gone by are the keynotes of this Victorian, gabled manor house near Richmond. It stands in extensive wooded grounds, secluded from the nearby A66, and the gardens contain several old and very rare trees and shrubs, the legacy of the Victorian gentlewoman who rebuilt the manor after a disastrous fire, and landscaped the grounds, with lawns, ponds and rockeries. Guests receive a personal welcome in the high-ceilinged entrance hall, and are taken up to their bedrooms, all of which have en suite bathrooms, and are individually and tastefully furnished, each with its own colour scheme. Colour television and tea-making facilities are provided. In cold weather, welcoming fires in the grates are an experience to be cherished, and the outlook on all sides is superb. The lounge is spacious and elegant, with comfortable sofas and window seats, and plenty of magazines to read.

The owner, Mrs Stainthorpe, is a Cordon Bleu chef, and the dinners leave nothing to be desired, as she uses fresh local produce whenever possible, and cooks all dishes to order. She and her family have done wonders with this rambling old house, making the most of its natural advantages, and creating a friendly, family atmosphere for her guests.

Full details of facilities and prices will be found in the gazetteer entry under West Layton

Priory Lodge Hotel

NEWQUAY·CORNWALL

The warm and friendly welcome guests receive when they book in at Priory Lodge is merely a foretaste of what they may expect throughout their stay. The large, attractive detached house is set in its own gardens and has been so well converted and extended by the owners, Mr and Mrs Pocklington, that you would never guess that it was once a vicarage although it retains all the charm and character of the original house, while providing modern standards of comfort.

The downstairs rooms are all pleasant to sit in, with good, comfortable seating in the cosy TV lounge, which opens on to a spacious dining room with lovely sea views. There is a good bar,

good comfortable beds, with duvets and curtains matching, and most have very nice en suite bath or shower rooms. Vases of fresh flowers add that personal touch that is so cheering after a long journey. In running this excellent small hotel, the Pocklingtons have certainly launched their new career in fine style, and we are sure that their guests will appreciate all their efforts.

Full details of facilities and prices will be found in the gazetteer entry under Newquay.

and leading off from it, a functions room where all kinds of entertainment can be organized, and there is also a separate games room, plus a sauna and solarium, not to mention the heated swimming pool in the garden. The food too is very good, efficiently served by friendly staff, and all cooked on the premises in the immaculate modern kitchens that the owners are justifiably proud to show to their guests.

On the upper floors, the bedrooms all have

Ardell House

MACHRIHANISH

Mr and Mrs Baxter have been running Ardell House, on the south-west of the lovely Kintyre peninsula, for the last six years, when they bought this roomy, stone-built Victorian house whose bow windows command magnificent views across the bay to the islands of Jura, Islay and Gigha. The house, distanced from the road by a well-manicured sweep of lawn is, as it were, caught between the hills and the sea. For golfers it is ideally placed, as the links lie between the house and the bay. Guests receive a friendly welcome on arrival and are shown to their rooms by way of a handsome oak staircase. All the doors are in the same natural wood, and reinforce the impression of solid family comfort to be expected from the spacious bedrooms. The lounge, also on the first floor, is a comfortable room, with a fine bay window, looking out to sea. There is a colour television, and a bar,

operated on a serve-yourself principle, and the chairs and settee are very comfortable. Dinner is a pleasurable occasion, with the food courteously and promptly served, featuring such Scottish delicacies as smoked Tobermory sea trout; freshly caught local fish is often on the

menu. China and glassware are such as one would like to have at home. Mr and Mrs Baxter work very hard to ensure their guests' comfort and have kept Ardell House as much like a family home as possible.

Full details of facilities and prices will be found in the gazetteer entry under Machrihanish.

FARMHOUSE FOOD

What do the words 'Farmhouse
Food' conjure up for most of us?
Succulent joints of roast meat,
home-made steak and kidney pies,
home-baked bread, scones and
pies, sizzling platters of
bacon and eggs with
all the trimmings?

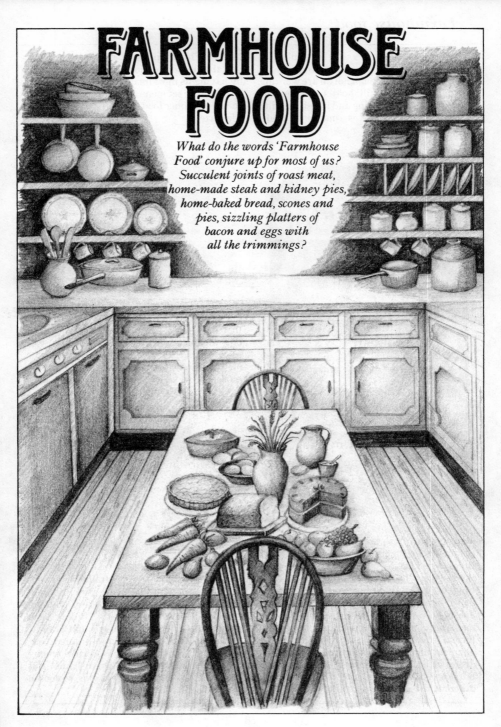

From our survey of 250 or so farmhouses you can expect all this and sometimes more. Our farmhouses, although not all are working farms any longer, still hold firmly to the tradition of home cooking and lavish catering – 'keeping a good table' is a matter of pride.

Indeed, **The Steppes** at Ullingswick turns the tables on conventional restaurant practice by having its most imaginative dishes as the set menu and a choice of plainer food as the à la carte.

Many of our farms are happy to cater for vegetarians or those on special diets, provided that they know in advance, and some serve only organically grown produce. But those of us to whom a holiday is definitely not a time for 'watching what we eat' will also be happy, especially when it comes to the sweet course.

Many use only fresh, home-produced or locally obtained ingredients, offering four and some-times five courses (almost never less than three except by request). Styles of cooking range from the traditional to the exotic and, depending on the individual farmhouse, guests may either eat with the family, or at one large communal dining table, or in more formal restaurant style, at separate tables. Some farmhouses offer quite a large choice of dishes at each meal, some have a set menu, but nearly all will be happy to cook something different if a guest really dislikes a set dish.

Puddings, ranging from the traditional child-hood favourites of treacle tart, trifle, jam roly poly, spotted dick, bread and butter pudding etc. to the most elaborate Cordon Bleu concoctions of cream, meringue and brandy, are in abundant supply and, according to our survey, in great demand, especially among the men who 'never get them at home'. But breakfast is where the day begins, so loosen your belts . . .

The Breakfast Table

Some of our farmhouses describe their breakfasts as 'a really challenging start to the day', and three, if not four, courses, counting the fruit juice, are the norm. **Holmhead Farm**, at Greenhead, on Hadrian's Wall, boasts the 'longest breakfast menu in the world', offering an overwhelming choice, including a Scandinavian-style cold table, which is a more imaginative and generous interpretation of 'Continental Breakfast' than many hotels can manage. **New Farmhouse** at Wix in Essex also interprets this in the northern European manner, to mean hard-boiled eggs and a selection of cheeses, rather than a croissant that has not travelled at all well since leaving France.

What can you expect to find on almost all the menus? Fruit juice, for a start, often a choice of three or four different kinds, usually served in large jugs on a help-yourself basis. This is sometimes an alternative, sometimes a prelude to the cereals course, where there will be several different kinds, including, perhaps, home-made muesli, and maybe a dish of stewed or fresh fruit in season. Porridge may well also be a choice at this stage of the meal for the serious breakfaster. The standard main course is what everyone associates with 'the great British Breakfast' and this will consist of at least bacon and eggs, with some of the following extras: fried bread, fried potatoes, potato cakes, mushrooms, sausages, tomatoes. If you cannot face this, you can usually have eggs cooked in a variety of other ways – Mrs Hackett-Jones at **Pipps Ford Farm**, Needham Market will even fry them in heart shapes for honeymooners if asked – or try

other traditional favourites like kippers or kedgeree (a mixture of rice, flaked smoked haddock and chopped hard-boiled eggs). At **Old Parsonage Farm** at Hanley Castle you may well be offered those Edwardian country-house favourites, devilled kidneys, or cods' roe on toast, especially if you bespeak them in advance. Of course, you can skip all this, and go straight to the toast and marmalade, and you are likely to find that the bread is home-made, as well as the marmalade, jam and honey, if your hosts keep bees, as some of them do.

But these are health-conscious days as well, and many of our farms will offer yoghurt, usually home-made, with fruit, as an alternative start to the day. **Fron Oleu Farm** at Trawsfynydd, for example, offers a totally cholesterol-free, fibre-rich breakfast, with goats' milk as an alternative to cows' milk.

It is not only in terms of generous quantities that our farms excel; most of them go out of their way to ensure that everything is of good quality as well, including on their breakfast menus quite a range of regional specialities. Things that are luxuries in the town become commonplace down on the farm. Almost all the places we have surveyed either keep their own hens or obtain free-range eggs locally, and some can even offer duck or goose eggs in season. Many also have suppliers of home-cured bacon, locally made sausages and, especially in the Midlands, the North and Scotland, excellent black puddings. Loch Fyne, oak-smoked kippers are the things to look for in Scotland, at **Pole Farm**, Lochgoilhead, when available. Failing kippers, a delicious alternative is a fresh herring fried in oatmeal, as served at **Gilchrist Farm**, Muir-of-Ord. At **Dalilea Farm** at Acharacle you will find Chanterelle mushrooms if you are there at the right time of year. Fresh field mushrooms will also be found in season at **Fallowfield Farm** at Kingston Bagpuize and **Middle Woodston Farm** at Lindridge. Regional specialities like Cumberland sausages are on the menu at Lakeland farms, like **Bessiestown** at Catlowdy and have indeed spread far beyond their native Cumbria; **Falicon Farm** at Longridge serves local Ribchester sausages; at **Village Farm** near

Sturton-by-Stow there are traditional Lincolnshire sausages; at **Ty'n Rhos Farm** at Llanddeiniolen they make their own; in Devon, hog's puddings are a seldom-encountered local dish you will find at **Holwell Farm**, Bampton, and **Wringworthy Farm** at Mary Tavy. Haggis, not commonly thought of as a breakfast dish, can be sliced and fried (and is at **Bishopfield Farm**, just south of the border at Allendale). In Scotland, needless to say, you will be offered properly made porridge almost everywhere and a wonderful variety of traditional baking. At **Traighmor Farm** at Ardfern large baskets of scones freshly baked that morning will be placed on the breakfast table. Staffordshire and Derbyshire farms – **High House** near Buxton, and **Whitelee Farm** at Sparrowpit; **Packhorse** and **Manor Farms** near Matlock, **Roston Hall Farm** at Roston, Ashbourne, and **Glenwood House Farm** at Ipstones – all serve the delicious local oatcakes (an oatmeal pancake, not a biscuit) hot with bacon.

After a feast on this scale to fortify you against the day, who could want lunch? When it comes to dinner, however, you will have recovered your appetite (it grows with eating, the French say), so read on . . .

The Dinner Table

For Starters

Home-made soups are the mainstay of many of our farmhouses, and these range from the usual mushroom, tomato and lentil to the more adventurous: lovage soup at **Fallowfield Farm**, Kingston Bagpuize; parsnip or beetroot soup as served at **Middle Woodston Farm** at Lindridge; walnut soup and curried parsnip soup at **Manor Farm**, Crackington Haven; cucumber, or carrot and coriander soup at **Close House**, Giggleswick; artichoke at **Abbey House**, Monk Soham; lettuce at **Moorend Court** near Malvern. Last but not least, are two Scottish classics, Cock a Leekie, at **Gall Farm**, Boreland and Scotch Broth at many farmhouses, including **Rovie Farm**, Rogart in Sutherland and **Pole Farm**, Lochgoilhead. Alas for those two great English favourites of British Rail fame, Brown Windsor and Mulligatawny. No farm seemed to favour them, and even oxtail was not mentioned; one or two farms had cheese soups – the most unusual being a chilled cider and cheese soup from **The Steppes** at Ullingswick. Among the many home-made pâtés, Farmhouse Whisky Pâté from **Gilchrist Farm** at Muir of Ord seemed tempting; salmon mousse at **Bessiestown Farm**, Catlowdy, and an interesting smoked haddock mousse made with apple, sour cream and lemon is a speciality of **Garreg Ganol** near Holywell. Avocado pears dressed with cranberries are an interesting variation on an old theme that you may find at **Struther Farm** at Dunlop,

or baked and filled with herbs, cheese and bacon at **Harrop Fold Farm**, Harrop Fold, in Lancashire. Some farmhouses lead you gently towards the main course by way of three preludes to the main event: at **University Farm**, Lew, you may find a choice of mixed hors d'oeuvres, followed by a soup, followed by a mango or other fruit sorbet to refresh you before the main course. If all this is too much, the really delicate appetite may be tempted by grapefruit soaked in crème de menthe as at **Village Farm**, Sturton-by-Stow in Lincolnshire, or by deep-fried camembert with fresh grapes at the **Old Mill Farm** at Hoarwithy.

The Main Course

Roast beef, roast lamb, roast pork: these, with gravy, roast potatoes, two or three different vegetables and appropriate sauces, are the traditional farmhouse fare all over the country. Some farmhouses concentrate exclusively on roasts – **University Farm** at Lew organizes all its dinners around the 'carvery' theme – and they could indeed be described as our national dishes, with steak and kidney pies and puddings as close runners-up. Yorkshire pudding with the roast beef has long been a national rather than a regional dish, and in fact regional dishes now seem to be the exception rather than the rule, so much so that one almost greets them with surprise. Welsh lamb, of course, is one of the great Welsh national dishes, and is offered at almost all our Welsh farmhouses: at **Cyfie Farm** in Llanfihangel-yng-Ngwynfa a lamb and leek pie combines the two national favourites into an appetising dish. Sewin, or Welsh sea trout, is another delicacy to be tasted at **Penrallt Ceibwr Farm** at Moylegrove, and **Cilpost Farm** at Whitland.

Salmon and venison are as closely associated with Scotland as beef or haggis, and several farm menus feature them, including **Dalilea Farm** at Acharacle, **Wester Moniack Farm** at Kirkhill, **Struther Farm** at Dunlop, **Baltier Farm** at Whithorn and **Rock Hill Farm** at Ardbrecknish, which makes a game pie with venison, hare and duck in red wine, and a fish pie with salmon, pike and trout in white wine; at **Pole Farm,** Lochgoilhead, salmon is served in a champagne sauce.

Game is also a speciality of some English farms, when in season, for example **Leigh Court Farm** at Leigh, where there is jugged hare and other game, or pike; or **Holbrook Farm** at Lydlinch where gougère (a type of cheesey *choux* pastry) is served with a pheasant

filling. Roasts are often stuffed or dressed in unusual ways – for example lamb with orange and coriander stuffing at **Frog Street Farm,** Beercrocombe, or coated with mustard, herbs and breadcrumbs at **Old Parsonage Farm**, Hanley Castle, or basted with apple juice at **Buckyette Farm**, Littlehempston. Chicken and turkey are perennial favourites – from the classic roast capon at **Elvey Farm** at Pluckley, where they also serve savoury Pivington Pie (turkey, ham, mushrooms and eggs in parsley sauce enclosed in shortcrust pastry) to a whole range of more complicated dishes: in a cream, almonds and Grand Marnier sauce at **Penwyn Farm** near Pontypool, or stuffed with crumbled Stilton, wrapped in bacon and cooked in red wine at **Garreg Ganol** near Holywell, or in cider and mushroom sauce at **Lower Upton Farm**, Little Vowchurch. Goats' milk cheese and yoghurt are nowadays quite commonly found, but roast kid is quite rare – though it is sometimes served at **Morar Farm** near Bampton (Oxfordshire). One or two farmhouses seek out historic recipes : at **Manor Farm**, Crackington Haven, Victorian Stew consists of beef, onions and carrots cooked with pickled walnuts, and Elizabethan Pork has more than 20 different ingredients.

It is not only in their meat that farmhouses take pride: the tradition of a good vegetable garden is also maintained. **Morar Farm** grows 27 different sorts, and at **Pipps Ford Farm**, Needham Market, they experiment with some very Old-English vegetables – for example Good King Henry, which has a flavour reminiscent of asparagus. The serving of vegetables is an art at **The Steppes** at Ullingswick, where cauliflower is often topped with a savoury meringue, and carrots are moulded into little castles, crowned with a mushroom.

The Croft at Vowchurch has three herb gardens; fennel and sea-kale are served at **Holwell Farm**, Bampton (Devon). Several farms concentrate on organically grown produce, for example, **Churchill Green Farm**, Churchill, near Bristol and **Wigham Farm** at Morchard Bishop, where the animals are also reared naturally. Many farmhouses now cater for vegetarians. **Tregynon Farm** at Pontfaen offers an excellent range of non-meat dishes: stuffed pancakes, curried Brazil-nut loaf, or chilli chick pea patties with goats' cheese sauce, and **Mount Pleasant Farm** at Mount near Bodmin offers a pasta and parsnip bake with tomatoes and cheese.

To Finish

Most farmhouses pride themselves on having a really tempting range of puddings and desserts, and your main course may be followed by one or more of the following: spotted dick, steamed sponges, treacle pudding, treacle tart (sometimes with bread-crumbs, sometimes with cream and egg yolks instead), bread and butter pudding, Bakewell tart, all kinds of fruit pies and crumbles, sherry trifle, chocolate and lemon mousses, home-made meringues, pavlovas, vacherins, fresh raspberries and strawberries in season,

suet-crust puddings filled with fruit (whole lemons, butter and demarara sugar at **Cold-wall Farm** at Blore), syllabubs (the rosé syllabub at **Close House**, Giggleswick is flavoured with rosé wine as well as lemon, and coloured faintly pink with a drop or two of colouring). To accompany all this there will certainly be clotted cream in Devon and Cornwall (at **Wigham Farm**, Morchard Bishop, they make their own clotted cream, as well as butter and yoghourt), and many farms keep a Jersey cow specially for the milk and cream.

So finally one comes to the coffee. This is one of the few things that cannot actually be grown on the farm, but some farmhouses triumph over this difficulty by offering home-made petit-fours or fudge to accompany it.

Just one last word to thank all the farms who helped us with material for this article. They are listed on pages 23–4.

N.B. Visitors should bear in mind that the dishes described above may possibly not happen to feature on the menu during their stay, as some are subject to seasonal availability, and most farms have a very wide repertoire of menus, planned on a weekly, fortnightly, or even longer rotation.

Index of farms

The farms listed here are those who kindly helped us with information for our feature on Farmhouse Food

Avon
Bishop Sutton, Overbrook Farm

Buckinghamshire
Kingsey, Foxhill Farm

Cheshire
Rushton, Barnswood Farm

Cornwall
Advent, Pencarrow Farm
Coombe, Treway Farm
Coverack Bridges, Boscadjack Farm
Crackington Haven, Manor Farm
Cury Cross Lanes, Polglase
Lanlivery, Treganoon Farm
Marshgate, Carleton Farm
Mount, Mount Pleasant Farm
Newquay,
  Mannets Farm
  Manuel's Farm
St Buryan, Boskenna Farm
Summercourt, Barlan Farm
Troon, Seaview Farm
Widemouth Bay, Kennacot Farm

Cumbria
Alston, Middle Bayles Farm
Appleby-in-Westmorland, Gale House Farm
Bassenthwaite
  Bassenthwaite Hall Farm
Catlowdy, Bessiestown Farm
Crook, Greenbank Farm
Greenhead, Holmhead Farm
Kirkcambeck, Cacrop Farm
Penrith, Highgate Farm
Penton, Craigburn Farm
St Johns-in-the-Vale, Shundraw Farm
Sebergham, Bustabeck Farm
Shap,
  Green Farm
  Southfield Farm
Thirlmere, Stybeck Farm
Troutbeck, Lanehead Farm

Derbyshire
Buxton, High House, Foxlow Farm
Hathersage, Highlow Farm

Matlock,
  Farley Farm
  Packhorse Farm
Roston, Roston Hall Farm
Sparrowpit, Whitelee Farm
Tissington, Bent Farm

Devon
Aveton Gifford, Court Barton Farm
Bampton, Holwell Farm
Bondleigh, Cadditon Farm
Bovey Tracey, Willmead Farm
Bridestowe,
  Little Bidlake Farm
  Week Farm
Buckland Brewer, Holwell Farm
Bulkworthy, Blakes Farm
Cheriton Fitzpaine, Brindwell Farm
Cullompton, Five Bridges Farm
Exbourne, Stapleford Farm
Harberton, Tristford Farm
Holne, Wellpritton Farm
Holsworthy, Leworthy Farm
Jacobstowe, Higher Cadham Farm
Littlehempston, Buckyette Farm
Lower Blakewell, Home Farm
Manaton, Langstone Farm
Mary Tavy, Wringworthy Farm
Morchard Bishop, Wigham Farm
Oakford, Newhouse Farm
Okehampton, Hughslade Farm
Ottery St Mary, Pitt Farm
Spreyton, East Hillerton Farm
Tavistock, Parswell Farm Bungalow
Throwleigh, East Ash Manor
Tiverton, Lower Collipriest Farm
Uffculme, Houndaller Farm
Upottery, Yarde Farm
Whiddon Down, South Nethercott Whiddon Farm

Dorset
Broadwindsor, Hursey Farm
Chedington, Lower Farm
Little Bredy, Foxholes Farm
Mappowder, Boywood Farm
Milborne Port, Venn Farm
Wareham, Luckford Wood Farm

Essex
Debden Green, Wychbars Farm
Margaret Roding, Greys Farm
Wix, New Farmhouse

Gloucestershire
Falfield, Green Farmhouse
Kelmscott, Manor Farm
Stonehouse, Welches Farm

Hampshire
Cadnam, Budds Farm
East Meon, Giants Farm

Hereford & Worcester
Eardisland, Elms Farm
Hanley Castle, Old Parsonage Farm
Hergest, Bucks Head Farm
Hoarwithy, Old Mill Farm
Kilpeck, Priory Farm
Leigh, Leigh Court Farm
Lindridge, Middle Woodston Farm
Little Dewchurch, Cwm Craig Farm
Marstow, Trebandy Farm
Mathon, Moorend Court Farm
Newton, Little Green Farm
St Owen's Cross, Aberhall Farm
Ullingswick, The Steppes
Vowchurch, Croft Farm
Wormbridge, Duffryn Farm

Isle of Wight
Ryde, Aldermoor Farm

Kent
Dover, Walletts Court
Egerton, Link Farm
Pluckley, Elvey Farm
Stone-in-Oxney, Tighe Farm

Lancashire
Longridge, Falicon Farm
Slaidburn, Parrock Head Farm

Leicestershire
Old Dalby, Home Farm
Thringstone, Talbot House

Lincolnshire
Gedney Hill, Sycamore Farm
Sturton-by-Stow, Village Farm
Whaplode, Guy Wells Farm

Norfolk
Garboldisham, Ingleneuk Farm
Loddon, Stubbs House Farm
Thurning, Rookery Farm

Northumberland
Allendale, Bishopfield Farm
Elsdon, Dunns Farm

Index of farms

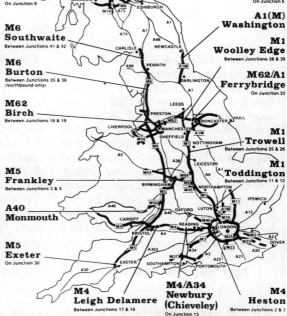

Using the Guide

This guidebook is for those travellers who are looking for the personal attention, comfortable accommodation and warm reception that are now more likely to be found in a good guesthouse, small hotel, farmhouse or inn than in many more expensive, but impersonal hotels. We list over 3,000 of these establishments all over Britain, and at each of them you can be assured that you will get good value for money, and that standards will be acceptable, because AA Inspectors visit each place regularly and we update our information every year.

Specially Recommended: In the 1987 edition of the guide, we are, for the first time, distinguishing the very best of the establishments by means of a special 'Recommended' box in the Gazetteer. These places have been selected by our inspectors as offering standards of cooking, accommodation and hospitality that are well above the normal requirement for an AA listing. In all, only about 120 establishments have been awarded the distinction for this year, and from this list of the élite, we have chosen our Guesthouse of the Year for 1986–7, announced in the colour feature on pages 7–16. There is also a special feature on farmhouse food (pages 17–24), with a list of all the farmhouses who have helped us in our research.

What is a Guesthouse?

The term *'guesthouse'* can lead to some confusion, particularly when many include the word *'hotel'* in their name. For our purposes we include small and private hotels in this category when they lack some of the requirements for our star classification system. This is not to say that they are inferior to hotels – just that they are different – and many offer a very high standard of accommodation. It is not unusual to be offered en suite bathrooms, for instance, or to find a colour television in your room. It is true that some guesthouses will only offer a set meal in the evening, but many provide a varied and interesting menu and a standard of service which one would expect of a good restaurant. At the other end of the scale, some guesthouses offer bed and breakfast only, and it would also be wise to check if there are any restrictions to your access to the house, particularly late in the morning and during the afternoon.

We do have certain basic requirements which establishments must meet if they are to be listed in the guide, although, as we have said, many will exceed these. Usually they must offer at least six bedrooms and there should be a general bathroom and toilet for every six bedrooms which do not have private facilities. Fully licensed premises are now considered for inclusion, although many have a residential or restaurant licence only. We also stipulate that parking facilities, if not on the premises, should be within a reasonable distance.

Guesthouses in the London section of the book are treated differently. They are actually all small hotels and so their entries are not accompanied by the **GH** symbol used throughout the rest of the book. Of course, London prices tend to be higher than those in the provinces, but those that we list provide cost-conscious accommodation, although bed and breakfast only is normally provided. To allow for all eventualities, we have also included a few which provide a full meal service and the charges for these will naturally be higher.

Staying at a Farmhouse

Farmhouse accommodation has a special quality and is particularly noted for being inexpensive and cosy with a high standard of good home cooking (see the feature on pp. 17–24). Those listed in our book are generally working farms and some farmers are happy to allow visitors to look around the farm or even to help feed the animals. However, we must stress that the modern farm is a potentially dangerous place, with all the machinery and chemicals involved, and visitors must be prepared to take great care, particularly if they bring children. Never leave children unsupervised around the farm. Some of the guest accommodation, on the other hand, is run as a separate concern from the farm on which it stands and visitors are discouraged from venturing beyond the house and garden. In some cases the land has been sold off, and although the gazetteer entry states the acreage and the type of farming carried out, it is advisable to check when booking to make sure that your requirements are met. To qualify for inclusion in the book, farms must have a minimum of two letting bedrooms, preferably fitted with washbasins, together with a bathroom with hot and cold running water and an inside toilet. As with the guesthouses, standards will vary considerably and are often far above what one would expect. Some of our farmhouses are grand ex-manor houses, furnished with antiques and offering a stylish way of life, and again some will have a residential or restaurant licence. All of the farmhouses are listed under town or village names, but obviously many will be some distance from other habitation. Proprietors will, of course, give directions when you book, and we publish a six figure map reference against the gazetteer entry which can be used in conjunction with Ordnance Survey maps.

Inns

What need we say? We all know what we can expect to find in a traditional inn – a cosy bar, convivial atmosphere, good beer and pub food. Nevertheless, we have a few criteria which must be met here too. There must be a minimum of three and ideally a maximum of fifteen letting bedrooms, each having washbasins with hot and cold running water. Most bedrooms should be served by a bathroom and toilet on the same floor and, although a residents' lounge is not essential, there must be a suitable breakfast room.

Breakfast is a must, of course, but the inn should also serve at least light meals during licensing hours. Our inn category may also include a number of small, fully licensed hotels and the character of the properties will vary according to whether they are pretty country inns or larger establishments in towns.

Common to all

Whatever the type of establishment, there are certain requirements common to all, including a well-maintained exterior; clean and hygienic kitchens; good standards of furnishing; friendly and courteous service; access to the premises at reasonable times; the use of a telephone; full English breakfast; an adequately heated sitting room when half-board is provided (except inns – see above); bedrooms equipped with comfortable beds, a wardrobe, a bedside cabinet, a washbasin with soap, towel, mirror and shaver socket and at least a carpet beside the bed; there should be no extra charge for the use of baths or lavatories, and heating should be un-metered.

NB Where an establishment shows the central heating symbol, it does not necessarily mean that it will be available all year round. Some places only use the central heating in winter, and then only at their own discretion.

The Money-off Voucher Scheme

In the front of this book you will find six £1 vouchers which can be redeemed against your bill for accommodation at any of the establishments which show the ⓥ symbol in the gazetteer. If you use all of the vouchers you will, in effect, be saving the cost of this book. Conditions for the use of the vouchers are printed on the reverse of each one. Remember that you cannot use the voucher if you are already being offered a discount price and that you can only use one voucher, even if you are settling a bill for more than one person.

How to find your Guesthouse, Farmhouse or Inn

If you know exactly in which town you intend to stay, you can turn straight to the

Using the guide

gazetteer where towns are listed in alphabetical order. A full explanation of how the gazetteer works is displayed on page **32**. Otherwise, you will need to refer to our location maps at the end of the book. Only the places for which we have a gazetteer entry are shown on the maps and the type of establishments you can expect to find there are distinguished as follows:

Places with guesthouses or inns are marked with a solid dot ●

Places with guesthouses and/or inns plus farmhouses are marked with a dot in an open circle ☉

Places with farmhouses only are marked with an open circle ○

Remember that farms may be some way outside the place under which they are listed.

We make every effort to ensure that the establishments are located accurately, but it is always wise to obtain more specific directions when booking.

Town Plans

For some of the main towns and holiday resorts we have included town plans within the gazetteer so that we can pinpoint the establishments for you. We do try to make these as up-to-date as possible, but as the plans must be produced before we complete the updating of the gazetteer, you may find that some of the last-minute entries to the book are not shown on the plans. Equally, there may still be establishments on the plans which we have deleted from the gazetteer for some reason. Where establishments are located just outside the town, or just off the edge of the plan, we identify the road you should follow.

Special Requirements for Disabled Persons

Establishments which can accommodate disabled people have the easily identifiable wheelchair symbol against their gazetteer entry. Of course, we cannot be specific in the space we have available, so it is advisable to check with the proprietor before making reservations, to be sure that a particular disability can be catered for. Details more relevant to disabled people are published in the AA _Travellers' Guide for The Disabled 1987_, available from AA offices (free to Members, £2.25 to non-members).

Children

Most of the establishments in the guide will accommodate children of all ages, but if not, a minimum age is stated in the gazetteer entry (nc8yrs = no children under eight). Even when children are accommodated, it does not automatically follow that any special facilities are available. If you intend to take very young children, find out before making a reservation what special amenities are available, such as cots, high chairs, laundry facilities etc. Establishments which do have special facilities are indicated by the symbol ⚘ and this means that all of the following amenities will be found: baby-sitting service or baby intercom system; play-room or playground; laundry facilities including drying and ironing; cots and high chairs; special meals. Children sharing a parent's room are usually accommodated at a reduced price.

Dogs

We can only indicate in the gazetteer those establishments which will not accept dogs – look for the symbol ✖. Other establishments may well impose certain restrictions, particularly on the size of dog – one establishment once specified Yorkshire Terriers only! Generally, dogs are not allowed into the dining room and sometimes they must sleep in their owners' cars. In the case of farmhouse

---

Symbols used in town plans

▬▬ Recommended route	✔ Tourist information centre	◀▭ Distances to guesthouse etc from edge of plan
▬ Other routes	AA AA service centre	**ASHFORD 16m** Mileages to towns from
■ ■ ▬ ▬ Restricted roads	P Car park	edge of plan (district plan)
✝ Church	⑥ Guesthouses, inns, etc	

28

accommodation in particular, it is essential that your pet should get along well with other animals – farms always have their own dogs and cats, and the livestock should not be worried in any way. Always check before booking whether your pet will be welcome and if you need to take anything with you for its care. Guide dogs for the blind may be an exception to the normal rules.

Prices and what they include

All prices quoted normally include VAT and service charge where applicable. Remember that in the United Kingdom and the Isle of Man, VAT is payable on both basic prices and on any service charge. VAT does not apply in the Channel Islands. Although we endeavour to provide up-to-date prices, they are liable to fluctuate and it is advisable to check when you book. In some cases proprietors have been unable to provide us with their 1987 charges, but to give you a rough guide, we publish the 1986 price, prefixed with an asterisk (*). It is also a good idea to ascertain exactly what is included in the price. Weekly

terms, for instance, vary from full board to bed and breakfast only, which we try to make clear in the text by the use of the symbols Ⱡ – no lunches and Ӎ – no main meals. Packed lunches and snacks may be available, though. You may also find that, at the height of the season, some establishments will offer accommodation only on a weekly basis – often Saturday to Saturday – and this, too, is indicated in the gazetteer. We cannot indicate whether or not you are able to book mid-week to mid-week, so if this is your intention, do check when making your reservation.

The hotel industry in Britain has a Voluntary Code of Booking Practice and its prime objective is to ensure that the customer is clear about the precise services and facilities he or she is buying, and what price he will have to pay, before he commits himself to a contractually binding agreement. If no written details of costs were received prior to arrival the guest should be handed a card at the time of registration detailing the total obligatory charge, and tariff details should also be displayed prominently, as per the

Tourism (Sleeping Accommodation Price Display) Order 1977 which applies where four or more bedrooms are available. Every effort is being made by the AA to encourage the use of the Voluntary Code in appropriate establishments.

Reservations, Deposits, Cancellations and Legal Obligations

Although it is possible for chance callers to find a night's accommodation, it is by no means a certainty, especially at peak holiday times and in the popular areas, so to be certain of obtaining the accommodation you require, it is always advisable to book as far in advance as possible. Some establishments will also require a deposit on booking. If you later find that you must cancel your visit, let the proprietor know at once because if the room you booked cannot be re-let, you may be held legally responsible for partial payment. Whether it is a matter of losing your deposit, or of being liable for compensation, you should seriously consider taking out cancellation insurance, such as AA Travelsure.

It is regretted that the AA cannot at the present time undertake to make any reservations.

Opening Dates and Low Season Restrictions

Unless otherwise stated, the establishments are open all year, but where dates are shown they are inclusive: eg Apr–Oct indicates that the establishment is open from the beginning of April to the end of October. Although some places are open all year, they may offer a restricted service during the less busy months, and we indicate this in the gazetteer by using the 'rs' abbreviation. This may mean that there is a reduction in meals served and/or accommodation available and, if you see this within the gazetteer, you should telephone in advance to find out the nature of the restriction.

About Food and Drink

In some parts of the country, such as the north east of Scotland, high tea is generally served in guesthouses, although dinner is often also available on request. On Sundays many establishments throughout the country will serve their main meal at midday and will

charge accordingly. However, it is possible that a cold supper will be available in the evening. If you intend to take dinner at the establishment, note that sometimes the meal must be ordered in advance of the actual meal time. In some cases this may be at breakfast time, or even at dinner on the previous evening. If you have booked for dinner, bed and breakfast terms, you may find that the tariff includes a set menu, but you can usually order from the à la carte menu, where one exists, and pay a supplement if you so desire.

Regarding beverages, the symbol ® means that tea- and coffee-making facilities are available in the bedrooms, although they may only be available on request. Sometimes this takes the form of a specially designed unit or it may consist of an electric kettle and a supply of tea bags, sachets of coffee etc. Some proprietors prefer the personal approach and will make tea and coffee for their guests on request.

If it is something a little stronger that you are after, you will be able to tell from the gazetteer entry whether or not the establishment is licensed to serve alcoholic drinks. Most places in the guesthouse category do not hold a full licence, but all inns do. Licensed premises are not obliged to remain open throughout the permitted hours and they may do so only when they expect reasonable trade. Note that in establishments which have registered clubs, club membership does not come into effect, nor can a drink be bought, until 48 hours after joining. For further information AA leaflet HR192 'The Law about Licensing Hours and Children/Young Persons on Licensed Premises' is available from AA offices.

Television

If the gazetteer entry shows 'CTV' or 'TV' it means that either colour or monochrome television is available in the lounge. Where televisions are quoted as being available in bedrooms, this means that they are permanently fixed or that they can be supplied by the management on request.

Advance Information and Complaints

We have tried to provide as much information as possible about the establishments in our gazetteer, but if you should require further information before deciding to book, you should write to the establishment concerned. Do remember to enclose a stamped, addressed envelope, or an international reply paid coupon if writing from overseas, and please quote this publication in any enquiry.

We sincerely hope that you will not have any cause for complaint, but if you do, you should inform the proprietor immediately so that the trouble can be dealt with promptly. If a personal approach should fail, members should inform the AA.

Fire Precautions

Many of the establishments listed in the guide are subject to the requirements of the Fire Precautions Act of 1971. As far as we can ascertain at the time of going to press, every one of these establishments has at least applied for, and has not been refused, a certificate. The Act does not apply to the Channel Islands or the Isle of Man, both of which have their own rules about fire precautions for accommodation units.

AA

GUIDE TO
NATIONAL TRUST
PROPERTIES IN BRITAIN

Hundreds of castles and historic houses; breathtaking gardens and parks; spectacular tracts of unspoilt countryside and coastline. The fascinating stories of all these places are told in this guide and there are nearly 200 specially commissioned photographs. Detailed maps show the locations of every property.

AA

WHERE·TO·GO IN·THE COUNTRYSIDE

For all lovers of rural Britain, this new AA guide, richly illustrated with colour photographs, exquisite watercolour paintings, and sensitive pencil studies, reveals the glories of our countryside and the secrets of the natural world.
There are details of 500 places to visit, ranging from national parks, nature reserves and beauty spots to farm parks, countryside museums and woodland gardens.
Special features include a month-by-month country calendar detailing many fascinating traditional events, country crafts, rural buildings, and species of wildlife.

Introducing the gazetteer

This gazetteer is listed alphabetically under place name throughout England, Scotland and Wales, the Isle of Man and the Channel Islands. Establishments on islands are listed under the appropriate island heading.

Some establishments in the gazetteer belong to the Guestaccom consortium and any bookings should be made through their Central Reservation Office: Guestaccom – tel Brighton (0273) 722833;

The example of a gazetteer entry shown below is to help you find your way through the entries. All the abbreviations and symbols are explained on the inside covers of the book. 'Using the Guide' on pages 26–31 gives further information.

Explanation of a Gazetteer Entry

County Name
The county in which the town is located appears, but this may not be the complete postal address. In the case of Scotland we use the Region name, followed by the former county name in *italics*.

Establishment Name
Where the name appears in *italics*, this indicates that particulars have not been confirmed by the proprietor in time for this edition.

Ordnance Survey Map Reference
This is shown for farmhouse entries only. As they are often in remote areas, we provide a six-figure map reference which can be used with Ordnance Survey maps.

Town Name
in alphabetical order

Map reference
The first figure is the map-page number; then follow the grid-square reference letters; the final two numbers refer to the sub-divisions of the grid square. Read first number across (left to right) and second figure vertically (bottom to top).

Telephone Number
Unless otherwise stated, the exchange is that of the gazetteer place name. In some areas, however, telephone numbers are likely to be changed by British Telecom during the currency of this publication. In case of difficulty, check with the operator.

LOOE
Cornwall
Map **2**   SX25

⊢⊣GH **Ram Hotel** *(ST075149)*🖀(07652)
768 Plan **9**
Etr–Oct

12hc (2⇔4🖦) Annexe: 2🖦 (1fb) CTV in 6 bedrooms ✖ Ⓡ B&b£7–£8 Bdi£12–£13 W£85–£105 LDO5pm
Lic �📺 CTV 9P nc7yrs
Credit cards ① ③

Accommodation for £8 or under
This symbol indicates that the establishment expects to provide bed and breakfast for under £8 per person per night during 1987, but remember that circumstances can change during the currency of the guide.

Town Plan
Where a town plan exists, we locate each establishment on the plan using numbers. The plan will appear as close to the relevant towns as possible within the gazetteer. See page 28 for town plan symbols.

Classification
Guesthouses are identified with '**GH**', Farmhouses with '**FH**' and Inns with '**INN**' – this is also the order in which they are listed beneath the town headings.

Annexes
If annexe rooms are shown, this indicates that their standard is acceptable. They may, however, lack some of the facilities available in the main building. If you are offered an annexe room, check facilities and charges before booking.

Credit Cards
The numbered boxes indicate the credit cards which the establishment will accept:
1 Access/Euro/Mastercard
2 American Express
3 Barclays/Visa
4 Carte Blanche
5 Diners

Specific Details
To interpret details of opening times, prices, facilities etc consult 'Symbols and Abbreviations' on inside covers. See also 'Using the Guide.'

Gazetteer

ABBERLEY
Hereford & Worcester
Map **7**   SO76

FH Mrs S Neath **Church** *(SO753678)*
☎Great Witley (029921) 316
Apr–Oct

An early Victorian farmhouse in the peaceful village of Abberley. Off A443 on B4202, in ¼m turn right into village.

2hc (1fb) ✖

TV 5P 2🚗 300acres arable beef

ABBOTS BROMLEY
Staffordshire
Map **7**   SK02

FH Mr & Mrs W R Aitkenhead **Fishers Pit** *(SK098244)* ☎Burton-on-Trent (0283) 840204

Early Victorian two-storey brick-built farmhouse, ½m from village on B5234.

5hc (3fb) ® ✱ B&b£9–£10 Bdi£12–£15 Wfr£95 ⎱ LDO6pm

CTV 8P nc3yrs 85acres dairy mixed

FH Mrs M K Hollins **Marsh** *(SK069261)*
☎Burton-on-Trent (0283) 840323
Closed Xmas

Large two-storey, cement-rendered farmhouse set in open countryside 1m from village.

2rm (1hc) (1fb) ✱B&b£8.50–£9.50 Bdi£13.50–£14.50 W£84–£87 ⎱ LDO5pm

⫿ CTV 6P 87acres mixed

ABERAERON
Dyfed
See **Pennant**

ABERDARE
Mid Glamorgan
Map **3**   SO00

GH *Cae-Coed Private Hotel* Craig St, off Monk St ☎(0685) 871190

A neat but modestly appointed guesthouse.

7hc (1fb) LDO4pm

Lic ⫿ CTV nc2½yrs

ABERDEEN
Grampian *Aberdeenshire*
Map **15**   NJ90

GH Alelanro 272 Holburn St ☎(0224) 575601

Neat and homely house with limited lounge facilities.

6hc (2fb) CTV in all bedrooms ®
✱B&b£8.50–£10

⫿ 🅿 ♨

GH Broomfield Private Hotel 15 Balmoral Pl ☎(0224) 588758

9hc ® ✱B&bfr£13 Bdifr£20 LDO5.30pm

⫿ CTV P

Ⓥ

GH La Casa 385 Great Western Rd ☎(0224) 313063

A well maintained house with pleasant bedrooms.

12hc (2⇌10⍟) (2fb) CTV in all bedrooms ® ✱B&b£16–£22 Bdi£23–£29 W£161–£203 ⎱ LDO6.30pm

Lic ⫿ 10P

GH Cedars Private Hotel 339 Great Western Rd ☎(0224) 583225

A well-decorated house with compact but well-equipped bedrooms.

13hc (2⇌2⍟) (4fb) CTV in all bedrooms ® ✱B&b£13–£20 W£100–£130 M

⫿ CTV 13P

Credit card ②

GH Klibreck 410 Great Western Rd ☎(0224) 316115
Closed Xmas & New Year

Well-appointed small hotel with some ground-floor bedrooms.

6hc (1fb) ✖ ✱B&b£10–£12 Bdi£15–£17 LDO3pm

⫿ CTV 3P

Ⓥ

GH Mannofield Hotel 447 Great Western Rd ☎(0224) 315888

10hc (3fb) CTV in 6 bedrooms ✱B&b£16–£21.85 Bdi£23–£28.85 W£161–£201.95 ⎱ LDO6pm

Lic ⫿ CTV 14P nc10yrs

Ⓥ

GH Open Hearth 349 Holburn St ☎(0224) 596888

Modest, cheerfully decorated house.

12hc (1fb) ⚡in 6 bedrooms CTV in all bedrooms ® ✱B&b£12.65–£13.80

⫿ CTV 6P

GH Strathboyne 26 Abergeldie Ter ☎(0224) 593400

A compact house with homely atmosphere.

6hc (2fb) ® ✱B&b£9.50–£10.50 Bdi£14–£15 LDO3.30pm

⫿ CTV

GH Tower Hotel 36 Fonthill Rd ☎(0224) 584050
Closed Xmas & New Year

Spacious, traditionally furnished hotel with a pleasant dining room. Caters for business clientele.

9hc (1⇌) (2fb) ✱B&b£15 Bdi£21.50

Lic ⫿ CTV 8P

ABERDOVEY
Gwynedd
Map **6**   SN69

GH Cartref ☎(065472) 273

Family-run guesthouse near beach and recreation area.

7hc (1⇌ 1⍟) (2fb) B&b£10 Bdi£15 W£102 ⎱

⫿ CTV 8P

ABEREDW
Powys
Map **3**   SO04

FH Mrs M M Evans **Danycoed** *(SO079476)* ☎Erwood (09823) 298
Etr–Oct

Stone-built, two-storey farmhouse. Pleasant situation on edge of River Wye.

3rm (2hc) ✖ LDO5.30pm

P 230acres sheep mixed

ABERFELDY
Tayside *Perthshire*
Map **14**   NN84

GH Balnearn Private Hotel Crieff Rd ☎(0887) 20431

Large house with modern bedroom wing.

13hc (2fb) TV in 1 bedroom ®
✱B&b£10.35–£11.50 Bdi£16.10–£17.25 W£112.70–£120.75 ⎱ LDO7.30pm

CTV 15P 2🚗 ♿

Ⓥ

GH Caber-Feidh 66 Dunkeld St ☎(0887) 20342

Very well-appointed little guesthouse above town-centre shops. Many attractive features.

6hc (2fb) ® ✱B&b£8–£8.50 Bdi£13–£13.50 W£90 ⎱ LDO9.30pm

⫿ CTV 3P

Ⓥ

--- *Recommended* ---

GH Guinach House Urlar Road ☎(0887) 20251
Mar–Oct

Attractive house standing in its own well tended gardens in a quiet spot close to the town centre.

7hc CTV in all bedrooms ®
✱B&b£18 Bdi£27 W£172 ⎱ LDO9pm

Lic ⫿ 10P 🚗 nc6yrs

GH Nessbank House Crieff Rd ☎(0887) 20214
Apr–Oct

A very comfortable little hotel with high standards throughout.

6hc (1fb) ✖ ® ✱B&b£11.50 Bdi£18 W£115 ⎱ LDO7pm

Lic CTV 6P 2🚗

Ⓥ

ABERGAVENNY
Gwent
Map **3** SO21

GH Belchamps 1 Holywell Rd (Guestacom) ☎(0873) 3204
Small, personally-run guesthouse with cosy bedrooms and comfortable lounge and dining room. Near to both town and river.
5hc (2fb) 🚫 [R] ✱B&b£9–£10 Bdi£14.50–£16 W£93–£106 🍽 LDO10am
♨ CTV 5P
[V]

GH *Llanwenarth House* Govilon ☎Gilwern (0873) 830289
Mar–Dec
Partly 16th-century, country house property in rural surroundings. Charm and elegance are keynotes of drawing- and dining-rooms; bedrooms are spacious.
5hc (3🛁 2🚿) (1fb) CTV in all bedrooms [R] LDO8pm
Lic ♨ CTV 10P 2🚗
Credit cards [2] [5]

GH Park 36 Hereford Rd ☎(0873) 3715
Closed 1–10 Jan
Proprietor-run small guest house offering a warm welcome.
7hc (1fb) ✱B&b£9.50–£10.50 Bdi£14–£15.50 W£95–£105 🍽 LDO4.30pm
Lic ♨ CTV 10P
[V]

FH Mrs D Miles **Great Lwynfranc** *(SO327193)* Llanvihangel Crucorney. (Off A465 3mN) ☎Crucorney (0873) 890418
Closed Dec & Jan
Near Abergavenny, a farmhouse of character with views over the Brecon Beacons. Bedrooms bright and airy; lounge and dining rooms elegantly furnished. Perfect for a tranquil holiday.
3hc (1fb) B&b£9–£9.50 Wfr£60 M
♨ CTV 12P ⌂ 154 acres mixed
[V]

FH Mrs D V M Nicholls **Newcourt** *(SO317165)* Mardy ☎(0873) 3734
16th-century, stone-built farmhouse with views of Sugar Loaf Mountain.
3hc 🚫 ✱B&bfr£10
♨ CTV P nc6yrs 160acres dairy

ABERHOSAN
Powys
Map **6** SN89

FH Mrs A Lewis ***Bacheiddon*** *(SN825980)* ☎Machynlleth (0654) 2229
Apr–Sep
From the windows there are lovely views of the surrounding mountains and countryside. Off unclassified road linking Machynlleth and Dyliffe/Staylittle (B4518).
3🚿 (1fb) 🚫
CTV P 850acres beef sheep mixed

ABERPORTH
Dyfed
Map **2** SN25

GH Ffynonwen Country ☎(0239) 810312
Rural guesthouse full of character.
10hc (3🛁) (2fb) ✱B&b£11–£12 Bdi£16–£17 Wfr£100.80 🍽
Lic ♨ 30P
[V]

ABERSOCH
Gwynedd
Map **6** SH32

GH Llysfor ☎(075881) 2248
Etr–Oct
Detached Victorian house near beach and shops.
8hc (1🛁) (2fb) [R] ✱B&b£10 Bdi£14.50 W£98 🍽 LDO4pm
Lic CTV 14P
[V]

ABERYSTWYTH
Dyfed
Map **6** SN58

GH Glan-Aber Hotel 7–8 Union St ☎(0970) 617610 Plan **1** *B2*
Closed Xmas
Victorian house in side street opposite the railway terminus.
14hc (3fb) CTV in 10 bedrooms TV in 4 bedrooms [R] B&b£12.50 Bdi£17.75 W£115.50 🍽 LDO10pm
Lic ♨ CTV
Credit card [1]

GH Glyn-Garth South Rd ☎(0970) 615050 Plan **2** *A2*
Closed 2 wks Xmas (rs Oct–Etr)
Victorian, mid-terrace property adjacent to beach, harbour and castle, ¼m from the shops.
10hc (4🛁 2🚿) (3fb) CTV in all bedrooms 🚫 [R] ✱B&b£10–£16 Bdi£17–£23 W£100–£138 🍽 LDO4pm
Lic ♨ CTV nc7yrs
[V]
See advertisement on page 36

GH Llety-Gwyn Llanbadarn Fawr (1mE A44) ☎(0970) 3965 Plan **3** *D2*
8hc (4🚿) Annexe: 6hc (1🛁 3🚿) (5fb) CTV in 11 bedrooms TV in 3 bedrooms [R] ✱B&b£11.50–£16 Bdi £17.50–£22.50 W£125–£144 🍽 LDO5pm
Lic ♨ CTV 55P
[V]
See advertisement on page 36

GH Plas Antaron Pen Parcau ☎(0970) 611550
Plan **3A** *B1*
A comfortable guesthouse situated about 1½m from the town centre and sea front.
11hc (6🚿) (1fb) CTV in 3 bedrooms B&b£9.50–£13.50 Bdi£14–£18 LDO6pm
Lic ♨ CTV 40P
Credit card [3]
See advertisement on page 36

GH Shangri La 36 Portland St ☎(0970) 617659 Plan **5** *B3*
Single-fronted, mid-terrace Victorian building adjacent to shops and ¼ mile from beach.

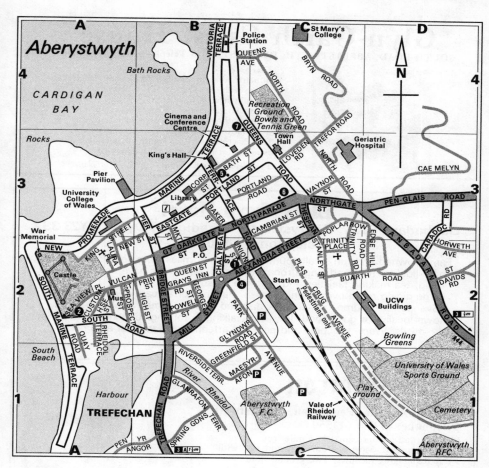

Aberystwyth

6hc (3fb) TV in all bedrooms ®
✳B&b£8.50 Bdi£11.50 W£80.50 ⅃
LDO4pm
⫘ CTV ⅌
Ⓥ

GH Swn-y-Don 40–42 North Pde
☎(0970) 612647 Plan **6** *C3*
*Double-fronted Victorian mid-terrace
house at end of shopping area.*
29hc (3fb)
⫘ CTV 7P

See advertisement on page 36

GH Windsor Private Hotel 41 Queens
Rd ☎(0970) 612134 Plan **7** *B4*
*Victorian mid-terrace house in residential
area adjacent to shops and beaches.*
9hc (2fb) ⅍ in 2 bedrooms TV in 3
bedrooms ® ✳B&b£8.75–£10 Bdi£12.45–
£14 W£78–£92 ⅃ LDO5pm
Lic ⫘ CTV ⅌
Ⓥ

INN *Railway Hotel* Alexandra Rd
☎(0970) 611258 Plan **4** *B2*
*Cosy and comfortable Victorian inn,
popular with families.*

4hc (1fb) ⚓ ®
⅌ ⇔

ABINGTON
Strathclyde *Lanarkshire*
Map **11**   NS92

FH Mrs M Hodge **Craighead** *(NS914236)*
☎Crawford (08642) 356
Apr–Oct

*Large farm building in courtyard design.
Set amid rolling hills on the banks of the
River Duneaton. Main buildings date from
1780. Off unclassified Crawfordjohn Road.
1m N of A74/A73 junc.*   →

35

Glyn-Garth Guest House
SOUTH ROAD, ABERYSTWYTH, DYFED SY23 1JS Telephone: (0970) 615050

Licensed
Situated adjacent to South Promenade. Many rooms with sea-view. All eleven bedrooms are centrally heated, have H&C, colour TV, and tea making facilities. Many rooms en-suite toilet, bath/shower. A good selection of wine available in dining room. Comfortable lounge. Cosy licensed bar. This family run guest house is noted for excellent food and service.

Proprietor: Mrs E. Evans   *SAE for brochure.*

Llety Gwyn Hotel
Llanbadarn Fawr, Aberystwyth, Ceredigion, Dyfed SY23 3SX
Telephone: (0970) 3965

Family owned and run small country house, 1½ miles from sea front on A44. Family, double, twin and single rooms available. All rooms have colour TV, clock radio, tea making facilities and 60% are en suite. Two lounges, 1 with TV. Large dining room overlooking garden. Parking for all cars in own grounds. Swings for children. Suitable for disabled visitors, ramps at all entrances. Known locally for good food. Ideal for walking & touring. Coaches catered for meals. Warm welcome and personal attention of family at all times.

Plas Antaron

Antaron Avenue, Penparcau, Aberystwyth
Telephone: (0970) 611550

Plas Antoran is approximately 1 mile from Town Centre. Licensed. Most bedrooms en suite and with TV & tea making facilities. Two ground floor bedrooms suitable for disabled guests. Cot available — Two TV lounges — Ample parking — Large dining room for functions — Evening dinner optional — **SAE for Brochure. Prop Mrs J Morgan**

SŴN-Y-DON Guest House
RESIDENTIAL GUEST HOUSE
40-42 North Parade, Aberystwyth SY23 2NF.
Telephone: Residents 615059, Reception 612647

A Fire Certificate has been granted.
Near shopping centre, sea front and railway station.
Full board — dinner — bed and breakfast. Open all year — Commercials welcome. Licensed bar. Private parties, wedding receptions and special dinners catered for. Colour TV in lounge. Hot and cold, shaving points in all bedrooms. Gas central heating in all rooms. Overnight parking on premises. Terms on request (SAE for reply). Every convenience for a comfortable and happy holiday. Under the personal supervision of the Proprietress, Mrs. A. M. Owen-Evans who wishes to thank all her regular clients for their continued support and extends a warm welcome to all new clients.

3rm (1fb) ® ✱B&b£7.50–£8 Bdi£11.50–£12 LDO5pm

🍴 CTV 6P 4🐄 ⌒ ⌀ 600acres mixed

FH Mr D Wilson *Crawfordjohn Mill* (NS897242) Crawfordjohn ☎Crawfordjohn (08644) 248 May–Sep

Two-storey, brown-brick farmhouse. Situated off the A74 1m SE of Crawfordjohn on an unclassified road.

2rm

🍴 CTV 180acres mixed

FH Mrs M E Hamilton *Kirkton* (NS933210) ☎Crawford (08642) 376 Jun–Sep

Stone-built farmhouse dating from 17th century and set amongst rolling hills overlooking the River Clyde. Situated 120 yds off A74, 2m S of Abington.

3rm ✖ ✱B&b£7.50–£8

🍴 CTV 3P nc4yrs 750acres beef sheep

---Recommended---

FH Mrs J Hyslop *Netherton* (NS908254) (on unclass road joining A74 & A73) ☎Crawford (08642) 321

Converted whinstone shooting lodge standing in sheltered hillside position. Spacious, comfortable bedrooms and attractive public areas.

3hc (1fb) ✖ ✱B&b£9–£10 Bdi£13–£14 W£78–£80 ⅃ LDO5pm

🍴 CTV 4P ⌀ 3000acres hill farm beef sheep

Ⓥ

ACASTER MALBIS
North Yorkshire
Map **8**   SE54

INN Ship ☎York (0904) 705609

18th-century riverside inn retaining many original features. Separate restaurant and good range of bar meals.

5hc (2fb) CTV in all bedrooms ✖ ®
✱B&b£10–£12 Bdi£15–£17 W£98–£107 ⅃
Bar lunch £1.45–£6.50 Dinner 9.30pm£6alc

🍴 40P ⌀

Credit cards ① ③ Ⓥ

See advertisement under York

Abington
Aldwark

ACHARACLE
Highland *Argyllshire*
Map **13**   NM66

FH Mrs M Macaulay *Dalilea House* (NM735693) ☎Salen (096785) 253 Etr–Oct

A splendid turreted house with surrounding grounds giving excellent views over farmland hills and Loch Shiel. A blend of ancient and modern.

6hc (1fb) ® LDO7pm

P 13000acres beef sheep fish

AINSTABLE
Cumbria
Map **12**   NY54

FH Miss K Pollock *Basco Dyke Head* (NY529450) Basco Dyke ☎Croglin (076886) 254 Mar–Oct

Simple accommodation in a cosy Cumbrian farmhouse.

3hc (2fb) LDO8.30pm

CTV P 2🐄 250acres arable beef dairy

AISLABY
North Yorkshire
Map **8**   NZ80

FH Mrs B A Howard *Cote Bank* (NZ827070) ☎Whitby (0947) 85314 Closed Xmas

A quiet farmhouse in a pleasant valley, near Whitby.

2hc (2fb) ✖ ✱B&b£8.50 Bdi£14 W£98 ⅃
LDOnoon

CTV 3P ⌀ 100 acres dairy mixed

Ⓥ

ALDEBURGH
Suffolk
Map **5**   TM45

GH Cotmandene 6 Park Ln ☎(072885) 3775

A double-fronted Victorian house, modernised but retaining its original character. Fresh home cooking

6hc TV in all bedrooms ® ✱B&b£12 Bdifr£17.75 Wfr£115 ⅃ LDO8.30pm

Lic 🍴 CTV ℙ

Credit cards ① ③

ALDERMINSTER
Warwickshire
Map **4**   SP24

FH Mr & Mrs V Miller *Alderminster* (SP219492) ☎(078987) 296 Mar–Oct

A Georgian farmhouse in lovely countryside, convenient to Stratford.

3rm (2hc) (1fb) ✖ ® ✱B&b£10–£15 W£70–£105 ⋈

🍴 CTV 6P ⌀ 250acres arable sheep

Ⓥ

ALDERSHOT
Hampshire
Map **4**   SU85

GH Cedar Court Hotel Eggars Hill ☎(0252) 20931 Closed 24 Dec–1 Jan

Large private house with comfortable annexe accommodation.

8hc (3🍴) Annexe: 4hc (1🍴 3🍴) (2fb) CTV in 8 bedrooms LDO3pm

Lic 🍴 CTV 14P

GH Glencoe Hotel 4 Eggars Hill ☎(0252) 20801 Closed Xmas

Friendly, nicely appointed private house with spacious bedrooms.

12hc (3🍴) (2fb) TV in 2 bedrooms ®
LDO7pm

Lic 🍴 CTV 12P

ALDWARK
Derbyshire
Map **8**   SK25

FH J N Lomas *Lydgate* (SK228577) ☎Carsington (062985) 250

Peace and comfort are assured in this delightful 17th-century stone farmhouse.

→

3rm (1fb) ✖ LDO3pm

♨ CTV 3P 2🚗 300acres beef dairy sheep

ALFRISTON
East Sussex
Map **5** TQ50

Recommended

FH Mrs D Y Savage **Pleasant Rise** *(TQ516027)* ☎(0323) 870545
Closed Xmas week

Very attractive farm with large, bright and clean accommodation, delightfully appointed. Badminton, cricket nets and extensive tennis facilities. Adjacent to B2108 Seaford road.

4hc (1🚿) (1fb) ✱B&b£9.50–£10.50

♨ CTV 8P nc5yrs 🎾 100acres mixed

ALKMONTON
Derbyshire
Map **7** SK13

FH Mr A Harris **Dairy House** *(SK198367)* ☎Great Cubley (033523) 359

16th-century brick farmhouse, comfortably modernised yet retaining character. Nature Reserve.

7hc (2fb) ✖ [R] ✱B&b£9–£10 Bdi£15–£16 W£107ⱡ LDO8pm

Lic ♨ CTV 8P 🏠 82acres dairy

[V]

ALLENDALE
Northumberland
Map **12** NY85

Recommended

FH Mr & Mrs Fairless **Bishopfield** *(NY826565)* (1m W) ☎(043483) 248

An 18th-century house, beautifully furnished, with charm and elegance – it is also a very comfortable and friendly place to stay. Excellent home cooking is a priority, meals are often served by candlelight in a dinner-party atmosphere. A well-established garden, a small nature reserve and trout fishing are added attractions on this 200-acre farm.

4hc (3🛁) CTV in all bedrooms ✱B&b£14–£18 Bdi£20–£24 W £140–£168ⱡ LDO8pm

Lic ♨ 15P 🎣 snooker 200acres mixed

[V]

ALNMOUTH
Northumberland
Map **12** NU21

GH Marine House Private Hotel 1 Marine Dr ☎Alnwick (0665) 830349
Feb–Oct

Friendly staff and home-cooking ensure a comfortable stay at this pleasant house overlooking the bay.

8hc (2🚿) (4fb) ✱B&b£12–£15 Bdi£18–£21.50 W£130–£143ⱡ

Lic ♨ CTV 8P 🏠

[V]

ALNWICK
Northumberland
Map **12** NU11

GH *Aln House* South Rd ☎(0665) 602265
Closed Xmas

Friendly, comfortable guesthouse serving home-cooked food.

8hc (2🛁) (2fb) TV in 2 bedrooms ✖ LDO9am

Lic ♨ CTV 8P

GH *Aydon House* South Rd ☎(0665) 602218

A comfortable house, with good bedrooms, on main road.

10hc (4fb) TV in 1 bedroom LDO5pm

Lic ♨ CTV 12P

Credit cards [1] [2] [3] [4] [5]

GH Bondgate House Hotel Bondgate
Without ☎(0665) 602025
rs Oct–Apr

Friendly, personally-run, town-centre house with quaint, comfortable rooms.

8hc (1 🛁) (3fb) CTV in all bedrooms ⓡ
✱B&b£8.50–£11 Bdi£14–£17 W£90–£110
⅃LDO4pm

Lic 🅟 8P

ⓥ

↦GH Hope Rise The Dunterns ☎(0665) 602930

In quiet residential area, house offers comfortable accommodation and a friendly atmosphere.

7hc (2fb) ✘ ⓡ ✱B&b£8–£8.50 W£55–£58 M
🅟 CTV 12P nc5yrs

Credit cards 🛚 🗿

FH Mrs A Davison **Alndyke** *(NU208124)*
☎(0665) 602193
May–Oct

Comfortable house offering good home-cooking.

3hc (1fb) ✘ ⓡ ✱B&b£10 Bdi£16 W£105⅃
(W only 18 Jul–29 Aug) LDOnoon

CTV 6P nc5yrs 320acres arable beef sheep mixed

ALSTON
Cumbria
Map **12** NY74

FH Mrs P M Dent **Middle Bayles**
(NY706451) ☎(0498) 81383
rs Xmas & New Year

Charming old-world hill farm overlooking South Tyne Valley. Attractive accommodation.

2hc (1fb) ✱B&b£7.20–£8 Bdi£10.80–£12
W£75.50⅃LDO4pm

🅟 CTV 2P 300acres beef sheep

ⓥ

ALTRINCHAM
Gt Manchester
Map **7** SJ78

GH Bollin Hotel 58 Manchester Rd
☎061-928 2390

Alnwick
–
Ambleside

Well-furnished small hotel on A56 near town centre.

10hc (2fb) ✱B&bfr£13.80 Wfr£96.60 M
🅟 CTV 10P ·

AMBLESIDE
Cumbria
Map **7** NY30
During the currency of the guide the Ambleside code is to change to (05394)

GH Chapel House Hotel Kirkstone Rd
☎(0966) 33143
Closed Jan & Feb

Former 16th-century cottages retaining old-world atmosphere. Very good food.

9hc (3🛁) (1fb) ✘ ✱B&b£17–£20.50
W£115–£125.50⅃LDO7pm

Lic 🅟 🅿

ⓥ

GH Compston House Hotel Compston
Rd ☎(0966) 32305

A spacious house near park and conveniently sited for town centre.

10hc (2fb) CTV in all bedrooms ✘ ⓡ
B&b£9.50–£9.95 Bdi£14.50–£14.95
W£96.50–£99.50⅃LDO5pm

Lic 🅟 CTV 🅿 nc2yrs

ⓥ

GH Gables Private Hotel Church Walk,
Compston Rd ☎(0966) 33272
Mar–Oct

Tudor-style house in central position overlooking the bowling green and tennis courts.

15hc (1🛁 2🛁) (5fb)ⓡ ✱B&bfr£10
Bdifr£15 Wfr£105⅃

Lic 🅟 CTV 8P

GH Gale Crescent Hotel Lower Gale
☎(0966) 32284

Peaceful, hill-top house with fine lakeland views.

8hc (1🛁1🛁) (3fb)✘ ⓡ ✱B&b£11–£13
Bdi£16.95–£19.95 W£107–£125.65
LDO5pm

Lic CTV 10P ⚿

ⓥ

Recommended

GH Grey Friar Lodge Country House Hotel Brathay (1m W off
A593) ☎(0966) 33158
Mid Mar–Oct

A delightful Lakeland stone country house set in its own gardens at the foot of Loughrigg Fell. The whole house is attractively decorated and comfortably furnished and the proprietors offer a personal service in a warm and friendly atmosphere. The food is excellent, from the hearty breakfast to a 5-course dinner based on traditional English cooking.

8hc (2🛁3🛁) (1fb) CTV in all bedrooms ⓡ B&b£12–£18.50
Bdi£21–£27.50 W£136.50–£179⅃
LDO7.30pm

Lic 🅟 12P nc10yrs

GH Hillsdale Hotel Church St ☎(0966)
33174

A homely, terraced town-centre guesthouse.

8hc (1🛁) (2fb) ✘ ⓡ B&b£10–£13
Bdi£16–£19 W£110–£130⅃ LDO5pm

Lic 🅟 CTV 🅿

GH Horseshoe Rothay Rd☎(0966)
32000
Closed 3 Jan–13 Feb

Town centre guesthouse overlooking park.

12hc (5🛁) (4fb) ✱B&b£11–£15 W£77–
£103 M

🅟 CTV 16P

ⓥ

See advertisement on page 40

↦GH Melrose Church St ☎(0966)
32500

An attractive slate-built house with feature marble fireplaces and basement dining room. →

6hc (2🛏) (3fb) TV in 3 bedrooms ®
B&b£8–£13.50 W£50.40–£85.05 M
🍴 CTV ⚟

GH *Oaklands Country House Hotel*
Millans Park ☎(0966) 32525
Feb–Nov

*Large house amidst rambling gardens
and woodland.*

8hc (2 ⇦ 3🛏) (3fb) CTV in all bedrooms
✕ ® LDO4pm
Lic 🍴 8P nc5yrs

GH Park House Compston Rd ☎(0966)
33542

Ambleside

*A small friendly house overlooking the
park in the town centre.*

6hc (2fb) TV in 4 bedrooms ®
✱B&b£8.50–£9.50 Bdi£13.50–£14.50
W£92–£99 ⅄

CTV ⚟
ⓥ

GH Romney Hotel Waterhead ☎(0966)
32219
Etr–Oct

---

*A tranquil country house atmosphere
prevails and the resident proprietors give
service in keeping.*

19hc (1⇦ 1🛏) (5fb) ✱B&bfr£13 Bdifr£20
Wfr£136.50 ⅄ LDO7pm
Lic CTV 20P 3🛌 ⚘
Credit card ③

GH Rothay Garth Hotel Rothay Rd
☎(0966) 32217

*Hotel offers very relaxing atmosphere and
comfortable accommodation.*

15hc (4⇦ 6🛏) (3fb) CTV in all bedrooms
® ✱B&b£13.50–£24.50 Bdi£21.50–£31.50
W£137–£204 ⅄ LDO7.30pm

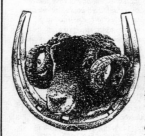

*John and Susan Horne welcome you to their spacious William IV
house enjoying panoramic mountain views.*

The ḢORŞEŞḢOE

Rothay Road, Ambleside. Telephone: 0966 32000

We offer a friendly relaxed atmosphere, 12 comfortably furnished
bedrooms, some with private facilities and access onto the spinning
gallery. Renowned for our traditional and wholefood breakfasts.
Ideal for walking and touring. What our guests say.
*"What a pleasant surprise to find such a warm welcome, super food
and comfy beds. Best breakfast in Britain."*
Private car park.   British Relais Routiers.

Church Street, Ambleside
Cumbria LA22 0BT
Telephone (0966) 32500
Proprietors
Rex & Jenny George.

Melrose Guest House

Melrose Guest House is situated in the centre of
Ambleside, close to all amenities. Spacious family
rooms, some with private facilities, caters for
walker's needs. We offer drying room, cycle shed,
packed lunches, tea and coffee making facilities in
all rooms. Log fires in winter, children half price
sharing. Pets welcome. Lovely fell walks from guest
house. Reduced rates for groups.

Oaklands Country House Hotel

Millans Park, Ambleside, Cumbria
Tel: (0966) 32525

Set in wooded grounds in a quiet position away from the main
roads in the heart of the Lake District. Oaklands has delightful
mountain views and our main concern is the comfort of our
guests. The hotel is fully centrally heated and all bedrooms have
television and tea/coffee making facilities; the majority have
bathroom-en-suite. There is a spacious lounge, intimate cocktail
bar and separate dining room. An interestingly varied menu
of good food and wine.

40

Lic ♨ CTV 16P
Credit cards [1] [2] [3] [5]
[V]

Recommended

GH Rydal Lodge Hotel (2m NW A590) ☎(0966) 33208
Closed Jan

A welcoming guesthouse on the main road between Ambleside and Rydal Water – just a 5-minute walk away. The proprietors pride themselves on their cooking. They offer good, freshly cooked English food and home-made sweets in the attractive dining room which overlooks the gardens. There are books and games in the spacious lounge and there is a separate TV lounge..

8hc (1fb) ✱B&b£13–£14.50 Bdi£19.85–£21 W£133–£140 ⱡ LDO6pm
Lic CTV 12P ⛳ 🌳
Credit cards [1] [3] [5]
[V]
See advertisement on page 41

GH Rysdale Hotel Kelsick Rd ☎(0966) 32140
Closed Xmas

House with pretty window boxes and a well-appointed dining room.

9hc (4fb) TV in all bedrooms ✖ B&b£9.50–£10.50 Bdi£14.50–£16 W£97–£107 ⱡ LDO5.30pm
Lic ♨ ⛔ nc3yrs
[V]

GH *Smallwood Hotel* Compston Rd ☎(0966) 32330
Mar–Oct

Cheerful and spacious detached house near town centre.

13hc (1🚿) (5fb) LDO5pm
♨ CTV 10P nc2yrs
See advertisement on page 41

GH Thrang House Compston Rd ☎(0966) 32112

A slate-built house serving good, hearty breakfasts.

6hc (2🚿) ✖ B&b£8.50–£11 Bdi£13.50–£16 W£95–£110 ⱡ LDO5pm
♨ CTV 5P nc5yrs

ANDOVERSFORD
Gloucestershire
Map **4** SP01

GH Old Cold Comfort Dowdeswell (1m W A436) ☎Cheltenham (0242) 820349

Small, attractive 17th-century hotel which serves good English food.

8hc (1🛁 1🚿) (2fb) CTV in all bedrooms ✖ [R] ✱B&b£13.50–£15.50 Bdi£21.50–£23.50 W£140–£150 ⱡ LDO7.45pm
Lic ♨ 10P 1🚗 🌳
Credit card [1]

ANNAN
Dumfries & Galloway *Dumfriesshire*
Map **11** NY16

GH Ravenswood Private Hotel St Johns Rd ☎(04612) 2158

Sandstone villa dating from 1880 standing in residential street close to town centre.

8hc (2fb) ✖ ✱B&b£11.50 Bdifr£16 Wfr£112 ⱡ LDO8.30pm
Lic ♨ CTV ⛔

APPLEBY-IN-WESTMORLAND
Cumbria
Map **12** NY62

GH Bongate House Bongate ☎(07683) 51245
Closed Xmas

Detached house in attractive garden offering high standard of accommodation.

7hc (1🛁 3🚿) (4fb) [R] B&b£10.30–£12 Bdi£15.50–£17.20 W£93–£103.20 ⱡ LDO6pm

Lic ♨ CTV 8P 2🚗

[V]

GH *Howgill House* ☎(0930) 51574
Etr–Oct

Spacious, detached house situated in an attractive garden ½m south of the town centre.

6hc (3fb) 🚫🐕

CTV 6P

FH Mrs M Wood **Gale House** *(NY695206)* ☎(07683) 51380
May–Sep

Farmhouse standing in small garden surrounding open fields. Traditional farmhouse furnishings. Facilities nearby include fishing, golf and bathing.

2rm (1fb) 🚫🐕 *B&b£8.50–£9

3P nc5yrs 167acres dairy

APPLEDORE
Kent
Map **5** TQ92

INN Red Lion 15 The Street ☎(023383) 206

Ivy-clad, roadside inn with well-equipped accommodation, and serving good, wholesome food.

3🛁 (1fb) CTV in all bedrooms [R] *B&b£12–£15 W£76–£95 M̸ Lunch £1.60–£4.90 & alc High tea 70p–£2.50 & alc Dinner 10.30pm £2.20–£7.70 & alc

♨ 6P 🚗̸ 🏡

ARBROATH
Tayside *Angus*
Map **12** NO64

GH Kingsley 29 Market Gate ☎(0241) 73933

Small and friendly family-run guesthouse close to harbour.

14hc (8fb) *B&b£9–£10 Bdi£12–£13 W£75–£80 L̸

Lic ♨ CTV P̸

[V]

ARDBRECKNISH
Strathclyde *Argyllshire*
Map **10** NN02

FH Mrs H F Hodge ***Rockhill*** *(NN072219)* ☎Kilchrenan (08663) 218
Etr–Sep

Loch-shore farm. Trout and perch fishing (free), and at the farm's private loch by arrangement.

6hc (3fb)

Lic CTV 8P nc7yrs 🎣 200acres sheep horses

See advertisement on page 137

ARDEN
Strathclyde *Dunbartonshire*
Map **10** NS38

FH Mrs R Keith **Mid Ross** *(NS359859)* ☎(038985) 655
Apr–Sep

Farmhouse pleasantly located close to Loch Lomond 3m N of Balloch off A82.

3hc (1fb) 🚫🐕 *B&b£8–£10 W£50–£60 M̸

♨ CTV 10P 40acres arable beef sheep mixed

ARDERSIER
Highland *Inverness-shire*
Map **14** NH85

FH Mrs L E MacBean **Milton-of-Gollanfield** *(NH809534)* ☎(0667) 62207
Apr–Oct

Stone farmhouse set on north side of A96 5m W of Nairn, 9m E of Inverness.

4rm (3hc) (1fb) 🚫🐕 *B&b£8–£11 W£56–£77 M̸

CTV P 360acres arable beef sheep mixed

ARDFERN
Strathclyde *Argyllshire*
Map **10** NM80

FH Mrs M C Peterson ***Traighmhor*** *(NM800039)* ☎Barbreck (08525) 228
Apr–Oct

Modern bungalow at loch-side with three small croft farms nearby.

3rm (1fb) LDO 3pm

CTV 6P 🏡 56acres mixed

ARDGAY
Highland *Sutherland*
Map **14** NH58

GH Croit Mairi Kincardine Hill ☎(08632) 504
Closed 2 wks mid Oct/Nov

Comfortable modern-style house in secluded location with pleasant views.

6hc [R] *B&b£8.50–£10.50 Bdi£13.50–£15.50 LDO6.45pm (later by arrangement)

Lic ♨ CTV 10P nc4yrs

Credit cards [1] [2] [3] [5]

ARDROSSAN
Strathclyde *Ayrshire*
Map **10** NS24

GH Ellwood House 6 Arran Pl ☎(0294) 61130

Bright and cheerful guesthouse close to sandy beach.

8hc (1fb) *B&b£7 W£49 M̸

CTV

[V]

ARINAGOUR
Coll (Island of) Strathclyde *Argyllshire*
Map **13** NM25

See **COLL (Island of)**

ARRAN, ISLE OF
Strathclyde *Buteshire*
Map **10**

CORRIE
Map **10** NS04

GH Blackrock House ☎(077081) 282
Closed Dec

Stone house dating from 1930 with modernised interior and good sea views.

9rm (8hc) (5fb) B&b£9.50 Bdi£14.50 W£98 L̸ LDO5pm

♨ CTV 8P

LAMLASH
Map **10** NS03

GH *Glenisle Hotel* ☎(07706) 258
Apr–Oct

Victorian house with extensions standing on main road in small village, with sea views. 9-hole putting green →

16hc (3🛁 2🚿) (3fb) [R] LDO6.30pm
CTV 18P 🏠

GH *Marine House Hotel* ☎(07706) 298
Mar–Oct
Converted and modernised coastguard building in own grounds of ¾-acre with views over to Holy Island.
18hc (6🚿) (6fb)
CTV 16P

LOCHRANZA
Map **10** NR95

GH Kincardine Lodge ☎ (077083) 267
Apr–Oct
Converted house dating from 1910, standing in own grounds overlooking the bay and castle.
6hc (4fb) ✱B&b£8–£9 Bdi£12–£13 W£84–£91 Ł
CTV 6P
[V]

SANNOX
Map **10** NS04

GH Cliffdene ☎Corrie (077081) 224
Closed Oct & Nov
Stone house built in 1900 on main road overlooking beach and sea.
5hc (3fb) 🐕 B&b£8.75 Bdi£12.25 W£85.75 Ł LDO6.30pm
CTV 5P
[V]

ARRETON
Isle of Wight
See **Wight, Isle of**

ARTHOG
Gwynedd
Map **6** SH61

GH Pen-y-Rodyn ☎Fairbourne (0341) 250659
4hc (1🛁 1🚿) TV in all bedrooms 🐕 [R]
✱B&b£10–£15 Bdi£17–£22 W£112–£143.50 Ł LDO9.15pm
Lic ♨ 30P nc11yrs
Credit card [3]

Arran, Isle of — Ashford

ARUNDEL
West Sussex
Map **4** TQ00

GH Arden 4 Queens Ln ☎(0903) 882544
Closed Xmas
Small house with friendly, homely atmosphere.
8hc (2🚿) (1fb) CTV in all bedrooms 🐕 [R]
✱B&b£9–£13 W£54–£78 M̸
♨ 6P

GH Bridge House 18 Queen St ☎(0903) 882142
Closed Xmas wk
Well-maintained with good homely atmosphere in attractive situation overlooking river and facing the castle.
11hc (4🚿) (6fb) CTV in 7 bedrooms [R]
✱B&b£12–£25 W£80.50–£119 M̸
♨ CTV 9P 4🚗
Credit cards [1] [3]

INN Swan Hotel High St ☎(0903) 882314
Georgian-style inn, overlooking the River Arun.
11hc (8🛁 3🚿) CTV in all bedrooms 🐕 [R]
LDO9.30pm
♨ P̸ 🚌
Credit cards [1] [2] [3] [4] [5] [V]

ASCOT
Berkshire
Map **4** SU96

GH *Highclere House* Kings Rd, Sunninghill ☎(0990) 25220
Well-appointed and-decorated property run by friendly young proprietor.
12hc (5🚿) (3fb) CTV in all bedrooms [R]
LDO8pm
Lic ♨ CTV 14P 2🚗 🏠

ASCOTT-UNDER-WYCHWOOD
Oxfordshire
Map **4** SP31

INN Wychwood Arms Hotel ☎Shipton-under-Wychwood (0993) 830271
Closed first 2 wks Jan
Attractive, Cotswold-stone, village inn offering antique-furnished bedrooms.
5🛁 CTV in all bedrooms 🐕 [R]
✱B&b£21.50–£27 Bdi£27.50–£35.50
W£192.50–£199.50 Ł Bar lunch£3.50alc
Dinner 10pm£10.75alc
♨ 30P 🚌 nc10yrs
Credit cards [1] [2] [3] [5] [V]

ASHBURTON
Devon
Map **3** SX77

GH Gages Mill Buckfastleigh Rd
☎(0364) 52391
Mar–Nov
Carefully restored 400-year-old mill in one acre of well-kept garden.
8hc (1🛁 3🚿) (1fb) 🐕 [R] ✱B&b£10–£12
Bdi£16.50–£18.50 W£106.75–£113.75 Ł
Lic CTV 10P nc5yrs

FH Mrs Young **Bremridge** *(SX785701)*
Woodland (2mE unclass towards Denbury) ☎(0364) 52426
Closed Xmas
4rm (3hc) (3fb) ✱B&b£11.50–£14.50
Bdi£13.50–£16.50 W£75–£90 Ł (W only mid Jul–Aug) LDO5.30pm
♨ CTV 4P 🏠 8 acres mixed

ASHFORD
Kent
Map **5** TR04

GH Croft Hotel Canterbury Rd, Kennington ☎(0233) 22140
Comfortable simple accommodation with more modern annexe.
15hc (2🛁 7🚿) Annexe: 13hc (8🛁 5🚿)
(4fb) CTV in all bedrooms [R]
✱B&b£13.75–£26.50 Bdi£20.25–£33
LDO8pm
Lic ♨ CTV 30P
Credit card [1]

GH Downsview Willesborough Rd, Kennington ☎(0233) 21953

16hc (3🚿) (2fb) CTV in all bedrooms [R] *B&b£12.30–£20.70 Bdi£18.80–£27.20 W£119.30–£169.70 K LDO8.30pm

Lic ♨ 20P

Credit cards [1] [3]

INN George High St ☎(0233) 25512
Closed Xmas Day

Small, olde-worlde inn with cosy well-decorated bedrooms.

14hc (1🛁 1🚿) (2fb) CTV in all bedrooms 🚫 [R] *B&bfr£18.15 Bdifr£24.15 Lunch£3–£8&alc Dinner 10pm (10.45pm wknds) £3–£8&alc

♨ CTV 5P 8🚗

Credit cards [1] [2] [3] [5]

ASHPRINGTON
Devon
Map **3** SX85

FH Mrs T C Grimshaw **Sharpham Barton** *(SX814583)* ☎Harbertonford (080423) 278

Modern farmhouse in 11 acres with well-appointed bedrooms.

3rm (2hc 1🚿) TV in all bedrooms *B&b£9–£10 Bdi£15–£16 W£105 K LDOday prior

♨ TV 3P 🏊heated 🎾grass U 11acres mixed non-working

[V]

ASHTON-UNDER-LYNE
Greater Manchester
Map **7** SJ99

GH Welbeck House Hotel 324 Katherine St ☎061-344 0751

A modern, well furnished, town-centre hotel, privately owned and run.

7🚿 (2fb) CTV in all bedrooms 🚫 [R] *B&b£22.50 Bdi£27 LDO9pm

Lic ♨ CTV 15P

Credit cards [1] [2] [3] [5]

ASHURST
Hampshire
Map **4** SU31

GH Barn 112 Lyndhurst Rd ☎(042129) 2531
Etr–Sep

Attractive detached house offering comfortable bedrooms.

6hc 🚫 *B&b£9–£9.50 W£63–£66.50 M

♨ CTV 8P 1🚗(charge)

[V]

See advertisement under Southampton

ASHWELL
Hertfordshire
Map **4** TL23

INN Three Tuns Hotel 6 High St ☎(046274) 2387

Country inn with pleasant individually-furnished bedrooms.

7hc Annexe: 5hc (1🛁 1🚿) (1fb) CTV in all bedrooms [R] *B&b£19.75–£27.50 W£75–£95 M Lunch£5alc Dinner 10.30pm £5alc

♨ 25P solarium

Credit cards [1] [2] [5]

ASKRIGG
North Yorkshire
Map **8** SD99

GH Winville Hotel ☎Wensleydale (0969) 50515
Mar–Nov

A comfortable house, in centre of picturesque village. Cheerful, friendly proprietors.

6🛁🚿 (3fb) CTV in all bedrooms 🚫 [R] B&b£13.75–£14.75 Bdi£20.50–£21.50 W£138 K

Lic ♨ 14P 2🚗 nc10yrs

Credit cards [1] [2] [3] [5] [V]

DOWNSVIEW HOTEL
Ashford, Kent
Licensed

An ideal base for touring the 'Garden of England' and for cross-Channel travellers.
Peacefully situated on the B2164 but with easy access to the A20 and A28- the Weald of Kent, Canterbury, and the coast are all within easy reach.
Downsview stands in an acre of mature grounds, adjoining orchards and has fine views across the Stour Valley to the North Downs.

Willesborough Road,
Kennington
Tel: Ashford (STD 0233) 21953

An ideal base for holidaymakers and businessmen

The Winville Hotel
LICENSED

IN THE HEART OF HERRIOT'S YORKSHIRE

A sympathetically converted c1800 gentleman's residence with every bedroom having en-suite bathroom, Colour TV, Tea & Coffee making facilities.
The ideal base for your exploration of Herriot's Yorkshire and the whole of the Dales and where Barbara and Michael Phelan ensure comfort, hospitality and good food.

Please write or phone for a brochure

Askrigg, Leyburn, North Yorkshire DL8 3HG.
Phone Wensleydale (0969) 50515

English Tourist Board

ASTBURY
Cheshire
Map **7** SJ86

INN Egerton Arms Hotel ☎Congleton (0260) 273946
Village inn with pleasant bedrooms and popular restaurant.
6hc (1fb) CTV in all bedrooms [R] B&b£15 Bdi£24 W£168 M Lunch£4.25 Dinner9.30pm£7.50
♨ 100P 🚌
Credit card [3]

ATHERSTONE
Warwickshire
Map **4** SP39

Recommended
GH Chapel House Friars Gate ☎(08277) 66238 (due to change to (0827) 716238)
Closed Xmas & New Year
A most charming and hospitable 18th-century house with walled garden and swimming pool. Pleasantly furnished bedrooms and lounge have a comfortable, welcoming atmosphere. A good set menu is served in the elegant dining room during the week, and on Fridays and Saturdays is open to non-residents also, with a well-chosen a la carte menu that is deservedly popular in the locality.
Midlands Regional Winner of the AA 1986/7 Guesthouse of the Year Award.
9hc (6🚿) CTV in all bedrooms ✖ ✱B&b£15–£25 Bdi£22–£32 LDO6pm
Lic ♨ 🏊 (heated)
Credit card [5] [V]

INN *Three Tuns Hotel* 95 Long St ☎(08277) 3161
14hc (5🛁 5🚿) TV in all bedrooms ✖ [R] LDO10.30pm
♨ CTV 20P
Credit cards [1] [2] [3] [5]

ATTLEBOROUGH
Norfolk
Map **5** TM09

INN Griffin Hotel Church St ☎(0953) 452149
A friendly inn, recently renovated, offering good fare.
7hc (1fb) TV in all bedrooms ✖ ✱B&b£15–£16 Bar lunch 75p–£2.50 Dinner 8.30pm £7.50alc
♨ 20P

AUCHENCAIRN
Dumfries & Galloway *Kirkcudbrightshire*
Map **11** NX75

FH Mrs D Cannon **Bluehill** *(NX786515)* ☎(055664) 228
Etr–Sep
A comfortable house with nice bedrooms and panoramic views towards Solway Firth.
4hc (1fb) ✖ [R] ✱B&b£9.50–£10
♨ CTV 6P nc12yrs 120acres dairy

AUDLEY
Staffordshire
Map **7** SJ75

FH Mrs E.E. Oulton **Domvilles** *(SJ776516)* Barthomley Rd ☎Stoke-on-Trent (0782) 720378
Large farmhouse overlooking Cheshire Plain. Dairy farm with pigs, geese and tropical birds, situated close to Junct. 16 of M6.
3rm (1🚿) (1fb) CTV in 1 bedroom ✖ B&b£9–£10 LDO6pm
Lic CTV 5P 👶 snooker 120 acres dairy mixed

AUSTWICK
North Yorkshire
Map **7** SD76

FH Mrs M Hird **Rawlinshaw** *(SD781673)* ☎Settle (07292) 3214
Etr–Sep
200-year-old farmhouse with attractive views to the front of the house.
2hc (2fb) ✖ [R] ✱ B&bfr£8 Wfr£55 M
♨ CTV P U 206acres dairy sheep

AVETON GIFFORD
Devon
Map **3** SX64

FH Mrs G M Balkwill **Court Barton** *(SX695477)* ☎Kingsbridge (0548) 550312
Closed Dec
6hc (2fb) ✖ ✱B&b£7–£9 W£49–£63 M
♨ CTV 10P 🏊 ⛳ 350acres arable
[V]

AVIEMORE
Highland *Inverness-shire*
Map **14** NH81

GH *Aviemore Chalets Motel* Aviemore Centre ☎(0479) 810624
Chalet-style accommodation in blocks of four units.
79🚿 (32fb) CTV in 47 bedrooms LDO10pm
Lic ♨ CTV 400P 🏊 (heated) ⛳ squash snooker sauna bath solarium gymnasium
Credit cards [1] [2] [3] [5]

GH *Corrour House* Inverdruie ☎(0479) 810220
Closed Nov
Stone-built house standing in tree-studded grounds ½m E of Aviemore on B970.
11rm (9hc) (5fb) [R] LDO6.30pm
Lic CTV 12P 👶
Credit card [3]

GH Craiglea Grampian Rd ☎(0479) 810210
Detached stone-house with garden and childrens play area.
11hc (1🚿) (4fb) B&b£9.50–£10.50 W£65–£72 M
CTV 12P sauna bath
[V]

GH Ravenscraig ☎(0479) 810278
Detached house on main road at north end of Aviemore, with annexe to the side.

The Griffin Hotel
Church Street, Attleborough, Norfolk NR17 2AH
Telephone: Attleborough (0953) 452149

A warm and friendly atmosphere awaits you at the Griffin Hotel, situated on the main A11 road midway between Norwich and Thetford. This 16th century Coaching Inn full of charm and character offers comfortable, centrally heated bedrooms, all with hot and cold water, black and white television and conveniently situated for bathroom, shower room and toilets, full English breakfast is served in the restaurant which is open 6 evenings a week and traditional 3-course Sunday lunch served between 12 noon and 2pm, also open to non-residents. Bar meals and traditional ales available in the two tastefully furnished bars. Regrettably no animals allowed.

6hc (1⌂) Annexe: 6⌂ (3fb) B&b£10.50–£11.50
♫ CTV 12P ⚙
Ⓥ

AXBRIDGE
Somerset
Map **3** ST45

FH Mr L F Dimmock **Manor** *(ST420549)* Cross ☎(0934) 732577
Closed Xmas

At junction of A38 and A371 roads.

7rm (2hc) (2fb) B&bfr£9 Bdifr£14.50 Wfr£99 ⫞ LDO5pm

CTV 10P ↻ 250acres beef sheep
Ⓥ

INN Lamb The Square ☎Weston-super-Mare (0934) 732253

Attractive and busy market-town inn with good facilities and an extensive menu.

4hc (1⇆ 2⌂) CTV in 1 bedroom TV in 3 bedrooms Ⓡ ✻B&b£9–£16 Lunch£6alc LDO9pm

♫ ✗
Ⓥ

AXMINSTER
Devon
Map **3** SY39

FH Mrs S Clist **Annings** *(SY299966)* Wyke ☎(0297) 33294
Etr–Sep

Large secluded farmhouse with modern furnishings. Situated in elevated position with fine views. Coast nearby. South of town on unclassified road between A35 and A358.

4rm (3hc) (2fb) ✗ LDO4.15pm

CTV 4P 🚲 ⌁ 54acres mixed

AYR
Strathclyde *Ayrshire*
Map **10** NS32

GH Clifton Hotel 19 Miller Rd ☎(0292) 264521

Detached sandstone house with rear gardens situated in residential area.

11hc (5⌂) (2fb) CTV in 5 bedrooms ✗ Ⓡ LDO6pm

Aviemore — Bakewell

Lic ♫ CTV 16P

Credit cards ① ③

GH Parkhouse 1A Ballantine Dr ☎(0292) 264151

Situated in a quiet residential area to the south of the town centre.

7hc (2fb) TV in all bedrooms ✗ Ⓡ ✻B&b£10

Lic ♫ CTV ✗
Ⓥ

GH Windsor Hotel 6 Alloway Pl ☎(0292) 264689
rs Nov

Victorian stone house on main road near seafront.

10hc (3fb) B&b£12.50–£13.50 Bdi£16.50–£17.50 W£110–£116 ⫞ LDO4.30pm

♫ CTV ✗

FH Mr & Mrs A Stevenson **Trees** *(NS386186)* ☎Joppa (0292) 570270
Closed Xmas & New Year

White farmhouse offering good quality accommodation at modest prices.

3hc (1fb) ✗ ✻B&b£8.50–£9 Bdi£14–£15 Wfr£98 ⫞ LDO4pm

lift ♫ CTV 5P 75acres grazing
Ⓥ

AYTON, GREAT
North Yorkshire
Map **8** NZ51

INN Royal Oak Hotel High Green ☎(0642) 722361

5hc (1⇆) CTV in all bedrooms Ⓡ ✻B&b£13–£22 Lunch£5.95&alc Dinner9.30pm£10.25&alc
♫

Credit cards ① ③ Ⓥ

BABELL
Clwyd
Map **7** SJ17

FH Mrs M L Williams **Bryn Glas** *(SJ155737)* ☎Caerwys (0352) 720493
Mar–Oct

Comfortable modern farmhouse situated in a quiet, rural area near Mold.

2hc (2fb) TV in all bedrooms ✗ Ⓡ

♫ CTV 2P 40acres beef sheep mixed

BACUP
Lancashire
Map **7** SD82

GH Burwood House Hotel Todmorden Rd ☎Rochdale (0706) 873466

Family-run town centre house with modern bedrooms.

11rm (6⇆) (2fb) LDO9pm

Lic ♫ CTV 12P

BAKEWELL
Derbyshire
Map **8** SK26

GH Cliffe House Hotel Monsal Head ☎Great Longstone (062987) 376

Pleasant house at the head of Monsal Dale.

7hc (2fb) ✗ Ⓡ LDO10am

Lic ♫ CTV P

— Recommended —

GH Merlin House Country Hotel Ashford Ln, Monsal Head ☎Great Longstone (062987) 475
Closed Xmas & New Year rs Nov–Feb

Merlin House stands in its own quiet grounds and attractive gardens close to the spectacular scenery of Monsal Head. Well-proportioned, comfortable bedrooms are fitted to a high standard; the lounge and conservatory have pleasant views over the garden and there is a small bar.

7hc (1⇆ 1⌂) ✗ Ⓡ B&b£14–£15.50 Bdi£19.50–£24 W£136.50–£150 ⫞ LDOnoon

Lic ♫ CTV 8P nc8yrs

BALA
Gwynedd
Map **6**   SH93

GH Frondderw ☎(0678) 520301
Closed Xmas

Large Georgian house with lawned gardens set high above village, overlooking lake.

9hc (1⇨ 1🛏) (3fb) ⊁ in 3 bedrooms ✖ ® B&b£9.50–£12.50 Bdi£15.50–£18.50 W£97.50–£118 ⅃LDO5pm

Lic 🍴 CTV 10P

Ⓥ

GH *Plas Teg* Tegid St ☎(0678) 520268

Semi-detached Victorian house in lane off High Street.

8hc (4fb) ® LDO8pm

Lic CTV 12P

FH Mrs E Jones **Eirianfa** *(SH967394)* Sarnau (4m N on A494) ☎Llandderfel (06783) 389
Mar–Nov

This modernised farmhouse rests on the edge of the Berwyn Mountains. Free trout fishing is available in the farm's private lake.

3hc (1fb) ✖ ® ✳B&b£8.50–£9 Bdi£12–£12.50 W£78–£80 ⅃ LDO6pm

🍴 CTV 3P ⚓ 150acres mixed

Ⓥ

FH Mr D Davies **Tytandderwen** *(SH944345)* ☎(0678) 520273
Etr–Oct

Two-storey, manor house style, farmhouse in open country. Stone-built and modernised in parts. Borders on the River Dee.

3rm (2hc) ✳B&bfr£7

🍴 CTV 3P ⚓ 40acres mixed

BALDOCK
Hertfordshire
Map **4**   TL23

GH Butterfield House Hotel Hitchin St ☎(0462) 892701

Small private hotel with spacious bedrooms and Victorian-style conservatory.

13⇨🛏 (1fb) CTV in all bedrooms ✖ ® ✳B&b£16.15–£28.18 Bdi£24.20–£36.23 LDO9pm

Lic 🍴 14P

Credit cards ① ② ③

BALLACHULISH
Highland *Argyllshire*
Map **14**   NN05

GH Lyn-Leven White St ☎(08552) 392
Closed Xmas

Comfortable and well-appointed modern bungalow, situated close to A82 overlooking Loch Leven.

8hc (6🛏) (1fb) ⊁ in 3 bedrooms CTV in 6 bedrooms ® ✳B&b£9–£14 Bdi£15–£20 W£105–£140 ⅃ LDO7.30pm

Lic 🍴 CTV 12P

Ⓥ

BALLANTRAE
Strathclyde *Ayrshire*
Map **10**   NX08

INN *Royal Hotel* 71 Main St ☎(046583) 204

Small and homely family-run inn.

5hc ® LDO10pm

CTV �'

BALLATER
Grampian *Aberdeenshire*
Map **15**   NO39

┌─ *Recommended* ─┐

GH Moorside Braemar Rd (Guestaccom) ☎(0338) 55492
Mar–Oct

Small tourist hotel with modern décor and furnishing throughout.

8hc (2⇨ 6🛏) (2fb) ® ✳B&b£11–£18 Bdi£18–£24 W£110–£150 ⅃ LDO6pm

Lic 🍴 CTV 10P

Fronndderw
Bala, Gwynedd LL23 7YD. N. Wales
Tel: Bala 520301 (STD code 0678)

FRONDDERW is a charming period mansion set on the hillside overlooking the town of Bala, with magnificent views of the Berwyn Mountains and Llyn Tegid (Bala Lake).

Guest accommodation includes one downstairs suite suitable for disabled visitors. All rooms decorated to a high standard with fitted carpets and central heating. Cots available on request with linens.

The front lounge is spacious and comfortable, with books and games for guests' use. There is a separate television lounge with colour tv and a large dining room.

Each bedroom is provided with tea and coffee making facilities. Ample parking space is available free of charge. No garage accommodation.

Sorry, no guests' pets allowed in the house.

Plas Teg Guest House   BALA

Tel: Bala 520268

Plas Teg Guest House is pleasantly situated on the outskirts of the charming little town of Bala and overlooks the lake. It has ample parking facilities and is within walking distance of the excellent and varied shops in the main street, yet is quiet and secluded itself.

If you are looking for a pleasant, peaceful holiday with excellent food and service and within easy reach of fine Welsh scenery with golf, sailing and fishing on your doorstep, this is the place.

Please see gazetteer entry for details of the tariff.

PLAS TEG
GUEST HOUSE
BALA

GH _Morvada_ ☎(0338) 55501
Apr–Oct

_A neat, well-maintained house set back
from the main street._

6hc (2🚿) ® LDO6pm
Lic 🍴 CTV 6P

GH _Netherley_ 2 Netherley Place ☎(0338)
55792
Feb–Oct

Cosy house with modern extension.

9hc (1⇘) (1fb) ✱B&bfr£9 Bdifr£15
Wfr£105 ⓀLDO6pm
🍴 CTV 🐾 nc4yrs

BALLAUGH
Isle of Man
See **Man, Isle of**

BALMACLELLAN
Dumfries & Galloway _Kirkcudbrightshire_
Map **11**　　NX67

FH Mrs P Porritt **_Craig_** _(NX682757)_ ☎New
Galloway (06442) 228

_Isolated but spacious farm mansion. 3m
SE of village._

3rm (1fb) ✖ ® ✱B&b£9.50 Bdi£15
Wfr£105 Ⓚ LDO7.30pm
🍴 CTV 6P ✈ 500acres beef sheep
Ⓥ

FH Mr & Mrs A Shaw **_High Park_**
_(NX644765)_ ☎New Galloway (06442) 298
Apr–Oct

_Neat roadside farmhouse with pleasant
bedrooms._

3hc (1fb) ✱B&b£7–£7.50 Bdi£10–£11
W£65–£70 Ⓚ LDO6pm
🍴 CTV 3P ♨ ⚓ 171acres beef dairy
sheep mixed
Ⓥ

BALMAHA
Central _Stirlingshire_
Map **10**　　NS49

GH _Arrochoile_ ☎(036087) 231
Apr–Oct

_Attractive white-painted house, set back
from the main road and looking west
across Loch Lomond._

6hc (2fb) ✖ ✱B&b£8 W£56 Ⓜ
🍴 CTV 12P 1🚗
Ⓥ

BAMPTON
Devon
Map **3**　　SS92

GH Bridge House Hotel Luke St
☎(0398) 31298

_Character hotel, approximately 250 years
old with local hunting, fishing and walking._

6hc (2⇘ 1🚿) (2fb) ✱B&b£10.75–£12
W£67.73–£75.60 Ⓜ LDO8pm
Lic 🍴 CTV 🐾
Credit cards ① ③

Ballater
–
Bantham

━ _Recommended_ ━

FH Mrs R A Fleming **Holwell**
_(SS966233)_ ☎(0398) 31452
Closed Xmas

_Devonshire longhouse with friendly
atmosphere offering traditional
home-produced country fare._

3hc ✖ ✱B&b£9.50–£10 Bdi£16–£17
LDO2pm
🍴 CTV 8P nc 25acres mixed

FH Mrs R Cole **Hukeley** _(SS972237)_
☎(0398) 31267
Apr–Oct

_16th-century farmhouse, on edge of
Exmoor with fine old beams. Rooms are
comfortable and well-decorated._

2hc (2fb) ® ✱B&b£8.50 Bdifr£13 Wfr£90
Ⓚ LDO4pm

CTV 4P 120acres arable beef sheep
mixed

BAMPTON
Oxfordshire
Map **4**　　SP30

FH Mrs J Rouse **Morar** _(SP312026)_ Weald
St (½m SW off A4095) ☎Bampton Castle
(0993) 850162
Closed 21–28 Dec

_Small modern farmhouse with
comfortable rooms and pleasant garden._

3hc ✖ ® B&b£9.50–£14.50 Bdi£17.80–
£22.80 W£124.60–£152.60 Ⓚ LDOnoon
🍴 CTV 4P nc6yrs 450acres arable beef
dairy mixed
Ⓥ

BANAVIE
Highland _Inverness-shire_
Map **14**　　NN17

FH Mrs A C MacDonald **Burnside**
_(NN138805)_ Muirshearlich ☎Corpach
(03977) 275
Apr–Oct

_Small, stone-built farmhouse with open
views over Caledonian Canal, Loch and
north face of Ben Nevis 3m NE off B8004._

3hc ✱B&b£7.50–£8.50 Bdi£10.50–£11.50
W£70–£75 Ⓚ LDO4pm
🍴 CTV 3P nc6yrs 60acres mixed

BANBURY
Oxfordshire
Map **4**　　SP44

GH Lismore Hotel & Restaurant
61 Oxford Rd (Guestaccom) ☎(0295)
67661
Closed 25 Dec–4 Jan

_Homely hotel offering comfortable
bedrooms and more than most in the way
of well-priced food._

14hc (8⇘ 1🚿) (3fb) CTV in all bedrooms
® B&b£14.50–£30 Bdi£19–£37.95
W£130.50–£266 Ⓚ LDO9pm
Lic 🍴 15P 1🚗(charge)
Credit cards ① ③ Ⓥ

GH Mill House North Newington (3m W
off B4035) ☎Wroxton St Mary (029573)
212
Closed 20–31 Dec

_Picturesque, part 16th-century Mill-house
with comfortable, well-appointed
bedrooms in converted Cotswold
cottages._

5hc (2⇘ 3🚿) (1fb) CTV in all bedrooms ®
B&b£16–£20 Bdi£24.50–£28.50 W£140–
£168 Ⓚ LDO4.45pm
Lic 🍴 9P ⏁(heated)
Credit card ① Ⓥ

GH Tredis 15 Broughton Rd ☎(0295)
4632

Small, cosy and welcoming guesthouse.

6hc (1fb) CTV in all bedrooms ®
✱B&b£9.50–£11 Bdi£14–£15.50 LDO2pm
🍴 3P ‒

BANFF
Grampian _Banffshire_
Map **15**　　NJ66

GH Carmelite House Hotel Low St
☎(02612) 2152

_Town house of historic interest in
conservation area._

8hc (2fb) ✱B&b£9.50–£10.50 Bdi£14.25–
£15.25 W£93.10–£98.40 Ⓚ LDO7.45pm
Lic CTV 6P
Ⓥ

GH _Ellerslie_ 45 Low St ☎(02612) 5888

_Nicely decorated, well-appointed
guesthouse occupying 1st floor and
above in terraced row on main shopping
street._

6hc (1fb) ✖ ® LDO5pm
Lic CTV 🐾

INN Tolbooth Hotel 1 Strait Path
☎(02612) 5034
Closed Xmas Day & New Years Day

_Completely renovated in 1986 to provide
modern, attractive bedroom. Meals are
modestly priced._

4hc (2fb) CTV in all bedrooms ✖ B&b£9–
£10 Bdi£12–£13 W£80 Ⓚ Lunch£2.50–£3
Dinner7pm£2.50–£3
🍴 🐾

BANTHAM
Devon
Map **3**　　SX64

INN Sloop ☎Kingsbridge (0548) 560489

5hc (4⇘) (2fb) CTV in all bedrooms ®
✱B&b£13–£14 Bdi£18–£21 W£119–£135 Ⓚ
Lunch £2.50–£6&alc Dinner10pm £3–
£7.50&alc
🍴 30P 🚲

49

BARHAM
Kent
Map **5** TR25

INN Old Coach House A2 Trunk Rd
☎Canterbury (0227) 831218
10hc (4fb) CTV in all bedrooms
✱B&b£11–£12.50 Bdi£16–£17.50 W£112–£122.50 Ł Lunch £5.50–£6.50&alc Dinner 10pm £5.50–£6.50 & alc
♨ 60P snooker
Credit cards [1] [2] [3] [5]

BARKESTONE-LE-VALE
Leicestershire
Map **8** SK73

FH Mrs S H Smart **The Paddocks** *(SK781351)* ☎Bottesford (0949) 42208
Closed Xmas
North of village off 'The Green'.
3hc Annexe: 2hc (2fb) TV in 3 bedrooms 🚫🐕 ✱B&b£9–£10 Bdi£15–£16 W£102–£107 Ł LDO4pm
♨ CTV 10P 🏊 (heated) 150acres arable sheep
[V]

BARMOUTH
Gwynedd
Map **6** SH61

GH Lawrenny Lodge ☎(0341) 280466
Etr–Oct
Detached Edwardian house on outskirts of town ½m from shops and beach.
9hc (1🛁 3🚿) (3fb) ✱B&b£10.60–£13 Bdi£16.35–£18.75 W£111.55–£128.10 Ł LDO5.30pm
Lic CTV 15P
[V]

GH Morwendon Llanaber ☎(0341) 280566
Mar–Nov
Detached Victorian house overlooking Cardigan Bay, located 1m N A496.
7hc (3🚿) (3fb) CTV in 6 bedrooms [R] ✱B&b£8.50–£10.50 Bdi£13–£15 W£92–£99 Ł LDO5pm
Lic ♨ CTV 7P 🏡
[V]

Barham — Barton-on-Sea

BARNSTAPLE
Devon
Map **2** SS53

GH Cresta 26 Sticklepath Hill ☎(0271) 74022
Closed Xmas
Detached house on main Barnstaple to Bideford road, 1 mile from Barnstaple town centre.
5hc (1🚿) Annexe: 1🛁 (1fb) CTV in all bedrooms 🚫🐕 [R] ✱B&b£10–£15 W£63–£84 M̸
♨ CTV 6P no babies
[V]

GH *Yeo Dale Hotel* Pilton Bridge ☎(0271) 42954
Blue- and white-fronted terraced house in Pilton overlooking the river.
12hc (3fb) 🚫🐕 LDO5pm
Lic ♨ CTV 3P

FH Mrs G Hannington **Fair Oak** *(SS530348)* Ashford ☎(0271) 73698
May–Oct
Modern Farmhouse in rural position overlooking Taw Estuary.
4rm (3hc) (3fb) 🚫🐕 [R] ✱B&b£8–£10 Bdi£12–£14 W£75–£80 Ł LDO3pm
♨ CTV 6P 🏡 89acres beef sheep mixed

FH Mrs J Stanbury **Halmpstone** *(SS595285)* Bishops Tawton. (2m SE Bishop's Tawton off unclass) ☎Swimbridge (0271) 830321
Excellent home cooking at handsome, stone-built farm. Rooms tastefully decorated and furnished.
4rm (2hc) (1🚿) (2fb) 🚭 in 2 bedrooms 🚫🐕 ✱B&b£10.50–£12 Bdi£18–£19.50 W£113.40–£122.85 Ł LDO9pm
Lic CTV 15P 🏡 235 acres dairy
[V]

FH Mrs M Lethaby **Home** *(SS555360)* Lower Blakewell, Muddiford ☎(0271) 42955
Mar–Oct
Farmhouse situated in peaceful North Devon countryside. Pony, many pets and Wendy House available for children.
4hc (3fb) TV in all bedrooms 🚫🐕 [R] ✱B&b£9 Bdi£12 W£75 Ł LDO6pm
♨ CTV 4P 🏡 90acres mixed
[V]

FH Mr & Mrs J Dallyn **Rowden Barton** *(SS538306)* Roundswell (2m SW B3232) ☎(0271) 44365
Modern farmhouse with glorious views. Friendly atmosphere.
2rm (2fb) 🚫🐕 ✱B&bfr£7.50
♨ CTV P 🏡 100 acres beef sheep
[V]

BARROW-IN-FURNESS
Cumbria
Map **7** SD16

GH Lisdoonie Private Hotel Abbey Rd ☎(0229) 27312
rs Xmas
12hc (6🛁 6🚿) (1fb) CTV in all bedrooms [R] B&b£18.50–£27 Bdi£23.50–£32 LDO7.30pm
Lic ♨ 43P
Credit cards [1] [2] [3]

BARRY
South Glamorgan
Map **3** ST16

GH Maytree 9 The Parade ☎(0446) 734075
Closed 2 wks Xmas
Victorian seafront house with lounge for residents at the front.
15hc (2🚿) (2fb) ✱B&b£9.20 Wfr£59.40 M̸
Lic ♨ CTV 3P

BARTON-ON-SEA
Hampshire
Map **4** SZ29

GH Cliff House Hotel Marine Drive West ☎New Milton (0425) 619333
Mar–Oct

Clifftop hotel with panoramic views, offering nicely-appointed bedrooms, spacious sunlounge and family-run restaurant.

10hc (3fl) CTV in 3 bedrooms
✱B&b£14.50–£15 Bdi£21–£22 W£132–£135 L LDO7pm

Lic 🛋 CTV 20P

Credit cards [1] [2] [3] [5]

GH Old Coastguard Hotel 53 Marine Drive East ☎New Milton (0425) 612987

8hc (3fl) [R] ✱B&b£13–£14 Bdi£18.50–£19.50 W£115–£125 L LDO5pm

Lic 🛋 CTV 10P nc12yrs

BASINGSTOKE
Hampshire
See **Sherfield-on-Loddon**

BASSENTHWAITE
Cumbria
Map **11** NY23

GH Link House Hotel ☎Bassenthwaite Lake (059681) 291
mid Mar–4 Nov

A Victorian house, comfortably converted to offer well-appointed bedrooms and cosy lounges.

7hc (6fl) (1fb) CTV in 6 bedrooms TV in 1 bedroom ✗ [R] ✱B&b£11–£14 Bdi£19.50–£21 W£125–£135 L LDO5pm

Lic 🛋 6P nc7yrs

[V]

GH Ravenstone Hotel ☎Bassenthwaite Lake (059681) 240
Mar–Oct

Charming country house, built in 1865 of local slate. Distant views of Bassenthwaite Lake; Spacious accommodation.

12hc (3⇌) [R] ✱B&b£13 Bdi£17 Wfr£119 L LDO6pm

Lic 🛋 CTV 15P snooker

[V]

FH Mrs A M Trafford **Bassenthwaite Hall (East)** *(NY231322)* ☎Bassenthwaite Lake (059681) 393
Mar–Oct rs Nov–Feb

Fully modernised 17th-century farmhouse in picturesque village close to quiet stream.

2hc (1fb) ✱B&b£8–£10 W£50–£70 M

🛋 CTV 6P ⌂ 200acres beef sheep poultry

[V]

FH Mrs D Mattinson ***Bassenthwaite Hall (West)*** *(NY228323)* ☎Bassenthwaite Lake (059681) 279
Apr–Nov

Traditional farmhouse in village centre with good mountain views.

3hc (1fb) ✗ LDO4pm

CTV 4P 135acres beef sheep

BATH
Avon
Map **3** ST76
See also **Keynsham** and **Timbury**
See plan on pages 52–53

GH *Arden Hotel* 73 Great Pulteney St ☎(0225) 66601 Plan **1** *E4*

12hc (1⇌ 3fl) (2fb) CTV in 10 bedrooms ✗ [R]

Lic 🛋 CTV nc3yrs

See advertisement on page 55

GH Arney 99 Wells Rd, Bathavon ☎Bath (0225) 310020 Plan **2** *B1*

8hc (1fl) (3fb) ✱B&b£10–£12 W£70–£84 M

🛋 CTV ₱

GH Ashley Villa Hotel 26 Newbridge Rd ☎(0225) 21683 Plan **3** *A3*
Closed 2 wks Xmas

15hc (3⇌ 6fl) (2fb) CTV in all bedrooms ✱B&b£15–£23 Bdi£25–£33 W£160–£208 L LDO9pm

Lic 🛋 10P ♿ ⛆ (heated)

Credit cards [1] [3] [V]

The Wessex House Hotel
Sherfield-on-Loddon, Basingstoke
Telephone: (0256) 882243
The hotel is an extension of an attractive old house and stands in an acre of land with ample parking space. All rooms have private bathroom, direct dial telephones, colour TV, tea/coffee-making facilities. Candle lit dining room. Licensed. Full breakfast with home-baked bread, farm produce, home-made marmalade etc. Personal attention of resident owners.

ravenstone hotel

Near Keswick, Cumbria CA12 4QG
Telephone: Bassenthwaite Lake 240
A well-appointed comfortable Country House Hotel on slopes of Skiddaw, with fine views over Bassenthwaite Valley and Lake, ideally situated for touring the Lake District and Cumbrian coast. Reductions for children sharing family rooms. Extensive grounds, Residential Licence, Games and Billiards Room, TV Lounge, Spacious Parking, Full Central Heating. Situated on the A591 road, Keswick to Scotland. *Personally managed by the Proprietors.*

GH Astor House 14 Oldfield Rd ☎(0225)
29134 Plan **3A** *B1*
Apr–Oct

*Bath-stone Victorian villa with friendly
atmosphere, overlooking the city.*

7rm ✠ ® B&b£10 W£63 M

Lic CTV 4P nc7yrs

GH Avon Hotel 9 Bathwick St ☎(0225)
65469 Plan **3B** *E4*
Closed Xmas

*Georgian end of terrace with well
furnished bedrooms. Ample parking and
close to shops and tourist sites.*

20hc (18🛏) (3fb) ✗ in 6 bedrooms CTV in
all bedrooms ® ✱B&b£13.50–£22
W£181–£264 M

Lic ㎖ CTV 20P

Credit cards ① ③

See advertisement on page 54

GH *Carfax Hotel* Great Pulteney St
☎(0225) 62089 Plan **4** *D4*
rs Xmas

Bath

35hc (18🛏 7🛏) (3fb) CTV in all bedrooms
✠ ® LDO8pm
Temperance lift ㎖ 13P 4🚗
Credit cards ① ② ③

GH Charnwood House 51 Upper Oldfield
Pk ☎(0225) 334937 Plan **5** *A1*

*Quietly-situated small hotel offering a
friendly welcome and well-appointed
bedrooms.*

8hc (1🛏 3🛏) (4fb) CTV in all bedrooms ✠
® B&b£12–£20 W£78–£126 M

㎖ 7P sauna bath
Ⓥ

GH Chesterfield Hotel 11 Great Pulteney
St ☎(0225) 60953 Plan **5A** *D4*
Closed 22 Dec–2 Jan

*Terraced Georgian building in wide,
elegant avenue. Close to tourist
attractions and shops.*

28hc (12🛏) (3fb) CTV in 8 bedrooms ✠
® ✱B&b£14–£22
Lic ㎖ CTV 8🚗(charge)
Credit cards ① ② ③ Ⓥ

See advertisement on page 55

GH Dorset Villa 14 Newbridge Rd
☎(0225) 25975 Plan **7** *A3*
Apr–Oct

6hc ✱B&b£9–£9.50
㎖ CTV 6P nc12yrs
Credit card ③

GH Eagle House Church St, Bathford
(3m NE A363) ☎(0225) 859946 Not on
plan
Closed 23 Dec–1 Jan

*Listed Georgian house set in own
grounds some 3½m from Bath. Spacious
public rooms and well fitted bedrooms.*

6hc (4🛏 1🛏) (2fb) CTV in all bedrooms ®
✱B&b£15–£24
Lic ㎖ 8P
Ⓥ

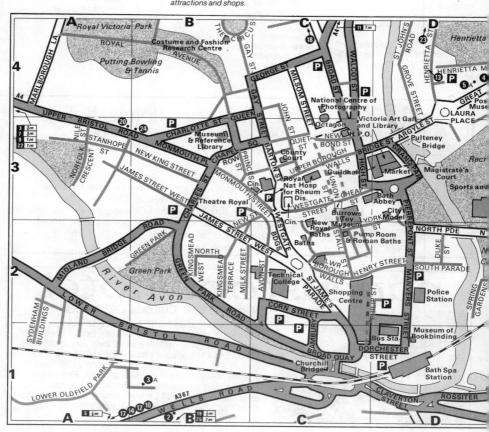

GH Edgar Hotel 64 Great Pulteney St ☎(0225) 20619 Plan **8** *E4*

Original Georgian town-house in historic city centre.

14🚿 (1fb) CTV in all bedrooms 🚫🐕 [R] ✱B&b£16–£22

Lic 🍽 CTV P̸

[V]

See advertisement on page 55

GH Fern Cottage 9 Northend, Batheaston (2½m NE off A4) ☎(0225) 858190 Not on plan

Bath-stone, Georgian cottage in quiet hamlet. Well converted and very comfortable.

8hc (2🛁 2🚿) CTV in all bedrooms [R] B&b£14–£19 Bdi£21–£26 W£147–£182 Ⱡ LDO8.30pm

Lic 🍽 8P nc10yrs

See advertisement on page 55

GH Gainsborough Hotel Weston Ln ☎(0225) 311380 Plan **9** *A3* Closed Xmas & first 2 wks Jan

Bath

Comfortable detached house in an acre of grounds with easy access to city centre.

16hc (12🛁 4🚿) (2fb) CTV in all bedrooms 🚫🐕 [R] ✱B&b£20–£22 Bdi£27.95–£29.95 W£174.65–£234.15 Ⱡ LDO8.15pm

Lic 🍽 18P

Credit cards [1] [2] [3]

See advertisement on page 56

GH Glenbeigh Hotel 1 Upper Oldfield Park ☎(0225) 26336 Plan **10** *B1* rs Xmas wk

12hc (2🚿) (3fb) CTV in 2 bedrooms [R] B&b£12.50–£17

Lic 🍽 CTV 7P 3🚗

[V]

GH *Grove Lodge* 11 Lambridge, London Road ☎(0225) 310860 Plan **11** *C4* Closed Oct

8hc (2fb) CTV in 7 bedrooms TV in 1 bedroom

Lic P̸

GH *Highways House* 143 Wells Rd ☎(0225) 21238 Plan **12** *B1* Closed Xmas

5hc (2🚿) [R]

🍽 CTV 6P nc13yrs

GH Kennard Hotel 11 Henrietta St ☎(0225) 310472 Plan **13** *D4* Closed Xmas

Pleasant Georgian house, close to city centre. Bedrooms compact, bright and fresh.

12hc (7🚿) (3fb) CTV in all bedrooms [R] ✱B&b£14–£20 W£88.20–£126 M̸

P̸ nc3yrs

Credit cards [1] [3] [V]

GH Leighton House 139 Wells Rd ☎(0225) 314769 Plan **14** *B1* Closed Xmas & New Year

A comfortable, enthusiastically-run hotel with good degree of hospitality.

7hc (2🛁 2🚿) (2fb) CTV in all bedrooms [R] ✱B&b£14–£28 W£88–£176 M̸

🍽 CTV 7P

Credit cards [1] [3]

See advertisement on page 56

GH Lynwood 6 Putleney Gdns ☎(0225) 26410 Plan **15** *E2* Closed Xmas

14hc (3fb) CTV in 12 bedrooms TV in 2 bedrooms 🚫🐕 [R] B&b£12.50–£14.50

🍽 3P 1🚗 nc3yrs

Credit cards [1] [2] [3] [5] [V]

GH Millers Hotel 69 Great Pulteney St ☎(0225) 65798 Plan **16** *E4* Closed Xmas wk

Bright, agreeable Georgian terraced house in historic part of city centre.

14hc (5🛁 1🚿) (3fb) CTV in 6 bedrooms 🚫🐕 ✱B&b£18–£28 LDO5pm

Lic 🍽 CTV P̸

[V]

Recommended

GH Orchard House Hotel Warminster Rd (A36), Bathampton ☎(0225) 66115 Plan **17A** *F4* rs Xmas

Modern and very comfortable small hotel, with welcoming atmosphere. Bedrooms offer plenty of space, and are very well equipped, with mini-bars and fridges, plus the usual tea- and coffee-making facilities. Small but satisfactory table d'hôte menu for dinner; attentive service.

14🛁🚿 (3fb) CTV in all bedrooms [R] ✱B&b£18–£20 Bdi£25.50–£27.50 W£160–£175 Ⱡ

Lic 🍽 14P sauna bath solarium

Credit cards [1] [2] [3] [5] [V]

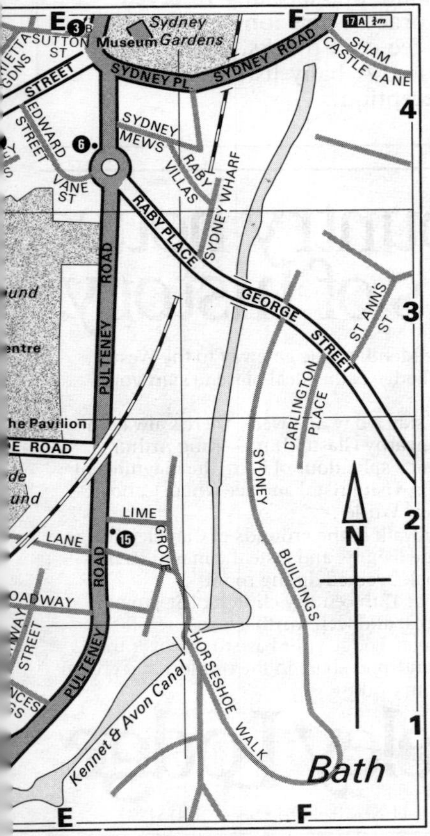

Bath

1 Arden Hotel
2 Arney
3 Ashley Villa Hotel
3A Astor House
3B Avon Hotel
4 Carfax Hotel
5 Charnwood House
5A Chesterfield Hotel
6 County Hotel (*Inn*)
7 Dorset Villa
8 Edgar Hotel
9 Gainsborough Hotel
10 Glenbeigh Hotel
11 Grove Lodge
12 Highways House
13 Kennard Hotel
14 Leighton House
15 Lynwood
16 Millers Hotel
17 Oldfields
17A Orchard House Hotel
18 Oxford Private Hotel
19 Paradise House Hotel
20 Hotel St Clair
22 Tacoma
23 Villa Magdala Private Hotel
24 Waltons
25 Wentworth House Hotel

GH *Oldfields* 102 Wells Rd ☎(0225) 317984 Plan **17** *A1*
Closed mid Dec–mid Jan
Detached house with garden promoting Victorian elegance and attentive service.
14hc (1🛁 7🚿) (2fb) TV in all bedrooms 🐕 [R]
🍴 8P
Credit cards [1] [3]

GH Oxford Private Hotel 5 Oxford Row, Lansdown Rd ☎(0225) 314039 Plan **18** *C4*
8hc (3🚿) (1fb) 🐕 ✱B&b£18–£20 W£108–£120 M
CTV 🅿
Credit cards [1] [2] [3] [5]

GH Paradise House Hotel Holloway (Guestaccom) ☎(0225) 317723 Plan **19** *B1*
Closed 15 Dec–15 Jan
An elegant, comfortably appointed hotel in cul-de-sac overlooking the city. Splendid walled garden.
8hc (5🛁 1🚿) (1fb) CTV in all bedrooms 🐕 [R] ✱B&b£15–£34 Bdi£23 W£95–£210 M
🍴 CTV 3P 3🚗
Credit cards [1] [3] [V]

GH Hotel St Clair 1 Cresent Gdns, Upper Bristol Rd ☎(0225) 25543 Plan **20** *A3*
10hc (2🚿) (1fb) CTV in all bedrooms [R] B&b£12–£20
Lic 🍴 🅿 nc3yrs
Credit card [3] [V]

GH Tacoma 159 Newbridge Hill ☎(0225) 310197 Plan **22** *A3*
Closed Xmas & New Year
8hc (3fb) 🐕 [R] ✱B&b£9–£12
🍴 CTV 5P
[V]

GH Villa Magdala Private Hotel Henrietta Rd ☎(0225) 66329 Plan **23** *D4*
Closed Jan
17hc (13🛁 4🚿) (3fb) CTV in all bedrooms 🐕 [R] ✱B&b£19.50–£21 (W only Nov–Mar)
🍴 14P 1🚗 nc6yrs

GH Waltons 17 Crescent Gdns ☎(0225) 26528 Plan **24** *B3*
16hc (2fb) B&b£11–£15 LDO4pm
Lic 🍴 CTV 🅿

GH Wentworth House Hotel 106 Bloomfield Rd ☎(0225) 339193 Plan **25** *B1*
20hc (6🛁 4🚿) (4fb) CTV in 10 bedrooms TV in 10 bedrooms [R] ✱B&b£11–£19 Bdi£17–£26.50 W£113.40–£166.95 L LDO6pm
Lic 🍴 CTV 20P 🏊
Credit cards [1] [3] [5] [V]
See advertisement on page 58

INN County Hotel 18–19 Pulteney Rd ☎(0225) 25003. Plan **6** *E4*
Closed Xmas
23hc (1🛁 11🚿) (1fb) CTV in 12 bedrooms ✱B&b£18.50–£32.50 W£116.55–£204.75 M Bar lunch £2alc Dinner 10pm £10alc
🍴 CTV 60P
Credit card [3]

BATTLE
East Sussex
Map **5** TQ71

FH Mrs A Benton ***Little Hemingfold*** *(TQ774149)* Telham (2½m SE on N side of A210) ☎(04246) 2910
Picturesque, part-17th-century farmhouse in 26 acres with lovely sheltered garden. Has peaceful, well-equipped bedrooms.
13🛁 CTV in all bedrooms [R]
Lic 🍴 20P nc12yrs 🎾 (grass) 🎣 26acres mixed
See advertisement on page 58

BEAMINSTER
Dorset
Map **3** ST40

Recommended

GH Hams Plot Bridport Rd ☎(0308) 862979
Apr–Sep
An elegant Regency country house with attractive bedrooms, majestic public areas and friendly service.
5hc (3⇌ 2fl) ✈ Ⓡ ✱B&b£13–£16 LDOnoon
Lic 🛏 CTV 7P nc10yrs ⛵ 🎾 (hard)

BEATTOCK
Dumfries & Galloway *Dumfriesshire*
Map **11** NT00

FH Mr & Mrs Bell ***Cogrie's*** *(NY106974)* (3m S off A74) ☎Johnstone Bridge (05764) 320
Mar–Nov
Tidy little house standing in a wooded copse.
2rm (1hc) (2fb) ✈ LDO7.30pm
🛏 CTV 4P 275acres dairy mixed

BEAULY
Highland *Inverness-shire*
Map **14** NH54

GH Chrialdon Station Rd ☎(0463) 782336
Mar–Dec
Detached house in own grounds on main road.
8hc (2fb) ✈ Ⓡ ✱B&bfr£9.50 Bdifr£15 Wfr£105 λLDO7pm
Lic 🛏 CTV 15P
Ⓥ

GH Heathmount Station Rd ☎(0463) 782411
Closed Xmas & New Year
Comfortable, well-appointed accommodation situated on a main road, close to shops.
5hc (2fb) ✱B&b£9–£9.50 Bdi£15–£15.50 W£105–£108.50 λLDO6pm
Lic 🛏 CTV 5P

FH Mrs M R Munro **Thornhill** *(NH531475)* ☎(0463) 782338
May–Sep
Attractive, well-appointed farm-house set back from main road near town.
3hc ✱B&b£8–£8.50 Bdi£12–£12.50 W£80 λLDO4pm
🛏 CTV 4P nc10yrs
100acres arable
Ⓥ

Recommended

FH Mrs E Munro **Tomich House** *(NH531480)* (1m N A862) ☎(0463) 782225
Apr–Oct
Beautifully furnished Georgian farmhouse near woodland.
3hc ✈ ✱B&b£10 Wfr£70 M
🛏 CTV P nc9yrs ✂ Ư
600acres arable beef sheep mixed
Ⓥ

BEAUMARIS
Gwynedd
Map **6** SH67

Recommended

INN Liverpool Arms ☎(0248) 810362
Attractive coaching inn, recently modernised but retaining its character.
10hc (8⇌ 2fl) CTV in all bedrooms ✈ Ⓡ ✱B&b£22–£30 Bar lunch £4alc Dinner 9.30pm £7.50alc
🛏 8P 🏨 nc5yrs
Credit cards 1 3 4 5 Ⓥ

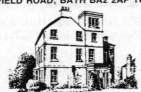

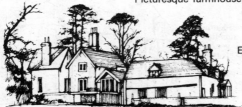

GH Sea View 10 West End ☎(0248) 810384
Closed Xmas
Single-fronted Victorian house at water's edge adjacent to the shops.
6hc ✖ ✱B&b£9–£10 Bdifr£17
CTV 5P nc10yrs

BECCLES
Suffolk
Map **5** TM49

GH Riverview House Ballygate (Guestaccom) ☎(0502) 713519
Closed 20 Dec–4 Jan
12rm (11hc) (1🚿) (2fb) CTV in all bedrooms [R] B&b£11.50–£14.50 Bdi£18–£21 W£120–£141 Ⱡ LDO10am
🍴 CTV P̸
[V]

BEDDGELERT
Gwynedd
Map **6** SH54

GH Sygyn Fawr Country House Hotel ☎(076686) 258
18th-century stone country house in own grounds ½m from village.
7hc (3🛁 3🚿) (1fb) [R] ✱B&b£13–£16.50 Bdi£20.35–£23.85 W£129–£150 Ⱡ LDO7.30pm
Lic CTV 30P
[V]

BEDFORD
Bedfordshire
Map **4** TL04

GH Clarendon House Hotel 25/27 Ampthill Rd ☎(0234) 66054
Closed 24 Dec–3 Jan
Comfortable Edwardian house run by young professional couple.
12hc (5🚿) (1fb) CTV in all bedrooms ✖ [R] ✱B&b£15–£25 Bdi£31–£41 W£217–£287 Ⱡ LDO7.45pm
Lic 🍴 CTV 16P
Credit cards [1] [2] [3] [5]

GH *Hurst House Hotel* 178 Hurst Gv ☎(0234) 40791
6hc (2fb) CTV in all bedrooms [R] LDO7.30pm
Lic 🍴 CTV 5P
Credit cards [1] [2] [3] [5]

GH Kimbolton Hotel 78 Clapham Rd ☎(0234) 54854
Closed 25–31 Dec
Three storey Victorian house, family-run on traditional lines.
15hc (2🛁 11🚿) CTV in all bedrooms ✖ [R] ✱B&b£16–£27.60 Bdi£23–£34.60 W£219 Ⱡ LDO8.30pm
Lic 🍴 CTV 15P nc3yrs
Credit card [3]
See advertisement on page 60

BEER
Devon
Map **3** SY28

GH Bay View Fore St ☎Seaton (0297) 20489
Etr–mid Oct
Property at end of village overlooking the beach and sea.
6hc (2fb) ✱B&b£9–£10 W£63 Ḿ
🍴 CTV P̸ nc5yrs

BEERCROCOMBE
Somerset
Map **3** ST32

FH Mrs V A Cole **Frog Street Farm** Frog St *(ST317197)* ☎Hatch Beauchamp (0823) 480430
Closed Xmas
Attractive stone and beamed farmhouse with swimming pool and trout stream. →

3hc (1⇄ 1🚿) (1fb) ✂ ® ✳B&b£11–£15
Bdi£19–£23 W£127–£155 ⅃ LDO4pm
♨ CTV 4P ♨ ⌷(heated) ♩
160acres mixed
Ⓥ

Recommended

FH Mrs C M Mitchem **Whittles**
(ST324194) ☎Hatch Beauchamp
(0823) 480301
15 Jan–10 Dec (rs 16 Jan–Feb &
Nov–9 Dec)

*Superb accommodation in peaceful
surroundings are assured at this
friendly farmhouse.*

4hc (3⇄🚿) (1fb) CTV in 3 bedrooms
TV in 1 bedroom ✂ ® ✳B&b£12.50–
£19.50 Bdi£19–£26 W£130.50–
£179.50 ⅃ LDO11.30am

Lic ♨ 6P nc12yrs 200acres dairy
Ⓥ
See advertisement under Taunton

BEESTON
Nottinghamshire
Map **8**   SK53

GH Brackley House Hotel 31 Elm Av
☎Nottingham (0602) 251787
rs no meals Sun

14hc (3⇄ 7🚿) (1fb) CTV in all bedrooms
✂ ✳B&b£22.50–£28 Bdi£32.50–£38

Beercrocombe
—
Belton

Lic ♨ CTV 20P
Credit cards ① ② ③ Ⓥ

GH Fairhaven Private Hotel 19 Meadow
Rd, Rylands ☎Nottingham (0602) 227509

*Large house 3½m SW of Nottingham and
close to Beeston Station. Simple but
comfortable accommodation.*

11hc (1fb) ✂ ✳B&b£7.50–£11 Bdi£10.50–
£14.50 W£73.50–£91 ⅃ LDOnoon

Lic ♨ CTV 12P

BELFORD
Northumberland
Map **12**   NU13

INN Black Swan Market Sq ☎(06683)
266

*Simple village inn with informal
atmosphere. Situated in village centre on
A1.*

9hc (1 ⇄) (3fb) ® LDO8pm
CTV 24P

BELL BUSK
North Yorkshire
Map **7**   SD95

GH Tudor ☎Airton (07293) 301

*This friendly hospitable little guesthouse
by the Settle–Carlisle line was once Bell
Busk station.*

6hc (2fb) TV in 1 bedroom ✂ ®
✳B&b£8.50 Bdi£13.25 W£75–£92 ⅃
LDO7pm

Lic ♨ CTV P nc5yrs

BELSTONE
Devon
Map **2**   SX69

INN Tors ☎Okehampton (0837) 840689

3hc (1fb) CTV in 2 bedrooms ® ✳B&b£9–
£10 Bdi£13.50–£14.50 W£95–£100 ⅃
Lunch £2.50–£3.75&alc High tea £1.50
Dinner 9.30pm £3.50–£5&alc
♨ CTV 10P

BELTON
Leicestershire
Map **4**   SK80

FH Mrs S L Renner **Old Rectory**
(SK814008) ☎(057286) 279

*Lovely old house incorporating a rural
museum, craft shop, a miniature farm and
a children's play area.*

4hc (2fb) CTV in all bedrooms ®
✳B&b£5–£9.50 Wfr£60 Ⓜ

lift ♨ CTV 10P 🚗 ♨ 30acres beef
pastural sheep

Kimbolton Hotel

"Small Enough To Care—Large Enough to Know How"

- SUPERB ROOMS AND GARDENS
- FULLY LICENSED BAR
- COLOUR TV's & SHOWERS
- TRADITIONAL ENGLISH CUISINE
- FRIENDLY PERSONAL SERVICE
- CLOSE TO ALL AMENITIES

THE PERFECT SETTING FOR:
WEDDINGS AND BUSINESS FUNCTIONS
BEDFORD (0234) 54854
76 CLAPHAM ROAD, BEDFORD

Brackley House Hotel

Hildegard's German Restaurant & Wine Bar
31 Elm Avenue, Beeston, Nottingham NG9 1BU
Telephone: 0602 251787

Situated 4 miles south west of Nottingham city centre, in quiet residential
surroundings, it is ideally suited for business or pleasure and is close to
East Midlands Airport and the University, off exit 25 of the M1 motorway.
The hotel stands in its own pleasant and extensive gardens, there are 14
bedrooms all with colour TV, video system and hot and cold water. A
comfortable residents' lounge with colour television and a separate licensed
bar lounge. The large dining room can also be used for conferences, parties,
wedding receptions and business meetings. Pool room. Antique jewellery
sold in hotel foyer. There are excellent parking facilities and a large garden
which can be enjoyed by its residents and non residents. The owner Mrs
Hildegard Ryan provides High Class standards with a friendly Continental
atmosphere.

TAS Listed   **BTB Listed**

BENSON
Oxfordshire
Map **4** SU69

INN Castle Castle Sq ☎Wallingford (0491) 35349
Small village inn with well-appointed bedrooms.
4hc (1fb) CTV in all bedrooms Ⓡ ✱B&b£15–£22 Bdi£20–£27 Lunch £4.50alc Dinner 9.45pm £5.50alc
♨ 15P 🚌
Credit cards [1] [2] [3] [5]

BEPTON (nr Midhurst)
West Sussex
Map **4** SU81

GH Park House Hotel ☎Midhurst (073081) 2880
Part-17th-century house with homely welcome and accommodation. Set in attractive lawns for croquet, putting and tennis.
9🛁🚿 Annexe: 2🛁🚿 (1fb) CTV in all bedrooms Ⓡ ✱B&b£28.75–£34.50 Bdi£37.50–£40.50 W£241.50–£257 Ⱡ LDO8pm
Lic ♨ CTV 20P 2🚗 🏊 (heated) 🎾 (grass)

BERKELEY
Gloucestershire
Map **3** ST69

FH Mrs B A Evans **Greenacres** *(ST713008)* Breadstone (2m E off A38) ☎Dursley (0453) 810348
16th-century house with beams and inglenook fireplaces.
4hc (1🛁 1🚿) (1fb) 🚫 Ⓡ B&b£11.50–£13.75 Bdi£18.75 W£75–£113 Ⱡ LDO6.30pm
♨ CTV 10P 47acres horse breeding
Ⓥ

BERRYNARBOR
Devon
Map **2** SS54

GH Lodge Country House ☎Combe Martin (027188) 3246
Closed Xmas

Benson — Bickington

6hc Annexe: 1hc (2fb) ✱B&b£9–£10 Bdi£13–£15 W£83–£90 Ⱡ LDO7pm
Lic ♨ CTV 7P nc2yrs
Ⓥ

See advertisement on page 130

BETHESDA
Gwynedd
Map **6** SH66

FH Mrs D Williams **Maes Caradog** *(SH635626)* Nant Ffrancon ☎(0248) 600266
Pleasant stone-farmhouse amidst mountain scenery.
2hc (1fb) 🚫 ✱B&b£7.50–£8 Bdi£11.50–£12 W£80–£84 Ⱡ LDO6.30pm
♨ CTV 10P 636acres sheep
Ⓥ

BETWS GARMON
Gwynedd
Map **6** SH55

GH *Bryn Gloch Farm* ☎Waunfawr (028685) 216
Converted farmhouse with glorious views, on edge of Snowdonia National Park.
3hc (1fb) LDO6pm
Lic CTV 8P 🎣

BETWS-Y-COED
Gwynedd
Map **6** SH75

GH Bryn Llewelyn Holyhead Rd (A5) ☎(06902) 601
Three-storey building near the village centre.
7hc (3fb) 🚫 ✱B&b£7.50–£9
♨ CTV 10P

GH Glenwood ☎(06902) 508
Feb–Oct
Attractive house with good standard of accommodation, set back from main road.
6hc (3fb) 🚫 ✱B&b£12–£14
♨ CTV 12P nc4yrs
Ⓥ

GH Hafan ☎(06902) 233
Detached Victorian house in rural surroundings, near centre of village.
7hc (4🚿) (4fb) CTV in 6 bedrooms 🚫 Ⓡ ✱B&b£9–£13.50 W£63–£94.50 M
Lic ♨ CTV 7P
Ⓥ

GH Henllys (Old Court) Hotel ☎(06902) 534
Converted police station and cells, adjacent to village centre.
11hc (3🛁 4🚿) (2fb) CTV in all bedrooms Ⓡ ✱B&b£13.50–£18.50 Bdi£22.45–£27.45 W£148.20–£183.20 Ⱡ LDO8.30pm
Lic ♨ 12P nc4yrs
Ⓥ

GH Mount Garmon Hotel ☎(06902) 335
Mar–Oct
Victorian semi-detached house alongside the A5 in the centre of village.
5hc (3🚿) 🚫 B&b£10–£17 Bdi£17–£24 W£115–£150 Ⱡ LDO4pm
Lic ♨ CTV 7P nc3yrs
Ⓥ

BEXHILL-ON-SEA
East Sussex
Map **5** TQ70

GH Chantry Close Hotel 13 Hastings Rd ☎(0424) 222024
Mar–Oct
Mock-Tudor house in own grounds with comfortable, well-appointed bedrooms.
7hc (1🛁 1🚿) (2fb) CTV 2 bedrooms 🚫 Ⓡ ✱B&b£12–£14 Bdi£17.50–£19.50 W£112.50–£125.50 Ⱡ LDO5pm
♨ CTV 6P nc3yrs

BICKINGTON (nr Ashburton)
Devon
Map **3** SX77

GH Privet Cottage ☎(062682) 319
May–Sep →

Attractive, white-stone, cottage-style house in central position for touring south Devon.

6hc ✗ ✱B&b£8.50–£9.50 Bdi£14.50–£15.50 LDO6.30pm

CTV 6P 🏠

FH Mr & Mrs Ross **East Burne** *(SX799711)* ☎(062682) 496
Closed Xmas & New Year

Isolated farmhouse of great charm with modern, fitted bedrooms.

3rm (2hc 1🚿) ✗ [R] ✱B&b£9–£10 Bdi£15–£16 W£95 Ł LDO24hrs notice

CTV 8P 🏊 (heated) 25acres mixed

[V]

BICKLEIGH (nr Tiverton)
Devon
Map **3** SS90

GH Bickleigh Cottage ☎(08845) 230
May–Sep rs Apr & Oct

10hc (2🛁 1🚿) ✗ [R] ✱B&b£10.50–£15 Bdi£16.25–£20.75 W£113.75–£145.25 Ł LDO5pm

CTV 10P nc10yrs 🎣

BIDEFORD
Devon
Map **2** SS42

GH *Edelweiss* 2 Buttgarden St ☎(02372) 72676
rs Jan (B&b only)

Proprietor-run guesthouse with à la carte restaurant.

8hc (2fb)

Lic 🍸 CTV 🚫 nc5yrs

Credit cards [1] [2] [3] [5]

GH Kumba Chudleigh Rd, East-the-Water ☎(02372) 71526

Comfortable, detached country-house, situated in private road overlooking the town and River Torridge.

9hc (1🚿) (5fb) 🚭 in 4 bedrooms ✱B&b£8.50–£10.50 Bdi£12.50–£14.50 W£80–£94 Ł LDO4pm

Lic CTV 10P 2🚗 🏠

[V]

GH *Mount Private Hotel* Northdown Rd ☎(02372) 73748

Detached Georgian house standing in attractive walled garden with terrace at front.

6hc (1🛁 2🚿) (2fb) TV in 2 bedrooms ✗ LDOnoon

Lic 🍸 CTV 4P

Bickington — Bideford

GH Pine's Farmhouse Hotel Eastleigh (3m E off A39 at East-the-Water) ☎Instow (0271) 860561
Mar–Oct

Delightful, friendly, Georgian house with large gardens and glorious views.

8hc (2fb) ✗ [R] ✱B&b£11.50–£14 Bdi£18–£19.50 W£116–£126.50 Ł LDO5pm

Lic 🍸 CTV nc4yrs

Credit cards [1] [3] [V]

GH Sonnenheim Hotel & Restaurant Heywood Rd, Northam ☎(02372) 74989

Comfortable manor house standing in its own grounds. Attractive bar and dining room, with small but interesting à-la-carte menu.

9hc (2🛁 1🚿) (2fb) CTV in all bedrooms [R] ✱B&b£12.50–£15 Bdi£19–£22.50 W£122.50–£133 Ł LDO9pm

Lic 🍸 CTV 12P

Credit cards [1] [3] [V]

GH *Tadworthy House Hotel* Tadworthy Rd, Northam (2m N off A386) ☎(02372) 74721

A 16th-century family-run hotel close to the sea and the Royal North Devon Golf Club.

6hc (1🚿) (2fb) CTV in 4 bedrooms TV in 2 bedrooms [R] LDO8.30pm

Lic CTV 10P

BIDFORD-ON-AVON
Warwickshire
Map **4** SP15

Recommended

FH Mrs T G N Windsor **Bidford Grange** *(SD117517)* ☎(0789) 773367

This charming Cotswold-stone farmhouse is situated on the banks of the River Avon in 500 acres of rolling Warwickshire countryside. This is the place to stay if you like luxurious, comfortable accommodation and warm, attentive hospitality in beautiful surroundings.

3🛁🚿 (1fb) CTV in all bedrooms 🐕 Ⓡ ✱B&b£13–£17.50 Bdi£22.50–£26.50 W£141.75–£166.95 Ł LDO8.30pm

🛋 CTV 100P 20🚗 nc7yrs 🏊 🎾(grass) ⛳ croquet sauna bath 500acres arable

Credit card [2]

BILLINGSHURST
West Sussex
Map **4** TQ02

GH Newstead Hall Adversane ☎(040381) 3196

7🛁🚿 (2fb) CTV in all bedrooms Ⓡ ✱B&b£15–£23 Bdi£22–£30 W£141–£194 Ł LDO10pm

Lic 🛋 CTV 17P

Credit cards [1] [2] [3] [5] Ⓥ

BINGLEY
West Yorkshire
Map **7** SE13

GH Hall Bank Private Hotel Beck Ln ☎Bradford (0274) 565296
Closed Xmas

Conversion of an old mill owner's house has provided large, comfortable rooms, plus conservatory, in lovely Aire valley setting.

8hc (2🛁 2🚿) Annexe: 2hc (2fb) CTV in all bedrooms Ⓡ ✱B&b£14–£19 Bdi£20–£25 W£120–£160 Ł LDO7.30pm

🛋 CTV 20P nc2yrs

Ⓥ

FH Mr & Mrs G Warin **March Cote** *(SE103374)* Cottingley (2m S B6146) ☎Bradford (0274) 487433
Closed Xmas & New Year

Extended and modernised 17th-century farmhouse retaining many original features.

2rm (1fb) CTV in 1 bedroom TV in 1 bedroom 🐕 Ⓡ ✱B&b£7.50–£9 Bdi£12–£13.50 W£80.50–£94.50 Ł LDO7pm

CTV 4P 1🚗 U 230acres beef dairy sheep

Ⓥ

BIRKENHEAD
Merseyside
Map **7** SJ38

GH Gronwen 11 Willowbank Rd, Devonshire Park ☎051-652 8306

Pleasantly furnished small guesthouse set in quiet residential area.

5rm Ⓡ ✱B&b£12 Bdi£17

🛋 CTV 🚫

BIRMINGHAM
West Midlands
Map **7** SP08

See plan on pages 64–65

GH Alexander 44 Bunbury Rd ☎021-475 4341 Plan **1**

12hc (2fb) ✱B&b£11.50–£12 Bdi£16.50–£17 Wfr£115.50 Ł

Lic 🛋 CTV 12P

GH Beech House Hotel 21 Gravelly Hill North, Erdington ☎021-373 0620 Plan **1A**
Closed 2 wks Xmas

Friendly, personally run Tudor-style hotel set back from main road.

10hc (2🛁 2🚿) (1fb) CTV in 1 bedroom ✱B&b£16–£18 Bdi£21–£23 W£147–£161 Ł LDOnoon

🛋 CTV 10P nc5yrs

GH *Bridge House Hotel* 49 Sherbourne Rd, Acocks Gn ☎021-706 5900 Plan **2**

18rm (12hc 6🛁 6🚿) (1fb) CTV in 2 bedrooms TV in 6 bedrooms Ⓡ LDO9.30pm

Lic 🛋 CTV P

GH *Cape Race Hotel* 929 Chester Rd, Erdington ☎021-373 3085 Plan **3**

Spacious converted private house with large rear garden containing lawns and hard tennis court.

8hc (4🚿) (2fb) CTV in all bedrooms Ⓡ LDO7pm

Lic 🛋 CTV 12P 🏊 🎾 hard

See advertisement on page 66

GH *Hagley Court Hotel* 229 Hagley Rd, Edgbaston ☎021-454 6514 Plan **4**
Closed Xmas

25hc (8🛁 6🚿) CTV in all bedrooms 🐕 Ⓡ LDO10pm

Lic 🛋 CTV 24P

Credit cards [1] [3]

GH *Heath Lodge Hotel* Coleshill Rd, Marston Green ☎021-779 2218 Plan **5**

15hc (2fb) 🐕 LDO9.30pm

Lic 🛋 CTV 15P

Credit cards [1] [3]

GH Hurstwood Hotel 775–777 Chester Rd, Erdington ☎021-382 8212 Plan **6**

10🚿 (2fb) CTV in all bedrooms 🐕 Ⓡ B&b£18.98 Bdi£25 W£125 Ł LDO9.15pm

Lic 🛋 CTV 15P

Credit cards [1] [2] [3] [5] Ⓥ

See advertisement on page 66

GH Kerry House Hotel 946 Warwick Rd, Acocks Gn ☎021-707 0316 Plan **7**
Closed Xmas

25hc (6🚿) (2fb) CTV in all bedrooms ✱B&b£17.25–£18.40 Bdifr£21 LDO6pm

Lic 🛋 25P nc3yrs

GH Linden Lodge Hotel 79 Sutton Rd, Erdington ☎021-382 5992 Plan **8**

6hc (1fb) 🐕 ✱B&b£10 Bdi£12.50 W£70 M LDO7pm

🛋 CTV 8P

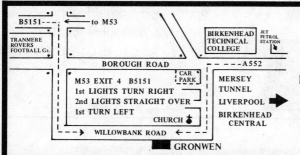

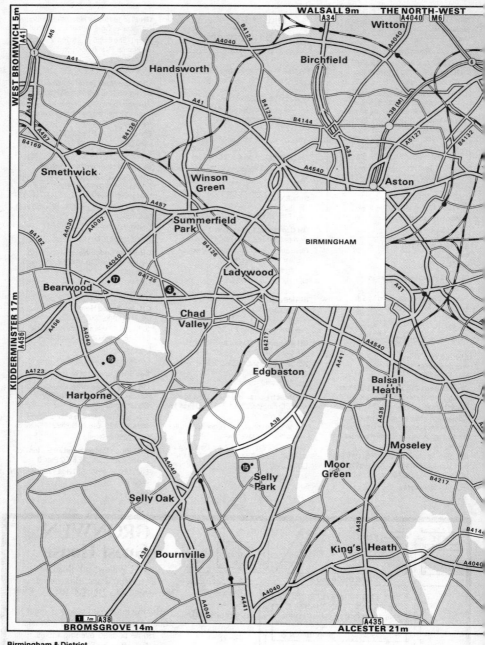

Birmingham & District

1	Alexander	**3**	Cape Race Hotel	**6**	Hurstwood Hotel
1A	Beech House Hotel	**4**	Hagley Court Hotel	**7**	Kerry House Hotel
2	Bridge House Hotel	**5**	Heath Lodge Hotel	**8**	Linden Lodge Hotel

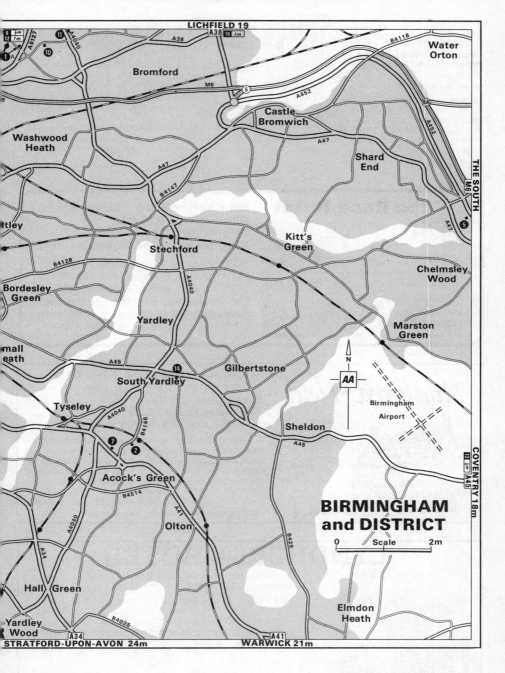

BIRMINGHAM and DISTRICT

Scale 0 — 2m

LICHFIELD 19

Water Orton

Bromford

Castle Bromwich

Washwood Heath

Shard End

Kitt's Green

Chelmsley Wood

Stechford

Bordesley Green

Yardley

Marston Green

Small Heath

South Yardley

Gilbertstone

Birmingham Airport

Tyseley

Sheldon

Acock's Green

Olton

Hall Green

Elmdon Heath

Yardley Wood

THE SOUTH

COVENTRY 18m

STRATFORD-UPON-AVON 24m

WARWICK 21m

10	Lyndhurst Hotel	**13**	Tri-Star Hotel
11	Rollason Wood Hotel	**14**	Welcome House
12	Stanbridge Hotel	**15**	Wentsbury Hotel
	(*Listed under Sutton Coldfield*)		

16	Wentworth Hotel
17	Westbourne Lodge
18	Willow Tree Hotel

65

GH Lyndhurst Hotel 135 Kingsbury Rd, Erdington ☎021-373 5695 Plan **10**

14hc (2🚿) (4fb) CTV in 8 bedrooms ✗ ✻B&b£14–£19 Bdi£20–£25 W£90–£120 M

♨ CTV 15P

Credit cards [1] [2] [3] [5] [V]

GH Rollason Wood Hotel 130 Wood End Rd, Erdington ☎021-373 1230 Plan **11**

35hc (1🛁 9🚿) (3fb) CTV in 10 bedrooms ✗ ✻B&b£8.25–£17.95 W£55.50–£96.60 M LDO9pm

Lic ♨ CTV 50P

Credit cards [1] [2] [3] [5]

Birmingham

GH Tri-Star Hotel Coventry Rd, Elmdon ☎021-779 2233

15hc (2🚿) (3fb) CTV in all bedrooms ✗ [R] ✻B&b£18.40–£23 Bdi£24.15–£28.75 W£169.05–£201.25 L LDO8pm

Lic ♨ CTV 20P

[V]

GH *Welcome House* 1641 Coventry Rd, Yardley ☎021-707 3232 Plan **14** Closed 24–26 Dec

7hc (1🚿) (1fb) CTV in 1 bedroom TV in 6 bedrooms ✗

♨ 8P nc

GH *Wentsbury Hotel* 21 Serpentine Rd, Selly Park ☎021-472 1258 Plan **15**

Large detached house with garden in residential area close to city centre.

9hc (2fb) CTV in 5 bedrooms LDO4pm

♨ CTV 15P 1🚗 🏠

Cape Race Hotel

929 Chester Road · Erdington
Birmingham B24 0HJ
Telephone: 021-373-3085
Proprietors: Brian & Shirley Ford

All bedrooms with colour TV and tea & coffee making facilities, most with shower/toilet. Licensed bar. Central heating. Ample car parking. Tennis Court. 10 minutes from National Exhibition Centre.

Hurstwood Hotel

and Heather's Licensed Restaurant

775/777 Chester Road, Erdington, Birmingham B24 0BY
Telephone: 021-382 8212
Near NEC plus M5 and M6 motorways

A family hotel offering high quality accommodation and service. Ten bedrooms each with shower and toilet en suite, colour TV and tea and coffee making facilities. Central heating. Television and reading lounge. Ample car parking. Morning coffee. Lunch. Afternoon tea. Dinner. Special weekly and weekend rates. Conference facilities, on the spot secretarial and photocopying service.

LYNDHURST HOTEL

135 Kingsbury Road, Erdington, Birmingham B24 8QT.
Telephone: 021-373-5695

★ Private & Commercial ★ Twenty Bedrooms — Some En Suite ★ Two Lounges (one with colour TV) ★ Portable TV's available ★ Centrally heated & modern throughout ★ Ten minutes City Centre ★ ½ mile "Spaghetti Junction" M6 Junc 6 ★ Easy reach National Exhibition Centre ★ On City bus route (No 114) ★ Free car park ★ Credit Cards Accepted.

Bed & Breakfast, Dinner optional

Resident Proprietor: Robert J. Williams

GH Wentworth Hotel 103 Wentworth Rd, Harbone ☎021–427 2839 Plan **16**
Closed Xmas wk

21hc (2⋒) (1fb) CTV in all bedrooms ®
✱B&b£15–£20 Bdi£21.50–£26.50
LDO8pm

Lic ⚄ CTV 14P 2☎

GH Westbourne Lodge 27–29 Fountain Rd, Edgbaston ☎021–429 1003 Plan **17**
Closed Xmas wk

18hc (8⊸5 2⋒) (1fb) CTV in 10 bedrooms
✱B&b£14.95–£24.15 Bdi£23–£32.20
W£146–£201.25 ⅃ LDO7pm

Lic ⚄ CTV 12P ⅋

Credit cards ① ③ ⓥ

GH Willow Tree Hotel 759 Chester Rd, Erdington ☎021-373 6388 Plan **18**
rs Xmas

Small, comfortable hotel on the outskirts of the City. Large rear garden.

7hc (5⋒) (2fb) CTV in all bedrooms ✖ ®
✱B&b£16.10–£21.28 Bdi£19.50–£30
W£131–£205 ⅃ LDO8.30pm

Lic ⚄ CTV 7P

ⓥ

BISHOP'S CLEEVE
Gloucestershire
Map **3**   SO92

GH Old Manor House 43 Station Rd
☎(024267) 4127

Birmingham

Blackpool

6hc (3fb) ✖ ® ✱B&bfr£9.50 Wfr£66.50 ₥
CTV 6P

BISHOP SUTTON
Avon
Map **3**   ST55

FH Mrs R M Shellard **Overbrook**
(ST585607) Stowey Bottom ☎Chew
Magna (0272) 332648
rs Xmas

Attractive, comfortable farmhouse with 3½acres of land. Trout fishing in Chew Valley Lake.

2hc ® B&b£8.50–£9 Bdi£14–£15
LDO11am

⚄ CTV 4P 1☎

3½acres sheep

ⓥ

BISHOPSTON
West Glamorgan
Map **2**   SS58

See also **Langland Bay** and **Mumbles**

GH *Winston Hotel* 11 Church Ln,
Bishopston Valley ☎(044128) 2074
Closed 24–29 Dec

Well-equipped small hotel with good indoor heated-pool, sauna and solarium.

14rm (3hc 3⋒) Annexe: 5hc (4⊸5 1⋒) (2fb) CTV in 5 bedrooms ®

Lic ⚄ CTV 20P ☐ (heated) snooker sauna bath

See advertisement under Swansea

BISHOP WILTON
Humberside
Map **8**   SE75

INN *Fleece* ☎(07596) 251

Village inn on edge of Yorkshire Wold with good standard of rooms. Bar meals or à-la-carte menu for lunch and dinner.

4hc ✖ LDO9pm

⚄ CTV 20P ⇷ nc12yrs

BLACKPOOL
Lancashire
Map **7**   SD33

See plan on page 68

GH Arandora Star Private Hotel
559 New South Prom ☎(0253) 41528
Plan **1** *A1*

Family-run seafront hotel.

18hc (3fb) ✱B&b£9.20–£10.50 Bdi£10.35–£11.50 W£72.35–£80.50 ⅃ LDO5pm

Lic ⚄ CTV 12P 8☎ (charge)

Credit cards ③ ⓥ

See advertisement on page 69

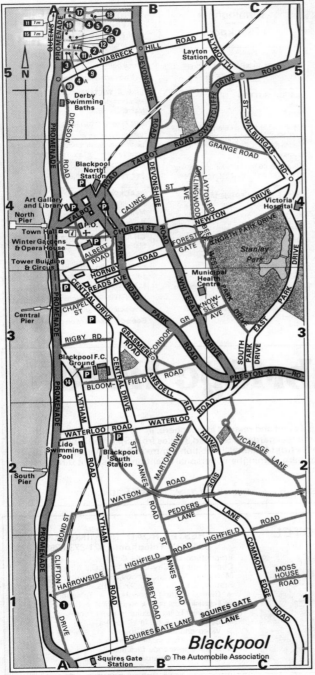

GH Arosa Hotel 18–20 Empress Dr
☎(0253) 52555 Plan **2** A5
Mar–Nov & Xmas

Well-furnished modern hotel just off the Promenade.

21hc (2⇨7🛏) (5fb) ®
✱B&b£12–£15 Bdi£13.80–£18.50 W£108–£130 ⅃

Lic 🎵 CTV 7P

GH Ashcroft Private Hotel 42 King
Edward Av ☎(0253) 51538 Plan **2A** A5
Apr–Oct

Attractively-furnished hotel, just off the Queens Promenade.

10hc (4fb) CTV in 5 bedrooms ®
B&b£8.50–£10.50 Bdi£10.50–£13.50
W£65–£83 ⅃ LDO2.30pm

Lic 🎵 CTV 5P

Ⓥ

GH Berwick Private Hotel 23 King
Edward Av ☎(0253) 51496 Plan **3** A5
Mar–Oct

Set in a quiet side road, this is a modern, well-furnished hotel with friendly atmosphere.

8hc (2fb) ✖ ® B&b£8.50–£12.50 Bdi£10–£14.50 W£70–£91 ⅃ LDO3pm

Lic 🎵 CTV 4P nc3yrs

GH Brabyns Hotel 1–3 Shaftesbury Av
☎(0253) 54263 Plan **4** A5

Detached modernised hotel in side road just off the Promenade.

22rm (19⇨3🛏) Annexe: 3hc (1⇨2🛏) (9fb) CTV in all bedrooms ® ✱B&b£18–£21 Bdi£21.50–£24.50 Wfr£130 ⅃ LDO6pm

Lic 🎵 CTV 12P

Credit cards ① ③

GH Brooklands Hotel 28–30 King
Edward Av ☎(0253) 51479 Plan **4A** A5
An attractive hotel set in a quiet side road off the North Promenade.

Blackpool

1 Arandora Star Private Hotel
2 Arosa Hotel
2A Ashcroft Private Hotel
3 Berwick Private Hotel
4 Brabyns Hotel
4A Brooklands Hotel
5 Burlees Hotel
7 Cliftonville Hotel
9 Denely Private Hotel
10 Derwent Private Hotel
11 Garville
11A Hartshead Hotel
12 Lynstead Private Hotel
14 Motel Mimosa
15 New Heathcot Private Hotel
16 North Mount Private Hotel
17 Sunnycliff
18 Sunray Private Hotel
19 Surrey House Hotel

16hc (4🛁) (3fb) CTV in 6 bedrooms ✗ ® ✱B&b£9.80–£13.80 Bdi£11–£17.95 LDO5pm

Lic ⌘ CTV 5P

GH Burlees Hotel 40 Knowle Av ☎(0253) 54535 Plan **5** *A5*
Apr–Nov (rs Etr–May)

Pleasantly situated family-run hotel a short walk from the Promenade.

10hc (2fb) ® ✱B&b£9.50–£10 Bdi£13.50–£14.50 W£90–£98 ⱡ

CTV 5P 1🚗 ⌂

Ⓥ

Blackpool

GH Cliftonville Hotel 14 Empress Dr, Northshore ☎(0253) 51052 Plan **7** *A5*
Apr–Nov & Xmas

A lift, and bedrooms with private facilities, are features of this private hotel near the sea front.

19🛁 (8fb) ✗ ® B&b£9–£16 Bdi£11–£18 W£79–£110 ⱡ LDO5pm

Lic lift ⌘ CTV 5P solarium

Credit cards 1 3 Ⓥ

GH Denely Private Hotel 15 King Edward Av ☎(0253) 52757 Plan **9** *A5*

A delightful, small, privately-run hotel in a quiet side road on the north shore.

9hc (1🛁) (2fb) ✗ ® ✱B&b£8.90–£9 Bdi £10.50–£10.65 W£73.50–£74.55 ⱡ LDO4.30pm

⌘ CTV 6P (charge)

See advertisement on page 70

GH Derwent Private Hotel 8 Gynn Av ☎(0253) 55194 Plan **10** *A5*

A friendly, well-furnished hotel occupying a middle terrace in a quiet road. →

12hc (4⑪) (2fb) ✳B&b£10–£12.50
Bdi£12.50–£15 W£80–£95 ⱡ (W only Jun–
Aug) LDO2pm
Lic ⑪ CTV 5P 1☎ nc3yrs

GH Garville 3 Beaufort Av, Bispham (2m
N) ☎(0253) 51004 Plan **11** *A5*
Closed Dec

*Attractive small hotel in side road of
Blackpool's north end.*

7hc (2⇄) (2fb) ⱡ in 1 bedroom ✳B&b£7
Bdi£9.75 Wfr£68.25 ⱡ LDO5pm

Lic ⑪ CTV 5P

GH Hartshead Hotel 17 King Edward Av
☎(0253) 53133 Plan **11A** *A5*

Blackpool

*A well-run, friendly house with good
furnishings. Set in a quiet side road just
off the promenade.*

10hc (1⇄ 1⑪) (2fb) ✠ Ⓡ ✳B&b£8–£9
Bdi£9.50–£12 W£66.50–£84 ⱡ LDO3pm

Lic ⑪ CTV 6P nc3yrs

Ⓥ

GH Lynstead Private Hotel 40 King
Edward Av ☎(0253) 51050 Plan **12** *A5*

Closed first 2 wks Jan

*The 'Tram Bar' is a unique feature of this
modern hotel in a quiet road.*

10hc (5⑪) (4fb) ✠ Ⓡ LDO3pm

Lic lift ⑪ CTV

GH Motel Mimosa 24A Lonsdale Rd
☎(0253) 41906 Plan **14** *A3*

*Small motel-style establishment with
spacious and comfortable bedrooms.*

15hc (9⇄ 6⑪) CTV in all bedrooms Ⓡ
B&bfr£9.95 Wfr£69 M

⑪ 12P 2☎ gymnasium

Credit cards ① ③ Ⓥ

Blackpool

GH New Heathcot Private Hotel
270 Queens Prom ☎(0253) 52083
Plan **15** *A5*
Closed Jan
A pleasant, small, family-run guesthouse on the North Shore overlooking the sea.
9hc (4fb) ✱B&b£8–£10 Bdi£11–£12
W£77–£84 Ⱡ LDO5pm
Lic Ⅲ CTV 6P
Ⓥ

GH North Mount Private Hotel
22 King Edward Av ☎(0253) 55937 Plan **16** *A5*
A charming, personally-run guesthouse on the north shore in peaceful surroundings.
8hc (2fb) Ⓡ ✱B&b£9–£10 Bdi£10.50–£12
W£70–£84 Ⱡ LDO3pm
Lic Ⅲ CTV 1P
Ⓥ

GH Sunnycliff 98 Queens Prom, Northshore ☎(0253) 51155 Plan **17** *A5*
Mar–Xmas
Seaside hotel with modern frontage, family-owned and run.
12hc (4fb) Ⓡ B&b£8.75–£9 Bdi£11–£12
W£77–£84 Ⱡ LDO5pm
Lic CTV 8P
Ⓥ

GH Sunray Private Hotel 42 Knowle Av, Queens Prom (Guestaccom) ☎(0253) 51937 Plan **18** *A5*
Closed Xmas & New Year
Comfortable small hotel in quiet residential area, close to Queens Promenade and Blackpool's many attractions.
→

9hc (1⇆8⦰) (2fb) CTV in all bedrooms ®
B&b£14–£16 Bdi£19–£23 W£133–£156 ₭
LDO2pm
⛨ CTV 6P

GH Surrey House Hotel
9 Northumberland Av ☎(0253) 51743
Plan **19** A5
Apr–Oct rs Mar & early Nov
Excellent hospitality is offered at this
small hotel in a quiet residential area.
11hc (2⇆7⦰) (2fb) ⚥ in 1 bedroom ®
✳B&b£7.50–£9.50 Bdi£10.75–£13 W£72–
£84 ₭ LDO4.30pm
⛨ CTV 6P 1⚘ nc3months
Ⓥ

Blackpool — Blairgowrie

BLACKWOOD
Gwent
Map **3**   ST19

INN *Plas* Gordon Rd ☎(0495) 224674
Comfortable and popular family-run inn
enjoying elevated location.
6rm (4⦰) CTV in all bedrooms ®
LDO9.45pm
⛨ 80P
Credit cards ① ③

BLAENAU FFESTINIOG
Gwynedd
Map **6**   SH74

GH *Don* 147 High St ☎(0766) 830403
Three-storey stone Victorian house near
centre of village.
6hc (3fb) ✈ LDO7pm
Lic ⛨ CTV 2P 2⚘

BLAIRGOWRIE
Tayside *Perthshire*
Map **11**   NO14

GH Glenshieling Hatton Rd, Rattray
☎(0250) 4605
Closed Nov & Dec

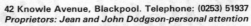
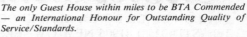

Comfortable accommodation in house standing in its own gardens.

6hc (2🚿) (2fb) TV in 1 bedroom [R] ✱B&b£10–£11 Bdi£16–£17 W£109–£115 k LDO7pm

Lic ♨ CTV 12P

[V]

GH Ivybank House Boat Brae, Rattray ☎(0250) 3056

A well-furnished, large, Victorian house standing in own grounds, with floodlit tennis court. Personally run.

6hc (2fb) CTV in all bedrooms [R] ✱B&b£9.50 Bdi£15 W£105 k LDO 7pm

♨ CTV 6P 🎾 (hard)

GH Rosebank House Balmoral Rd ☎(0250) 2912

Jan–Oct

Lovely privately-owned Georgian house set in own attractive gardens.

7hc (5🚿) (2fb) 🚫 CTV in 1 bedroom [R] B&b£11–£12 Bdi£17.95–£18.95 W£123–£130 k LDO6pm

Lic ♨ CTV 12P nc10yrs

[V]

GH St Ninan's 126 Perth Rd ☎(0250) 2443

On the outskirts of the town, a spacious Victorian house with pleasant, comfortable rooms.

6hc (2fb) [R] B&b£8.50–£9 Bdi£12.50–£13 W£87.50–£91 k LDO6pm

♨ CTV 6P

BLETCHINGLEY
Surrey
Map **4** TQ35

INN Whyte Harte ☎Godstone (0883) 843231

Popular roadside inn, dating from 1388, with compact modern character bedrooms and a good restaurant.

9hc (4🛁) 🚫 ✱B&b£17–£21 Lunchfr£6.50&alc Dinner10pm fr£11.50

CTV 40P 🚌

Credit cards [1] [2] [3] [4] [5] [V]

Blairgowrie — Bognor Regis

BLORE
Staffordshire
Map **7** SK14

FH M A Griffin **Coldwall** *(SK144494)* Okeover ☎Thorpe Cloud (033529) 249

Etr–Oct

Stone-built farmhouse approximately 200 years old. Good views of the surrounding hills. 4 miles NW of Ashbourne.

2hc (2fb) 🚫 ✱B&b£8–£9 Bdi£12–£12.50 LDO6pm

CTV 6P 280acres dairy sheep mixed

[V]

BLUE ANCHOR
Somerset
Map **3** ST04

GH Camelot ☎Dunster (0643) 821348

7hc (2fb) ✱B&b£8.50 Bdi£11.50–£14 Wfr£85 k LDO8pm

Lic ♨ CTV 7P

[V]

BOAT OF GARTEN
Highland *Inverness-shire*
Map **14** NH91

GH Moorfield House Hotel Deshar Rd ☎(047983) 646

Closed Nov

Village-centre hotel within lovely Spey Valley.

6hc (3🚿) (2fb) [R] ✱B&b£10.50–£13 Bdi£16–£18.50 W£105–£125 k LDO6pm

Lic ♨ CTV 12P

[V]

BODEDERN
Gwynedd
Map **6** SH38

INN Crown Hotel ☎Valley (0407) 740734

Old country coaching inn with pleasant homely atmosphere, situated a few miles from holiday beaches and the Irish car ferry terminal.

5hc (2fb) CTV in 2 bedrooms TV in 3 bedrooms 🚫 ✱B&b£10.50 LDO10pm

♨ 150P

[V]

BODLE STREET GREEN
East Sussex
Map **5** TQ61

FH Mr & Mrs R Gentry **Stud Farm** *(TQ163658)* ☎Herstmonceux (0323) 833201

A small, homely farmhouse in picturesque countryside.

3hc (1🚿) 🚫 [R] B&b£9.50–£10.50 Bdi£15–£16 W£101.50–£108.50 k

♨ CTV 3P

70 acres beef sheep

[V]

BODMIN
Cornwall
See **Roche**

BOGHEAD
Strathclyde *Lanarkshire*
Map **11** NS74

FH I McInally **Dykehead** *(NS772417)* ☎Lesmahagow (0555) 892226

Rough cast, two-storey farmhouse just 50 yards from Strathaven/Lesmahagow Road. On A726.

3rm (1fb) ✱B&b£7.50–£8 W£52–£56 M

♨ CTV 4P 60acres sheep

Credit cards [1] [2] [3] [5] [V]

BOGNOR REGIS
West Sussex
Map **4** SZ99

GH *Lansdowne Hotel* 55–57 West St ☎(0243) 865552

Modernised property incorporating cottage-style restaurant, set in a quiet residential area near the sea front.

8hc (5fb) 🚫 LDO10pm

Lic CTV no babies

Credit cards [1] [2] [3] [5]

See advertisement on page 74

Bollington — Bonsall

BOLLINGTON
Cheshire
Map **7** SJ97

INN Turners Arms 1 Ingersley Rd
☎(0625) 73864

A small, well-run village pub with a good range of food.

4hc (2fb) CTV in all bedrooms
✱B&b£12.50–£22.50 Bdi£13–£30 W£80–£91 🍴 Lunch £3.50alc Dinner 9.30pm £4alc

🛋 2P

BOLNEY
West Sussex
Map **4** TQ22

GH Bolney Grange House Hotel
☎Burgess Hill (04446) 45164

Country house, set in rural surroundings with swimming pool, fishing lakes and horse riding available.

15hc (1fb) CTV in 9 bedrooms [R]
✱B&b£23–£35.65 LDO9.30pm

Lic 🛋 CTV 50P 🏊 (heated) 🎾 (hard) 🎣 sauna bath

Credit cards [1] [2] [3] [5]

BOLTON LE SANDS
Lancashire
Map **7** SD46

FH Mrs A Ireland ***Thwaite End***
(SD507697) ☎Carnforth (0524) 732551
Mar–Oct

17th-century farmhouse with old beams.

3hc ✖ [R]

🛋 CTV 4P nc10yrs 75acres beef sheep

BOMERE HEATH
Shropshire
Map **7** SJ41

↦**FH** Mrs D M Cooke **Grange**
(SJ200484) ☎(0939) 290234
Closed Xmas

Large house with attractive gardens and open rural views.

2hc (1fb) ✖ B&b£7–£9 Bdi£12–£14 Wfr£84 🍴 LDO3pm

🛋 CTV 4P 🏠 360acres arable dairy

BONDLEIGH (nr North Tawton)
Devon
Map **3** SS60

FH Mrs M C H Partridge **Cadditon**
(SS644050) ☎North Tawton (083782) 450
Mar–Nov

Attractive, friendly farmhouse with old beams and fireplaces.

1¼m W unclassified road.

2hc (2fb) ✖ [R] Wfr£91 🍴 LDO7pm

🛋 CTV P 147acres beef dairy

BO'NESS
Central *West Lothian*
Map **11** NS98

Recommended

FH Mrs B Kirk **Kinglass** *(NT006803)*
Borrowstoun Rd ☎(0506) 822861

A charming sandstone farmhouse overlooking the Firth of Forth, where the style of operation and standard of amenities are comparable to those provided by a private hotel. Well-equipped and decorated bedrooms, very comfortably furnished public areas and a smart little dining room all help to make this a pleasant place to stay.

7rm (6hc) (1fb) TV in all bedrooms [R]
✱B&b£9–£10 Bdi£12–£16 LDO6pm

Lic 🛋 CTV 20P 120acres arable

[V]

BONSALL
Derbyshire
Map **8** SK25

GH Sycamore 76 High St, Town Head
☎Wirksworth (062982) 3903
Mar–Dec

Stone-built former farmhouse dating from the early 18th century.

6hc (3fb) ® ✱B&bfr£10.50 Bdifr£15.50 Wfr£105 ⚹ LDO5.30pm

Lic ⊞ CTV 6P

See advertisement under Matlock

GH *Town Head Farmhouse* 70 High St ☎Wirksworth (062982) 3762

200-year old stone-built farmhouse with attached converted barns, located on edge of village.

6hc ®

⊞ 8P nc10yrs

See advertisement under Matlock

BONTDDU
Gwynedd
Map **6**　SH61

INN *Halfway House Hotel* ☎(034149) 635

Half timbered inn in centre of small village.

3hc Annexe: 1↪ LDO9pm

⊞ CTV 12P 2🐾

BOOT
Cumbria
Map **7**　NY10

GH Brook House ☎Eskdale (09403) 288
Closed Nov–28 Dec

Bonsall
—
Borrowdale

Good home-cooking, with some dishes for vegetarians, in a spacious comfortable house.

6hc (2⎕) (2fb) TV in all bedrooms
✱B&b£10–£19 Bdi£16–£25 W£105–£168 ⚹ LDO8.30pm

Lic ⊞ CTV 14P

Ⓥ

BORELAND
Dumfries & Galloway *Dumfriesshire*
Map **11**　NY19

FH Mrs I Maxwell **Gall** *(NY172901)*
☎(05766) 229
Apr–Oct

Well-appointed modern farmhouse with delightful views across rolling countryside and distant hills.

3hc (2fb) ® ✱B&b£8–£9.50 Bdi£13–£14.50 Wfr£90 ⚹

⊞ CTV 3P 2🐾 1066acres beef sheep

BOROUGHBRIDGE
North Yorkshire
Map **8**　SE36

GH Farndale Horsefair ☎(09012) 3463
Closed 19 Dec–3 Jan

Restored Edwardian building with spacious attractive lounge and separate TV area.

13hc (2↪ 2⎕) (3fb) B&b£10–£14 Bdi£14–£18 W£88–£103 ⚹ LDO8.30pm

Lic ⊞ CTV 12P

BORROWDALE
Cumbria
Map **11**　NY21

GH Greenbank Country ☎(059684) 215
Closed Dec

Delightful family-run country guesthouse with good home cooking.

10hc (7↪ 2⎕) (1fb) ✖ Bdi£19.50–£20.50 W£129.50 ⚹ LDO5pm

Lic ⊞ CTV 15P

GH Langstrath Hotel ☎(059684) 239
mid Mar–Oct

Small, comfortable hotel with lots of character and peaceful setting.

15hc (2⎕) (3fb) B&bfr£16 Bdifr£21 Wfr£140 ⚹ LDO3pm

Lic ⊞ 20P

Ⓥ

The Halfway House Hotel

BONTDDU, DOLGELLAU, NORTH WALES
Tel: Bontddu 635. (STD 034 149)

Picturesque village. Coaching Inn set in spectacular mountain scenery.
Completely modernised bedroom accommodation. Intimate, candle-lit dining room specialising in Welsh lamb, local salmon and seafood.

Resident proprietors: Maggie and Bill Hutchinson

The Grange ~ Bed & Breakfast
Grange-in-Borrowdale,
Near Keswick, Cumbria CA12 5UQ
Telephone: 059 684 251

Owned and managed by Mr & Mrs G Jenkinson

The Grange is a small, friendly hotel in the village of Grange in one of the loveliest valleys, Borrowdale in the Lake District. This is an excellent centre for walking, rock-climbing, boating and touring, and for less energetic occupations.
There are 6 bedrooms, 3 bathrooms (one private) all rooms have central heating and lovely views. Guests are sure of personal attention. Ample parking space.
Dogs are accommodated at the management's discretion.

The Grange

GH Mary Mount Hotel ☎(059684) 223
Telex no 64305
Feb–Nov
Magnificent views from the elegant dining room. Comfortable, well-appointed bedrooms.
7🚿 Annexe: 5🛁 CTV in all bedrooms 🐕 [R] B&bfr£18
Lic ♨ 40P

BORTH
Dyfed
Map **6** SN68

GH Glanmor Princess St ☎(097081) 689
Etr–Sep
A sea-front hotel with comfortable accommodation, good food and warm hospitality.
7hc (2🚿) (3fb) 🐕 [R] ✱B&b£10 Bdi£14–£18 W£91 Ɏ LDO 10pm
Lic CTV 6P
Credit cards [1] [2] [3] [5]
[V]

BOSCASTLE
Cornwall
Map **2** SX09

GH *St Christophers Country House Hotel* High St (Guestaccom) ☎(08405) 412
Mar–Oct
8hc (4🚿) LDO7pm
Lic ♨ CTV 7P

BOSHAM
West Sussex
Map **4** SU80

GH White Barn Crede Ln (Guestaccom) ☎(0243) 573113
Closed 21 Dec–14 Jan
5hc (1🛁 2🚿) (1fb) 🐕 [R] ✱B&b£14–£15 Bdi£23–£25 W£150–£165 Ɏ
♨ CTV 5P 2🚗
[V]

Borrowdale — Bournemouth

BOUGHTON MONCHELSEA
Kent
Map **5** TQ75

Recommended

GH Tanyard Wierton Hill
☎Maidstone (0622) 44705
Mar–Oct
Set in an acre of well-tended gardens, the Tanyard is a beautifully preserved 14th-century timbered house, offering every comfort and excellent food.
National Winner of the AA 1986/7 Guesthouse of the Year Award.
5hc (3🛁 1🚿) (1fb) CTV in all bedrooms 🐕 [R] ✱B&b£23–£34.50 Bdi£36.80–£48.30 W£257.60–£338.10 Ɏ LDO7.30pm
Lic ♨ 10P nc6yrs
Credit cards [1] [2] [3] [5]
See advertisement on page 263

BOURNEMOUTH AND BOSCOMBE
Dorset
Map **4** SZ09

See **Key Map** (p 77), **Central Plan** (pages 78–79), **Boscombe** and **Southbourne** Plan (pages 80–81) and **Westbourne** & **Branksome** Plan (page 85)

For additional guesthouses see **Poole** and **Christchurch**

GH Albemarle Private Hotel 123 West Hill Rd ☎(0202) 21351
Central plan **1** *A1*
Small, comfortable terraced hotel, near town centre, offering excellent food and hospitality.
12hc (3🚿) (4fb) CTV in all bedrooms (charge) [R](charge) ✱B&b£9–£12 Bdi£13–£16 W£71.50–£92 Ɏ LDO6pm
Lic ♨ CTV 2P
Credit cards [1] [2]

GH *Alum Bay Hotel* 19 Burnaby Rd, Alum Chine ☎(0202) 761034 Westbourne & Branksome plan **80** *B2*
Victorian house within a few minutes walk of Alum Chine and the beach.
12hc (1🚿) (4fb) [R] LDO6pm
Lic ♨ CTV 10P

GH *Alum Grange Hotel* 1 Burnaby Rd, Alum Chine ☎(0202) 761195 Westbourne & Branksome plan **82** *B2*
Within two minutes walking distance of the sea.
14hc (4🛁 6🚿) (5fb) CTV in all bedrooms 🐕 [R]
Lic ♨ 9P nc3yrs

GH Bay Tree Hotel 17 Burnaby Rd, Alum Chine ☎(0202) 763807 Westbourne & Branksome plan **84** *B2*
Adjacent to Alum Chine, a few minutes from beach.
12hc (2🚿) (4fb) [R] ✱B&b£7.50–£13.50 Bdi£11.50–£17.50 W£69–£116 Ɏ LDO4pm
Lic CTV 8P

GH Blinkbonnie Heights Hotel 26 Clifton Rd, Southbourne ☎(0202) 426512 Boscombe & Southbourne plan **30** *F1*
Apr–Oct
12hc (1🛁) (5fb) [R] ✱B&b£8.50–£12 Bdi£11–£14.50 W£76–£97 Ɏ
Lic ♨ CTV 8P ⌂
[V]

GH Blue Cedars Hotel Portchester Pl ☎(0202) 26893 Boscombe & Southbourne plan **30A** *A3*
13hc (3fb) CTV in all bedrooms 🐕 ✱B&b£8–£11 Bdi£12–£15 W£59–£79 Ɏ (W only Jul & Aug) LDO6pm
Lic ♨ 9P
[V]

GH *Borodale Hotel* 10 St Johns Rd, Boscombe ☎(0202) 35285 Boscombe & Southbourne plan **31** *B2*
Mar–Nov
Short distance from Boscombe pier with nearby shopping complex.
16hc (1🛁 2🚿) (6fb)
Lic ♨ CTV 20P

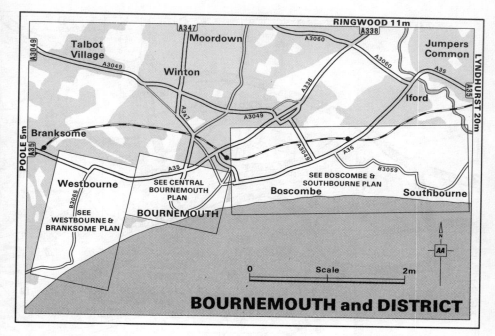

BOURNEMOUTH and DISTRICT

↤→**GH Braemar Private Hotel** 30 Glen Rd, Boscombe ☎(0202) 36054 Boscombe & Southbourne plan **33** *C2*

Simple accommodation is offered at this gabled hotel near Boscombe Pier.

11hc (1⇄ 2🛏) (5fb) ✗ ® B&b£8–£11.50 Bdi£10–£15 W£65–£90 ⅄ (W only Jun–Aug)

Lic 🍴 CTV 6P

Ⓥ

GH Hotel Bristol Terrace Rd ☎(0202) 27007 Central plan **2** *B2*

Central popular hotel convenient to theatres.

28hc (6⇄ 2🛏) (6fb) ✗ LDO7.30pm

lift 🍴 CTV 2P

GH Britannia Hotel 40 Christchurch Rd ☎(0202) 26700 Boscombe & Southbourne plan **34** *A2* Closed Xmas

On main Christchurch road into Bournemouth.

28hc ✗

🍴 CTV 30P nc3yrs

GH Brun-Lea Hotel 94 Southbourne Rd ☎(0202) 425956 Boscombe & Southbourne plan **35** *E2*

Detached, well-run house in Southbourne area, just off main shopping street.

15hc (4🛏) (2fb) ✗ ® LDO8pm

Lic 🍴 CTV 12P nc8yrs

GH Bursledon Hotel 34 Gervis Rd ☎(0202) 24622 Central plan **3** *E3*

Central position on East Cliff within short walking distance of shops and theatres.

23hc (2⇄ 7🛏) (4fb) LDO6.30pm

🍴 CTV 14P 5🐾 nc3yrs

Credit card ③

GH Carisbrooke Hotel 42 Tregonwell Rd ☎(0202) 290432 Central plan **4** *C1* mid Mar–Dec

Modern family run hotel near the Winter Gardens.

24hc (4⇄ 8🛏) (4fb) CTV in all bedrooms ✗ ® ✳B&b£11.50–£17 Bdi£16–£21 W£89–£123 ⅄ LDO7pm

Lic CTV 19P

Credit cards ① ② ③ Ⓥ

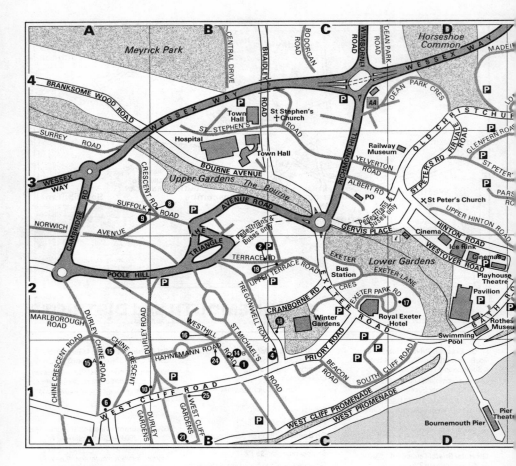

GH *Charles Taylor Hotel* Knyveton Gdns, 40–44 Frances Rd ☎(0202) 22695 Boscombe & Southbourne plan **37** *A2* Mar–Nov

Named after owner who personally supervises. Pleasant location overlooking bowling greens.

28hc (11⇌) (9fb) ® LDO6.30pm

Lic ♨ CTV 12P nc3yrs

GH Chequers Hotel 17 West Cliff Rd ☎(0202) 23900 Central plan **6** *A1* Closed Jan

Personally supervised, corner-sited hotel near Durley Chine.

27hc (7⇌ 10㎜) (4fb) CTV in all bedrooms ✖ ✱B&b£13.50–£15 Bdi£16.50–£23 W£98.50–£135 ⅃ LDO6.30pm

Lic ♨ CTV 28P

ⓥ

GH Chilterns Hotel 44 Westby Rd, Boscombe ☎(0202) 36539 Boscombe & Southbourne plan **38** *C2* Apr–Oct

Gabled guesthouse within easy walking distance of beach and Boscombe centre.

19hc (8fb) LDO5pm

Lic CTV 17P 2🏠

GH Chineside Private Hotel 15 Studland Rd, Alum Chine ☎(0202) 761206 Westbourne & Branksome plan **85** *B2* Etr–mid Oct

Modern, well-appointed hotel near sea front.

13hc (3㎜) (4fb) ✖ ® LDO6pm

♨ CTV 13P nc4yrs

⊢⟶**GH Cintra** 10–12 Florence Rd, Boscombe ☎(0202) 36103 Boscombe & Southbourne plan **39** *C2* Etr–Oct & Xmas

Within walking distance of pier and shopping centre.

39hc (4⇌ 5㎜) (13fb) ® B&b£7.50–£11.50 Bdi£9–£15.75 W£63–£110 ⅃ LDO6pm

Lic ♨ CTV 12P ♿

---**Recommended**---

GH Cliff House Hotel 113 Alumhurst Rd, Westbourne ☎(0202) 763003 Westbourne & Branksome plan **86** *B2* Apr–1 Nov

High standard of accommodation and some fine sea views are offered at this hotel adjacent to Alum Chine.

10hc (2⇌ 6㎜) (3fb) CTV in all bedrooms ✖ ® ✱B&b£13.50–£14.50 Bdi£19.50–£21.50 W£125–£136 ⅃ LDO6.30pm

Lic lift ♨ 12P nc7yrs snooker

GH Clifton Court Hotel 30 Clifton Rd ☎(0202) 427753 Boscombe & Southbourne plan **40** *F1*

Well-furnished guesthouse with modern extension.

78

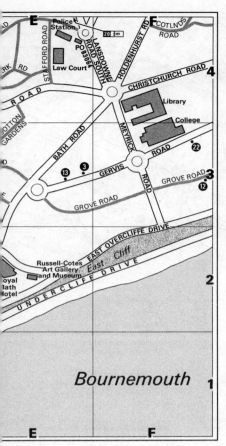

Bournemouth

Central Bournemouth

1	Albermarle Private Hotel
2	Hotel Bristol
3	Bursledon Hotel
4	Carisbrooke Hotel
6	Chequers Hotel
8	Crescent Grange Hotel
9	Cresta Court Hotel
10	Croham Hurst Hotel
12	East Cliff Cottage Private Hotel
13	Gervis Court Hotel
14B	Hollyhurst Hotel
15	Kensington Hotel
15A	Langton Hall Hotel
16	Mae-Mar Private Hotel
17	Monreith Hotel
18	Mount Stuart Hotel
19	Hotel Restormel
20	Silver Trees Hotel
21	Tower House Hotel
22	Tudor Grange Hotel
24	West Leigh
25	Whitley Court Hotel

12hc (5⇄ 5fll) (2fb) CTV in 10 bedrooms ® ✳B&b£9.20–£12.65 Bdi£13.80–£16 W£74.75–£97.75 ⩊

Lic CTV 10P

Credit cards ① ③ Ⓥ

GH *Crescent Grange Hotel*
6–8 Crescent Rd, The Triangle ☎(0202) 26959 Central plan **8** *B3*

Backing onto central gardens and convenient to shops and theatres.

19hc (16⇄ 3fll) (2fb) CTV in all bedrooms ® LDO5pm

Lic 岬 CTV 24P nc3yrs

Credit cards ① ③

GH Cresta Court Hotel 3 Crescent Rd ☎(0202) 25217 Central plan **9** *A3*

18hc (2⇄ 1fll) (4fb) CTV in 15 bedrooms ® ✳B&b£11–£13 Bdi£16–£19 W£105–£125 ⩊ LDOnoon

Lic 岬 CTV 20P nc4yrs

Ⓥ

GH Croham Hurst Hotel 9 Durley Rd, West Cliff ☎(0202) 22353 Central plan **10** *B1*
Etr–Nov

26hc (17⇄ 3fll) (7fb) CTV in all bedrooms ✖ ® ✳B&b£11.70–£16.50 Bdi£14.20–£19 W£99–£129 ⩊ LDO6pm

Lic CTV 20P

See advertisement on page 80

GH *Crossroads Hotel* 88 Belle Vue Rd, Southbourne ☎(0202) 426307 Boscombe & Southbourne plan **42** *G2*

Pleasant, detached property near cliff-top at Southbourne. Comfortable, personally-run.

10hc (4fll) (6fb) ✖
Lic 岬 CTV 12P nc5yrs

GH *Derwent House* 36 Hamilton Rd, Boscombe ☎(0202) 309102 Boscombe & Southbourne plan **44** *B2*

Detached property with Mansard roof, close to Boscombe shops.

10hc (2fll) (5fb) CTV in all bedrooms
Lic 岬 CTV 10P ⚶

12hc (2⇄) (3fb) ® B&b£9.50–£13.50 Bdi£13–£16 W£85–£110 ⩊
Lic 岬 CTV 10P
Credit cards ① ③

GH Cransley Private Hotel 11 Knyveton Rd, East Cliff ☎(0202) 290067 Boscombe & Southbourne plan **41** *A2*
Apr–Nov

Boscombe & Southborne

30 Blinkbonnie Heights Hotel
30A Blue Cedars Hotel
31 Borodale Hotel
33 Braemar Private Hotel
34 Britannia Hotel
35 Brun-Lea Hotel
37 Charles Taylor Hotel
38 Chilterns Hotel
39 Cintra
40 Clifton Court Hotel
41 Cransley Private Hotel
42 Crossroads Hotel
44 Derwent House
45 Eglan Court Hotel
46 Farlow Private Hotel
46A Florida Hotel
50 Hawaiian Hotel
52 Highlin Private Hotel
55 Kingsley Hotel
56 Linwood House Hotel
57 Lyntnwaite Hotel
59 Mariner's Hotel
59A Mayfield Private Hotel
60 Myrtle House Hotel
61 Naseby-Nye Hotel
61A Norland Private Hotel
62 Oak Hall Private Hotel
64 Pine Beach Hotel
65 St John's Lodge Hotel
67 St Wilfreds Private Hotel
68 Sandelheath Hotel
69 Sea Shells
71 Sea View Court Hotel
71A Sherbourne Hotel
72 Hotel Sorrento
73 Stonecroft Hotel

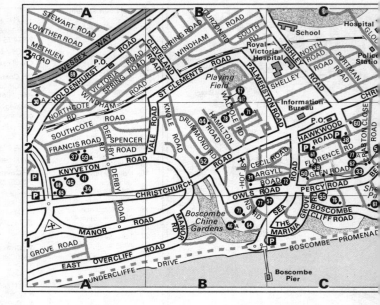

74 Stratford Hotel
76 Valberg Hotel
76A Vine
77 Waldale

77A Weavers Hotel
78 Wenmaur House Hotel
79 Wood Lodge Hotel
79A Woodside Private Hotel

GH Earlham Lodge 91 Alumhurst Rd,
Alum Chine ☎(0202) 761943 Westbourne
& Branksome plan **88** *B2*
Feb–Oct & Xmas

*Neat, modern house, a few minutes walk
from Alum Chine and beach.*

14hc (6fl) (4fb) CTV in all bedrooms ✗ ®
✱B&b£10.50–£14 Bdi£15.50–£18.50
W£115–£125 ⫝ LDO6pm

Lic CTV 9P

GH East Cliff Cottage Private Hotel
57 Grove Rd, East Cliff ☎(0202) 22788
Central plan **12** *F3*
Etr–Oct

Cottage in quiet area near East Cliff.
10hc (3⟶1fl) (1fb) ® LDO4.30pm
⋈ CTV 8P nc5yrs

GH Egerton House Private Hotel 385
Holdenhurst Rd, Queens Park Not on plan
☎(0202) 34024

8hc (3fb) ✗
⋈ CTV 8P

GH Eglan Court Hotel 7 Knyveton Rd
☎(0202) 290093 Boscombe &
Southbourne plan **45** *A2*

Located in pine clad avenue near to sea.
15hc (4⟶4fl) (2fb) CTV in 12 bedrooms
® LDO2pm

Lic ⋈ CTV 10P nc5yrs

GH Farlow Private Hotel 13 Walpole Rd,
Boscombe ☎(0202) 35865 Boscombe &
Southbourne plan **46** *B2*
Closed Dec

*Well-maintained hotel with sound
furnishings and personal service.*

12hc (2fb) ✗ ✱B&b£8–£10 Bdi£12–£14
W£80–£95 ⫝ LDO4pm

CTV 12P nc3yrs

Credit card ① ⓥ

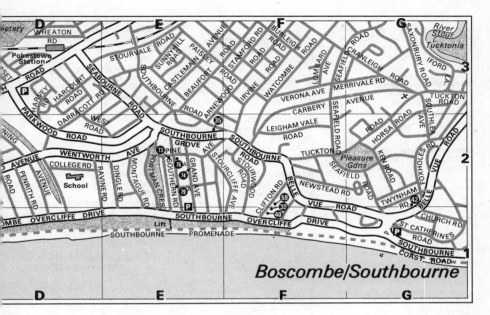

Boscombe/Southbourne

GH Florida Hotel 35 Boscombe Spa Rd
☎(0202) 34537 Boscombe &
Southbourne plan **46A** *B1*
Mar–Dec

*Detached hotel with sea views
overlooking Bournemouth bay.*

26hc (7⇄9🏠) (4fb) ® ✱B&b£10–£15
Bdi£14.50–£19.50 W£75–£119 ⅟ LDO6pm

Lic 🍴 CTV 12P

Credit cards ① ③

GH Gervis Court Hotel 38 Gervis Rd
☎(0202) 26871 Central plan **13** *E3*
Etr–Oct

Amidst pines on East Cliff.

16hc (4⇄3🏠) (3fb) ✖ ® B&b£10.50–
£12.50 Bdi£17–£19 W£90.27–£113 ⅟
LDO7.15pm

Lic CTV 15P

ⓥ

GH Golden Sands Hotel 83 Alumhurst
Rd ☎(0202) 763832 Westbourne &
Branksome plan **88A** *B2*
Feb–Nov

*Attractive guesthouse close to Alum
Chine. Good standard of furnishings and
very comfortable bedrooms.*

9hc (5⇄4🏠) (1fb) CTV in all bedrooms ✖
® LDO6.30pm

Lic CTV 10P nc4yrs

GH Gordons Hotel 84 West Cliff Rd,
Alum Chine ☎(0202) 765844 Westbourne
& Branksome plan **89** *B2*
Mar–Oct

Within walking distance of beach.

15hc (4🏠) (2fb) ✖ ® ✱B&b£10–£14
Bdi£15–£19 W£78–£115 ⅟ LDO11am

Lic CTV 12P 🐾

GH Hawaiian Hotel 4 Glen Rd ☎(0202)
33234 Boscombe & Southbourne plan **50**
C2
Mar–Oct rs Feb & Nov

*Nice, bright property near Boscombe Pier
and shops.*

13hc (4⇄1🏠) (3fb) ✖ ® ✱B&b£7.50–£11
Bdi£10.50–£14.50 W£68–£95 ⅟

Lic 🍴 CTV 8P nc4yrs

ⓥ

GH Highclere Hotel 15 Burnaby Rd,
Alum Chine ☎(0202) 761350 Westbourne
& Branksome plan **89A** *B2*
Etr–Oct

*Neat, well-maintained hotel with sea
views. Easy walk to Alum Chine and
beach.*

→

81

9hc (4🛁 5🚿) (5fb) CTV in all bedrooms [R] ✱B&b£12.20–£13.40 Bdi£17.12–£18.86 W£104.86–£118.23 Ⱡ LDO5pm

Lic 🍴 CTV 7P solarium

[V]

GH *Highlin Private Hotel* 14 Knole Rd ☎(0202) 33758 Boscombe & Southbourne plan **52** *B2*

In a quiet area near Boscombe Chine.

12hc (1🛁) (8fb) 🚫🐕 [R] LDO4pm

Lic CTV 8P 1🚗

GH Hollyhurst Hotel West Hill Rd ☎(0202) 27137 Central plan **14B** *B1*
Mar–Nov & Xmas

24hc (4🛁 11🚿) (10fb) CTV in 12 bedrooms [R] ✱B&b£8.50–£10.50 Bdi£12.50–£14.50 W£75–£89 Ⱡ LDO6pm

Lic CTV 24P 2🚗 ⛪

Credit cards [1] [2] [3] [5]

GH *Holmcroft Hotel* 5 Earle Rd, Alum Chine ☎(0202) 761289 Westbourne & Branksome plan **90** *B2*
Mar–Dec

Neat, well-maintained accommodation, close to Alum Chine woods and beach.

21hc (2🛁 6🚿) (6fb) CTV in all bedrooms LDO5pm

Lic CTV 12P nc2yrs

Credit cards [1] [2] [3] [5]

Bournemouth

GH *Kensington Hotel* Durley Chine Rd, West Cliff ☎(0202) 27434 Central plan **15** *A1*
Etr–Oct

Detached hotel within walking distance of West Cliff. Attractive dining room with adjoining bar.

26hc (2🛁 19🚿) (3fb) 🚫🐕 [R] LDO7pm

Lic 🍴 CTV 26P

GH *Kingsley Hotel* 20 Glen Rd, Boscombe ☎(0202) 38683 Boscombe & Southbourne plan **55** *C2*

Few minutes walk from Boscombe Pier and shops.

12hc (1🛁 2🚿) (3fb) 🚫🐕 LDO4.30pm

Lic 🍴 CTV 6P ⛪

Credit cards [1] [3]

GH Langton Hall Hotel 8 Durley Chine Rd, West Cliff ☎(0202) 25025 Central plan **15A** *A1*

22hc (7🛁 3🚿) (5fb) CTV in all bedrooms [R] ✱B&b£14–£18 Bdi£18–£22 W£89–£125 Ⱡ (W only Jul & Aug)

Lic 🍴 CTV 22P

Credit cards [1] [2] [3] [V]

GH Linwood House Hotel 11 Wilfred Rd ☎(0202) 37818 Boscombe & Southbourne plan **56** *C2*
Mar–Oct

Attractively-decorated guesthouse in quiet road near beach and Boscombe town centre.

10hc (2🚿) (3fb) CTV in 2 bedrooms TV in 2 bedrooms [R]

Lic 🍴 CTV 7P nc5yrs

[V]

GH Lynthwaite Hotel 10 Owls Rd, Boscombe ☎(0202) 38015 Boscombe & Southbourne plan **57** *B2*

Comfortable small hotel with good bedrooms, friendly atmosphere and easy parking.

14hc (6🛁 1🚿) (4fb) CTV in 7 bedrooms 🚫🐕 [R] B&bfr£8.50 Bdifr£13 Wfr£50 M LDO4pm

Lic CTV 17P

Credit card [3]

GH *Mae-Mar Private Hotel* 91–93 West Hill Rd, West Cliff ☎(0202) 23167 Central plan **16** *B2*

In the heart of West Cliff hotel area.

28hc (7fb) LDO6.30pm

Lic lift 🍴 CTV 🅿̸

Bournemouth

GH Mariners Hotel 22 Clifton Rd, Southbourne ☎(0202) 420851 Boscombe & Southbourne plan **59** *F2*
Mar–Oct

Close to cliff top and Southbourne zig-zag path to beach.

15hc (2fb) ✱B&b£8–£9.50 Bdi£11.50–£13 W£75–£90 Ł LDO6.15pm

♨ CTV 20P ⌂

Ⓥ

GH Mayfield Private Hotel 46 Frances Rd, Knyveton Gdns ☎(0202) 21839 Boscombe & Southbourne plan **59A** *A2*

Situated in quiet area with easy walk to beach.

8hc (2🚿) (1fb) Ⓡ ✱B&b£6.50–£9 Bdi£9.50–£12 W£61–£81 Ł (W only last Wk Jul & 1st Wk Aug)

Lic ♨ CTV 5P nc7yrs

Ⓥ

GH Monreith Hotel Lower Gdns, 6 Exeter Park Rd ☎(0202) 290344 Central plan **17** *D2*
Mar–Oct

In own grounds overlooking bandstand, and central gardens.

29hc (6fb) ✖ Ⓡ B&b£12–£14.50 Bdi£16–£18.50 W£87–£120 Ł LDO6.30pm

Lic ♨ CTV 24P nc4yrs

GH *Mount Lodge Hotel* 19 Beaulieu Rd, Alum Chine ☎(0202) 761173 Westbourne & Branksome plan **91** *B2*

Adjacent to Alum Chine.

11hc (1🛁 1🚿) (3fb) ✖ Ⓡ LDO7pm

Lic ♨ CTV 6P ⌂

Credit card [1]

GH Mount Stuart Hotel 31 Tregonwell Rd ☎(0202) 24639 Central plan **18** *C2*
Mar–Nov rs Dec

Behind the Winter Gardens on West Cliff.

18hc (1🛁 11🚿) (6fb) CTV in all bedrooms ✖ Ⓡ B&b£11–£19 Bdi£15.50–£23.50 W£89–£130 Ł LDO7pm

Lic ♨ CTV 18P

Credit cards [1] [2] [3] Ⓥ

GH Myrtle House Hotel 41 Hawkwood Rd, Boscombe ☎(0202) 36579 Boscombe & Southbourne plan **60** *C2*

Short distance from Boscombe shops and pier.

10hc (1🛁 2🚿) (5fb) ✖ ✱B&b£9–£13 Bdi£11–£16 W£70–£105 Ł LDO4pm

Lic ♨ CTV 8P

Credit card [1] Ⓥ

Recommended

GH *Naseby-Nye Hotel* Byron Rd, Boscombe ☎(0202) 34079 Boscombe & Southbourne plan **61** *C1*

Large detached house set in gardens close to cliff-top. Comfortable, well-appointed rooms.

13hc (3🛁) (4fb)

Lic ♨ CTV 12P nc5yrs

GH Newfield Private Hotel 29 Burnaby Rd, Alum Chine ☎(0202) 762724 Westbourne & Branksome plan **92** *B2*

Short distance from beach in Alum Chine area.

12hc (1🛁 3🚿) (3fb) CTV in all bedrooms Ⓡ ✱B&b£9.50–£12.50 Bdi£15–£19 W£94–£132 Ł LDOnoon

Lic ♨ CTV 5P

Ⓥ

GH Norland Private Hotel 6 Westby Rd, Boscombe ☎(0202) 36729 Boscombe & Southbourne plan **61A** *C2*

Semi-detached Victorian building by Boscombe Pier.

8hc (1🛁 2🚿) (3fb) ✖ ✱B&b£7.50–£9.50 Bdi£11–£13 W£66–£85 Ł LDO4pm

Lic ♨ CTV 7P

Credit cards [1] [3]

GH Northover Private Hotel 10 Earle Rd, Alum Chine ☎(0202) 767349 Westbourne & Branksome plan **93** *B2*
Etr–Nov

Overlooking Alum Chine, 400 yds from sea.

11hc (5🚿) (5fb) Ⓡ ✱B&b£11–£16 Bdi£16–£21 W£99–£130 Ł LDO4pm

Lic lift ♨ CTV 11P

GH Oak Hall Private Hotel 9 Wilfred Rd, Boscombe ☎(0202) 35062 Boscombe & Southbourne plan **62** *C2*
Closed 6 Dec–12 Jan

Situated within easy reach of shops and Boscombe Pier and less than 5 minutes walk to Overcliff.

10hc (3fb) Ⓡ ✱B&b£10–£12 Bdi£12–£16 W£72–£98 Ł (W only Jul & Aug) LDO1pm

Lic ♨ CTV 8P nc6yrs

See advertisement on page 84

GH *Pine Beach Hotel* 31 Boscombe Spa Rd, Boscombe ☎(0202) 35902 Boscombe & Southbourne plan **64** *B1*

Situated in a quiet, elevated position overlooking Boscombe Pier and the sea.

21hc (4fb) LDO6pm

Lic CTV 17P nc4yrs

GH Ravenstone Hotel 36 Burnaby Rd, Alum Chine ☎(0202) 761047 Westbourne & Branksome plan **94A** *B2*

Handsome villa near Alum Chine with pleasant garden and games room for children.

9hc (5🛁 4🚿) (3fb) CTV in all bedrooms Ⓡ ✱B&b£13.50–£17.50 Bdi£16.50–£20.50 W£94–£124 Ł (W only mid Jul & Aug) LDO5pm

Lic ♨ CTV 6P

Ⓥ

GH *Hotel Retormel* Upper Terrace Rd ☎(0202) 25070 Central plan **19** *C2*

Centrally located for the theatre and shops.

18hc (1🛁 1🚿) (2fb) CTV in 8 bedrooms LDO7pm

Lic ♨ CTV 8P ♿

Credit cards [1] [2] [3] [4] [5]

GH *St John's Lodge Hotel* 10 St Swithun's Rd ☎(0202) 290677 Boscombe & Southbourne plan **65** *A2* →

Close to shops and within walking distance of the Chine and pier.

19hc (2fl) (4fb) ✖ Ⓡ LDO4.30pm

Lic CTV 16P

GH *St Wilfreds Private Hotel* 15 Walpole Rd, Boscombe ☎(0202) 36189 Boscombe & Southbourne plan **67** *B3*

Near the shops and within walking distance of the Chine and sea.

7hc (4fb) ✖ LDO6pm

CTV 6P ⌂

GH *Sandelheath Hotel* 1 Knyveton Rd, East Cliff ☎(0202) 25428 Boscombe & Southbourne Plan **68** *A2*

Situated in a pine-clad avenue in a quiet area of Lansdowne.

15hc (4fb) ✖ Ⓡ LDO7pm

Lic ꟾ CTV 12P

GH *Sea-Dene* 10 Burnaby Rd, Alum Chine ☎(0202) 761372 Westbourne & Branksome plan **96** *B2*

Mar–Nov

Pleasant, detached house with forecourt parking, close to beach at Alum Chine.

7hc (4fl) (3fb) Ⓡ LDO7.30pm

Lic ꟾ CTV 4P nc5yrs

GH Sea Shells 203–205 Holdenhurst Rd ☎(0202) 292542 Boscombe & Southbourne plan **69** *A3*

Bournemouth

Located near to shops on main road.

12hc (7fb) CTV in 1 bedroom TV in 8 bedrooms B&b£9.20–£10.35 W£58–£68 M̸

CTV 12P

Credit cards 1 3 Ⓥ

GH *Sea View Court Hotel* 14 Boscombe Spa Rd ☎(0202) 37197 Boscombe & Southbourne plan **71** *B1*

Mar–Oct

Two minutes walk from Boscombe Pier, an attractive gabled house with good bedrooms.

18hc (8⇌ 7fl) (7fb) Ⓡ

Lic ꟾ CTV 25P

GH Sherbourne Hotel 6 Walpole Rd, Boscombe ☎(0202) 36222 Boscombe & Southbourne plan **71A** *B2*

Nicely-furnished detached hotel near Boscombe's main shopping street.

10hc (5fb) ✖ ✱B&b£7.50–£9.25 Bdi£11.25–£12.75 W£67.50–£85 Ł LDO5.30pm

Lic CTV 8P ⌂ sauna bath

GH Silver Trees Hotel 57 Wimborne Rd ☎(0202) 26040 Central plan **20** *F4*

A modernised, late Victorian house standing in its own grounds and offering comfortable accommodation.

9hc (1⇌ 4fl) (2fb) CTV in all bedrooms ✖ ✱B&b£13–£15 Bdi£20–£22 W£133–£141 Ł LDO2pm

ꟾ 10P nc3yrs

Credit cards 1 3

GH Hotel Sorrento 16 Owls Rd, **Boscombe** ☎(0202) 34019 Boscombe & Southbourne plan **72** *C2*

Etr–Oct

Attractive hotel adjacent to Boscombe shopping centre and easy walk from beach and pier.

19hc (4fl) (4fb) Ⓡ B&b£9–£15 Bdi£13.50–£20 W£50–£76 M̸ LDO4pm

Lic CTV 16P

Ⓥ

GH *Hotel Sorrento* 8 Studland Rd, **Alum Chine**, Westbourne ☎(0202) 762116 Westbourne & Branksome plan **98** *B2*

Mar–Nov

The resident proprietors offer a friendly atmosphere and good cuisine.

19hc (9⇌ 8fl) (3fb) CTV in 2 bedrooms Ⓡ LDO5.30pm

Lic ꟾ CTV 15P nc5yrs

GH Stonecroft Hotel 6 Wollstonecraft Rd, Boscombe Manor ☎(0202) 309390 Boscombe & Southbourne plan **73** *E2*

Feb–Oct

An attractive building in pleasant gardens, with comfortable rooms, 2 minutes from Boscombe Pier.

8⋔ (3fb) Ⓡ ✱B&b£8.50–£10 Bdi£13–£14 W£80–£91 Ⱡ

Lic CTV 7P

Ⓥ

GH Stratford Hotel 20 Grand Av, Southbourne ☎(0202) 424726 Boscombe & Southbourne plan **74** *E2*
Etr–Oct

13hc (5⇌) (7fb) ✱B&b£10.50–£12 Bdi£13–£14 W£89.70–£103.50 Ⱡ (W only Jul & Aug) LDOnoon

Lic ♛ CTV 8P nc2yrs

Ⓥ

GH Tower House Hotel West Cliff Gdns ☎(0202) 290742 Central plan **21** *B1*
Apr–Oct & Xmas

Large detached property on West Cliff offering neat bedrooms and friendly service.

34hc (15⇌ 4⋔) (8fb) CTV in 31 bedrooms Ⓡ ✱B&b£11–£17.50 Bdi£13–£19.50 W£82.50–£127.50 Ⱡ LDO4.45pm

Lic lift ♛ CTV 32P nc5yrs

Bournemouth

GH Trent Private Hotel 12 Studland Rd ☎(0202) 761088 Westbourne & Branksome plan **99** *B2*
Closed Jan & Feb

12hc (6⋔) (3fb) CTV in 10 bedrooms ✖ ✱B&b9.50–£12.50 Bdi£14–£17 W£93–£115 Ⱡ (W only 19 Jul & Aug)

Lic CTV 9P nc4yrs

GH Tudor Grange Hotel 31 Gervis Rd ☎(0202) 291472 Central plan **22** *F3*

Centrally located mock Tudor house with neat grounds.

12hc (3⇌) (4fb) ✱B&b£11.50–£17 Bdi£16.50–£22 W£103–£139 Ⱡ LDO7pm

Lic ♛ CTV 8P

Ⓥ

⊢⊣ **GH Valberg Hotel** 1A Wollstonecraft Rd, Boscombe ☎(0202) 34644 Boscombe & Southbourne plan **76** *C1*

Well-appointed detached house in quiet road near Boscombe Pier.

10⋔ (2fb) ✖ Ⓡ B&b£8–£11 W£52–£72 M

♛ CTV 9P

GH Vine 22 Southern Rd, Southbourne ☎(0202) 428309 Boscombe & Southbourne plan **76A** *E2*
Closed New Year

Double-fronted villa in quiet surroundings and leading to cliff top at Southbourne.

7⋔ ✱B&b£9–£12.50 Bdi£12.50–£16.50 W£78–£98 Ⱡ

Lic ♛ CTV 7P nc

GH Waldale 37–39 Boscombe Spa Rd ☎(0202) 37744 Boscombe & Southbourne plan **77** *B1*
Mar–Oct

Well-maintained house at Boscombe with good sea views.

21hc (8⇌) (5fb) Ⓡ ✱B&b£10–£14 Bdi£14–£20 W£95–£135 Ⱡ (W only Jun–Sep) LDO3pm

Lic ♛ CTV 19P 8🚗 nc5yrs

Ⓥ

GH Weavers Hotel 14 Wilfred Rd, Boscombe ☎(0202) 37871 Boscombe & Southbourne plan **77A** *C2*
Apr–Oct

In quiet residential area close to sea. A small friendly hotel offering good cooking.

7hc (1fb) ✖ Ⓡ ✱B&b£9–£12 Bdi£12–£14 W£80–£90 Ⱡ (W only Jul, Aug) LDO5pm

Lic ♛ CTV 7P nc7yrs

Ⓥ

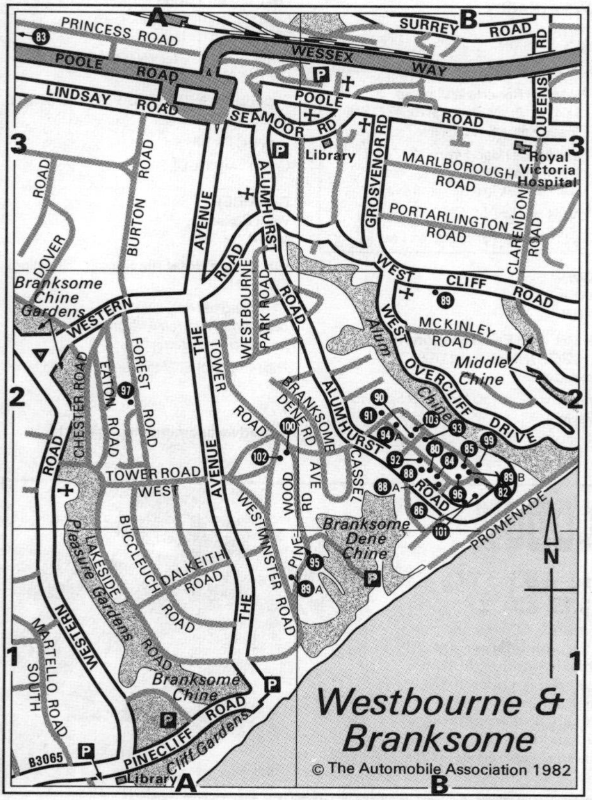

Westbourne & Branksome

80 Alum Bay Hotel
82 Alum Grange Hotel
83 Avoncroft Private Hotel
84 Bay Tree Hotel
85 Chineside Private Hotel
86 Cliff House Hotel
88 Earlham Lodge
88A Golden Sands Hotel
89 Gordons Hotel
89A Grovefield Hotel
89B Highclere Hotel
90 Holmcroft Hotel
91 Mount Lodge Hotel
92 Newfield Private Hotel
93 Northover Private Hotel
94A Ravenstone Hotel
95 Redcroft Private Hotel (*listed under Poole*)
96 Sea-Dene
97 Sheldon Lodge (*listed under Poole*)
99 Trent Private Hotel
100 Twin Cedars Hotel (*listed under Poole*)
101 West Dene Private Hotel
102 Westminster Cottage Hotel (*listed under Poole*)
103 Woodford Court Hotel

GH *Wenmaur House Hotel* 14 Carysfort Rd, Boscombe ☎(0202) 35081 Boscombe & Southbourne plan **78** *B2*
Closed New Year

Enjoying quiet location near to Boscombe shops.

12hc (7fb) ✗ LDOnoon

Lic 📺 CTV 10P 🏠

GH West Dene Private Hotel
117 Alumhurst Rd, Alum Chine ☎(0202) 764843 Westbourne & Branksome plan **101** *B2*

Overlooking sea at foot of Alum Chine.

17hc (5🛁 7🚿) (4fb) CTV in all bedrooms ✗ Ⓡ *B&b£13.50–£23 Bdi£17.50–£27 W£112–£177 Ł LDO5pm

Lic 📺 CTV 17P

Credit cards [1] [2] [3] [5] Ⓥ

GH *West Leigh* 26 West Hill Rd ☎(0202) 292195 Central plan **24** *B1*

Neat, detached house with swimming pool in rear garden. Easy walk to West Cliff.

31rm (28hc 20🛁 8🚿) (8fb) CTV in 3 bedrooms LDO7.15pm

Lic lift CTV 30P 🏠 🏊 (heated)

Credit cards [1] [2] [3] [5]

GH *Whitley Court Hotel* West Cliff Gdns ☎(0202) 21302 Central plan **25** *B1*
Closed 10 Nov–15 Dec

Situated in the West Cliff area enjoying ideal location for shops and sea.

15rm (2🚿) (6fb) LDO4pm

Lic 📺 CTV 12P

GH *Woodford Court Hotel* 19–21 Studland Rd, Alum Chine ☎(0202) 764907 Westbourne & Branksome plan **103** *B2*
Mar–Nov

Overlooking Alum Chine enjoying a quiet location near beach.

26hc (11🛁 5🚿) (7fb) CTV in all bedrooms Ⓡ LDO6.15pm

Lic 📺 CTV 12P nc2yrs

Credit card [1]

GH Wood Lodge Hotel 10 Manor Rd, East Cliff ☎(0202) 290891 Boscombe & Southbourne plan **79** *A1*
Etr–Oct

Peaceful and elegant house opposite East Cliff with attentive service and good accommodation.

15hc (7🛁 7🚿) (5fb) CTV in all bedrooms Ⓡ B&b£10.25–£18.25 Bdi£13.75–£21.75 W£95.25–£140 Ł LDO6pm

Lic 📺 CTV 12P

Credit cards [1] [3] Ⓥ

GH Woodside Private Hotel 29 Southern Rd, Southbourne ☎(0202) 427213 Boscombe & Southbourne plan **79A** *E2*
Etr–Oct

9hc (1🚿) ✗ *B&b£9–£11.50 Bdi£12.50–£14.50 W£87.50–£101.50 Ł LDO5pm

Lic 📺 CTV 5P nc12yrs

Credit card [3]

BOVEY TRACEY
Devon
Map **3** SX87

Recommended

FH Mrs H Roberts **Willmead** *(SX795812)* ☎Lustleigh (06477) 214
Closed Xmas & New Year

Farmhouse dating from 1327 and situated on the edge of Dartmoor National Park in a delightful valley.

3hc ✗ *B&b£14 W£98 M̸

📺 CTV P nc10yrs 32acres beef

BOW
Devon
Map **3** SS70

FH Mrs V Hill **East Hillerton House** *(SX725981)* Spreyton ☎(0633) 393
Closed Xmas

The farm is located 2m NE of Spreyton village.

3hc (1fb) ✗ Ⓡ *B&bfr£7 Bdifr£12 Wfr£75 Ł

📺 CTV 🚗 180acres arable beef sheep mixed

Ⓥ

BOWNESS-ON-WINDERMERE
Cumbria
Map **7** SD49

Guesthouses are listed under **Windermere**

BRADFORD
West Yorkshire
Map **7** SE13

GH *Maple Hill* 3 Park Dr, Heaton ☎(0274) 44061

Large, comfortable Victorian house with many original features.

11rm (10hc) (2fb) CTV in all bedrooms ✗ Ⓡ

Lic 📺 CTV 15P 2🚗

BRAEMAR
Grampian *Aberdeenshire*
Map **15** NO19

GH Callater Lodge Hotel 9 Glenshee Rd (Guestaccom) ☎(03383) 275
26 Dec–mid Oct

Small friendly hotel set in own grounds with hill views.

9hc (1fb) Ⓡ *B&b£12 Bdi£20 W£134.70 Ł LDO7.30pm

Lic 📺 CTV 10P

Credit cards [1] [3]

BRAMBER
West Sussex
Map **4** TQ11

INN *Castle Hotel* The Street ☎Steyning (0903) 812102

Charming old hotel with well-appointed bedrooms. Garden with small swimming pool and play area.

7hc (4🚿) (2fb) CTV in 5 bedrooms Ⓡ LDO9.30pm

📺 P

See advertisement on page 361

CALLATER LODGE

Braemar, Aberdeenshire AB3 5YQ
Telephone: Braemar (033 83) 275

A small, comfortable hotel situated in grounds of over one acre on the south side of Braemar, with accommodation for 18 persons. All rooms have pleasant views of surrounding hills, hot & cold water, electric fires, razor sockets, tea & coffee making facilities and comfortable beds. An ideal centre for climbing, fishing, touring, ski-ing, hang-gliding and an 18-hole golf course nearby. Glenshee Ski Centre — nine miles and Balmoral — eight miles. Ample car parking. *Under the personal supervision of the proprietors — Mr & Mrs W J O Rose.*

BRAMPTON
Cumbria
See **Castle Carrock** and **Kirkcambeck**

BRANSCOMBE
Devon
Map **3**   SY18

GH The Bulstone ☎(029780) 446
Feb–Nov

6hc (4fb) B&b£9.99–£11.50 Bdi£17–
£19.25 W£105–£132.50 ⅄ LDO7.30pm
Lic ♨ CTV 12P ⚿

BRAUNTON
Devon
Map **2**   SS43

GH Brookdale Hotel 62 South St
☎(0271) 812075
*A personally run guesthouse, situated
only 200 yds from the village centre.*

8hc (3fb) ✖ LDO9.30pm
Lic ♨ CTV P 1🐎

FH Mr & Mrs Barnes **Denham** (SS480404)
North Buckland ☎Croyde (0271) 890297
Mar–Dec

*Large farmhouse, parts of which date
from the 18th century, set in lovely
countryside, 2 miles from Croyde and
within easy reach of Barnstaple and
Ilfracombe.*

7hc (3fb) ✖ ✱B&bfr£8.50 Bdifr£14 (W
only Spring Bank Hol, end Jul–Aug)
Lic CTV 3P 4🐎 160acres beef

Brampton
—
Bredwardine

BRECHIN
Tayside
Map **15**   NO56

—Recommended—
FH Mrs M Stewart **Blibberhill**
(NO553568) (5m WSW off B9134)
☎Aberlemno (030783) 225

*Spacious, well-appointed farmhouse
in peaceful surroundings.*

3hc (1⇘) ✖ ℝ ✱B&bfr£8 Bdifr£13
♨ CTV 4P 300acres arable beef
mixed
Ⓥ

—Recommended—
FH Mrs J Stewart **Wood of Auldbar**
(NO554556) Aberlemno
☎Aberlemno (030783) 218

*Fairly large farmhouse well back from
road amidst wooded land, 5m SW on
unclassified road, between B9134
and A932.*

3rm (1fb) ✖ ✱B&bfr£8 Bdifr£12
Wfr£84 ⅄
♨ TV 4P ⚿ 187acres arable mixed
Ⓥ

BRECON
Powys
Map **3**   SO02

GH Beacons 16 Bridge St ☎(0874) 3339
*Georgian house with secluded garden
beside the River Usk.*

12hc (2🛏) (7fb) ✱B&b£8.50–£12 Bdi£13–
£16.50 W£91–£115.50 ⅄ LDO6pm
Lic ♨ CTV 12P

BREDWARDINE
Hereford & Worcester
Map **3**   SO34

GH Bredwardine Hall ☎Moccas (09817)
596
Mar–Nov

*Elegant early 19th-century manor-house in
tranquil garden setting.*

5hc (3⇘) (1fb) CTV in all bedrooms ✖ ℝ
✱B&b£10.50–£15 Bdi£18–£22.50 W£121–
£152.50 ⅄ LDO6.30pm
Lic ♨ 7P nc10yrs
Ⓥ

INN Red Lion ☎Moccas (09817) 303
Mar–Oct (rs Nov–Feb party bookings
only)

*Charming, comfortable inn which also
offers fishing and organised shoots.*   →

7hc (4🛁) Annexe: 3hc (2🛁 1🚿) (1fb) CTV in 5 bedrooms [R] ✱B&b£11.50–£24 Bdi£15–£34.50 W£133–£195 Ł Bar lunch £2.25alc Dinner8.30pm £10.50

♨ 35P 3🚗 ♩

Credit cards [1] [2] [3] [5]

BRENCHLEY
Kent
Map **5** TQ64

INN *Rose & Crown* High St ☎(089272) 2107

Historic, 16th-century inn with an interesting menu; well-furnished bedrooms with en-suite facilities.

3🛁 (1fb) CTV in all bedrooms ⋈ LDO9pm

♨ 20P

Credit cards [1] [2] [3] [5]

BRENDON
Devon
Map **3** SS74

GH Brendon House ☎(05987) 206

Standing in ¾acre of walled gardens, ideally situated for walking or riding through wooded valleys. Stabling for two horses.

5hc (1🛁) (1fb) B&b£10–£12 Bdi£16–£18 W£98–£105 Ł LDO6pm

Lic ♨ CTV 5P ♩

[V]

FH Mrs C A South ***Farley Water*** *(SS744464)* ☎(05987) 272
May–Oct

Comfortable farmhouse adjoining the moors. Good home-cooking and freedom for children.

3rm (2hc) (2fb)

CTV P ♩ 220acres beef sheep mixed

BRENT ELEIGH
Suffolk
Map **5** TL94

FH Mrs J P Gage **Street** *(TL945476)* ☎Lavenham (0787) 247271
Apr–Oct

A most beautiful period house, tastefully-furnished to a high standard.

3rm (2hc) ⋈ [R] ✱B&b£11–£11.50

♨ CTV 3P nc12yrs 143acres arable

BRICKHILL, GREAT
Buckinghamshire
Map **4** SP93

INN Duncombe Arms 32 Lower Way ☎(052526) 226
rs Sun evening

Cosy, comfortable and well equipped. Extensive garden leisure facilities including putting green.

(3🚿) (1fb) CTV in all bedrooms ⋈ [R] ✱B&b£25–£30 Bdi£31.75–£45 Wfr£222.25 Ł L£6.75&alc D10pm £6.75–£10&alc

♨ 15P 2🚗 🏠 petanque

Credit cards [1] [3] [V]

BRIDESTOWE
Devon
Map **2** SX58

FH Mrs M A Down **Little Bidlake** *(SX494887)* ☎(083786) 233
Whit–Oct

Neat, clean and efficient farmhouse adjacent to A30 between Bridestowe and Launceston.

2hc ⋈ ✱B&b£8 Bdi£12.50 Wfr£80 Ł LDO9am

♨ CTV P 🏠 ♩ 150acres arable beef dairy

[V]

FH Mrs J Northcott **Town** *(SX504905)* ☎(083786) 226
May–Oct

Attractive Devonshire farmhouse situated in the centre of a typical Dartmoor village. Offers comfortable accommodation and friendly service.

3hc (1fb) ⋈ [R] ✱B&b£8–£9 Bdi£12–£13 Wfr£80 Ł LDO7pm

♨ CTV 4P 160acres dairy

FH Mrs M Hockridge **Week** *(SX519913)* ☎(083786) 221

Large 17th-century stone-built farmhouse set in peaceful Devonshire countryside ¾ mile from A30.

6hc (4fb) ⋈ [R] ✱B&b£9–£9.50 Bdi£13–£13.50 W£88 Ł LDO3pm

CTV 10P 163acres dairy sheep mixed

[V]

See advertisement under Okehampton

BRIDGERULE
Devon
Map **2** SS20

FH Mrs S A Gardener **Buttsbeer Cross** *(SS266043)* ☎(028881) 210
May–Sep

Modernised farmhouse dating from 15th century. Within easy reach of Bude and North Cornish coast.

4rm (3hc) ⋈ ✱B&b£7–£7.50 Bdi£10–£10.50 W£70–£72 Ł LDO1pm

CTV 3P nc6yrs 230acres mixed

BRIDGNORTH
Shropshire
Map **7** SO79

GH Croft Hotel St Mary's Street (Guestaccom) ☎(07462) 67155
Closed Xmas

Lovely 18th-century house, tastefully preserved and modernised.

12hc (4🛁 6🚿) (2fb) ✱B&b£13–£16 Bdi£20.95–£23.95 Wfr£114 Ł LDO7.30pm

Lic ♨ CTV 🏠

Credit cards [1] [3] [V]

GH Severn Arms Hotel Underhill St, Low Town ☎(07462) 4616
rs Nov–Mar

A homely and convivial atmosphere in this early Victorian house near the River Severn.

10hc (6fb) [R] ✱B&b£11.50–£14 Bdi£17–£18.50 W£92–£103.50 Ł LDO7.30pm

Lic ♨ CTV *P* 🏠

INN King's Head Hotel Whitburn St ☎(07462) 2141

An authentic 17th-century coaching inn close to town centre.

5hc (3fb) CTV in all bedrooms ✈ [R] ✱B&b£12.50–£13 Lunch £2–£6 Dinner 8pm £3–£8

♨ 8P 🚗

[V]

BRIDLINGTON
Humberside
Map **8** TA16

GH Bay Ridge Hotel Summerfield Rd ☎(0262) 673425
Closed Oct & Nov

Spacious, well-designed conversion of two semi-detached houses, close to South Bay.

14hc (5🛁 5🚿) (5fb) CTV in 8 bedrooms ✱B&b£10–£11 Bdi£12.80–£13.80 W£80–£90 Ł LDO4pm

Lic ♨ CTV 6P ⌂

[V]

GH Langdon Hotel Pembroke Ter ☎(0262) 673065
May–Oct rs Mar, Apr & Nov

Comfortable hotel with smart, cosy lounge and sea views.

21hc (9🚿) (6fb) TV in 6 bedrooms ✈ ✱B&b£11–£13 Bdi£15–£18 W£85–£96 Ł (W only Jun–Sep) LDO6pm

Lic ♨ CTV ₱

GH Shirley Private Hotel 48 South Marine Dr ☎(0262) 672539

Comfortable, well-furnished guesthouse with spacious lounge and attractive dining room.

41hc (2🛁 12🚿) (4fb) [R] ✱B&b£12–£13 Bdi£16–£17 W£90.85–£115 Ł LDO10pm

Lic lift ♨ CTV 7P

Credit cards [1] [3] [V]

GH *Southdowne Hotel* South Marine Dr ☎(0262) 673270

Bright and cheerful house facing the sea.

10hc (2fb) ✈ [R] LDO6pm

Lic ♨ CTV 10P

Bridgnorth — Brighton & Hove

BRIDPORT
Dorset
Map **3** SY49

GH Bridge House East St ☎(0308) 23371

Spacious, 18th-century, detached building on A35 on outskirts of town. Comfortable accommodation and friendly service.

11rm (10hc 6🛁 2🚿) (3fb) [R] ✱B&b£10–£12 Bdi£15.50–£17.50 W£117 Ł LDO9pm

Lic ♨ CTV 13P

See advertisement on page 90

GH Britmead House 154 West Bay Rd (Guestaccom) ☎(0308) 22941
Closed Jan

Between Bridport and West Bay harbour.

6hc (4🛁) (1fb) CTV in all bedrooms [R] B&b£12–£15 Bdi£19–£22.50 W£122.50–£147 Ł LDO5pm

Lic ♨ 6P nc5yrs

Credit cards [1] [3] [V]

See advertisement on page 90

INN King Charles Tavern 114 St Andrews Rd ☎(0308) 22911

Situated a short distance from the town centre alongside the Beaminster to Yeovil road.

4hc TV in 2 bedrooms ✈ ✱B&b£9–£10 Bdi£11–£14 W£75–£85 Ł Lunch £4–£6 Dinner 7.30pm £5–£8

CTV 6P 🚗

Credit card [3] [V]

BRIGHTON & HOVE
East Sussex
Map **4** TQ30

See plans **Brighton** and **Hove** on pp 91 & 92

For additional guesthouses see **Rottingdean** and **Saltdean**

Recommended

GH Adelaide Hotel 51 Regency Sq ☎(0273) 205286 Brighton plan **1** *B1*
Closed Jan

Good bedrooms with modern facilities. Cosy lounge and bar.

11hc (2🛁 9🚿) (1fb) CTV in all bedrooms ✈ [R] B&b£22.50–£35 Bdi£29.50–£42 W£206.50–£294 Ł

Lic ♨ ₱

Credit cards [1] [2] [3] [5]

GH Ascott House 21 New Steine, Marine Pde ☎(0273) 688085 Brighton plan **2** *E2*

Small Victorian guesthouse run by friendly proprietors, only a short walk from shops and sea front.

10hc (4fb) CTV in all bedrooms ✈ [R] ✱B&b£10–£12.50 W£63–£77 M

Lic ♨ ₱

Credit cards [1] [2] [3]

GH *Cavalaire House* 34 Upper Rock Gdns, Kemptown ☎(0273) 696899 Brighton plan **3** *E2*
Closed Xmas

Cheerful little terraced house away from the sea front.

9hc (2🚿) (4fb) CTV in all bedrooms [R]

♨ CTV ₱ nc3yrs

GH *Charlotte House* 9 Charlotte St ☎(0273) 692849 Brighton plan **4** *F1*

Family-run commercial hotel within easy reach of the city centre.

9hc (3🚿) (1fb) CTV in all bedrooms [R]

♨ ₱

GH *Corner Lodge Hotel* 33 Wilbury Gdns, Hove ☎(0273) 775931 Hove plan **1** *B3*

A small, family-run residence, standing in its own grounds.

15🛁 🚿 (7fb) CTV in all bedrooms LDO8.30pm

Lic lift ♨ CTV P solarium

Credit cards [1] [2] [3] [5]

Bridge House Hotel

East Street, Bridport, Dorset DT6 3LB
Telephone: Bridport (0308) 23371

A spacious 18th-century hotel of character ideally located. The hotel is situated on the A35 close to the historic town of Bridport. West Dorset is an area of outstanding natural beauty with West Bay a mere 1½ miles, a quaint fishing harbour that is not over commercialised. We offer excellent home cooking and an informal relaxed atmosphere. Ample car parking. Open all year. The hotel is very popular and highly recommended.
Proprietors: John & Carole Horne.

Britmead House Hotel

This small hotel is an ideal base for touring West Dorset beauty spots and the Hardy Country. Pleasant location with level walks to beach, harbour and shops.
Full central heating, licensed, lounge. All bedrooms have Colour TV, tea & coffee making and electric blankets. Private bathrooms available.
All cooking and service by resident proprietors Roy and Dot Beckhelling who assure their guests of good food and every comfort.
Mid-week bookings taken at all times. Ample Parking

Brochure on request:
154, West Bay Road, Bridport, Dorset. DT6 4EG. Tel: Bridport (0308) 22941

The Marquis of Lorne

Nettlecombe, Nr Bridport, Dorset
Telephone: Powerstock 236

16th century Country Inn, 6 miles from the coast. Beautiful walking country. Large childrens' adventure play area. Warm comfortable bars and cosy restaurant. Traditional and French dishes cooked by chef/proprietor. Log fires and warm welcome. Eight rooms, four en suite and three family.

If you like warm comfortable rooms, happy atmosphere and superb food, please phone or write for details.

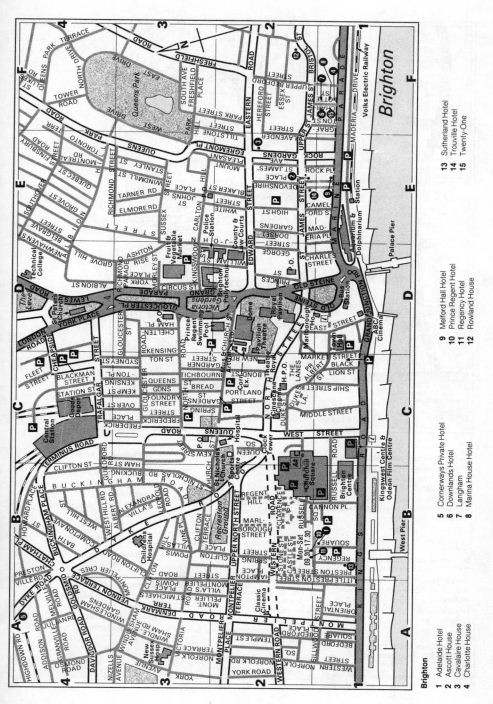

Brighton

1 Adelaide Hotel
2 Ascott House
3 Cavalaire House
4 Charlotte House

5 Cornerways Private Hotel
6 Downlands Hotel
7 Langham
8 Marina House Hotel

9 Melford Hall Hotel
10 Prince Regent Hotel
11 Regency Hotel
12 Rowland House

13 Sutherland Hotel
14 Trouville Hotel
15 Twenty-One

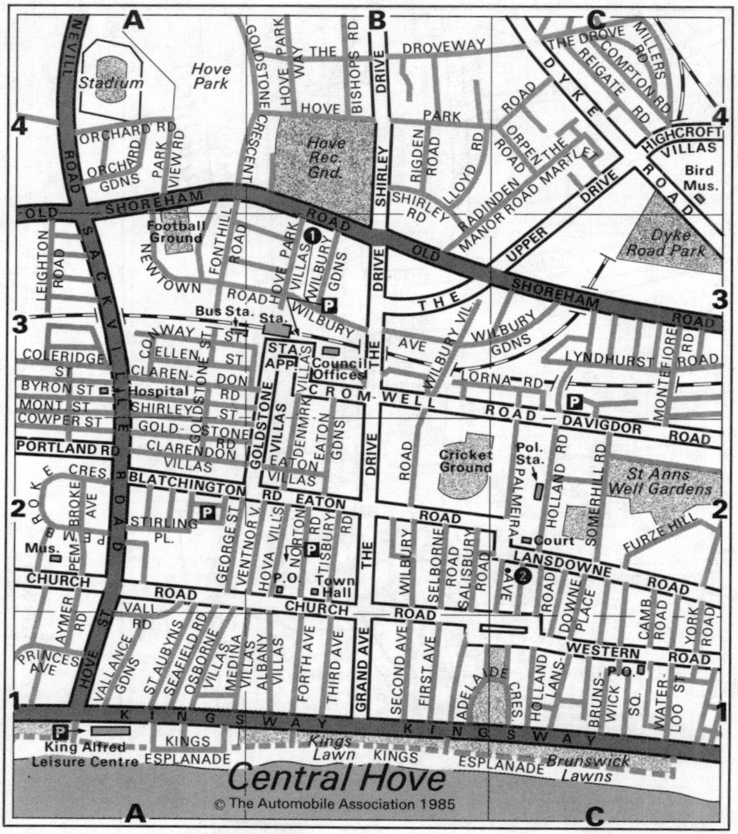

Hove

1 Corner Lodge Hotel
2 Croft Hotel

Recommended

GH *Cornerways Private Hotel*
20 Caburn Rd, Hove ☎(0273) 731882
Brighton plan **5** *A4*

Small comfortable house with modern bedrooms and limited lounge facilities.

10hc (2fb) [R] LDO4pm

Lic CTV 🚫🅿

GH Croft Hotel 24 Palmeira Av, Hove ☎(0273) 732860 Hove plan **2** *C2*

Well-established guesthouse, pleasantly situated within easy walking distance to the beach.

11hc (3fb) B&b£12.25–£15

Lic 🍴 CTV 🚫🅿

[V]

GH *Downlands Hotel* 19 Charlotte St ☎(0273) 601203 Brighton plan **6** *F1*
Closed Xmas

A five-storey Victorian house run by young friendly couple, near shops and sea front.

11hc (2fb) CTV in 5 bedrooms TV in 6 bedrooms [R] LDO10am

🍴 CTV 🚫🅿

Credit cards [2] [3]

GH Langham 16 Charlotte St ☎(0273) 682843 Brighton plan **7** *F1*
Closed Dec

Victorian terraced house, comfortable and well-run establishment, just off sea front.

9hc (3fb) 🚫🐕 *B&b£10–£11

CTV nc7yrs

Recommended

GH *Marina House Hotel* 8 Charlotte St, Marine Pde ☎(0273) 605349
Brighton plan **8** *F1*

Five-storey terraced Victorian hotel, with well-equipped accommodation, near sea front.

11hc (4🚿) (1fb) CTV in 8 bedrooms TV in 3 bedrooms [R] LDOnoon

Lic 🍴 CTV 🚫🅿

GH Melford Hall Hotel 41 Marine Pde ☎(0273) 681435 Brighton plan **9** *E1*
Closed Xmas–1st Jan

Situated on sea front with well-appointed accommodation.

12hc (8fb) CTV in all bedrooms
*B&b£16–£24

Lic CTV 12P

Credit cards [1] [2] [3] [5] [V]

GH Prince Regent Hotel 29 Regency Sq ☎(0273) 29962 Brighton plan **10** *B2*

Very comfortable Regency town house, with friendly attentive staff.

18🚿 CTV in all bedrooms 🚫🐕 [R]
*B&b£20–£30 W£126 M̸

Lic CTV 🚫🅿 nc12yrs

Credit cards [1] [3] [5] [V]

GH *Birkdale Hotel* 11 Ashgrove Rd,
Redland ☎(0272) 733635 Plan **4** *C5*
Closed Xmas

Commercial hotel off Whiteladies Road.

18hc (4⇆5fl) CTV in all bedrooms ℗
LDO7.55pm

Lic ㎩ 12P snooker

Credit cards ① ③

See advertisement on page 96

Bristol

GH Cavendish House Hotel
18 Cavendish Rd, Henleaze ☎(0272)
621017 Plan **6** *C5*

*Small, comfortable, friendly guesthouse in
residential area near Henleaze shopping
centre.*

8hc (3fb) CTV in all bedrooms ✳B&bfr£13
Wfr£91 ₥

㎩ 5P

ⓥ

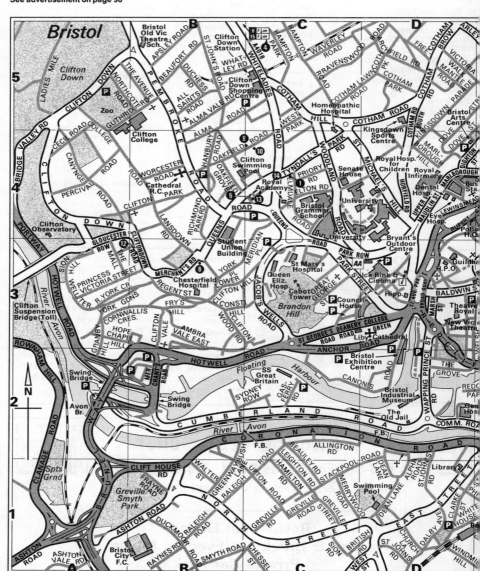

GH Chesterfield Hotel 3 Westbourne Pl, Clifton ☎(0272) 734606 Telex no 449075 Plan **5** *C4*
Closed wknds & Xmas
Pleasant small commercial hotel convenient to Clifton and local restaurants.
13hc CTV in all bedrooms [R]
*B&b£10.25–£13.50
🍴 P̸
Credit cards [1] [3] [V]

Bristol

Recommended

GH *Glenroy Hotel* 30 Victoria Sq, Clifton ☎(0272) 739058 Plan **8** *B3*
Closed Xmas wk
Pleasing private hotel in Clifton near to restaurants.
31hc (6🛁 13🚿) Annexe: 17 🚿 (9fb) CTV in all bedrooms [R]
Lic 🍴 16P
Credit cards [1] [3]

GH Oakdene Hotel 45 Oakfield Rd, Clifton ☎(0272) 735900 Plan **9** *C4*
Closed Xmas wk
Small, proprietor-run hotel.
14hc (2fb) CTV in all bedrooms ✗ [R]
*B&b£15 Bdi£19 Wfr£124 ⱡ LDO6.30pm
🍴 1P
See advertisement on page 96

GH *Oakfield Hotel* 52–54 Oakfield Rd, Clifton ☎(0272) 735556 Plan **10** *C4*
Closed 23–31 Dec
Personally-run, private hotel.
27hc (4fb) LDO7pm
🍴 CTV 4P 2🚗
See advertisement on page 97

GH Rodney Hotel 4 Rodney Pl, Clifton ☎(0272) 735422 Plan **12** *B3*
Closed Xmas
In Clifton village near to restaurants.
25hc (6fb) ✗ *B&b£15
🍴 CTV P̸
[V]

GH *Seeleys Hotel* 19–27 St Pauls Rd, Clifton ☎(0272) 738544 Plan **13** *C4*
Closed Xmas wk
Lively hotel conveniently situated for city centre.
40rm (26hc 9🛁 17🚿) Annexe: 20rm (9hc 6🛁 3🚿) (22fb) CTV in all bedrooms ✗ [R] LDO10.30pm
Lic 🍴 12P 18🚗 ⌂
Credit cards [1] [2] [3]

GH Washington Hotel 11–15 St Pauls Rd, Clifton ☎(0272) 733980 Telex no 449075 Plan **14** *C4*
Closed Xmas
Pleasant small hotel.
34hc (10🛁 8🚿) (6fb) CTV in all bedrooms [R] *B&b£13–£23 Bdi£17.50–£30 W£82–£145 M LDO9pm
Lic 🍴 13P
Credit cards [1] [2] [3] [5]

GH *Westbury Park Hotel*
37 Westbury Rd, Westbury-on-Trym ☎(0272) 620465 Plan **15** *C5*
A high standard of both accommodation and home-cooking can be enjoyed at this hotel.
9hc (2🛁 3🚿) CTV in all bedrooms B&b£13.25–£24 Bdi£21.15–£31.95 LDO8pm
Lic 🍴 6P

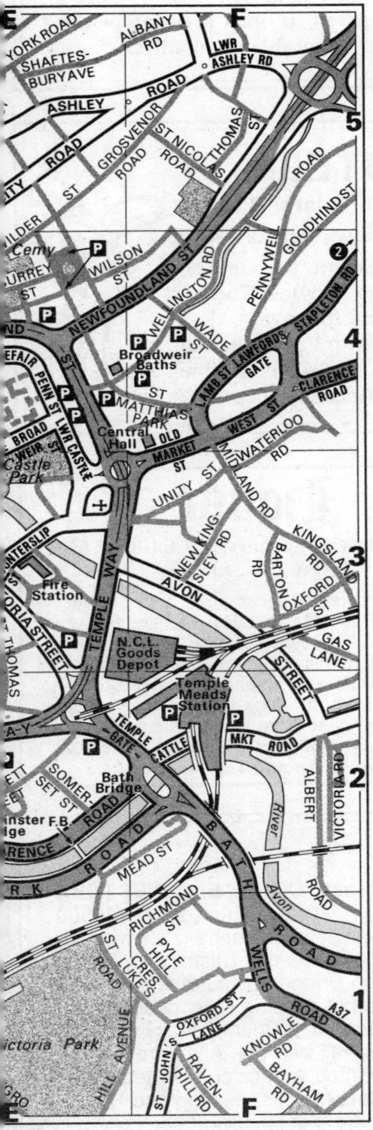

Bristol

1 Alandale Hotel
2 Alcove
4 Birkdale Hotel
5 Chesterfield Hotel
6 Cavendish House Hotel
8 Glenroy Hotel
9 Oakdene Hotel
10 Oakfield Hotel
12 Rodney Hotel
13 Seeleys Hotel
14 Washington Hotel
15 Westbury Park Hotel

Brixham

1 Cottage Hotel
2 Harbour View Hotel
3 Harbour Side
4 Raddicombe Lodge
5 Ranscambe House Hotel
6 Sampford House
7 Torbay Heights Hotel

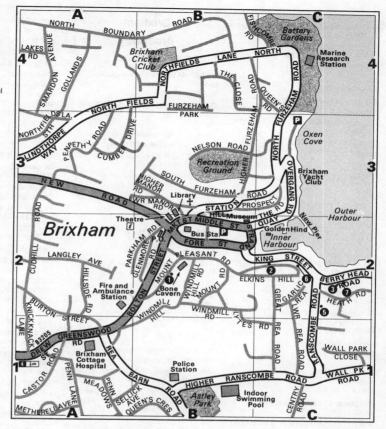

BRIXHAM
Devon
Map **3** SX95
See plan

GH *Cottage Hotel* Mount Pleasant Rd
☎(08045) 2123 Plan **1** *B2*

8hc (3fb) ✠
Lic ⬚ CTV 5P nc2yrs

GH Harbour Side 65 Berry Head Road
☎(08045) 58899 Plan **3** *C2*

*Friendly guesthouse overlooking harbour
and coastline.*

6hc (3fb) ® ✱B&b£7.50–£9 Bdi£12.50–
£13.50 W£87.50–£94.50 ⅙ LDOnoon
CTV ⬚ 🅿
ⓥ

GH Harbour View Hotel 65 King St
☎(08045) 3052 Plan **2** *C2*

10hc (3fb) CTV in 4 bedrooms TV in 6
bedrooms ✠ ® B&b£8.50–£14.50
Bdi£13.50–£19.50 W£94–£135 ⅙
CTV 2P

Credit cards ① ③

GH Raddicombe Lodge 105 Kingswear Rd ☎(08045) 2125 Plan **4** *A1*

9hc (2fb) ✖ *B&b£9.55–£11.65 Bdi£14.50–£17.70 W£101.50–£112.70Ⱡ LDO4.30pm

Lic CTV 10P

Credit cards [1] [3] [V]

GH *Ranscambe House Hotel*
Ranscambe Rd ☎(08045) 2337 Plan **5** *C2*

Country-house-style property with friendly service.

10hc (7🛁 3🚿) (4fb) [R] LDOnoon

Lic 🍴 CTV 14P

GH Sampford House 57–59 King St ☎(08045) 7761 Plan **6** *C2*
Apr–Oct

Small, personally-run residence. Spotless, comfortable bedrooms.

6hc (4fb) ✖ *B&b£7.50–£8.50 Bdi£12.45–£13.45 LDO7.30pm

CTV Ᵽ

[V]

GH Torbay Heights Hotel Berry Head Rd ☎(08045) 4738
Etr–Oct rs Nov–7 Jan & Mar–Etr

Small, friendly guesthouse offering good home cooking.

10hc (1🛁) (3fb) [R] *B&b£9–£11 Bdi£14.50–£16.50 W£98–£110Ⱡ LDO7.15pm

Lic 🍴 CTV 9P nc6yrs

Credit cards [1] [3] [5]

BROAD CHALKE
Wiltshire
Map **4** SU02

INN Queens Head ☎Salisbury (0722) 780344

4🛁 CTV in all bedrooms ✖ [R] B&b£19.50 Lunch £5–£8&alc Dinner 9pm £5–£8&alc

Lic 🍴 40P ⧣ nc14yrs

Credit card [3]

BROADFORD
Isle of Skye, Highland *Inverness-shire*
See **Skye, Isle of**

Brixham — Broadway

BROAD HAVEN (nr Haverfordwest)
Dyfed
Map **2** SM81

GH Broad Haven Hotel ☎(043783) 366
Telex no 57515
Mar–Oct

Large, lively family hotel facing beach.

39hc (32🛁 3🚿) (12fb) CTV in all bedrooms [R] *B&b£10–£20 Bdi£16–£26 W£105–£156Ⱡ LDO7.30pm

Lic CTV 100P 🏊 (heated) solarium

Credit cards [1] [2] [3] [5] [V]

BROAD MARSTON
Hereford & Worcester
Map **4** SP14

GH Broad Marston Manor ☎Stratford-upon-Avon (0789) 720252
Mar–Nov

7hc (1🛁) TV in all bedrooms ✖ B&b£16–£17

🍴 CTV 20P nc12yrs

See advertisement under Stratford upon Avon

BROADSTAIRS
Kent
Map **5** TR36

GH Bay Tree Hotel 12 Eastern Esp ☎Thanet (0843) 62502

Well-run, comfortable hotel with spacious bedrooms and sea views.

10hc (3🛁 1🚿) (2fb) CTV in 9 bedrooms TV in 1 bedroom [R] B&b£11.75–£13.75 Bdi£16.50–£17.75 W£106–£118.50Ⱡ LDO1pm

Lic 🍴 CTV 10P

[V]

GH *Cornerways Hotel* 49–51 Westcliff Rd ☎Thanet (0843) 61612

12hc (5fb) CTV in 4 bedrooms [R] LDO7pm

Lic CTV 14P

GH *Dutch House Hotel* 30 North Foreland Rd ☎Thanet (0843) 62824

Homely house with simple accommodation. Overlooking the sea.

10hc ✖ LDO6.30pm

Lic 🍴 CTV 6P

GH *East Horndon Hotel*
4 Eastern Esp ☎Thanet (0843) 68306

Well-managed hotel with well-equipped bedrooms, most facing the sea, complemented by a good choice of home-cooking, and friendly hospitable service.

10hc (2🛁 2🚿) (3fb) CTV in 2 bedrooms TV in 8 bedrooms [R] LDO7pm

Lic 🍴 CTV Ᵽ

Credit cards [1] [3] [5]

GH Keston Court Hotel 14 Ramsgate Rd ☎Thanet (0843) 62401

Comfortable, homely accommodation offering choice of menu.

9hc (2fb) ✖ [R] *B&b£10.50–£12.50 Bdifr£16.50–£17.50 W£90–£102Ⱡ LDO2pm

Lic 🍴 CTV 7P nc5yrs

Credit card [2] [V]

GH *Rothsay Private Hotel*
110 Pierremont Av ☎Thanet (0843) 62646

Detached double-fronted house with nicely-appointed rooms and run by the proprietor and his wife.

14hc (5🚿) (4fb) [R]

Lic 🍴 CTV Ᵽ

GH *St Augustines Hotel* 19 Granville Rd ☎Thanet (0843) 65017

Cheerful and bright modern bedrooms complemented by small lounge with bar. Near the sea.

15hc (4🚿) (5fb) CTV in all bedrooms [R] Ⱡ LDO7pm

Lic 🍴 1P

Credit cards [1] [3]

BROADWAY
Hereford & Worcester
Map **4** SP03

GH Leasow House Laverton Meadows ☎Stanton (038673) 526
(For full entry see **Laverton**)

GH Old Rectory Church St ☎Evesham (0386) 853729
(For full entry see **Willersey**)

GH Olive Branch 78–80 High St ☎(0386) 853440
Closed Xmas
8hc (2➦) (2fb) ✗ B&b£10–£12
CTV 8P
Ⓥ

BROADWINDSOR
Dorset
Map **3** ST40

FH Mrs C Poulton **Hursey** (ST433028)
☎(0308) 68323
Closed Xmas & New Year

Broadway
—
Brockweir Common

Comfortable and well-designed farmhouse accommodation enjoying quiet location in rolling Dorset countryside.
2hc ✗ Ⓡ ✳B&bfr£9 Bdifr£14 Wfr£85 ⅃
LDOnoon
🍴 TV 2P nc5yrs 2½acres non-working
Ⓥ

BROCKWEIR COMMON
Gloucestershire
Map **3** SO50

FH Mrs M L Hitchon **Sylvia** (SO 544024)
☎(02918) 514
Closed Jan

16th-century farmhouse with magnificent views over surrounding countryside. Comfortable rooms.
3hc (1fb) ✗ ✳B&bfr£9.50 Bdifr£15.50
Wfr£65 ℳ
CTV 6P
14 acres livestock

Rothsay Private Hotel

110 PIERREMONT AVENUE, BROADSTAIRS, KENT Telephone (0843) 62646

Comfortable family hotel offering all modern facilities.
Only 2 minutes from main beaches and all amenities.
Pleasant modern bedrooms some with shower and toilet en suite and all offering tea or coffee making facilities and Radio/Intercom/Baby Alarm System.
Spacious Licensed Restaurant. Five course evening dinner offering choice of Menu, or Bed and Breakfast if preferred.
Children welcome at reduced terms.
Open all year.
We specialise in Off Season Breaks.
Full Central Heating.

Leasow House

Laverton Meadows, Broadway, Worcestershire WR12 7NA
Telephone: Stanton (0386 73) 526

Tranquilly situated approximately one mile off the A46 and some three miles south of Broadway, making it ideally situated as a centre for touring the Cotswolds and the Vale of Evesham.

We offer spacious accommodation with all the refinements of the 20th century. All bedrooms have private shower/bathroom en suite, colour television, tea and coffee making facilities.

Leasow House is personally run by your hosts:
BARBARA & GORDON MEEKINGS
See gazetteer under Laverton

The Old Rectory

WILLERSEY, Nr. BROADWAY, WORCS.

High Class Bed & Breakfast
Delightful Accommodation
Every Facility
Ideal for touring the Cotswolds

Free Brochure on request
Evesham (0386) 853729
John & Helen Jones

BROMLEY
Gt London
London plan **4** *F2*
(page 247)

GH Bromley Continental Hotel
56 Plaistow Ln ☎01-464 2415
Plainly furnished detached Victorian house with own garden.
23hc (1🛁) CTV in 6 bedrooms ✕
✱B&b£10.50–£27.50 W£73.50–£192.50 M
Lic ♨ CTV 14P
Credit cards [1] [3] [4]

GH Glendevon House 80 Southborough Rd, Bickley (2m E off A22)
☎01-467 2183
10hc (1🚿) (1fb) CTV in 5 bedrooms
✱B&b£12.25–£15 Bdi£13.50–£16.50
Wfr£75 M LDO9pm
♨ CTV 7P
Credit cards [1] [3] Ⓥ

BROMPTON REGIS
Somerset
Map **3** SS93

FH Mrs G Payne **Lower Holworthy**
(SS978308) ☎(03987) 244
Closed Xmas
Small 18th-century hill farm overlooking and bordering Wimbleball Lake in Exmoor National Park.
3hc ✕ Ⓡ ✱B&b£10 Bdi£16
♨ CTV 6P ⌂ 200acres beef sheep
Ⓥ

BROMSGROVE
Hereford & Worcester
Map **7** SO97

INN Forest 290 Birmingham Rd ☎(0527) 72063
9hc CTV in all bedrooms Ⓡ ✱B&b£16.50
Lunch £2.80alc Dinner 9.15pm £4alc
♨ 70P
Credit cards [1] [3]

BROUGH
Cumbria
Map **12** NY71

FH Mrs J M Atkinson **Augill House**
(NY814148) ☎(09304) 305
Closed Xmas & New Year
Fine Victorian house in pleasant rural surroundings offering comfortable accommodation and good home-cooking.
3hc TV in all bedrooms Ⓡ ✱B&b£8.50
Bdi£14 LDO4pm
♨ CTV 6P nc12yrs 40acres dairy

BROUGHTON IN FURNESS
Cumbria
Map **7** SD28

INN High Cross Inn ☎(06576) 272
Closed Xmas
Built in 1660. Spectacular views from the attractive restaurant.
7hc (1🛁 2🚿) (2fb) CTV in all bedrooms Ⓡ
✱B&b£10–£15 Bdi£14–£17 W£98–£120 L
Lunch £3–£6&alc Dinner 9.30pm £4–£8&alc
♨ CTV 40P ⌂
Credit cards [1] [3]

BRUAR
Tayside *Perthshire*
Map **14** NN86

INN Bruar Falls Hotel ☎Calvine (0796) 83243
Family-run hotel in picturesque setting just off the A9. Simple accommodation with all-day meal service.
7rm (1fb) Ⓡ ✱B&b£10.50 Lunch £4.50alc
High Tea £4.50alc Dinner 9pm £9alc
♨ CTV 80P
Credit cards [1] [2] [3] [5] Ⓥ

BRUTON
Somerset
Map **3** ST63

GH *Fryerning* Frome Rd, Burrowfield
☎(0749) 812343
4hc (3🛁 1🚿) CTV in 2 bedrooms TV in 2 bedrooms Ⓡ LDO7pm
Lic ♨ CTV 6P nc12yrs

BRYNGWYN
Powys
Map **3** SO14

FH Mrs H E A Nicholls **Newhouse**
(SO191497) ☎Painscastle (04975) 671
200-year old, two-storey, stone-built farmhouse set in rolling countryside.
2hc ✕ Ⓡ ✱B&b£7.50–£8.50 Bdi£14–£16
W£95–£108 L LDO5.30pm
♨ CTV 2P nc8yrs ♪ 150acres beef sheep mixed
Ⓥ

BUCKFASTLEIGH
Devon
Map **3** SX76

GH *Black Rock* Buckfast Rd, Dart Bridge (at Buckfast 1m N) ☎(0364) 42343
10hc (3🚿) (3fb) Ⓡ ✱B&b£12–£14
Bdi£17.50–£19 W£122.50–£133 L
LDO9pm
Lic ♨ CTV 43P ♪
Credit cards [1] [3] Ⓥ

BUCKLAND BREWER
Devon
Map **2** SS42

FH Mrs M Brown **Holwell** *(SS424159)*
☎Langtree (08055) 288
May–Oct
16th-century farmhouse with a friendly and homely atmosphere.
5hc (3fb) ✱B&b£9 Bdi£13 W£75 L (W only Jul & Aug) LDO5pm
CTV P 300acres mixed
Ⓥ

BUCKNELL
Shropshire
Map **7** SO37

FH Mrs B E M Davies **Bucknell House**
(SO355735) ☎(05474) 248
Mar–Nov
Mellow, listed Georgian house in secluded grounds on fringe of village, overlooking picturesque Teme Valley.
2🛁 ✱B&b£9.50–£11 W£66.50–£73.50 M
♨ CTV 3P nc13yrs 🎾(hard) ♪ 70acres grazing

FH Mrs C Price **Hall** *(SO356737)*
☎(05474) 249
Feb–Nov

A large Georgian farmhouse providing homely accommodation in peaceful rural surroundings close to village centre.

3rm (2hc) (1fb) ✗ ✱B&b£9 Bdi£14 W£90 ⫽ LDO10am

CTV 6P nc7yrs 225acres arable sheep

BUDE
Cornwall
Map **2**   SS20
See plan on page 102

GH Atlantic Beach 25 Downs View
☎(0288) 3431 Plan **1** *B5*

Edwardian mid-terrace house overlooking the golf course, 300 yards from beach.

9hc (4🏶) (3fb) CTV in all bedrooms ®
✱B&b£6.50–£9 Bdi£10.50–£11 W£60–£82 ⫽ LDO6.30pm

Lic 🏵 CTV 1P

Credit cards 1 2 3 Ⓥ

GH Cliff Hotel Maer Down, Crooklets
☎(0288) 3110 Plan **2** *B5*
Apr–Oct

15⇔ (10fb) CTV in all bedrooms
B&b£10.50–£13.50 Bdi£14.50–£17.50 W£95–£117 ⫽ LDO6.30pm

Lic CTV 15P ⋒ ⌇ (heated) ♪ (hard)
Ⓥ

Bucknell
—
Bude

GH Dorset House Hotel 47 Killerton Rd
☎(0288) 2665 Plan **2A** *C3*

Charming building offering traditional English fare.

6hc (1⇔) (2fb) ✗ ✱B&b£10–£14 Bdi£12–£15 W£70–£95 ⫽ LDO2pm

Lic 🏵 CTV 6P
Ⓥ

GH Kisauni 4 Downs View ☎(0288) 2653 Plan **3** *C5*
Closed Xmas

A convivial atmosphere and home-cooking distinguish this semi-detached guesthouse.

6hc (3fb) ✗ ® ✱B&b£8–£9.50 Bdi£12.50–£14 W£80–£90 ⫽ LDO9am

CTV 5P nc2yrs
Ⓥ

GH Links View 13 Morwenna Ter
☎(0288) 2561 Plan **4** *C4*
Closed 2 wks Xmas

7hc (2fb) CTV in all bedrooms ✗ ®
✱B&b£8–£9.50 Bdi£12–£13.50 W£65–£78 ⫽ LDO6pm

Lic 🏵 CTV 2P 1🎖
Ⓥ

⇤GH Pencarrol 21 Downs View
☎(0288) 2478 Plan **5** *C5*
Closed Xmas

Double-fronted, end of terrace Victorian house overlooking the downs and close to beaches.

9rm (8hc) (2fb) B&b£7–£8 Bdi£10.50–£11.50 W£67.50–£77 ⫽ LDO5pm

CTV 1🎖
Ⓥ

GH Surf Haven 31 Downs View ☎(0288) 2998 Plan **7** *B5*
Closed Dec

10hc (5fb) CTV in 5 bedrooms ®
LDO5.30pm

Lic CTV 6P

GH Sweeney's 35 Downs View ☎(0288) 2073 Plan **6** *B5*
Mar–Oct

Friendly guest house a short way from Crooklets Beach.

11hc (5fb) ✗ LDO5pm

Lic CTV 10P nc3yrs snooker

GH Wayfarer Hotel 23 Downs View
☎(0288) 2253 Plan **8** *B5*
Closed Xmas

11hc (2⇔ 6🏶) (5fb) CTV in all bedrooms ® ✱B&b£10–£12.50 Bdi£15–£17.50 W£95–£110 ⫽ LDO6.30pm

Lic 🏵 CTV 2P ⋒
Ⓥ

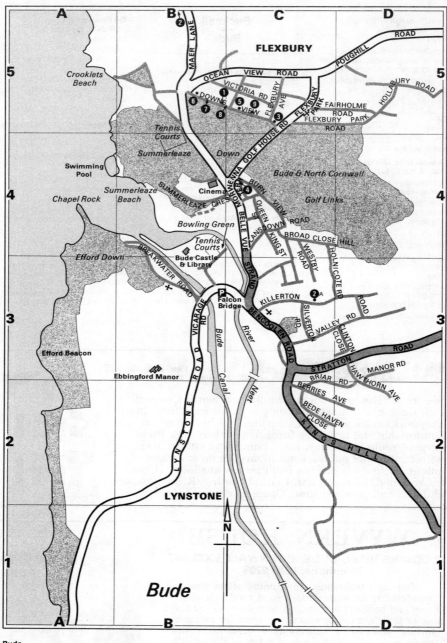

Bude

1	Atlantic Beach	**4**	Links View	**8**	Wayfarer Hotel
2	Cliff Hotel	**5**	Pencarrol	**9**	Wyvern House
2A	Dorset House Hotel	**6**	Sweeneys		
3	Kisauni	**7**	Surf Haven		

⊢→**GH Wyvern House** 7 Downs View ☎(0288) 2205 Plan **9** *C5*

Privately run guesthouse with sea views.

8hc (3fb) ✖ B&b£8–£10 Bdi£13–£15 W£91–£105 ⱡ LDO8pm

Lic 🛋 CTV 4P

See advertisement on page 101

BUDLEIGH SALTERTON
Devon
Map **3** SY08

GH Copperfields Hotel 7 Upper Stoneborough Ln ☎(03954) 3430

6hc (1fb) Ⓡ *B&bfr£11.50 Bdifr£17.50 Wfr£70 M LDO7pm

Lic CTV P

GH Long Range Hotel Vale's Rd ☎(03954) 3321
Spring–Autumn

9hc (1🛁 1🚿) (1fb) CTV in all bedrooms ✖ Ⓡ *B&b£12–£13 Bdi£18–£19 W£112–£120 ⱡ

🛋 CTV 8P 2🚗 (charge) nc4yrs

GH Tidwell House Country Hotel ☎(03954) 2444
Closed Xmas

Beautiful Georgian manor in extensive gardens.

8hc (3🛁 3🚿) (6fb) Ⓡ *B&b£14.50 Bdi£18.75 W£115 ⱡ LDO9.15pm

Lic 🛋 CTV 16P 4🚗 🏠

GH Willowmead 12 Little Knowle ☎(03954) 3115

6hc Ⓡ *B&b£8.50–£10 Bdi£14.50–£16 Wfr£90 ⱡ

🛋 CTV 6P nc5yrs

BUILTH WELLS
Powys
Map **3** SO05

FH Mrs Z E Hope **Cae Pandy** *(SO023511)* Garth Rd (1m W A483) ☎(0982) 553793

Cosy farmhouse near the River Irfon.

3hc (1fb) B&b£7.50–£8 Bdi£11–£11.50 W£77–£80.50 ⱡ

🛋 CTV 10P 50acres mixed

Credit cards [1] [2] [3] Ⓥ

BULKWORTHY
Devon
Map **2** SS31

FH Mrs K P Hockridge **Blakes** *(SS395143)* ☎Milton Damerel (040926) 249
Etr–Sep

Pleasant, comfortable and well-decorated house in peaceful setting close to the River Torridge. Ideal touring centre for Devon and Cornwall.

2hc (1fb) ✖ B&bfr£8.50

CTV 6P nc12yrs 150acres arable beef sheep

BURFORD
Oxfordshire
Map **4** SP21

GH Corner House Hotel High St ☎(099382) 3151
Mar–Nov

Charming Cotswold stone building in picturesque High Street. Comfortable antique furnished bedrooms.

9hc (5🛁 4🚿) (2fb) CTV in all bedrooms *B&b£17–£19 LDO9pm

Lic 🛋 CTV 🚫P

BURGH ST PETER
Norfolk
Map **5** TM49

FH Mrs R M Clarke **Shrublands** *(TM473926)* ☎Aldeby (050277) 241

1m SSW unclass rd.

3hc (1fb) ✖ *B&b£8.50–£9.50 W£59.50–£66.50 M

CTV 6P nc5yrs 🎾 (hard) 🎣 350acres arable beef mixed

Ⓥ

BURNSALL
North Yorkshire
Map **7** SE06

GH Manor House ☎(075672) 231
Closed Jan

Small private hotel whose gardens run down to River Wharfe.

7hc (2fb) ✖ B&b£10 Bdi£14 W£98 ⱡ LDO5pm

Lic 🛋 CTV 7P 🎣 [U] solarium

BURNTISLAND
Fife
Map **11** NT28

GH Forthaven 4 South View, Lammerlaws ☎(0592) 872600

Homely guesthouse looking out across the Firth of Forth.

4hc (2fb)

CTV

Ⓥ

BURTON UPON TRENT
Staffordshire
Map **8** SK22

GH Delter Hotel 5 Derby Rd ☎(0283) 35115

5hc (1fb) CTV in all bedrooms *B&bfr£12.50 Bdi£17.50–£19.50 W£122.50–£136.50 ⱡ LDO8pm

Lic 🛋 8P 1🚗 🏠

BURWASH
East Sussex
Map **5** TQ62

FH Mrs E Sirrell **Woodlands** *(TQ656242)* ☎(0435) 882794
Etr–Oct

Comfortably furnished, 16th-century cottage-style farmhouse, 1/3m down track from main road.

4rm ✖ *B&b£9–£10 Bdi£13.50–£14.50 LDOam

🛋 CTV 4P

55 acres mixed

Ⓥ

INN Admiral Vernon Etchingham Rd ☎(0435) 882230

Small 16th-century inn with beautiful gardens, overlooking Rother Valley.

5hc (2fb) CTV in 2 bedrooms TV in 2 bedrooms *B&b£12 Bdi£18 W£98 ⱡ Lunch £4 Dinner 8.45pm £6.50

CTV 30P 2🚗 nc10yrs

Credit card [2]

INN Bell Hign St ☎(0435) 882304
rs Tue

5hc ✖ Ⓡ *B&b£12.50–£15 Bdi£17.50–£20 W£122.50–£140 ⱡ Lunch £5–£8.50 Dinner £5–£8.50 LDO9.30pm

Lic 15P

Credit cards [1] [3] Ⓥ

INN Burwash Motel High St ☎(0435) 882540

17th-century inn, skilfully extended to provide spacious, well-equipped bedrooms. Imaginative home-cooking.

8🛁 (8fb) CTV in all bedrooms Ⓡ *B&b£13–£19 Lunch £3–£8&alc Dinner 10pm £3–£8&alc

🛋 CTV P 8🚗

Credit cards [1] [2] [3] [4] [5]

BURY ST EDMUNDS
Suffolk
Map **5** TL86

GH Chantry 8 Sparhawk St ☎(0284) 2157

Recent conversion of a listed Georgian house a short walk from centre. (Major refurbishment taking place, to be completed early 87, details shown here may change).

8hc (2fb) B&b£11–£16 Bdi£17–£22 LDO8pm

🛋 CTV 8P

GH Dunstow 8 Springfield Rd ☎(0284) 67981

Well-extended, Victorian house with bright, well-equipped rooms.

12hc (2🚿) (5fb) CTV in all bedrooms ✖ Ⓡ *B&bfr£14 Bdifr£20.50 LDO6pm

Lic CTV 12P 🏠

GH White Hart 35 Southgate St ☎(0284) 5547

Old Tudor inn with original beams and chimneys, restored and converted to a guesthouse.

7hc (2🛁 1🚿) (2fb) CTV in all bedrooms Ⓡ *B&b£11–£12.50

Lic 🛋 CTV 7P

Ⓥ

Butleigh — Buxton

BUTLEIGH
Somerset
Map **3** ST53

FH Mrs J M Gillam **Dower House** *(ST517333)* ☎Baltonsborough (0458) 50354
Apr–Oct
Attractive 18th-century farmhouse with friendly atmosphere.
3hc (1🛁) Annexe: 2hc (1fb) 🐕
✱B&b£8.50–£9.50 Bdi£12–£13 W£84–£91 ⊬ LDO6pm
🍴 CTV 6P 8acres beef, calves small holding
[V]

BUTTERLEIGH
Devon
Map **3** SS90

FH Mrs B J Hill **Sunnyside** *(ST975088)*
☎Bickleigh (08845) 322
Closed Xmas
Friendly service and comfortable rooms in this Devon farmhouse 4m from M5 at Cullompton (junct 28).
5hc (3fb) 🐕 ✱B&b£7.50–£9 Bdifr£12.50 Wfr£80 ⊬
CTV P 140acres mixed
Credit card [3] [V]

BUXTON
Derbyshire
Map **7** SK07

⟼**GH Buxton Lodge** 28 London Rd
☎(0298) 3522
Spacious bedrooms, cosy lounge and dining area, forecourt parking. Near to town centre.
6hc (2fb) CTV in all bedrooms [R] B&b£8–£9 Bdi£12–£13 W£80–£85 ⊬ LDO5pm
🍴 CTV 4P

GH Fairhaven 1 Dale Ter ☎(0298) 4481
Victorian, end-of-terrace, town house with good home comfort near town centre.
7hc (3fb) TV in all bedrooms [R] ✱B&b£8 Bdi£11 W£74 ⊬
🍴 P

GH Griff 2 Compton Rd ☎(0298) 3628
Beautifully proportioned and furnished rooms in large Victorian semi-detached house in residential area on edge of centre.
7hc (1fb) [R] ✱B&b£7.50–£8.50 Bdi£10.50–£12.50
🍴 CTV 6P
[V]

GH Hawthorn Farm Fairfield Rd ☎(0298) 3230
Mar–Oct
Charming 16th-century farmhouse retaining original features. Annexe in converted barns.
5hc Annexe: 7hc (2fb) ✱B&b£9–£10 W£60–£66.50 M
🍴 CTV 12P 2🚗 ⛺
[V]

GH Hill House 54 London Rd ☎(0298) 4468
Closed Xmas rs Jan & Feb
Detached Victorian house standing in own gardens a short distance from centre. Smartly furnished with lounge-bar and seminar facilities.
7hc (2fb) 🐕 [R] B&b£9.50–£10 Bdi£16.50–£17.50 W£104–£110 ⊬ LDO6.30pm
Lic 🍴 CTV 9P nc12yrs

GH Kingscroft 10 Green Ln ☎(0298) 2757
Mar–Nov rs Dec
Large stone-built town house in a suburban area.
7hc (4fb) CTV in all bedrooms [R] ✱B&b£8.50 Bdi£12 W£75 ⊬ LDO4pm
Lic 🍴 CTV 9P 2🚗 nc5yrs
[V]

GH Old Manse 6 Clifton Rd, Silverlands ☎(0298) 5638
Feb–Nov
Spacious Victorian house in quiet side-road.
8hc (4🚿) (2fb) 🐕 [R] ✱B&b£9–£10 Bdi£14–£15 LDO4pm
Lic 🍴 CTV 4P

GH Roseleigh Private Hotel 19 Broad Walk ☎(0298) 4904
rs Dec/Jan–Mar
Spacious accommodation overlooking the lake and Pavilion Gardens.
13hc (2🚿) (2fb) ✱B&b£10.50–£11.50 Bdi£16–£17 W£105–£115 ⊬ LDO5pm
Lic CTV 12P nc7yrs

GH *Templeton* 13 Compton Rd ☎(0298) 5275
Mar–Oct
On edge of centre, Victorian house of character with good-sized, well-appointed rooms.
6hc LDO5.30pm
🍴 CTV 10P nc5yrs

GH Thorn Heyes Private Hotel 137 London Rd (Guestaccom) ☎(0298) 3539
Closed last 2 wks Nov
Local stone-built house dating from 1860, once a gentlemans residence, it still retains a Victorian theme throughout. Set in gardens.
8🚿 (2fb) CTV in all bedrooms [R] B&bfr£14.50 Bdifr£21.25 Wfr£122 ⊬ LDO5.30pm
Lic 🍴 CTV 11P

GH Westminster Hotel 21 Broadwalk ☎(0298) 3929
Feb–Nov & Xmas
Overlooking Pavilion Gardens lake, a large, double-fronted, Victorian town house with good, well-furnished rooms.
12hc (4🛁 8🚿) (2fb) CTV in all bedrooms [R] ✱B&b£12.50–£15.50 Bdi£18–£21 Wfr£120 ⊬ LDO3pm
Lic 🍴 CTV 10P
Credit cards [1] [2] [3] [5] [V]

FH Mrs C Heathcote **High House** *(SK065714)* Foxlow Farm, Harpur Hill ☎(0298) 4219
Mar–Oct
Modern stone-built farmhouse offering spacious accommodation in fine upland setting.

3rm (1fb) ✗ *B&b£9–£12 Bdi£15–£18 Wfr£105 ȽLDO9pm

♨ CTV 6P ⌂ 275acres beef dairy pigs

FH Mrs M A Mackenzie ***Staden Grange*** *(SK075717)* Staden Ln (1½m SE off A515) ☎(0298) 4965

Friendly proprietors run this well-converted, hillside farmhouse, offering spacious accommodation. Good scenic views.

4hc (1🛁) (1fb) [R] ȽLDO4pm

Lic ♨ CTV 20P 1🚗 ⌂ 🐴 250acres mixed

CADGWITH
Cornwall
Map **2** SW71

INN Cadgwith Cove ☎The Lizard (0326) 290513

Unspoilt 17th-century inn dating back to smuggling days, but offering modern comforts. Local fish a speciality.

5hc ✗ [R] *B&b£9–£12 W£50–£84 M̸ (W only 19 Jul–Aug) Lunch £3–£5.50 Dinner 9.30pm £6.50alc

CTV P̸

Credit cards [1] [3] [V]

CADNAM
Hampshire
Map **4** SU21

FH Mrs A M Dawe **Budds** *(SU310139)* Winsor Rd, Winsor ☎Southampton (0703) 812381
Apr–Oct

Picturesque dairy farm with thatched roof and attractive gardens, adjacent to the New Forest.

2hc (1fb) ✗ *B&b£9–£10 W£60–£65 M̸

♨ CTV 3P 200acres dairy

[V]

FH Mr & Mrs R D L Dawe **Kents** Winsor Rd, Winsor ☎Southampton (0703) 813497
May–Sep

Picturesque thatched farmhouse, recently renovated. Accommodation of a high standard. 2m NE unclass rd.

2hc (1🛁 1🚿) (1fb) ✗ *B&b£9–£9.50 W£63 M̸

♨ CTV 6P nc2yrs 200acres beef dairy

CAERNARFON
Gwynedd
Map **6** SH46

GH Bryn Idan Hotel North Rd ☎(0286) 2282

A carved oak fireplace is a feature of the dining room of this comfortable guesthouse overlooking the Menai Strait.

8hc (1fb) CTV in all bedrooms [R] B&b£11 Bdi£17 W£112 ȽLDO7pm

Lic ♨ 8P

GH Caer Menai 15 Church St ☎(0286) 2612
Mar–Dec

Mid-terrace Victorian building situated a short walk from the castle.

7hc (3fb) *B&b£8.50–£9.50

CTV P̸ solarium

[V]

GH Menai View Hotel North Rd ☎(0286) 4602

Single-fronted mid-terrace Victorian building overlooking the Menai Straits.

6hc (2fb) ✗ *B&b£8.50–£9.50 Bdi£14–£15 W£87.50–£94.50 ȽLDO6.30pm

Lic ♨ CTV P̸

Credit card [1]

GH Plas Treflan Motel Caethro ☎(0286) 2542
Mar–Nov

2🚿 Annexe: 7🚿 (2fb) CTV in all bedrooms [R] *B&b£8.75–£11 Bdi£14–£17 W£95–£145 ȽLDO9pm

Lic CTV 15P ⛳grass solarium

Credit cards [1] [2] [3] [V]

INN *Black Boy* Northgate St ☎(0286) 3604
Closed 23 Dec–1 Jan

14th-century inn in the centre of town.

12hc (6🚿) (3fb) LDO9pm

CTV 8P

Credit card [1]

CAERSWS
Powys
Map **7** SO09

FH Mrs J Williams **Cefn-Gwyn** Trefeglwys (3m W along B4569) *(SO993923)* ☎Trefeglwys (05516) 648

2hc (1fb) *B&b£7.50–£8.50 Bdi£11.50–£12.50 W£77–£84 ȽLDO7pm

♨ CTV 12P 2🚗 ⌂

80 acres mixed

Credit cards [1] [2] [3] [4] [5] [V]

CAIRNRYAN
Dumfries & Galloway *Wigtownshire*
Map**10** NX06

INN Loch Ryan Hotel ☎(05812) 275

A nicely appointed, friendly establishment at the Cairnryan-Larne ferry terminal.

12hc (4🚿) CTV in 4 bedrooms [R] *B&bfr£15 Bdifr£18.50 Bar lunch fr£3.50 Dinner 10.30pm fr£3.50

Lic CTV 50P

CALDBECK
Cumbria
Map **11** NY33

GH High Greenrigg House ☎(06998) 430

Delightful 17th-century farmhouse offering good standard of accommodation. Well-equipped games room.

8hc (2🛁 1🚿) ✗ B&b£13.50–£16.50 Bdi£22.50–£25.50 W£135–£153 Ƚ LDO5pm

Lic ♨ CTV 8P

[V]

FH Mrs D H Coulthard **Friar Hall** *(NY324399)* ☎(06998) 633
Mar–Oct

Modernised two-storey stone-built farmhouse, well-decorated and containing good quality furniture. Overlooks river and village church.

→

3hc (2fb) ⋈ ✳B&b£9–£10 Bdi£14.50–£15.50

CTV 3P 140acres dairy sheep

ⓥ

CALLANDER
Central *Perthshire*
Map **11**   NN60

GH Abbotsford Lodge Stirling Rd
☎(0877) 30066

Large stone house on main street in its own grounds, at S entrance to the town.

18hc (2⇌) (7fb) ⓡ ✳B&bfr£9 Bdifr£16 Wfr£105 ⚡LDO7pm

Lic 🍴 CTV 20P

⤷ **GH Annfield** 18 North Church St
☎(0877) 30204
Mar–Nov

Attractive stone-built house on quiet street in the town centre.

8hc (2fb) B&b£7.50 Wfr£52.50 ⋈
🍴 CTV 8P

ⓥ

GH Arden House Bracklinn Rd
☎(0877) 30235
Feb–Nov

Attractive stone house standing on hillside close to golf course, formerly used in the making of 'Dr Finlay's Casebook'.

Caldbeck
—
Callander

9hc (2🛏) (3fb) ⓡ ✳B&b£8.50–£9.50 Bdi£14–£15.50 W£90–£100 ⚡LDO6pm

🍴 CTV 12P ⚿

ⓥ

GH Brook Linn Country House Leny Feus ☎(0877) 30103
Etr–Oct

Country house in own grounds with fine views over town and surrounding hills specialising in wholefood and vegetarian cooking.

7hc (2🛏) (2fb) ⓡ ✳B&b£8.50–£9 Bdi£15.50–£16 W£104–£108 ⚡LDO6pm

🍴 CTV 10P

GH Edina 111 Main St ☎(0877) 30004

Pleasant stone-built guesthouse in main street.

9hc (1⇌) Annexe: 2hc (1⇌ 1🛏) (1fb) ⓡ ✳B&b£8–£8.50 Bdi£12.30–£13 W£80–£85 ⚡LDO6.30pm

CTV 8P

ⓥ

GH Greenbank 143 Main St
☎(0877) 30296

Pleasant house standing in the main street.

6hc (2fb) ✳B&b£8.50 Bdi£13.50 W£90 ⚡LDO7pm

Lic 🍴 CTV 6P nc5yrs

ⓥ

— Recommended —
GH Highland House Hotel South Church St ☎(0877) 30269
Apr–Oct

This charming, white-painted house is situated in a quiet street in the centre of town. Friendly and attentive service, cosy public areas, bright, attractive bedrooms and carefully prepared and varied cuisine are the main attractions here.

10hc (3🛏) (1fb) ✳B&b£10–£11.75 Bdi£19.50–£21.25 W£130–£142.50 ⋈ LDO6.30pm

Lic 🍴 CTV

GH Kinnell 24 Main St ☎(0877) 30181
Friendly house in main street, also functions as a tea room.

7hc (2fb) ✳B&b£8.75–£9 W£14–£14.25 W£95–£96 ⚡LDO7pm

CTV 7P

GH Riverview House Private Hotel Leny Rd ☎(0877) 30635
Etr–Oct

6hc (2🛏) (2fb) ⓡ B&b£9 Bdi£15.50 W£108.50 ⚡LDO7.15pm

Lic 🍴 CTV 8P

Friar Hall
Caldbeck, Wigton, Cumbria
Telephone: Caldbeck (069 98) 633
Mrs. D. Coulthard

Friar Hall is a very old farmhouse with oak beams in most rooms. Situated in a peaceful position in the village of Caldbeck overlooking the river and Caldbeck Falls. Ideal situation for touring. English Lakes, Scottish Border and Roman Wall, also for fellwalks and fishing. This is a dairy and sheep farm a good place for people to stay when breaking their journey to and from Scotland.
2 double rooms and one family room.

𝕰𝖉𝖎𝖓𝖆 𝕲𝖚𝖊𝖘𝖙 𝕳𝖔𝖚𝖘𝖊

111 Main Street, Callander, Perthshire
Telephone: Callander (0877) 30004

Edina is a friendly family run guest house, offering home-cooking with choice of menu. All bedrooms have heating, tea/coffee making facilities, hot and cold water, some rooms with private bath.
There is a comfortable TV lounge and a large car park at the heart of the building.

GH *Rock Villa* 1 Bracklinn Rd ☎(0877) 30331
May–Sep
Detached house in corner site set back from the main road.
7hc (1fb) ⋈
♨ 7P

CALSTOCK
Cornwall
Map **2** SX46

INN Boot Fore St ☎Tavistock (0822) 832331
4hc (1🛁) (1fb) CTV in 2 bedrooms ⋈ [R] B&b£12.50–£16 Bdi£17–£20.50 Lunch fr £6 Dinner 9.30pm fr £6&alc
♨ 7P
Credit cards [1] [2] [3] [5] [V]

CALVINE
Tayside *Perthshire*
Map **14** NN86

FH Mrs W Stewart **Clachan of Struan** *(NN802654)* ☎(079683) 207
rs Oct–Etr
½m S on B847
2rm (1fb) ⋈ *B&bfr£7.50 Wfr£52.50 M
CTV 10P 10,000acres sheep

CAMBO
Northumberland
Map **12** NZ08

Callander — Cambridge

FH Mrs S Robinson-Gay **Shieldhall** *(NZ026827)* Wallington (2½m S of B6342 towards A696) ☎Otterburn (0830) 40387
Apr–Oct
A most tastefully appointed farmhouse arranged around a courtyard.
6hc (2🛁 4🚿) (1fb) ⋈ [R] *B&bfr£11 Bdifr£17 Wfr£119 ⊭ LDO10am
♨ CTV 10P 10acres beef
[V]

CAMBORNE
Cornwall
Map **2** SW64

GH Pendarves Lodge Ramsgate ☎(0209) 712691
Late Georgian stone-built house in its own grounds.
8hc (2fb) TV in 2 bedrooms ⋈ *B&b£10.50 Bdi£16 W£110 ⊭ LDO9.30pm
Lic CTV 16P 1🚗 ⌂
Credit card [2]

GH Regal Hotel Church Ln ☎(0209) 713131
(closed 25 Dec–3 Jan) rs Sun
Small hotel in the heart of town, adjacent to church.
13hc (2🛁) CTV in 4 bedrooms TV in 2 bedrooms ⋈ *B&b£11–£15 Bdi£17–£21 W£69.30–£94.50 M LDO9.15pm
Lic ♨ CTV 12P
[V]

CAMBRIDGE
Cambridgeshire
Map **5** TL45

Antwerp 36 Brookfields ☎(0223) 247690
Converted period house with modern extension.
9hc (3fb) TV in all bedrooms ⋈ [R] *B&b£10–£15 Bdi£13–£18 W£91–£126 ⊭ LDO6pm
Lic ♨ CTV 8P nc2yrs
[V]

GH Ayeone Cleave 95 Gilbert Rd ☎(0223) 63387
6hc (2🚿) (1fb) 🚭 in 1 bedroom CTV in all bedrooms ⋈ [R] *B&b£11.50–£13
♨ CTV 7P

GH Belle Vue 33 Chesterton Rd ☎(0223) 351859
Closed Xmas
7hc (2fb) CTV in all bedrooms [R] B&b£9.50–£11
♨ 4P 2🚗

GH Fairways 143 Cherryhinton Rd
☎(0223) 246063
Closed 24–26 Dec

14hc (4🛏) (4fb) CTV in all bedrooms ✗ ®
✱B&b£11–£12.50

卿 CTV 20P

See advertisement on page 107

GH Hamilton Hotel 156 Chesterton Rd
☎(0223) 65664
Closed Xmas

Detached house in busy city road with car-parking at rear.

10hc (5🛏) (3fb) CTV in all bedrooms ✗ ®
✱B&b£11.50–£21 Bdi£18–£20 W£126–
£187 ⅄ LDOnoon

Lic 卿 10P nc4yrs

GH *Helen's Hotel* 167–169 Hills Rd
☎(0223) 246465

(23🛏) Annexe: 6hc (3🛏) (2fb)
CTV in all bedrooms LDO7.30pm

Lic 卿 CTV 20P

Credit cards 1 3

GH Lensfield Hotel 53 Lensfield Rd
☎(0223) 355017
Closed 20 Dec–6 Jan

36hc (4🛏 28🛏) (4fb) CTV in all bedrooms
✗ ✱B&b£20–£32 Bdi£26.50–£38.50
W£185.50–£269.50 ⅄ (W only Nov–Feb)
LDO9pm

Lic 卿 CTV 5P 2🚗

Credit cards 1 2 3 5

GH Sorrento Hotel 196 Cherry Hinton Rd
☎(0223) 243533

A family-run hotel in a residential area with ample private parking.

26hc (5🛏 21🛏) (6fb) CTV in all bedrooms
B&b£24–£28 Bdi£30.50–£38.50
LDO9.30pm

Lic CTV 26P ₼

Credit card 3

GH Suffolk House Private Hotel
69 Milton Rd ☎(0223) 352016
8hc (1⇨) (2fb) CTV in all bedrooms ✖ ⓡ
✱B&b£11.25–£16
⌂ CTV 8P

CAMELFORD
Cornwall
Map **2**   SX18

GH Sunnyside Hotel Victoria Rd
☎(0840) 212250
Closed Nov

*An impressive stone-built hotel standing
on the outskirts of the small market town.*

10hc (2⇨) (6fb) CTV in all bedrooms
B&b£11.50–£13.50 Bdi£17.50–£20.50
W£95–£110 ⅄ LDO7pm
Lic ⌂ CTV 16P
ⓥ

GH Warmington House 32 Market Pl
☎(0840) 213380

*Creeper-hung, large double-fronted house
set in the middle of Camelford.*

7hc ✖ ✱B&b£8.50–£9.50 Bdi£13.50–£14.50
W£84–£94 ⅄ LDO9.30pm
Lic ⌂ CTV 2P 2🐾 ♨
Credit cards ① ③

FH Mrs R Y Lyes **Pencarrow** (SX108825)
Advent ☎(0840) 213282
Apr–Nov

---

*Large stone farmhouse in pretty hamlet,
1½miles from Camelford.*

2hc ✖ ✱B&b£6.50–£7.50 W£44–£49 M
TV 2🐾 40acres dairy
ⓥ

CAMPBELTOWN
Strathclyde *Argyllshire*
Map **10**   NR72

Seafield Private Hotel Kilkerran Rd
☎(0586) 54385

*Small private hotel, quietly situated
overlooking Campbeltown Loch to Davaar
Island.*

6hc (1🛏) CTV in all bedrooms ⓡ
✱B&b£13–£15 Bdi£20–£22 W£126–
£138.60 ⅄ LDO7.30pm
Lic ⌂ CTV 12P nc14yrs

CANTERBURY
Kent
Map **5**   TR15

GH Abba Hotel Station Road West
☎(0227) 464771
Closed Xmas wk

*Comfortable, modern, well-maintained
accommodation with cellar restaurant.*

19hc (2⇨) (5fb) ✱B&b£11.50–£15
Bdi£15–£25 W£95–£116 ⅄ LDO9.30pm
Lic lift ⌂ CTV 6P (charge)
ⓥ

See advertisement on page 110

GH Castle Court 8 Castle St ☎(0227)
463441

*Georgian-style building in city centre with
delightful coffee lounge and walled patio
garden. Peaceful position yet close to
Cathedral, shops and gardens.*

12hc B&b£9.50–£11.50

CTV 🚫 nc2yrs
Credit cards ① ③ ⓥ

GH Ebury Hotel New Dover Rd ☎(0227)
68433
Closed 24 Dec–14 Jan

*Large Victorian gabled building in three
acres of grounds. Cheerfully decorated
spacious well-equipped accommodation.*

17hc (15⇨ 2🛏) (4fb) CTV in all bedrooms
ⓡ ✱B&b£18–£28 Bdi£21.25–£38 W£120–
£140 ⅄ LDO8.30pm
Lic ⌂ CTV 20P ♨
Credit cards ① ② ③ ⓥ

GH *Ersham Lodge* 12 New Dover Rd
☎(0227) 463174 Telex no 965536
Apr–Oct

*Comfortable modern accommodation with
well-equipped bedrooms and some very
compact annexe rooms.*   →

14hc (2🛁 7🚿) Annexe: 11hc (1🛁) (5fb) CTV in 4 bedrooms TV in 21 bedrooms

Lic ♨ CTV 17P 2🚗

GH Highfield Hotel Summer Hill, Harbledown ☎(0227) 462772
Mar–Nov

Georgian-style country house, family-run and providing value for money.

10hc (2🚿) (2fb) 🚫 ✱B&b£10–£15

Lic ♨ 10P nc4yrs

Credit cards [1] [3]

GH *Kingsbridge Villa Hotel* 15 Best Ln ☎(0227) 66415

Modern guesthouse with 'Il Pozzo' basement restaurant and lounge bar.

12hc (1🛁) (4fb) CTV in 4 bedrooms 🚫 LDO9pm

Lic ♨ CTV 6P

GH Magnolia House 36 St Dunstans Ter ☎(0227) 65121

Small, homely house offering simple but comfortable accommodation.

6hc (3fb) 🚫 [R] ✱B&b£9–£10 W£63–£70 M

♨ 3P

[V]

GH *Pilgrims* 18 The Friars ☎(0227) 464531

Compact city-centre guesthouse with simple but comfortable accommodation. Smoking is not encouraged.

14hc (2🚿) 🚫 (2fb)

♨ CTV 2P 4🚗

GH Pointers Hotel 1 London Rd ☎(0227) 456846
Closed 23 Dec–20 Jan

Tastefully furnished and well-equipped Regency-style hotel.

14hc (2🛁 1🚿) (2fb) CTV in all bedrooms [R] B&b£18–£28 Bdi£26–£34 W£126–£147 Ⱡ LDO8.30pm

Lic ♨ 10P

Credit cards [1] [2] [3] [5]

GH St Stephen's 100 St Stephen's Rd ☎(0227) 462167

Tudor-style building with modern extension to rear.

10hc ✱B&b£10

Lic ♨ CTV 8P 3🚗 (charge)

Credit cards [2] [3] [V]

CAPUTH

Tayside *Perthshire*
Map **11** NO04

FH Mrs R Smith **Stralochy** *(NO086413)* ☎(073871) 250
May–Oct

Situated in lovely spot looking down a valley with trees merging in Sidlaw hills.

3rm (1fb) 🚫 ✱B&bfr£7 Bdifr£10 Wfr£70 Ⱡ TV 3P 239 acres arable beef sheep

CARDIFF

South Glamorgan
Map **3** ST17

GH *Ambassador Hotel* 4 Oakfield St Roath ☎(0222) 491988
Closed Xmas

A friendly but modestly-appointed hotel; bar for residents.

16hc (3fb) 🚫 LDOnoon

Lic ♨ CTV 12P

GH Balkan Hotel 144 Newport Rd ☎(0222) 463673

Modest commercial hotel convenient to city.

13hc (2🛁 3🚿) (3fb) CTV in 8 bedrooms 🚫 ✱B&b£12–£15 Bdi£16.60–£19.60 Wfr£70 Ⱡ LDO6pm

♨ CTV 18P

Credit cards [2] [3]

GH Clayton Hotel 65 Stacey Rd, Roath ☎(0222) 492345
Closed Xmas & New Year

Commercial guest house just off the main Newport road.

10hc (1fb) ✖ [R] B&b£10–£15 Bdi£16–£21 W£112–£147 ₤ LDOnoon

Lic 🛋 CTV 6P nc3yrs

[V]

GH *Domus* 201 Newport Rd ☎(0222) 495785

A personally run guest house with small bar.

10hc (2🚿) (2fb) ✖ LDOnoon

Lic 🛋 CTV 10P

GH *Dorville Hotel* 3 Ryder St ☎(0222) 30951

Closed Etr & Xmas

Cardiff

Personally run establishment within walking distance of the city centre.

13hc (3fb) ✖

🛋 CTV

GH Ferrier's (Alva Hotel) 130/132 Cathedral Rd ☎(0222) 383413

rs Fri, Sat & Sun closed 2 wks Xmas

Well-equipped and comfortable family-run hotel offering a good standard of service.

27hc (1⇔) (4fb) CTV in all bedrooms ✱B&b£14–£29.50 LDO7.45pm

Lic 🛋 CTV 12P 🚗

Credit cards [1] [2] [3] [5]

GH Princes 10 Princes St, Roath ☎(0222) 491732

Proprietor run guest house.

6hc (2fb) ✖ ✱B&b£9–£10 Bdi£13.50–£14.50 LDOnoon

🛋 CTV 3P nc1yr

GH Tane's Hotel 148 Newport Rd ☎(0222) 491755

Within easy distance of the city centre, a proprietor-run establishment. →

9hc (1fb) ✘ ✱B&b£12–£14 Bdi£16–£18
W£83–£93½ LDO7pm
♨ CTV 9P nc3yrs
Ⓥ

CARDIGAN
Dyfed
Map **2**   SN14

GH Brynhyfryd Gwbert Rd ☎(0239)
612861

Small guesthouse run by enthusiastic
family on pleasant outskirts of town.

6hc ✘ B&b£8.50–£9 Bdi£12.50–£13.50
W£80–£90½
♨ CTV ⚘
Ⓥ

Cardiff
–
Carlisle

CAREY
Hereford & Worcester
Map **3**   SO53

INN *Cottage of Content* ☎(043270) 242
Closed Xmas Day

Lovely old inn, full of character, offering
high standard of accommodation and
food.

3hc CTV in all bedrooms Ⓡ LDO9.30pm
♨ 30P

Credit card ①
See advertisement on page 193

CARLISLE
Cumbria
Map **12**   NY45

GH Angus Hotel 14 Scotland Rd
☎(0228) 23546
Closed Xmas & New Year

A neat, mid-terrace house on N side of
centre.

9hc (2fb) ✱B&b£7.50–£11 Bdi£13–£16.50
LDO4.15pm
Lic ♨ CTV ⚘

GH *East View* 110 Warwick Rd ☎(0228) 22112
Closed Jan
Family-run, friendly guesthouse offering good value.
9hc (3fb) LDO5pm
🍴 CTV ⅌

GH *Georgian House* 40–44 London Rd ☎(0228) 23805
Closed Xmas Day & New Years Day
Simple and business-like guesthouse with interesting 'Movie Bar'.
14hc (5fb) LDO8.30pm
Lic 🍴 CTV 9P

GH *Kenilworth Hotel* 34 Lazonby Ter ☎(0228) 26179
Small, friendly, guesthouse, family-run.
6hc (2fb) ⑧ ✱B&b£8–£10 Wfr£56 M
🍴 CTV 5P

CARLOPS
Borders *Peeblesshire*
Map **11**   NT15

┝━┥**FH** Mrs J Aitken **Carlophill** (NT155556) (¼m SW unclass) ☎West Linton (0968) 60340
Jun–mid Oct (rs May)
Compact, homely bungalow with attractive residents' lounge. Reached by private track at S end of village.
3rm ✖ ✱B&b£8–£10 Wfr£54
🍴 CTV 6P 2000acres beef sheep mixed
Ⓥ

CARNO
Powys
Map **6**   SN99

FH P M Lewis **Y Grofftydd** (SN981965) ☎(05514) 274
Farmhouse is situated off A470 overlooking typical mid-Wales scenery. Ideal centre for walking. Sporting clay-pigeon shooting on premises.
3hc (2fb) ✖ ✱B&bfr£9 Bdifr£14 Wfr£98 ⅃
🍴 CTV 4P 180acres beef sheep
Ⓥ

Carlisle
—
Carrutherstown

CARRADALE
Strathclyde *Argyllshire*
Map **10**   NR83

GH *Ashbank Hotel* ☎(05833) 650
Adjacent to golf course offering comfortable but compact accommodation.
6hc (3🍴) (1fb) ⑧ ✱B&b£9–£10.50 Bdi£15.50–£16.50 W£85–£90 ⅃ LDO7.45pm
Lic CTV 10P

GH *Drumfearne* ☎(05833) 710
May–Sep
Detached stone house in own grounds on a hill behind the harbour.
6rm (5hc) (2fb) ✖ ✱B&b£7 Bdi£10.50–£11 Wfr£70 ⅃ LDO6pm
CTV P
Ⓥ

GH *Dunvalanree* Portrigh ☎(05833) 226
Etr–Oct
Large house with attractive rockery garden beside small sandy bay to the south of Carradale Harbour.
12hc (3fb) ✖ ✱B&b£8.50–£9 Bdi£11.50–£12 W£77–£84 ⅃ LDO4pm
Lic 🍴 CTV 9P
Ⓥ

CARRBRIDGE
Highland *Inverness-shire*
Map **14**   NH92

GH *Ard-na-Coille* Station Rd ☎(047984) 239
6hc (2fb) ✱B&b£8.50 Bdi£12.50 W£84 ⅃ LDO 6pm
Lic 🍴 CTV 10P
Ⓥ

GH *Carrmoor* Carr Rd ☎(047984) 244
A charming little house where you will get a warm welcome from the owners, with bright, airy cottage-style bedrooms and comfortable lounge in which to relax. Good home-cooking.
4hc (1fb) ⑧ ✱B&b£8.50 Bdi£13 W£80 ⅃ LDO5.30pm
Lic 🍴 CTV 4P

GH *Mountain Thyme Country* Station Rd ☎(047984) 696
Closed Nov–27 Dec
A comfortable and nicely-appointed country guesthouse. Situated ½m W of Carrbridge station.
6hc (1fb) ✖ ⑧ ✱B&b£9.50–£14.50 Bdi£14.50–£16.50 LDO6pm
🍴 CTV 7P
Ⓥ

GH *Old Manse Private Hotel* Duthil ☎(047984) 278
Jan–Oct
Personally-run, modernised, country manse in secluded setting with attractive, comfortable rooms.
8hc (2fb) ⑧ LDO1pm
Lic 🍴 CTV 9P

CARRONBRIDGE
Central *Stirlingshire*
See **Denny**

CARRUTHERSTOWN
Dumfries & Galloway *Dumfriesshire*
Map **11**   NY17

┝━┥**FH** Mrs J Brown **Domaru** (NY093716) ☎(038784) 260
Apr–Oct
Modern farmhouse set back from main road. Good home-cooking by Mrs Brown, a highly qualified chef.
3rm (2hc) TV in all bedrooms B&b£8 Bdi£12 LDO8pm
🍴 3P 150acres dairy
Ⓥ

Castle Carrock — Cawood

CASTLE CARROCK
Cumbria
Map **12** NY55

FH B W Robinson **Gelt Hall** *(NY542554)* ☎Hayton (022870) 260

An olde-worlde farmhouse built around a courtyard directly off the main street of this tiny village.

3rm (1🛁) (1fb) TV in 1 bedroom 🚫🐕 ✱B&b£9–£9.50 Bdi£14–£14.50 LDO6pm

CTV P 🚗 120acres mixed

[V]

CASTLE DONINGTON
Leicestershire
Map **8** SK42

GH Delven Hotel 12 Delven Ln ☎Derby (0332) 810153

7hc (1fb) CTV in all bedrooms ✱B&b£11.64–£14.38 Bdi£16.14–£18.88 LDO11pm

Lic 🍴 3P 2🚗

Credit cards [1] [3] [V]

GH *Four Poster* 73 Clapgun St ☎Derby (0332) 810335

Tastefully restored and modernised old ivy-clad house in quiet street.

7hc (1fb) 🚫🐕 LDO1pm

🍴 CTV 10P 4🚗 🏊(heated)

FH Mr J C G Shields **Park** *(SK417253)* Melbourne Rd (1½m S A453) ☎Melbourne (Derbys) (03316) 2409
Closed Xmas

Impressive half-timbered farmhouse dating from the 18th-century.

6hc (2🚿) (3fb) [R] ✱B&b£13–£20 W£65–£100 M̸ LDO8.30pm

Lic 🍴 CTV 20P 40acres non-working

Credit cards [1] [2] [3] [5] [V]

CATLOWDY
Cumbria
Map **12** NY47

FH Mr & Mrs Lawson **Craigburn** *(NY474761)* ☎Nicholforest (022877) 214

Attractive farmhouse dating from 1760 with friendly atmosphere and good home-cooking.

7hc (4🛁 3🚿) (4fb) [R] ✱B&b£9–£9.50 Bdi£14.50–£15.50 W£99–£103 L̸ LDO6pm

Lic CTV 12P ⌂ ⚲ 250acres beef sheep

[V]

See advertisement on page 112

Recommended

FH Mr & Mrs J Sisson ***Bessiestown*** *(NY457768)* ☎Nicholforest (022877) 219

Mr and Mrs Sissons provide a friendly welcome and good home-cooking at their lovely farmhouse. Bedrooms are exceptionally comfortable and attractively decorated, with lots of pretty ornaments adding to their charm. The spacious, quiet lounge, with bar, is also comfortable and there is a separate small TV lounge.

8rm (6hc 3🛁 3🚿) (1fb) 🚫🐕 LDO4pm

Lic 🍴 CTV 20P 🏊(heated) 🐴 55acres beef sheep mixed

CAWOOD
North Yorkshire
Map **8** SE53

GH Compton Court Hotel ☎Selby (075786) 315
rs Sat & Sun

Converted, late-Georgian residence in village centre. Comfortable bedrooms and cosy lounge-bar/dining room with separate TV lounge.

9hc (2🛁) (1fb) TV in all bedrooms [R] ✱B&b£9–£18.50 Bdi£23.50–£28.50 Wfr£98 L̸ LDO9pm

Lic 🍴 CTV 8P

Credit cards [1] [3] [5]

CEMMAES
Powys
Map **6** SH80

FH Mrs D Evans-Breese **Rydygwiel** *(SH826056)* ☎Cemmaes Road (06502) 541

Remote, detached, stone-built farmhouse on north side of the Dovey Valley with attractive gardens to rear of the house.

3rm (1fb) ✱B&b£7–£8.50

P 200acres beef sheep

CENARTH
Dyfed
Map **2** SN24

FH B & J Swalton **Penwernfach** *(SN266438)* Pont Hirwaun (1½m N off B4570) ☎Newcastle Emlyn (0239) 710694

Small-holding, with own ducks, goats & donkeys, offering comfortable accommodation.

3hc 🚫🐕 Ⓡ B&bfr£9 Wfr£59 M̸

📺 20P 🏠 🎣

6acres non-working

CHAGFORD
Devon
Map **3** SX78

GH Bly House Nattadon Hill ☎(06473) 2404
Feb–Oct

Lavishly furnished with antiques, this elegant former rectory is set in five acres of grounds.

8hc (5🛁) Ⓡ ✱B&b£11–£14 Bdi£17–£20 W£115–£133 M̸ LDO7pm

📺 CTV 10P nc10yrs

GH Glendarah ☎(06473) 3270
Closed Jan & Feb

7hc Annexe: 1🛁 (2fb) CTV in 1 bedroom Ⓡ ✱B&b£9.50–£11 Bdi£16–£18 W£108.50–£122.50 M̸ LDO6.30pm

Lic 📺 CTV 9P 🏠

[V]

INN *Globe* ☎(06473) 3485

Friendly inn of character in the centre of this small Devonshire town.

3🛁 CTV in all bedrooms Ⓡ LDO9pm

📺 🚫P 🚫🛁

CHALE
Isle of Wight
See **Wight, Isle of**

CHANNEL ISLANDS
Map **16**

GUERNSEY

L'ANCRESSE VALE

GH *Lynton Private Hotel* Hacsé Ln ☎(0481) 45418
mid May–Sep

14hc (3🛁 7🚿) (2fb) 🚫🐕 Ⓡ LDO6.45pm

Lic 📺 CTV 20P nc5yrs

GRANDES ROCQUES

GH La Galaad Hotel Rue Des Français ☎(0481) 57233
Etr–Oct

Only 10 mins walk from the sea, a modernised hotel in quiet residential area.

12hc (2🛁 10🚿) (3fb) CTV in all bedrooms ✱B&b£10–£17 Bdi£13–£20 W£91–£140 M̸ LDO5.30pm

Lic 📺 CTV 14P ♿ nc4yrs

GH *Hotel le Saumarez* Rue de Galad ☎(0481) 56341
Apr–Oct

Detached hotel in residential area, with spacious bar, separate lounge and modest bedrooms.

21hc (10🛁 5🚿) (10fb) Ⓡ LDO7pm

Lic 📺 CTV 25P 🎾

ST MARTIN

GH *Triton* Les Hubits ☎(0481) 38017

Clean and comfortable guesthouse in rural surroundings near St Peter Port.

14hc (4🛁) (2fb) 🚫🐕 LDO6.30pm

CTV 10P nc4yrs

ST PETER PORT

GH Baltimore House Hotel Les Gravees ☎(0481) 23641
Mar–Oct

Pleasant Georgian house with walled garden. Bright and clean with comfortable, well furnished rooms.

12hc (1🛁 7🚿) (3fb) Ⓡ ✱B&b£7.50–£12.50 Bdi£10.50–£17 W£73.50–£119 M̸ LDO7.15pm

Lic CTV 7P 🏠

Credit cards [1] [2] [3] [4] [5] [V]

GH Changi Lodge Hotel Les Baissieres ☎(0481) 56446
Apr–Oct

13hc (2🛁 5🚿) (7fb) 🚫🐕 Ⓡ ✱B&b£8.50–£13.50 Bdi£12.50–£17.50 W£87.50–£122.50 M̸ LDO7pm

Lic 📺 CTV 15P 🏊(heated)

Credit card [3] [V]

Recommended

GH Midhurst House Candie Rd ☎(0481) 24391
Mar–Oct

5hc (2🛁 3🚿) (2fb) CTV in all bedrooms 🚫🐕 Ⓡ ✱B&b£14–£18 Bdi£19–£23 W£134–£161 M̸ LDO7pm

Lic 📺 🚫P nc8yrs

ST SAMPSON'S

GH Ann-Dawn Private Hotel Route Des Capelles ☎(0481) 25606
Etr–12 Oct

Traditional Guernsey house with informal atmosphere, large lawned and landscaped gardens.

14hc (2🛁 8🚿) CTV in all bedrooms 🚫🐕 Ⓡ ✱B&b£10.50–£12.50 Bdi£15–£17 W£84–£119.50 M̸

Lic 📺 12P nc5yrs

[V]

ST SAVIOUR

GH La Girouette House Hotel ☎ (0481) 63269
mid Mar–Oct

→

14hc (4🛁 8🚿) (2fb) CTV in all bedrooms ✖ [R] *B&b£16–£19 Bdi£21.25–£24.25 W£148.75–£170 ℓ LDO7.30pm

Lic 🍴 14P nc5yrs

Credit cards [1] [2] [3] [V]

JERSEY

GOREY

GH Royal Bay Hotel ☎(0534) 53318
May–Sep

Family-run hotel near the beach in this picturesque village.

16hc (6🛁 10🚿) (2fb) ✖ *B&b£11.18–£16.64 Bdi£12.95–£18.36 W£90.65–£128.52 ℓ (W only Jul & Aug) LDO7.30pm

Lic 🍴 CTV P nc6yrs

ST AUBIN

GH Panorama St Aubin High St ☎(0534) 42429 Telex No 4192341
Mar–Nov

Family-run hotel with beautiful views over the bay.

16hc (7🛁 9🚿) (3fb) CTV in all bedrooms ✖ [R] B&b£14–£30 W£98–£210 M (W only Jul & Aug)

🍴 P̸ nc5yrs

Credit cards [1] [2] [3] [5] [V]

Channel Islands

ST CLEMENT

GH Belle Plage Hotel Green Island ☎(0534) 53750
Etr–Oct

Family-run hotel backing onto beach in a lovely part of the island.

20hc (4🛁 16🚿) (2fb) B&b£17–£21 Bdi£18–£22

Lic CTV 18P nc8yrs 🏊

Credit cards [1] [3]

ST HELIER

GH Almorah Hotel La Pouquelaye ☎(0534) 21648
Etr–Oct

Small, well-appointed hotel overlooking the bay with oak-panelled lounge and Breton dining room.

16hc (11🛁) (4fb) ✖ B&b£11–£18 Bdi£13–£20 (W only low season) LDO6.30pm

Lic lift 🍴 CTV 10P ⛳

GH *Cliff Court Hotel* St Andrews Rd, First Tower ☎(0534) 34919
Apr–Nov

Good, comfortable accommodation and lovely views over the bay.

11🛁🚿 (4fb) ✖ LDO7.30pm

Lic 🍴 CTV 10P 🏊(heated)

GH Runneymede Court Hotel 46–52 Roseville St ☎(0534) 20044
mid Mar–5 Nov

Large family-run hotel wihtin walking distance of town centre.

57hc (41🛁 16🚿) (8fb) CTV in 30 bedrooms ✖ B&b£10–£18 Bdi£13–£22 W£91–£154 ℓ LDO6.30pm

Lic lift 🍴 CTV P̸ nc5yrs

Credit card [3] [V]

ST MARTIN

GH Le Relais de St Martin ☎(0534) 53271
mid Apr–mid Oct

12hc (2🛁 3🚿) (2fb) [R] B&b£12–£16 Bdi£15.50–£20

Lic 🍴 CTV P 🏊

ST PETER'S VALLEY

GH Midvale Private Hotel ☎(0534) 42498
Etr–Oct

Impressive 19th-century hotel in beautiful woodlands and water meadows.

20hc (7🛁) (4fb) ✖ *B&b£11.85–£14.60 Bdi£14.85–£17.60 W£103.95–£123.20 ℓ (W only Jul & Aug) LDO6.30pm

Lic CTV 15P nc3yrs

[V]

Channel Islands — Cheltenham

TRINITY

GH *Highfield Country Hotel* Route du Ebenezer ☎(0534) 62194
25hc (14🛁) (4fb) LDO9.30pm
Lic CTV 25P 1🚗 🌳 🏊
Credit cards [1] [2] [3] [5]

CHAPELHALL
Strathclyde *Lanarkshire*
Map **11** NS76

GH *Laurel House Hotel* 101 Main St ☎Airdrie (02364) 63230
A comfortable house with good standards, run by friendly proprietors.
6rm (5hc) (1fb)
Lic ♨ CTV 6P

CHAPELTON
Strathclyde *Lanarksire*
Map **11** NS64

FH Mrs E Taylor ***Millwell*** *(NS653496)* ☎East Kilbride (03552) 43248
Small, 18th-century farmhouse set in tree-studded land.
3rm (1fb) LDO5pm
♨ CTV 5P 94acres dairy

CHAPMANSLADE
Wiltshire
Map **3** ST84

FH Mrs M Hoskins **Spinney** *(ST839480)* ☎(037388) 412
Two-storey stone-built farmhouse surrounded by fields and woodland.
3hc (1fb) [R] ✱B&b£9–£9.50 Bdi£15–£15.50 W£87.50–£94.50Ł LDO4pm
♨ TV 12P 1🚗 4acres poultry
[V]

CHARD
Somerset
Map **3** ST30

GH Watermead 83 High St ☎(04606) 2834
9hc (1fb) ✱B&b£9–£10 Bdi£13.50–£14.50 W£91.50–£96.50Ł LDO1pm
Lic ♨ CTV 9P 2🚗 🌳
[V]

CHARFIELD
Gloucestershire
Map **3** ST79

INN Huntingford Mill Hotel ☎Dursley (0453) 843431
Pleasant converted mill, enthusiastically-run and having a good steak restaurant.
5hc (1fb) CTV in all bedrooms ✖ [R] ✱B&b£14–£16 Bdi£24.95–£26.95 W£169–£182Ł Lunch £10.95&alc Dinner 10pm £10.95&alc
♨ 25P 🚗🚗 🌳 🎣
Credit cards [1] [2] [3] [V]

CHARLTON
West Sussex
Map **4** SU81

GH Woodstock House Hotel ☎Singleton (024363) 666
mid Feb–mid Nov
Country house dating back to the 18th century with antique furnishings throughout and beautiful well-kept gardens.
11hc (2🛁 4🚿) ✖ ✱B&b£17–£19 Bdi£25.50–£27.50 W£155–£170Ł LDO7.30pm
Lic ♨ CTV 11P nc9yrs

CHARLTON MUSGROVE
Somerset
Map **3** ST72

FH Mrs A Teague **Lower Church** *(ST721302)* ☎Wincanton (0963) 32307
Apr–Oct
18th-century brick-built farmhouse with inglenook fireplace and beams.
2hc (1fb) [R] ✱B&b£8.50 Bdi£13.50 W£85Ł LDO10am
CTV 4P 60acres dairy sheep

CHARLWOOD
Surrey
Map **4** TQ24
For accommodation details see under **Gatwick Airport**

CHARMOUTH
Dorset
Map **3** SY39

GH *Newlands House* Stonebarrow Ln ☎(0297) 60212
Mar–Oct
Standing in own grounds on edge of village, minutes walk from beach.
12hc (7🛁 4🚿) (2fb) CTV in all bedrooms [R] LDOnoon
Lic ♨ CTV 12P 🌳

CHEDINGTON
Dorset
Map **3** ST40

FH Lt Col & Mrs E I Stanford **Lower Farm** *(ST485054)* ☎Corscombe (093589) 371
Closed Xmas
16th-century thatched farmhouse with extensive views over unspoilt Dorset and Somerset countryside. Jacob sheep, Suffolk Punch horses and ornamental waterfowl can be seen. Boating available on farm lakes.
3hc ✖ ✱B&b£12 Wfr£77 M
♨ CTV 4P nc5yrs 🎣 120acres beef pig sheep

CHELMSFORD
Essex
Map **5** TL70

GH Beechcroft Private Hotel 211 New London Rd ☎(0245) 352462
Closed Xmas–New Year
Friendly, traditional-style guesthouse.
24hc (2🚿) (2fb) B&b£17.60 W£123.20 M
♨ CTV 15P

Recommended

GH Boswell House Hotel 118–120 Springfield Rd ☎(0245) 287587
Closed 10 days Xmas
Recently renovated to provide a good modern standard, yet retaining traditional charm.
13hc (9🛁 4🚿) (2fb) CTV in 9 bedrooms [R] ✱B&b20–£27.50 Bdi£25.50–£33 W£178.50–£231Ł LDO7pm
Lic ♨ CTV 15P 1🚗
Credit cards [1] [2] [3] [5] [V]

GH *Tanunda Hotel* 219 New London Rd ☎(0245) 354295
Closed Xmas wk
Fairly large modern hotel with good restaurant facilities and effective management.
20hc (2🛁 9🚿) CTV in 11 bedrooms LDO7.30pm
Lic ♨ CTV 20P

CHELTENHAM
Gloucestershire
Map **3** SO92
See also **Bishop's Cleeve**

GH Askham Court Hotel Pittville Circus Rd ☎(0242) 525547
Regency house within walking distance of the town centre.
19hc (4🛁 2🚿) (4fb) CTV in 6 bedrooms [R] ✱B&b£16–£22 Bdi£22–£30 W£145–£185Ł LDO6.30pm
Lic ♨ CTV 25P
[V]

GH Beaumont House 56 Shurdington Rd ☎(0242) 45986
Substantial Regency house with garden, and spacious attractive bedrooms.
8hc (2fb) B&b£11–£12 Bdi£16.50–£17.50 W105Ł LDO5pm
Credit cards [1] [3]

GH Beechworth Lawn Hotel 133 Hales Rd ☎(0242) 522583
Closed Xmas
Pleasantly furnished detached Victorian town-house with good parking.
6hc (2🚿) (2fb) B&b£11–£14 Bdi£16–£19 W£73–£93 M LDO4pm
♨ CTV 12P
[V]

See advertisement on page 118

GH *Bowler Hat Hotel* 130 London Rd ☎(0242) 523614

Proprietor-run guesthouse.

6hc (1🛁) (2fb) CTV in all bedrooms 🚫 LDOam

Lic 🍴 8P

GH Carrs Hotel 42 Clarence St ☎(0242) 524003
Closed Xmas

15hc (2🚿) (3fb) CTV available in bedrooms [R] ✱B&b£11–£17 Bdi£16–£22 LDO6pm

Lic CTV 🚸

Credit cards [1] [2] [3] [5] [V]

GH Central Hotel 7/9 Portland St ☎(0242) 582172

Recently refurbished and altered town-centre hotel.

17hc (8🚿) (2fb) CTV in 8 bedrooms B&b£13–£21 Bdi£19–£27 W£130–£180 Ⱡ

Lic CTV 4P 🏠

Credit cards [1] [2] [3] [5] [V]

GH Cleevelands House 38 Evesham Rd ☎(0242) 518898

15hc (1🛁 1🚿) (2fb) CTV in 14 bedrooms TV in 1 bedroom [R] B&b£11–£15 W£85–£100 M LDO7pm

Lic 🍴 CTV 10P ♿

[V]

Cheltenham

GH Cotswold Grange Hotel Pittville Circus Rd ☎(0242) 515119
Closed Xmas wk

Cotswold-stone house, attractively appointed.

27hc (9🛁 7🚿) (4fb) CTV in 16 bedrooms [R] ✱B&b£18–£25 LDO7.15pm

Lic 🍴 CTV 27P 🏠

Credit card [3]

GH Hallery House 48 Shurdington Rd ☎(0242) 578450

Corner-sited, Georgian villa on main Stroud road out of town. Friendly atmosphere.

16hc (3🚿) (3fb) 🚭 in 2 bedrooms [R] ✱B&b£9.50–£12.50 Bdi£14–£17 W£85–£105 Ⱡ LDO8.30pm

🍴 CTV 20P 3🚗 🏠

[V]

GH Hannaford's 20 Evesham Rd ☎(0242) 515181

Attractive, comfortable, terrace house, near centre and public car park. Personally-run.

11hc (1🛁 7🚿) (3fb) 🚭 in 4 bedrooms CTV in all bedrooms 🚫 [R] B&b£14–£17 Bdi£21.50–£24.50 W£135–£150 Ⱡ (W only 2 wks in Mar) LDO4pm

Lic 🍴 CTV 🚸 nc7yrs

Credit cards [1] [3]

GH Hollington House Hotel 115 Hales Rd ☎(0242) 519718
Closed Xmas

Attractive Cotswold-stone detached house in small pleasant gardens.

7hc (3🚿) (2fb) CTV in all bedrooms [R] ✱B&b£14–£20 Bdi£21.25–£27.95 LDO6pm

Lic 🍴 CTV 10P

[V]

GH *Ivy Dene* 145 Hewlett Rd ☎(0242) 521726

Proprietor-run guesthouse, modestly appointed.

9hc (2fb) [R]

🍴 CTV 9P

GH Knowle House 89 Leckhampton Rd ☎(0242) 516091
Closed 22 Dec–3 Jan

Double-fronted, red-brick house in residential suburb. Bright, neat interior.

5hc (1fb) ✱B&b£10 Wfr£65 M

🍴 CTV 6P

[V]

GH Lawn Hotel 5 Pittville Lawn ☎(0242) 526638

9hc (2fb) CTV in 4 bedrooms TV in 1 bedroom ⓡ ✱B&b£9.75–£10.75 Bdi£14.75–£15.75 W£96–£105 ⅃ LDO11am

Lic ♔ CTV 8P

ⓥ

GH Milton House 12 Royal Pde, Bayshill Rd ☎(0242) 582601

Elegant Georgian terraced house, recently converted, with comfortable bedrooms.

9hc (1⇌3⑩) (4fb) CTV in all bedrooms ⓡ ✱B&b£12–£15 W£75.60–£94.50 ⋈ ♔ 2P

Cheltenham

GH North Hall Hotel Pittville Circus Rd ☎(0242) 520589

Closed Xmas

Detached house with large bedrooms.

19hc (5⇌5⑩) (1fb) CTV in all bedrooms ⓡ B&b£12.94–£18.40 Bdi£18.11–£26.34 W£108.68–£158.01 ⅃ LDO6.30pm

Lic ♔ CTV 20P

Credit cards ① ③

GH Regency 50 Clarence Sq ☎(0242) 582718

rs Xmas

8⑩ CTV in all bedrooms ⓡ ✱B&b£12–£13 Bdi£18–£19 W£110–£120 ⅃ LDO4pm

Lic ♔ 3P nc3yrs

GH *Wellington House Hotel* Wellington Sq ☎(0242) 521627

Semi-detached house of local stone, with large bedrooms.

10hc (3fb) ✈ ⓡ LDO7.30pm

Lic ♔ CTV 6P 1⌂

GH Willoughby 1 Suffolk Sq ☎(0242) 522798
Closed Xmas & New Year
Proprietor run Regency house.
11hc (5🚿) (1fb) CTV in all bedrooms [R]
✱B&b£13–£15.50 Bdi£17.50–£20 W£110–£130 Ł LDO4pm
🛋 CTV 10P

CHEPSTOW
Gwent
Map **3** ST59

GH First Hurdle Hotel 9 Upper Church St ☎(02912) 2189
Pleasing hotel with pretty bedrooms equipped with Edwardian furniture.
10hc (2🛁 1🚿) CTV in all bedrooms
✱B&b£13–£16 Bdi£18–£24 W£156–£196 Ł LDO9.30pm
Lic 🛋 CTV 🚫🐕
Credit cards [1] [2] [3]

CHERITON FITZPAINE
Devon
Map **3** SS80

FH Mrs D M Lock **Brindiwell** *(SS896079)* ☎(03636) 357
Period farmhouse with oak beams and panelling; on the side of a valley with views of the Exe Valley and Dartmoor.

Cheltenham — Chester

4rm ✘ [R] ✱B&b£8.50–£10 Bdi£12–£15 W£84 Ł LDO5pm
CTV 4P ⌂ 120acres sheep
[V]

CHESTER
Cheshire
Map **7** SJ46

GH Brookside Private Hotel 12 Brook Ln (Exec Hotels) ☎(0244) 381943
Closed Xmas wk
Large, well-furnished hotel with attractive restaurant and Victorian-style lounges.
24hc (15🛁 7🚿) (5fb) CTV in all bedrooms [R] ✱B&b£14–£18 Bdi£20.95–£24.95 W£131.98–£157.18 M̸ LDO8.30pm
Lic 🛋 CTV 14P
Credit card [3]

GH Cavendish Hotel 44 Hough Green ☎(0244) 675100
Comfortable, elegantly furnished Victorian house in own grounds.
20hc (4🛁 12🚿) CTV in all bedrooms B&b£19.50–£29.50 Bdi£27–£37 LDO9pm
Lic 🛋 CTV 30P ⌂
Credit cards [1] [2] [3] [5]

GH *Chester Court Hotel* 48 Hoole Rd ☎(0244) 20779
Closed Xmas wk
Modern, motel-style rooms behind well-appointed house with good restaurant.
8hc (4🚿) Annexe: 12hc (6🛁 6🚿) (8fb) CTV in all bedrooms LDO8pm
Lic 🛋 30P
Credit cards [1] [2] [3] [5]

GH *Devonia* 33–35 Hoole Rd ☎(0244) 22236
A small establishment catering for tourists and business people. On A56, ½m from city centre.
10hc (6fb) CTV in all bedrooms [R] LDO4pm
Lic 🛋 CTV 15P

GH Eaton Hotel 29 City Rd ☎(0244) 312091
Family-run canal-side hotel close to city centre and station.
21hc (5🛁 7🚿) (3fb) CTV in all bedrooms [R] B&b£12–£19 W£75.60–£133 M̸ LDO8pm
Lic 🛋 CTV 9P
Credit cards [1] [2] [3] [5] [V]

GH Egerton Lodge Hotel 57 Hoole Rd, Hoole ☎(0244) 20712
Attractive and well-furnished Victorian terraced house close to city centre.

6🚿 (4fb) CTV in all bedrooms 🐕 ✱B&b£12.50–£14.50 W£87.50–£101.50 M

Temperance 5P nc6yrs

[V]

GH Elizabeth Park Hotel 78 Hoole Rd ☎(0244) 310213

Charming, well-furnished house in own grounds, with good service only 1 mile from city.

7hc (2🛁 5🚿) (3fb) [R] ✱B&bfr£14 Bdifr£20 Wfr£140 Ⱡ LDO6.30pm

🛋 20P 1🚗

GH Eversley Private Hotel 9 Eversley Park (Guestaccom) ☎(0244) 373744

Small, privately owned hotel with relaxing atmosphere.

8hc (4🛁) (3fb) CTV in all bedrooms 🐕 [R] ✱B&b£13–£14 LDO4pm

Lic 🛋 CTV 10P ⌂

GH *Gables* 5 Vicarage Rd, Hoole ☎(0244) 23969

Modern guesthouse in quiet road outside the city centre.

7hc (3fb) [R]

🛋 CTV 7P

GH *Hamilton Court* 5–7 Hamilton St ☎(0244) 45387

Closed Xmas wk

A comfortable, family-run hotel in a quiet side road.

Chester — Chichester

12hc (4fb) CTV in bedrooms [R] LDO7pm

Lic 🛋 CTV 10P

GH Malvern 21 Victoria Rd ☎(0244) 380865

Conveniently situated guesthouse opposite Northgate.

8hc (2fb) 🐕 [R] ✱B&b£8–£10 Bdi£11–£13 W£70–£84 Ⱡ LDO5pm

🛋 CTV 🅿 nc2yrs

[V]

GH Redland Private Hotel 64 Hough Green ☎(0244) 671024

Mar–23 Dec

Attractive, well-furnished house in own grounds with comfortable sitting rooms.

10hc (2🚿) (3fb) 🐕 ✱B&b£14.50–£23

Lic 🛋 CTV 12P 2🚗 billiards

[V]

GH Riverside Pensione 19 City Walls ☎(0244) 311498

Closed 2wks Xmas

Small hotel with good facilities, newly furnished, on Roman Wall.

10hc (4🛁 6🚿) (2fb) CTV in all bedrooms [R] ✱B&b£14.50–£21 Bdi£19.50–£26 W£122.50 Ⱡ

15P

[V]

See advertisement on page 122

GH Riverside Private Hotel 22 City Walls, off Lower Bridge St ☎(0244) 26580

Well-furnished modern hotel on City Walls next to the River Dee.

14hc (11🛁) (3fb) CTV in 12 bedrooms TV in 2 bedrooms [R] ✱B&b£14–£17 Bdi£21–£24 W£147–£168 Ⱡ LDO9pm

Lic 🛋 CTV 25P

[V]

See advertisement on page 122

CHICHESTER

West Sussex

Map **4** SU80

GH Bedford Hotel Southgate ☎(0243) 785766

Small comfortable hotel. Personally run.

27hc (2🚿) (2fb) CTV in all bedrooms ✱B&b£17–£20 W£156–£175 Ⱡ LDO9pm

Lic 🛋 CTV 6P ⌂

Credit cards [1] [2] [3] [5] [V]

CHICKERELL
Dorset
Map **3** SY68

INN Turks Head 6–8 East St
☎Weymouth (0305) 783093
Closed 23 Dec–3 Jan

Converted cottage extension to small village inn, only 3 miles from Weymouth, offers comfortable bedrooms with own bathrooms.

5🛁 (1fb) CTV in all bedrooms [R]
✱B&b£15–£17 Bdi£22.50–£24.50 W£135–£150 🍴 Lunch £5–£7 Dinner £6.50–£7.50&alc

♨ 60P 🚌 nc5yrs

Credit cards [1] [3] [V]

CHICKLADE
Wiltshire
Map **3** ST93

GH Old Rectory ☎Hindon (074789) 226
Closed Xmas

7hc (2fb) ✱B&b£10–£13 Bdi£16–£18 W£90–£100 🍴 LDO9pm

Lic ♨ CTV 14P 🏠

Credit card [1] [V]

CHIDEOCK
Dorset
Map **3** SY49

GH Betchworth House Hotel ☎(0297) 89478

6hc (3🚿) (1fb) 🐕 ✱B&b£11.50–£14 Bdi£18.50–£21 W£109–£126 🍴 LDO6pm

Lic ♨ CTV 15P nc7yrs

[V]

CHIPPENHAM
Wiltshire
Map **3** ST97

GH Oxford Hotel 32/36 Langley Rd
☎(0249) 652542
rs Xmas & New Year

Tidy, detached guesthouse on edge of town on Swindon Road.

13hc (7🚿) (1fb) CTV in all bedrooms 🐕
✱B&b£12–£17 Bdi£17–£22 W£72–£102 M
LDO5.30pm

Lic ♨ 9P

Credit cards [1] [2] [3] [5] [V]

CHIPPING SODBURY
Avon
Map **3** ST78

GH *Moda Hotel* 1 High St ☎(0454) 312135

On High Street, a large well-maintained Georgian house, personally-run.

8hc Annexe: 3hc CTV in all bedrooms 🐕
[R] LDO7.30pm

Lic ♨ CTV 20P

CHIRNSIDE
Borders *Berwickshire*
Map **12** NT85

INN *Mitchell's Hotel* West End
☎(089081) 507

Small, friendly family-run inn. Modern conversion of six stone houses.

4hc (1fb) TV in all bedrooms 🐕
LDO9.30pm

♨ CTV 15P

CHISELBOROUGH
Somerset
Map **3** ST41

FH Mrs E Holloway **Manor** *(ST468151)*
☎(093588) 203
Apr–Oct

Comfortable 19th-century house built of ham stone with well appointed rooms.

3hc (1fb) 🐕 [R] ✱B&b£10–£11 Bdi£15.50–£16.50 W£99–£105 🍴 LDO5pm

CTV 4P 🌾 450acres mixed

[V]

Chiseldon — Christchurch

CHISELDON
Wiltshire
Map **4** SU17

FH Mrs M M Hughes **Parsonage** *(SU185799)* ☎Swindon (0793) 740204

16th-century building with spacious rooms. Pleasant lawned gardens back on to church.

5hc (1🛁 1🚿) 🐕 [R] ✱B&b£12.50–£25 W£75–£100 M

🍴 CTV 4P 2🚗 🏠 🎣

400acres arable sheep

[V]

CHISLEHAMPTON
Oxfordshire
Map **4** SU59

INN Coach & Horses Stadhampton Rd ☎Stadhampton (0865) 890255

Hospitable, old-world country inn with very pleasant bedrooms.

9hc (2🛁 7🚿) CTV in all bedrooms 🐕 (except guide dogs) [R] ✱B&b£21.50–£35 Bdi£29–£42.50 W£179–£240 ɫ Lunch £8.25–£9.90&alc Dinner 10pm £8.25–£9.90&alc

42P

Credit cards [1] [2] [3] [5] [V]

CHRISTCHURCH
Dorset
Map **4** SZ19
For additional guesthouses see **Bournemouth**

GH Belvedere Hotel 59 Barrack Rd ☎(0202) 485978

Large Victorian hotel on main Christchurch to Bournemouth road.

10hc (3fb) ⚡ in 2 bedrooms CTV in 2 bedrooms TV in 8 bedrooms ✱B&b£8.50–£10.50 Bdi£14.50–£16.50 Wfr£105 ɫ LDO7pm

Lic 🍴 CTV 12P 1🚗 🏠 🎣

[V]

GH *Broomway Hotel* 46 Barrack Rd ☎(0202) 483405
Closed Xmas

On main road near to town centre and convenient to Bournemouth.

9hc (3fb)

Lic CTV 12P nc2yrs

GH Park House Hotel 48 Barrack Rd ☎(0202) 482124
Closed Xmas

Attractive, well-appointed house on main road out of town.

9hc (1🚿) (4fb) CTV in 4 bedrooms [R] ✱B&b£12.50–£15 W£75–£90 M

Lic 🍴 CTV 12P nc3yrs

Credit cards [1] [3]

GH Pines Private Hotel 39 Mudeford Rd ☎(0202) 482393

Quiet location close to Mudeford Quay and beaches.

14hc (6🚿) (2fb) CTV in 6 bedrooms [R] ✱B&b£13.50–£14 Bdi£17.50–£18 W£105–£110 ɫ LDO6pm

Lic 🍴 CTV 14P 🏠

GH Sea Witch Hotel 153/5 Barrack Rd ☎(0202) 482846

Friendly and efficient guesthouse on main Bournemouth road.

9hc (2fb) ✱B&b£10–£11 Bdi£15–£16 W£98 ɫ LDO2pm

Lic 🍴 CTV 15P

[V]

GH Shortwood House Hotel 1 Magdalen Ln ☎(0202) 485223

Attractive, detached house in own garden in a cul-de-sac off main Bournemouth Road.

7hc (1🛁 3🚿) Annexe: 2🚿 (4fb) CTV in 6 bedrooms 🐕 ✱B&b£10–£15 Bdi£15–£20 W£84–£110 ɫ LDO5pm

Lic 🍴 CTV 12P

[V]

CHURCHILL
Avon
Map **3** ST45

FH Mrs S Sacof **Churchill Green**
(ST429602) ☎(0934) 852438

*Modernised 16th-century farmhouse still
retaining its character, the large garden
faces south overlooking the foothills of the
Mendips.*

7hc (1🏠) (2fb) 🗶 ® B&b£11.85 Bdi£17.77
W£85 ⌿ LDOnoon

Lic 🍴 TV 50P ॐ ➔ ∪ 25acres beef

CHURCHINFORD
Somerset
Map **3** ST21

FH M Palmer **Hunter Lodge** *(ST212144)*
☎Churchstanton (082360) 253

*Detached, two-storey farmhouse with
slate roof and large garden. Set in the
Blackdown Hills.*

4rm (3hc) (2fb) ✱B&b£6.50–£7 Bdi£9.50–
£10 W£70 ⌿ LDO4pm

CTV 6P ➔(heated) ∪ 30acres mixed
Ⓥ

CHURCH STOKE
Powys
Map **7** SO29

FH Mrs C Richards **Drewin** *(SO261905)*
☎(05885) 325
Apr–Oct rs Etr

*A border farmhouse with beams and
inglenook fireplace. Fine views of
surrounding countryside. Offa's Dyke
footpath runs through the farm.*

2hc (1fb) CTV in 1 bedroom TV in 1
bedroom 🗶 ® ✱B&b£8–£9 Bdi£12–£14
W£84–£90 ⌿ LDO7.30pm

🍴 CTV 10P ॐ 104acres mixed
Ⓥ

CHURCH STRETTON
Shropshire
Map **7** SO49

GH Dudgeley Mill All Stretton (2mN
B4370) (Guestaccom) ☎(0694) 723461

*Tastefully modernised old mill in peaceful,
picturesque setting.*

Churchill
—
Cirencester

7hc (1fb) 🗶 ® B&b£11.50–£12
Bdi£17.50–£18 W£115 ⌿ LDO6pm

Lic 7P ॐ Ⓥ

GH Mynd House Private Hotel Ludlow
Rd, Little Stretton (2m S B4370) ☎(0694)
722212 Closed Jan

13hc (3⇔) ® B&b£10–£15.50
Bdi£16.50–£22 W£115–£136 ⌿ LDO8pm

Lic 🍴 CTV 16P nc10yrs

Credit cards ① ③ Ⓥ

FH Mrs C J Hotchkiss **Olde Hall Farm**
(SO509926) Wall-under-Heywood
☎Longville (06943) 253 Feb–Nov

*Beautifully preserved Elizabethan
farmhouse with cruck timbers and fine
Jacobean staircase.*

3rm (2hc) (1fb) 🗶 ® ✱B&b£9 W£56 M

CTV 4P ♪ 190acres dairy

FH Mrs J C Inglis **Hope Bowdler Hall**
(SO478925) Hope Bowdler (1m E B4371)
☎(0694) 722041 Mar–Oct rs Nov

*17th-century manor-house which has
recently been modernised to a high
standard. Set on the edge of the tiny
village of Hope Bowdler and surrounded
by hills.*

3hc (1fb) 🗶 B&b£9–£10

🍴 6P nc10yrs ♪(hard) 22acres sheep Ⓥ

--- *Recommended* ---

FH Mrs J A Davies **Rectory**
(SO452985) Woolstaston (3¼m off
B4370 at All Stretton) ☎Leebotwood
(06945) 306
Closed Nov

3⇔ 🗶 ✱B&b£9–£11 Wfr£63 M

🍴 CTV 10P nc12yrs 170acres beef
dairy

CINDERFORD
Gloucestershire
Map **3** SO61

GH Overdean 31 St White's Rd ☎Dean
(0594) 22136

A small, pleasant guesthouse.

5hc (2fb) ✱B&b£8.50–£9.50 W£59.50–£63
M

🍴 CTV 6P

Ⓥ

INN White Hart Hotel St White's Rd,
Ruspidge (B4227) ☎Dean (0594) 23139

*Satisfactory inn with good-value
restaurant.*

4hc (2⇔) (2fb) CTV in all bedrooms ®
✱B&b£12.50–£15 Bdi£17.50–£20 Lunch
£5alc Dinner 9.45pm £5alc

CTV P

Credit card ① Ⓥ

CIRENCESTER
Gloucestershire
Map **4** SP00

GH Raydon House Hotel 3 The Avenue
(Guestaccom) ☎(0285) 3485
Closed Xmas & New Year

*Pleasant, small guesthouse, run by
proprietors.*

16hc (4⇔ 4🏠) (4fb) ⚡ in 1 bedroom CTV
in 12 bedrooms TV in 4 bedrooms 🗶 ®
✱B&b£15–£20 Bdi£24–£29 W£148–£165 ⌿
LDO8.30pm

Lic 🍴 CTV 12P

Credit cards ① ③

GH Rivercourt Beeches Rd ☎(0285)
3998

*Comfortable homely guesthouse in
pleasant garden setting.*

6hc Annexe: 4hc (1fb) ® B&bfr£10.35 Bdi
fr£16.35 Wfr£110 ⌿ LDO6pm

Lic 🍴 CTV 10P 2🚗

GH La Ronde 52–54 Ashcroft Rd
☎(0285) 4611

*An enthusiastically run comfortable
guesthouse with attractive dining room.*

10hc (1⇔ 5🏠) (3fb) CTV in 3 bedrooms 🗶
® ✱B&b£13.25–£16.75 Bdi£20.25–£24.25
Wfr£145 ⌿ LDO8pm

Lic 🍴 CTV 9P

Ⓥ

Mynd House Hotel
Little Stretton, Church Stretton
Shropshire SY6 6RB   Telephone (0694) 722212
A warm welcome and friendly service ensured by the
resident proprietors at this comfortable small hotel set
in terraced gardens in the Shropshire Hills.
Highly recommended cooking, cosy bar, licensed
Restaurant. Centrally heated throughout, some
bedrooms en suite, some with showers. Residents'
lounge, colour TV lounge, games room, private car
park. **Write or telephone John or Judy Keatinge.**

124

La Ronde Hotel

GH Wimborne 91 Victoria Rd ☎(0285) 3890

A neat and modestly appointed guesthouse.

5⇆ CTV in all bedrooms ✗ ⓡ ✱B&b£11–£12.50 Bdi£17.50–£19 Wfr£118 ⅃ LDOnoon

🍴 6P nc5yrs

Ⓥ

CLACTON-ON-SEA
Essex
Map **5**   TM11

GH Chudleigh Hotel Agate Rd ☎(0255) 425407

Well-kept family hotel near sea and shops.

11hc (1⇆ 4🛏) (4fb) CTV in all bedrooms ⓡ ✱B&b£12.50–£15.50 Bdi£19.50–£22.50 W£100–£120 ⅃ LDO6.30pm

Lic 🍴 CTV 7P

Credit cards ① ② ③ Ⓥ

GH *Sandrock Hotel* 1 Penfold Rd ☎(0255) 428215

Detached house close to pier offering sound accommodation.

6hc (4🛏) (3fb) ✗ ⓡ LDO6pm

Lic 🍴 CTV 6P

GH *Stonar Private Hotel* 19 Agate Rd ☎(0255) 426554

Small beautifully kept hotel, close to the sea and pier.

Cirencester
—
Cleobury Mortimer

9hc (1fb) ⓡ LDO4pm

🍴 CTV 3P nc5yrs

CLAVERDON
Warwickshire
Map **4**   SP16

FH Mr & Mrs F E Bromilow **Woodside** *(SP186644)* Langley Rd (¾m S of B4095) ☎(092684) 2446
Closed Xmas

3hc (1fb) CTV in 1 bedroom ⓡ B&b£9–£12 Bdi£17.50–£20.50 W£112–£135 ⅃ LDO2pm

🍴 CTV 12P 1🏊 ⌓ 22acres Bee hives dogs

CLAWDDNEWYDD
Clwyd
Map **6**   SJ05

FH Mrs G Williams **Maestyddyn Isa** *(SJ054535)* ☎(08245) 289
Apr–Nov

Old farmhouse in rural setting on the outskirts of Cleanog Forest. Situated 1m off the B5015.

3hc (1fb) ✗

🍴 CTV nc3yrs 365acres mixed

CLEARWELL
Gloucestershire
Map **3**   SO50

GH Tudor Farm ☎Dean (0594) 33046
Closed Jan

Farmhouse dates back to the 13th century and features oak beams, panelling and inglenook fireplace.

6hc (1⇆ 1🛏) Annexe: 1hc (2fb) ✗ ⓡ ✱B&b£11.50–£17.50 Bdi£19–£25 W£115–£157 ⅃ LDO5pm

Lic 🍴 CTV 15P 2🏊

Ⓥ

INN Wyndham Arms ☎Dean (0594) 33666
Closed Xmas

A comfortable inn with good atmosphere.

5⇆ 🛏 CTV in all bedrooms ⓡ ✱B&b£24.75–£33 Bdi£35.75–£44 Lunch£6–£8.50&alc Dinner10pm£14.50&alc

🍴 30P 1🏊 ⌗

Credit card ① Ⓥ

CLEOBURY MORTIMER
Shropshire
Map **7**   SO67

INN Talbot Hotel High St ☎(0299) 270205

Half-timbered, town-centre inn some 400 years old.

4🛁🚿 (4fb) CTV in all bedrooms ⊘ [R] B&b£18–£35 W£70–£80 ℓ Lunch£1–£8&alc Dinner9.30pm£6.50–£9.50&alc

🛋 CTV 25P

Credit cards [1] [3]

CLEVEDON
Avon
Map **3** ST47

GH Amberley 146 Old Church Rd ☎(0272) 874402
Closed Xmas

A comfortable stone-built house enthusiastically run by proprietor.

8hc (2🛁 3🚿) CTV in all bedrooms ⊘ [R] ✱B&b£12.50–£14.50 Bdi£18.50–£20.50 W£129.50–£143.50 ℓ LDO7pm

Lic 🛋 CTV 2P

Credit card [2]

See advertisement on page 96

CLIFTONVILLE
Kent
Map **5** TR37

See **Margate**

CLITHEROE
Lancashire
Map **7** SD74

INN Swan & Royal Castle St ☎(0200) 23130

Town centre inn with good, all-round furnishings. Reputedly one of the oldest buildings in Clitheroe.

5hc (3🛁) (3fb) CTV in all bedrooms [R] ✱B&b£13.30–£17.25 Bdi£18.30–£22.25 W£115.30–£140.05 ℓ Lunch£3.75&alc Dinner10pm£4.95&alc

🛋 P̸ solarium

Credit cards [1] [2] [3] [5]

INN *White Lion Hotel* Market Pl ☎(0200) 26955

Reputed to be the oldest alehouse in Clitheroe, now a well-furnished and comfortable inn.

6hc (1fb) CTV in all bedrooms [R] LDO10pm

🛋 CTV 9P solarium

CLOVELLY
Devon
Map **2** SS32

FH Mrs E Symons ***Burnstone*** *(SS325233)* Higher Clovelly ☎(02373) 219

Large, comfortably furnished farmhouse with open fires in spacious lounge. Good farmhouse fare.

2hc (1fb) ⊘ LDO5pm

🛋 CTV 2P 500acres arable dairy mixed

Credit cards [1] [2] [3]

INN New Inn Main St ☎(02373) 303

4hc ⊘ ✱B&b£10.50–£12.50 Bdi£15.50–£17.50 W£108.50–£115 ℓ Lunch 95p–£2.40 Dinner9.30pm£3.25–£5.95

CTV P 🏠 snooker

Credit card [1]

Cleobury Mortimer — Coll (Island of)

INN Red Lion The Quay ☎(02373) 237
Apr–Oct

10hc (1🚿) ⊘ [R] ✱B&b£12.50 Bdi£20.50 Lunchfr£2.95 Dinner8pmfr£8.50

🛋 CTV 6P

Credit cards [1] [3]

CLOVENFORDS
Borders *Selkirkshire*
Map **12** NT43

INN Thornilee House ☎(089685) 350

18th-century stone-built inn situated in landscaped gardens. Good home cooking using fresh produce.

4hc [R] B&bfr£12 Bdifr£17 Lunch fr£3.50&alc Dinner10pmfr£5&alc

Lic CTV 20P 🎣

CLUN
Shropshire
Map **7** SO38

Recommended

INN *Sun* ☎(05884) 559

This comfortable and friendly inn dating back, in parts, to the 15th century, is full of character, with stone fireplaces and lots of exposed beams. Bar meals are available at most times or try the popular restaurant for a more formal meal.

4hc Annexe: 3🚿 ⊘ LDOpm

🛋 CTV 8P 🚗 nc7yrs

Credit card [1]

CLUNTON
Shropshire
Map **7** SO38

FH Mrs J Williams **Hurst Mill** *(SO318811)* ☎Clun (05884) 224

Stone-built farmhouse in picturesque setting with a river running through, surrounded by tree-clad hills. Friendly atmosphere.

4rm (2hc) (1fb) ✱B&b£8–£8.50 Bdi£12–£12.50 W£87 ℓ LDO6pm

CTV 6P 2🚗 🏠 🎣 U 105acres mixed

[V]

CLYST ST MARY
Devon
Map **3** SX99

FH Mrs A Freemantle **Ivington** *(SX985912)* ☎Topsham (039287) 3290

Large brick-built farmhouse surrounded by lawns and gardens, situated 200yds from A3052.

3hc (2fb) [R] ✱B&b£8–£10 Wfr£56 M̸

CTV 4P 200acres arable beef dairy

[V]

COCKERMOUTH
Cumbria
Map **11** NY13

GH Low Hall Country Brandlingill (3m S on unclass off A5086) ☎(0900) 826654
Mar–Dec

A charming house in peaceful setting with good accommodation.

6hc (1🛁 2🚿) ⊘ [R] B&b£11.50–£15 Bdi£18–£21.50 W£119–£143 ℓ LDO5.30pm

Lic 🛋 CTV 10P nc10yrs

Credit cards [1] [3]

CODSALL
Staffordshire
Map **7** SJ80

FH Mrs D E Moreton **Moors** *(SJ859048)* Chillington Ln ☎(09074) 2330

Modernised and extended old farmhouse in pleasant rural location.

6hc (1🚿) (3fb) ⊘ [R] B&b£11–£18 Bdi£17.50–£24.50 W£120–£170 ℓ LDO9pm

Lic CTV 20P nc4yrs 100acres dairy mixed

Credit card [1]

COLESHILL
Warwickshire
Map **4** SP28

INN George & Dragon 154 Coventry Rd ☎(0675) 62249

Large half-timbered roadside inn near M6 Junction 4.

4hc (3fb) TV in all bedrooms ⊘ ✱B&bfr£11 Bdifr£14 W£98 ℓ Lunch£1.50–£5.95 Dinner9.45pm£1.50–£5.95

🛋 50P 🚗

[V]

COLL (Island of)
Strathclyde *Argyllshire*
Map **13** NM25

Car Ferry from Oban. (Some services via Lochaline/Tobermory. Also linking with Tiree)

GH Tigh-na-Mara Arinagour ☎(08793) 354
Feb–Oct

A modern guesthouse beautifully situated, with commanding views towards Mull and the Treshnish Isles. The house is tastefully decorated and furnished and has a relaxed and friendly atmosphere. Facilities include cycle and boat hire, sea-angling trips, with putting and croquet on the front lawn.

8hc (3fb) 🚭 in 1 bedroom TV in 2 bedrooms [R] ✱B&b£11.50–£12.50 Bdi£18–£20.50 W£119–£136.50 ℓ LDO6.30pm

Lic 🛋 CTV 10P 🎣

COLLYWESTON
Northamptonshire
Map **4** TF00

INN *Cavalier* Main St ☎Duddington
(078083) 288

7rm (5hc 3⇌ 2⌗) CTV in all bedrooms ®
LDO9.30pm

⊕ 60P

Credit card ①

COLMONELL
Strathclyde *Ayrshire*
Map **10** NX18

FH Mrs G B Shankland **Burnfoot**
(NX162862) ☎(046588) 220
Apr–Oct

*Welcoming farmhouse in peaceful country
setting beside River Stinchar.*

2rm (1hc) (1fb) ✱B&b£7.50–£8 Bdi£11–
£12 W£70–£77 ⚡LDO5.30pm

CTV 2P

157acres beef dairy
ⓋN

COLNE
Lancashire
Map **7** SD84

FH Mrs C Mitson **Higher Wanless**
(SD873413) Red Ln ☎(0282) 865301
Closed Dec

*Attractive, well-furnished, comfortable
farmhouse, with friendly owners.*

2hc (2fb) CTV in 1 bedroom ✱ ®
B&b£11–£12.50 Wfr£80 ⚡

⊕ CTV 4P

25acres sheep shire horses
Ⓥ

COLWYN BAY
Clwyd
Map **6** SH87
See plan

GH Cabin Hill Private Hotel College Av,
Rhos-on-Sea ☎(0492) 44568 Plan **1** *A4*
Mar–Oct

*Detached Edwardian house in residential
area, off Marine Drive.*

10hc (3⌗) (5fb) CTV in all bedrooms ✱ ®
B&b£10–£13 Bdi£14–£17 Wfr£86 ⚡
LDO5pm

Lic ⊕ CTV 6P

GH Grosvenor Hotel 106–108
Abergele Rd ☎(0492) 30798 Plan **2** *B1*

*Detached Victorian house set back from
the A55 and adjacent to shops.*

18hc (2⇌) (8fb) ® ✱B&bfr£12.65
Bdifr£17.25 Wfr£120.75 ⚡LDO10pm

Lic ⊕ CTV 16P ⚭

Credit card ③

Colwyn Bay

1 Cabin Hill Private
  Hotel
2 Grosvenor Hotel
4 Northwood Hotel
4A Silver Howe Hotel
5 Southlea
6 Sunny Downs
  Private Hotel

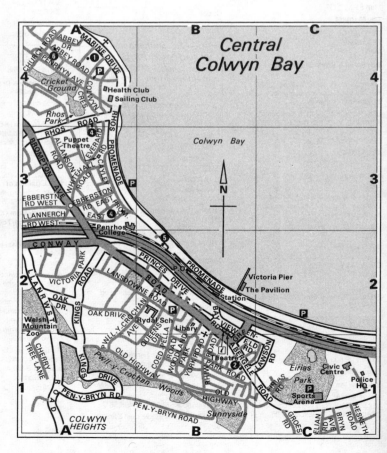

Central
Colwyn Bay

GH Northwood Hotel 47 Rhos Rd, Rhos-on-Sea ☎(0492) 49931 Plan **4** A4
Mar–Dec

Detached hotel, a short walk from shops and beach.

14hc (1⇆3🚿) (4fb) CTV in 4 bedrooms TV in 4 bedrooms ✖ ® LDO6pm
Lic 🅿 CTV 12P

GH Silver Howe Hotel Llanerch Road East, Rhos-on-Sea ☎(0492) 44593 Plan **4A** A3

16hc (2fb) B&bfr£11.50 Bdifr£15.50 Wfr£80.50 ⓜ LDO4.30pm
Lic CTV 6P ♨

GH Southlea 4 Upper Prom ☎(0492) 532004 Plan **5** B1

Single-fronted mid-terrace Victorian house adjacent to beach.

10hc (5fb) ® ✱B&b£10–£11 Bdi£14–£15 LDO6.30pm
Lic 🅿 CTV 🅿
Ⓥ

GH Sunny Downs Private Hotel 66 Abbey Rd, Rhos-on-Sea ☎(0492) 44256 Plan **6** A4

Detached Edwardian house in residential area.

17hc (4🚿) (4fb) ® LDO4pm
Lic 🅿 CTV 12P nc3yrs

Colwyn Bay
—
Combe Martin

COLYFORD
Devon
Map **3** SY29

---Recommended---

GH Swallows Eaves Hotel Swan Hill Rd ☎Colyton (0297) 53184

Comfortable accommodation in attractive gabled property in village centre.

6hc (5⇆1🚿) (2fb) CTV in all bedrooms ✖ ® B&b£12–£14.50 Bdi£24–£29 LDO7.30pm
Lic 10P ♨

COLYTON
Devon
Map **3** SY29

GH Old Bakehouse Lower Church St ☎(0297) 52518

Former 17th-century bakery with attractive beamed dining room. Personal service and good food.

6hc (3⇆) (1fb) CTV in all bedrooms ®
LDO9.45pm
Lic 🅿 10P
Credit card ③

COMBE MARTIN
Devon
Map **2** SS54

GH 'Almaza' 3 Woodlands ☎(027188) 3431

Friendly, family-run guesthouse, 150 yds from beach and local amenities.

7hc (2fb) ✖ ✱B&b£6.50–£8.50 Bdi£10.50–£12.50 W£70–£85 ⅃ LDO6.30pm
Lic CTV 5P

GH Channel Vista ☎(027188) 3514
Apr–Oct

Comfortable and well-maintained guesthouse 150 yds from Newberry Beach.

8hc (2🚿) (4fb) ✖ ✱B&b£7.50–£8.50 Bdi£11.50–£12.50 W£73–£81 ⅃ LDO5.30pm
Lic CTV 10P 2🚗
Credit card ①

GH Firs Woodlands ☎(027188) 3404
Mar–Oct

9hc (4fb) ✖ LDO5pm
Lic 🅿 CTV 10P ♨

GH Mellstock House Woodlands ☎(027188) 2592
Mar–15 Nov

6hc (1fb) ✖ ✱B&b£8–£9 Bdi£13–£15 W£77–£87 ⅃ (W only Jun–Sep) LDO4.30pm
Lic 🅿 CTV 5P 1🚗 nc3yrs

GH Miramar Hotel Victoria St ☎(027188) 3558

10hc (4🚿) (5fb) LDO6pm

Lic 🛋 CTV 9P 2🚗 ⛺ 🏊(heated)

GH *The Woodlands* 2 The Woodlands ☎(027188) 2769

Mar–Nov

Comfortable, family-run guesthouse offering good home cooking.

8hc (2fb) 🐕 LDO5pm

Lic CTV 7P 2🚗 nc5yrs

Credit card [3]

FH Mrs M A Peacock **Longlands** *(SS614451)* Easterclose Cross ☎(027188) 3522

Mar–Oct

Situated in unspoilt woods and valleys with fine views.

6hc (2fb) *B&b£9–£11 Bdi£12–£16 W£75–£105 ⱡ LDO6.30pm

Lic 🛋 CTV 15P ⛳ 27acres sheep mixed

COMPTON
Berkshire
Map **4** SU57

INN Swan Hotel ☎(063522) 269

Friendly warm atmosphere with bar and restaurant menus.

3hc (1fb) [R] *B&b£15 Bdifr£19 Lunch £2.50–£5.50&alc Dinner8.15pm£3.50–£8.50&alc

TV 40P 🍷

Credit cards [1] [2] [3] [5]

COMRIE
Tayside *Perthshire*
Map **11** NN72

GH Mossgiel Burrell St ☎(0764) 70567

Etr–Oct

A homely and cosy little house on the western outskirts of town.

6hc *B&b£7–£7.50 Bdi£11 W£70 ⱡ LDO5.30pm

🛋 CTV 6P nc3yrs

Credit cards [1] [2] [3] [4] [5]

FH Mrs J H Rimmer **West Ballindaloch** *(NN744262)* Glenlednock ☎(0764) 70282

Mar–Nov

Cosy, small farmhouse with neat garden set amid hills in secluded glen, 4m from Comrie.

2rm (1fb) 🐕 [R] *B&b£8–£8.50

CTV 3P 1500acres sheep hill farm

[V]

CONISTON
Cumbria
Map **7** SD39

INN Crown ☎(0966) 41243

Cheerful village inn near lake.

7hc (3fb) TV in 1 bedroom CTV in 6 bedrooms [R] *B&b£13–£15 Bdi£22–£25 W£150–£190 ⱡ Lunch£3.50–£5.50&alc High tea £1–£5 Dinner 8pm £8.50–£10.50&alc

🛋 CTV 30P 2🚗 ⛺

Credit cards [1] [2] [3] [5] [V]

CONSTANTINE
Cornwall
Map **2** SW72

INN *Trengilly Wartha* Nancenoy ☎Falmouth (0326) 40332

6hc (4🛁) [R] LDO9.30pm

🛋 60P

Credit cards [1] [2] [3]

See advertisement on page 167

CONWY
Gwynedd
Map **6** SH77

GH Cyfnant Private Hotel Henryd Rd, Gyffin (1m S B5106) ☎(049263) 2442 (due to change to (0492) 592442)

Apr–Oct

Large, semi-detached house close to castle and town. Bright, clean accommodation.

6hc (2fb) TV in all bedrooms ✗ ✱B&b£8.95–£9.95 Bdi£13.55–£14.55 W£91.35–£98.35 ⅃
Lic CTV 6P
Ⓥ

GH Llys Gwilym 3 Mountain Rd, off Cadnant Park ☎(049263) 2351 (due to change to (0492) 592351)

Semi-detached house ¼m from the Castle.

6hc (3fb) ✗ ✱B&b£8–£9 Bdi£11.50–£12.50 Wfr£75 ⅃ LDO6pm
Lic ᵐ CTV 3P
Ⓥ

⊢⊷**GH Sunnybanks** Llanrwst Rd, Woodlands ☎(049263) 3845 (due to change to (0492) 593845)
Etr–Oct

Semi-detached house in quiet residential area.

5hc (2fb) ✱B&bfr£7.50 Bdifr£12 Wfr£70 ⅃ LDO8pm
Lic ᵐ TV 6P
Ⓥ

FH Mrs C Roberts **Henllys** (SH767758) Llechwedd (2m W unclass rd) ☎(049263) 3269 (due to change to (0492) 593269)
Apr–Oct

Large, stone-built farmhouse, signposted from main road.

2rm (1fb) ✱B&b£7.50–£9 Bdi£11.50–£13 W£70–£90 ⅃
CTV 3P 140acres sheep mixed
Ⓥ

COOKLEY
Suffolk
Map **5**   TM37

FH Mr & Mrs A T Veasy **Green** (TM337772) ☎Linstead (098685) 209
Mar–Oct

17th-century farmhouse with exposed timbers. Situated in an area of rural peace and quiet. Friendly atmosphere.

Conwy
—
Countisbury

3hc (1fb) ✗ B&bfr£9.25 Bdifr£14 Wfr£98 ⅃ LDO3.30pm
CTV 3P nc8yrs 45 acres mixed

COOMBE
Cornwall
Map **2**   SW95

FH Mrs J Scott **Treway** (SW935505) ☎St Austell (0726) 882236

Pleasant, comfortable farmhouse in isolated rural setting approx 8m from St Austell.

3rm (2hc) (2fb) ✱B&b£7.15–£8.65
ᵐ CTV 3P ๛ 180acres arable beef dairy
Ⓥ

COPMANTHORPE
North Yorkshire
Map **8**   SE54

GH Duke of Connaught Copmanthorpe Grange (Guestaccom) ☎Appleton Roebuck (090484) 318
Mar–Dec

Nicely converted former stables in open rural surroundings.

8ᵐ (1fb) ⚿ in 1 bedroom CTV in 5 bedrooms ✗ ® ✱B&b£12–£13.50 Bdi£18–£19.50 W£126–£136.50 ⅃ LDO5pm
Lic ᵐ CTV 40P
Ⓥ

COPPLESTONE
Devon
Map **3**   SS70

FH Mrs J A King **Elston Barton** (SS784025) (1m E on unclass) ☎(03634) 397
Jul–Sep

3rm (1hc) ®
CTV 4P 1🐾 non-working

CORRIE
Isle of Arran, Strathclyde *Buteshire*
See **Arran, Isle of**

CORTACHY
Tayside *Angus*
Map **15**   NO35

FH Mrs J Grant **Cullew** (NO387609) ☎(05754) 242
Apr–Sep

Substantial stone farmhouse in lovely hill country.

2rm (1fb) LDO9pm
ᵐ CTV 3P ✦ 850acres mixed

CORWEN
Clwyd
Map **6**   SJ04

GH Coleg-y-Groes ☎(0490) 2169

Small, Christian guesthouse, originally 19th-century almshouses, in quiet part of town.

6hc (2fb) B&bfr£9.50 Bdifr£13.50 Wfr£60 M CTV 7P ๛

GH Corwen Court Private Hotel London Rd ☎(0490) 2854
Mar–Oct rs Nov–Feb

10hc (4↩ 4ᵐ) ✱B&b£9.50–£10 Bdi£14–£15 W£93–£98 ⅃ LDO6pm
ᵐ CTV ✗
Ⓥ

COTHERIDGE
Hereford & Worcester
Map **3**   SO75

FH Mr & Mrs V A Rogers **Little Lightwood** (SP798554) ☎(090566) 236
Feb–Nov

Welcoming and relaxed farmhouse offering good home-cooking.

3hc (1fb) ✗ ✱B&b£7.50–£9 Bdi£12–£13.50 W£82–£88 ⅃ LDO10am
ᵐ CTV 6P ๛ 60acres dairy

COUNTISBURY (nr Lynton)
Devon
Map **3**   SS74

FH Mrs R Pile **Coombe** (SS766489) ☎Brendon (05987) 236
Apr–Oct rs Nov–Dec

5hc (3fb) ✗ ® ✱B&b£9–£11 Bdi£16–£20 W£95–£105 ⅃ LDO5pm
Lic ᵐ CTV 6P 365acres hill-stock

COVENTRY
West Midlands
Map **4** SP37

GH Croft Hotel 23 Stoke Gn, off Binley Rd ☎(0203) 457846

12hc (1☆⋒) (1fb) CTV in 5 bedrooms ✱B&b£16.10–£20.12 Bdi£22.42–£26.44 W£156.94–£185.08 ⊬ LDO6.15pm

Lic ⋒ CTV 20P solarium

ⓥ

GH Fairlight 14 Regent St ☎(0203) 24215
Closed 24 Dec–2 Jan

Victorian terraced house near city centre and railway station.

11hc (3fb) ⓡ B&b£9–£10 W£63–£70 ᴹ

⋒ CTV 7P

GH Hearsall Lodge Hotel 1 Broad Ln ☎(0203) 74543

Large detached house with modern bedroom extension. Close to common and town centre.

13hc (2fb) CTV in all bedrooms ⓡ ✱B&b£15 Bdi£20 W£140 ⊬ LDO7.30pm

Lic ⋒ CTV 13P

ⓥ

GH Northanger House 35 Westminster Rd ☎(0203) 26780

Comfortable, welcoming, Victorian terrace house near city centre.

9hc (3fb) ⓡ B&b£9–£10 W£63–£70 ᴹ

⋒ CTV 1☎

GH *Spire View* 36 Park Rd ☎(0203) 51602

Large and comfortable Victorian house near City centre.

7hc (2⋒) (3fb) CTV in 4 bedrooms ✖ LDO10am

⋒ CTV 3P

GH Trinity House Hotel 28 Lower Holyhead Rd ☎(0203) 555654

Tall, bay-windowed house with bright modern interior, situated in a cul-de-sac, close to the town centre.

7hc (1fb) TV in 1 bedroom ✖ ⓡ ✱B&b£11–£12.50 Bdifr£17 Wfr£107.10 ⊬ LDO9.30pm

---

Lic ⋒ CTV 2P nc5yrs

ⓥ

COVERACK BRIDGES (nr Helston)
Cornwall
Map **2** SW63

FH Mr & Mrs E Lawrance **Boscadjack** *(SW673311)* ☎Helston (0326) 572086
Etr–Oct

Modernised farmhouse situated in Cober Valley amidst delightful unspoilt countryside.

4hc (2fb) ✖ ✱B&b£8–£9 Bdi£13–£14 W£85–£98 ⊬

⋒ CTV P 92acres dairy

COWDENBEATH
Fife
Map **11** NT19

GH Glenbank House 36 Foulford Rd ☎(0383) 515466

Detached house in elevated position in residential area.

5hc (3fb) ⓡ ✱B&b£8–£10 Bdi£12–£15 W£80–£100 ⊬ LDO9pm

Lic ⋒ CTV 10P

ⓥ

GH Struan Bank Private Hotel 74 Perth Rd ☎(0383) 511057

A small pleasantly-appointed hotel on outskirts of town.

8hc ✖ B&b£10 Bdi£15 W£105 ⊬ LDO7pm

Lic ⋒ CTV 8P

ⓥ

CRACKINGTON HAVEN
Cornwall
Map **2** SX19

FH Mrs M Knight **Manor** *(SX159962)* ☎St Gennys (08403) 304

Dating from the 12th century and mentioned in the Domesday Book. Attractive gardens with beautiful view, in secluded position. Guests are not permitted to smoke in the house.

4hc (2⇌) ✖ ✱B&b£11–£12 Bdi£16–£17 W£112–£119 ⊬ LDO5pm

⋒ CTV 6P nc14yrs snooker 40acres arable beef

CRAFTHOLE
Cornwall
Map **2** SX35

INN *Finnygook* ☎St Germans (0503) 30338

Well-modernised, country inn with pleasant views and comfortable bedrooms.

6hc (5⇌⋒) CTV in 5 bedrooms ✖ ⓡ

⋒ 30P 2☎ nc14yrs

CRAIL
Fife
Map **12** NO60

GH Caiplie 51–53 High St ☎(0333) 50564
Mar–Sep

Neatly maintained guesthouse in main street, with well-furnished bedrooms, shower-rooms and bistro-style dining room.

7hc (1fb) ⓡ ✱B&b£10.50–£12.50 W£105–£119 ⊬ LDO4pm

Lic ⋒ CTV ₽

GH Hazelton Private Hotel 29 Marketgate ☎(0333) 50250

Comfortable, welcoming house off main street.

5hc (1fb) ✱B&b£8–£10.50 Bdifr£13 LDO8pm

Lic ⋒ CTV ₽

CRAVEN ARMS
Shropshire
Map **7** SO48

FH Mrs C Morgan **Strefford Hall** *(SO444856)* ☎(05882) 2383
Etr–Oct

Large, comfortable, stone-built, Victorian farmhouse, north of town off A49.

3rm (1fb) ✗ ✱B&b£7.50–£8.50 W£52.50–£56 M
CTV 3P ⏚
350acres mixed
Ⓥ

CRAWLEY
West Sussex
Map **4** TQ23

For accommodation details see **Gatwick Airport**

CREDITON
Devon
Map **3** SS80

Craven Arms
—
Creetown

FH Mr & Mrs M Pennington **Woolsgrove** (SS793028) Sandford ☎Copplestone (03634) 246
Mar–Oct

17th-century farmhouse overlooking grassland. 3m NW on unclass road and 1m N of A377.

3rm (2hc) (2fb) ✱B&bfr£8.50 Bdifr£12.50 Wfr£87.50 ⨍ LDO4pm

CTV P 150acres mixed
Ⓥ

CREETOWN
Dumfries & Galloway *Kirkcudbrightshire*
Map **11** NX45

INN Creetown Arms Hotel St Johns Street ☎(067182) 282

Neat, spotlessly clean village inn run by dedicated proprietor.

5hc (2fb) ⓑ ✱B&b£10–£12 Bdi£15–£20 Lunch95p–£5 Dinner 8pm £3.50–£10
🍴 CTV 16P 🚗

𝔐anor 𝔉arm
Crackington Haven, Nr. Bude, N. Cornwall

Welcome to our beautiful secluded 12th-Century Manor now a delightful farmhouse, one mile from sea. The Domesday List recorded in 1086 that the Manor was held by the Earl of Mortain, the half-brother of William the Conqueror. It has since been tastefully restored and adapted to provide an elegant, peaceful setting for a perfect holiday. We offer charming accommodation double ensuite and single rooms and excellent home-cooking using our own farm and garden produce. The games room includes a full-sized snooker table. Regret no children and no-smoking in the house. Open all year.
Mrs M. Knight   Tel: St Gennys 304

CRIANLARICH
Central *Perthshire*
Map **10**　NN32

GH Glenardran ☎(08383) 236

Stone house in village with good accommodation.

6hc (3fb) B&b£8.50 Bdi£14.10 W£84.60 ⌀ LDO6.30pm

Lic ⁍ CTV 8P

Credit cards ① ③ Ⓥ

See advertisement on page 133

GH Moungreenan ☎(08383) 286

Friendly little guesthouse with good views of Ben More.

5hc (1fb) ⤬ ✱B&bfr£9 Bdi£14–£14.50 W£95–£101.50 ⌀ LDO4pm

⁍ CTV 8P gymnasium

Ⓥ

CRICCIETH
Gwynedd
Map **6**　SH53

GH Glyn-y-Coed Private Hotel
Portmadoc Rd ☎(076671) 2870
Closed Xmas & New Year

10hc (5fb) Ⓡ B&bfr£10 Bdifr£15 Wfr£100 ⌀ LDO6pm

Lic CTV 12P

Ⓥ

Crianlarich — Crieff

GH *Kairon Hotel* Marine Ter ☎(076671) 2453

10hc Ⓡ LDO7pm

Lic CTV 14P

GH Min-y-Gaer Private Hotel
Porthmadoc Rd ☎(076671) 2151
Apr–Oct

Substantial Victorian semi-detached house with coastal views.

10hc (4fb) Ⓡ B&b£9.50–£11 Bdi£14.50–£16 W£99–108 ⌀ LDO4pm

Lic ⁍ CTV 12P

Ⓥ

GH Moorings 20 Marine Ter ☎(076671) 2802
Mar–Oct (rs Mar & Oct)

Victorian mid terrace on the front, adjacent to the castle.

6hc TV in 1 bedroom ⤬ ✱B&bfr£9.50 Bdifr£13.50 LDO6pm

Lic CTV 20P

Ⓥ

GH Môr Heli Hotel Marine Ter ☎(076671) 2878
Mar–Oct (rs Mar & Oct)

Victorian mid terrace house on the sea front, ¼ mile from shops.

10hc (1⬱) (4fb) ✱B&bfr£9.50 Bdifr£13.50 LDO6pm

Lic CTV 20P

GH Neptune Hotel Marine Ter (Guestaccom) ☎(076671) 2794
Mar–Oct (rs Mar & Oct)

Victorian mid-terrace house on sea front adjacent to the castle.

10hc (3fb) ✱B&bfr£9.50 Bdifr£13.50 Wfr£94.50 ⌀ LDO6pm

Lic CTV 20P ⌂

Ⓥ

CRICKHOWELL
Powys
Map　SO21

GH Dragon Country House Hotel High St ☎(0873) 810362

Friendly, informal hotel catering for tourists and commercial trade. Vegetarian meals served.

11rm (7hc 2⬱ 1⁍) (1fb) CTV in 7 bedrooms ⤬ Ⓡ ✱B&b£11.50–£22.50 W£96.50–£148.50 ⌀ LDO8.30pm

Lic ⁍ CTV 15P ⚿

Credit cards ① ③ Ⓥ

CRIEFF
Tayside *Perthshire*
Map **11**　NN82

GH Comely Bank 32 Burrell St ☎(0764) 3409
Mar–Oct rs Nov–Feb
Small, pleasantly furnished terrace guesthouse on main road.
7hc (2fb) ✱B&b£8–£8.50 Bdi£11.50–£12 W£70–£73.50₤ LDO6pm
CTV 🚫P

GH Heatherville 29–31 Burrell St ☎(0764) 2825
Comfortable, privately owned house forming part of a terrace.
5hc (2fb) ✱B&b£8–£8.50 Bdi£12–£12.50 W£79–£83₤ LDO5pm
Lic 📺 CTV 5P nc2yrs
[V]

GH Keppoch House Hotel Perth Rd ☎(0764) 4341
Closed 4 Jan–22 Feb
Small hotel with modern bedrooms offering a choice of Scottish or gourmet speciality meals.
6hc (4🛁) (2fb) 🚭 in 2 bedrooms CTV in all bedrooms 🚫 [R] ✱B&b£13.50–£21 Bdi£19.50–£28.50 W£130–£190₤ LDO9.30pm
Lic 📺 CTV P
Credit cards [2] [3]

Crieff — Cromer

CROESGOCH
Dyfed
Map **2** SM83

GH Cwmwdig Water Berea ☎(03483) 434
Bedrooms have charm and individuality in this lovely converted farmhouse overlooking the sea.
3hc Annexe: 8hc (3fb) [R] ✱B&b£11.50–£14 Bdi£15.50–£17.80 W£105–£118₤(W only 26 Jul–30 Aug) LDO7.30pm
Lic 📺 CTV 15P ⌂
Credit cards [1] [2] [3] [5] [V]

FH Mrs A Charles **Torbant** *(SM845307)* ☎(03483) 276
Etr–Sep (rs Oct–Etr, except closed Xmas–New Year)
Larger than average farm guesthouse in pleasant position overlooking open country.
10hc (1🛁) (4fb) 🚫 ✱B&b£9.50–£10.50 Bdi£14–£15 W£95–£99₤ LDO6pm
Lic 📺 CTV 40P 110acres dairy
[V]
See advertisement on page 332

FH Mrs M B Jenkins **Trearched** *(SM831306)* ☎(03483) 310
Cosy character farmhouse overlooking St George's Channel. Reading room and patio gardens.
7hc ✱B&b£10 Bdi£15 W£105₤ LDOnoon
📺 CTV 10P 100acres arable
[V]

CROMER
Norfolk
Map **9** TG24

GH *Brightside* 19 Macdonald Rd ☎(0263) 513408
Apr–Oct
7hc (3fb) 🚫 LDO3.30pm
Lic 📺 CTV nc5yrs

GH Chellow Dene 23 Macdonald Rd ☎(0263) 513251
7hc (2fb) CTV in all bedrooms [R] ✱B&bfr£8.50 Bdifr£13.50 Wfr£73₤
Lic 📺 6P
Credit card [1]

GH Ivy House Hotel 2 Vicarage Rd ☎(0263) 514179
6hc (1🛁) CTV in all bedrooms B&b£10.50–£13 Bdi£14.50–£19 LDO9.30pm
CTV
Credit cards [1] [3]

Neptune & Môr Heli Hotels
Min-y-Môr, Criccieth, Gwynedd LL52 0EF
Telephone: 2794/2878 - STD 076671
Two, well-established, family-run hotels situated on sea-front, noted for good food and friendly atmosphere. Comfortably furnished throughout with an attractive licensed bar for guests and diners.
Some rooms en-suite.
For brochure and terms contact resident proprietors:
WJJ & E Williams.
Fire certificate granted
Licensed
Car Park

CRAFT WORKSHOPS IN THE ENGLISH COUNTRYSIDE
A completely new and up-dated edition of the ever-popular CoSIRA directory of hundreds of craft workshops, craft centres and craft galleries.
AA
If your roof needs thatching, or your family heirloom restoring, or if you like to see skilled craftsmen at work, this book is your guide.

GH Morden 20 Cliff Av ☎(0263) 513396
Mar–Nov & Xmas

Smart late Victorian house in a quiet residential avenue.

7hc (2🚿) (2fb) *B&b£9–£9.50 Bdi£13.50–£14.50 W£84–£91 ⁄ LDO5pm

Lic 🛋 CTV 3P ⌂

[V]

GH Sandcliffe Private Hotel Runton Rd ☎(0263) 512888
Closed 10 Dec–5 Jan

Friendly-run private hotel situated on the coast road, conveniently placed for access to town centre.

22hc (4🛁 10🚿) (8fb) CTV in 9 bedrooms [R] *B&b£13.20–£14.20 Bdi£17–£18 Wfr£90 ⁄

Lic CTV 10P

GH Westgate Lodge Private Hotel 10 Macdonald Rd ☎(0263) 512840
Closed Xmas

12hc (6🚿) (5fb) CTV in all bedrooms ✖ *B&bfr£11.50 Bdifr£17.25 Wfr£103.50 ⁄ LDO7pm

Lic 🛋 14P nc3yrs

Credit cards [1] [3]

CROMHALL
Avon
Map **3** ST69

FH Mrs S Scolding **Varley** *(ST699905)* Talbot End ☎Wickwar (045424) 292
Etr–Sep (rs Oct–mid Apr) Closed Xmas

Spacious, two-storey stone-built farmhouse with garden. Well-maintained and neatly decorated throughout.

4hc (4fb) 🚭 in 2 bedrooms ✖ *B&b£9–£11 Bdi£13–£13.90 W£87 ⁄ LDO3pm

🛋 CTV 5P 75acres dairy

[V]

CROOK
Cumbria
Map **7** SD49

FH Mrs I D Scales **Greenbank** *(SD462953)* ☎Staveley (0539) 821216

Good home-cooking is a feature of this attractive, comfortable farmhouse.

5hc (1🚿) (3fb) [R] *B&b£10.75–£11.25 Bdi£19.75–£20.50 Wfr£130 ⁄ LDO4pm

Lic 🛋 CTV 20P nc12yrs 14½acres mushrooms

Credit card [3]

CROSCOMBE
Somerset
Map **3** ST54

FH Mrs Keen **Upper Thrupe** Maesbury *(ST604457)* (1½m NE of Croscombe unclass) ☎Shepton Mallet (0749) 2697

Comfortable accommodation at a peaceful dairy farm.

3rm (2hc) 🚭 in 2 bedrooms ✖ *B&bfr£8

160acres dairy

CROSSGATES
Powys
Map **3** SO06

GH Guidfa House ☎Penybont (059787) 241

Exquisite country house offering very agreeable accommodation.

6hc (2🚿) (2fb) ✖ [R] *B&b£10–£11.50 Bdi£17–£18.50 W£105–£115 ⁄

Lic 🛋 CTV 8P ⌂

[V]

CROYDE
Devon
Map **2** SS43

GH Moorsands House Hotel Moor Ln ☎(0271) 890781
Apr–Oct

8hc (3fb) ✖ *B&b£10–£12 Bdi£15–£18 Wfr£98 ⁄ LDO1pm

Lic 🛋 CTV 8P nc4yrs

INN *Thatched Barn* ☎Barnstaple(0271) 890349

16th-century, thatched free house in centre of pretty village.

4hc (1🚿) (1fb) ✖ LDO10.15pm

🛋 30P

CROYDON
Gt London
London plan **4** D1 (pages 246–247)

GH *Friends* 50 Friends Rd ☎01-688 6215

Victorian house run by Maltese family plainly furnished, friendly atmosphere.

11hc (5fb) TV in 2 bedrooms ✖

🛋 CTV 5P

Credit card [3] [V]

GH Lonsdale Hotel 158 Lower Addiscombe Rd ☎01-654 2276
Closed 24 Dec–8 Jan

Family-run guesthouse with a warm, homely atmosphere.

10hc (1🛁) (2fb) CTV in all bedrooms ✖ [R] *B&b£21 Bdi£28.50 W£145 ⁄ LDO6.30pm

Lic 🛋 CTV 10P snooker

[V]

GH Markington Hotel 9 Haling Park Rd ☎01-688 6530
Closed Xmas

Well-equipped family run guesthouse with relaxing atmosphere.

16hc (1🛁 14🚿) (4fb) 🚭 in 4 bedrooms CTV in all bedrooms ✖ [R] *B&b£22–£32 LDO8pm

Lic 🛋 CTV 7P

Credit cards [1] [2] [3] [4] [V]

GH *Oakwood Hotel* 69 Outram Rd ☎01-654 2835

Near town centre, Victorian house with bay windows, offering comfortable rooms.

14hc (8🛁 6🚿) (4fb) CTV in all bedrooms [R] LDO8pm

Lic 🛋 CTV 7P ⌂ sauna bath solarium

Credit cards [1] [2] [3] [5]

CRUCKTON
Shropshire
Map **7** SJ41

FH Mrs M L Birchall ***Woodfield*** *(SJ432108)* ☎Shrewsbury (0743) 860249

Large, modern detached farmhouse with neat gardens.

3rm ✖

🛋 CTV P 84acres

CUCKLINGTON
Somerset
Map **3** ST72

FH Mrs P David **Hale** *(ST765277)* Hale Ln ☎Wincanton (0963) 33342
Mar–Oct

2hc (1fb) [R] ✱B&bfr£8 Bdifr£12 Wfr£75 🍴 LDO10am

CTV 2P 🏠

55½acres mixed

CULLEN
Grampian *Banffshire*
Map **15** NJ56

GH Wakes Hotel Seafield Pl ☎(0542) 40251

23rm (22hc) (5fb) LDO7.30pm

Lic CTV 20P 🏠

[V]

CULLODEN MOOR
Highland *Inverness-shire*
Map **14** NH74

FH Mrs E M C Alexander **Culdoich** *(NH755435)* ☎Inverness (0463) 790268
Apr–Oct

18th-century farmhouse in a position near Culloden battlefield and Clava standing stones

2hc (1fb) 🚫 ✱B&b£8–£9 Bdi£12–£13 W£80–£85 🍴 LDO4.30pm

CTV P 🏠 200acres mixed

[V]

CULLOMPTON
Devon
Map **3** ST00

FH Mrs A C Cole **Five Bridges** *(ST026095)* ☎(0884) 33453
Closed Xmas

Well-maintained, brick-built farmhouse.

4hc (3fb) ✱B&b£7 Bdi£11 W£74 🍴

CTV 6P 1🚗 🎣 22acres non-working

[V]

CULROSS
Fife
Map **11** NS98

Cucklington — Dalwood

INN *Red Lion* Low Causeway ☎Newmills (0383) 880225

Neat and homely inn with modestly priced meals, set in conservation village.

6hc

CTV

CURY
Cornwall
Map **2** SW62

FH Mrs M F Osborne **Polglase** *(SW686213)* Cross Lanes (1m E) ☎Mullion (0326) 240469
Etr–Sep

Comfortable working farm with modern accommodation and good food. 5m from Helston.

6rm (5hc) (2fb) 🚫 ✱B&b£8 Bdi£13 W£91 🍴 LDO6.30pm

CTV P 60acres mixed

Credit card [3]

FH Mrs H Lugg **Tregaddra** *(SW701219)* ☎Mullion (0326) 240235
Mar–Oct

A delightful 18th-century stone farmhouse with glorious views.

5hc (2🛁) (2fb) 🚫 B&b£8–£9.50 Bdi£12–£15 W£84–£105 🍴 LDO10am

CTV 8P 🏊

120acres arable beef

CWMBACH (nr Builth Wells)
Powys
Map **3** SO13

GH *Rhydfelin Farm* Builth Rd ☎Builth Wells (0982) 553678
Closed 26–30 Dec

6hc (1fb) LDO8.45pm

Lic ♨ CTV 12P 🏠

Credit cards [1] [3]

CWMBRAN
Gwent
Map **3** ST29

FH Mrs B Watkins **Glebe** *(ST325965)* Croes-y-Ceiliog (1½m E unclass towards Tredunnock) ☎Tredunnock (063349) 251
Feb–Dec

Modern ranch-house-style building in lovely countryside, offering a friendly welcome.

3rm 2hc 🚫 ✱B&b£9–£10

♨ TV P

100acres beef dairy mixed

[V]

CWMDUAD
Dyfed
Map **2** SN33

GH Neuadd-Wen ☎Cynwyl Elfed (026787) 438

A welcoming, family-run rural guesthouse, in village set in wooded valley. An ideal base for seeing West Wales.

5hc (2fb) ✱B&b£7.50–£9.50 Bdi£12–£14 W£67–£88 🍴 LDO10pm

Lic ♨ CTV 12P 🏠 🎣

[V]

DALMALLY
Strathclyde *Argyllshire*
Map **10** NN12

GH *Orchy Bank* Stronmilchan Rd ☎(08382) 370
Apr–Oct

White house in rural setting by River Orchy. Friendly proprietor is bilingual.

9rm (8hc) (2fb) [R]

CTV 8P ♿

DALWOOD (nr Axminster)
Devon
Map **3** ST20

FH Mr & Mrs Cobley **Elford** *(ST258004)* ☎Axminster (0297) 32415
Mar–Oct

Listed farmhouse of historic interest with parts dating from the 12th century. Panoramic and pastoral views.

5hc (2🚿) (2fb) 🚫 ✱B&b£8.50–£10 Bdi£12.50–£14 W£84–£90 🍴 LDO5pm

Lic ♨ CTV 8P 15acres dairy

[V]

DARLINGTON
Co Durham
Map **8** NZ21

GH *Raydale Hotel* Stanhope Road South ☎(0325) 58993
Closed 24 Dec–1 Jan
Impressive house with friendly and relaxed atmosphere, standing within walled garden.
11hc (3fb) TV in 1 bedroom LDO3pm
Lic 🛋 CTV 12P
Credit cards [1] [3] [5]

DARTINGTON
Devon
Map **3** SX76

INN Cott ☎Totnes (0803) 863777
6hc ✕ [R] B&b£18.50 Bdi£27 W£182 Ɫ Lunch£5.25–£7.75 Dinner 9.30pm £8.75–£11.75&alc
CTV 40P nc8yrs
Credit cards [1] [2] [3] [5] [V]

DARTMOUTH
Devon
Map **3** SX84

GH Orleans 24 South Town ☎(08043) 2967
Listed Georgian terraced house overlooking estuary. Simply furnished with warm, relaxed atmosphere.

Darlington — Dawlish

5hc ✕ *B&b£10–£11 W£66–£69 M̸
🛋 CTV 🚫P

DAVENTRY
Northamptonshire
Map **4** SP56

GH Abercorn Hotel Warwick St ☎(0327) 703741
Commercial hotel in residential street a short way from town centre
32hc (2🛁 30🚿) (1fb) CTV in all bedrooms ✕ *B&b£25 Bdi£34 LDO8.30pm
Lic 🛋 CTV 20P

DAVIOT
Highland *Inverness-shire*
Map **14** NH73

FH Mrs E M MacPherson **Lairgandour** *(NH720376)* ☎(046385) 207
Etr–Oct
In a quiet location near to Culloden Moor, Loch Ness and the Cairngorms. Situated east of A9 at junction with B9154.
5rm (4hc) (3fb) *B&bfr£7.50 Bdifr£11
CTV P 1000acres mixed

DAWLISH
Devon
Map **3** SX97

GH Broxmore Private Hotel
20 Plantation Ter ☎(0626) 863602
Closed Jan & Feb
8hc (3fb) ✕ [R] *B&b£8.20–£9.50 Bdi£12.50–£14 W£80–£92 Ɫ LDO4pm
Lic 🛋 CTV 🚫P nc5yrs
Credit cards [1] [3] [V]

GH Lynbridge Private Hotel Barton Villas ☎(0626) 862352
Etr–Oct
8hc (1fb) ✕ *B&b£9.50–£10 Bdi£13–£14 W£84–£88 Ɫ LDO5pm
🛋 CTV 6P nc2yrs

GH Mimosa 11 Barton Ter ☎(0626) 863283
8hc (1🚿) (4fb) ✕ *B&b£6.50–£7.50 Bdi£9.50–£10.50 W£60–£69 Ɫ LDO2pm
CTV 4P nc3yrs
[V]

GH Radfords Hotel Dawlish Water ☎(0626) 863322
mid Mar–Oct
Fine, old-world, thatched building with modern extension, ideal for family holidays.
34🛁 (34fb) [R] *B&bfr£20 Bdifr£22 W£140–£176 Ɫ (W only Jun–Sep) LDO7pm

Lic 🍺 CTV 50P ⌂ ⌷(heated) snooker
solarium
Ⓥ

DEBDEN GREEN
Essex
Map **5**   TL53

FH Mrs K M Low **Wychbars** *(TL564313)*
☎Bishop's Stortford (0279) 850362

*Moated farmhouse in 3½ acres. Down
unclassified Debden Green road, off
B1051. Farmhouse through Scotts Farm.*

2rm CTV in all bedrooms ✱B&b£9.50–£10
lift 🍺 CTV 10P ♿ 600acres arable
Ⓥ

DEDHAM
Essex
Map **5**   TM03

─────── *Recommended* ───────

GH Dedham Hall ☎Colchester
(0206) 323027
rs mid Dec–Feb

*Beautiful timber-framed house in six
acres of grounds providing
comfortable accommodation and
good home-cooking.*

7hc (3⇄) ✖ Ⓡ LDOnoon
Lic 🍺 CTV 12P 2🐾

───────────────────────────

┌─────────────────────┐
│   **Dawlish**   │
│   —   │
│   **Derby**   │
└─────────────────────┘

DENBIGH
Clwyd
Map **6**   SJ06

GH Cayo 74 Vale St ☎(074571) 2686
5hc (2fb) CTV in 1 bedroom ✱B&b£9–
£9.50 Bdi£13–£13.50 W£91 ⌿ LDO4pm
Lic 🍺 CTV P

DENNY
Central *Stirlingshire*
Map **11**   NS88

FH Mrs J Morton **Lochend** *(NS759856)*
☎(0324) 822778
Closed Apr (rs Oct–Mar)

*4m W along B818, then turn right at
Carronbridge on unclass road for 2 miles.*

2hc ✖ Ⓡ ✱B&b£8.50 Bdi£14 Wfr£95 ⌿
LDO3pm
🍺 CTV P nc3yrs
650acres sheep
Ⓥ

DERBY
Derbyshire
Map **8**   SK33

GH Ascot Hotel 724 Osmaston Rd
☎(0332) 41916

───────────────────────────

20hc (1fb) CTV in 2 bedrooms TV in 4
bedrooms ✖
Lic 🍺 CTV 15P

GH Dalby House 100 Radbourne St
☎(0332) 42353

*Lovely old house in residential area.
Popular with tourists and business
travellers.*

9hc (2fb) CTV in all bedrooms ✖ Ⓡ
✱B&b£9.70–£13 Bdi£15.20–£18.50
W£106.40–£129.50 ⌿ LDO6pm
🍺 CTV 9P 1🐾
Ⓥ

GH Georgian House Hotel 32/34
Ashbourne Rd ☎(0332) 49806
rs Xmas & New Year

*Beautifully maintained house offering a
high standard of accommodation.*

18hc (2⇄ 2🚿) (6fb) CTV in all bedrooms
✱B&b£11.50–£23 Bdi£18.90–£30 ⌿
LDO7.30pm
Lic 🍺 CTV 20P
Ⓥ

GH Kerrance Hotel 115 London Rd
☎(0332) 45242
Closed Xmas

*Simple, keenly priced hotel popular with
business people.*

12hc (1fb)
🍺 CTV ⚑

GH *Rangemoor Hotel* 67 Macklin St
☎(0332) 47252
Closed Xmas day

Simple accommodation in a terraced house near town centre.

12hc Annexe: 8hc (3fb) CTV in 1 bedroom
🛋 CTV 15P

DERSINGHAM
Norfolk
Map **9** TF63

GH Westdene House Hotel 60 Hunstanton Rd ☎(0485) 40395
rs Nov–Feb

5hc (1🛁) (1fb) [R] ✱B&b£11–£13.50 Bdi£16–£18 W£105–£115 ⊬ LDO9pm
Lic 🛋 CTV 12P

DEVIL'S BRIDGE
Dyfed
Map **6** SN77

FH Mrs E E Lewis ***Erwbarfe*** *(SN749784)*
☎Ponterwyd (097085) 251
Apr–Oct

A traditional stone-built farmhouse with oak-beamed ceiling in the lounge. 2m NE of Devil's Bridge on A4120.

2hc ✖ [R]
🛋 CTV 4P nc5yrs 400acres mixed

DEVIZES
Wiltshire
Map **4** SU06

Derby — Diddlebury

INN Castle Hotel New Park St ☎(0380) 2902
Closed Boxing Day

17hc (2🛁) (2fb) CTV in all bedrooms [R] ✱B&b£14–£22 Bdi£18–£22 W£126–£154 ⊬ Lunch fr£6&alc Dinner10pm £8.50alc
🛋 8🚗
Credit cards [1] [2] [3] [5] [V]

DEVORAN
Cornwall
Map **2** SW73

GH Driffold Hotel 8 Devoran Ln (Guestaccom) ☎(0872) 863314
rs Dec & Jan

Attractive small hotel overlooking Devoran Creek. Friendly, personally-run and good food.

7hc (2🚿) ✖ B&b£11–£13.50 Bdi£16–£18 W£108.50–£122.50 ⊬ LDO7pm
Lic 🛋 CTV 12P

See advertisement under Truro

DIBDEN
Hampshire
Map **4** SU40

⊢✱⊣**GH Dale Farm** Manor Rd
☎Southampton (0703) 849632
Closed Xmas

18th-century farmhouse on edge of the New Forest with modern bedrooms and fresh home-cooking.

6hc (1fb) ✖ [R] B&b£7.50–£11 Bdi£11.50–£16 W£76.50–£101 ⊬ LDO11am
🛋 CTV 10P 🐕 🐎

DIDDLEBURY
Shropshire
Map **7** SO58

Recommended

FH Mrs E Wilkes **Glebe** *(SO507856)*
☎Munslow (058476) 221
Mar–7 Nov (closed 10 days early Jun)

'Pride of Place' national winner in 1983 Glebe Farm is a Tudor farmhouse in the village centre. Rooms are divided between the main house with its ancient timbers and a cottage annexe recently converted to provide more modern surroundings. British country cooking is a speciality, with warm, friendly service.

3hc (1🚿) Annexe: 3hc (1🚿) ✖ [R] ✱B&b£15–£19 Bdi£25.50–£30.50 W185.50–£192 ⊬ LDO6pm
Lic 🛋 CTV 10P 2🚗 nc10yrs 123acres mixed
[V]

The Glebe Farm

1983 National Winner
AA Pride of Place
Good Hotel Guide 1986
Licensed

**The Glebe Farm, Diddlebury,
Craven Arms, Shropshire SY7 9DH.
Telephone: Munslow (058476) 221**

The Glebe Farm is a working farm. The Elizabethan farmhouse is set in the centre of the tiny village of Diddlebury. The old house is in a peaceful and quiet setting between the stream which runs through the beautiful garden and the Saxon Church with its fortified tower. Whilst you sit in the garden time stops; one can hear nothing but country sounds.

Michael, Eileen and Adrian Wilkes, the owners, are on hand to greet their visitors who are welcomed as houseguests. The farmhouse has a friendly atmosphere and is warm and comfortable. Each bedroom has an electric heater, a wash basin with hot and cold water also tea and coffee making facilities. Full English or Continental breakfast and dinner with choices are served in the flag stoned and oak beamed dining room. Whilst enjoying the delights of English traditional cooking, guests may look across the well tended Shropshire country garden.

DINDER
Somerset
Map **3** ST54

FH Mrs P J Keen **Crapnell** *(ST597457)* ☎Shepton Mallet (0749) 2683
Mar–Oct
Pleasant farm with comfortable bedrooms and friendly atmosphere.
3hc (1fb) ✗ [R] ✱B&b£8.50–£9.50 Bdi£15–£16.50 LDOnoon
♨ CTV P ⌂ ≈ snooker 300acres dairy mixed

DIRLETON
Lothian *East Lothian*
Map **12** NT58

INN Castle ☎(062085) 221
Closed Xmas & New Year
Plain but comfortable inn in attractive setting on village green.
4hc Annexe: 4hc [R] ✱B&b£13–£16 Bdi£19–£22 W£126–£150 ⊮ Bar lunch £1.50–£3.50 Dinner 8.30pm £7.50alc
♨ CTV 20P
Credit card [2] [V]

DITCHLING
East Sussex
Map **4** TQ31

INN Bull Hotel 2 High St ☎Hassocks (07918) 3147
Beautifully restored country inn with comfortable accommodation and welcoming bars.
3🛁 CTV in all bedrooms [R] B&bfr£27.50 Bar lunch 70p–£5.25 Dinner 9.30pm 70p–£5.25
♨ 50P 🚌
Credit cards [1] [2] [3] [5]

DOCKLOW
Hereford & Worcester
Map **3** SO55

FH Mrs M R M Brooke **Nicholson** *(SO584581)* ☎Steens Bridge (056882) 269
Etr–Xmas
Typical Herefordshire farmhouse, about 350 years old.
2rm (1fb) ✱B&b£8.50–£9 Bdi£12.50–£13 Wfr£87 ⊮
♨ CTV P 🎣 200acres dairy
Credit card [1]

DODDISCOMBSLEIGH
Devon
Map **3** SX88

INN *Nobody* ☎Christow (0647) 52394
rs Sun & Mon (closed Xmas Day)
Attractive inn dating from the 16th century retaining many original features.
4hc (1🛁 3🚿) Annexe: 2🛁 🚿 (3fb) CTV in all bedrooms ✗ [R] LDO9.30pm
50P 🚌 nc14yrs
Credit cards [1] [3]

DOLGELLAU
Gwynedd
Map **6** SH71

GH Clifton Private Hotel Smithfield Sq ☎(0341) 422554
6hc (2fb) ✗ ✱B&b£9.50–£12 Bdi£13–£18.50 W£87.50–£122.50 ⊮ LDO9.30pm
♨ CTV 3P
[V]

FH Mrs E W Price ***Glyn*** *(SH704178)* ☎(0341) 422286
Etr–Nov (rs Aug)
Stone-built farmhouse of historical interest with oak beams, floors and doors. Well-situated for coastal resorts.
5rm (4hc) (2fb) LDOprevious day
♨ CTV 10P 150acres mixed

FH Mrs C Tudor-Owen ***Rhedyncochion*** *(SH693156)* Llanfachreth (3m NE unclass) ☎Rhydymain (034141) 600
Etr–Oct
→

100-year-old, stone-built farmhouse with extensive views of surrounding countryside and mountains.

2rm (1hc) (1fb) ✹ ✱B&b£8 Bdi£12 W£84 ⫫
🍴 CTV P 120acres mixed

DOLWYDDELAN
Gwynedd
Map **6** SH75

INN Gwydyr ☎(06906) 209
rs Oct–May

Victorian detached inn in centre of village, set in peaceful valley.

3hc CTV in all bedrooms ✱B&b£9–£10 W£70 ⫫ Bar lunch 60p–£3.25 Dinner 10pm£2.80–£7
🍴 CTV 6P nc

DORNIE
Highland *Ross & Cromarty*
Map **14** NG82

FH Mrs M Macrae **Bungalow** *(NG871272)*
Ardelve ☎(059985) 231
Etr–Oct

Farmhouse situated on main A87.

3hc (2fb) ✹ ✱B&b£7.50–£8.50 Bdi£11–£12
6P 10acres mixed

DORSINGTON
Warwickshire
Map **4** SP14

Dolgellau
~
Dover

FH Mrs M J Walters **Church** *(SP132495)*
☎Stratford-upon-Avon (0789) 720471

Homely Georgian house on village outskirts.

3hc (1fb) ✹ ✱B&bfr£9 Bdifr£15 LDO6pm
🍴 CTV 3P ⚗ 127acres arable beef horse

DOUGLAS
Isle of Man
See **Man, Isle of**

DOVER
Kent
Map **5** TR34

GH Beaufort House 18 Eastcliff, Marine Pde ☎(0304) 202573
Closed Dec

6hc (2fb) ✹ ® ✱B&b£12–£24 Bdi£18–£29 W£82–£144 ⫫ LDOnoon
Lic 🍴 CTV 7P

GH Beulah House 94 Crabble Hill, London Rd ☎(0304) 824615

Cosy, homely compact accommodation with limited lounge facilities. Extensive lawns and gardens to rear with open aspect.

7hc (3fb) ✹
🍴 8P 2🚗

GH Castle 10 Castle Hill Rd ☎(0304) 201656
Closed Xmas

6hc (2🚿) (1fb) CTV in all bedrooms ✹ ®
✱B&bfr£9–£12 W£100–£130 ⫫ LDO7pm
Lic 🍴 3P 1🚗(charge)
Credit card ③ ⓥ

GH Dell 233 Folkestone Rd ☎(0304)202422

Victorian terraced house with good family accommodation.

6hc (4fb) ✹ ® ✱B&b£9–£11 W£63–£77 ⫫
🍴 CTV 6P
ⓥ

GH Dover Stop 45 London Rd, River (2m NW A256) ☎(0304) 822751

Cheerful modern accommodation with limited louge facilities.

7hc Annexe: 4hc (6fb) LDO9pm
Lic 🍴 CTV 14P sauna bath

GH Gateway Hovertel Snargate St ☎(0304) 205479
Closed 23 Dec–Feb

27hc (4⇄ 23🚿) (7fb) CTV in all bedrooms ✹ ✱B&b£16–£23 LDO6pm
Lic 🍴 CTV 22P
ⓥ

See advertisement on page 141

GH Kernow 189 Folkestone Rd ☎(0304) 207797

6hc (2fb) CTV in all bedrooms ℜ ✱B&b£9–£11 (W only Jan–Apr)

📺 4P 2🚗 (charge)

Credit card ③ Ⓥ

See advertisement on page 141

GH Number One 1 Castle St ☎(0304) 202007

Conveniently situated, nicely furnished, friendly and efficient establishment complemented by a cosy Victorian atmosphere.

5hc (1⇨ 3🗊) (2fb) CTV in all bedrooms 🗶 ℜ ✱B&b£11.50–£13

📺 2P 4🚗 (charge)

Ⓥ

GH Peverall House Hotel 28 Park Av ☎(0304) 20573
Closed Dec

Comfortable, well-appointed accommodation and a cheerful, pleasant welcome.

6hc (2fb) 🗶 ℜ ✱B&b£12–£15 Bdi£18–£21 LDOnoon

Lic 📺 CTV 6P

GH St Brelades 82 Buckland Av ☎(0304) 206126

Family accommodation with friendly attentive service.

Dover
—
Downton

8hc (4fb) CTV in 4 bedrooms TV in 1 bedroom 🗶 ℜ ✱B&b£9–£11 Bdi£13.50–£15.50

Lic 📺 CTV 6P

GH St Martins 17 Castle Hill Rd ☎(0304) 205938
Closed Xmas

8hc (2fb) CTV in all bedrooms 🗶 ℜ ✱B&b£8–£12 W£56–£84 🅜

Lic 📺 1🚗

Credit card ① Ⓥ

GH Walletts Court West Cliffe, St Margarets-at-Cliffe (1½m NE of A2/A258 junction, off B2058) ☎(0304) 852424
Closed Xmas & Boxing Day

A restored 17th-century farmhouse with large beamed bedrooms, inglenooks and oak staircase. Situated on the white cliffs of Dover, 3m from harbour.

3hc (2⇨ 1🗊) Annexe: 4🗊 (3fb) 🗶 ℜ ✱B&b£13–£22 Bdi £21–£30 LDO7pm

Lic 📺 CTV 16P ♠

DOWNHAM MARKET
Norfolk
Map **5** TF60

GH Cross Keys Riverside Hotel Hilgay (Guestaccom) ☎(0366) 387777
Closed 24 Dec–22 Jan

Once a coaching inn, now a small attractive and comfortable hotel, adjacent to the A10 and on the banks of the River Wissey. 3m S off A5012.

3⇨ Annexe: 2⇨ (1fb) CTV in all bedrooms 🗶 ℜ ✱B&b£15.40–£16.17 Bdi£20.50–£21.50 W£125–£131.25 ⏛ LDO8.30pm

Lic 📺 10P ♪

Ⓥ

DOWNTON
Wiltshire
Map **4** SU12

GH Warren High St ☎(0725) 20263
Closed 15 Dec–15 Jan

A charming period house, comfortably furnished, with a warm welcome.

7hc (1⇨) (1fb) ℜ ✱B&b£11.50–£12.50 W£80.50–£87.50 🅜

📺 CTV 8P nc5yrs

Ⓥ

See advertisement on page 340

DROXFORD
Hampshire
Map **4** SU61

GH Little Uplands Country Motel
Garrison Hill ☎(0489) 878507 Telex no 477046
Closed Xmas & New Year
Annexe: 16hc (14🛁) (1fb) CTV in all bedrooms ✗ [R] ✱B&b£17.25 LDO9pm
Lic 🛋 CTV 25P 🏊(heated) 🎾(hard) 🎣 snooker sauna bath solarium gymnasium
Credit cards [1] [2] [3] [5] [V]

DRUMNADROCHIT
Highland *Inverness-shire*
Map **14** NH53

INN *Lewiston Arms* Lewiston ☎(04562) 225
A comfortable and cosy old inn with a friendly relaxed atmosphere.
4rm (3hc) Annexe: 4hc LDO8.30pm
🛋 CTV 30P 🚌
Credit card [3]

DRYSLWYN
Dyfed
Map **2** SN52

FH Mrs M Wilson ***Pant-y-Fen*** *(SR548226)*
☎(05584) 481
Apr–Oct
Cosy, small farmhouse with views over the Towy Valley. Bright modern bedrooms.
2rm (1fb)
🛋 CTV 4P 66acres dairy

DULVERTON
Somerset
See **Oakford**

DUMFRIES
Dumfries & Galloway *Dumfriesshire*
Map **11** NX97

GH Fulwood Private Hotel 30 Lovers Walk ☎(0387) 52262
Compact neat homely villa lying opposite railway station.
6hc (2fb) ✗ ✱B&b£9–£10 W£50–£70 M̸
CTV 1🚗
[V]

GH Newall House 22 Newall Ter
☎(0387) 52676
Neatly appointed house with spacious airy bedrooms in residential area between station and town centre.
7rm (6hc) (3fb) TV in 3 bedrooms [R]
B&b£9 Bdi£13.50 LDO5pm
Lic 🛋 CTV 7P
[V]

DUNBAR
Lothian *East Lothian*
Map **12** NT67

GH Courtyard Woodbush Brae ☎(0368) 64169
Closed 2wks Jan
Delightful modernised guesthouse in cobbled courtyard on sea-front. It offers excellent home-cooking and has well-equipped bedrooms.
6hc CTV in all bedrooms [R] ✱B&b£11–£17 Bdi£20.95–£26.95 W£66–£102 M̸
LDO9pm
Lic 🛋 6P
Credit cards [1] [3]

GH Marine 7 Marine Rd ☎(0368) 63315
Seaside guesthouse, in terraced row in quiet residential area on west side of town.
10hc (3🛁) (3fb) ✱B&b£9–£10 Bdi£13–£14 W£85–£90 L̸ LDO5pm
🛋 CTV 6P
[V]

GH Springfield House Edinburgh Rd
☎(0368) 62502
Apr–Oct
Attractive, family-run detached house set in own grounds a short walk from the town centre.
6hc (2fb) CTV in all bedrooms [R]
✱B&b£11–£11.50 Bdi£18–£18.50 W£108 L̸
LDO5pm

Lic ⅡⅡ 7P ⌂

Credit cards [1] [3]

Recommended

GH *St Beys* 2 Bayswell Rd ☎(0368) 63571

This attractive, well-appointed guesthouse though close to the centre of town, still enjoys spectacular sea views. Public areas are homely and comfortable, the lounge has a log-burning stove and the dining room has matching soft furnishings. The bedrooms are fresh, smartly decorated and well-equipped with extras.

6hc (4fb) CTV in all bedrooms ⊠ Ⓡ LDO6pm

ⅡⅡ CTV

Credit card [3]

DUNDEE
Tayside *Angus*
Map **11** NO43

GH Beach 22 Esplanade, Broughty Ferry ☎(0382) 76614

Compact, friendly tourist/commercial guesthouse with well-equipped, modern bedrooms.

4hc (1fb) CTV in all bedrooms Ⓡ B&b£10 Bdi£14 LDO4.30pm

ⅡⅡ P̸

Dunbar — Dunure

DUNLOP
Strathclyde *Ayrshire*
Map **10** NS44

FH Mr & Mrs R B Wilson **Struther** *(NS412496)* ☎Stewarton (0560) 84946

Large farmhouse in its own gardens. On edge of Dunlop village.

6hc (2fb) ✱B&b£9.50 Bdi£19.50 W£100 Ⱡ LDO8.30pm

CTV 16P 35acres non-working

Ⓥ

DUNOON
Strathclyde *Argyllshire*
Map **10** NS17

GH Cedars Hotel 51 Alexandra Pde, East Bay ☎(0369) 2425

Small family hotel on seafront. Home-cooking and warm welcome.

13hc (4⇌ 5fl) (2fb) ⊠ Ⓡ ✱B&b£11–£18 Bdi£17–£24 W£99–£155 Ⱡ LDO6.30pm

Lic ⅡⅡ CTV P̸

Credit cards [1] [3] Ⓥ

DUNS
Borders *Berwickshire*
Map **12** NT75

INN *Black Bull Hotel* Black Bull St ☎(0361) 83379

Informally run hotel in side street in town centre.

4hc Ⓡ LDO9.30pm

ⅡⅡ CTV 10p

Credit cards [1] [2] [3]

DUNSYRE
Strathclyde *Lanarkshire*
Map **11** NT04

FH Mrs L Armstrong **Dunsyre Mains** *(NT074482)* ☎(089981) 251
Mar–Oct

Two-storey stone farmhouse dating from 1800 in courtyard-style with splendid views and small garden.

3hc (1fb) ⊠ Ⓡ ✱B&b£8.50–£9 Bdi£13–£14 Wfr£91 Ⱡ LDO6pm

ⅡⅡ CTV P ⌂ 400acres beef sheep

DUNURE
Strathclyde *Ayrshire*
Map **10** NS21

FH Mrs R J Reid **Lagg** *(NS281166)* ☎(029250) 647
Apr–Oct rs Nov & Mar

Extensively renovated and modernised farmhouse overlooking the coast.

3hc ⊠ ✱B&b£8.50–£10 Bdifr£13 Wfr£56 M LDOnoon

ⅡⅡ CTV 6P 480acres dairy sheep

Ⓥ

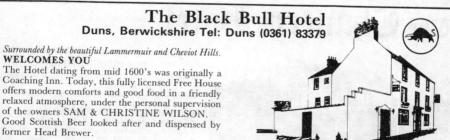

DUNVEGAN
Isle of Skye, Highland *Inverness-shire*
See **Skye, Isle of**

DURHAM
Co Durham
Map **12** NZ24

INN Croxdale Croxdale (3m S A167)
☎Spennymoor (0388) 815727

Comfortable inn offering spacious and attractive bedrooms and friendly service.

6hc (1fb) CTV in all bedrooms
✱B&b£12.50–£15 W£80–£95 Ⓜ

6P ⇔ ✔
Ⓥ

DURSLEY
Gloucestershire
Map **3** ST79

FH Mrs C M St John-Mildmay
Drakestone House *(ST734977)*
Stinchcombe (2½m W off B4060) ☎(0453) 2140
Apr–Oct

Charming country house on the edge of beechwoods with superb views, gardens, and a warm welcome.

3rm (2hc 1🛏) ✘ ✱B&b£12 Bdi£20.50
W£140 ⅃

🍴 5P 10acres sheep & rare breed cows
Ⓥ

Dunvegan
—
Eardisland

FH Mrs E Pain **Park** *(ST745970)*
Stancombe Park ☎(0453) 45345
Apr–Oct

Comfortable farmhouse surrounded by beech woods. Off B4060 Wotton-under-Edge to Cam road. Turn at sign marked Millend/Waterly Bottom.

2hc (1fb) ✱B&b£10 W£70 Ⓜ

CTV 4P 140acres sheep
Ⓥ

DYFFRYN-ARDUDWY
Gwynedd
Map **6** SH52

FH Mrs J Bailey **Cors-y-Gedol Hall**
(SH601230) ☎(03417) 231
RS Dec

Carefully modernised 18th-century farmhouse.

3hc (2🛏) (1fb) TV in 2 bedrooms ✘
✱B&b£7.50–£9.50 Bdi£12.50–£14.50
W£78–£95 ⅃ (W only Jul–Aug)

CTV 10P nc6yrs ✔ 4,000acres mixed
Ⓥ

DYLIFE
Powys
Map **6** SN89

INN Star ☎Llanbrynmair (06503) 345

This inn is well-situated for activity holidays. Own pony-trekking centre.

7hc (2🛏) (1fb) ✱B&b£9.50–£10.50
Bdi£11.50–£15.50 W£72.45–£97.65 ⅃
Lunch £2–£6 Dinner 10.30pm £6

🍴 CTV 30P ⏾
Ⓥ

DYMCHURCH
Kent
Map **5** TR12

GH Chantry Hotel Sycamore Gdns
(Guestaccom) ☎(0303) 873137

8hc (2🛏 1🛏) (4fb) ✘ B&b£12–£13
Bdi£18–£19 W£95–£106 ⅃ (W only end Jul–Aug) LDO6pm

Lic 🍴 CTV 8P nc 3yrs
Ⓥ

GH Waterside 15 Hythe Rd ☎(0303) 872253

7hc (3fb) ✘ ✱B&b£9–£9.50 Bdi£15–£15.50 W£97.50–£101 ⅃ LDO3pm

Lic 🍴 CTV 9P ⚬
Ⓥ

EARDISLAND
Hereford & Worcester
Map **3** SO45

FH Mrs F M Johnson **The Elms**
(SO418584) (Guestaccom) ☎Pembridge (05447) 405
Closed Jan–Feb

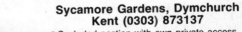
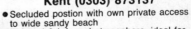

4hc ✖ ✱B&b£10–£11 W£66.50–£70 M
6P nc10yrs 33acres mixed

EARLSWOOD
Gwent
Map **3** ST49

FH Mrs G Powell **Parsons Grove** *(ST 452943)* ☎ Shirenewton (02917) 382
A modern farmhouse, complete with swimming pool, situated in quiet countryside. Newly planted vineyard.

3hc (2⇌ 1⚭) (2fb) CTV in all bedrooms ®
✱B&b£10–£12 W£60–£75 M
🍴 CTV 10P ⌣(heated) 17 acres beef vineyards

Eardisland
—
Eastbourne

EASTBOURNE
East Sussex
Map **5** TV69
See plan on pages 148–149

GH Avalon Private Hotel 64–66
Pevensey Rd ☎(0323) 22695
Plan **1A** *D2*

Meals prepared by the chef-patron himself ensure a pleasant stay in this extended terraced house away from the sea front.

14hc (2fb) CTV in all bedrooms ®
✱B&b£9.77–£12.07 Bdi£12.65–£14.37
W£67.85–£80.50 ◄ (W only Jun–Sep)
LDO6pm
Lic 🍴
Ⓥ

GH Beachy Rise 20 Beachy Head Rd,
☎(0323) 639171 Plan **2** *C1*
Closed Xmas

Small but homely and friendly establishment.

6hc (2fb) ✱B&b£8.50–£10.50 Bdi£11.25–
£13.25 W£69–£77 ◄ LDO7pm
🍴 CTV ⚐

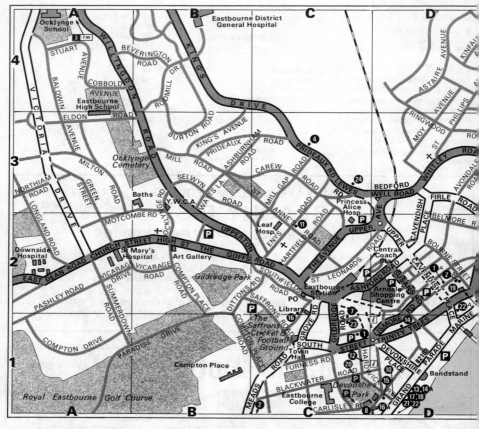

GH Bourne House Private Hotel 16
Bourne St ☎(0323) 21981

Charming guesthouse just off the front.

9hc ✖ ® ✱Bdi£12 W£80.50 ⅃ (W only
winter) LDO6pm

Lic ▥ CTV ⌿ nc2yrs ✦

┌─── **Recommended** ───┐

GH Chalk Farm Hotel & Restaurant
Coopers Hill, Willingdon (2m NNE)
☎(0323) 503800 Plan **3** A4

9hc (2⇆) (1fb) ✖ LDO8.30pm

Lic ▥ CTV 30P nc2yrs

Credit card ①

See advertisement on page 147

GH Delladale Lodge 35 Lewes Rd
☎(0323) 25207 Plan **4** C3
Apr–Oct

*Tastefully appointed guesthouse with the
accent on comfort and informal
atmosphere.*

10hc (6㎙) (1fb) ✖ ® ✱B&b£11–£14
Bdi£15–£18.50 W£85–£110

Lic ▥ CTV 10P nc5yrs ⌓(heated)

GH Edmar 30 Hyde Gdns ☎(0323) 33024
Plan **7** C1
Apr–Oct

*A homely, family-run guesthouse with a
bright dining room.*

9hc (2⇆ 1㎙) (1fb) ✖ ® ✱B&b£10.50–
£11.50 Bdi£12.85–£16 W£75.95–£105.95 ⅃
LDO6pm

CTV ⌿

GH Ellesmere Hotel 11 Wilmington Sq
☎(0323) 31463 Plan **8** D1

13hc (2⇆ 7㎙) (2fb) CTV in all bedrooms
® ✱B&b£15–£16.50 Bdi£21–£22.50
W£110–£136

Lic lift ▥ ⌿ nc5yrs

GH Fairlands Hotel 15–17 Lascelles Ter
☎(0323) 33287 Plan **10** D1
late Mar–mid Oct

*Warm, friendly, delightfully modernised
guesthouse*

25hc (16⇆) (2fb) ® LDO6.15pm

Lic CTV ⌿

GH Far End Hotel 139 Royal Pde
☎(0323) 25666 Plan **9** E3

*Large house with bright and comfortable
accommodation, on sea front on eastern
outskirts of town.*

10hc (2㎙) (1fb) ✖ ® ✱B&b£10–£12
Bdi£12–£15 W£80–£89 ⅃ LDO4pm

Lic ▥ CTV 6P 2☎ nc5yrs

GH Flamingo Private Hotel 20 Enys Rd
(Guestaccom) ☎(0323) 21654 Plan **11** C2

Closed Jan & Nov

*Large Victorian house in residential area
with comfortable rooms and friendly
atmosphere.*

12hc (5⇆ 7㎙) CTV in all bedrooms ✖ ®
B&b£13–£15 Bdi£18–£20.50 W£108–£123
⅃ LDO4.30pm

Lic ▥ CTV ⌿ nc8yrs

Credit cards ① ③ Ⓥ

See advertisement on page 147

GH Hanburies Hotel 4 Hardwick Rd
☎(0323) 30698 Plan **12** C1

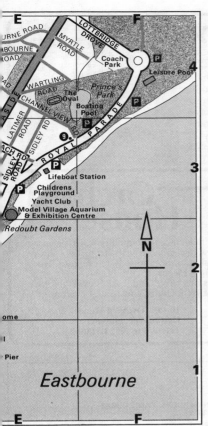

Eastbourne

Eastbourne

- **1A** Avalon Private Hotel
- **2** Beachy Rise
- **2A** Bourne House Private Hotel
- **3** Chalk Farm Hotel & Restaurant
- **4** Delladale Lodge
- **7** Edmar
- **8** Ellesmere Hotel
- **9** Far End Hotel
- **10** Fairlands Hotel
- **11** Flamingo Private Hotel
- **12** Hanburies Hotel
- **13** Little Crookham Private Hotel
- **14** Hotel Mandalay
- **14A** Merton Private Hotel
- **15** Mowbray Hotel
- **16** Orchard House
- **16A** Park View Hotel
- **17** Rosforde Private Hotel
- **18** Saffrons Hotel
- **19** St Clare
- **20** Somerville Private Hotel
- **21** South Cliff House
- **22** Southcroft
- **22A** Stirling House Hotel
- **23** Traquair Private Hotel
- **24** Wynstay Private Hotel

Small family-run guesthouse nicely situated, near Devonshire Park, theatres and sea front.

14hc (10⇆) CTV in 11 bedrooms ✘ ®
✳B&b£13.50–£16.50 Bdi£15.50–£18.50 W£98–£125 ⅃ LDO6pm

Lic ㎒ CTV 4P nc12yrs

Ⓥ

─ Recommended ─

GH Little Crookham Private Hotel 16 Southcliffe Av ☎(0323) 34160 Plan **13** *D1*
Apr–Oct

Homely and welcoming guesthouse, five minutes walk from the sea.

8hc (1fb) ® ✳B&b£11 Bdi£15 W£96 ⅃ (W only Jun–Sep)

㎒ CTV ✗ nc4yrs

GH Hotel Mandalay 16 Trinity Trees ☎(0323) 29222 Plan **14** *D1*

A comfortable house with a warm and friendly atmosphere.

12hc (8㎡) (1fb) CTV in all bedrooms ✘ ®
✳B&b£13.50–£19.50 Bdi£16–£23 W£105–£145 ⅃ LDO10.30pm

Lic ㎒ 20P nc5yrs

Credit cards ① ③

See advertisement on page 150

GH Merton Private Hotel 49 Jevington Gdns ☎(0323) 21943 Plan **14A** *D1*

7hc (2fb) ✘ ®

Lic CTV ✗

GH Mowbray Hotel 2 Lascelles Ter ☎(0323) 20012 Plan **15** *D1*
Apr–Dec

Large four-storey Victorian house, adjacent to Devonshire Park and theatres.

16hc (4㎡) (1fb) CTV in all bedrooms ®
✳B&b£11.75–£12.75 Bdi£17.50–£18.50 W£115–£122 ⅃ LDO5.30pm

lift CTV ✗ nc6yrs

Credit cards ① ③

GH Orchard House 10 Old Orchard Rd ☎(0323) 23682 Plan **16** *C2*

Well-appointed semi-detached Victorian house near town centre and railway station. Run by charming young couple.

8rm (5⇆ 3㎡) (2fb) CTV in all bedrooms ✘ ® ✳B&b£13–£15 Bdi£15–£19 W£93–£107 ⅃ LDO6pm

Lic ㎒ 3P nc5yrs

Ⓥ

See advertisement on page 150

─ Recommended ─

GH *Park View Hotel* Wilmington Gdns ☎(0323) 21242 Plan **16A** *D1*

Well-appointed family-run hotel with good home-cooking.

13hc (3⇆ 9㎡) CTV in all bedrooms ✘ ® LDO8pm

Lic lift 10P nc2yrs

Credit cards ① ② ③

GH *Rosforde Private Hotel* 51 Jevington Gdns ☎(0323) 32503 Plan **17** *D1*

Well-run, clean and comfortable accommodation.

13hc (4㎡) (4fb) ✘ ® LDO4pm

Lic CTV ✗

GH Saffrons Hotel 30–32 Jevington Gdns ☎(0323) 25539 Plan **18** *D1*
Apr–Oct rs Mar

Comfortable, large accommodation within this Victorian building, situated in gardens close to town centre.

25hc (7⇆ 6㎡) CTV in all bedrooms ®
✳B&b£15–£19.50 Bdi£20.50–£25 W£131.50–£160 ⅃ LDO6pm

Lic CTV ✗

See advertisement on page 150

GH St Clare 70 Pevensey Rd ☎(0323) 29483 Plan **19** *D2*

Family house with friendly atmosphere, five minutes from the sea.

8hc (1fb) ✘ ® ✳B&b£9–£10 Bdi£12–£14 W£65–£80 ⅃ LDO4pm

Lic ㎒ CTV ✗

Ⓥ

See advertisement on page 150

GH Somerville Private Hotel 6 Blackwater Rd ☎(0323) 29342 Plan **20** *C1*
Mar–Dec

Small private hotel convenient for Devonshire Park and the Winter Gardens.

12hc (3㎡) (2fb) ✘ ® ✳B&b£11.50–£14.50 Bdi£16.50–£19.50 W£99–117 ⅃

Lic CTV ✗

GH South Cliff House 19 South Cliff Av ☎(0323) 21019 Plan **21** *D1*

Small and cheerful guesthouse in quiet situation some distance from the sea.

7hc (1fb) ® ✳B&bfr£11 Bdifr£14 W£85 ⅃

Lic ㎒ CTV ✗ nc5yrs

See advertisement on page 151

GH Southcroft 15 South Cliff Av ☎(0323) 29071 Plan **22** D1

Attractively appointed and well-maintained guesthouse.

6hc (4⇶2🛏) ✹ ® ✱B&bfr£12–£14 Bdifr£16–£18 W£99–£110 ⚹ LDOnoon 🕮 CTV ✗ nc12yrs

GH Stirling House Hotel 5–7 Cavendish Pl ☎(0323) 32263 Plan **22A** D2

A cosy, personally-run house not far from sea or shops.

21hc (7🛏) (3fb) CTV in 7 bedrooms ✹ ® ✱B&b£11–£13.50 Bdi£16–£18.50 W£80–£100 ⚹ LDO9am

Lic CTV ✗
Ⓥ

GH Traquair Private Hotel 25 Hyde Gdns ☎(0323) 25198 Plan **23** C1

Clean, colourful and comfortable accommodation where cooking is taken seriously.

11hc (6🛏) (3fb) CTV in all bedrooms ® ✱B&b£10–£13 Bdi£17–£20 W£90–£115 ⚹ LDO6.30pm

Lic 🕮 CTV ✗
Credit cards 1 2 3 5

GH Wynstay Private Hotel 13 Lewes Rd ☎(0323) 21550 Plan **24** C3

Closed Xmas & New Year

Simple homely hotel about ½ mile from town centre.

7hc (6🛏) (1fb) CTV in all bedrooms ✹ ® B&b£12.50–£16.50 Bdi£16.50–£20.50 W£96–£118 ⚹ LDO2pm

🕮 7P nc4yrs
Ⓥ

South Cliff House

19 South Cliff Avenue, Eastbourne, East Sussex BN20 7AH
Telephone: Eastbourne (0323) 21019

Quiet road, close to the sea, theatres, and a short walk along the seafront to the Bandstand and Pier (East). Beachy Head to the West. Noted for good home-cooked food and a friendly atmosphere. Tea and coffee-making facilities, comfortable lounge with colour TV. Own keys and access to rooms at all times. Four-course evening dinner. Separate tables in dining-room. Payphone for guests. Unrestricted parking. Bed & Breakfast from £11 per day. From £68 per week. Bed, Breakfast and Evening Dinner from £14 per day. From £85 per week. Open Christmas & Easter. Conference delegates welcome.

'Southcroft' Private Hotel

15, South Cliff Avenue, Meads, Eastbourne, East Sussex.
Telephone: (0323) 29071

A small select private hotel situated in a quiet residential area within easy reach of the beach, shopping centre and theatres. The well furnished bedrooms are equipped with en suite facilities and full central heating, plus tea/coffee making facilities. Known for good food and comfort there is a television lounge and residential licence. Street parking. Conference delegates catered for.
Proprietors: Mr and Mrs K Hambleton.

TRAQUAIR PRIVATE HOTEL

25 Hyde Gardens Eastbourne

East Sussex BN21 4PX Telephone (0323) 25198

A first class small privately owned hotel. Town Centre. Minutes from the theatres parks sea & new shopping centre. Renowned for its warm and friendly atmosphere, good traditional English cooking, vegetarian & special diets catered for. Luxurious ground floor suite. All rooms have colour TV, radio alarm clocks and tea-making facilities. Most rooms are en suite. Full central heating. Adequate parking. Fire certificate. American Express, Barclay cards, Access & Diners Club accepted.

EAST CALDER
Lothian *Midlothian*
Map **11**   NT06

FH Mr & Mrs D R Scott **Whitecroft**
(NT095682) 7 Raw Holdings ☎Mid Calder
(0506) 881810

*Compact roadside bungalow attached to
smallholding ½m E on B7015.*

3hc (1fb) ✻ ✱B&b£9–£10 W£63 ⋈

📺 CTV 6P ⚲ 5acres arable

___

EAST CHINNOCK
Somerset
Map **3**   ST41

GH Barrows Country House Weston St
☎ West Coker (093586) 2390
Closed 24 Dec–1 Jan

*Small, quiet, personally-run house on the
edge of this pleasant village.*

6hc ✻ B&b£10–£12 Bdi£16–£18 W£100–
£110 ⵏ LDOnoon

Lic 📺 CTV 6P nc5yrs croquet
Ⓥ

___

EAST COWTON
North Yorkshire
Map **8**   NZ30

INN Beeswing ☎North Cowton (032578)
349

*A friendly village inn offering comfortable
accommodation. Wholesome, home-
cooking available in the dining room and
bars.*

4⇆ CTV in all bedrooms ✻ Ⓡ LDO10pm
📺 17P

___

EAST GRINSTEAD
West Sussex
Map **5**   TQ33

GH Cranfield Hotel Maypole Rd ☎(0342)
21251

*Homely, comfortable private hotel in quiet
residential area.*

11hc (2📺) Annexe 9hc (1⇆ 6📺) (3fb) CTV
in all bedrooms Ⓡ ✱B&b£13.80–£23
Bdi£21.30–£30.50 LDO8pm

Lic 📺 CTV 11P
Ⓥ

___

EAST MEON
Hampshire
Map **4**   SU62

FH Mrs P M Berry **Giants** *(SU696207)*
Harvesting Ln ☎(073087) 205
Mar–Oct

*Modern farmhouse, set in ½acre with
views from all rooms of the surrounding
countryside. Queen Elizabeth Country
Park of 1,400 acres, with facilities for
pony-trekking and grass skiing is nearby.*

3hc (2⇆) TV in all bedrooms ✻ Ⓡ
B&b£9–£12 W£60–£80 ⋈

📺 CTV 4P 30acres sheep poultry

___

EAST MEY
Highland *Caithness*
Map **15**   ND37

FH Mrs M Morrison **Glenearn** *(ND307739)*
☎Barrock (084785) 608
Etr–Oct

*Small croft situated on the main coast
road; Thurso 15 miles.*

3hc (1fb) ✻ ✱B&b£7–£9 Bdi£11–£13
Wfr£74 ⵏ LDOnoon

📺 CTV 3P 7½acre sheep
Ⓥ

FH Mr & Mrs N Geddes **Island View**
☎Barrock (084785) 254
Apr–Oct

*Snug modernised croft house about five
miles from John O'Groats.*

2hc (1fb) ✱B&b£7–£7.50 Bdi£11.50–£12
Wfr£80 ⵏ

9acres non-working
Ⓥ

___

EAST PRESTON
West Sussex
Map **5**   TQ00

___

INN South Strand ☎ Rustington (0903)
785086

14hc (3⇆) (1fb) ✱B&bfr£16 Bdifr£24
Wfr£168 ⵏ Lunch£8&alc
Dinner7.45pm£8&alc

📺 CTV 25P ⇱

___

EAST WITTERING
West Sussex
Map **4**   SZ79

GH Wittering Lodge Hotel Shore Rd
☎Bracklesham Bay (0243) 673207
Etr–Oct

*Small well-appointed and comfortable
hotel offering good food.*

9hc (1⇆) (3fb) LDO7.30pm

Lic 📺 CTV 12P 2🛏

Credit card ③

___

EBBERSTON
North Yorkshire
Map **8**   SE88

GH Foxholm Hotel (on B1258)
☎Scarborough (0723) 85550
Mar–Nov & Xmas

*Small, family-run country hotel in a
peaceful setting. York, the moors, dales
and sea all within easy reach.*

10hc (1⇆ 3📺) (1fb) B&b£13–£15
Bdi£19.50–£21.50 W£130–£144 ⵏ
LDO7pm

Lic 📺 CTV 12P 2🛏
Ⓥ

___

EDINBURGH
Lothian *Midlothian*
Map **11**   NT27
See **Central Plan** (pages 154–155) and
District Plan (pages 156–157)

GH Adam Hotel 19 Landsdowne Cres
☎031-337 1148 District Plan **6**
Closed Xmas & New Year

*Comfortable accommodation in quiet,
residential area.*

9hc (2fb) CTV in all bedrooms ✻
✱B&b£13.50–£14

Lic 📺 CTV ⫽
Ⓥ

___

Whitecroft
East Calder

½ mile from East Calder on B7015

A modern bungalow, centrally heated
throughout, and all bedrooms with hot & cold
water. Surrounded by farmland, yet only 10
miles from Edinburgh City centre.
5 miles Ingliston, Edinburgh Airport. Ideally
situated for the M9 and M8 motorways (only
3 miles away) and Livingston New Town (5
miles). Fire Certificate. Whitecroft is a 5 acre
farm and Mrs Scott runs a Farm shop on the
farm. Sorry no pets.
Telephone: Midcalder (STD 0506) 881810

GH *Adria Hotel* 11–12 Royal Ter ☎031-556 7875 Central plan **1** *F6*
Closed Dec
Part of a Georgian terrace close to Princes Street. Spacious, well-decorated accommodation.

20hc (2⇄4🛁) (6fb) ✱B&b£27.60–£36.80
🎬CTV
Ⓥ

GH Allison House 15/17 Mayfield Gdns
☎031-667 8049 District plan **6A**
Closed Xmas & New Year
A conversion of two terraced houses.

Edinburgh

24hc (18🛁) (8fb) CTV in all bedrooms ®
B&b£11.50–£21 W£72–£130 Ⓜ
Lic 🎬 12P
Ⓥ

GH Ben Doran Hotel 11 Mayfield Gdns
☎031-445 1994 District plan **7**
Closed 20–27 Dec
Situated in a terraced row, with modest bedrooms.

9hc (5fb) CTV in all bedrooms ®
✱B&b£10–£14
🎬 8P

GH Boisdale Hotel 9 Coates Gdns
☎031-337 1134 District plan **8**
10hc (4⇄2🛁) (4fb) TV in 2 bedrooms ®
✱B&b£16.10–£18.20 Bdi£22–£24
LDO10am
Lic 🎬 CTV ⚟

GH *Bonnington* 202 Ferry Rd ☎031-554 7610 District plan **8A**
6hc (3fb) ✈ LDO1pm
🎬 CTV 12P

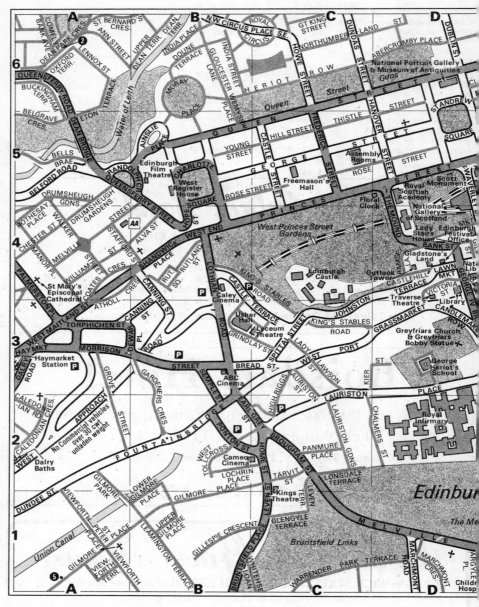

GH Brunswick 7 Brunswick St ☎031-556 1238 District plan **8B**

A newly converted property with spacious bedrooms, convenient for Princes St and city centre.

7hc (4⚑) (2fb) CTV in all bedrooms ✖ ✱B&b£9–£16 W£56–£105 ₥

🍴 🅿 nc2yrs

ⓥ

See advertisement on page 153

GH Buchan Hotel 3 Coates Gdns ☎031-337 1045 District plan **9**

Carefully decorated and furnished Victorian guesthouse in terraced row.

10hc (1⚑) (6fb) CTV in 7 bedrooms ✱B&b£11.50–£14 Bdi£17–£20 W£119–£140 ⧸ LDO10am

🍴 CTV 🅿

ⓥ

Edinburgh Central
1 Adria
2 Galloway
3 Greenside Hotel
4 Halcyon Hotel
5 Kariba

GH Clans Hotel 4 Magdala Cres ☎031-337 6301 District plan **10**

The hotel occupies three storeys of a residential block.

7hc (1🚿) (2fb) ✖ ✱B&b£12–£16
Lic 🍴 CTV ₽
See advertisement on page 158

GH Dorstan Private Hotel 7 Priestfield Rd ☎031-667 6721 District plan **11**
Closed 2 wks Xmas

A well-appointed and comfortable house in a residential area.

14hc (5🛏 4🚿) (1fb) CTV in all bedrooms Ⓡ ✱B&b£13–£17 Bdi£18.50–£22.50 LDO6pm
🍴 CTV 8P
Ⓥ

See advertisement on page 158

GH Dunstane House 4 West Coates ☎031-337 6169 District plan **11A**
Closed Xmas–4 Jan

Comfortable and spacious accommodation. All rooms with private shower.

15hc (5fb) CTV in all bedrooms Ⓡ ✱B&b£18–£23.50 W£113–£148 M
Lic 🍴 CTV 10P
Credit card ③

GH Galloway 22 Dean Park Cres ☎031-332 3672 Telex no 72165 Central plan **2** *A6*

Handsome Victorian town house close to city centre.

10hc (3🛏 1🚿) (6fb) Ⓡ ✱B&b£12–£30 Bdi£16–£34 W£72–£180 M LDO5pm
🍴 CTV
Ⓥ

GH Glenisla Hotel 12 Lygon Rd ☎031-667 4098 District plan **13**

A very attractively appointed and well-maintained house in a residential area.

8hc (2fb) ✱B&b£13–£15 Bdi£18.50–£19.50 W£122.50 ⫽LDO3pm
🍴 CTV P

GH Greenside Hotel 9 Royal Ter ☎031-557 0022 Central plan **3** *F6*
Jan–Oct

Neat and well-maintained with nice spacious bedrooms.

12hc (4🛏 4🚿) (3fb) ✖ B&b£18.40–£24 W£128–£168 M
🍴 CTV ₽ nc5yrs

GH Grosvenor 1 Grosvenor Gdns, Haymarket ☎031-337 4143 District plan **14**

A Victorian town house with a peaceful atmosphere.

7hc (1🛏 1🚿) (3fb) CTV in all bedrooms ✖ Ⓡ
🍴 ₽

See advertisement on page 158

GH Halcyon Hotel 8 Royal Ter ☎031-556 1033 Central plan **4** *F6*
Closed Feb & New Year

Forms part of a large Regency terraced row.

16hc (4fb)
🍴 CTV ₽ ♪(hard)

GH Heriott Park 256 Ferry Rd ☎031-552 6628 District plan **15**

Smart, recently converted house on main road in north part of the city.

7hc (3fb) TV in all bedrooms ✱B&b9–£12
🍴 CTV 7P snooker

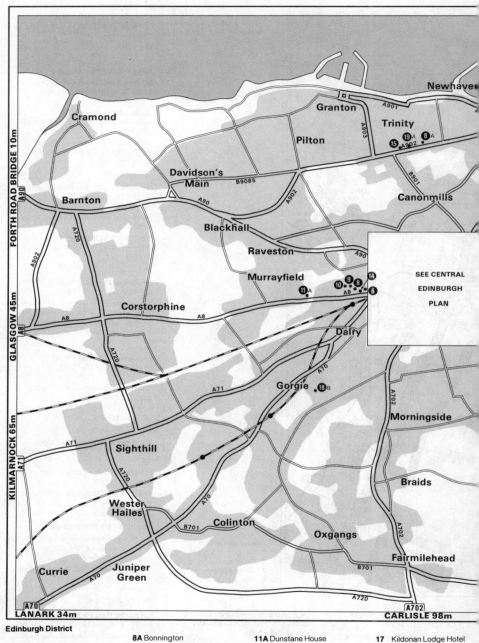

SEE CENTRAL
EDINBURGH
PLAN

Edinburgh District

6	Adam Hotel	**8A**	Bonnington	**11A**	Dunstane House	**17**
6A	Allison House	**8B**	Brunswick	**13**	Glenisla Hotel	**18**
7	Ben Doran Hotel	**9**	Buchan Hotel	**14**	Grosvenor	**18A**
8	Boisdale Hotel	**10**	Clans Hotel	**15**	Heriott Park	**18B**
		11	Dorstan Private Hotel	**16**	Hillview	**18C**

17 Kildonan Lodge Hotel
18 Kingsley
18A Kirtle House
18B Lindsay
18C Marchhall Hotel

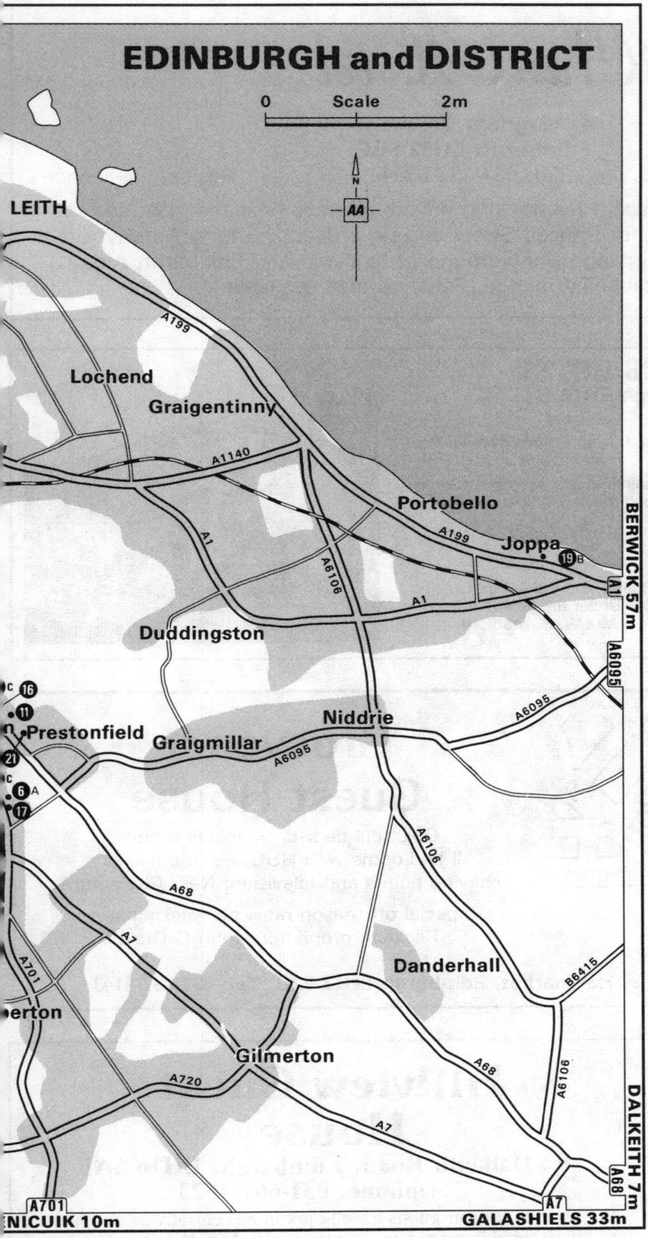
EDINBURGH and DISTRICT
0 Scale 2m
N
AA
LEITH
Lochend
Graigentinny
Portobello
Joppa
Duddingston
Niddrie
Prestonfield
Graigmillar
Danderhall
Gilmerton
A199
A1140
A1
A6106
A6095
A68
A7
A701
A720
B6415
BERWICK 57m
DALKEITH 7m
GALASHIELS 33m
NICUIK 10m
erton

18D Marvin
19 Newington
19A Ravensdown
19B Rockville Hotel
19C St Margaret's Hotel
20 Salisbury Hotel
22 Sherwood
23 Southdown
24 Thrums Private Hotel
25 Tiree

GH Hillview 92 Dalkeith Rd ☎031-667 1523 District plan **16**

Situated close to the Commonwealth swimming pool.

9hc (1🛁 1🚿) (4fb) CTV in all bedrooms 🐕 Ⓡ ✱B&b£9.50–£15 Bdi£15.50–£22 Wfr£65 M̸ LDO9am

♨ 3P nc5yrs

See advertisement on page 158

GH Kariba 10 Granville Ter ☎031-229 3773 Central plan **5** *A1*

8hc (2fb) CTV in all bedrooms 🐕 Ⓡ ✱B&b£12–£55 W£75.60–£94.50 M̸

♨ CTV 3P

Credit card [2] Ⓥ

GH Kildonan Lodge Hotel 27 Craigmillar Pk ☎031-667 2793 District plan **17**

The hotel incorporates a most attractive restaurant and cocktail lounge. (Residents and diners only).

9hc (5fb) CTV in all bedrooms ✱B&b£9.50–£12.50 Bdi£19–£21 LDO9.30pm

Lic ♨ 20P

Credit card [2]

See advertisement on page 159

GH Kingsley 30 Craigmillar Pk, Newington ☎031-667 8439 District plan **18**

A pleasant, homely house on main road to the S of the city.

7hc (4fb) Ⓡ ✱B&b£8.50–£10.50

♨ CTV 7P

See advertisement on page 159

GH Kirtle House 8 Minto St ☎031-667 2813 District plan **18A**

Neat terraced house to the south of the city centre.

7hc (4🚿) (2fb) CTV in all bedrooms Ⓡ ✱B&b£10–£14

♨ CTV 5P

Credit cards [1] [2] [3] [5]

GH Lindsay 108 Polwarth Ter ☎031-337 1580 District plan **18B**

6hc (2fb) CTV in all bedrooms Ⓡ ✱B&b£9–£12 W£63–£84 M̸

6P

Ⓥ

GH Marchhall Hotel 14–16 Marchhall Cres ☎031-667 2743 District plan **18A**

11hc (2🚿) (4fb) CTV in all bedrooms Ⓡ ✱B&b£12–£15 LDO6.30pm

Lic ♨ CTV P̸

GH Marvin 46 Pilrig St ☎031-554 6605 District plan **18B**

Neat family-run guesthouse in terraced row.

7hc (4🛁 4🚿) (2fb) CTV in 4 bedrooms TV in 3 bedrooms Ⓡ B&b£10–£17 W£65–£109 M̸

♨ CTV 6P

Ⓥ

Clans Hotel

4, Magdala Crescent
Edinburgh EH12 5BE

Bed & Breakfast   **Tel: 031-337 6301**   Residential licence

Situated in a quiet Crescent overlooking private gardens near the west end of Edinburgh. Convenient for Princes Street and on a direct route to Murrayfield Rugby Ground, Royal Highland Showground at Ingliston and Edinburgh Airport. Comfortable TV lounge. Family rooms available.

DORSTAN PRIVATE HOTEL

7 Prestfield Road, Edinburgh EH16 5HJ
Tel: 031-667 6721

Private car park. Off Dalkeith Road. Near Commonwealth Pool. Modernised to a high standard.

Fitted wardrobes, H & C, razor points in all bedrooms. (Some bedrooms with Private Bath). 2 bathrooms, TV lounge. Full central heating.

Reduced terms for children.

Fire precautions carried out.

Member of the Scottish Tourist Board, and Edinburgh Guest House & Private Hotel Association. Under the personal supervision of the Proprietors: Mr & Mrs W. S. Bradford. Send for SAE for brochure.

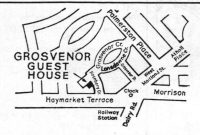

Grosvenor Guest House

Quiet cul-de-sac. Spacious rooms. All bedrooms with H&C, electric blankets, shaving points and television. Near City centre.

Special off-season rates on weekly basis. Resident proprietor: John G Gray.

1 Grosvenor Gardens, Haymarket, Edinburgh EH12 5JU. Tel: 031 337 4143

EDINBURGH

Hillview Guest House

92 Dalkeith Road, Edinburgh, EH16 5AF
Telephone: 031-667 1523

We provide for our guests a well-appointed centrally-heated house, nicely situated in a residential area, on the A68. We are a few yards from the Commonwealth Pool and Holyrood Park and under a mile from the Castle, Palace and City Centre shops. There is limited car parking space but ample off-street parking nearby. We are open all year. Dinners are by arrangement. SAE for terms and brochure.

GH *Newington* 18 Newington Rd ☎031-667 3356 District plan **19**

A house of character and appeal well-appointed and thoughtfully equipped

8hc (3🚿) (3fb) CTV in 1 bedroom TV in 7 bedrooms

♨ CTV 3P

GH Ravensdown 248 Ferry Rd ☎031-552 5438 District plan **19A**

Comfortable, well appointed house with views over the city and its imposing castle.

7hc (5fb) 🐕 ✱B&b£9–£11

Lic ♨ CTV 4🚗

Edinburgh

GH Rockville Hotel 2 Joppa Pans, Joppa (2m E off A1) ☎031-669 5418 District plan **19B**

5🛁 (2fb) CTV in all bedrooms 🐕 [R] ✱B&bfr£19 Bdifr£26 LDO10pm

Lic ♨ CTV 10P 2🚗 🏠

Credit cards [1] [2] [3] [5] [V]

GH St Bernards 22 St Bernards Cres ☎031-332 2339 Central plan **6** *A6*

10hc (3fb) 🚭 in 2 bedrooms CTV in 4 bedrooms 🐕 ✱B&b£11–£13 W£70–£83 M

♨ CTV 🅿 🏠

Credit cards [1] [3] [V]

GH *St Margaret's*

18 Craigmillar Pk ☎031-667 2202 District plan **19A**

A neatly maintained house in terraced row. Coach tours taken early in season.

8hc (3fb) CTV in all bedrooms [R]

♨ CTV 6P

GH Salisbury Hotel 45 Salisbury Rd
☎031-667 1264 District plan **20**

A neatly decorated combination of two
Georgian town houses close to a
shopping suburb.

12hc (1⇔3🛁) (4fb) CTV in 3 bedrooms Ⓡ
✱B&b£10–£15 W£50–£90 M
Lic �🍴 CTV 12P
Ⓥ

GH Sherwood 42 Minto St ☎031-667
1200 District plan **22**
Closed Xmas & New Year

A friendly, well-maintained terraced house
south of the city centre

6hc (3fb) Ⓡ B&b£9–£12.50
🍴 3P
Ⓥ

GH Southdown 20 Craigmillar Pk ☎031-
667 2410 District plan **23**

A neatly maintained house, part of a
terraced row, which especially caters for
groups in early season.

8hc (2fb) TV in all bedrooms ✖(except
guide dogs) Ⓡ B&b£10.50–£12.50 W£65–
£75 M
🍴 CTV 8P

GH Thrums Private Hotel 14 Minto St,
Newington ☎031-667 5545 District plan
24
Closed Xmas & New Year

A neat, compact house with gardens to
front and rear.

7hc (1🛁) (2fb) CTV in 2 bedrooms TV in 2
bedrooms Ⓡ LDO7pm
Lic CTV 6P

GH Tiree 26 Craigmillar Pk ☎031-667
7477 District plan **25**

Tidy, well-decorated house with good
bedroom facilities.

7hc (3🛁) (2fb) CTV in all bedrooms Ⓡ
✱B&b£8.50–£16
🍴 CTV 7P

EGERTON
Kent
Map **5**   TQ94

FH Mrs D Boardman **Link** (TQ898470)
☎(023376) 214
Apr–Oct

1m SW off unclass rd.

3rm (1⇔) ✖ ✱B&bfr£10 Bdifr£16 W£112
⅃ LDO7pm
🍴 CTV 2P 3🐎 nc9yrs 10acres arable

EGGLESTON
Co Durham
Map **12**   NY92

INN Moorcock Hill Top ☎Teesdale
(0833) 50395

A charming country inn with comfortable
accommodation. Good food served in bar
and restaurant.

6hc CTV available in bedrooms Ⓡ
LDO10pm
🍴 60P

EGLINGHAM
Northumberland
Map **12**   NU11

─── *Recommended* ───

FH Mrs A I Easton **West Ditchburn**
(NU131207) ☎Powburn (066578) 337
Mar–Oct

A handsome stone house standing in
its own walled garden in the heart of
the farm. The charming bedrooms
are all colour coordinated and
equipped with thoughtful extras.
Hearty English breakfasts and good
wholesome dinners, using local
produce, are served in the
impressive dining room.

4hc (2fb) CTV in all bedrooms Ⓡ
B&b£11.50–£12.50 Bdi£16.50–£17.50
W£112.50–£119.50 ⅃ LDO6pm
🍴 CTV 7P nc5yrs 1000acres beef
sheep

Credit cards ① ② ③ ⑤

Southdown Guest House

20 Criagmillar Park, Edinburgh, EH16 5PS
Tel: 031-667 2410   Proprietors: Anne and Allan Paterson

Situated in residential area only 10 minutes from Princes Street on
main bus route. Golf courses, the Commonwealth Pool, the Castle
and Holyrood Palace are within easy reach. All home comforts and
full Scottish breakfast with home produce our speciality. All rooms
with showers, TVs and tea/coffee-making facilities. Residents'
lounge with colour TV. Full central heating, Fire Certificate and
private car park. Own key access all day. Reduced rates for
groups and families. Weekly terms available.
Under the personal supervision of Anne and Allan Paterson.

EGREMONT
Cumbria
Map **11** NY01

INN Royal Oak Hotel Beckermet (2½m S off A595) ☎ Beckermet (094684) 551

Old inn with low ceilings and open-fires. Bedrooms are modern.

8⇌ CTV in all bedrooms Ⓡ ✱B&b£22 Bdi£30 W£190 Ⱡ Bar lunch £1–£3 Dinner 9.45pm £8

♨ 20P

ELIE
Fife
Map **12** NO40

GH Elms Park Pl ☎(0333) 330404
Feb–Nov

A neatly appointed house with garden to rear.

6hc (1⇌) (2fb) 🐕 Ⓡ ✱B&b£9.50–£10 Bdi£15–£15.50 W£95–£98 Ⱡ LDO6pm

Lic ♨ CTV P̸ ⌂

ELSDON
Northumberland
Map **12** NY99

FH Mrs T M Carruthers **Dunns** *(NY937969)* ☎Rothbury (0669) 40219

Old farmhouse in quiet position amongst the Cheviot Hills and Coquet Valley.

3rm (2hc) (2fb) 🐕 Ⓡ ✱B&b£8–£9

CTV 6P 1000acres mixed

Ⓥ

ELY
Cambridgeshire
Map **5** TL58

GH Castle Lodge Hotel 50 New Barns Rd ☎(0353) 2276

10hc (1⇌ 2🚿) (1fb) CTV in all bedrooms 🐕 ✱B&b£14–£15 Bdi£20.50–£21.40 W£123–£128.40 Ⱡ LDO7.30pm

Lic ♨ 8P

Credit cards [1] [3] Ⓥ

GH Nyton 7 Barton Rd ☎(0353) 2459

11hc (1⇌ 10🚿) (3fb) Ⓡ B&b£15.50–£20 W£98–£126 M

Lic ♨ CTV 12P

Ⓥ

See advertisement on page 162

EMPINGHAM
Leicestershire
Map **4** SK90

INN *White Horse* High St ☎(078086) 221

Warm and welcoming village inn whose food enjoys a good local reputation.

3hc (1fb) CTV in all bedrooms Ⓡ LDO9.45pm

♨ 30P 5🚗 ⛳

Credit cards [1] [2] [3] [5]

EMSWORTH
Hampshire
Map **4** SU70

GH Jingles Hotel 77 Horndean Rd ☎(0243) 373755

Large Victorian house with simple bedroom appointments, run by pleasant and friendly proprietors.

10hc (2🚿) (1fb) Ⓡ B&b£12–£14.95 Bdi£16–£18.95 W£108–£128 Ⱡ LDO6pm

Lic ♨ CTV 10P

Credit cards [1] [3] Ⓥ

GH *Merry Hall Hotel* 73 Horndean Rd ☎(02434) 2424
Closed Xmas–New Year

9hc (6⇌) (2fb) TV in all bedrooms 🐕 LDO8pm

Lic ♨ P

Credit cards [1] [3]

See advertisement on page 317

The Moorcock Inn

The Moorcock Inn is situated in the heart of Teesdale, one of the most picturesque valleys in Britain.

All bedrooms are fitted with vanity units, central heating, radios, Colour TV and tea & coffee facilities.

Bar snacks are available every lunchtime and evening. In addition, a new, intimate, dining room is now open, for residents and passing trade.

A la Carte and set menu available.

Eggleston, Near Barnard Castle, Teesdale.
Telephone: Teesdale 50395

Fully Licensed

Castle Lodge Hotel

New Barns Road, Ely, Cambridgeshire
Telephone: Ely (0353) 2276

The Castle Lodge Hotel is a small family run hotel nicely furnished and decorated with Full Central Heating, Full Dining Facilities and a Comprehensive Wine List. Bathrooms or Shower and Toilets and Colour Television are available in some bedrooms. Function room available with fitted bar. The Castle lodge is situated just off the City Centre in a quiet residential area. Three minutes walk to the Market Square and seven minutes walk to the Cathedral. Joyce & Drew McIntyre are residential proprietors, on hand at most times to ensure you have a comfortable stay.

ERLESTOKE
Wiltshire
Map **3** ST95

FH Mrs P Hampton **Longwater Park** *(ST966541)* ☎Bratton (0380) 830095
Closed Xmas

3🚿🛁(1fb) TV in 2 bedrooms [R]
B&b£9.50–£10 Bdi£14–£15 W£97–£105 Ⱡ
LDO5pm

♨ CTV 6P ⌂ 🎣 166 acres dairy

[V]

ERWOOD
Powys
Map **3** SO04

FH N M Jones **Ty-Isaf** *(SO101425)*
☎(09823) 607

3hc (2fb) ✱B&b£7.50–£8 Bdi£10.50–£11.50 W£73.50–£80 Ⱡ LDO7.30pm

♨ CTV P 340acres sheep mixed

[V]

ETON
Berkshire
Map **4** SU97

GH Christopher Hotel High St
☎Windsor (0753) 852359
rs Xmas

Well-furnished free-house, with modern, very well-equipped chalets, and complemented by the well-run Peacock Restaurant.

21🛁 (6fb) CTV in all bedrooms [R]
✱B&b£45–£47 Bdi£59–£69 LDO10pm

Lic ♨ 16P

Credit cards [1] [2] [3] [5]

ETTINGTON
Warwickshire
Map **4** SP24

FH Mrs B J Wakeham **Whitfield** *(SP265506)* Warwick Rd ☎Stratford-upon-Avon (0789) 740260
Closed Dec

Pleasant house set in active farm with a wide variety of animals for interest.

3hc (1fb) ⋈ ✱B&b£7.25–£7.50

♨ CTV 3P 220acres mixed

EVESHAM
Hereford & Worcester
Map **4** SP04

GH Waterside Family Hotel 56/59 Waterside ☎(0386) 2420

Modernised hotel with a genial atmosphere. Close to the river.

9hc (2🚿 4🛁) Annexe: 4hc (2🚿 2🛁) (4fb)
CTV in all bedrooms [R] B&b£14–£23
Bdi£21.50–£30.50 W£147–£160 Ⱡ
LDO9.30pm

Lic ♨ 30P 🎣

Credit cards [1] [2] [3]

EXBOURNE
Devon
Map **2** SS60

FH Mrs S J Allain **Stapleford** *(SS580039)*
☎(083785) 277

17th-century Devon longhouse, modernised to high standard of comfort. 2m SE unclass rd.

Closed Xmas & New Year

2rm (1hc) ⋈ [R] ✱B&b£10 Bdi£15 Wfr£95
Ⱡ LDO5pm

CTV 2P 2🚗 nc12yrs 🎣 80acres sheep

[V]

EXETER
Devon
Map **3** SX99
See plan on pages 164–165

GH Braeside 21 New North Rd ☎(0392) 56875 Plan **1** *B4*

9hc 🚭 in 2 bedrooms CTV in all bedrooms
⋈ ✱B&b£10–£15 W£60–£70 M

♨ CTV 🅿̸ nc16yrs

[V]

Exeter

GH Dunmore Hotel 22 Blackall Rd
☎(0392) 31643 Plan **1A** *C4*
Closed Xmas & New Year

7hc (2🚿) (4fb) CTV in 5 bedrooms TV in 2 bedrooms [R] ✱B&b£9–£12 W£70–£84 M̸

🛋 CTV P̸

[V]

GH Hotel Gledhills 32 Alphington Rd
☎(0392) 30469 Plan **2** *B1*
Closed Xmas

Friendly, traditional, small hotel standing in own grounds, close to city and St Thomas' Station.

12hc (3fb) TV in all bedrooms 🐕 [R] ✱B&b£13–£16.45 Bdi£17.60–£21.05 W£110.20–£130.90 Ł LDO6.30pm

Lic 🛋 CTV 9P 3🚗

Credit cards [1] [2] [3] [5]

GH Park View Hotel 8 Howell Rd
☎(0392) 71772 Plan **3** *B4*
Closed Xmas

Attractive Georgian property in quiet position. Friendly service and well equipped bedrooms.

10hc (2🛁 2🚿) Annexe: 7hc (1🛁 1🚿) (3fb) CTV in all bedrooms [R] ✱B&b£12–£17 Bdi£17–£22

🛋 CTV 6P 🏠

Credit cards [1] [3] [V]

GH Radnor Hotel 79 St Davids Hill
☎(0392) 72004 Plan **4** *A4*
Closed Xmas & New Year

8hc (2🚿) (7fb) CTV in 2 bedrooms [R] B&b£10–£12 Bdi£15–£17 W£105–£119 Ł LDO4pm

🛋 CTV 7P

[V]

GH *Sunnymede* 24 New North Rd
☎(0392) 73844 Plan **7** *B3*

Georgian property, recently refurbished, close to shopping area. Comfortable, modern bedrooms and welcoming atmosphere.

8hc 🐕

🛋 CTV P̸ nc

GH Sylvania House Hotel 64 Pennsylvania Rd (Guestaccom) ☎(0392) 75583 Plan **8** *D4*
Closed 22 Dec–4 Jan

8hc (1🛁 4🚿) (2fb) CTV in all bedrooms 🐕 [R] ✱B&b£10–£12.50 Bdi£14.50–£17 W£100–£110 Ł

Lic 🛋 CTV 4P

Credit card [3] [V]

GH *Telstar Hotel* 77 St Davids Hill
☎(0392) 72466 Plan **9** *A4*
Closed Xmas

Friendly, family-run guesthouse with cosy bedrooms. Close to colleges and central station.

(8hc) (2🚿) (2fb) 🐕 LDO1pm

🛋 CTV 5P

GH Trees Mini Hotel 2 Queen's Cres, York Rd ☎(0392) 59531 Plan **10** *D4*
Closed Xmas

Small, personally run guesthouse in quiet crescent. Convenient for cathedral, university and theatres.

12hc (1fb) 🐕 B&b£9–£10 W£59.50–£66.50 M̸

🛋 CTV 1P nc3yrs

[V]

See advertisement on page 164

GH Trenance House Hotel 1 Queen's Cres, York Rd ☎(0392) 73277 Plan **11** *D4*

14hc (1🛁) (2fb) CTV in all bedrooms [R] ✱B&b£9.50–£12 Bdi£15–£17.50 W£105–£122.50 Ł LDO1pm

🛋 CTV 8P

Credit cards [1] [3] [V]

See advertisement on page 165

GH *Westholme Hotel* 85 Heavitree Rd
☎(0392) 71878 Plan **12** *F2*
Closed mid Dec–mid Jan

7hc (1fb) [R] LDO7.45pm

CTV 9P

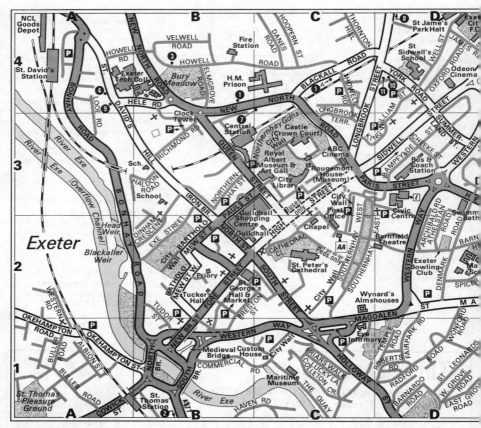

GH Willowdene Hotel 161 Magdalen Rd
☎(0392) 71925 Plan **13** *F2*

*Georgian house with neat garden
frontage. Within walking distance of town
centre and tourist attractions.*

6hc (1fb) ✠ ✳B&b£10 W£70 M
CTV 1P

EXFORD
Somerset
Map **3**   SS83

GH Exmoor House ☎(064383) 304
Mar–Oct

5hc Annexe: 12hc (2fb) B&b£10.35
Bdi£16.10 W£112 ⅃ LDO6pm
🅟 CTV 12P

EXMOUTH
Devon
Map **3**   SY08

GH *Blenheim* 39 Morton Rd ☎(0395)
264230
Closed Xmas

6hc (2fb) CTV in 4 bedrooms ✠ ®
LDO5pm

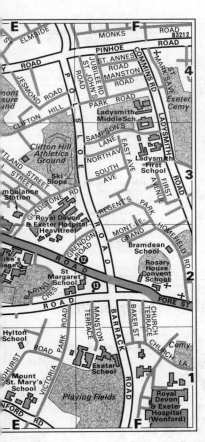

Exeter

1 Braeside
1A Dunmore
2 Hotel Gledhills
3 Park View Hotel
4 Radnor Hotel
7 Sunnymede
8 Sylvania House Hotel
9 Telstar Hotel
10 Trees Mini Hotel
11 Trenance House Hotel
12 Westholme Hotel
13 Willowdene Hotel

FH Mrs A J Skinner *Maer* *(SY018803)*
Maer Ln ☎(0395) 263651
Etr–Oct

*In large garden which has views of sea
and Haldon Hills, 5 minutes walk to beach
and 20 minutes walk to town.*

3rm (1hc) (2fb) ✱ ®

🍴 CTV 3P ᴁ 300acres arable beef dairy

FH Mrs J Reddaway *Quentance*
(SY037812) Salterton Rd ☎Budleigh
Salterton (03954) 2733
Apr–Oct

*Superior-style farmhouse with bedrooms
overlooking south-east Devon coastline.*

3hc (1fb) ✱ LDO7pm

CTV 3P 2🐎 nc3yrs 260acres arable dairy
mixed

FALFIELD
Avon
Map **3**   ST69

GH Mr & Mrs Bryant **Green Farm**
☎(0454) 260319

*14th-century, former farmhouse, carefully
modernised, with tennis court and
swimming pool in grounds. Extensive
dinner menu.*

8hc (1⇆) (1fb) ✱B&b£9–£14 Bdi£14–£21
W£98–£147 ⅃ LDO10pm
🍴 CTV 10P ⏋ ♪(hard)

FALMOUTH
Cornwall
Map **2**   SW83
See plan on page 166

GH Bedruthan 49 Castle Dr, Sea Front
☎(0326) 311028 Plan **1** *D2*

*Occupying a fine seafront position, close
to Pendennis Castle and offering
panoramic sea views.*

8hc (1🚿) (1fb) ✱ ® ✱B&b£8.75–£9.25
Bdi£13.50–£14 W£94.50–£99.75 ⅃ (Nov–
Apr) LDO3pm

Lic 🍴 CTV 3P(charge) nc10

GH Cotswold House Private Hotel
49 Melvill Rd ☎(0326) 312077
Plan **3** *C1*

*A small, private hotel pleasantly located
close to Gyllyngvase Beach and the town
and harbour.*   →

Lic 🍴 CTV ♪ nc4yrs
Credit cards ① ③

GH *Carlton Lodge Hotel* Carlton Hill
☎(0395) 263314

6hc (2⇆ 2🚿) (3fb) CTV in all bedrooms ®
LDO9pm

Lic 🍴 8P nc3yrs (Jun–Sep)

GH *Clinton House* 41 Morton Rd
☎(0395) 271969

*A house dating from the 1920s, just off the
seafront, near beach and ½ mile from the
town centre.*

8hc (2fb) CTV in all bedrooms ✱ LDO5pm

🍴 CTV ♪ nc3yrs

11hc (2⇄ 3⋔) (2fb) ✘ ✱B&b£9.50–£11
Bdi£14.50–£16 W£83–£99 ⚓
Lic CTV 10P

GH Hotel Dracaena Dracaena Av
☎(0326) 314470 Plan **4** *B3*

*A detached, private hotel, commercially
orientated.*

10hc (3⇄ 3⋔) (6fb) CTV in all bedrooms
® ✱B&b£14 Bdi£19.50 W£115 ⚓
LDO6.30pm

Lic CTV 18P ⚲

Credit cards ① ② ③ ⓥ

GH Evendale Private Hotel 51 Melvill Rd
☎(0326) 314164 Plan **5** *C1*
May–Oct

*A small hotel pleasantly located close to
the beach, Princess Pavilion and
Gardens.*

10hc (3⇄) (3fb) ® ✱B&b£9–£10.50
Bdi£14–£15.50 W£85–£99 ⚓ LDO6.30pm

CTV 10P

ⓥ

Falmouth

GH Gyllyngvase House Hotel
Gyllyngvase Rd ☎(0326) 312956 Plan **6**
C1

*The hotel stands in its own grounds
ideally situated for the beaches, town,
parks and pavilion.*

16hc (5⇄ 8⋔) (3fb) CTV in all bedrooms
B&b£11.50–£15 Bdi£16–£18 W£112–£126
⚓ LDO7pm

Lic ⋓ CTV 15P

ⓥ

GH Harbour Hotel 1 Harbour Ter
☎(0326) 311344 Plan **7** *C3*

*Small, family-run guesthouse overlooking
the harbour.*

6hc (2⋔) (2fb) ® ✱B&b£8–£10
Bdi£10.50–£13 W£57–£92 ⚓ LDO6pm

Lic ⋓ CTV ⚐

ⓥ

GH Langton Leigh 11 Florence Pl
☎(0326) 313684 Plan **8** *C2*
Apr–Oct

*Attractive character terraced property in
an elevated position with views of
Falmouth Bay.*

8hc (3⋔) (4fb) B&b£8.50–£11 Bdi£12.50–
£15 W£73–£87.50 ⚓ LDO4.30pm

Lic ⋓ CTV 6P 1🐕

ⓥ

GH *Maskee House* Spernen Wyn Rd
☎(0326) 311783 Plan **9** *C1*
Etr–Oct

*Fine, well-appointed small hotel near sea,
with peaceful, well-tended gardens.*

6hc (4fb) CTV in all bedrooms ✘ ®
⋓ CTV 6P 3🐕

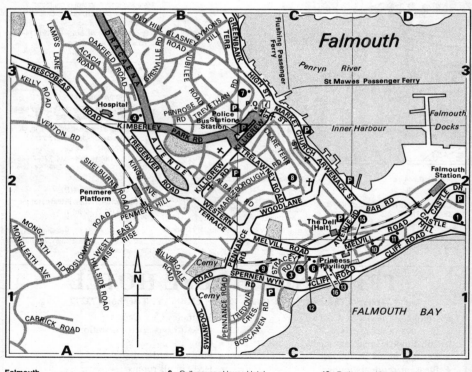

GH Milton House 33 Melvill Rd ☎(0326) 314390 Plan **10** *D1*

Small semi-detached residence positioned close to beaches, town and pavilion.

6hc (2fb) ✱B&b£7.50–£8.50 Bdi£10.50–£12 W£70–£80 ⱡ LDO3pm

🍽 CTV 6P nc3yrs

GH Penty Bryn Hotel 10 Melvill Rd ☎(0326) 314988 Plan **11** *D2*
Feb–Oct

Small, select hotel with high standard of facilities. Close to local amenities.

7rm (6hc 4fl) (3fb) CTV in all bedrooms [R] B&b£8.75–£10.50 Bdi£13–£15.50 W£80–£96 ⱡ LDO5pm

Lic 🍽 CTV 2P nc6yrs

Credit cards [1] [3] [V]

GH Rathgowry Hotel Gyllyngvase Hill ☎(0326) 313482 Plan **12** *C1*
Mar–Oct

10hc (2⇨ 8fl) (6fb) CTV in 8 bedrooms [R] ✱B&b£11–£15 Bdi£13–£18 W£90–£117 ⱡ LDO5pm

Lic 🍽 CTV 10P

GH *Rosemary Hotel* 22 Gyllyngvase Ter ☎(0326) 314669 Plan **13** *C1*
Closed Xmas

Cosy, family-run guesthouse close to town centre and beaches.

Falmouth — Farrington Gurney

11hc (5fb) CTV in 3 bedrooms ✈ LDO6.30pm

🍽 CTV 4P

GH Tregenna House 28 Melvill Rd ☎(0326) 313881 Plan **14** *D2*

Semi-detached, friendly hotel positioned close to the beaches, town and pavilion.

6hc (2fb) TV in 2 bedrooms ✱B&b£8–£9 Bdi£12–£13.50 W£84–£92 ⱡ LDO4pm

Lic 🍽 CTV 7P nc2yrs

Credit cards [1] [3] [4] [5] [V]

GH Wickham 21 Gyllyngvase Ter ☎(0326) 311140 Plan **16** *C1*
Apr–Oct

Small guesthouse pleasantly situated in a quiet road, close to beaches.

10hc (2fb) ✈ [R] ✱B&b£8.50–£10 Bdi£12.50–£13.50 W£82–£86 ⱡ LDO5pm

CTV 3P nc3yrs

FAREHAM
Hampshire
Map **4** SU50

GH Catisfield Hotel Catisfield (2m W A27) ☎Titchfield (0329) 41851

Modern, well furnished bedrooms on 2 floors above Catisfield Wine Stores in quiet residential area.

20hc (16⇨ 2fl) (12fb) CTV in all bedrooms [R] B&b£10–£18 Bdi£14.50–£22.50 W£91–£145 ⱡ LDO5pm

Lic 🍽 CTV 150P 🏠

FARNHAM
Surrey
Map **4** SU84

INN Eldon Hotel 43 Frensham Rd, Lower Bourne ☎Frensham (025125) 2745

Popular, privately-managed hotel with modern, well-equipped bedrooms, good leisure facilities plus restaurant.

14hc (8⇨ 4fl) CTV in 12 bedrooms [R] ✱B&b£20–£30 Bdi£25–£45

🍽 CTV 70P 🚗 squash

Credit cards [1] [2] [3] [5] [V]

FARRINGTON GURNEY
Avon
Map **3** ST65

FH Mrs J Candy **Cliff** *(ST633547)* Rush Hill (½m S over county boundary in Somerset) ☎Chewton Mendip (076121) 274

Guest accommodation has been converted from former dairy and cheese room. →

The Gyllyngvase house hotel

Gyllyngvase Road, FALMOUTH, Cornwall Tel: (0326) 312956 Visitors 311319

Ashley Courtenay

A small privately run Hotel in own grounds, ideally situated as a touring centre for local beauty spots and town etc. For overnight or weekly stay — business or holiday visitor. Central heating — own car park — particular attention to comfort and good home-cooking. Open all year.

Brochure sent on application.

Trengilly Wartha Inn

Nancenoy, Constantine, Nr. Falmouth, Cornwall Tel: Falmouth (0326) 40332

Set in extensive grounds amid glorious countryside, near the Helford River, and Beaches.
Add the hospitality of our inn (real ale included!), to our excellent cuisine ranging from restaurant "á la carte" to extensive bar snacks; then consider the comfort of our en-suite accommodation (all bedrooms colour TV) and make us your choice when visiting this delightful area.

Prices Moderate *See gazetteer under Constantine*

2hc (1⇌ 1🛏) (1fb) ✖ ® ✱B&b£10–£12
Bdi£16–£18W£112–£126⫽LDOnoon
🍴 CTV 6P 186acres dairy

FAR SAWREY
Cumbria
Map **7**　SD39

GH West Vale 🏠Windermere (09662)
2817

*Small, well-furnished, guesthouse where
home-cooking is a speciality.*

8hc (5🛏) (3fb) ® B&b£11–£12.75
Bdi£18.25–£20 W£113.75–£126⫽
LDOnoon

Lic 🍴 CTV 8P
Ⓥ

FAZELEY
Staffordshire
Map **4**　SK20

GH Buxton Hotel 65 Coleshill St
🏠Tamworth (0827) 285805
Closed Xmas

15hc (1⇌ 8🛏) (4fb) CTV in 13 bedrooms
TV in 2 bedrooms LDO5pm

Lic 🍴 CTV 16P

Credit cards ① ③

FELINDRE (nr Swansea)
West Glamorgan
Map **2**　SN60

FH Mr F Jones *Coynant* (SN648070)
🏠Ammanford (0269) 2064 & 5640

*Secluded house in elevated position at
head of valley. 4m N of Felindre off
unclass road linking M4 jct 46 &
Ammanford.*

6hc (2🛏) (3fb) CTV in 3 bedrooms ✖ ®
🍴 CTV 10P ♻ 150acres livestock

FELMINGHAM
Norfolk
Map **9**　TG22

GH Felmingham Hall 🏠Swanton
Abbott(069269) 228
Mar–Dec

*Large, interesting old manor house.
Remote but near North Walsham. Big
rooms comfortably appointed.*

12hc (11⇌ 1🛏) CTV in all bedrooms ✖
® B&b£27.50–£33.50 Bdi£32.50–£38.50
W£227.50–£255.50⫽LDO8.30pm

Lic 🍴 40P 10🚗 nc12yrs ⌇(heated)
🏌grass

Credit cards ① ②

FENITON
Devon
Map **3**　SY19

GH Colestocks House Colestocks (1m N
unclass rd) 🏠Honiton (0404) 850633

*Large 16th-century thatched country
house in own gardens. Comfortable
accommodation, friendly service,
traditional French and English cooking.*

Farrington Gurney — Folkestone

7hc (4⇌ 1🛏) (1fb) CTV in all bedrooms ✖
® LDO9pm

Lic 🍴 CTV 8P nc10yrs

FENSTANTON
Cambridgeshire
Map **4**　TL36

INN Tudor Hotel High St 🏠Huntingdon
(0480) 62532

*Mock Tudor inn situated in small village of
Fenstanton off busy A604 Hunstanton–
Cambridge bypass.*

6⇌ (1fb) CTV in all bedrooms ®
✱B&b£13.50–£20 W£84–£112 M
Lunch£8alc Dinner9.30pm £8alc

Lic 🍴 50P

Credit cards ① ③ Ⓥ

FERNDOWN
Dorset
Map **4**　SU00

GH Broadlands Hotel West Moors Rd
🏠(0202) 877884

17hc (4⇌ 3🛏) (2fb) ✱B&b£15–£20
Bdi£21–£26 LDO6pm

Lic 🍴 CTV 15P

FFESTINIOG
Gwynedd
Map **6**　SH64

GH Newborough House Hotel Church
Sq 🏠(076676) 2682
Mar–Dec (rs early & late season)

*Stone-built Georgian house on edge of
village.*

6hc (1🛏) (3fb) TV in 1 bedroom B&b£11–
£15 Bdi£17–£21 W£112–£145⫽

Lic 🍴 CTV 6P nc7yrs
Ⓥ

FIDDLEFORD
Dorset
Map **3**　ST81

INN Fiddleford 🏠Sturminster Newton
(0258) 72489
Closed Xmas Day

*Situated near Sturminster Newton on
main Blandford to Sherborne road.*

4hc (1⇌ 1🛏) LDO9.30pm

🍴 50P

FILEY
North Yorkshire
Map **8**　TA18

GH Downcliffe Hotel The Beach
🏠Scarborough (0723) 513310
Apr–Oct

*Detached sea-front hotel offering a
special welcome to families.*

17hc (6🛏) (9fb) CTV in 6 bedrooms ®
✱B&b£11.50–£13.50 Bdi£12.50–£15.75
W£87.50–£110.25⫽LDO6pm

Lic 🍴 CTV 8P 2🐕

GH Seafield Hotel 9–11 Rutland St
🏠Scarborough (0723) 513715
Feb–Nov

*Spacious accommodation close to sea
and town centre.*

14hc (1⇌ 1🛏) (7fb) ✖ ® B&b£9.50–
£10.50 Bdi£13–£14.50 W£80–£87.50⫽
LDOnoon

Lic 🍴 CTV 6P
Ⓥ

FINTRY
Central *Stirlingshire*
Map **11**　NS68

FH Mrs M Mitchell **Nether Glinns**
(NS606883) 🏠(036086) 207
Apr–Sep

*Well-maintained farmhouse situated
among rolling hills. Signposted drive.*

3rm (1fb) ✂ in 1 bedroom ✱B&b£7.50–£8
CTV 4P 150acres beef dairy

FISHGUARD
Dyfed
Map **2**　SM93

GH Glanmoy Country House Goodwick
(1m NW on A40) 🏠(0348) 872844

*Secluded country house with friendly
personal service and exceptionally well-
appointed bedrooms.*

3⇌ CTV in all bedrooms ✖ ®
✱B&b£16.50–£18.50 Bdi£19.50–£21
W£136–£145⫽LDO9pm

Lic 🍴 40P nc7yrs
Ⓥ

FLAX BOURTON
Avon
Map **3**　ST56

INN Jubilee Farleigh Rd 🏠(027583) 2741

4hc ✱B&b£15–£16 Lunch£6–£7alc
Dinner10pm£6–£7alc

CTV 52P 🚗 nc16yrs

FLUSHING
Cornwall
Map **2**　SW83

GH Nankersey Hotel St Peters Rd
🏠Falmouth (0326) 74471
Closed Nov

*Grade II listed building beautifully
positioned within character fishing village.*

8hc (2fb) ✖ ® ✱B&b£11–£12.50 Bdi£17–
£18.50 W£98⫽ (W only Jul & Aug)
LDO5pm

Lic 🍴 CTV 🏌

Credit cards ① ② ③

FOLKESTONE
Kent
Map **5**　TR23

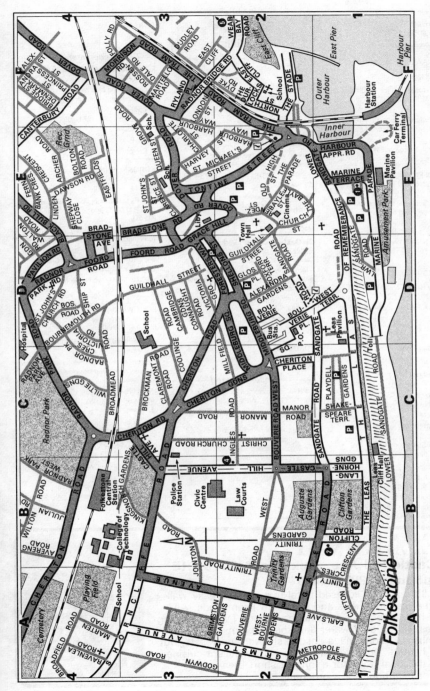

Folkestone

1 Argos Private Hotel
2 Arundel Hotel
4 Belmonte Private Hotel

5 Wearbay Hotel
6 Westwood Hol

Folkestone

GH *Argos Private Hotel* 6 Marine Ter ☎(0303) 54309 Plan **1** *E1*

Homely little house, close to the ferry terminal.

9hc (2fb) 🚫 LDO9pm

Lic 🛋 CTV nc3yrs

GH *Arundel Hotel* The Leas, 3 Clifton Rd ☎(0303) 52442 Plan **2** *B1*
Mar–Oct

Spacious, comfortable accommodation on four floors, with friendly and efficient service.

13hc (4fb) TV in 1 bedroom 🚫 LDO3pm

Lic 🛋 CTV

GH Belmonte Private Hotel 30 Castle Hill Av ☎(0303) 54470 Telex no 15701001 Plan **4** *B2*

Comfortable family run hotel central and quiet with homely and courteous atmosphere.

9hc (1🛁 2🚿) (2fb) CTV in all bedrooms [R] B&b£14–£16.50 Bdi£19–£21.50 W£114–£129⊬ LDO6pm

Lic 🛋 3P

Credit cards [1] [2] [3] [5] [V]

GH Wearbay Hotel 23/25 Wearbay Cres ☎(0303) 52586 Plan **5** *F2*

Old-fashioned, friendly accommodation.

12hc (1🛁) (1fb) CTV in 3 bedrooms B&b£10–£16 Bdi£16.50–£22.50 W£108.50–£157.50⊬ LDO11pm

Lic 🛋 CTV 1🚗(charge)

Credit cards [1] [2] [3] [5] [V]

GH Westward Ho! 13 Clifton Cres ☎(0303) 52663 Plan **6** *A1*

11hc (1🚿) (6fb) ✱B&b£12.50–£13.50 Bdi£16.50–£17.50 W£99–£105⊬ LDO5pm

Lic lift 🛋 CTV 🚫🅿

Credit cards [1] [3] [V]

FONTHILL BISHOP
Wiltshire
Map **3** ST93

INN Kings Arms ☎Hindon (074789) 523
Closed Xmas & Boxing Day

3hc 🚫 [R] ✱B&b£12–£16 Bdi£18–£22 W£119–£126⊬ Lunch £4.50–£8alc Dinner9.30pm £4.50–£8alc

🛋 CTV 20P

Credit card [1]

FONTMELL MAGNA
Dorset
Map **3** ST81

GH Estyard House ☎(0747) 811460
Closed Nov & Xmas

A warm welcome is assured at this pleasant detached guesthouse.

6hc B&b£10.75–£11.75 Bdi£15.75–£16.75 W£101⊬ LDO3pm

🛋 8P nc8yrs

FORDINGBRIDGE
Hampshire
Map **4** SU11

GH Oakfield Lodge 1 Park Rd ☎(0425) 52789
Closed Xmas

A family-run hotel offering a warm welcome with a high standard of service and accommodation.

10hc (1🚿) (2fb) B&b£10–£11 Bdi£12–£17 Wfr£74⊬

Lic 🛋 CTV 8P 2🚗 🏠

[V]

FORDOUN
Grampian *Kincardineshire*
Map **15** NO77

Recommended

FH Mrs M Anderson **Ringwood** *(NO743774)* ☎Auchenblae (05612) 313
Apr–Oct

Small, modernised villa in open setting amidst farmland and with its own neat garden and outhouse. Very high standard of décor and furnishings. 1½ miles off A94 on B966.

4hc (1fb) 🚫 [R] ✱B&b£8–£10 W£50–£65 M

🛋 CTV 4P 16acres arable

[V]

FORFAR
Tayside *Angus*
Map **15** NO45

Recommended

INN *Queen's Hotel* 12–14 The Cross ☎(0307) 62533

Small stone-built hotel with good bedrooms, home-cooking and friendly service.

6🛁 (2fb) CTV in all bedrooms 🚫 LDO8pm

🛋 🚫🅿

Credit card [2]

FORGANDENNY
Tayside *Perthshire*
Map **11** NO01

FH Mrs M Fotheringham **Craighall** *(NO081176)* ☎Bridge of Earn (0738) 812415

Large bungalow-type farmhouse tastefully furnished, with friendly atmosphere. ½m W off B935 Bridge of Earn–Forteviot road.

3hc (1fb) 🚫 ✱B&b£7–£9 Bdi£12–£14 W£84–£98⊬ LDO9pm

🛋 CTV 3P 1000acres beef sheep

[V]

FORT WILLIAM
Highland *Inverness-shire*
Map **14** NN17

GN Benview Belford Rd ☎(0397) 2966
Mar–Nov

Detached stone-built house with modern extension situated beside A82 just N of town centre.

15hc (1🚿) (1fb) ✱B&b£10.35–£13.50 Bdi£14.95–£16.10 W£100–£112⊬ LDO7pm

🛋 CTV 20P

[V]

GH Gulsachan Alma Rd ☎(0397) 3797
Closed 20 Dec–4 Jan

Comfortable, well-maintained house in an elevated residential area.

15hc (1🛁 3🚿) (3fb) 🚫 ✱B&b£9–£15 Bdi£14–£23 W£98–£161⊬ LDO5.30pm

Lic 🛋 CTV 15P

GH Hillview Achintore Rd ☎(0397) 4349

A friendly, comfortable and nicely appointed guesthouse situated beside the A82 overlooking Loch Linnhe.

9hc (2fb) ✖ ⓡ B&b£7.50–£8.50
Bdi£12.50–£13.50
🏠 9P
Ⓥ

GH Innseagan Achintore Rd ☎(0397) 2452

Apr–Oct

Large stone-built house with modern extensions, situated on the A82 South of the town, overlooking Loch Linnhe.

26hc (12⇋) (2fb) ✖ ✱Bdi£13.50–£17.75
W£94.50–£124.25 ⅃ LDO7pm
Lic 🏠 CTV 30P
Ⓥ

GH Lochview Heathcroft, Argyll Rd
☎(0397) 3149

Etr–Oct

A comfortable modern-style guesthouse.

6hc (1⇋ 3🏠) (2fb) ✱B&b£8.50–£10
Bdi£13.50–£15 W£89–£96 ⅃ LDO6.30pm
🏠 CTV 7P

GH Orchy Villa Alma Rd ☎(0397) 2445

Smartly decorated house, situated on a hillside above the town, with compact bedrooms.

6hc (4fb) ✖ ✱B&b£9.50
🏠 CTV 6P

GH Rhu Mhor Alma Rd ☎(0397) 2213

Etr–Sep

A traditional style guesthouse in a quiet residential area.

7hc (2fb) ✖ ✱B&b£8.50–£9 Bdi£13–
£13.50 LDO5pm
🏠 CTV 7P
Ⓥ

GH Stronchreggan View Achintore Rd
☎(0397) 4644

Apr–Oct

Comfortable and well-appointed modern house.

Fort William
—
Framlingham

7hc (3fb) ✖ Bdi£14–£15 W£98–£105 ⅃
LDO7pm
🏠 7P
Ⓥ

FOURCROSSES
Powys
Map **7**   SJ21

FH Mrs J E Wigley **Maerdy** (SJ259168)
(½m SW of A483 signed Penrhos)
☎Guilsfield (093875) 202
Apr–Sep

Warm, friendly old farmhouse full of beams and polished floors.

2hc (1🏠) (1fb) ✖ ✱B&bfr£9 Bdifr£13
Wfr£91 ⅃ LDO2.30pm
TV P 157acres dairy mixed

FOVANT
Wiltshire
Map **4**   SU02

INN Cross Keys ☎(072270) 284
4hc (1fb) ✖ ✱B&b£12 Bdi£17–£19
Lunch£7alc Dinner 9.30pm£8alc
Lic 🏠 CTV 30p
Credit cards 1 3

FOWEY
Cornwall
Map **2**   SX15

GH Ashley House Hotel 14 Esplanade
☎(072683) 2310
Etr–Oct

8hc (1🏠) (4fb) ⓡ ✱B&b£11–£13 Bdi£16–
£20 W£105–£126 ⅃ LDO6pm
Lic 🏠 CTV ✗
Ⓥ

GH Carnethic House Lambs Barn
☎(072683) 3336
Etr–Oct

8hc (6🏠) (2fb) ✗ in 1 bedroom CTV in all
bedrooms ✖ ⓡ ✱B&b£11–£18.50
Bdi£18–£25 W£120–£167 ⅃ LDO6.45pm

Lic 🏠 20P nc12yrs ⇗(heated) snooker
Credit cards 1 2 3 5

GH Wheelhouse 60 Esplanade
☎(072683) 2452

There are magnificent views from this small, family-run guesthouse.

6hc (2🏠) (1fb) ✗ in 3 bedrooms ✖ ⓡ
B&b£11–£17.50 Bdi£19–£25.50 W£133–
£178.50 ⅃ LDOnoon
Lic 🏠 CTV ✗ nc12yrs
Credit card 1 Ⓥ

FH Mrs R. Dunn **Trezare** (SX112538)
☎(072683) 3485
Apr–Sep

Conveniently situated 1m from Fowey, pleasant atmosphere and good farmhouse fare.

3rm (2hc) ✖ CTV 4P 2🐄 230acres arable
beef dairy sheep mixed

FOWNHOPE
Hereford & Worcester
Map **3**   SO53

GH Bowens Farmhouse ☎(043277) 430
Feb–mid Dec

8hc (2⇋ 3🏠) (3fb) ⓡ ⓡ ✱B&bfr£12.75
Bdifr£19.75 Wfr£115 ⅃ LDO7.30pm
Lic 🏠 CTV 10P nc10yrs putting green
Ⓥ

FRADDON
Cornwall
Map **2**   SW95

GH St Margaret's Country Hotel
☎St Austell (0726) 860375

Small family-run hotel on main A30.

11hc (5fb) ⓡ B&b£9–£12 Bdi£12–£15
W£78–£99 ⅃ LDO7pm
Lic 🏠 CTV 15P
Ⓥ

FRAMLINGHAM
Suffolk
Map **5**   TM26

FH Mrs S F Stocker **Broadwater**
(TM289614) Woodbridge Rd ☎(0728)
723645
Closed Xmas & New Year   →

Fine Georgian house in large garden. Wine produced from 4-acre vineyard here, is available at dinner.

5rm (2hc 1🛁) (1fb) *B&b£9.50–£11 Bdi£15.50–£17 W£98.50–£109 ⊬ LDO10am

Lic 🛋 CTV 6P 28acres sheep ponies

[V]

FRESHWATER
Isle of Wight
See **Wight, Isle of**

FRESSINGFIELD
Suffolk
Map **5** TM27

FH Mrs R Willis ***Priory House*** *(TM256770)* Priory Rd ☎(037986) 254

Attractive 400-year-old brick-built farmhouse with beamed interior and quality furniture. Secluded garden.

4rm (3hc) ✈

🛋 CTV 6P nc10yrs 2acres non-working

FRINTON-ON-SEA
Essex
Map **5** TM21

GH Forde 18 Queens Rd ☎(02556) 4758

Traditional-style seaside guesthouse run by friendly proprietors.

6hc (1fb) ✈ *B&b£10.50 Bdi£15 W£83 ⊬ LDOnoon.

🛋 CTV 1P nc5yrs

[V]

Recommended

GH Montpellier Private Hotel
2 Harold Gv ☎(02556) 4462

Situated in residential area and recently renovated, with spacious bedrooms.

6🛁 🚿 (1fb) CTV in all bedrooms [R] *B&b£18–£20 Bdi£25–£30 Wfr£175 ⊬ LDO7pm

Lic 🛋 7P

Credit card [3]

Framlingham — Garforth

FROGMORE
Devon
Map **3** SX74

INN Globe ☎(054853) 351

17th-century village inn, personally run with relaxed, informal atmosphere.

5hc (1fb) CTV in all bedrooms [R] *B&b£12.60–£15.50 W£78–£84 ⊬

Lic 🛋 CTV 20P

Credit cards [1] [2] [3] [5] [V]

GAIRLOCH
Highland *Ross & Cromarty*
Map **14** NG87

GH Eilean View ☎(0445) 2272

There are fine views over Gairloch Bay from this modern, timber-clad bungalow.

3hc *B&b£8.50–£9 Bdi£13.50–£14 W£94.50–£98 ⊬ LDO6pm

🛋 CTV 4P

Recommended

GH Horisdale House Strath ☎(0445) 2151
May–Sep rs Apr & Oct

Modern, elegant, comfortable and well-equipped guesthouse.

9hc (3fb) ✈ [R] *B&b£10–£11.50 Bdi£17–£18.50 LDO9am

🛋 12P nc7yrs

GH Kerrysdale House ☎(0445) 2292

Family-run country house with pretty bedrooms, lying 1 mile south of Gairloch.

4hc (1fb) ✈ *B&b£9–£11 Bdi£14–£16 LDO7pm

🛋 CTV 3P ⛺

GALASHIELS
Borders *Selkirkshire*
Map **12** NT43

GH Buckholmburn Edinburgh Rd ☎(0896) 2697

Detached house sitting high above the Galawater on the A7 on the northern outskirts of the town.

8hc (3fb) *B&b£12 Bdi£17–£22 W£107–£142 ⊬ LDO7pm

Lic 🛋 CTV 20P

Credit cards [1] [2] [3] [5]

GALSTON
Strathclyde *Ayrshire*
Map **11** NS53

FH Mrs J Bone **Auchencloigh** *(NS535320)* ☎(0563) 820567
Apr–Oct

A comfortable, traditional farmhouse with a friendly atmosphere. 5m S off B7037 – Scorn road.

2rm (1fb) ✈ *B&b£8–£9 Bdi £13–£13.50 W£90–£95 ⊬ LDO6pm

🛋 CTV 4P 4🚗 ⛺ sauna bath 240acres beef sheep mixed

GARBOLDISHAM
Norfolk
Map **5** TM08

FH Mr & Mrs D Atkins **Ingleneuk Guesthouse** *(TM002804)* Hopton Rd (Guestaccom) ☎(095381) 541

Modern bungalow set in ten acres of quiet wooded countryside.

6hc (5🚿) (1fb) CTV in all bedrooms [R] B&b£10.50–£16.80 Bdi£18.40–£24.70 W£121.80–£165.90 ⊬ LDO2pm

Lic 🛋 10P ⛳ 10acres soft fruit small-holding

[V]

GARFORTH
West Yorkshire
Map **8** SE43

GH Coach House Hotel 58 Lidgett Ln ☎Leeds (0532) 862323
Closed 23 Dec–2 Jan

Spacious breakfast room and main lounge in main building with modern bedrooms and small lounge in former stables opposite.

6hc Annexe: 5rm (4hc) (1fb) [R] *B&b£14

🛋 CTV 8P 2🚗

[V]

Gargrave — Gatwick Airport

GARGRAVE
North Yorkshire
Map **7** SD95

GH Kirk Syke 19 High St ☎ (075678) 356

Large stone house in village, with pleasant modern bedrooms.

3hc (2🛁 1🚿) Annexe: 6hc (4🛁 2🚿) (1fb) CTV in 4 bedrooms Ⓡ ✱B&b£11–£12 Bdi£17–£18 W£110–£117 Ⱡ LDOnoon

Lic 🍴 CTV 10P

[V]

GARSTANG
Lancashire
Map **7** SD44

FH Mrs J Higginson **Clay Lane Head** Cabus (2m N on A6) *(SD490474)* ☎(09952) 3132
2 Jan–21 Dec

A comfortable farmhouse of some character, with fine furniture and log fires.

3hc ✱B&b£8.50–£9.50 W£56–£63 M

CTV 4P U 30acres beef

[V]

FH Mrs J Fowler **Greenhaigh Castle** *(SD501452)* Castle Ln ☎(09952) 2140
Etr–Oct

17th-century character farmhouse, overlooked by ruins of Greenhaigh Castle. ½m E unclass rd.

3hc 🚫 Ⓡ ✱B&b£8.50 Wfr£56 M

CTV 3P 2🚗 200acres beef dairy sheep

GATEHEAD
Strathclyde *Ayrshire*
Map **10** NS33

INN *Old Rome Farmhouse* ☎Drybridge (0563) 850265

4hc (1fb) 🚫 Ⓡ

🍴 CTV 20P ⛳

GATWICK AIRPORT, LONDON
West Sussex
Map **4** TQ24

GH Barnwood Hotel Balcombe Rd, Pound Hill, Crawley ☎Crawley (0293) 882709 Telex no 877005

Modern private hotel with comfortable lounge and bar.

40hc (3🛁 37🚿) (20fb) CTV in all bedrooms 🚫 Ⓡ ✱B&b£32–£36 LDO9pm

Lic 🍴 45P

Credit cards [1] [2] [3] [4] [5]

GH Gainsborough Lodge 39 Massetts Rd, Horley (2m NE of airport adjacent A23) ☎Horley (0293) 783982

Extended victorian house with comfortable, compact accommodation.

12hc (4🛁 7🚿) (3fb) CTV in all bedrooms 🚫 Ⓡ ✱B&b£16.25–£18

🍴 16P

Credit cards [1] [3] [V]

See advertisement on page 174

GH *Gatwick Skylodge Motel* London Rd, County Oak, Crawley (2m S of airport on A23) ☎Crawley (0293) 544511

45🛁 🚿 (7fb) CTV in all bedrooms Ⓡ LDO9.45pm

Lic 🍴 60P (charge)

Credit cards [1] [2] [3]

See advertisement on page 174

GH Trumble's Hotel & Restaurant Stanhill, Charlwood (Exec Hotels) ☎Crawley (0293) 862212

Overlooking Gatwick and incorporating an attractive restaurant serving home-made teas.

5hc (3🛁 2🚿) CTV in all bedrooms 🚫 Ⓡ ✱B&b£25–£32.50

Lic 🍴 25P

Credit cards [1] [2] [3] [5] [V]

See advertisement on page 174

GH Woodlands 42 Massetts Rd, Horley
☎Crawley (0293) 782994
7hc (2🚿) (2fb) 🚭 in 5 bedrooms CTV in all bedrooms 🐕 [R] ✱B&b£13–£18
🛋 CTV 14P
Credit card [1] [V]

GAYHURST
Buckinghamshire
Map **4** SP84

FH Mrs K Adams **Mill** *(SP852454)*
☎Newport Pagnell (0908) 611489
17th-century stone-built farmhouse with the River Ouse running through the grounds from which fishing is available. 1m S off B526 unclass road to Haversham.
3hc (1🚿) (1fb) TV in all bedrooms [R] ✱B&b£12.50 Bdi£18 W£120 ⊭ LDO5pm
🛋 CTV 10P 3🚗 🏊 🎣 🐎 550 acres mixed
[V]

GEDNEY HILL
Lincolnshire
Map **8** TF31

FH Mrs C Cave ***Sycamore*** *(TF336108)*
☎Holbeach (0406) 330445
Closed Xmas wk
Situated on the B1166 in the village. The farmhouse is over 100 years old.
3rm (1fb) TV in 1 bedroom [R] LDO4pm
🛋 CTV 6P 80acres beef mixed

Gatwick Airport — Gilwern

GIGGLESWICK
North Yorkshire
Map **7** SD86

Recommended

GH Woodlands The Mains ☎Settle (07292) 2576
Closed Xmas & New Year
A handsome Georgian-style house in an elevated position with splendid views over the surrounding countryside. The bedrooms are comfortable and there is an elegant, inviting lounge. Dinners are cooked to order by Margaret Callan who, with her husband Roger, ensures that guests are well looked after during their stay.
8hc (2🛁 1🚿) CTV in 3 bedrooms 🐕 B&b£17–£19 Bdi£25.50–£27.50 W£170.50–£184.50 ⊭ LDOnoon
Lic 🛋 CTV 10P nc12yrs
[V]

INN Black Horse Hotel Church St
☎Settle (07292) 2506
A secluded village inn dating back to 1663. Well furnished bedrooms and good home-cooking.
3hc (1🛁 2🚿) (1fb) 🐕 ✱B&b£10 Bar lunch £2–£5.50
🛋 CTV 20P
Credit cards [1] [5] [V]

Recommended

FH Mrs B T Hargreaves **Close House** *(SD801634)* ☎Settle (07292) 3540
May–Sep
This charming house, dating back to 1676, is a delightfully relaxing place to stay. The bedrooms are comfortable and Mrs Hargreaves produces a fine dinner which is served in the attractive dining room.
3hc 🐕 [R] ✱B&b£17.50–£18.50 Bdi£28.50–£29.50 Wfr£108.50 M LDOnoon
Lic 6P nc 230acres dairy sheep

GILWERN
Gwent
Map **3** SO21

FH Mrs J C Harris **Wenallt** *(SO245138)*
☎(0873) 830694
Carefully restored, 16th-century Welsh longhouse, standing in 50 acres, with magnificent views over the Usk Valley. The plentiful catering is of a high standard.
→

7hc (2⇌ 3🛏) (1fb) ✖ ⓡ B&b£10–£12
Bdi£16–£18 W£105–£120 ⏣ LDO9pm
🎨 CTV 10P

50acres beef sheep

GISLINGHAM
Suffolk
Map **5**   TM07

─ Recommended ─
GH Old Guildhall Mill St ☎Mellis
(037983) 361

Fine 15th-century, timbered guildhall,
with extensive landscaped gardens.
Comfortable, well-appointed
bedrooms, and two attractive lounge
areas, one equipped with writing
desk. Adjacent to the ground-floor
lounge is a snooker table and an
electric organ.

4hc (3⇌) CTV in all bedrooms ✖ ⓡ
B&bfr£17.50 Bdifr£22.50 Wfr£115 M
LDO8pm

GLAN-YR-AFON (nr Corwen)
Gwynedd
Map **6**   SJ04

FH Mrs G B Jones *Llawr-Bettws*
(*SJO16424*) Bala Rd ☎Maerdy (049081)
224

Rambling, stone-built farmhouse with
pleasant, homely atmosphere. At Druid
traffic lights on A5 follow A494 Bala road
for 2m.

3hc (2fb) ✖ LDO6.30pm

CTV 6P 🐾 62acres beef sheep mixed

GLASBURY
Powys
Map **3**   SO13

FH Mrs B Eckley *Fforddfawr* (*SO192398*)
☎(04974) 332
Apr–Oct

17th-century farmhouse bordered by the
River Wye. 3m from Hay-on-Wye.

2hc ✖ ⓡ

CTV 4P 280acres mixed

GLASFRYN
Clwyd
Map **6**   SH95

FH Mr C Ellis *Growine* (*SH927502*)
☎Cerrigydrudion (049082) 447
Apr–Oct

Modernised and extended farmhouse at
end of drive. N of A5, E of village.

2rm ✖ ✱B&bfr£8.50 Bdifr£12.50 Wfr£84 ⏣
LDO2pm

🎨 CTV 3P 70acres mixed

Credit cards ① ② ③

Glasgow

1   Dalmeny Hotel
2   Kelvin Private Hotel
3   Linwood Hotel
4   Marie Stuart Hotel
5   Smith's Hotel

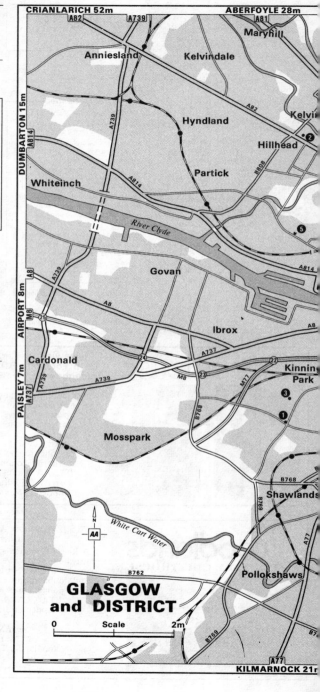

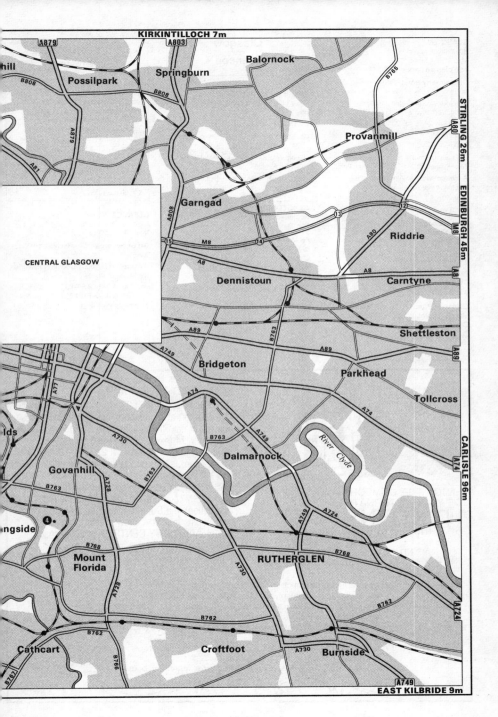

GLASGOW
Strathclyde *Lanarkshire*
Map **11** NS56
See plan on pages 176–177

GH Dalmeny Hotel 62 St Andrews Dr,
Nithsdale Cross ☎041-427 1106 Plan **1**
A friendly, comfortable and nicely appointed private hotel.
10hc (3⇨ 2㎡) (1fb) CTV in all bedrooms
® B&b£21
Lic ㎜ CTV 20P

GH Kelvin Private Hotel 15 Buckingham Ter, Hillhead ☎041-339 7143 Plan **2**
A terrace house in West End, close to Botanical Gardens.
15hc (1fb)
㎜ CTV 6P

GH Linwood Hotel 356 Albert Dr,
Pollokshields ☎041-427 1642 Plan **3**
Mar–Nov
Nicely appointed house with tidy garden, in quiet residential area.
11hc (1fb) CTV in 4 bedrooms ✖
B&b£12–£13
㎜ CTV 7P

GH Marie Stuart Hotel 46–48 Queen Mary Av, Cathcart ☎041-424 3939 Plan **4**
Closed Xmas Day & New Year's Day
Private hotel with modern extension.

Glasgow
Glencoe

31hc (8⇨ 1㎡) (4fb) CTV in 8 bedrooms
TV in 1 bedroom ✱B&b£14.50–£32
Bdi£21.50–£39 LDO7pm
Lic ㎜ CTV 40P

GH Smith's Hotel 963 Sauchiehall St
☎041-339 6363 Plan **5**
A long-established private hotel in the West End.
26hc (7fb) ✖ ✱B&b£9.80–£13.80
㎜ CTV ₽

GLASTONBURY
Somerset
Map **3** ST53

FH Mrs H T Tinney **Cradlebridge** *(ST477385)* ☎(0458) 31827
Closed Xmas
Large, renovated farmhouse with vegetable and fruit garden.
4hc (1fb) ✱B&b£10 Bdi£17 W£102 ⱡ
LDOnoon
㎜ CTV 6P 200acres dairy
ⓥ

GLENCOE
Highland *Argyllshire*
Map **14** NN15

GH Scorrybreac ☎Ballachulish (08552) 354
A modern guesthouse, comfortable and well-appointed.
5hc (1fb) ✱B&b£8.50–£9.50 Bdi£13.50–£14.50 W£94.50–£101.50 ⱡ LDO10pm
㎜ CTV 8P nc8yrs ♪
ⓥ

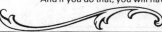
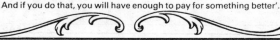

GLENMAVIS

Strathclyde *Lanarkshire*
Map **11**   NS76

FH Mrs M Dunbar **Braidenhill** *(NS742673)*
☎Glenboig (0236) 872319

300-year-old farmhouse on the outskirts of Coatbridge. About ½m from town boundary, N off B803.

3hc (1fb) ✱B&b£8.50–£9

🍴CTV 4P 50acres arable sheep mixed

GLENRIDDING

Cumbria
Map **11**   NY31

GH *Bridge House* ☎(08532) 236
Mar–Oct

Friendly little guesthouse overlooking the lake.

6hc (5fb) Ⓡ

🍴CTV 7P

GLOSSOP

Derbyshire
Map **7**   SK09

GH Colliers Hotel & Restaurant 14 High St East ☎(04574) 63409

6hc CTV in all bedrooms ✱B&b£12.50–£15 LDO8.30pm

Lic 🍴CTV ⟋

Glenmavis — Goathland

GLOUCESTER

Gloucestershire
Map **3**   SO81

GH Alma 49 Kingsholm Rd ☎(0452) 20940

A well-maintained guesthouse offering a warm welcome.

8hc (2fb) TV in 1 bedroom ⋈ ✱B&bfr£13

🍴CTV 6P 1🏤

Credit card ③

GH Claremont 135 Stroud Rd ☎(0452) 29540

7hc (1🚿) (2fb) CTV in all bedrooms ⋈ ✱B&b£9.50–£12 W£56–£59.50 Ⓜ

🍴CTV 6P

Ⓥ

GH *Lulworth* 12 Midland Rd ☎(0452) 21881
Closed Xmas

8hc (2fb) CTV in all bedrooms Ⓡ

🍴CTV 8P

See advertisement on page 180

GH Rotherfield House Hotel 5 Horton Rd ☎(0452) 410500

9hc (1↤⊐ 2🚿) (1fb) CTV in all bedrooms Ⓡ ✱B&b£12.65–£13.80 Bdi£18.40–£21.55 W£122.36–£142.17 ⥮ LDO5pm

Lic 🍴 9P nc5yrs

Credit cards ① ② ③ Ⓥ

GOATHLAND

North Yorkshire
Map **8**   NZ80

GH Heatherdene Hotel ☎Whitby (0947) 86334

Simple but comfortable accommodation on outskirts of village.
→

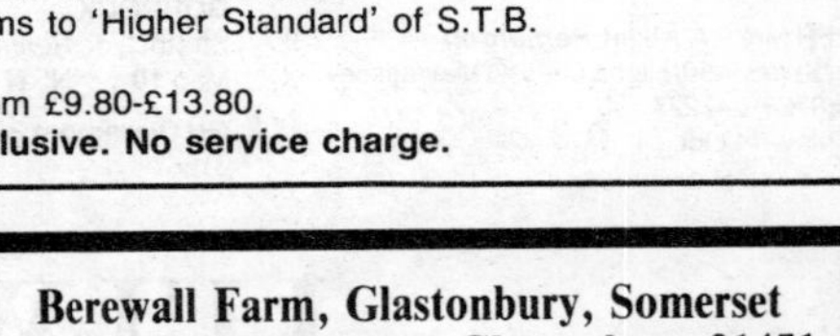

7hc (2⇌) (3fb) [R] ✱B&b£12.50–£13.50 Bdi£17–£18 (W only Oct–Mar) LDO6pm

Lic ♨ CTV 10P solarium

GOLSPIE
Highland *Sutherland*
Map **14** NH89

GH *Glenshee* Station Rd ☎(04083) 3254

Small, homely guesthouse near beach and golf course.

6hc (3fb)

♨ CTV 10P

Recommended

INN Stag's Head Hotel Main St ☎(04083) 3245

A comfortable and well-appointed, town-centre inn.

5⇌ CTV in all bedrooms ⋈ [R] ✱B&b£12.50 Bdi£20 W£141.75 ⱡ Bar lunch £2–£4 Dinner £7.50 LDO7.30pm

♨ CTV Ᵽ

Credit cards [1] [2] [3] [4] [5]

GOMSHALL
Surrey
Map **4** TQ04

INN Black Horse ☎Shere (048641) 2242

Well-maintained modern bedrooms, comfortable lounge and good bar facilities are complemented by efficient friendly service.

4hc ⋈ [R] ✱B&b£16.10 Wfr£112.70 M Lunch £6.95&alc Dinner 9.30pm £7&alc

CTV 60P 🚗 nc12yrs

Credit cards [3] [5]

GOREY
Jersey, Channel Islands
See **Channel Islands**

GORRAN
Cornwall
Map **2** SW94

FH Mrs P A Atkins ***Pentargon*** *(SW985450)* High Lanes ☎Mevagissey (0726) 842227
May–14 Oct

2hc (1fb) ⋈ [R] in 2 bedrooms

♨ CTV 2P 5½acres market-gardening

GORRAN HAVEN
Cornwall
Map **2** SX04

GH Perhaver ☎Mevagissey (0726) 842471
Apr–early Oct

Situated on top of cliffs, 500 yds from village.

5hc ⋈ [R] ✱B&b£10 Bdi£14–£14.50 W£86–£89 ⱡ LDO5pm

Lic CTV 5P nc18yrs

[V]

INN Llawnroc Hotel ☎Mevagissey (0726) 843461
Closed Xmas Day & Boxing Day

Pleasant inn with large garden and modern bedrooms in new extension.

6hc (3⇌ 3fl) (2fb) CTV in 2 bedrooms TV in 4 bedrooms [R] ✱B&b£12–£20 W£70–£98 M Lunch £4–£7 Dinner 9.45pm £4–£7

♨ CTV 40P 🚗 🏠

Credit cards [1] [2] [3] [5] [V]

GOUDHURST
Kent
Map **5** TQ73

INN Vine High St ☎(0580) 211261

Small country inn of character with interesting restaurant.

5hc (2⇌) ⋈ ✱B&b£15–£20 Bdi£23–£25.50 Wfr£140 ⱡ Bar lunch 70p–£4 Dinner 10pm £7–£9&alc

CTV 15P

Credit cards [1] [3]

GOUROCK
Strathclyde *Renfrewshire*
Map **10** NS27

GH Claremont 34 Victoria Rd ☎(0475) 31687

Stone-house on hillside overlooking the Clyde Estuary.

6hc (2fb) TV in all bedrooms ✱B&b£10.50 W£73.50 M

♨ CTV 4P

GRAMPOUND
Cornwall
Map **2** SW94

FH Mrs L M Wade **Tregidgeo** *(SW960473)* ☎St Austell (0726) 882450
May–Sep

Comfortably furnished farmhouse in a beautiful, secluded and peaceful setting.

5rm (4hc) (2fb) ⋈ ✱B&b£7–£7.50 Bdi£11–£12 W£73–£79.50 ⱡ LDO10am

CTV 4P 216acres mixed

GRAMPOUND ROAD VILLAGE
Cornwall
Map **2** SW95

INN *Midway* ☎St Austell (0726) 882343
Apr–Oct

4hc (3fb) ⋈ [R] Dinner 6pm

♨ CTV 4P 🚗

GRANDES ROCQUES
Guernsey, Channel Islands
See **Channel Islands**

GRANGE (in Borrowdale)
Cumbria
Map **11** NY21

GH Grange ☎Borrowdale (059684) 251
Mar–Oct

Attractive house of lakeland slate set in its own gardens.

7hc (1⇌ 1fl) (1fb) ⋈ [R] ✱B&b£9.50–£10.75 W£66–£71.50 M

♨ 8P

Credit cards [1] [2] [3]

See advertisement on page 75

GRANGE-OVER-SANDS
Cumbria
Map **7** SD47

GH Corner Beech Methven Ter, Kents Bank Rd ☎(04484) 3088

Bright and cheerful guesthouse with a pleasant front garden.

9hc (2fb) ® B&b£9–£10.50 Bdi£12.50–£14.50 W£82–£92 ⊬ LDO4.30pm

🏠 CTV ⋗

ⓥ

GH Elton Private Hotel Windermere Rd ☎(04484) 2838

A stone-built, traditional-style guesthouse offering good-value accommodation.

10hc (3fb)

CTV 8P

GH Grayrigge Private Hotel Kents Bank Rd ☎(04484) 2345

Large family owned hotel with spacious rooms.

27hc (3⤳) Annexe: 9hc (13fb) CTV in 14 bedrooms ✱B&b£11–£13 Bdi£16–£19 W£112–£140 ⊬

Lic 🏠 CTV 60P 6🐾

GH Thornfield House Kents Bank Rd ☎(04484) 2512

Apr–Oct

A pleasant and comfortable guesthouse with good views over Morecambe Bay.

6hc (2fb) TV in all bedrooms ✖ ®
B&bfr£8.50 Bdifr£12.50 Wfr£80 ⊬ LDO5pm

🏠 6P nc5yrs

Grange-over-Sands
—
Grantown-on-Spey

GRANTOWN-ON-SPEY
Highland *Morayshire*
Map **14**   NJ02

⊢–**GH Dar-Il-Hena** Grant Rd ☎(0479) 2929

Etr–Oct

This well appointed property has a friendly atmosphere, elegant lounge and comfortable bedrooms.

7hc (3fb) B&bfr£8 Bdifr£13.50 Wfr£85 ⊬ LDO7pm

🏠 CTV 10P

GH Dunachton Coppice Court (off Grant Rd) ☎(0479) 2098

Comfortable, well appointed house in a quiet residential area.

8hc (1⤳) (2fb)

Lic 🏠 CTV 10P

GH Dunallan Woodside Av ☎(0479) 2140

May–Nov

Late Victorian house in quiet, residential location with several family bedrooms.

5hc (2fb) LDO4pm

🏠 CTV 5P

⊢–**GH Firhall** ☎(0479) 3097

A secluded, residential location for this house of character with fine woodwork and elaborate ceilings. Comfortable bedrooms and spacious public rooms.

7hc (3fb) ✖ ® B&b£8 Bdi£13 W£85 ⊬ LDO7pm

🏠 CTV 10P

GH Kinross House Woodside Av ☎(0479) 2042

Closed Xmas & New Year

Stone-built house in quiet residential part of town.

6hc (2fb) ® ✱B&bfr£8.30 Bdifr£13 Wfr£89 ⊬ LDO7pm

Lic 🏠 CTV 6P

ⓥ

GH Pines Hotel Woodside Av ☎(0479) 2092

Etr–Sep

Traditional style house with spacious rooms, conveniently situated for shops.

10hc (2fb) ✱B&bfr£8.50 Bdifr£14 Wfr£87.50 ⊬ LDO5pm

CTV 4P

ⓥ

⊢–**GH Ravenscourt** Seafield Av ☎(0479) 2286

Jan–Oct

Offers comfortable and spacious accommodation.

→

6hc (2fb) B&b£7–£7.75 Bdi£11–£12.25 W£70–£80 ⊬ LDO7pm

Lic 🍴 CTV 15P

⊢ **GH Riversdale** Grant Rd ☎(0479) 2648

Detached house with small garden at front and lawn at rear.

7hc (2fb) B&b£7.75–£8 Bdi£12–£12.50 W£80.50–£84 ⊬ LDO6pm

🍴 CTV 8P ♿

[V]

GH Umaria Woodlands Ter ☎(0479) 2104
Closed Nov & Dec

Situated on main road at the south end of town.

8hc (4fb) [R] ✱B&b£8.50 Bdi£13.50 LDO6.30pm

Lic CTV 8P

GRASMERE
Cumbria
Map **11** NY30

GH Beck Steps College St ☎(09665) 348
Mar–Nov

Friendly, family-run guesthouse overlooking green specialising in home-cooked English food.

10hc (2🛁 2🚿) (3fb) 🚫 [R] ✱Bdi£18.50–£19.50 W£124 ⊬ LDO5pm

Lic 🍴 8P nc4yrs

GH Bridge House Hotel Stock Ln ☎(09665) 425
Mar–mid Nov

Lovely village centre house standing within its own gardens beside the river.

12hc (5🛁 1🚿) (1fb) 🚫 [R] B&b£17–£21.50 Bdi£23–£27.50 W£154–£178.50 ⊬ LDO7.30pm

Lic 🍴 CTV 20P

Credit cards [1] [3] [V]

GH Lake View Lake View Dr ☎(09665) 384
Mar–Nov

A comfortable, detached house with lovely gardens leading down to the lake.

6hc (2🚿) [R] ✱B&b£11.50 Bdi£18.50 W£120 ⊬ LDOnoon

CTV 11P nc10yrs

[V]

GH Titteringdales Pye Ln ☎(09665) 439
Apr–1 Nov

A pleasant house in 2½ acres of gardens with good views over the surrounding fells.

7hc (2🚿) ✱B&b£12–£12.50 Bdi£18.50–£19 W£125–£135 ⊬ LDO4pm

Lic 🍴 CTV 8P

GRASSINGTON
North Yorkshire
Map **7** SE06

GH Ashfield House Hotel ☎(0756) 752584
Apr–Oct

Secluded, comfortable 17th century house, offering splendid food.

7hc (1🚿) (2fb) 🚫 [R] ✱B&b£11.60–£14 Bdi£18.60–£21.40 W£123.60–£150.50 ⊬ LDO5.30pm

Lic 🍴 CTV 7P

[V]

GH *Lodge* ☎(0756) 752518
Mar–Oct

Family run house with good furnishings, in village centre.

7hc (1fb) LDO5pm

🍴 CTV 8P nc5yrs

Credit card [3]

GRAVESEND
Kent
Map **5** TQ67

GH Cromer 194 Parrock St ☎(0474) 61935
Closed 24 Dec–2Jan

Victorian corner house with well-furnished bedrooms and tastefully-appointed restaurant.

11hc (1🛁) (3fb) CTV in all bedrooms 🚫 ✱B&b£8.75–£9.50

🍴 CTV 15P nc12yrs

Credit card [3]

GH *Overcliffe Hotel* 15–16 The Overcliffe ☎(0474) 22131

Tastefully decorated hotel with very well-equipped bedrooms and a separate restaurant.

19🚿 CTV in all bedrooms [R]

Lic P

Credit cards [1] [2] [3] [5]

GREAT
Placenames incorporating the word 'Great', such as Gt Malvern and Gt Yarmouth, will be found under the actual placename, *ie* Malvern, Yarmouth.

GREENHEAD
Northumberland
Map **12** NY66

FH Mrs P Staff **Holmhead** *(NY659661)* ☎Gilsland (06972) 402

A traditional Northumbrian farmhouse offering warmth and comfort. The Roman wall runs beneath the house and Thirlwall Castle is behind. ½m N of unclassified road.

4hc (1fb) 🚫 ✱B&b£9.50–£11.50 Bdi£15.50–£17.50 W£93 ⊬ LDO4pm

Lic 🍴 CTV 6P 🏠 solarium 300acres beef & sheep breeding non-working

Credit cards [2] [3] [V]

GRETNA
Dumfries & Galloway *Dumfriesshire*
Map **11** NY36

GH Surrone House Annan Rd ☎(0461) 38341

Nicely appointed former farmhouse with attractive modern bedrooms.

6hc (5🛁 🚿) (4fb) CTV in all bedrooms [R] ✱B&b£13.80–£17.25 Bdi£19.55–£23 W£210 ⊬ LDO8pm

Lic 🍴 CTV 16P 🏠

[V]

INN ***Crossways*** Annan Rd ☎(04613) 465
Tidy little inn with well equipped, compact bedrooms.
6🚿 CTV in all bedrooms ✈ [R] LDO9.45pm
♨ 30P
Credit cards [1] [3] [4]

GRETNA GREEN
Dumfries & Galloway *Dumfriesshire*
Map **11** NY36

GH Greenlaw ☎Gretna (0461) 38361
Compact homely villa. The majority of bedrooms are small.
8hc (1fb) ✱B&b£8.50–£9 Bdi£12.50–£14 W£84–£93.50 L̸ LDO6pm
♨ CTV 8P 1🚗 ⌂
[V]

GUERNSEY
See **Channel Islands**

GUILDFORD
Surrey
Map **4** SU94

GH Blanes Court Hotel Albury Rd ☎(0483) 573171
Closed Xmas wk
Quietly situated, elegant accommodation, with well equipped bedrooms and homely atmosphere.
21hc (1🛁 10🚿) (2fb) CTV in all bedrooms [R] ✱B&b£16–£21 W£96–£126 M̸
Lic ♨ CTV 20P ⌂
Credit cards [1] [2] [3] [V]

GH Quinns Hotel 78 Epsom Rd (Guestaccom) ☎(0483) 60422
A fine Victorian house, stylishly decorated and furnished.
10hc (3🛁 4🚿) (2fb) CTV in all bedrooms [R] B&b£24–£35 W£144–£210 M̸
Lic ♨ 14P
Credit cards [1] [2] [3] [5] [V]

GUNNISLAKE
Cornwall
Map **2** SX47

GH Hingston House St Anns Chapel ☎Tavistock (0822) 832468
A country house built originally for the captain of the local tin mines, now providing comfortable accommodation and friendly service.
8hc (1🛁 1🚿) (1fb) [R] ✱B&b£11–£13.50 Bdi£18.75–£21 W£119–£133.25 L̸ LDO8.30pm
Lic ♨ CTV 10P ⌂
Credit cards [1] [3] [V]

GWYSTRE
Powys
Map **3** SO06

FH Mrs M A Davies **Bryn Nicholas** *(SJ075658)* (½m E on N side of A44) ☎Penybont (059787) 447
Apr–Oct
Cosy farmhouse accommodation in this convenient touring location.
3hc [R] ✱B&bfr£8 Bdifr£13 Wfr£84 L̸ LDO4pm
♨ CTV 6P 161acres beef sheep
[V]

FH Mrs C Drew **Gwystre** *(SO070656)* ☎Penybont (059787) 316
Mar–Oct
Modestly appointed small farmhouse.
2rm [R] ✱B&b£7.50–£7.75 Bdi£12.50 Wfr£87 L̸ LDO4pm
CTV P̸ 160acres beef sheep mixed
[V]

HALFORD
Warwickshire
Map **4** SP24

INN Halford Bridge Fosse Way ☎Stratford-upon-Avon (0789) 740382
Cheerful, character-inn, built of local Cotswold stone, on Fosse Way. →

5rm (4hc) (1fb) CTV in all bedrooms
✳B&bfr£13 Bdifr£21.50 Wfr£129.50 ⌇
Lunch £3.50–£7.75&alc High tea £3.50–
£7.75&alc Dinner 9.45pm£3.50–£7.75&alc
60P

Credit card ① ⓥ

HALFWAY HOUSE
Shropshire
Map **7**   SJ31

FH Mrs E Morgan **Willows** *(SJ342115)*
☎(074378) 233 (due to change to
Shrewsbury (0743) 884233)
Mar–Oct

*Farm house in pretty garden, well situated
for those travelling to Wales. It is
surrounded by Long Mountain and
Middlebar Hills.*

3rm (1hc) (1fb) ✗ ✳B&b£7.50–£8.50
Bdi£10–£11 W£70–£80 ⌇ LDO4pm
🍴 TV 10P 35acres arable beef

HALIFAX
West Yorkshire
Map **7**   SE02

INN Stump Cross Stump Cross ☎(0422)
66004
rs Xmas Day

*Large period building beside the A58 1m
from Halifax in the attractive Shibden
Valley. 1m E A58/A6036 junction.*

Halford
—
Haltwhistle

12hc (6⇄) (1fb) CTV in 6 bedrooms TV in
2 bedrooms ✳B&b£12–£24 Bdi£17–£34
Lunch £3.50–£5.50&alc Dinner 9.45pm
£3.50–£5.50&alc
🍴 40P nc5yrs

HALSTOCK
Dorset
Map **3**   ST50

— Recommended —

FH Mr W Budd **Old Mill** *(ST530086)*
Higher Halstock ☎Corscombe
(093589) 278
Mar–Oct

*Comfortable 17th-century mill with
friendly atmosphere and interesting
food, in peaceful rural setting. 2m W
unclass rd.*

4⇄ (1fb) CTV in all bedrooms ®
B&b£14–£23 Bdi£21.50–£30.50
W£140.70–£197.40 ⌇ LDO9pm
Lic 🍴 CTV 10P nc5yrs 10acres
mixed

Credit cards ① ③

HALTWHISTLE
Northumberland
Map **12**   NY76

GH Ashcroft ☎(0498) 20213
Closed 30 Dec–6 Jan

*Carefully modernised former Victorian
vicarage with spacious rooms and tranquil
atmosphere.*

8hc (3fb) ✗ in 1 bedroom ✗ ✳B&b£9–
£10 Bdi£13–£14 W£78–£84 ⌇ LDO3pm
CTV 14P ♨
ⓥ

— Recommended —

FH Mrs J Brown **Broomshaw Hill**
(NY706654) Willia Rd ☎(0498) 20866

*Although close to the town centre,
this 18th-century, stone-built
farmhouse is in an attractive rural
setting just 1 mile from Hadrian's
Wall. It has been enlarged and
modernised over the years but still
retains much of its original character.
Comfortable accommodation
includes an impressive sitting room,
elegant dining room and spacious
bedrooms.*

3hc (1fb) TV in 1 bedroom ®
✳B&b£8.50–£9.50 Bdi£12.50–£13.50
W£80–£85 ⌇
🍴 CTV 4P 2🐎 7acres livestock
horses
ⓥ

FH Mrs M Dawson **Park Burnfoot**
(NY 687619) Featherstone Pk ☎(0498)
20378
May–Sep

Attractive stone-built farmhouse of 1740
situated on the banks of the South Tyne.

2hc (1fb) ✻ ® ✽B&b£8–£8.50
CTV 3P nc3yrs 220acres dairy mixed
Ⓥ

FH Mrs J I Laidlow **Ald White Craig**
(NY713649) Shield Hill ☎(0498) 20565
Mar–Oct

Modernised, croft-style farmhouse, with
bright, modern bedrooms but retaining an
olde worlde atmosphere in the
comfortable lounge.

3hc (1⇌ 1🚻) CTV in all bedrooms ✻ ®
B&b£9.50–£13 Bdifr£15 Wfr£103 M
LDOnoon
🛏 3P nc7yrs 60acres mixed
Ⓥ

HALWELL
Devon
Map **3**   SX75

GH Stanborough Hundred Hotel
☎East Allington (054852) 236
Mar–5 Jan

6hc (2⇌) Annexe: 1⇌ (4fb) ✼ in 1
bedroom ✻ ® B&b£14–£17 Bdi£22–£25
W£115–£135 ⅃LDO9pm
Lic 🛏 CTV 10P
Ⓥ

HAMBLEDEN
Buckinghamshire
Map **4**   SU78

INN Stag & Huntsman ☎Henley-on-
Thames (0491) 571227

Small country inn offering simple but
comfortable accommodation and warm,
informal atmosphere.

3hc ✻ ®
🛏 P 🐾 nc18yrs
Credit cards ① ③

HAMILTON
Strathclyde *Lanarkshire*
Map **11**   NS75

Haltwhistle
—
Harlech

FH Mr R Hamilton **East Drumloch**
(NS678521) Chapelton (3m SW off A723)
☎Chapelton (03573) 236

Large stone-built farmhouse with a
modern, well-furnished interior.
Signposted from A723 and A726.

3rm (1hc) (2fb) ✽B&b£6.50 Bdi£9.50
Wfr£66.50 ⅃ LDO9am
🛏 CTV 10P 260acres beef mixed

HANLEY CASTLE
Hereford & Worcester
Map **3**   SO84

Recommended

FH Mr & Mrs Addison
Old Parsonage *(SO840413)*
☎Hanley Swan (0684) 310124
Closed 11 Dec–2 Jan

If you want the comfort and amenities
of a hotel, combined with personal
service, then this Georgian house
should fit the bill. Mr and Mrs
Addison offer three extremely
comfortable bedrooms with private
facilities, interesting and varied
meals and a good wine list. Fly
fishing and shooting can be arranged
or just relax in the 1½ acres of
grounds.

3hc (2⇌) (1fb) TV in 1 bedroom
✽B&b£13.75–£15.50 Bdi£23.25–£25
W£162.75–£175 ⅃
Lic 🛏 CTV 6P nc6yrs 1½acres non-
working
Credit card ② Ⓥ

HANMER
Clwyd
Map **7**   SJ44

FH C Sumner & F Williams-Lee **Buck**
(SJ435424) ☎(094874) 339

On A525 Whitchurch (7m) to Wrexham
(9m) road this accommodation, for non-
smokers, is an ideal touring base. Good
cooking.

4hc ✻ ✽B&b£10–£10.50 Bdi£17–£17.50
W£112–£115 ⅃
🛏 CTV 12P 8acres small-holding
Ⓥ

HARBERTON
Devon
Map **3**   SX75

FH Mrs I P Steer **Preston** *(SX777587)*
☎Totnes (0803) 862235
Apr–Oct

Old farmhouse on outskirts of quaint and
attractive village. Totnes about 2¼m.

3hc (1fb) ✻ ® ✽B&b£10 Bdi£14.50 W£95
⅃ (W only Aug)

CTV 3P nc5yrs 250acres dairy mixed
Ⓥ

FH Mr R Rose **Tristford** *(SX775587)*
☎Totnes (0803) 862418

Charming house with 'olde worlde'
atmosphere. Good centre for touring the
coast between Plymouth and Torbay.

3hc ✻
🛏 CTV 4🐾 150acres mixed

HARDSTOFT
Derbyshire
Map **8**   SK46

INN Shoulder of Mutton ☎Chesterfield
(0246) 850276

A much-extended inn, originally a
farmhouse with a tap room, dating from
1660. Well-equipped accommodation and
extensive facilities for functions.

7rm (6hc 2🚻) (1fb) CTV in all bedrooms ®
✽B&bfr£25 Bdifr£32 LDO9.30pm
🛏 150P

HARLECH
Gwynedd
Map **6**   SH53

GH Gwrach Ynys Country Guest House
Ynys, Talsarnau ☎(0766) 780742

Beautifully restored Edwardian country-
house situated in own grounds, close to
Harlech.

7hc (6⇌) (3fb) ® ✽B&b£11 Bdi£16.50
W£77 M LDO6pm
CTV 8P nc2yrs

FH Mrs E A Jones **Tyddyn Gwynt** *(SH601302)* ☎(0766) 780298

2½m off B4573 (A496).

4rm (3hc) (2fb) ✱B&bfr£8 Bdifr£11 Wfr£75 ₭

CTV 6P 30acres sheep smallholding

[V]

INN Rum Hole Hotel ☎(0766) 780477

Two-storey inn at lower end of village.

8hc (3🚿) (6fb) CTV in 3 bedrooms [R] ✱B&b£10–£15 W£60–£90 ₥ Bar lunch 50p–£4 LDO 9pm

CTV 25P

[V]

Harlech — Harrogate

8hc (3🛁 4🚿) Annexe: 8hc (1🛁 5🚿) (4fb) CTV in all bedrooms ✖ [R] ✱B&b£13–£16 Bdi£21–£24 W£125–£144 ₭ LDO2pm

Lic ♨ CTV 18P

Credit cards [1] [3] [V]

HARROGATE

North Yorkshire
Map **8** SE35

GH *Abbey Lodge* 31 Ripon Rd ☎(0423) 69712

Smart, stylish house with very comfortable bedrooms and pleasant public areas.

8hc (1🛁 4🚿) (1fb) ✖ [R] LDOnoon

Lic ♨ CTV 14P 2🚗 ⌂

GH Alexa House & Stable Cottages 26 Ripon Rd ☎(0423) 501988
Closed Xmas wk

Guesthouse of distinction with bedrooms of a very high quality.

GH Alphen Lodge 2 Esplanade ☎(0423) 502882
Closed Xmas

Imaginatively decorated town house with elevated terrace garden.

11hc (6🛁 1🚿) (2fb) CTV in all bedrooms [R] ✱B&b£16.50–£30 Bdi£23.50–£37 Wfr£147 ₭ LDO7.30pm

Lic ♨ 11P

Credit cards [1] [2] [3] [V]

GH Ashley House Hotel 36–40 Franklin Rd ☎(0423) 507474
Closed Xmas

Nicely appointed combination of three town houses with spacious public rooms.

18hc (3🚿) (2fb) TV in all bedrooms ✖ [R] ✱B&b£11–£13 W£70–£84 ₥

Lic ♨ CTV 9P nc3yrs

Credit cards [1] [3] [V]

GH Aston Hotel Franklin Mount ☎(0423) 64262

Smart and stylish hotel in residential area.

16hc (12🚿) (1fb) ⊬ in 4 bedrooms CTV in 6 bedrooms TV in 10 bedrooms [R] ✱B&b£11–£14.50 Bdi£17–£20.50 W£101.50–£113.40 ₭ LDO4pm

Lic ♨ CTV 10P 1🚗

GH Aygarth 11 Harlow Moor Dr ☎(0423) 68705

Simple and homely accommodation overlooking Valley Gardens.

7hc (3fb) CTV in 5 bedrooms TV in 2 bedrooms [R] ✱B&b£12–£15 Bdi£18–£21 W£126–£147 ₭ LDO4pm

♨ CTV ₱

[V]

GH Cavendish Hotel 3 Valley Dr ☎(0423) 509637

Conveniently placed guesthouse with nicely equipped bedrooms.

11hc (1🛁 9🚿) (5fb) CTV in all bedrooms [R] ✱B&b£14.50–£20.50 Bdi£19–£25 W£130–£175 ₭ LDO6.30pm

Lic ♨ CTV ₱

Credit cards [1] [2] [3] [5] [V]

GH Coppice Hotel 9 Studley Rd ☎(0423) 69626

A stone-built town house in a quiet area close to local facilities and Conference Centre.

6hc (1🛁) (3fb) TV in 1 bedroom [R] ✻B&b£9.50 Bdi£13.50–£15 W£91 ⅊ LDO4.30pm

♨ CTV P̸

Credit card [5]

GH Craigleigh 6 West Grove Rd ☎(0423) 64064
rs Xmas & New Year

Charming and cosy Victorian town house close to the Conference Centre.

6hc (1fb) CTV in 1 bedroom TV in 1 bedroom [R] ✻B&b£8.50–£10.50 Bdi£15.50–£17.50 W£108.50–£122.50 ⅊

♨ CTV 2P 🏠

[V]

GH Croft Hotel 42–46 Franklin Rd ☎(0423) 63326

Spacious public rooms well appointed accommodation are offered in this hotel close to town centre.

16hc (3🚿) (7fb) CTV in all bedrooms [R] ✻B&b£13.50–£16 Bdi£21–£23.50 W£133–£150.50 ⅊ LDOnoon

Lic ♨ CTV 14P 🏠

GH Garden House Hotel 14 Harlow Moor Dr ☎(0423) 503059

8hc (6🛁) CTV in all bedrooms [R] B&b£15–£17 Bdi£21–£23 LDOnoon

Lic ♨ P

Credit card [1]

Harrogate

GH Gillmore Hotel 98 Kings Rd ☎(0423) 503699

An imaginative and well-organised conversion of two terraced houses.

25hc (6🛁 6🚿) (9fb) CTV in 10 bedrooms ✻B&b£10.50–£12.50 Bdi£15.25–£17.25 W£106.75–£120.75 (W only Oct–Apr)

Lic ♨ CTV 20P snooker

[V]

GH Grafton Hotel 1–3 Franklin Mount ☎(0423) 508491
Closed Xmas & New Year

Stone town houses, restored and providing comfortable modern accommodation.

17hc (1🛁 10🚿) (1fb) CTV in 11 bedrooms ✖ [R] ✻B&b£11–£15.75 Bdi£17–£21.75 W£110–£150 ⅊ LDO4pm

Lic ♨ CTV P̸

Credit cards [1] [2] [3] [V]

GH *Kingsway* 36 Kings Rd ☎(0423) 62179

Three-storey town house offering modest, comfortable accommodation opposite Conference Centre.

7hc (1🛁 6🚿) (1fb) LDO11.55am

Lic ♨ CTV 2P 1🚗

GH Lamont House 12 St Mary's Walk ☎(0423) 67143
Closed Xmas

Late Victorian town house near town centre and Spa Baths.

8hc (2fb) ✻B&b£10.50–£12 Bdi£16.50–£18 LDO6pm

Lic ♨ CTV P̸ 🏠

GH *Manor Hotel* 3 Clarence Dr ☎(0423) 503916

Well planned bedrooms and spacious public areas in a Victorian stone building with interesting architectural features. Near town centre.

14hc (8🛁 6🚿) (1fb) CTV in all bedrooms ✖ [R] LDO8.30pm

Lic ♨ CTV 8P

GH *Moorland Private Hotel* 34 Harlow Moor Dr ☎(0423) 64596
Closed Dec

Victorian town house, overlooking Valley Gardens, having homely accommodation.

11hc (1🛁 5🚿) (2fb) [R] LDO7pm

Lic ♨ CTV 3P

GH Mowbray House 18 Harlow Moor Drive ☎(0423) 63350

A sturdy Victorian town house, overlooking Valley Gardens, with simply furnished bedrooms. →

8hc (2fb) CTV in all bedrooms ✱B&b£8–£12 Bdi£12.50–£16.50 Wfr£105 ⅃ LDO6pm

Lic 🏴 CTV ⚡

GH Norman Hotel 41 Valley Dr ☎(0423) 502171

Tall town house overlooking Valley Gardens with small comfortable lounge bar and attractive dining room.

18hc (4⇆ 3🏴) (4fb) ✱B&b£14.50–£16.50 Bdi£21–£23 W£135–£140 ⅃ LDOnoon

Lic CTV ⚡

Ⓥ

GH Oakbrae 3 Springfield Av ☎(0423) 67682

Closed Xmas

Small, picturesque semi, near Conference Centre, with well-proportioned lounge and breakfast room, and pleasant bedrooms.

6hc (1⇆ 1🏴) (2fb) CTV in 2 bedrooms Ⓡ ✱B&b£10.50–£12 Bdi£16–£18 Wfr£105 ⅃ LDO5pm

🏴 CTV 6P

GH Prince's Hotel 7 Granby Rd ☎(0423) 883469

Victorian house of style and character offering comfortable accommodation.

8hc (1⇆ 2🏴) (1fb) ✂ in 1 bedroom CTV in all bedrooms 🗙 Ⓡ B&b£10–£17.50 Bdi£16–£23.50 W£105–£152 ⅃ LDO9am

---

Harrogate

Lic 🏴 CTV ⚡ nc3yrs

Ⓥ

GH Roan 90 Kings Rd ☎(0423) 503087

Closed Xmas

Town house near Conference Centre with charming bedrooms and spacious public areas.

7hc (3🏴) (1fb) 🗙 Ⓡ ✱B&bfr£10 Bdifr£15.50 LDO4.30pm

🏴 CTV ⚡ nc7yrs

Ⓥ

GH *Rosedale* 86 Kings Rd ☎(0423) 66630

Three-storey Victorian house with good bedrooms, a cosy bar and separate lounge; near Conference Centre.

7hc (1🏴) (2fb) 🗙 Ⓡ LDO4pm

Lic 🏴 CTV 6P 1🚘 nc5yrs

GH *Shelbourne* 78 Kings Rd ☎(0423) 504390

Closed Xmas wk

Good, clean, comfortable, town centre guesthouse.

7hc (2fb) Ⓡ LDO2pm

Lic 🏴 CTV 1P

Credit card ③

GH Strayend 56 Dragon View, Skipton Rd ☎(0423) 61700

An interesting house with bright, cheerful bedrooms and welcoming staff.

6🏴 (1fb) TV in 2 bedrooms Ⓡ ✱B&b£11.50–£13.50 Bdi£16–£17.50 LDO9am

🏴 CTV 6P

GH Wharfedale House 28 Harlow Moor Dr ☎(0423) 522233

Closed Dec

Large town house overlooking Valley Gardens. Wholefood dishes and vegetarian breakfasts are available.

7hc (1⇆ 6🏴) (1fb) CTV in all bedrooms Ⓡ ✱B&b£13.50–£16 Bdi£19.60–£21.50 W£121.20–£134.50 ⅃ LDO8.30pm

Lic 🏴 3P nc3yrs

Ⓥ

GH Woodhouse 7 Spring Grove ☎(0423) 60081

Closed 24 Dec–2 Jan

Stylish Victorian house with lovely dining room featuring co-ordinated crockery and decor.

9hc (3⇆ 3🏴) (2fb) CTV in all bedrooms 🗙 Ⓡ ✱B&b£12–£13 Bdi£19–£20 W£117.60–£124.90 ⅃ LDOnoon

Lic CTV 2P

Ⓥ

HARROP FOLD
Lancashire
Map **7** SD74

─ Recommended ─

FH Mr & Mrs P Wood **Harrop Fold Country Farmhouse Hotel**
(SD746492) (Guestaccom) ☎Bolton-by-Bowland (02007) 600 Telex No 635562

A 17th century Lancashire longhouse, situated in peaceful surroundings, lovingly furnished with antiques by Peter and Victoria Wood. Good home cooking makes the most of local produce and recipes. The lounge and dining room are quite delightful and the bedrooms are provided with thoughtful extras.

6hc (4⇄) Annexe: 1⇄ 1🛏 CTV in all bedrooms ✖ ® ✱B&b£16–£20 Bdi£26–£30 W£95–£133 ℳ
Lic ⚒ 15P nc 280acres sheep
Credit cards ① ③ Ⓥ

HARROW
Gt London
London plan **4**   B5 *(pages 246–247)*

GH Central Hotel 6 Hindes Rd ☎01-427 0893

Edwardian house in residential area of town centre.

Harrop Fold
─
Harwich

9hc (2🛏) (3fb) CTV in all bedrooms ✖
✱B&b£18.50–£28 W£129–£196 ℳ
⚒ CTV 9P
Credit cards ① ② ③
See advertisement on page 190

GH Hindes Hotel 8 Hindes Rd ☎01-427 7468

Homely and nicely appointed hotel under personal supervision of the owners.

13hc (1🛏) (2fb) CTV in all bedrooms ✖ ®
✱B&b£14–£19.50
⚒ CTV 6P
Credit cards ① ③

GH Kempsford House Hotel 21–23 St Johns Rd ☎01-427 4983
Closed 2 wks Xmas

Family-run private hotel offering basic but comfortable accommodation.

30hc (8🛏) (6fb) CTV in 18 bedrooms TV in 12 bedrooms ✖ ✱B&b£16.10–£31.05
W£112.70–£217.35 ℳ
Lic ⚒ CTV 30P
Credit cards ① ③ Ⓥ

GH *Lindal Hotel* 2 Hindes Rd ☎01-863 3164

Small and welcoming family-run guesthouse with simple accommodation.

9hc (1🛏) Annexe: 4hc (2⇄ 2🛏) (3fb) CTV in all bedrooms ✖ LDO8.30pm
Lic ⚒ CTV 20P
Credit card ③

HARTLAND
Devon
Map **2**   SS22

GH Fosfelle ☎(02374) 273

Former manor house dating from the 17th century amidst open countryside.

7hc (2fb) ✱B&b£9.50–£11.50 Bdi£15–£17 W£86.50–£96.50 ℒ LDO9pm
Lic CTV 20P ⋙ snooker

HARWICH
Essex
Map **5**   TM23

GH Hotel Continental 28/29 Marine Pde, Dovercourt Bay ☎(0255) 503454

Small private hotel run by friendly and hospitable owners.

15hc (5🛏) (5fb) CTV in all bedrooms
B&b£14–£17 Bdi£20–£23 LDO8.30pm
Lic ⚒ 6🚗
Credit cards ① ③

HASTINGS & ST LEONARDS
East Sussex
Map **5** TQ80

GH Argyle 32 Cambridge Gdns ☎(0424) 421294
Closed Xmas
Homely and well situated guesthouse near the sea front and local amenities.
8hc (2🚪) (3fb) ✗ ⓡ ✱B&b£8.50–£10.50 Bdi£12.50–£14.50 W£80.50–£94.50 ½ LDOnoon
🍴CTV 🅿 nc5yrs

GH *Chimes Hotel* 1 St Matthews Gdns, Silverhill, St Leonards (Guestaccom) ☎(0424) 434041

Hastings & St Leonards

Relaxing Edwardian house with good home cooking and friendly proprietors.
9hc (2🚪 2🚪) (2fb) CTV in 9 bedrooms ✗ ⓡ B&b£11–£13 Bdi£18–£20 W£119–£136 ½ S% LDO2pm
Lic 🍴 CTV 🅿
Ⓥ

GH Eagle House 12 Pevensey Rd, St Leonards ☎(0424) 430535

Situated in residential area, offering comfortable modern accommodation and period bar-lounge.
15hc (2🚪 10🚪) (2fb) CTV in all bedrooms ⓡ ✱B&b£16–£19 Bdi£26–£29 W£154–£203 ½ LDO8pm
Lic 🍴 14P nc5yrs
Credit cards ① ② ③

GH Gainsborough Hotel 5 Carlisle Pde ☎(0424) 434010
Well-maintained sea-front house with modern well-equipped bedrooms and comfortable public rooms.

190

12hc (3⇌ 5⋔) (2fb) CTV in all bedrooms
® ✱B&b£10.50–£14 Bdi£15.30–£18.30
W£104–£131.50 ⏴ LDO9pm
Lic ⅏ ⏀

ⓥ

GH Harbour Lights 20 Cambridge Gdns
☎(0424) 423424
Closed 4 days Xmas

*Small, conveniently situated town centre
guesthouse.*

8hc (1fb) CTV in all bedrooms ✖ ®
✱B&bfr£9.50 Wfr£60 ⋈
⅏ CTV ⏀

GH Tower 28 Tower Rd West, St
Leonards ☎(0424) 427217

*A quiet and very comfortable house well
away from the sea front. Unrestricted
street parking.*

9hc (1⋔) (2fb) ® ✱B&b£8–£9.50 Bdi£12–
£13.50 W£72–£81 ⏴ LDO4pm
⅏ CTV ⏀ ⚗

ⓥ

GH Waldorf Hotel 4 Carlisle Pde
☎(0424) 422185

*Homely, friendly accommodation with
nicely appointed restaurant and lounge.*

12hc (1⇌ 2⋔) (4fb) CTV in all bedrooms
✖ ® ✱B&b£10–£15 Bdi£15–£20
W£92.50–£106.50 ⏴ LDO6.30pm
Lic ⅏ CTV ⏀

ⓥ

HASWELL PLOUGH
Co Durham
Map **12**   NZ34

GH The Gables Front St ☎091-526 2982

*A comfortable house with very friendly
proprietors. Dinner, in the public
restaurant, can be especially
recommended.*

4hc (2fb) CTV in all bedrooms ✖
B&b£11.50–£12.50 W£75–£90 ⋈
LDO10.30pm
Lic ⅏ 20P
See advertisement on page 146

HATHERLEIGH
Devon
Map **2**   SS50

INN Bridge Bridge St ☎Okehampton
(0837) 810357

4hc (1fb) ® ✱B&b£10.50–£13.50 Lunch
£6.95–£7.50 Dinner 9.30pm £7.50&alc
⅏ CTV 20P nc5yrs

ⓥ

HATHERSAGE
Derbyshire
Map **8**   SK28

FH Mrs T C Wain **Highlow Hall**
(SK219802) ☎Hope Valley (0433) 50393
Apr–Oct

*16th-century house of character with well-
furnished interior in isolated position
south of Hathersage.*

Hastings & St Leonards
—
Hawkshead

6hc (2fb) ® ✱B&bfr£12.50 Bdifr£19
W£126 ⏴
Lic CTV 12P 900acres sheep

HATTON
Warwickshire
Map **4**   SP26

─── Recommended ───

FH Mrs S M Fishwick **Northleigh**
(SP225693) Five Ways Rd ☎Haseley
Knob (092687) 203

*This farmhouse offers sincere
hospitality combined with a very high
standard of food and
accommodation. Sylvia Fishwick
serves superb breakfasts (which set
you up for the day), and dinners
prepared to suit individual
requirements. The house is set in
mature gardens and bedrooms have
views across open farmland where
Mrs Fishwick keeps rare breeds of
sheep.*

4hc (2⇌ 2⋔) CTV in all bedrooms ®
✱B&b£14–£20 Bdi£21.50–£27.50
⅏ CTV 5P 16acres sheep

ⓥ

See advertisement on page 396

HAUGH OF URR
Dumfries & Galloway *Kirkcudbrightshire*
Map **11**   NX86

FH Mrs G J MacFarlane **Markfast**
(NX817682) ☎(055666) 220

*A comfortable house offering a nice mix of
traditional and modern, spacious
bedrooms. 1m E of village.*

3hc (2fb) ✖ ® ✱B&bfr£8 Bdifr£12 Wfr£84
⏴ LDO4pm
CTV 3P 140acres mixed

HAVERFORDWEST
Dyfed
Map **2**   SM91

GH Elliotts Hill Hotel Camrose Rd
☎(0437) 2383

*Comfortable accommodation in property
situated in its own grounds.*

18hc (3fb) CTV in 2 bedrooms TV in 1
bedroom ® in 3 bedrooms LDO9pm
Lic ⅏ CTV 25P 2 ⚗ ⚗ ⏀hard ⏀
Credit card ③

HAWES
North Yorkshire
Map **7**   SD88

GH Rookhurst Georgian Country Hotel
West End, Gayle ☎(09697) 454

*Large Georgian house with lots of
character in quiet Pennine village.*

6hc (1fb) CTV in 1 bedroom TV in 5
bedrooms ✖ ® LDO7pm
Lic ⅏ 8P ⚗

HAWKSHEAD
Cumbria
Map **7**   SD39

GH Greenbank Hotel ☎(09666) 497
Mar–Nov

*Charming and friendly little hotel in 17th
century former farmhouse.*

9hc (2⋔) (1fb) ✖ ® ✱B&b£13–£14
Bdi£17–£21 W£119–£133 ⏴ LDO5pm
Lic ⅏ CTV 13P nc12yrs

ⓥ

GH Highfield House Hotel Hawkshead
Hill ☎(09666) 344

*Delightful lakeland house with spacious
rooms.*

12hc (3⇌) (3fb) CTV in 3 bedrooms
LDO6.30pm
Lic ⅏ CTV 15P

GH Ivy House ☎(09666) 204
15 Mar–9 Nov

Attractive, well furnished Georgian house.

6hc (1⇌ 2⋔) Annexe: 5hc (4fb) ®
B&b£11–£13 Bdi£17–£19 W£98–£112 ⏴
S% LDO5pm
Lic CTV 14P

ⓥ

GH Rough Close Country House
☎(09666) 370
Apr–Oct rs Mar

*Fine house overlooking Esthwaite Water,
comfortably furnished and having good
home cooking.*

6hc (2fb) ✖ ® ✱B&b£12.50 Bdi£19.50–
£20.50 W£129.50 ⏴ LDO6pm
Lic ⅏ CTV 12P nc5yrs

ⓥ

GH Summer Hill Cottage Hawkshead
Hill ☎(09666) 311

*17th-century country residence
transformed into comfortable and friendly
little hotel, serving good home cooking.*

7hc (3⋔) (3fb) CTV in 6 bedrooms ✖ ®
B&b£11–£14 Bdi£18–£21 W£113–£133 ⏴
LDO7pm
Lic ⅏ 10P nc8yrs

ⓥ

INN King's Arms Hotel ☎(09666) 372

*16th-century inn with oak beams and
open fire, overlooking the village square.*

7hc (2fb) CTV in all bedrooms ®
✱B&b£10–£16 W£76–£81 ⋈ Lunch £2–£6
Dinner 9pm£2–£12
⅏ ⏀ ⚗

ⓥ

INN Queen's Head Hotel ☎(09666) 271
rs mid–end Dec

*Charming 17th-century inn with beams
and oak panelling, particularly noted for
its good food.* ⟶

9hc (1🛁) (2fb) 🚫🐕 ✱B&b£16–£26 Bar lunch £4alc Dinner 9pm £10alc

♨ CTV 🚫🅿 🚫🚌 nc10yrs

Credit cards [1] [2] [3] [4] [5] [V]

HAWNBY
North Yorkshire
Map **8** SE58

INN Hawnby Hotel ☎Bilsdale (04396) 202

A stone-built country inn of some age and character standing on a hillside position in the centre of an unspoilt village in the North York Moors.

4🛁 CTV in all bedrooms [R] ✱B&b£19 Bdi£25 W£154 Ⱡ Bar lunch 80p–£3.50 Dinner 8pm £8.50

♨ 8P ⛳

[V]

HAWORTH
West Yorkshire
Map **7** SE03

GH Ferncliffe Hebden Rd ☎(0535) 43405

Modern style house/restaurant situated in elevated position overlooking the Worth valley.

6🚿 (1fb) CTV in all bedrooms 🚫🐕 [R] ✱B&b£13.50–£17.50 Bdi£18.75–£22.75 W£131.25–£159.25 Ⱡ LDO9.30pm

Lic ♨ CTV 12P

Credit cards [3] [5] [V]

HAYFIELD
Derbyshire
Map **7** SK08

INN Sportsman Kinder Rd ☎New Mills (0663) 42118

Traditional country inn, with well-furnished, modern bedrooms, in valley of the River Set on the approach to Kinder Scout.

7hc (5🚿) (1fb) CTV in all bedrooms [R] ✱B&b£13.50–£18.50 Bdi£20–£35 Lunch £5–£7&alc High tea £2.50–£5 Dinner 10.30pm £5–£7&alc

♨

Credit cards [1] [3] [V]

HAY-ON-WYE
Powys
Map **3** SO24

GH York House Hardwick Rd, Cusop (1m SE in England) ☎(0497) 820705

Comfortable, reasonably priced accommodation in large Victorian house in extensive gardens with views of Black Mountains.

6hc (1fb) ✱B&b£9–£11.50 Bdi£14–£17.50 W£88.20–£110.25 Ⱡ LDO5pm

♨ CTV 8P

[V]

FH Mrs J Harris **Crossway** *(SO216459)* Clyro (1¼m N off A438 at Clyro) ☎(0497) 820567
Mar–Sep

Small farm situated in the hills in quiet and peaceful surroundings.

2rm (1fb) 🚫🐕 ✱B&b£7.50 Bdi£11 Wfr£75 Ⱡ LDO10am

CTV 6P 3🚗 nc5yrs 50acres mixed

[V]

HAZLEHEAD
South Yorkshire
Map **7** SE10

INN Flouch ☎Barnsley (0226) 762037
Closed Xmas Day

Large country inn on the crossroads of the A628/A616 in a rural semi moorland area. Very good accommodation with inviting bars and a separate dining room.

5hc (4🛁 1🚿) (2fb) CTV in all bedrooms [R] ✱B&b£17.50 Lunch £2.80–£5.35&alc Dinner 10pm£11alc

♨ 50P

Credit card [1]

HEACHAM
Norfolk
Map **9** TF63

GH St Annes 53 Neville Rd ☎(0485) 70021
Mar–Oct

4rm (3hc) Annexe: 2 🚿 (1fb) CTV in 2 bedrooms B&b£9.50–£12.50 W£64.75–£84 M̸

♨ CTV 6P

HEASLEY MILL
Devon
Map **3** SS73

GH Heasley House ☎North Molton (05984) 213
Closed Jan

Georgian style building, full of atmosphere and antiques, overlooking mill stream.

10hc (3🛁 3🚿) ✱B&b£9.50–£10.50 Bdi£15.20–£16.20 W£99–£106 Ⱡ LDO6pm

Lic ♨ CTV 11P

[V]

HEDDON'S MOUTH
Devon
Map **3** SS64

INN Hunters ☎Parracombe (05983) 230

10hc (8🛁) (1fb) CTV in all bedrooms [R] ✱B&b£16–£18 W£172–£186.50 Ⱡ Bar lunch £1.95–£4 LDO9pm

♨ CTV 400P nc5yrs ⛳ snooker

Credit cards [1] [3] [5]

HELSBY
Cheshire
Map **7** SJ47

GH Poplars Private Hotel 130 Chester Rd ☎(09282) 3433
Closed 25–31 Dec

Large detached house in own grounds.

6hc (2fb) TV in all bedrooms 🚫🐕 ✱B&b£10–£13 W£63–£84 M̸

♨ CTV 10P

HELSTON
Cornwall
Map **2** SW62

Within a short radius of this town there are AA-listed farmhouses at the following locations: (see appropriate gazetteer entry for full details) **Coverack Bridges & Trenear**

GH Hillside Godolphin Rd ☎(0326) 574788

Small stone-built residence, a few minutes walk from town centre.

7hc (3fb) 🚫🐕 ✱B&b£7.50–£8.50 Bdi£10.50–£11.50 W£73.50–£80.50 Ⱡ LDOam

Lic ♨ CTV 6P

GH Strathallan Monument Rd ☎(0326) 573683

On the edge of town, a recently extended, Georgian house, with friendly atmosphere.

7hc (3🚿) (2fb) CTV in all bedrooms [R] ✱B&bfr£7.50 Bdifr£13

CTV 7P

GH Wheal Tor Hotel 29 Godolphin Rd ☎(03265) 61211

Situated on a main road, two minutes walk from the town centre.

8hc (1🚿) (2fb) CTV in 5 bedrooms ✱B&b£8.50–£12 Bdi£12.50–£16.50 Wfr£87.50 Ⱡ LDO7pm

Lic ♨ CTV 🚫🅿 ⌂ snooker

HEMEL HEMPSTEAD
Hertfordshire
Map **4** TL00

GH Southville Private Hotel 9 Charles St ☎(0442) 51387

Comfortable family hotel in residential road.

14hc (3fb) TV in all bedrooms [R] ✱B&b£13.50–£17.50 Wfr£100 M̸

Lic ♨ CTV 9P

Credit card [2] [V]

HENFIELD
West Sussex
Map **4** TQ21

FH Mrs M Wilkin **Great Wapses** *(TQ243192)* Wineham (Guestaccom) ☎(0273) 492544

Part 16th-century and part Georgian farmhouse set in rural surroundings, with horses, calves and chickens. 3m NE off B2116.

3hc (2🛁 1🚿) (2fb) CTV in all bedrooms [R]
*B&b£10–£15
♨ 7P 1🚗 33acres mixed

HENLEY-IN-ARDEN
Warwickshire
Map **7** SP16

GH Ashleigh House Whitley Hill
☎(05642) 2315

Comfortable and welcoming hotel in peaceful area. Interesting gardens.

6hc (5🚿) TV in all bedrooms *B&bfr£15
♨ CTV 11P nc5yrs
[V]

HENLEY ON THAMES
Oxfordshire
Map **4** SU78

GH Flohr's Hotel & Restaurant
Northfield End ☎(0491) 573412

Simply furnished modern bedrooms together with a high quality formal restaurant.

9hc (1🛁 2🚿) (4fb) CTV in all bedrooms [R]
*B&b£19.50–£21.50 LDO10pm

Lic ♨ CTV 6P
Credit cards [1] [2] [3] [5] [V]

HENSTRIDGE
Somerset
Map **3** ST71

FH Mrs P J Doggrell **Toomer** *(ST708192)*
Templecombe ☎Milborne Port (0963) 250237

200-year-old stone-built farmhouse with large walled garden with an Elizabethan dovecote. 1½m W then S off A30.

3rm (2hc) (2fb) CTV in 1 bedroom TV in 1 bedroom ⋈ [R] *B&b£8.50–£9 Wfr£56 M
♨ CTV 6P 🚜 400acres arable dairy
[V]

HEREFORD
Hereford & Worcester
Map **3**   SO54

GH *Breinton Court* Lower Breinton
☎(0432) 268156
Apr–Oct

Peaceful and relaxing accommodation on the banks of the River Wye.

6hc (1fb) TV in all bedrooms ✠ ⓡ

🍴 CTV 8P ♬grass ✦

GH Ferncroft Hotel 144 Ledbury Rd
☎(0432) 265538
Closed mid Dec–1st Jan

11hc (3⇔) (2fb) CTV in all bedrooms ✠
✱B&b£13–£17 Bdi£20–£27 W£130–£150 ⅃ LDO7pm

Lic 🍴 CTV 8P

Credit cards ① ③

GH Munstone House Munstone
☎(0432) 267122
Apr–Oct

2m N unclass rd off A49.

6hc (3fb) ✠ ✱B&b£9–£9.50

CTV 10P

Ⓥ

GH White Lodge Hotel 50 Ledbury Rd
☎(0432) 273382

Modest, competitive hotel offering personal service and Corden Bleu cuisine.

7hc (1⇔ 2🍴) CTV in all bedrooms ✠
✱B&b£12.50–£16.50 Bdi£18.50–£23
W£120–£155 ⅃ LDO8.45pm

Lic 🍴 12P nc12yrs

Credit card ③

HERNE BAY
Kent
Map **5**   TR16

GH *Northdown Hotel* 14 Cecil Park
(Guestaccom) ☎(0227) 372051

Friendly small hotel with good bedrooms and quite spacious ground floor facilities.

5hc (2fb) ✠ ⓡ LDOam

Lic 🍴 CTV 8P ⚓

Hereford — Higham

HERSTMONCEUX
East Sussex
Map **5**   TQ61

GH Cleavers Lyng Country Hotel
(Guestaccom) ☎(0323) 833131
Closed Xmas rs Jan

Comfortable rooms and restaurant are features of this 16th-century house in rural setting near the Royal Greenwich Observatory.

8hc ✱B&b£11.25–£12 Bdi£15.95–£16.95
W£99.75–£108.50 ⅃ LDO6pm

Lic 🍴 CTV 15P

HESKET NEWMARKET
Cumbria
Map **11**   NY33

GH Denton House ☎Caldbeck (06998) 415

Large 17th century house with new restaurant extension.

6hc (2fb) ✱B&b£8–£8.50 Bdi£12–£12.50
W£80–£85 Ⅿ LDO8pm

Lic CTV 6P

HEWISH
Avon
Map **3**   ST46

⊢⊣**GH Kara** ☎Yatton (0934) 834442

Small, personally run, period house with an attractive garden. 3m from Weston-Super-Mare.

5hc (2fb) TV in 1 bedroom ⓡ B&b£8–£9.50 Bdi£13–£14.50 W£84–£91 ⅃ LDO4pm

Lic 🍴 CTV 5P 1⚓

See advertisement on page 401

HEXHAM
Northumberland
Map **12**   NY96

GH Westbrooke Hotel Allendale Rd
☎(0434) 603818

Detached Victorian house with a pretty little garden. Well-appointed and comfortable bedrooms.

7hc (1🍴) (1fb) CTV in 1 bedroom ⓡ
✱B&b£13.50

Lic CTV 4P snooker

HEYSHAM
Lancashire
Map **7**   SD46

GH Carr-Garth Bailey Ln ☎(0524) 51175
Etr–Oct

A family-owned house of character with small walled garden.

10hc (3fb) ✱B&b£8.25–£9.25 Bdi£10.50–£11.50 W£66–£72 ⅃ LDO4pm

CTV 8P

HICKLING
Norfolk
Map **9**   TG42

GH Jenter House Town St ☎(069261) 372
Mar–Nov

10hc (1fb) ⅃ in 1 bedroom TV in 1 bedroom ✱B&b£11 Bdi£15 W£84–£90 ⅃ LDO4pm

🍴 CTV 10P ⚓

HIGHAM
Suffolk
Map **5**   TM03

─── *Recommended* ───

GH Old Vicarage ☎(020637) 248

Featured as one of the best newcomers in 1985, this timber-framed 16th-century house is located just 1 mile from the A2. Bedrooms in both the house and its adjoining barn annexe have excellent private facilities, most are en-suite. Breakfast is a feature here with a 'help-yourself' farmhouse family-style platter. Evening meals are not served.

3hc (2⇔) Annexe: 2hc (1⇔ 1🍴) (1fb) CTV in all bedrooms ⓡ B&b£16–£24

🍴 CTV 12P ⚓ ➔ ♬(hard) ✦

Ⓥ

HIGH CATTON
North Yorkshire
Map **8** SE75

FH Mrs S Foster **High Catton Grange** *(SE128541)* ☎Stamford Bridge (0759) 71374
mid Jan–Nov
Substantial, well-kept farmhouse with an attractive garden.
3rm (1hc) ✱B&bfr£9
♨ TV 6P ⌂ 300acres mixed

HIGH WYCOMBE
Buckinghamshire
Map **4** SU89

GH Amersham Hill 52 Amersham Hill ☎(0494) 20635
Small, friendly place to stay.
7hc CTV in all bedrooms 🚫 [R] ✱B&b£17–£20
♨ 9P

GH Clifton Lodge Private Hotel
210 West Wycombe Rd ☎(0494) 40095
Closed 10 days Xmas
Private hotel with modern bedrooms and relaxing lounge and bar.
20hc (5🛁) (2fb) CTV in all bedrooms 🚫 ✱B&b£17.25–£27.60 Bdi£27.50–£38.10 W£192.50–£266.70 L̸ LDO8.15pm
Lic ♨ CTV 15P
Credit cards [1] [2] [5]

High Catton — Hoarwithy

GH *Drake Court Hotel* London Rd ☎(0494) 23639
A friendly, family-style hotel, ½m from town centre, with separate lounge and bar.
20hc (1🚿) (5fb) CTV in all bedrooms 🚫 [R] LDO8.30pm
Lic ♨ CTV 30P 🏊 (heated)
Credit cards [1] [2] [3] [5] [V]
See advertisement on page 196

HIMBLETON
Hereford & Worcester
Map **3** SO95

FH Mrs P Harvard **Phepson** *(SO941599)* ☎(090569) 205
Apr–Nov
Children are especially welcome at this peaceful, family-run stock farm in the heart of the English countryside.
3hc (1fb) B&bfr£9.50 Wfr£60 M̸
CTV 6P ⌂
170acres beef sheep

HINCKLEY
Leicestershire
Map **4** SP49

GH *Kings Hotel & Restaurant* 13–19 Mount Rd ☎(0455) 637193
7hc (2🛁 5🚿) CTV in all bedrooms 🚫 [R] LDO10pm
Lic ♨ 10P 1🚗
Credit cards [1] [2] [3] [5]

HITCHAM
Suffolk
Map **5** TL95

FH Mrs B Elsden **Wetherden Hall** *(TL971509)* ☎Bildeston (0449) 740412
Closed Jan & Dec
Part Tudor style farmhouse close to the ruins of a former hall offering friendly accommodation. 1m W of unclass road to Kettlebaston.
3rm (1fb) 🚫 ✱B&b£8–£9.50 W£55–£60 M̸
♨ CTV 4P nc10yrs 300acres arable mixed
[V]

HOARWITHY
Hereford & Worcester
Map **3** SO52

FH Mrs C Probert **Old Mill** *(SO546294)* ☎Carey (043270) 602
Small, white, cottage-style farmhouse in village centre with traditional English country front garden. →

4rm ⅟ in 2 bedrooms ✱B&b£7.50–£8.50 Bdi£11.50–£12.50 W£75–£80 Ⱡ

P ⌂

6acres calf rearing

HOCKHAM, GREAT
Norfolk
Map **5** TL99

FH Mrs E M Morfoot **Church Cottage** *(TL957946)* Breckles (1m N A1075) ☎(095382) 286

Farmhouse-style accommodation in 2-acre smallholding. Gardens, paddock and outdoor pool, with access to nearby coarse-fishing lake.

4hc ✖ B&b£9.50–£10

CTV 10P ⛱(heated) ✔

2acres smallholding

HOLBETON
Devon
Map **2** SX65

FH Mrs J A Baskerville **Keaton** *(SX595480)* ☎(075530) 255
Apr–Sep

Large, stone-built and well-maintained farmhouse in isolated rural position. Yachting at Newton Ferrers 3m away.

3rm (1fb) ✖ ✱B&b£9–£10 Wfr£55 M

CTV 3P nc5yrs 117acres beef

Ⓥ

HOLLYBUSH
Strathclyde *Ayrshire*
Map **10** NS31

⊢⊣**FH** Mrs A Woodburn **Boreland** *(NS400139)* ☎Patna (0292) 531228
Jun–Sep

Two-storey farmhouse with roughcast exterior, situated on the banks of the River Doon. West off A713 south of village.

3rm (2fb) ✖ Ⓡ ✱B&b£8–£9

𝍢 CTV 6P ⌂ ✔ 126acres dairy

HOLMFIRTH
West Yorkshire
Map **7** SE10

INN White Horse Scholes Rd, Jackson Bridge ☎(0484) 683940
Closed Xmas Eve, Xmas Day & New Years Eve

Warm and welcoming inn of traditional Pennine stone, close to a stream. 3m E A616 towards Sheffield.

5hc (3fb) TV in all bedrooms Ⓡ ✱B&b£13 Bdi£18 Lunch £2.20–£5.95 Dinner 10pm

𝍢 12P 1🚗

Credit card ③

HOLMROOK
Cumbria
Map **6** SD09

GH Carleton Green Saltcoats Rd ☎(09404) 608
Mar–Oct (normally closed Nov–Feb)

A delightful house in rural setting, run by a local couple

6hc (2⇌ 1⊓) (1fb) Ⓡ ✱B&b£9–£10 Bdi£14.50–£15.50 W£86–£93 Ⱡ

Lic 𝍢 CTV 6P

HOLNE
Devon
Map **3** SX76

Recommended

FH S Townsend **Wellpritton** *(SX716704)* ☎Poundsgate (03643) 273
Closed Xmas

Tastefully modernised farmhouse in Dartmoor National Park. There are panoramic views and the farm has its own swimming pool.

5hc (1⇌ 3⊓) ✖ Ⓡ B&b£9–£10 Bdi£12.50–£15 Wfr£91 Ⱡ (W only Jul & Aug)

𝍢 CTV 5P ⌂ ⛱ 15acres goats pigs sheep mixed

Ⓥ

INN *Church House* ☎Poundsgate (03643) 208

6hc CTV in 5 bedrooms TV in 1 bedroom Ⓡ Dinner 9.30pm

𝍢 7P nc5yrs

Credit cards ① ③

HOLNEST
Dorset
Map **3** ST60

FH Mrs J Mayo **Almhouse** *(ST651082)* (S off A352 on unclass road towards Hermitage) ☎(096321) 296
Mar–Oct

3hc (1fb) ✖ Ⓡ ✱B&b£8–£10 Bdi£12–£14 LDO2pm

CTV P snooker

140acres dairy

Ⓥ

HOLSWORTHY
Devon
Map **2** SS30

GH Coles Mill ☎(0409) 253313
Etr–Oct

Comfortable and well equipped converted mill house.

5⊓ TV in all bedrooms ✖ Ⓡ B&b£9.50–£12 Bdi£15.50–£18 W£87.50–£107 Ⱡ LDO5pm

Lic CTV 12P nc6yrs

FH Mr & Mrs E Cornish **Leworthy** *(SS323012)* ☎(0409) 253488

Low, white-fronted farmhouse with attractive garden facing open country.

12hc (3⊓) (5fb) ✖ ✱B&b£10–£12 Bdi£15–£20 W£100–£120 Ⱡ LDO6pm

Lic CTV 20P 2🚗 ⌂ ዖ ✔ U 240acres mixed

HOLT
Clwyd
Map **7** SJ35

⊢⊣**FH** Mrs G M Evans **New** *(SJ394538)* Commonwood ☎Farndon (0829) 270358

Small, comfortable and cosy farm.

2rm ✖ B&b£8–£8.50 Wfr£52.50 M

𝍢 CTV 4P 92acres dairy sheep

HOLT
Norfolk
Map **9**   TG03

GH Lawns Hotel Station Rd ☎(0263) 713390

This Georgian house, previously part of Gresham Public School, offers fresh home cooking.

12hc (2⇆) (2fb) ® ✱B&b£13.15–£16.10 Bdi£17.85–£24.15 W£125 ⫽ LDO8pm Lic ᵐᵐ CTV 12P
ⓥ

Holt
—
Holywell

HOLYHEAD
Gwynedd
Map **6**   SH28

GH The Witchingham Guest House
20 Walthew Av ☎(0407) 2426

Large, personally run house close to town centre and port. Bright, comfortable rooms.

6rm (3hc 1🛏) (3fb) LDO3pm
ᵐᵐ CTV 3P

HOLYWELL
Clwyd
Map **7**   SJ17

FH Mrs D E Masterman **Garreg Ganol** *(SJ157771)* Lloc ☎Mostyn (0745) 560488 Etr–Sep

19th-century farmhouse with well-planned extension, providing good, comfortable accommodation. 3m west of Holywell.

2hc CTV in 1 bedroom TV in 1 bedroom ✱B&b£10 Bdi£16.50 LDO6.45pm
ᵐᵐ P nc8yrs

10acres beef smallholding

197

FH Mrs M D Jones **Green Hill** *(SJ188769)*
☎(0352) 713270
Closed Dec–Jan

15th-century farmhouse completely
modernised to provide comfortable
accommodation, overlooking the Dee
estuary.

5hc (1⇄) (3fb) ✗ ✱B&bfr£8.50
Bdifr£13.50 W£94 ⅃ LDO previous day
CTV 6P ⮽ 120acres dairy mixed

HONITON
Devon
Map **3**   ST10
See also **Feniton**

GH Hill House Country Hotel Combe
Raleigh ☎(0404) 3371
Etr–Oct

2m NE unclass rd.

6hc (1🏠) (1fb) ® ✱B&b£12.50–£17
Bdi£17.50–£22 W£108.50–£138 ⅃
LDO7pm

Lic ㎖ CTV 12P ℘(grass)

FH Mrs I J Underdown **Roebuck**
(ST147001) (western end of Honiton-by-
pass) ☎(0404) 2225

Modern farm 8 miles from the coast.

4hc (1⇄ 1🏠) (1fb) ✱B&b£8–£8.50 Bdi£12
Wfr£84 ⅃

㎖ CTV P 180acres dairy
Credit cards 🔲 ③ ⓥ

INN Monkton Court Monkton (2m E A30)
☎(0404) 2309

8hc (3⇄) (2fb) TV in 5 bedrooms CTV in 3
bedrooms ✱B&b£15–£18 Lunch £2–
£6.95&alc Dinner 10pm£6.95&alc

㎖ 100P 3🐎
ⓥ

HOOK
Hampshire
Map **4**   SU75

GH Oaklea London Rd (Guestaccorn)
☎(025672) 2673

Detached Victorian house with friendly
service and good home cooking.

10hc (3🏠) (2fb) ✱B&b£16.50–£25
Bdi£24.50–£33 W£171.50–£231 ⅃
LDOnoon

Lic CTV 10P
ⓥ

HOPE COVE
Devon
Map **3**   SX63

GH Beacon House Hotel ☎Kingsbridge
(0548) 561304

Comfortable hotel in an elevated position.

9hc (3🏠) (2fb) ® ✱B&b£12–£15 Bdi£17–
£21 W£115–£145 ⅃ LDO9.30pm

Lic ㎖ CTV 6P ⮽

Credit cards 🔲 ③

GH Fern Lodge ☎Kingsbridge (0548)
561326
Mar–Oct

Small, friendly house in elevated position
overlooking Hope Cove and surrounding
countryside. Two bedroom, self-catering
flat also available.

5hc Annexe: 3hc (2fb) ✱B&b£7.50–£9
Bdi£13–£15 W£92.95–£99 ⅃ LDO5pm

Lic ㎖ CTV 8P ⮽

GH Sand Pebbles Hotel ☎Kingsbridge
(0548) 561673
Mar–Nov

Small, private hotel overlooking Hope
Cove, with compact, modern bedrooms.

10hc (5⇄ 4🏠) (2fb) ® LDO8pm

Lic CTV 10P nc5yrs sauna bath

HOPTON
Derbyshire
Map **8**   SK25

GH Henmore Grange ☎Carsington
(062985) 420
rs Xmas Day

Tastefully and cleverly converted farm
buildings provide high quality
accommodation.

10hc (6🛁 1🚿) (4fb) [R] ✱B&b£12–£17 Bdi£20–£25 W£130–£165 Ł LDO6pm

🛋 CTV 16P 1🚗 ⌂

HORLEY
Surrey
For accommodation details see under
Gatwick Airport

HORNS CROSS
Devon
Map **2** SS32

FH Mrs B Furse **Swanton** *(SS355227)*
☎Clovelly (02373) 241
Closed Dec

Modern dormer-style bungalow pleasantly situated overlooking the Bristol Channel.

3rm (2hc) (2fb) ✗ ✱B&bfr£7 Bdifr£11 Wfr£70 Ł LDO2pm

CTV P 60acres dairy

HORNSEA
Humberside
Map **8** TA24

GH Hotel Seaforth Esplanade ☎(04012) 2616

A large house overlooking the bowling green with sea views from the front. Cosy atmosphere.

6hc (2fb) CTV in 4 bedrooms [R] ✱B&b£8.50 Bdi£13.75 Wfr£90 Ł LDO5pm

Lic 🛋 CTV 4P

HORSHAM
West Sussex
Map **4** TQ13

GH *Blatchford House* 52 Kings Rd
☎(0403) 65317
rs Xmas

A converted Georgian house under the personal supervision of the owners who offer comfortable accommodation and a warm, homely atmosphere.

6hc (1fb) [R]

🛋 CTV 12P sauna bath solarium gymnasium

GH Wimblehurst Hotel
6 Wimblehurst Rd ☎(0403) 62319

Detached house with modern bedrooms, also catering for non smokers.

Hopton — Howey

14hc (1🛁 4🚿) (3fb) ✗ ✱B&b£14.99–£38.99 Bdi£24.98–£48.98 LDO6.45pm

CTV 14P ⌂

Credit cards [1] [3]

GH Winterpick Corner Winterpit Ln, Manning's Heath ☎(0403) 53882

2m SE of town off A281.

4hc (1fb) ✗ [R] ✱B&b£14–£16

🛋 CTV 4P 2🚗 🏊(heated) putting green croquet

Ⓥ

HORSHAM ST FAITH
Norfolk
Map **9** TG21

GH Elm Farm Chalet Hotel Norwich Rd
☎Norwich (0603) 898366
rs Xmas

6rm (3hc) Annexe: 13🚿 (1fb) CTV in all bedrooms ✗ [R] B&b£17–£19.50 Bdi£24–£26.50 W£161–£185.50 Ł LDO8pm

Lic CTV 20P

Credit cards [1] [3] Ⓥ

HORSMONDEN
Kent
Map **5** TQ74

FH Mrs S M Russell **Pullens** *(TQ689389)*
Lamberhurst Rd ☎Brenchley(089272) 2241
Mar–Nov

Black and white farmhouse with warm atmosphere.

3rm (2hc) (1fb) ✗ ✱B&b£9.50–£12 Bdi£16–£18 W£65–£70 Ł

🛋 CTV 3P 200acres arable hops

HORTON
Dorset
Map **4** SU00

INN *Horton* Cranborne Rd
☎Witchampton (0258) 840252
Closed Xmas night

Large detached inn on crossroads. Good food and very well-equipped bedrooms.

5rm (3hc 2🛁) CTV in all bedrooms ✗ [R] LDO9.45pm

🛋 100P 🚫

Credit cards [1] [2] [3] [5]

HORTON-IN-RIBBLESDALE
North Yorkshire
Map **7** SD87

INN Crown Hotel ☎(07296) 209

An attractive Dales pub offering warm and comfortable accommodation

10hc (5fb) ✱B&b£12.08 Bdi£18.40 W£120.75 Ł Bar lunch £2.50–£5 Dinner 7pm£6.50

🛋 CTV 15P

Credit card [5] Ⓥ

HOUNSLOW
Gt London
London plan **4** B3
(page 246)

GH *Shalimar Hotel* 219–221 Staines Rd
☎01-572 2816

Modest and informal guesthouse offering friendly personal service.

15hc (5🚿) (5fb) CTV in all bedrooms [R]

🛋 CTV 6P

Credit cards [1] [2] [3] [5]

See advertisement on page 200

HOVE
East Sussex
Map **4** TQ20
See **Brighton & Hove**

HOWEY (nr Llandrindod Wells)
Powys
Map **3** SO05

GH Corven Hall Country ☎Llandrindod Wells (0597) 3368
Closed Xmas

7hc (4🚿) (5fb) [R] B&b£8.50–£9.50 Bdi£13.25–£14.25 W£83–£89 Ł LDO6.30pm

Lic 🛋 CTV 9P 2🚗 ⌂

FH Mrs C Nixon **Brynhir** *(SJ067586)*
☎Llandrindod Wells (0597) 2425
Mar–Nov →

Blatchford House

A Grade II Listed Georgian Guest House conveniently situated for the station and town centre and, only 20 minutes from Gatwick.

6 spacious, centrally heated rooms, each with shower & basin and tea/coffee making facilities. A large TV lounge. Ample car parking. A sauna, hydro-message bath, gymnasium, solarium and relaxation lounge.

Open year round with limited service at Christmas.

Write for Brochure: **Blatchford House, 52 Kings Rd. Horsham, Sussex RH13 5PR. Tel: 0403 65317.**

Remote 17th-century hill farm, traditionally furnished. Pony for children to ride. 1m E on unclass road.

7hc (2⇆ 2🛁) (2fb) ✕ ✻B&b£8–£8.50 Bdi£12–£12.50 W£84–£87 ⅃ (W only Jun, Jul & Aug)

🍴 P ♨ 150acres hill farm

ⓥ

FH Mrs R Jones **Holly** *(SJ045593)* ☎Llandrindod Wells (0597) 2402 Apr–Nov

18th century building close to the A483, on the edge of the village, surrounded by open country.

3hc (1fb) ✕ ✻B&b£8–£9 Bdi£12–£13 Wfr£84 ⅃ LDO5pm

🍴 CTV P 70acres beef sheep

FH Mr & Mrs R Bufton **Three Wells** *(SO062586)* ☎Llandrindod Wells (0597) 2484

Set in beautiful countryside overlooking lake. Detached farmhouse with modern bedrooms and cosy bar. Good food. Fishing available.

12hc (7⇆ 5🛁) (4fb) CTV in all bedrooms ✕ ® B&b£9–£10 Bdi£13.50–£14 W£89– £99 ⅃ LDO6pm

Lic lift 🍴 CTV 20P ♨ ✔ ♈

50acres beef sheep mixed

ⓥ

HOYLAKE
Merseyside
Map **7** SJ28

GH Sandtoft Hotel 70 Alderley Rd ☎051-632 2204

Small guesthouse in a quiet side road close to the Dee estuary.

9hc (1🛁) (1fb) ✻B&b£13.50–£15 Bdi£17– £20 Wfr£120 LDO6.30pm

Lic 🍴 CTV 6P 3🛉

HUBBERHOLME
North Yorkshire
Map **7** SD97

INN George Kirk Gill ☎Kettlewell (075676) 223
Closed Christmas Day evening

Howey
— Hunstanton

Old Dales hostelry in attractive rural surroundings, offering home produced food.

3hc ® ✻B&b£11.50–£12.50 W£63–£66.50 Ⓜ Bar lunch £4.45 Dinner 9pm£8alc

Lic 🍴 20P 🚸 nc8yrs ✔

ⓥ

HUGHLEY
Shropshire
Map **7** SO59

FH Mrs E Bosworth **Mill** *(SO565978)* ☎Brockton (074636) 645

Lovely old house in pleasant rural area beneath Wenlock Edge.

2hc (1🛁) (1fb) CTV in 1 bedroom ✕ ✻B&b£9–£11 Wfr£60 Ⓜ

CTV 4P ✔ ♈ 250acres arable beef

ⓥ

HULL
Humberside
Map **8** TA02

GH Ashford 125 Park Av ☎(0482) 492849
Closed 25 & 26 Dec rs Fri–Sun

Well furnished, comfortable bedrooms are a feature of this end of terrace building in a tree lined street.

6hc (1fb) ✕ ✻B&b£11–£11.50 Bdi£15.50– £16.50 Wfr£88 ⅃ LDO10am

🍴 CTV 4P

GH Earlesmere Hotel 76–78 Sunny Bank, Spring Bank West ☎(0482) 41977

15hc (5🛁) (4fb) CTV in all bedrooms ® ✻B&b£14.95–£24.15 Bdi£20.95–£30.15 W£146.65–£211.05 ⅃ LDO6.30pm

Lic 🍴 CTV ✗

ⓥ

GH Parkwood Hotel 113 Princes Av ☎(0482) 445610

Terraced town house on bus route with well fitted comfortable bedrooms.

8hc (1fb) CTV in all bedrooms ® ✻B&b£11.25–£12.50 Bdi£17–£18.75 W£110–£125 ⅃ LDO8pm

Lic 🍴 CTV ✗

HUNA
Highland *Caithness*
Map **15** ND37

GH Haven Gore ☎John O'Groats (095581) 314

Modernised cottage with matching extension and sea views to Stroma and Orkney Isles.

5hc (3fb) ✻B&b£7–£7.50 Bdi£11–£11.50 W£77–£80 ⅃ LDO3pm

🍴 CTV 8P

ⓥ

HUNNINGHAM
Warwickshire
Map **4** SP36

FH Mrs R Hancock **Snowford Hall** *(SP386666)* ☎Marton (0926) 632297

3hc ✕ B&bfr£10 Bdifr£17.50
LDO previous day

🍴 CTV 3P

250acres arable beef

HUNSTANTON
Norfolk
Map **9** TF64

GH Caley Hall Motel ☎(04853) 33486

20⇆ (4fb) CTV in all bedrooms ® ✻B&b£17.50–£19.50 Bdi£25.75–£27.75 W£162–£174 ⅃ LDO9.30pm

Lic 🍴 50P

Credit card ③

GH Claremont 35 Greevegate ☎(04853) 33171
Closed Dec

7hc (2fb) ✕ ® LDO6.30pm

Lic 🍴 CTV 3P nc5yrs

GH Deepdene Hotel 29 Avenue Rd ☎(04853) 2460

Victorian building constructed from local Carstone stone.

9hc (1⇆) (3fb) ✕ ® ✻B&b£14 Bdi£20 W£130 ⅃ LDO7pm

CTV 12P [img](heated) sauna bath solarium gymnasium

GH Sunningdale 3 Avenue Rd ☎(04853) 2562

Small comfortable establishment in a residential road close to the town centre.

11hc (2⇨ 5🚿) CTV in 5 bedrooms ✕ ✱B&b£10–£11.50 Bdi£14.50–£16 W£67–£78 M̶ LDO7pm

Lic 🆓 CTV 🐾 nc10yrs

Credit cards ① ③ Ⓥ

GH *Sutton House Hotel* 24 Northgate ☎(04853) 2552

Family-run house in a quiet residential road close to town.

10hc (2fb) ✕ ® LDO1pm

Lic 🆓 CTV 6P nc5yrs

GH *Tolcarne Private Hotel* 3 Boston Sq ☎(04853) 2359
Mar–Oct

Large detached house in quiet square off sea front. Golfing visitors will find Links courses nearby.

11hc (3🚿) (1fb) TV in all bedrooms ✕ ® LDO9pm

Lic 🆓 8P nc10yrs

HUNTINGDON
Cambridgeshire
Map **4**   TL27

INN *Black Bull* Post St, Godmanchester ☎(0480) 53310

1m S B1043.

10hc TV in 3 bedrooms LDO9.50pm

🆓 CTV 20P 8🍴

HURSLEY
Hampshire
Map **4**   SU42

INN Kings Head Hotel ☎Winchester (0962) 75208
Closed Xmas Day

Popular roadside Charrington's house with good-size bedrooms and cosy lounge. Bar serves bistro-type food.

5hc (1fb) ✕ ® ✱B&b£15–£25 Bdi£18–£32.50 Lunch 70p–£1.50 Dinner 9.30pm£4–£7.50

Hunstanton
—
Ilford

CTV 25P

Credit cards ① ③

HUSTHWAITE
North Yorkshire
Map **8**   SE57

FH Mrs E Smith **Baxby Manor** *(SE512753)* ☎Coxwold (03476) 572
Closed Xmas

Unspoilt stone-built 13th-century manor with old beams, exposed stone walls and feature fireplace.

3hc (1fb) ✕ ® ✱B&b£8.50–£9 W£54–£63 M̶

Lift 🆓 CTV 3P ⚓ 110acres mixed

HUTTON-LE-HOLE
North Yorkshire
Map **8**   SE79

--- *Recommended* ---

GH Barn ☎Lastingham (07515) 311
Etr–Oct

Quaint, stone-built hotel and tea shop in the village centre. The bedrooms are comfortable and attractive and the lounge boasts an enormous feature fireplace. A good range of light meals is served in the tea shop.

9hc (2🚿) CTV in 2 bedrooms ✕ ® ✱B&b£12.50–£16

Lic 🆓 CTV 14P nc12yrs

ICKLESHAM
East Sussex
Map **5**   TQ81

GH Snailham House Broad St ☎Hastings (0424) 814556
Etr–Oct

350-year-old, beamed farmhouse surrounded by quiet countryside. Skilfully modernised, providing comfortable accommodation and friendly service.

7hc (1fb) ✕ ® ✱B&b£10–£10.50 Bdi£14.50–£15 W£91.50–£95 ⏝ LDO5.30pm

Lic 🆓 CTV 7P

IDOLE
Dyfed
Map **2**   SN41

FH Mr & Mrs A Bowen **Pantgwyn** *(SN419157)* ☎Carmarthen (0267) 235859
Apr–Sep

Spacious rebuilt farmhouse, 3m S of Carmarthen.

2rm (1fb) ✕

🆓 CTV P 35acres dairy

ILAM
Staffordshire
Map **7**   SK15

FH Mrs S Prince **Beechenhill** *(SK129525)* ☎Alstonefield (033527) 274
Closed Xmas

Two-storey, stone-built farmhouse with exposed beams, built around 1720. Situated in unspoilt rural area with panoramic views.

2hc (1fb) ✕ ® ✱B&b£8.50–£10

🆓 CTV 3P 92acres dairy sheep

ILFORD
Gt London
London plan **4**   F4
(page 247)

GH Cranbrook Hotel 24 Coventry Rd ☎01-554 6544

Situated in residential area, near shopping centre.

16hc (13🚿) (7fb) CTV in all bedrooms ✱B&b£17.25–£24.15 Bdi£21.75–£30.65 W£160.30–£200.50 ⏝ LDO8.30pm

Lic 🆓 CTV 12P 2🍴

Credit cards ① ② ③ Ⓥ

GH Park Hotel 327 Cranbrook Rd ☎01-554 9616

Modern, family accommodation overlooking Valentines Park.   →

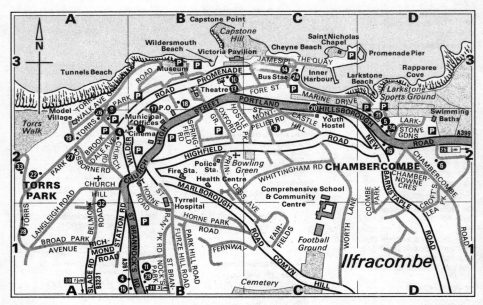

Ilfracombe

1 Avenue Private Hotel
3 Briercliffe Hotel
4 Carbis Private Hotel
4A Chalfont Private Hotel
5 Collingdale Hotel
6 Combe Lodge Hotel
8 Cresta Private Hotel
10 Dèdès Hotel
11 Earlsdale Hotel
13 Glendower

14 Headlands Hotel
15 Lantern House Hotel
16 Laston House Private Hotel
17 Lympstone Private Hotel
18 Marlyn
19 Merlin Court Hotel
20 Bristol Merchant Hotel
21 Cavendish Hotel
22 Norbury
24 Royal Britannia *(Inn)*
25 Rosebank Hotel

26 Seven Hills Hotel
27 Southcliffe Hotel
28 South Tor Hotel
29 Strathmore Private Hotel
30 Sunny Hill
31 Sunnymeade Country House Hotel
   (listed under West Down)
32 Wentworth House Private Hotel
33 Westwell Hall Hotel
34 Wilson

21hc (5⇄ 6🚿) (3fb) CTV in all bedrooms
✱B&b£20–£26 Bdi£25.50–£31 LDO8pm
Lic 🆇 CTV 23P
Credit cards ① ③

ILFRACOMBE
Devon
Map **2**   SS54
See plan

For additional accommodation see
Berrynarbor and **West Down**

GH *Avenue Private Hotel* Greenclose
Rd ☎(0271) 63767 Plan **1** *B2*
Apr–6 Nov
24hc (3⇄ 3🚿) (7fb) ✱ LDO7pm
Lic 🆇 CTV 15P
Credit cards ① ③

GH Briercliffe Hotel 9 Montpelier Ter
☎(0271) 63274 Plan **3** *C2*
Closed Nov
10hc (5fb) B&b£9 Bdi£13 W£80.50–£91 Ӿ
(W only last 2 wks Jul, first 2 wks Aug)
LDOam
Lic 🆇 CTV 5P
Ⓥ

Ilfracombe

GH *Bristol Merchant Hotel*
10 Hillsborough Ter ☎(0271) 62141
Plan **20** *C2*

12hc (1fb) CTV in 10 bedrooms LDO8pm

Lic 4P 3🚗 nc12yrs

[V]

GH Cavendish Hotel (formerly New Cavendish) 9–10 Larkstone Ter ☎(0271) 63994 Plan **21** *D2*
Etr–Oct

Family-owned private hotel close to town centre. Well-equipped bedrooms with CTV in all rooms.

23hc (15🚿) (5fb) CTV in all bedrooms [R] ✱B&b£8.75–£13 Bdi£13.25–£17.50 W£67.50–£105 Ł LDO4pm

Lic lift CTV 24P

GH Chalfont Private Hotel 21 Church Rd ☎(0271) 62224 Plan **4A** *A2*
Etr–Oct

Small, friendly hotel in quiet residential area.

13hc (3🚿) (6fb) [R] B&b£9–£10 Bdi£13–£14 W£80–£93 Ł LDO5pm

Lic 🍴 CTV ⓟ

Credit cards [1] [3] [V]

GH Collingdale Hotel Larkstone Ter ☎(0271) 63770 Plan **5** *D2*
Jan–Oct

9hc (3fb) ✈ [R] ✱B&b£9–£10 Bdi£12.50–£13.50 Wfr£80–£85 Ł (W only Jul–Aug)

Lic 🍴 CTV ⓟ

Credit cards [1] [3]

GH Combe Lodge Hotel
Chambercombe Park Rd ☎(0271) 64518
Plan **6** *D2*
Closed Xmas

9hc (1🚿) (3fb) ✱B&b£7.50–£9 Bdi£12–£13.50 W£82–£89 Ł LDO3pm

Lic 🍴 CTV 7P ♧

[V]

GH Cresta Private Hotel Torrs Park ☎(0271) 63742 Plan **8** *A2*
mid May–Sep (rs first half May & first half Oct)

24hc (2🚿) (10fb) [R] ✱B&b£10–£14 Bdi£14–£16 W£98–£120 Ł LDO6.30pm

Lic lift 🍴 CTV 30P

⟼**GH Dèdés Hotel** 1–3 The Promenade ☎(0271) 62545 Plan **10** *B3*
Etr–Oct rs Nov–Etr

17hc (7🛁) (6fb) B&b£7.75–£11.50 Bdi£12.50–£16.25 W£87.50–£113.75 Ł LDO10pm

Lic CTV P

Credit cards [1] [2] [3] [5] [V]

See advertisement on page 204

⟼**GH Earlsdale Hotel** 51 St Brannocks Rd ☎(0271) 62496 Plan **11** *B1*

11hc (4🚿) (4fb) CTV in 4 bedrooms ✈ B&b£8–£9 Bdi£12.50–£13.50 W£80–£90 Ł LDO6.30pm

Lic 🍴 CTV 11P

[V]

GH *Glendower* Wilder Rd ☎(0271) 65711 Plan **13** *B3*
Closed Jan

Three-storey balconied guesthouse overlooking Jubilee gardens.

11hc (2fb) CTV in 2 bedrooms ✈

🍴 CTV 12P

GH Headlands Hotel Capstone Cres ☎(0271) 62887 Plan **14** *C3*
Mar–Oct, Xmas & New Year

20hc (5🛁 3🚿) (3fb) [R] ✱B&b£9.95–£11.50 Bdi£13.50–£18 W£85–£115 Ł LDO4.15pm

Lic CTV 12🚗(charge) ♧

Credit cards [1] [3] [V]

See advertisement on page 204

GH Lantern House Hotel
62 St Brannocks Rd ☎(0271) 64401
Plan **15** *B1*

10hc (4fb) ✱B&b£8–£9 Bdi£12–£13 W£69–£84 Ł LDO5pm

Lic 🍴 CTV 8P

Credit card [3] [V]

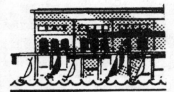

GH Laston House Private Hotel Hillsborough Rd ☎(0271) 62627 Plan **16** *D2*

11hc (5🛁 1🚿) (5fb) CTV in 9 bedrooms [R] *B&b£10–£16 Bdi£15–£20 W£99–£128 ⱡ LDO6pm

Lic ♨ CTV 20P 🏠

Credit cards [1] [3]

GH Lympstone Private Hotel 14 Cross Park ☎(0271) 63038 Plan **17** *B2* Mar–Oct

15hc (7🚿) (4fb) [R] *B&b£7.50–£8.50 Bdi£10.50–£11.50 W£70–£80 ⱡ LDO5pm

Lic ♨ CTV 5P

[V]

GH Marlyn 7 & 8 Regent Pl ☎(0271) 63785 Plan **18** *B3* Etr–Oct

12hc (2fb) *B&b£7.25–£8.25 Bdi£10.75–£11.75 W£74–£81 ⱡ LDO4pm

Lic ♨ CTV 8🚗

Credit card [1] [V]

GH *Merlin Court Hotel* Torrs Park ☎(0271) 62697 Plan **19** *A2* Apr–Oct

14hc (1🛁) (4fb) 🐕 [R] LDO6.45pm

Lic ♨ CTV 12P

GH *Norbury* Torrs Park ☎(0271) 63888 Plan **22** *A2* Apr–Sep

9hc (3🚿) (3fb)

Lic CTV 9P

GH *Rosebank Hotel* 26 Watermouth Rd, Hele Bay ☎(0271) 66488 Plan **25** *D2* Closed Oct

7hc (2🛁) (2fb) LDO8.30pm

Lic ♨ CTV 🏠 billiards

GH Seven Hills Hotel Torrs Park ☎(0271) 62207 Plan **26** *A2* Apr–Sep

14hc (5🛁) (4fb) B&b£9.50–£10.75 Bdi£13.50–£14.75 W£80.50–£90.50 ⱡ LDO6.30pm

CTV 12P nc3yrs

GH Southcliffe Hotel Torrs Park ☎(0271) 62958 Plan **27** *A2* Spring Bank Hol–Sep

19hc (11🚿) (9fb) 🐕 *B&b£11.50–£12.65 Bdi£16.10–£18.40 W£89.70–£95.45 ⱡ (W only Aug) LDO6pm

Lic CTV 12P 🏠

GH South Tor Hotel Torrs Park ☎(0271) 63750 Plan **28** *A1* Apr–Dec

15hc (9🚿) (3fb) [R] *B&b£7–£11.50 Bdi£11.50–£16.50 W£65–£103 ⱡ

Lic CTV 10P 2🚗

[V]

↦**GH Strathmore Private Hotel** 57 St Brannocks Rd ☎(0271) 62248 Plan **29** *B1*

Modest guesthouse run by friendly owners.

9hc (3🚿) (5fb) CTV in 8 bedrooms [R] B&b£8–£9 Bdi£13–£14 W£86.50–£93 ⱡ LDO5pm

Lic ♨ 7P

Credit cards [1] [2] [3] [V]

GH Sunny Hill Lincombe ☎(0271) 62953 Plan **30** *A1* Mar–Nov

2m SW off B3231.

6hc (2🚿) (1fb) *B&b£11.50–£13.50 Bdi£15.50–£17.50 W£99–£110 ⱡ LDO8pm

Lic ♨ CTV 6P nc5yrs

GH Wentworth House Private Hotel Belmont Road ☎(0271) 63048 Plan **32** *A1* Closed Xmas

11hc (1🚿) (4fb) *B&b£7.50–£8.50 Bdi£9.50–£10.75 W£59–£72 ⱡ

Lic CTV 11P

[V]

GH Westwell Hall Hotel Torrs Park ☎(0271) 62792 Plan **33** *A2* Mar–Dec

14hc (5🛁 9🚿) (2fb) CTV in all bedrooms [R] B&b£15–£17.50 Bdi£20–£22.50 W£140–£157.50 ⱡ LDO8pm

Lic ♨ CTV 12P nc4yrs

[V]

GH Wilson 16 Larkstone Ter ☎(0271) 63921 Plan **34** *D2*

Victorian terrace with glorious views over the harbour.

9hc (6fb) 🐕 [R] *B&b£7.50–£9 Bdi£11–£12.50 W£70–£85 ⱡ LDO5.30pm

Lic ♨ CTV 🚫🅿

[V]

INN *Royal Britannia* The Quay ☎(0271) 62939 Plan **24** *C3*

12hc (2fb) CTV in all bedrooms LDO10pm

CTV 🚫🅿 🏠

Credit cards [1] [3]

See advertisement on page 206

ILKLEY
West Yorkshire
Map **7** SE14

GH *Moorview House Hotel* 104 Skipton Rd (Guestaccom) ☎(0943) 600156 Closed Xmas

Large Victorian house overlooking valley of the River Wharfe. Lounge furnished with antiques and paintings; good-sized bedrooms.

11hc (5🚿) (6fb) CTV in 7 bedrooms TV in 4 bedrooms 🐕 [R] LDO5pm

Lic ♨ CTV 12P

INGHAM
Suffolk
Map **5** TL87

INN *Cadogan Arms* The Street ☎Culford (028484) 226

Fairly modern village pub situated on the A134.

4hc (2fb) CTV in 3 bedrooms TV in 1 bedroom 🐕 [R] LDO9.30pm

♨ 80P

Credit cards [1] [2] [3] [4] [5]

See advertisement on page 104

INGLEBY GREENHOW
North Yorkshire
Map **8**   NZ50

FH Mrs M Bloom **Manor House**
(NZ586056) ☎Great Ayton (0642) 722384

*Comfortable accommodation in a
traditional farming atmosphere at the foot
of the Cleveland Hills. Ideal for walking
and relaxation.*

3rm (1fb) ✖ ✱B&b£11.50–£12.50 Bdi£20–
£21 W£140–£147 ⊭LDO7pm
Lic ⊯ CTV 30P 6🐎 nc12yrs ➴ 164acres
arable sheep
ⓥ

INGLETON
North Yorkshire
Map **7**   SD67

GH Oakroyd Private Hotel Main St
☎(0468) 41258

*Formerly the Vicarage, now a small family
run hotel with comfortable
accommodation and a friendly
atmosphere.*

7hc (6fb) B&bfr£9 Bdifr£13.75 Wfr£90 ⊭
LDO8pm
Lic ⊯ CTV 9P

GH Springfield Private Hotel Main St
☎(0468) 41280
Jan–Oct

Ingleby Greenhow
Invergarry

*Large Victorian villa. Family-run hotel with
homely atmosphere and panoramic views
at rear.*

6hc (4⊞) (4fb) CTV in all bedrooms
✱B&b£9–£10 Bdi£13.75–£14.75 W£90–
£97 ⊭LDO4.30pm
Lic ⊯ CTV 12P
ⓥ

├↦┤**FH** G W & M Bell **Langber** *(SD689709)*
☎(0468) 41587
Closed Xmas

*A large detached property in open
countryside in an elevated position
situated in a quiet country lane about 1m
south of Ingleton village. Turn off A65 at
'Mason's Arms'.*

6hc (4fb) B&b£7.75–£9 Bdi£10.95–£12
W£73–£81 ⊭LDO5.30pm
⊯ CTV 6P ✿ 59acres sheep

INGLEWHITE
Lancashire
Map **7**   SD54

FH Mrs R Rhodes **Park Head** *(SD542395)*
☎Brock (0995) 40352

---

*A well-furnished farmhouse with old oak
beams and offering true Lancashire
hospitality.*

2rm (1fb) ✖ ✱B&b£8 Bdi£12 W£80 ⊭
⊯ CTV 4P
214acres dairy sheep
ⓥ

INSTOW
Devon
Map **2**   SS43

GH Anchorage Hotel The Quay ☎(0271)
860655
Mar–Nov

*Private hotel on quay, facing river and
beach. Excellent views.*

11hc (10⊞) (6fb) ✱B&b£13–£15
Bdi£18.50–£20 W£111–£120 ⊭ (W only
May–Sep) LDO9pm
Lic ⊯ CTV 9P ✿
Credit cards ①②③④

INVERGARRY
Highland *Inverness-shire*
Map **14**   NH30

GH Craigard ☎(08093) 258
Mar–Nov

*Detached house with spacious bedrooms
and comfortable lounges.*

206

7hc ® ✳B&b£9.50–£10 Bdi£15–£15.50
W£95–£100 ⏰ LDO7pm
Lic CTV 6P
Ⓥ

GH Forest Lodge South Laggan (3m SW
A82) ☎(08093) 219
Apr–Oct

7hc (2fb) ® B&bfr£8.50 Bdifr£13.50
Wfr£90 ⏰ LDO7.30pm
🍴 CTV 10P

⊢•⊣**GH Lundie View** Aberchalder
☎(08093) 291
Closed Xmas & New Year

*Modernised roadside cottage with
extension overlooking pleasant hill and
woodland scenery. 3m NE A82.*

5hc (3fb) ® B&b£8–£8.50 Wfr£55 M
Lic 🍴 CTV 8P ♿
Ⓥ

FH Mr & Mrs R Wilson **Ardgarry**
(NH286015) Faichem ☎(08093) 226

*A comfortable and homely traditional
farmhouse, now operating as a small
holding. Located about 1m from
Invergarry off the A87—signed Faichem.*

1hc Annexe: 3hc (1fb) ✖ ® ✳B&b£8.50
Bdi£13 W£90 ⏰ LDO4pm
🍴 CTV 10P nc5yrs 10acres sheep mixed

Invergarry
—
Inverness

FH Mr & Mrs O'Connell **Faichem Lodge**
(NH286014) ☎(08093) 314
Mar–Nov

*Beautiful, modernised old stone house
with cosy bedrooms and lounge.
Although not a working farm the house is
set in 1½ acres of farmland and owners
keep ducks and hens in the garden. A
non-working farm but has access to one.*

3hc (1fb) ® LDO7pm
🍴 CTV 5P 1½acres non-working

INVERKEITHING
Fife
Map **11**   NT18

GH Forth Craig Private Hotel 90 Hope St
☎(0383) 418440

*Modern and well appointed split-level villa
with river views.*

5🍴 CTV in all bedrooms ® ✳B&b£12.50–
£15 Bdi£16–£18.50 W£108.50–£126 ⏰
LDO7pm
Lic 🍴 8P
Ⓥ

INVERNESS
Highland *Inverness-shire*
Map **14**   NH64
See plan on page 208

GH Abermar 25 Fairfield Rd ☎(0463)
239019 Plan **1** A2

*Compact modern detached house with
extension to rear set in residential area.*

11hc (3⇄) (3fb)
🍴 CTV 9P
Credit cards ①②③④

GH Ardnacoille House 1A Annfield Rd
☎(0463) 233451 Plan **2** D1
Apr–Oct

*Semi-detached house with lovely lounge,
in own gardens. Nicely appointed and
very well maintained.*

6hc (2fb) ✖ ✳B&b£9–£10 W£61–£67 M
🍴 CTV 8P nc10yrs

GH Arran 42 Union St ☎(0463) 232115
Plan **3** B2

*Set in upper floors of tenement building in
central location between shops.*

7hc (2fb) ✳B&b£9–£9.50
🍴 TV ✦

GH Brae Ness Hotel 16–17 Ness Bank
☎(0463) 231732 Plan **4** B1
Apr–Nov rs Feb & Mar   →

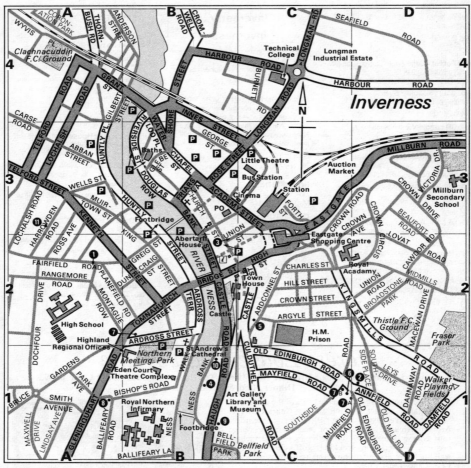

Inverness

1 Abermar	**4** Brae Ness Hotel	**7A** Ivybank	**10** Riverside House Hotel
2 Ardnacoille House	**5** Craigside House	**7B** Leinster Lodge	**11** St Ann's Hotel
3 Arran	**6** Four Winds	**8** Lyndale	
	7 Glencairn	**9** Moray Park Hotel	

Family run accommodation, situated beside the River Ness and close to town centre.

15hc (11🚿) (3fb) [R] B&b£11.50–£15 Bdi£17.50–£21.50 W£105–£135 k LDO7pm

Lic ♨ CTV 8P

Recommended

GH Craigside House 4 Gordon Ter (Guestaccom) ☎(0463) 231576 Plan **5** *C2*
May–Sep (rs Mar–Apr & Oct)

This welcoming Victorian house is situated in a quiet residential area overlooking the castle. The bright, cheerful bedrooms, four of which have en-suite facilities, are tastefully furnished and thoughtfully equipped. Well-filled bookshelves and magazines are provided for guests seeking quiet relaxation in the comfortable lounge.

6hc (1🛁 3🚿) (1fb) TV in all bedrooms 🚫 [R] ✱B&b£11.50–£15 Bdi£18–£21 W£120–£135 k LDO5pm

♨ 4P nc14yrs

GH *Four Winds* 42 Old Edinburgh Rd ☎(0463) 230397 Plan **6** *C1*
Closed Xmas & New Year

Detached lodge set in own grounds in residential suburb.

7hc (2fb)

♨ CTV 12P

GH Glencairn 19 Ardross St ☎(0463) 232965 Plan **7** *B2*
Closed 2 wks Xmas/New Year

Nicely appointed house in residential street.

11hc (2fb) ✱B&b£8.50–£9 W£59.50–£63 M

♨ CTV 3P 2🚗

GH Ivybank 28 Old Edinburgh Rd ☎(0463) 232796 Plan **7A** *C1*

A small, comfortable family-run guesthouse.

4hc (1🛁) [R] B&bfr£9

♨ CTV 5P

Inverness — Ipswich

GH *Leinster Lodge* 27 Southside Rd ☎(0463) 233311 Plan **7B** *C1*

Large town house with gardens, in a residential ara.

6hc (2fb)

CTV 8P

GH Moray Park Hotel Island Bank Rd ☎(0463) 233528 Plan **9** *B1*

Stone villa looking out across River Ness.

7hc (1🛁 2🚿) (2fb) CTV in all bedrooms 🚫 [R] B&b£10–£14 Bdi£17.50–£21.50 W£115–£143 k LDO6.30pm

Lic ♨ 7P nc9yrs solarium

Credit card [1]

GH Riverside House Hotel 8 Ness Bank ☎(0463) 231052 Plan **10** *B1*

Pleasantly situated beside river. Friendly service and comfortable accommodation.

10hc (5🚿) (5fb) CTV in all bedrooms [R] ✱B&b£12–£16 Bdi£18–£23 W£126–£161 k LDO5pm

Lic ♨ P̸

[V]

GH St Ann's Hotel 37 Harrowden Rd ☎(0463) 236157 Plan **11** *A3*

Nicely appointed guesthouse in a quiet, residential part of town.

6hc (1🛁 4🚿) (2fb) [R] ✱B&b£9–£11.75 Bdi£14.50–£17.25 W£90–£115 k LDO4.30pm

♨ CTV 3P

IPSTONES
Staffordshire
Map **7** SK04

FH Mrs J Brindley **Glenwood House** *(SK006488)* ☎(053871) 294
Closed 25 & 26 Dec

Large house approx 100 years old, built of dressed sandstone blocks in very picturesque and peaceful rural surroundings.

3hc (1fb) 🚫 [R] ✱B&b£9.50–£10.50 Bdi£15–£16 W£101.50–£108.50 k LDO2pm

♨ CTV 6P 🎾(hard) 58acres beef

IPSWICH
Suffolk
Map **5** TM14

GH Bentley Tower Hotel 172 Norwich Rd ☎(0473) 212142

Friendly, family-run establishment in large detached house.

10🚿 (2fb) CTV in all bedrooms 🚫 [R] ✱B&b£25 Bdi£32.50 W£227.50 k LDO9.30pm

Lic ♨ 10P

Credit cards [1] [2] [3] [5]

GH Gables Hotel 17 Park Rd ☎(0473) 54252

12hc ✱B&b£11.50–£13 Bdi£15.25–£16.75 W£80.50–£91 M

Lic ♨ CTV 10P

[V]

ISLE OF ARRAN
Strathclyde *Buteshire*
Map **10**
See **Arran, Isle of**

ISLE OF COLL
Strathclyde *Argyllshire*
Map **13**
See **Coll, Isle of**

ISLE OF LEWIS
Western Isles, Ross & Cromarty
Map **13**
See **Lewis, Isle of**

ISLE OF MAN
Map **6**
See **Man, Isle of**

ISLE OF MULL
Strathclyde *Argyllshire*
Map **10** & **13**
See **Mull, Isle of**

ISLE OF SKYE
Highland *Inverness-shire*
Map **13**
See **Skye, Isle of**

ISLE OF SOUTH UIST
Western Isles *Inverness-shire*
Map **13**
See **South Uist, Isle of**

ISLE OF WIGHT
Hampshire
Map **4**
See **Wight, Isle of**

ISLE ORNSAY
See **Skye, Isle of**

ISLES OF SCILLY
(No map)
See **Scilly, Isles of**

ISLEWORTH
Gt London
London plan **4** B3
(pages **246***)*

GH Kingswood Hotel 33 Woodlands Rd ☎01-560 5614

11hc CTV in all bedrooms ⋈ ✱B&b£14.95–£18.40 W£104.65–£128.80 M̸

Lic 🛋 CTV 5P 1🚗 nc6yrs

[V]

IVER HEATH
Buckinghamshire
Map **4** TQ08

GH Bridgettine Convent Fulmer Common Rd ☎Fulmer (02816) 2073

An unusual establishment, a convent run by nuns, offering simple, comfortable accommodation in a friendly, peaceful atmosphere.

22hc (7🛁) (4fb) ⋈ ✱B&b£11 Bdi£14.50 LDO6pm

🛋 CTV 30P 1🚗

JACOBSTOWE
Devon
Map **2** SS50

FH Mrs J King **Higher Cadham** *(SS585026)* ☎Exbourne (083785) 647
Mar–Nov (rs Mar & Nov, only one bedroom available)

Well-decorated and comfortably furnished 16th-century farmhouse. Ideal base for touring.

4hc (1fb) ⋈ [R] ✱B&b£8 Bdi£12 W£77 Ł (W only Aug) LDO5pm

Lic 🛋 CTV 6P nc3yrs 🎣 139acres beef sheep mixed

[V]

JEDBURGH
Borders *Roxburghshire*
Map **12** NT62

GH Ferniehirst Mill Lodge ☎(0835) 63279
Apr–Oct

Modern, purpose-built lodge in secluded position beside the River Jed. 3m S of Jedburgh off A68. Horse-riding holidays are a speciality.

11hc (5🛁 3🚿) [R] ✱B&b£17.50 Bdi£28.50 W£189.50 Ł LDO8.30pm

Lic 🛋 16P nc12yrs 🎣 U

[V]

GH Kenmore Bank Oxnam Rd ☎(0835) 62369

Compact house perched high above the Jed Water and looking across to the town.

6hc (2fb) CTV in all bedrooms ⋈ [R] ✱B&b£10–£12 Bdi£15–£17 W£105–£119 Ł LDO9pm

Lic 🛋 6P

[V]

GH The Spinney Langlee (2m S on A68) ☎(0835) 63525
Etr–Oct

Converted country cottages, now modernised and tastefully furnished. 2m S of Jedburgh on the A68.

3rm (2🛁) [R] ✱B&b£12–£13 W£84–£91 M̸

🛋 CTV P 🎣

[V]

JERSEY
Channel Islands
Map **16**
See **Channel Islands**

KEITH
Grampian *Banffshire*
Map **15** NJ45

FH Mrs J Jackson **The Haughs** *(NJ416515)* ☎(05422) 2238
May–Oct

Traditional stone-built farmhouse, with pleasant views, 1m from Keith off A96.

4hc (1fb) 🚭 in 2 bedrooms ⋈ [R] ✱B&b£8–£8.50 Bdi£13.50–£14 W£93–£96 Ł LDO3pm

🛋 CTV 9P 2🚗 🏠 220acres arable mixed

[V]

FH Mrs E C Leith **Montgrew** *(NJ453517)* ☎(05422) 2852
Apr–Oct

Stone-built house situated in valley within easy reach of beaches, hills and the Cairngorms. 2m E off A95.

4rm (1hc) (1fb) ✱B&bfr£8 Bdifr£12.50 Wfr£87.50 Ł LDO7pm

🛋 CTV 4P 🎣 211acres arable beef

Credit card [1] [V]

FH Mrs G Murphy **Tarnash House** *(NJ442490)* ☎(05422) 2728
May–Oct

Two-storey, stone farmhouse with well maintained garden to the front. 1m S off A96.

4hc (1fb) ✱B&b£8–£8.50

🛋 CTV 10P 100acres arable

Credit cards [1] [2] [3] [4] [5] [V]

KELMSCOTT
Oxfordshire
Map **4** SU29

FH Mrs A Amor **Manor Farm** *(SU253995)* ☎Faringdon (0367) 52620

An attractive Cotswold Farm (National Trust property) on edge of peaceful village of Kelmscott.

2hc (2fb) ⋈ [R] ✱B&b£9.50–£15 Bdi£15–£23 W£105–£160 Ł

🛋 CTV 6P 315acres arable dairy

[V]

KELSO
Borders *Roxburghshire*
Map **12** NT73

GH Bellevue Bowmont St ☎(0573) 24588
Apr–Oct

Attractive house with good standard throughout. Ten minutes walk from the town centre.

8hc (2🚿) (2fb) ⋈ B&b£9.50–£11 Bdi£14–£15.50 W£94.50–£105 Ł LDO5pm

Lic 🛋 CTV 8P

KENDAL
Cumbria
Map **7** SD59
See also **Brigsteer** & **Crook**

⊢⊣**FH** Mrs S Beaty **Garnett House** *(SD500959)* Burneside ☎(0539) 24542
Closed Xmas & New Year

15th-century stone-built farmhouse situated in an elevated position overlooking Howgill Fells, close to Windermere and Kendal.

5hc (2fb) ⋈ [R] B&b£8–£9 Bdi£11.75–£12.75 LDO5pm

CTV 6P 🏠 270acres dairy sheep

FH Mrs J Ellis **Gateside** *(NY494955)* Windermere Rd ☎(0539) 22036
Closed Xmas

16th-century farmhouse of great charm and character.

4hc (1fb) CTV in 3 bedrooms TV in 1 bedroom [R] ✱B&b£8.50–£9 Bdi£13–£14 LDO4.30pm

🛋 CTV 7P 280acres beef dairy sheep mixed

[V]

FH Mrs E M Gardner **Natland Mill Beck** *(SD520907)* (1m from Kendal on A69) ☎(0539) 21122
Mar–Oct

17th-century, local stone-built farmhouse with original beams, doors and cupboards. Large well-furnished rooms. Attractive walled garden.

3rm (2hc) [R] ✱B&b£8–£9

🛋 CTV 3P 🏠 100acres dairy

Credit cards [1] [2] [3] [4] [V]

FH Mrs S K Bell **Oxenholme** *(SD529905)*
Oxenholme Rd ☎(0539) 27226
*A delightfully furnished farmhouse dating
back to 1540. Many natural beams and
features an inglenook fireplace. 2m SE
B6254.*
3hc (1fb) ✻ ✱B&b£8–£8.50 W£50–£55 M
ᵐ CTV 4P nc3yrs 180acres dairy sheep
soft fruit
ⓥ

KENILWORTH
Warwickshire
Map **4**　SP27

GH Enderley 20 Queens Rd ☎(0926)
55388
5hc ✻ ® ✱B&b£10.50–£19
Lic ᵐ CTV 2P
ⓥ

GH Ferndale 45 Priory Rd ☎(0926)
53214
Closed Xmas & New Year
7hc (1fb) ✻ ✱B&b£9.50–£12.50
ᵐ CTV 8P
ⓥ

GH Hollyhurst 47 Priory Rd ☎(0926)
53882
Closed Xmas Day
*Large semi-detached house with well-
decorated bedrooms and comfortable
lounge.*

Kendal
—
Keswick

9hc (3fb) ® ✱B&b£9.50–£12 Bdi£14.50–
£17 LDO1pm
Lic ᵐ CTV 10P

GH Nightingales Hotel & Restaurant
95–97 Warwick Rd ☎(0926) 53594
*Modest hotel with interesting menus
which include fresh seasonal fare and
selected wines.*
10hc (1fb) LDO9.30pm
Lic ᵐ CTV 🅿
Credit cards ① ② ③

KENNFORD
Devon
Map **3**　SX98

⊩►**FH** Mrs R Weeks **Holloway Barton**
(SX893855) ☎Exeter (0392) 832302
Closed Xmas
*Well appointed house retaining its old
charm and offering panoramic views.
Situated just off the M5 & A38. Central for
two racecourses, coast and moors.*
4hc (1fb) ® in 2 bedrooms LDO4pm
ᵐ CTV 4P 1🎱 billiards 360acres arable
beef dairy

KENTALLEN
Highland *Argyllshire*
Map **14**　NN05

FH Mrs D A MacArthur **Ardsheal Home**
(NN996574) ☎Duror (063174) 229
Apr–Oct
*Tastefully decorated house with a tidy
garden, standing in sheltered position.*
3rm (1hc 1⇆) (1fb) ® ✱B&b£7.50–
£8.50 Wfr£56 M
ᵐ CTV 5P 1000acres beef dairy sheep
mixed
ⓥ

KESWICK
Cumbria
Map **11**　NY22
See plan on page 212

GH Acorn House Hotel Ambleside Rd
☎(07687) 72553
Plan **1** *C2*
*Large detached house with pleasant
garden in quiet part of town.*
10hc (1🖭) (2fb) ® ✱B&b£9.50–£10.50
Bdi£14.50–£15 W£96.50–£100 ⱡ LDO4pm
Lic ᵐ CTV 9P
ⓥ

GH Allerdale House 1 Eskin St
☎(07687) 73891 Plan **2** *C1*
Closed Dec　　　　　　　　　　→

Acorn House Hotel

**AMBLESIDE ROAD, KESWICK,
CUMBRIA, CA12 4DL
Telephone: Keswick (07687) 72553**
A converted Georgian House set in a large
garden with enclosed car parks, and convenient
for town centre and lake. All rooms have
washbasin, shaver socket, tea-making facilities,
electric blankets and clock radios. TV lounge,
Full central heating, Home cooking, Licensed.
Fred and Mary Lewis hope to welcome you to
Acorn House.

Acorn House Built in the early 19ᵗʰ Century.

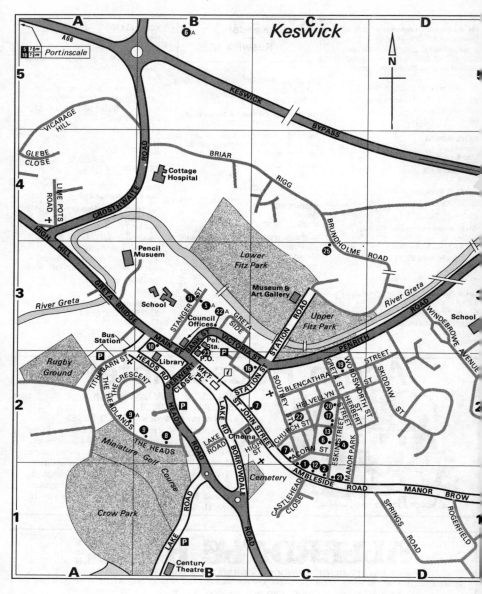

Keswick

Striking Lakeland slate house in quiet location. Some rooms with en suite facilities.

6hc (2⇨ 1🚿) (2fb) CTV in all bedrooms ℝ ✱B&b£10–£11 Bdi£15–£16 W£105–£112 ⏣ LDO5pm

Lic 🍴 CTV 4P nc2yrs

GH Clarence House 14 Eskin St ☎(07687) 73186 Plan **4** *C2*

A very comfortable Lakeland residence renowned for its good food and hospitality. Most bedrooms have en-suite facilities.

8hc (5🚿) (2fb) ✕ in 2 bedrooms ℝ ✱B&b£10.20–£11.60 Bdi£15.50–£16.90 W£102–£108 ⏣ LDO6pm

Lic 🍴 CTV ⏣

Ⓥ

GH *Derwent Lodge* Portinscale ☎(07687) 72746 Plan **5** *A5* Mar–Nov

Country house in mature gardens 1 mile from town centre.

8hc (1⇨) (2fb) ⏣ LDO7.15pm

Lic 🍴 CTV 20P

⤚•GH Fell House** 28 Stranger St ☎(07687) 72669 Plan **5A** *B3*

Warm and welcoming guesthouse with spacious and comfortable bedrooms.

Keswick

6hc (2fb) TV in 1 bedroom CTV in 5 bedrooms ✕ ℝ ✱B&b£9–£10 Bdi£13.50–£14.50 W£92.50–£95 ⏣ LDO3.30pm

🍴 CTV 4P nc4yrs

GH Foye House 23 Eskin St ☎(07687) 73288 Plan **6** *C2*

Pleasant and compact guesthouse in residential area.

6hc (2fb) ℝ B&b£9 Bdi£13.50 W£90 ⏣ LDO5.30pm

Lic 🍴 CTV ⏣

GH Gale Hotel Underskiddaw ☎(07687) 72413 Plan **6A** *B5* Etr–4 Nov

A lovely, spacious, comfortable house set in large attractive gardens with good views of Borrowdale.

14hc (5⇨ 4🚿) (3fb) ✕ ℝ ✱B&b£13–£15.50 Bdi£20–£22.50 LDO6pm

Lic 🍴 CTV 10P

Credit card ① Ⓥ

GH Greystones Ambleside Rd ☎(07687) 73108 Plan **7A** *C1*

An attractive and spacious end-terrace house serving good home-cooking.

10hc (2🚿) (2fb) ✕ ℝ ✱B&b£9–£11 Bdi£14–£16 LDO5pm

Lic 🍴 CTV 4P 2🏍

GH Hazeldene Hotel The Heads ☎(07687) 72106 Plan **8** *B2* 10 Mar–6 Nov

Large guesthouse with some lovely views of lake and surrounding fells.

23hc (15🚿) (10fb) ℝ ✱B&b£10.50–£14.30 Bdi£16.80–£20.50 W£112–£137 ⏣ LDO4.30pm

Lic 🍴 CTV 18P

Ⓥ

GH Highfield The Heads ☎(07687) 72508 Plan **9** *B2* Apr–Oct

Spacious family run guesthouse offering a high standard of accommodation.

19hc (2⇨ 13🚿) (3fb) ✱B&b£11–£14 Bdi£18.50–£21.50 W£129.50–£150.50 ⏣ LDO7.30pm

Lic 🍴 CTV 19P nc5yrs

Ⓥ

GH Holmwood House The Heads ☎(07687) 73301 Plan **9A** *A2* mid Mar–mid Nov

A well-appointed, comfortable house with fine views across Derwent Water. ⟶

7hc (1fb) ✗ B&b£11.50–£12 Bdi£16.50–£17 W£112.50 ⊬ LDO4pm
Lic ₩ CTV ✗ nc5yrs
Ⓥ

GH Lincoln House Stanger St ☎(07687) 72597 Plan **11** *B3*
Mar–Dec rs Jan & Feb
Terraced house in an elevated position close to centre of town.
6hc (2fb) ✗ ✱B&b£8.50–£9 Bdi£12.50–£13 W£87.50–£91 ⊬ LDO4pm
Lic ₩ CTV 4P

GH Lynwood Private Hotel
12 Ambleside Rd ☎(07687) 72081
Plan **12** *C1*

150-year-old end terraced house built of Lakeland stone, with pretty front garden in a residential area.
7hc (2fb) ✗ Ⓡ ✱B&b£9–£10 Bdi£14–£16 W£98–£112 ⊬ LDO5pm
Lic ₩ CTV ✗ nc8yrs
Ⓥ

GH Melbreak House 29 Church St ☎(07687) 73398 Plan **13** *C2*

A traditional, grey-slate building, cleverly converted from two corner houses in quiet residential area.
12hc (5fb) CTV in 6 bedrooms Ⓡ ✱B&b£9.50 Bdi£13.50 W£90 ⊬ LDO5.30pm
Lic CTV ✗
Ⓥ

GH Ravensworth 29 Station St ☎(07687) 72476 Plan **16** *C2*
Comfortable guesthouse near town centre with basement shop selling continental and home-made chocolates.
9hc (1⇦2⏰) (1fb) ✗ Ⓡ B&b£10.50–£17 Bdi£15–£22 W£103–£128 ⊬ LDO9pm

LINCOLN HOUSE

23 STANGER STREET, KESWICK CA12 5JX
Telephone: Keswick (07687) 72597
LINCOLN HOUSE is in an elevated position near the centre of town in a quiet cul-de-sac with parking available, with excellent views from all windows. Highly recommended for the excellence of it's catering and the attention given to the comfort of guests, comfortable lounge with colour TV. Guests' own rooms and lounge available at all times. Overnight visitors welcome.
S.A.E. for Brochure & Tariff to proprietors
Norman & Margaret Wise.

Lynwood Guest House

12 Ambleside Road, Keswick-on-Derwentwater, Cumbria CA12 4DL Telephone: Keswick (07687) 72081
Quietly and pleasantly situated 800 yards from Derwentwater and 350 yards from the town, is a small guesthouse with a residential licence where a high standard of comfort, cuisine and personal attention are ensured. All the bedrooms are centrally heated, tastefully furnished, have hot and cold water, shaver points and facilities for making hot drinks. Good home cooked food can be enjoyed in the friendly, relaxed atmosphere of the spacious dining room. Wholesome packed lunches can be provided & special diets catered for. Drying facilities and a lock up cycle store are available and ample street parking is close-by. Open all year. Special 3 day Christmas break.

Melbreak House
29 Church Street, Keswick CA12 4DX Telephone: (07687) 73398
Melbreak is a large, traditional grey-slate, Lakeland building in a peaceful yet convenient area of this lovely old market town which provides an ideal base for discovering the delights of the Lake District.
We provide all the usual amenities and a high standard of cuisine, comfort and service in an informal relaxed atmosphere.
Our emphasis is on good value for money, our rates are reasonable with generous reductions for children.
Residential Licence.
Brochure with pleasure on request.

Lic 🛋 CTV 5P
Credit cards [1] [2] [3] [5] [V]

GH Richmond House 37–39 Eskin St ☎(07687) 73965 Plan **17** *C2*

A comfortable private hotel set in a residential area close to town centre.

12hc (3🚿) (1fb) ✖ [R] ✱B&b£9.50–£11.50 Bdi£14.50–£16.50 W£95–£110 ⊬ LDO5pm
Lic 🛋 CTV P̸ nc10yrs
Credit cards [1] [2] [3] [5] [V]

Recommended

GH Rickerby Grange Portinscale (Guestaccom) ☎(07687) 72344 Plan **18** *A5*
Closed 23–28 Dec

Peacefully situated in the pretty little village of Portinscale, Rickerby Grange is an attractive detached house standing in its own grounds. The bedrooms are well-decorated and furnished and there is a cosy bar and comfortable lounge. A good home-cooked, four-course dinner is served every evening.

11hc (2🛁 7🚿) (2fb) B&b£12.50–£16.25 Bdi£18.50–£22.75 W£122–£147 ⊬ LDO6pm
Lic 🛋 15P
[V]
See advertisement on page 216

Keswick

GH Silverdale Hotel Blencathra St ☎(07687) 72294 Plan **19** *C2*

Large detached house in residential area.

13hc (2fb) ✖ B&b£10.50 Bdi£15 W£98 ⊬ LDO5.30pm
Lic 🛋 CTV 4P
[V]

GH Squirrel Lodge 43 Eskin St ☎(07687) 73091 Plan **20** *C2*

Lovely little family-run guesthouse with well-appointed bedrooms and good food.

7hc CTV in all bedrooms [R] ✱B&bfr£9.50 Bdifr£14.50 Wfr£97.50 ⊬ LDO6pm
Lic 🛋 CTV P̸ nc10yrs
Credit cards [1] [3]

GH Stonegarth 2 Eskin St ☎(07687) 72436 Plan **21** *C1*
Mar–Oct

A large corner terrace house in residential area, which the proprietors run on a homely basis.

9hc (3fb) [R] ✱B&b£9.75–£10.25 Bdi£14.50–£15 W£100–£103 ⊬ LDO6pm
Lic 🛋 CTV 9P nc3yrs
[V]
See advertisement on page 216

GH Sunnyside 25 Southey St ☎(07687) 72446 Plan **22** *C2*

A bright and comfortable family-run guesthouse.

8hc (2fb) CTV in all bedrooms ✖ [R] ✱B&b£8–£10 W£48–£55 M̸
🛋 8P
Credit card [1]

GH Swiss Court 25 Bank St ☎(07687) 72637 Plan **22A** *B3*

Victorian terraced house in town centre.

7hc ✖ ✱B&b£9
🛋 CTV 3P nc6yrs
See advertisement on page 216

GH Thornleigh 23 Bank St ☎(07687) 72863 Plan **23** *B3*

A comfortable house in the centre of town run by very friendly proprietors.

7hc ✖ [R] ✱B&b£8.95–£10.95 Bdi£14.95–£17.45 W£93.95–£109.95 ⊬ LDO5.30pm
🛋 CTV 3P nc15yrs
Credit cards [1] [3] [V]
See advertisement on page 216

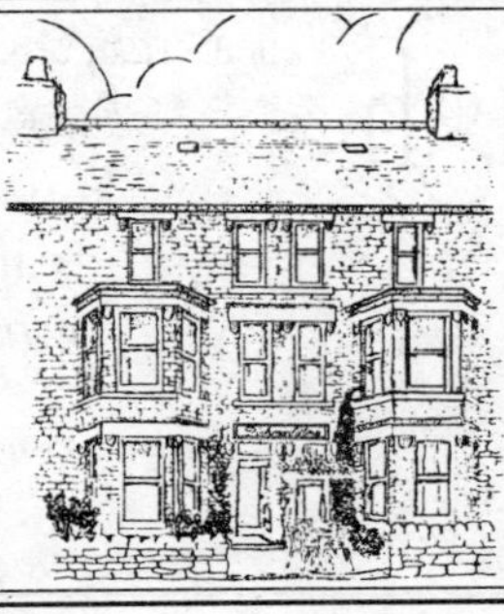

216

GH Woodlands Brundholme Rd
(07687) 72399 Plan **25** *C3*
1 wk before Etr–Oct

Charming, stone-built, country house in quiet location in own grounds.

4hc (1fb) ✗ ✱B&b£10.25–£11 Bdi£15.50–£16.25 W£95–£102 ⌀ LDO10am

🍴 CTV 7P nc6yrs

Ⓥ

INN George Hotel St Johns Street
(Mount Charlotte) ☎(07687) 72076
Plan **7** *C2*

16th-century coaching inn full of charm and character, with restaurant and bar meals.

17hc (3fb) Ⓡ ✱B&b£14–£15 Bdi£18–£19 W£126–£133 ⌀ Lunch £3.90–£4.50 High tea £3.85–£4.20 Dinner8.30pm £7.50–£8.50&alc

CTV 11P

Credit cards ① ② ③ ⑤ Ⓥ

INN Kings Arms Hotel Main St ☎(07687) 72083 Plan **10** *B3*
Closed Jan

An 18th-century coaching inn with attractively decorated and furnished bedrooms. Good food served in restaurant, pizzeria and bar.

13hc (2⇔ 11🚿) CTV in all bedrooms ✗ Ⓡ B&bfr£18 Wfr£154 ⌀ LDO9.30pm

Lic 🍴 CTV ⌗

Ⓥ

Keswick
—
Keynsham

KETTLEBURGH
Suffolk
Map **5**   TM26

FH Mrs I A Pearce **Rookery** *(TM273606)*
Framlingham ☎Framlingham (0728) 723248
rs Nov–Feb

Georgian farmhouse standing in 1½ acres of well kept gardens. Situated ¾m N of Kettleburgh.

3hc (1fb) ✗ B&b£9.50–£10.50 Bdi£14.50–£15.50 W£63–£70 ⋈ LDO6pm

🍴 CTV 3P nc10yrs 350acres arable

KETTLEWELL
North Yorkshire
Map **7**   SD97

GH Dale House ☎(075676) 836
Etr–Nov & Winter wknd breaks

Charming stone built village house close to the River Wharfe.

6hc (3🚿) Ⓡ B&b£14.50 Bdi£21.50 W£132 ⌀

Lic 🍴 CTV 6P nc ↻

Credit cards ① ③

GH Langcliffe House ☎(075676) 243
Mar–1 Jan

Charming, relaxed house on the edge of the village.

6hc (1⇔ 2🚿) CTV in 1 bedroom TV in 1 bedroom Ⓡ B&b£13–£14 Bdi£20–£21 W£130–£137 ⌀ LDO7pm

Lic 🍴 CTV 4P 2🚘

Credit cards ① ③ Ⓥ

KEXBY
North Yorkshire
Map **8**   SE75

FH Mrs K R Daniel **Ivy House** *(SE691511)*
☎York(0904) 489368 Telex no 57842

Brick-built farmhouse adjacent to A1079 York–Pocklington road. Snug accommodation of neat and modest proportions.

3rm (1fb) ✗ ✱B&b£8–£8.50 Wfr£50 ⋈

🍴 CTV 6P 135acres mixed

KEYNSHAM
Avon
Map **3**   ST66

FH Mrs L Sparkes **Uplands** *(ST663664)*
Wellsway ☎(02756) 5764

8hc (1⇔) (4fb) CTV in 1 bedroom ✱B&b£12.50–£15 Bdi£18.50–£21 W£105–£125 ⌀ LDO10am

🍴 CTV 25P 200acres dairy

GEORGE HOTEL

St John Street, Keswick, Cumbria
Telephone: (07687) 72076

A 16th century coaching Inn situated in the centre of Keswick, a pleasant market town tucked neatly in the folds of the fells. Originally a coaching house, the hotel still has a homely, cheerful appearance and is famous for its good food and hospitality. The bedrooms are well furnished and the bar is a popular meeting place with open fires that offers guests a warm friendly welcome.

King's Arms Hotel

Keswick-on-Derwentwater, English Lakes
Tel: Keswick (07687) 72083

18th-century Coaching Inn in centre of popular tourist town. Ideal base for touring, walking, climbing. All bedrooms with tea/coffee facilities, residents lounge with colour TV, oak beamed bar. The Beefeater restaurant provides a set menu or à la carte with comprehensive wine list. Extensive bar snacks lunch and evening. Loose Box bar and Pizzeria. Open all year round. Summer/winter breaks. Christmas/New Year programme. Brochure on request.

KIDDERMINSTER
Hereford & Worcester
Map **7** SO87

GH Cedars Hotel Mason Rd ☎(0562) 745869 Telex no 334994

Set in a residential area easily accessible to town centre and ring road: A Georgian house well equipped with modern facilities.

10🚿 (3fb) CTV in all bedrooms [R] B&bfr£21

Lic 21P

Credit cards [1] [2] [3] [5]

KIDLINGTON
Oxfordshire
Map **4** SP41

Recommended

GH Bowood House 238 Oxford Rd ☎(08675) 2839
Closed 25 & 26 Dec

Well-kept family house with modern bedroom facilities.

9hc (2🛁 3🚿) (2fb) CTV in all bedrooms 🐕 [R] B&b£12.50–£15.75 Bdi£22–£25.25 LDO4pm

Lic 🍸 CTV 12P 🏊(heated)

Credit cards [1] [3]

KILGETTY
Dyfed
Map **2** SN10

GH Manian Lodge Begelly ☎(0834) 813273

Family hotel beautifully situated near Tenby and Saundersfoot

6🚿 (4fb) [R] ✱B&b£10–£12 Bdi£14–£16 W£90–£105 ⱡ

Lic CTV 15P ⛍

[V]

FH Mrs S A James **Little Newton** *(SN122073)* ☎Saundersfoot (0834) 812306
May–Sep

Small farm with modern house of character.

9hc (6fb) 🐕 ✱B&b£7.50–£9 Bdi£11–£13 W£77–£91 ⱡ (W only Jul & Aug)

🍸 CTV 10P ⛍ 10acres non-working

[V]

KILKHAMPTON
Cornwall
Map **2** SS21

INN *London* ☎(028882) 343
3hc LDO9pm
CTV 4P nc10yrs
Credit card [3]

KILLIECRANKIE
Tayside *Perthshire*
Map **14** NN96

GH Dalnasgadh House ☎Pitlochry (0796) 3237
Apr–Oct

Attractive house standing on the outskirts of this village.

6hc (1fb) 🚭 in 4 bedrooms 🐕 ✱B&b£9.50–£10

🍸 CTV 10P nc12yrs

KILMARTIN
Strathclyde *Argyllshire*
Map **10** NR89

INN Kilmartin Hotel ☎(05465) 250

A white painted inn with attractive hanging baskets, on the main A816, it is a popular eating place.

5hc (1fb) [R] ✱B&b£11–£11.50 Bdi£16–£16.50 Wfr£105 ⱡ Bar lunch £3.50alc Dinner 9pm £9.50–£10.50&alc

CTV 13P 🏨

[V]

KILPECK
Hereford & Worcester
Map **3** SO43

FH Mrs I J Pike **Priory** *(SO446302)*
☎Wormbridge (098121) 366
Apr–Oct

2hc 🚫 [R] ✱B&b£10 W£70 M

CTV 4P 2🚗 small-holding mixed

KILVE
Somerset
Map **3** ST14

INN Hood Arms ☎Holford (027874) 210
Closed Xmas Day

5hc (3🛁 2🚿) CTV in all bedrooms [R]
B&b£18–£20 Bdi£24–£27 W£152–£171 Ł
Bar lunch £4.50alc Dinner 10pm £8alc

📺 12P ⛿ nc7yrs

Credit cards [1] [3] [V]

KINCRAIG
Highland *Inverness-shire*
Map **14** NH80

GH March House Lagganlia ☎(05404)
388
Closed Nov

Modern guesthouse with well-appointed rooms and magnificent views.

6hc (3🛁) (1fb) 🚭 in 4 bedrooms
✱B&b£9–£10 Bdi£14–£15 W£95–£100 Ł
LDO6pm

📺 8P

[V]

KINGHAM
Oxfordshire
Map **4** SP22

GH Conygree Gate Church St
(Guestaccom) ☎(060871) 389
Mar–Oct

Attractive Cotswold-stone house situated in charming, peaceful village, with modern amenities. Kept spotlessly clean and run by two very English ladies providing good home cooking.

6rm (5hc) (1fb) 🚫 ✱B&b£15 Bdi£20
W£133 Ł LDO5pm

Lic 📺 CTV 2P 5🚗 nc7yrs

KINGHORN
Fife
Map **11** NT28

INN *Long Boat* 107 Pettycur Rd ☎(0592)
890625

Large modern villa looking out across the Firth of Forth decorated and furnished to the highest standards.

6🚿 (1fb) CTV in all bedrooms [R]
LDO10pm

Lic 📺 35P

Credit cards [1] [2] [3] [5]

KINGSBRIDGE
Devon
Map **3** SX74

Kilpeck — Kingston

GH Ashleigh House Ashleigh Rd,
Westville ☎(0548) 2893
May–Sep

8hc (1fb) [R] B&b£10–£11 Bdi£15–£16.25
W£100–£110 Ł LDO4pm

CTV 6P nc5yrs

GH Harbour Lights Hotel Ebrington St
☎(0548) 2418
Etr–Oct

Friendly, personal service at this converted 18th-century property in the heart of Kingsbridge.

5hc ✱B&b£10.50–£12.50 Bdi£18.50–
£20.50 W£115–£125 Ł LDO8pm

Lic CTV 6P

GH *Hotel Kildare* Balkwill Rd ☎(0548)
2451

9hc (4fb) LDO7.15pm

Lic CTV 7P 🏠

Credit card [1]

KINGSDOWN
Kent
Map **5** TR34

GH Blencathra Country Kingsdown Hill
☎Deal (0304) 373725

Friendly, modern, country guesthouse with use of a croquet lawn.

5hc (3fb) CTV in 2 bedrooms 🚫 [R]
✱B&b£10 Bdi£15 W£95 Ł LDO6pm

Lic 📺 CTV 7P

KINGSEY
Buckinghamshire
Map **4** SP70

Recommended

FH Mr N M D Hooper **Foxhill**
(SP748066) ☎Haddenham (0844)
291650
Feb–Nov

17th-century farmhouse with spacious, comfortable bedrooms. Delightful garden with pool and pond.

3hc 🚫 ✱B&b£11.50–£12 W£80.50–
£84 M

📺 CTV 40P nc5yrs 🏊(heated)
4acres small-holding sheep

[V]

KINGSGATE
Kent
Map **5** TR37

GH Marylands Hotel Marine Dr ☎Thanet
(0843) 61259
May–Oct

Friendly hotel overlooking the sea with direct access to the beach.

10hc (1🛁) (3fb) [R] ✱B&b£10–£12
Bdi£14.50–£16.50 W£90–£100 Ł LDOnoon

Lic CTV 10P

[V]

KINGSLAND
Hereford & Worcester
Map **3** SO46

FH Mrs F M Hughes ***Tremayne***
(SO447613) ☎(056881) 233
Apr–Nov

Deceptively large, two-storey building on one of the main roads to Leominster.

3hc (1fb)

📺 CTV 3P 40acres sheep mixed

KING'S LYNN
Norfolk
Map **9** TF62

GH Havana 117 Gaywood Rd ☎(0553)
772331

Family run guesthouse offering simple, good- value accommodation.

7hc (1🚿) (2fb) CTV in 5 bedrooms TV in 2
bedrooms 🚫 [R] B&b£9–£10 Bdi£14–£15
W£98–£105 Ł LDO1pm

📺 CTV 8P

[V]

See advertisement on page 220

GH Marantha 115 Gaywood Rd
☎(0553) 774596

Large semi-detached house on busy town road.

6hc (1fb) ✱B&b £8 Bdi £11 W£77 Ł
LDO6pm

Lic 📺 CTV 5P 🏠 🏊

GH Russet House Hotel 53 Goodwins
Rd ☎(0553) 773098
Closed Xmas–New Year

11hc (3🛁 4🚿) (2fb) CTV in all bedrooms
[R] B&b£18–£26.50 Bdi£23.95–£32.45
LDO7pm

Lic 📺 CTV 12P

Credit cards [1] [3] [5]

See advertisement on page 220

KINGSTON
Devon
Map **2** SX64

GH Trebles Cottage Private Hotel
(Guestaccom) ☎Bigbury-on-Sea (0548)
810268
Mar–Oct

6hc (3🛁) 🚫 [R] B&b£11.50–£14.50
Bdi£17–£20 W£110.25–£131.25 Ł
LDO6pm

Lic 📺 CTV 10P nc12yrs

[V]

KINGSTON BAGPUIZE
Oxfordshire
Map **4** SU49

FH Mrs A Y Crowther **Fallowfields**
(SU393979) Fallow Field Southmoor
☎Longworth (0865) 820416
Telex 83388
Etr–Sep

4hc (1fб) (1fb) ® ✳B&b£13.50–£17
Bdi£24–£27.50 Wfr£157.50 ⌡ LDO6.30pm
Lic 艸 CTV 15P nc10years ⌇(heated)
12 acres sheep

INN Hinds Head Witney Rd
☎Longworth (0865) 820204

Kingston Bagpuize
—
Kingston upon Thames

Small roadside inn with comfortable, modern bedrooms.
3hc B&b£12 P

KINGSTONE
Hereford & Worcester
Map **3** SO43

FH Mrs G C Andrews **Webton Court**
(SO421365) ☎Golden Valley (0981) 250220

Georgian farmhouse amidst large farm buildings. Located off B4348.

6hc (2fb) ® ✳B&b£8–£10 Bdi£13–£14.50 W£88 ⌡ LDO7pm
Lic 艸 CTV 10P ♪ ♫ ♉ snooker
280acres arable beef horse sheep mixed

KINGSTON UPON THAMES
Gt London
London plan **4** B2
(page 246)

GH *Hotel Antoinette* 26 Beaufort Rd
☎01-546 1044

A friendly family run commercial hotel with most bedrooms en-suite and attractive garden. Situated in quiet residential area.

115hc (50⇐ 50🛁) (20fb) CTV in 30 bedrooms TV in 85 bedrooms ® in 20 bedrooms LDO9.30pm

Lic 🍽 CTV 70P

Credit cards ① ③

KINGSWELLS
Grampian *Aberdeenshire*
Map **15**   NJ80

FH Mrs M Mann **Bellfield** *(NJ868055)*
☎Aberdeen (0224) 740239
Closed Dec

Modern farmhouse on quiet road set amid farmlands. 4m W of Aberdeen city centre off A944.

3hc (2fb) CTV in 1 bedroom ✳B&b£9.50–£10

🍽 CTV P ⮑ 200acres arable dairy

Ⓥ

KINGTON
Hereford & Worcester
Map **3**   SO25

FH Mrs E E Protheroe **Bucks Head** *(SO265550)* Upper Hergest ☎(0544) 231063

2m SW on unclass Gladestry rd.

5hc (2fb) ✖ ✳B&b£8–£8.50 Bdi£13.50–£14 W£92–£95 ⏸ LDO9pm

🍽 CTV 6P ⮑ 290acres arable beef sheep

Ⓥ

FH Mrs M Eckley **Holme** *(SO339553)*
Lyonshall ☎ Lyonshall (05448) 216
Etr–Oct

Fully-modernised farmhouse standing on outskirts of village, 2m E of Kington.

4rm (3hc) (1fb) ✖ B&b£9.50 Bdi£15 W£101.50 ⏸ LDOam

🍽 CTV P nc 270acres arable dairy sheep mixed

FH J A Layton **Park Gate** *(SO332575)*
Lyonshall ☎Lyonshall (05448) 243
Closed Xmas

Two-storey, stone-built farmhouse with land overlooking Wales. Offa's Dyke runs through part of the farm. 2m E of Kington

2hc (1fb) ✖

🍽 CTV P ⮑ 230acres sheep mixed

Kingston upon Thames
—
Kirkconnel

KINGUSSIE
Highland *Inverness-shire*
Map **14**   NH70

— Recommended —
GH Homewood Lodge Newtonmore Rd ☎(05402) 507

Victorian house amidst tree-studded grounds with splendid views.

5hc (4🛁) (4fb) ✖ ® ✳B&b£12–£14 Bdi£21–£23 W£140–£155 ⏸ LDO7.30pm

Lic 🍽 CTV 10P

GH Sonnhalde East Ter ☎(05402) 266

Attractive grey stone detached house located in terrace in elevated position behind main street.

7hc (2fb) ✳B&b£8.50–£9 Bdi£13–£13.50 W£84–£90 ⏸ LDO2pm

🍽 CTV 8P 1🐎 ⮑

Ⓥ

KINVER
Staffordshire
Map **7**   SO88

INN Kinfayre Restaurant 41 High St ☎(0384) 872565

5⇐🛁 (1fb) ✖ ® ✳B&b£15 W£70 Ⓜ
Lunch£2.95–£4.95&alc Dinner 10pm fr£2

🍽 CTV 15P ⌷(heated)

KIPPEN
Central *Stirlingshire*
Map **11**   NS69

⊢⊶**FH** Mrs J Paterson **Powblack** *(NS670970)* ☎(078687) 260
Apr–Oct

Pleasant farmhouse near the River Forth on the Kippen to Doune road.

2hc (1fb) ✖ B&bfr£8 Wfr£50 Ⓜ

🍽 CTV P ◗ 300acres arable sheep

KIRKBEAN
Dumfries & Galloway *Dumfriesshire*
Map **11**   NX95

GH Cavens House ☎(038788) 234

Charming guesthouse in 10 acres of grounds; good hospitality and excellent home cooking. Ideally constructed to suit disabled persons.

6hc (4⇐ 2🛁) (1fb) ® LDO6.45pm

Lic 🍽 CTV 20P ⅙ ⮑

KIRKBY LONSDALE
Cumbria
Map **7**   SD67

GH Abbot Hall ☎(0468) 71406
Mar–Oct

A charming, 17th-century farmhouse with character, warmth and comfort.

6hc (1⇐ 4🛁) (1fb) ✖ ✳B&b£11.50–£12.50 Bdi£17.50–£18.50 W£122.50–£129.50 ⏸ LDO7pm

🍽 CTV 10P 2⮑ solarium

KIRKCAMBECK
Cumbria
Map **12**   NY56

FH Mrs M Stobart **Cracrop** *(NY521697)*
☎Roadhead (06978) 245
Closed Dec & Jan

Delightful farmhouse with very spacious and comfortable bedrooms.

2hc (2fb) ✖ ® ✳B&b£9 Bdi£15 Wfr£90 ⏸

🍽 CTV 3P 425acres mixed

Ⓥ

KIRKCONNEL
Dumfries & Galloway *Dumfriesshire*
Map **11**   NS71

FH Mrs E A McGarvie **Niviston** *(NS691135)* ☎(06593) 346
May–Oct

Pleasant, well maintained farm delightfully set overlooking River Nith. (NB washing facilities are on ground floor).

2rm (1fb) ✳B&b£8.50 Wfr£57 Ⓜ

🍽 TV 5P 1🐎 ◗ 345acres sheep stock

KIRKHILL
Highland *Inverness-shire*
Map **14** NH54

FH Mrs C Munro **Wester Moniack** *(NH551438)* ☎Drumchardine (046383) 237
Small, comfortable farmhouse. Follow signs 'Highland Vineries' from A862 and watch for farm sign.
2hc (1fb) ✱B&b£7–£7.50 Bdi£11–£12 W£77–£84 🍴LDO6pm
♨ CTV 3P 600acres arable beef
[V]

KIRKOSWALD
Cumbria
Map **12** NY54

Recommended

GH Prospect Hill Hotel (Guestaccom) ☎Lazonby (076883) 500
Closed Feb
An 18th-century farm complex, tastefully converted into a hotel of charm and character, where oak beams, stone walls and antiques are featured throughout. Each bedroom is comfortably and individually decorated and furnished and several boast beautiful brass beds. Good dinners, chosen from an extensive à la carte menu, are served.
9hc (3🛁 1🚿) (1fb) ✖ [R] ✱B&b£15–£22 LDO8.45pm
Lic ♨ CTV 20P ⛳
Credit cards [1] [2] [3] [5] [V]

KIRKOSWALD
Strathclyde *Ayrshire*
Map **10** NS20

INN *Kirkton Jeans Hotel* 45 Main St ☎(06556) 220
Small and welcoming inn with all bedrooms in annexe to the rear.
Annexe: 9🚿 CTV in all bedrooms [R] LDO9.30pm
♨ 60P

Kirkhill — Knowstone

KIRKWHELPINGTON
Northumberland
Map **12** NY98

FH Mrs J B White **Horncastle** *(NY986847)* (1m W of village off A696) ☎Otterburn (0830) 40247
Apr–Oct
Attractive farmhouse with tasteful décor and a high standard of comfort.
3hc (2🛁 1🚿) (1fb) ✖ [R] ✱B&b£11–£13 Bdi£17–£19 W£119–£130 🍴LDO9am
♨ CTV 6P 🏠 ⛳ squash snooker 310acres arable beef sheep mixed
[V]

KIRTLING
Cambridgeshire
Map **5** TL65

INN Queens Head ☎Newmarket (0638) 730253
3rm [R] ✱B&b£12.50 Bdi£17–£22 Wfr£84 M Bar lunch£2.30–£3 Dinner9.30pm£6–£10&alc
40P nc
[V]

KIRTON
Nottinghamshire
Map **8** SK66

GH Old Rectory Main St ☎Mansfield (0623) 861540
Closed Dec
Lovely old Georgian house with spacious gardens in village centre.
10hc (1🚿) ✖ ✱B&b£12.75–£13.50 Bdi£18.75–£19.50 W£121–£126 🍴 LDO6pm
Lic ♨ CTV 18P
[V]

KNARESBOROUGH
North Yorkshire
Map **8** SE35

GH Newton House 5–7 York Pl. ☎Harrogate (0423) 863539
A converted Georgian town house with archway access to inner courtyard car park. Dining room usually has à la carte menu available.
8hc (1🛁 3🚿) (2fb) CTV in 4 bedrooms [R] ✱B&b£10–£15 Bdi£15.95–£20.95 W£104–£139 🍴LDO7pm
Lic ♨ CTV 8P

KNIGHTON
Powys
Map **7** SO27

FH R Watkins **Heartsease** *(SO343725)* ☎Bucknell (05474) 220
Apr–Oct
Georgian, mellow-stone farmhouse with country house atmosphere and large garden.
3rm (1hc 1🛁) (1fb) ✱B&b£10–£12 Bdi£17 Wfr£110 🍴LDO9pm
♨ CTV 6P 3🚗 🏠 ⛳ snooker 800acres mixed
Credit card [3]

KNOWSTONE
Devon
Map **3** SS82

GH Knowstone Court ☎Anstey Mills (03984) 457
Tastefully decorated and furnished stone-built rectory in heart of Devonshire countryside. Imaginative, interesting menu.
9hc (4🛁 4🚿) CTV in all bedrooms ✖ [R] B&b£10–£20 Bdi£22–£32 LDO8pm
Lic ♨ 12P nc14yrs
Credit cards [1] [3] [V]
See advertisement on page 383

INN Masons Arms ☎Anstey Mills (03984) 231
Closed Xmas Day evening
An historic thatched inn on the edge of Exmoor.

4hc (1🚿) Annexe: 1🚿 CTV in all bedrooms [R] ✻B&b£14–£21 Bdi£21–£28 W£129.50–£150 Ⱡ Bar lunch 70p–£5.75 Dinner 9.30pm £8.45&alc

🛋 10P ⛟ ⌂

KNUTSFORD
Cheshire
Map **7** SJ77

GH Longview Private Hotel
55 Manchester Rd ☎(0565) 2119
Closed Xmas & New Year

Personal service is assured at this small family run hotel overlooking the common. A small menu of good home cooking is offered in the pleasant dining room.

14hc (2🚿) (1fb) CTV in all bedrooms [R] ✻B&b£13.50–£28 Bdi£20.25–£34.75 LDO9pm

Lic 🛋 CTV 20P

[V]

LAIRG
Highland *Sutherland*
Map **14** NC50

GH Carnbren ☎(0549) 2259
Apr–Oct

Modern detached house in roadside location overlooking Loch Shin.

3hc ✻B&bfr£8

🛋 CTV 3P

Knowstone — Lancing

FH Mrs M Mackay ***Alt-Na-Sorag*** *(NC547123)* 14 Achnairn ☎(0549) 2058
May–Sep

Attractive farmhouse with good views of Loch Shin. Situated 100 yards off the A838 and 5m from Lairg.

3rm (1fb)

🛋 CTV 3P 1🚗 250acres arable beef sheep

FH Mrs V Mackenzie **5 Terryside** *(NC570110)* ☎(0549) 2332
May–Sep

Two-storey stone farmhouse on roadside with distant views of Loch Shin. 2½m N off Lairg on unclassified road off the A838.

3rm (2hc 1🛁 1🚿) ✻B&bfr£7

🛋 CTV P 58acres mixed

FH Mrs M Sinclair ***Woodside*** *(NC533147)* West Shinness ☎(0549) 2072
Jun–Aug

Homely house overlooking Loch Shin with Ben More in the background. Situated 7m from Lairg on the A838.

3rm (1🛁) 🚫

CTV 4P 360acres arable beef sheep mixed

LAMBERHURST
Kent
Map **5** TQ63

INN Chequers School Hill ☎(0892) 890260

4🛁 (1fb) CTV in all bedrooms [R] ✻B&b£15.75–£21.50 Lunch £4.50&alc Dinner 10pm £3–£8.50&alc

🛋 60P ⛳

Credit cards [1] [2] [3] [5]

LAMLASH
Isle of Arran
See **Arran, Isle of**

LANCING
West Sussex
Map **4** TQ10

GH Beach House Hotel 81 Brighton Rd ☎(0903) 753368
Closed Xmas

Homely, comfortable seafront guesthouse.

6hc (1fb) 🚫 [R] ✻B&b£7.50–£8.50 W£49–£56 M̸

🛋 CTV 6P

INN Sussex Pad Hotel Old Shoreham Rd ☎Shoreham (0273) 454647

A modern, well-appointed inn with elegant restaurant. →

Lancing — Launceston

6🛁 (1fb) CTV in all bedrooms [R]
✻B&b£29 Lunch £9.50–£13 Dinner £9.50–£13
♨ 🅿
Credit cards [1] [2] [3] [5]

L'ANCRESSE VALE
Guernsey
See **Channel Islands**

LANGDALE, GREAT
Cumbria
Map **11** NY30

GH Long House ☎(09667) 222
Closed Xmas & Jan
A peacefully situated 17th-century cottage with oak beams, open fires and stained glass windows.
3🛁 ✕ ✻B&b£12.25–£13.75 Bdi£18.50–£20 W£126–£136.50 Ⱡ LDO5pm
♨ CTV 7P nc8yrs

INN Three Shires Little Langdale ☎(09667) 215
rs 15 Nov–8 Feb (Closed Xmas Day)
Small, friendly, family run inn with bright, attractive bedrooms, set in peaceful lakeland valley.
8hc (1🚿) (1fb) ✕ ✻B&b£15.75 Bdi£25–£27 W£161 Ⱡ Lunch £4–£8 Dinner 9pm £10.75
♨ CTV 20P 2🚗 ⊞ nc5yrs
See advertisement on page 42

LANGHO
Lancashire
Map **7** SD73

GH *Mytton Fold Farm* Whalley Rd (Guestaccom) ☎Blackburn (0254) 48255
Old stables have been converted to form this well-appointed guesthouse on a dairy farm.
12🛁🚿 (2fb) CTV in all bedrooms ✕ [R] LDO9.30pm
Lic ♨ 30P
Credit cards [1] [3]

LANGLAND BAY
West Glamorgan
Map **2** SS68
See also **Bishopston** and **Mumbles**

GH *Brynteg Hotel* 1 Higher Ln ☎Swansea (0792) 66820
Closed Xmas
10hc (2🛁) (5fb) [R] LDO5pm
Lic ♨ CTV 10P

GH Wittemberg Hotel 2 Rotherslade Rd ☎Swansea (0792) 69696
Closed Xmas
Small family-run hotel within walking distance of sea.
11hc (9🚿) (2fb) 🚭 in 4 bedrooms CTV in all bedrooms ✕ [R] ✻B&b£13–£20 Bdi£20–£27 W£135–£180 Ⱡ (W only Jul & Aug)
Lic ♨ CTV 11P nc5yrs
[V]

LANHYDROCK
Cornwall
Map **2** SX06

FH Mrs P A Smith **Treffry** *(SW073637)* ☎Bodmin (0208) 4405
Apr–Sep
Large, 18th-century farmhouse with garden in quiet location on working farm, 7 miles from coast.
3hc (1fb) ✕ [R] ✻B&b£8–£9 Bdi£12–£13 W£52–£59 Ⱡ (W only Jul & Aug) LDO11am
♨ CTV 4P nc3yrs 170acres dairy
[V]

LANLIVERY
Cornwall
Map **2** SX05

FH Mr & Mrs J Linfoot **Treganoon** *(SX065589)* ☎Bodmin (0208) 872205
Apr–Oct
Farmhouse with small garden in fairly isolated position and beautiful countryside.
6hc (2fb) [R] ✻B&b£7–£8 Bdi£12–£14 W£68–£78 Ⱡ LDO7pm
Lic CTV 8P 88acres beef

LAPWORTH
West Midlands
Map **4** SP17

FH Mr & Mrs Smart **Mountford** *(SO164714)* Church Ln ☎(05643) 3283
Tudor house with outdoor swimming pool and duck pond.
3rm (1hc) TV in 1 bedroom ✕ ✻B&b£10–£17
♨ CTV 3P 2🚗 nc10yrs 🏊(heated) 30acres arable mixed water fowl [V]

LARGS
Strathclyde *Ayrshire*
Map **10** NS25

GH Carlton 10 Aubery Cres ☎(0475) 672313
Apr–Oct
Friendly, family-run guesthouse on the sea front.
6hc (2fb) [R] ✻B&b£8.50–£9 Bdi£12.50–£13 W£87.50–£91 Ⱡ LDO4pm
CTV 6P [V]

LATHERON
Highland *Caithness*
Map **15** ND13

FH Mrs C B Sinclair **Upper Latheron** *(ND195352)* ☎(05934) 224
May–Oct
Two-storey farmhouse in elevated position with fine views across the North sea. The farm runs its own Ponies of Britain Pony Trekking Centre.
4rm (1fb) 🚭 in 3 bedrooms ✕ ✻B&bfr£7 Bdifr£10 Wfr£70 Ⱡ
CTV 4P U 200acres stock rearing mixed
Credit cards [1] [2] [3] [V]

LAUNCESTON
Cornwall
Map **2** SX38

GH Eagle House Hotel ☎(0566) 2036
Closed Xmas
17hc (5🛁 3🚿) (3fb) ✻B&b£9.50–£11.50 Bdi£13.50–£15.50 LDO9pm
Lic ♨ CTV 50P
Credit cards [3] [5] [V]

LAVERTON
Gloucestershire
Map **4** SP03

GH Leasow House Laverton Meadows (2m SW of Broadway off A46) ☎Stanton (038673) 526

Converted 18th-century Cotswold stone house with attractive garden in peaceful countryside 2½m SSW of Broadway.

6hc (3🛁 3🚿) (2fb) CTV in all bedrooms [R] ✱B&b£13.50–£18 W£90–£120 M̸

♨ 12P

Credit cards [1] [3] [V]

See advertisement on page 99

LAXTON
Nottinghamshire
Map **8** SK76

FH Mrs L S Rose **Moorgate** *(SK726665)* ☎Tuxford (0777) 870274

¼m S unclass rd.

3rm (1fb) 🚫 ✱B&b£7.50–£8 Bdi£11–£12 W£70–£80 Ł LDO8.15pm

CTV 8P 145acres arable beef

[V]

See advertisement on page 280

LEAMINGTON SPA (ROYAL)
Warwickshire
Map **4** SP36
See plan on page 226

GH Buckland Lodge Hotel 35 Avenue Rd ☎(0926) 23843 Plan **2** *C2*
Closed Xmas

11hc (4🛁) (2fb) ✱B&b£11–£12 Bdi£17–£18 W£101–£108 Ł LDOnoon

Lic ♨ CTV 12P

GH Glendower 8 Warwick Pl ☎(0926) 22784 Plan **3** *B3*
Closed Xmas–New Year

End terrace Victorian house offering comfortable bed-and-breakfast accommodation. Evening meals by prior arrangement.

8hc (1🚿) (3fb) [R] ✱B&b£9.50–£10.50

♨ CTV P̸

GH Warwick Place Hotel 1 Milverton Ter ☎(0926) 28335 Plan **4** *B3*
Closed Xmas day

12hc (2🛁 2🚿) (2fb) CTV in 8 bedrooms TV in 4 bedrooms [R] B&b£13–£17 Bdi£20–£24 W£133–£160 Ł LDO7pm

Lic ♨ 6P

[V]

GH *Westella Hotel* 26 Leam Ter ☎(0926) 22710 Plan **5** *D2*

Large, brightly painted Georgian terraced house near town centre.

10hc (3fb) LDO7pm

♨ CTV 10P

Credit cards [1] [3]

FH Mrs R Gibbs **Hill** *(SP343637)* Lewis Rd, Radford Semele ☎(0926) 37571
Closed Xmas

Farmhouse situated in large attractive garden. 2½m SE off A425.

3hc (1fb) 🚫 [R] B&b£9–£11 Bdi£15–£17 W£105–£119 Ł LDO9am

♨ CTV 4P 🏠 350acres arable beef sheep mixed

FH Mrs N Ellis **Sharmer** *(SP359624)* Fosse Way, Radford Semele (3m E A425 then ½m S on Fosse Way) ☎Harbury (0926) 612448
Apr–Nov

2hc (1fb) 🚫 ✱B&b£9–£12 W£63–£80 M̸

♨ CTV 3P 1🚗 120acres arable beef

LEEDS
West Yorkshire
Map **8** SE33

GH Aragon Hotel 250 Stainbeck Ln, Meanwood ☎(0532) 759306
Closed Xmas

Detached stone building with pleasant garden in suburban area.

13hc (7🛁 2🚿) (1fb) CTV in all bedrooms [R] ✱B&b£12.60–£23.25 Bdi£18.45–£29.10 LDO6pm

Lic ♨ 21P

Credit cards [1] [3] [5]

GH Ash Mount Hotel 22 Wetherby Rd, Roundhay ☎(0532) 658164
Closed Xmas wk

Large detached Victorian house in quiet residential area.

14hc (1🚿) (1fb) 🚫 [R] ✱B&b£13.25–£14.50

♨ CTV 11P

GH Clock Hotel 317 Roundhay Rd, Gipton Wood ☎(0532) 490304

Practical accommodation in convenient position for business people.

22hc (2🛁 2🚿) (1fb) [R] ✱B&b£10.50–£17 Bdi£15.50–£23.50 LDO8pm

Lic ♨ CTV 16P

GH Highfield Hotel 79 Cardigan Rd, Headingley ☎(0532) 752193

Modest three-storey house with nicely fitted bedrooms.

10hc (1fb) ✱B&b£12.65

♨ CTV 7P

[V]

GH Oak Villa Hotel 57 Cardigan Rd, Headingley ☎(0532) 758439

Large Victorian semi-detached house with walled garden.

13hc (3fb) CTV in 12 bedrooms TV in 1 bedroom [R] ✱B&b£11.50–£13 Bdi£17–£18.50 W£69–£78 M̸ LDO10.30am

♨ CTV 10P

GH Trafford House Hotel 18 Cardigan Rd, Headingley ☎(0532) 752034

Pair of Victorian town houses with spacious dining room, lounge bar and good bedrooms. Near Headingley cricket ground.

15hc (4fb) 🚫 LDO3pm

♨ CTV 9P

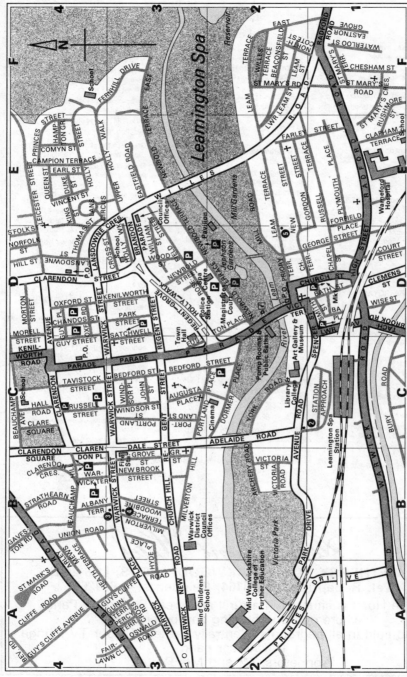

Leamington Spa

Leamington Spa (Royal)

2 Buckland Lodge Hotel
3 Glendower
4 Warwick Place Hotel
5 Westella Hotel

LEEK
Staffordshire
Map **7** SJ95

GH Peak Weavers Hotel King St
☎(0538) 383729

*Built in 1828, this former convent provides
simple accommodation close to town
centre.*

11hc (3⇄ 1🏠) (2fb) TV in all bedrooms ✖
® ✻B&b£11.50–£17 Bdi£18.25–£23.75
W£115–£150 ⊮ LDO8pm

Lic 🐃 CTV 8P 4🚗

Credit cards ① ③ ⓥ

FH Mrs D Needham **Holly Dale**
(SK019556) Bradnop ☎(0538) 383022
Apr–Oct

*Two-storey, stone-built farmhouse typical
of the area. 2m SE on unclass road off
A523.*

2hc ✖ ® ✻B&b£7–£7.50 W£45 ⋈
🐃 CTV 2P 72acres dairy

LEE-ON-THE-SOLENT
Hampshire
Map **4** SU50

GH Ash House 35 Marine Parade West
☎(0705) 550240

*Quiet house overlooking the Solent with
many antique items of interest in all
rooms.*

6hc (2fb) ✻B&b£9–£10.50
🐃 CTV 6P nc6yrs

LEICESTER
Leicestershire
Map **4** SK50

GH *Alexandra Hotel* 342 London Rd,
Stoneygate ☎(0533) 703056
Closed Xmas rs Etr

*Recently modernised guesthouse popular
with business people.*

18hc (3⇄ 5🏠) (3fb) ✖ LDO5pm

Lic 🐃 CTV 16P

Credit cards ① ③

GH *Burlington Hotel* Elmfield Av
☎(0533) 705112

17hc (1🏠) (1fb) CTV in 10 bedrooms ✖ ®
LDO7.30pm

Lic 🐃 CTV 18P

Credit card ①

GH Daval Hotel 292 London Rd ☎(0533)
708234

*Predominantly commercial hotel in large
Victorian building.*

14hc (3fb) CTV in all bedrooms
✻B&b£11–£20 Bdi£16.25–£25.25
LDO7pm

Lic 🐃 CTV 12P
ⓥ

GH Old Tudor Rectory Main St, Glenfield
☎(0533) 312214

3m W A50.

17hc (3⇄ 2🏠) (5fb) CTV in all bedrooms
® ✻B&b£13.80–£16.10 Bdi£20.70–£23
LDO10pm

Lic 🐃 35P

Credit cards ① ③

GH Scotia Hotel 10 Westcotes Dr
☎(0533) 549200
Closed Xmas & New Year

*Pleasant, predominantly commercial hotel
in side street.*

9hc Annexe: 6hc (2fb) CTV in all
bedrooms ® B&b£15–£16 Bdi£23–£25
LDO5pm

Lic 🐃 5P

GH Stanfre House Hotel 265 London Rd
☎(0533) 704294
Closed Xmas wk

12hc (1fb) ✻B&b£13

Lic 🐃 CTV 6P

GH Stoneycroft Hotel 5/7 Elmfield Av
☎(0533) 707605

*In a residential area just a few minutes
from city centre, large hotel with high
proportion of single rooms.* →

49hc (2fb) CTV in all bedrooms ✗ ®
✳B&b£11.50–£15 Bdi£18–£21.50 W£126–
£150.50 ⅃ LDO9pm

Lic ♔ CTV 20P

Credit cards ① ③ Ⓥ

LEIGH
Hereford & Worcester
Map **3**   SO75

FH Mrs F S Stewart **Leigh Court**
(SO784535) ☎Leigh Sinton (0886) 32275
27 Mar–8 Oct

3hc (1fb) ✗ ® B&b£10–£14 Bdi£18–£22
W£121–£149 ⅃ LDO9am

♔ CTV 6P ✔ 270acres arable sheep
cereals

Ⓥ

LEINTWARDINE
Hereford & Worcester
Map **7**   SO47

FH Mrs Y Lloyd **Upper Buckton**
(SO384733) (Guestaccom) ☎(05473) 634
Mar–Nov

1½m SW off A4113.

3hc ✗ (W only Aug)

CTV P nc4yrs 285acres mixed

LEOMINSTER
Hereford & Worcester
Map **3**   SO45

**GH Broadward Lodge Guesthouse &
Restaurant** Hereford Rd ☎(0568) 2914

*A Georgian Lodge on the main
Leominster-Hereford road with
comfortable rooms and restaurant-style
evening meals.*

6hc (3fb) ✗ ✳B&b£11–£13 Bdi£17–£19
W£103–£125 ⅃ LDO9.30pm

Lic ♔ CTV 12P

Credit card ①

FH Mrs Y Conad **Eye Court** *(SO495638)*
Eye (3m N between B4361 & A49)
☎(0568) 5718
end Mar–Oct

*Part 14th-century farmhouse, now fully
modernised, situated in peaceful hamlet;
friendly atmosphere.*

Leicester
⎯
Lewis, Isle of

2hc (2fb) TV in 2 bedrooms ✗ ®
✳B&b£8–£9

Lic CTV P ♨ ♋ 210acres arable dairy
sheep mixed

Credit cards ① ② ③

FH M J & S W Lloyd **Menalls** *(SO528611)*
Kimbolton (3m NE A4112) ☎(0568) 2605

2hc (2fb) ✗ ® ✳B&bfr£8 Bdifr£13 Wfr£84
⅃ LDO3pm

CTV P 40acres mixed

Ⓥ

FH Mrs E M Morris **Park Lodge** Eye (3m N
between B4361 & A49) *(SO502643)*
☎Leominster (0568) 5711

2hc (1fb) ✗ ✳B&b£8.50 Bdi£12.50 W£70–
£84 ⅃ LDO6.30pm

♔ CTV 6P 2♠ snooker 200acres mixed

FH Mrs S J Davenport **Stagbatch**
(SO465584) ☎(0568) 2673
Closed Xmas

*A small, half-timbered farmhouse with a
small patio and large stableyard.*

3⇆ (1fb) ✗ ✳B&b£9–£10

♔ CTV 6P nc10yrs 30acres mixed racing
stables

FH A P Black **Wharton Bank** Wharton
Bank *(SO508556)* ☎(0568) 2575

*Stone built hill-top farmhouse of 18th
century date, surrounded by attractive
Herefordshire countryside.*

4hc (1⇆) ✗ ® ✳B&b£9–£11 Bdi£16.50–
£19

♔ CTV 5P ⌣ ♬(grass) 174acres dairy

LERWICK
Shetland
See **Shetland**

LEW
Oxfordshire
Map **4**   SP30

LEWDOWN
Devon
Map **2**   SX48

GH *Stowford House Hotel* ☎(056683)
415

*Spacious and friendly former rectory in an
acre of gardens.*

6hc (2⇆ 2♛) (2fb) ✗ LDO8.30pm

Lic ♔ CTV 12P ♋

FH Mrs M E Horn **Venn Mill** *(SX484885)*
☎Bridestowe (083786) 288
Etr–Oct

*Large modern bungalow set in peaceful
surroundings with river fishing and private
trout lake. 400 yards from the A30.*

4rm (3hc) (1fb) ✗ LDO4pm

CTV 4P 4♠ ♨ ✔ 160acres beef sheep

LEWIS, ISLE OF
Western Isles *Ross & Cromarty*
Map **13**

STORNOWAY
Map **13**   NB43

GH Ardlonan 29 St Francis Street
☎(0851) 3482
Closed Xmas & New Year

*A pleasantly appointed house just off
town centre. Communal breakfast tables.*

5hc (1fb) ✗ ✳B&b£8.50

♔ CTV ♬

Ⓥ

LEYBURN
North Yorkshire
Map **7** SE19

GH Eastfield Lodge St Matthews Ter ☎Wensleydale (0969) 23196

Comfortable house with spacious accommodation and jovial proprietors.

8hc Annexe: 2rm (2fb) CTV in 8 bedrooms TV in 2 bedrooms ✱B&b£10–£12 Bdi£15–£17 W£105–£119 Ł LDO8.30pm

Lic 🍴 CTV 10P

LICHFIELD
Staffordshire
Map **7** SK10

GH *Oakleigh House Hotel* 25 St Chads Rd (Guestaccom) ☎(05432) 22688

11hc (2🛁 4🚿) CTV in all bedrooms 🐕 Ⓡ in 5 bedrooms LDO9.30pm

Lic 🍴 20P nc5yrs

Credit card [1]

LIFTON
Devon
Map **2** SX38

GH Mayfield House Tinhay ☎(0566) 84401

Detached house in good-sized gardens off main A30. Personally run with friendly, informal atmosphere, and good food.

Leyburn — Lindridge

6hc (2fb) CTV in all bedrooms Ⓡ B&b£9.50 Bdi£14.50–£16.50 LDO5pm

Lic CTV 9P 1🚗 ⌂

See advertisement on page 224

LINCOLN
Lincolnshire
Map **8** SK97

GH Brierley House Hotel 54 South Park ☎(0522) 26945
Closed last 2 wks Dec & first 2 wks Jan

Large house with good quality accommodation in quiet cul de sac overlooking park. Large family run hotel.

11rm (5hc 2🛁 4🚿) CTV in 8 bedrooms TV in 3 bedrooms 🐕 ✱B&b£10–£12.50 Bdi£15 LDO4.30pm

Lic 🍴 CTV P nc5yrs

GH D'Isney Place Hotel Eastgate ☎(0522) 38881

This small luxury hotel in the older part of the city has individually designed bedrooms, some with four-poster beds; substantial breakfasts served to the rooms.

16rm (12🛁 2🚿) (2fb) CTV in all bedrooms Ⓡ ✱B&b£33–£36 Wfr£233 M

🍴 7P

Credit cards [1] [2] [3] [5] [V]

GH Tennyson Hotel 7 South Park ☎(0522) 21624

Pair of Victorian houses, extensively modernised to provide good accommodation.

8hc (2🛁 6🚿) (1fb) CTV in all bedrooms 🐕 Ⓡ B&b£17.50–£20 Bdi£25–£28 LDO7.45pm

Lic 🍴 8P

Credit cards [1] [3] [V]

LINDRIDGE
Hereford & Worcester
Map **7** SO66

FH Mrs J M May **Middle Woodston** *(SO673696)* ☎Eardiston (058470) 244
Etr–Oct

A comfortable farmhouse with extensive views across the beautiful Teme Valley. Home-made bread a speciality.

3hc (1fb) 🐕 Ⓡ B&b£8.50–£10 Bdi£14–£15.50 W£90–£100 Ł LDO5pm

🍴 CTV 6P nc5yrs 10acres beef fruit mixed

[V]

See advertisement on page 376

LINLITHGOW
Lothian *West Lothian*
Map **11** NS97

FH Mrs A Hay **Belsyde House** *(NS976755)* Lanark Rd ☎(0506) 842098
Closed Xmas

Well maintained Georgain farmhouse in tree studded grounds above town. 1½m SW A706.

4hc (1fb) 🚫 Ⓡ B&b£8.50–£9 Bdi£14.50–£15 W£80–£100 Ⱡ LDOnoon

🛋 CTV 10P 🏠 106acres beef sheep

Ⓥ

FH Mrs W Erskine **Woodcockdale** *(NS973760)* Lanark Rd ☎(0506) 842088

Modern two-storey house lying approximately 50 yards from farmyard and outbuildings. 1½ miles SW of A706.

4rm (1fb) 🚫 ✱B&bfr£8 Bdifr£14 Wfr£56 M̸

🛋 CTV 12P 🏠 700acres dairy sheep mixed

Ⓥ

LISKEARD
Cornwall
Map **2** SX26

GH Elnor 1 Russell St ☎(0579) 42472

6hc (1🚿) (1fb) 🚫 B&b£9–£11 Bdi£13.50–£15.50 W£87.50–£101.50

Lic CTV 6P

Ⓥ

FH S A Kendall **Tencreek** *(SX265637)* ☎(0579) 43379

A well-kept 16th-century listed farmhouse set in beautiful countryside, 1m from Liskeard.

2hc 🚫 Ⓡ ✱B&b£8.50–£10 W£57–£63 M̸

CTV 2P 250acres mixed

LITTLE BREDY
Dorset
Map **3** SY58

FH Mrs D M Fry ***Foxholes*** *(SY582882)* ☎Long Bredy (03083) 395
Closed 20–27 Dec

2m E of village.

6rm (5hc) (6fb) Ⓡ in 4 bedrooms LDO4.15pm

Lic 🛋 CTV 8P 🏠 390acres dairy mixed

LITTLE DEWCHURCH
Hereford & Worcester
Map **3** SO53

FH Mrs G Lee **Cwm Craig** *(SO535322)* ☎(043270) 250

Spacious Georgian farmhouse in quiet wooded surroundings. Hereford 6 miles, Ross-on-Wye 7 miles. Few minutes drive from the Wye Valley.

3hc (1fb) 🚫 Ⓡ ✱B&b£8–£9 W£49–£56 M̸

🛋 CTV P 190acres arable beef mixed

Ⓥ

LITTLE EVERSDEN
Cambridgeshire
Map **5** TL35

FH Mrs F Ellis **Five Gables** *(TL371535)* Bucks Ln ☎Comberton (022026) 2236
May–Sep

A listed farmhouse, parts of which date from the 15th and 17th centuries, with oak beams and inglenook fireplace.

2hc (1fb) 🚫 B&b£13–£14

CTV 3P nc12yrs 240acres arable

Ⓥ

LITTLEHAMPTON
West Sussex
Map **4** TQ00

GH Old Windmill House 83 South Ter ☎(0903) 724939

Comfortable seafront house with friendly atmosphere.

7hc (2fb) 🚫 Ⓡ ✱B&b£8.75–£12 W£59.50–£82 M̸

Lic 🛋 CTV ₱

Credit cards [1] [2] [3] [5]

GH Regency Hotel 85 South Ter ☎(0903) 717707
Closed Xmas

Small, neatly-furnished house on seafront with a friendly atmosphere.

8hc (3fb) CTV in all bedrooms Ⓡ ✱B&b£10–£15 Bdi£15–£20 Wfr£75 M̸ LDO6.30pm

Lic 🛋 CTV ₱

Ⓥ

LITTLE HAVEN
Dyfed
Map **2** SM81

GH Pendyffryn Private Hotel ☎Broad Haven (043783) 337 (due to change to Broadhaven (0437) 781337)
mid May–Sep

Pleasant detached house in elevated position.

9hc (8fb) TV in 7 bedrooms 🚫 ✱B&b£10.35 Bdi£16.10 Wfr£97.75 Ⱡ LDO6.45pm

Lic 🛋 CTV 6P nc4yrs

LITTLEHEMPSTON
Devon
Map **3** SX86

FH Mrs E P Miller ***Buckyette*** *(SX812638)* ☎Staverton (080426) 638
May–Sep

7rm (6hc) (4fb) 🚫 LDO7pm

CTV 8P 🏠 51acres grassland

Ⓥ

LITTLE HEREFORD
Hereford & Worcester
Map **7** SO56

FH Mrs H Williams **Lower Upton** *(SO547663)* Lower Upton (1½m S of A456) ☎Brimfield (058472) 322
Closed Xmas & New Year

Impressive Victorian farmhouse set in peaceful, picturesque surroundings; offering friendly service and choice of meals.

3hc (1fb) 🚫 ✱B&b£8 Bdi£11.50–£12.50 W£80–£85 Ⱡ LDO7pm

🛋 CTV 4P 160acres mixed

LITTLE MILL
Gwent
Map **3** SO30

FH Mrs A Bradley **Pentwyn** *(SO325035)* ☎(049528) 249
Closed Dec & Jan

A 16th-century, traditional Welsh long house set in ½acre garden with swimming pool situated off A472, ½m E of junction with A4042.

4hc (1fb) 🚫 Ⓡ ✱B&b£9–£9.50 Wfr£90 Ⱡ LDOnoon

Lic 🛋 CTV P nc4yrs 🏊(heated) 120acres arable

Ⓥ

LITTLE TORRINGTON
Devon
Map **2** SS41

GH Smytham Manor ☎(0805) 22110
Closed Dec

12hc (4🛁) (2fb) 🚭 in 2 bedrooms CTV in 2 bedrooms Ⓡ ✱B&b£9.50–£12.50 Bdi£14–£17.50 W£64–£84 M̸ LDO9.30pm

Lic CTV 20P 🏊

Credit cards [1] [3]

FH Mrs E J Watkins **Lower Hollam** *(SS501161)* ☎Torrington (0805) 23253
Etr–Sep

Historic house situated in a peaceful, picturesque position. Good play facilities for children.

3hc (2fb) 🚫 Ⓡ ✱B&b£6.50–£8 Bdi£10.50–£12.50 W£66.50–£72 Ⱡ LDO5pm

CTV 4P 🏠 230 acres mixed

Ⓥ

LITTON
Derbyshire
Map **7** SK17

FH Mrs A Barnsley **Dale House** *(SK160750)* ☎Tideswell (0298) 871309
Closed Xmas

Large, stone-built Edwardian farmhouse situated on edge of picturesque village off B6049.

3rm (1fb) 🚫 ✱B&b£8–£8.50 W£53–£56 M̸

🛋 TV 6P nc5yrs 100acres sheep

Litton — Llandeloy

LITTON
North Yorkshire
Map **7** SD97

GH Park Bottom ☎Arncliffe (075677) 235
Mar–Nov
Stone-built house in beautiful scenery offering modern accommodation and good service.
7hc (6🚿) (1fb) [R] ✱B&b£14–£16 Bdi£17–£19 W£105.10–£119.70 ⅃ LDO6pm
Lic CTV 10P

LIVERPOOL
Merseyside
Map **7** SJ39

GH Aachen Hotel 91 Mount Pleasant ☎051-709 3477
Cosy little hotel with well equipped rooms and competitive prices.
17hc (1🛁) (6fb) CTV in all bedrooms ✗ [R] ✱B&b£12–£16 Bdi£17–£21 W£119–£147 ⅃ LDO9.30pm
Lic ♨ CTV 2P(charge) 3🚗(charge)
Credit cards [1] [2] [3] [5]

GH New Manx Hotel 39 Catherine St ☎051-708 6171
Listed Victorian building with modern facilities.
15hc (3fb) ⚑ in 5 bedrooms CTV in 10 bedrooms [R] ✱B&b£11–£13 Wfr£60 M̸
♨ CTV P̸
Credit cards [1] [2] [3] [4] [5] [V]

LIZARD
Cornwall
Map **3** SW71

GH *Mounts Bay Hotel* Penmenner Rd (Guestaccom) ☎(0326) 290305
Closed Xmas, Jan & Feb rs Nov, Dec & Mar
Secluded family residence standing in own grounds overlooking Kynance Cove.
10rm (2hc) (5fb) [R] LDO6pm
Lic CTV 12P 🏠

GH *Parc Brawse House* ☎(0326) 290466
Mar–Oct
Comfortable character house, friendly attention from family. Property overlooks sea across farmland.
6hc [R] LDO7pm
Lic CTV 6P nc7yrs

GH Penmenner House Hotel Penmenner Rd ☎(0326) 290370
Mar–Oct
Friendly family hotel. Home cooking including local produce, fresh fish, Cornish cream.
8hc (5🚿) (2fb) [R] B&bfr£11.50 Bdifr£17 Wfr£108.50 ⅃ LDO6pm
Lic ♨ CTV 10P 🏠

LLANBERIS
Gwynedd
Map **6** SH56

GH *Lake View Hotel* Tan-y-Pant ☎(0286) 870422
Cottage-style guesthouse alongside A4086 overlooking Llyn Padarn. 1m NW of town.
10hc (7🚿) (3fb) CTV in 7 bedrooms ✗ [R] in 7 bedrooms LDO9.30pm
Lic ♨ CTV 10P

LLANBOIDY
Dyfed
Map **2** SN22

FH Mrs B Worthing **Maencochyrwyn** *(SN181243)* Login ☎Hebron (09947) 283
Apr–Oct
Small isolated farmhouse in elevated position overlooking its own farmland and hills. 3½m WNW of Llanboidy on unclass road to East Login/Llanglydwen road.
3rm (1fb) ⚑ in 2 bedrooms ✱B&b£8–£9 Bdi£12.50–£13.50 W£80–£85 ⅃ LDO4pm
CTV P 2🚗 🏠 80acres dairy
[V]

FH Mrs M A E Lewis **Maesgwyn Isaf** *(SS203229)* ☎(09946) 385
Apr–Oct
A bright, modern farmhouse neatly tucked away in a secluded valley.
3rm (1fb) ✗ ✱B&b£8–£8.50 Bdi£12.50–£13 W£87.50–£91 ⅃ LDO5pm
♨ CTV 4P 🏠
180acres beef dairy
[V]

LLANDDEINIOLEN
Gwynedd
Map **6** SH56

Recommended

FH Mrs Kettle ***Ty'n-Rhos*** *(SH548672)* Seion (Guestaccom) ☎Port Dinorwic (0248) 670489
Closed Xmas & New Year
Farm has been extended to provide modern hotel comforts while retaining farm atmosphere. ½m N unclass rd.
9🛁 (3fb) ✗ [R] LDO7pm
Lic ♨ 9P 72acres dairy mixed

LLANDEILO
Dyfed
Map **2** SN62

FH N & J Card **Llwyndewl Farm Guesthouse** *(SN658177)* Trapp (3m SE off A483) ☎Llandybie (0269) 850362
Closed Xmas
A warm welcome and good home cooking are assured at this delightful old farmhouse.
4rm (1hc) (1fb) ✗ ✱B&b£8.50–£9.50 Bdi£11.50–£12.50 Wfr£87.50 ⅃ LDO7.30pm
Lic ♨ CTV 12P ⛵ 6acres small holding

LLANDELOY
Dyfed
Map **2** SM82

FH Mrs M Jones **Upper Vanley** *(SM862245)* ☎Croesgoch (03483) 418
Friendly Welsh farmhouse where good home cooking is a speciality. Vegetarians are well-catered for. Useful play area for children.
7hc (5fb) CTV in all bedrooms Wfr£84 ⅃
♨ CTV P 🏠 150acres dairy
See advertisement on page 352

LLANDINAM
Powys
Map **6** SO08

FH Mrs M C Davies **Trewythen** *(SJ003901)* ☎Caersws (068684) 444
May–Sep
Farmhouse dating from 1820 situated 2m SW of Caersws, on unclass road off B4569.
2hc (1🚿) (1fb) ✱B&b£8.50–£9.50 Bdifr£13 Wfr£86 ⱡ
♨ CTV P arable beef sheep mixed
[V]

LLANDOGO
Gwent
Map **3** SO50

GH *Brown's Hotel & Restaurant*
☎Dean (0594) 530262
Feb–Nov
Proprietor-run tea rooms and guesthouse. Walking distance of the river.
7hc (1🚿) LDO7.30pm
Lic CTV 20P

Recommended

INN Sloop ☎Dean (0594) 530291
Former mill overlooking Wye Valley with modern extension providing charming, beautifully furnished bedrooms of character.
4hc (3🚿 1🛁) CTV in 3 bedrooms TV in 1 bedroom [R] ✱B&b£13–£19 Bdi£18–£27 W£126–£189 ⱡ Lunch 75p–£7&alc LDO10pm
♨ 45P 🚫🚌 nc12yrs
Credit cards [1] [2] [3] [5] [V]

LLANDOVERY
Dyfed
Map **3** SN73

GH Llwyncelyn ☎(0550) 20566
Closed Xmas
Proprietor-run comfortable guesthouse with grounds running down to river.
6hc (3fb) B&b£12–£13 Bdi£19.50–£20.50 W£124.90–£129.50 ⱡ LDO7.30pm

Llandinam — Llandudno

Lic ♨ CTV 12P 🎣
[V]

LLANDRINDOD WELLS
Powys
Map **3** SO06

GH Griffin Lodge Hotel Temple St (Guestaccom) ☎(0597) 2432
Closed Jan
Attractive Victorian house with cosy modern bedrooms and intimate restaurant.
8hc (4🛁) [R] ✱B&b£12–£14 Bdi£17.50–£19.50 W£118.50–£133 (W only 3rd wk Jul) ⱡ LDO9pm
Lic ♨ CTV 8P
Credit cards [1] [2] [3] [V]

FH Mrs P Lewis ***Bailey Einon*** *(SO078616)* Cefnllys ☎(0597) 2449
Etr–Sep
Stone-built Georgian farmhouse, part of which dates back to the 17th-century. 2m E of town on unclass road.
3hc 🚫🐕 [R] LDO4pm
♨ CTV 3P nc14yrs 280acres beef sheep mixed

FH Mrs D Evans **Dolberthog** *(SO048602)* Dolberthog Ln ☎(0597) 2255
Apr–Oct
Victorian stone farmhouse on outskirts of town.
3hc (2fb) 🚫🐕 ✱B&b£8 Bdi£12 W£75–£80 ⱡ LDO3pm
♨ TV 3P 🎣 250acres mixed

FH Mrs S A Evans **Highbury** *(SO044628)* Llanyre (1m W off A4081) ☎(0597) 2716
Apr–Oct
3rm (2hc) (1fb) 🚫🐕 ✱B&b£7.50–£8.50 Bdi£11.50–£12.50 W£80–£85 ⱡ LDO4pm
♨ CTV 3P
20acres sheep
[V]

LLANDRINIO
Powys
Map **7** SJ21

FH Mrs G M Wigley **New Hall** *(SJ296171)* ☎Llanymynech (0691) 830384
Apr–Sep
Modernised farmhouse, partly dating from 16th century.
2hc (1🛁) (2fb) 🚫🐕 ✱B&b£9–£10 Bdi£13–£14 W£91–£98 ⱡ LDO5pm
CTV P 🎣 snooker 265acres arable beef dairy

FH Mrs S M Pritchard **Rhos** *(SO276174)* ☎Llanymynech (0691) 830785
3rm (1hc 1🚿) (1fb) 🚭 in 2 bedrooms CTV in 1 bedroom ✱B&b£9–£10 Bdi£13–£14 W£85–£90 ⱡ (W only Oct–Apr) LDO5.30pm
♨ CTV 8P 265acres arable beef
Credit card [4] [V]

LLANDUDNO
Gwynedd
Map **6** SH78
See plan on pages 234–235

GH Braemar Hotel 5 St Davids Rd ☎(0492) 76257 Plan **2** *B3*
Edwardian house in residential area 5 minutes from beach and shops.
9hc (3fb) 🚭 in 2 bedrooms CTV in 1 bedroom ✱B&b£8–£8.50 Bdi£11.50–£12 W£75–£80 ⱡ (W only Jul & Aug) LDO4.30pm
♨ CTV 🚫P nc7yrs
[V]

GH Brannock Private Hotel 36 St Davids Rd ☎(0492) 77483 Plan **3** *B3*
Edwardian house in residential area 5 minutes from beach and shops.
6hc (1fb) 🚫🐕 ✱B&b£8–£9 Bdi£11–£12.50 W£75–£85 ⱡ
Lic ♨ CTV 5P nc4yrs

GH Brigstock Private Hotel 1 St David's Pl ☎(0492) 76416 Plan **4** *B3*
Mar–Oct
In corner position in quiet residential area 5 minutes to shops and beach.

10hc (2⇄) (2fb) ✻ ® ✱B&b£10–£11
Bdi£13.50–£14.50 W£80–£92.50 ⊬
LDO4.30pm
Lic ㎜ CTV 8P nc3yrs

GH Britannia Hotel 15 Craig-y-Don Pde
☎(0492) 77185 Plan **5** *E3*
Closed Xmas

*Single-fronted Victorian terraced house
on Promenade, ¾ mile from main shopping
area.*

9hc (4🛏) (5fb) CTV in all bedrooms ®
✱B&b£8–£10 Bdi£11.50–£14 W£80–
£91 ⊬ LDO5pm

㎜ CTV ⨏

GH Bryn Rosa 16 Abbey Rd ☎(0492)
78215 Plan **6** *B4*

*Listed Victorian semi-detached house
with friendly atmosphere. Short walk to
sea and town centre.*

7hc (2fb) ✱B&b£7.50–£8.50 Bdi£10.50–
£12 W£75 ⊬ LDO4pm

㎜ CTV 4P nc2yrs
Ⓥ

GH Bryn-y-Mor Private Hotel North Pde
☎(0492) 76790 Plan **7** *C4*
Mar–Oct

*Semi-detached Victorian house on
Promenade 2 minutes from shops.*

17hc (3⇄ 1🛏) (5fb) ✻ ® ✱B&b£10–£12
Bdi£13.50–£15 W£81–£105 ⊬ LDO6pm
Temperance ㎜ CTV ⨏ ⚲
Ⓥ

Llandudno

Recommended

GH Buile Hill Private Hotel 46 St
Mary's Rd ☎(0492) 76972 Plan **8** *B3*
Etr–Oct

*Edwardian house in corner position in
residential area. Short walk to shops
and beach.*

13hc (3⇄ 4🛏) ✻ ® ✱B&b£10–£16
Bdi£14–£20 W£90–£120 ⊬ LDO4pm
Lic ㎜ CTV 6P

GH Capri Hotel 70 Church Walks
☎(0492) 79177 Plan **9** *B4*
Etr–Oct

*Victorian terraced house offering a warm
welcome and bright comfortable
bedrooms. Situated within easy reach of
shops and promenade.*

8hc (3fb) TV in 1 bedroom ✻ ✱B&b£8.50–
£9.50 Bdi£11–£12 W£77–£84 ⊬ LDO6pm
Lic ㎜ CTV 8P nc4yrs

GH Carmel Private Hotel 17 Craig-y-Don
Pde, Promenade ☎(0492) 77643 Plan **10**
E3
Etr–Nov

*Terraced Victorian house on Promenade,
¾m from main shopping area.*

10hc (5🛏) (4fb) CTV in 3 bedrooms ®
✱B&b£8.25–£8.75 Bdi£11.75–£12.50
Wfr£85.75 ⊬ LDO6.30pm
㎜ CTV 7P nc4yrs
Ⓥ

GH Hotel Carmen Carmen Sylva Rd,
Craig-y-Don ☎(0492) 76361 Plan **10A** *E3*

15hc (1⇄) (4fb) CTV in 7 bedrooms
✱B&b£8.75–£11.25 Bdi£12.75–£15.25
W£85.95–£93.45 ⊬ LDO6.45pm
Lic ㎜ CTV ⨏
Ⓥ

GH Cleave Court Private Hotel
1 St Seiriol's Rd ☎(0492) 77849 Plan **11**
B2
Apr–Oct

*Edwardian house in residential area. Short
walk to shops and beach.*

9hc (2fb) ✻ ✱B&b£7.50–£8.50 Bdi£10–
£11 W£70–£77 ⊬

CTV 8P 1⚲ nc3yrs
Credit card ③ Ⓥ

GH Cliffbury Private Hotel 34 St Davids
Rd ☎(0492) 77224 Plan **12** *B3*
Closed Xmas

*Semi-detached house in quiet residential
area, a short walk to shops and beach.*

6hc (1⇄) (2fb) CTV in all bedrooms ®
✱B&b£8.50–£9 Bdi£11.10–£12.10 W£77–
£83 ⊬ LDO6pm
㎜ 6P nc5yrs
Ⓥ

LLWYNCELYN GUEST HOUSE

LLANDOVERY, DYFED,
SA20 0EP

Tel: 0550-20566

*Proprietors:
Mr & Mrs D. C. Griffiths.*

Ideal Holiday Centre. Our Guest House with
its rural, riverside setting, full central heating
and homely atmosphere offers Bed &
Breakfast, or Dinner, Bed & Breakfast at
moderate rates.

Buile Hill Hotel
St Mary's Road, Llandudno   AA
Tel: (0492) 76972   Specially recommended

Well situated, detached and in own grounds. Only
minutes' walk from two shores, rail and coach
stations. First class service and every modern comfort.
Lounge with colour TV, large dining room with
separate tables. Choice of menus at each meal. Most
bedrooms have en suite facilities, all have tea making
facilities included in terms. Hotel is open throughout
the day with access to all rooms. Car park.
We cater for bed, breakfast and dinner or just bed
and breakfast. Central Heating. Fire Certificate.
Brochure on request — Jill and Bill Caldwell.

233

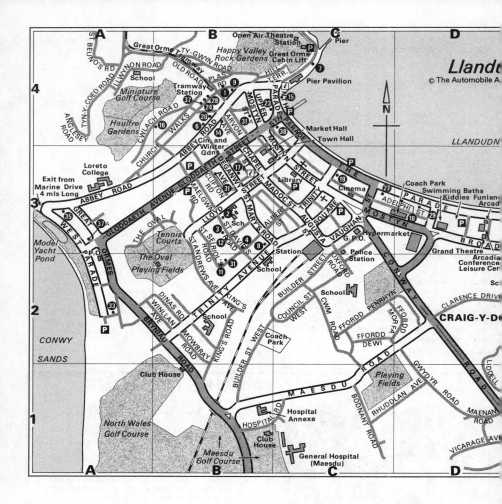

E

1982

4

Llandudno

Llandudno

2	Braemar Hotel
3	Brannock Private Hotel
4	Brigstock Private Hotel
5	Britannia Hotel
6	Bryn Rosa
7	Bryn-y-Mor Private Hotel
8	Buile Hill Private Hotel
9	Capri Hotel
10	Carmel Private Hotel
10A	Hotel Carmen
11	Cleave Court Private Hotel
12	Cliffbury Private Hotel
14	Craig Ard Private Hotel
14A	Craiglands Private Hotel
15	Cumberland Hotel
16	Cwlach Private Hotel
17	Grafton Hotel
17A	Granby
18	Heath House Hotel
19	Lynwood Private Hotel
20	Mayfair Private Hotel
22	Minion Private Hotel
23	Montclare Hotel
24	Nant-y-Glyn
26	Orotava Private Hotel
28	Plas Madoc Private Hotel
29	Puffin Lodge Hotel
31	Rosaire Private Hotel
31A	Rose Tor
31B	St Davids
32	St Hilary Hotel
33	Sandilands Private Hotel
34	Stratford Hotel
35	Tan-y-Marian Private Hotel
36	Tilstone Private Hotel
37	Warwick Hotel
38	Wilton Hotel

GH Craig Ard Private Hotel Arvon Av
☎(0492) 77318 Plan **14** *B4*

Semi-detached Victorian house in quiet residential street adjacent to beaches and shops.

17hc (5fb) ® ✱B&b£10 Bdi£14 W£98 ⅃ LDO4pm

Lic ⁇ CTV 12P

Ⓥ

GH Craiglands Private Hotel 7 Carmen Sylva Rd, Craig Y Don ☎(0492) 75090 Plan **14A** *E2*
Mar–Nov

Situated in a quiet part of town, but close to the Promenade.

6🛏 (1fb) CTV in all bedrooms ® ✱B&b£9–£10.50 Bdi£12.95–£14.95 W£90–£115 ⅃ LDO5.30pm

⁇ CTV ⅌ nc2yrs

GH Cumberland Hotel North Parade
☎(0492) 76379 Plan **15** *C4*

Victorian mid-terrace by Central Promenade and adjacent shops.

18hc (1🛏) (10fb) CTV in all bedrooms ✱B&b£9–£10 Bdi£12–£13 W£84–£91 ⅃ LDO6.30pm

Lic ⁇ CTV 3P

Ⓥ

GH Cwlach Private Hotel Cwlach Rd
☎(0492) 75587 Plan **16** *B4*

Detached Victorian house set high over town on the Orme.

8hc (5fb) ⚡ ✱B&b£7.50–£8.50 Bdi£10.50–£11.50 W£73.50–£80.50 ⅃

Lic CTV ⅌

GH Grafton Hotel 13 Craig-y-Don Pde
☎(0492) 76814 Plan **17** *E3*
Feb–Nov

Double-fronted Victorian mid-terrace on Promenade. ¾m from main shopping area.

20hc (4⇔ 14🛏) (1fb) CTV in all bedrooms ® B&b£14.50–£16.50 Bdi£21–£23 W£140–£155 ⅃ LDO5.30pm

Lic ⁇ 15P pool table

Credit cards ① ③ Ⓥ

GH Granby Deganwy Av ☎(0492) 76095
Plan **17A** *B3*
Apr–Oct

Bright, well appointed guesthouse in quiet residential area.

8hc (5fb) ✖ ® ✳B&b£9.50–£10 Bdi£12–
£12.75 W£77–£78.75 ½ LDO5pm

Lic CTV 6P

Credit card ③ ⓥ

GH Heath House Hotel Central Prom
☎(0492) 76538 Plan **18** *D3*
rs Oct–Mar (closed Jan)

Restored and extended Victorian building with sea and mountain views.

22hc (14fb) ✖ B&b£9.90–£12 Bdi£14.40–
£17 W£98.10–£109 ½ LDO4pm

Lic 卿 CTV 2P

ⓥ

GH Lynwood Private Hotel Clonmel St
☎(0492) 76613 Plan **19** *C3*
Mar–Nov & Xmas

Four-storey single-fronted mid-Victorian terrace just off Promenade near shops.

12hc (1卿) (8fb) ® B&b£9–£11 Bdi£12–£14
W£70–£85 ½

Lic 卿 CTV ✗

ⓥ

GH Mayfair Private Hotel 4 Abbey Rd
☎(0492) 76170 Plan **20** *B4*
Mar–Oct

13hc (6⇄2卿) (7fb) CTV in all bedrooms
® LDO6pm

Lic 卿 CTV 2P

GH Minion Private Hotel 21–23 Carmen
Sylva Rd, Craig-y-Don ☎(0492) 77740
Plan **22** *E2*
Etr–mid Oct

Detached Edwardian house in quiet residential area adjacent to beach.

16hc (6卿) (4fb) LDO5pm

Lic CTV 8P

GH Montclare Hotel North Pde ☎(0492)
77061 Plan **23** *B4*
Mar–Oct

Victorian mid-terrace overlooking bay adjacent to shops & pier.

Llandudno

16hc (10fb) CTV in all bedrooms ®
✳B&b£10 Bdi£13 W£85 ½ LDO6pm

Lic CTV 4P

ⓥ

GH Nant-y-Glyn 59 Church Walks
☎(0492) 75915 Plan **24** *B4*
Closed Dec & Jan

Semi-detached house on high ground just a short distance from the sea and town centre.

10hc (3fb) ✖ ✳B&b£7.50–£8.50 Bdi£11–
£12 W£74.50–£81.50 ½ LDO5.30pm

卿 CTV ✗ nc5yrs

ⓥ

GH Orotava Private Hotel 105 Glan-y-
Mor Rd, Penrhyn Bay ☎(0492) 49780
Plan **26** *E3*
Etr–Oct

Detached Edwardian house, 2 miles from town below Little Orme.

6hc ✖ ✳B&b£9.95 Bdi£14.75 W£103.25 ½
LDO6.30pm

CTV 6P nc6yrs

ⓥ

GH Plas Madoc Private Hotel 60 Church
Walks ☎(0492) 76514 Plan **28** *B4*

Semi-detached Victorian house, close to shops and Promenade.

9hc (2fb) ✖ ® ✳B&b£8–£8.50 Bdi£11–
£11.50 W£75–£79 ½ LDO4pm

Lic 卿 CTV 6P nc3yrs

ⓥ

GH Puffin Lodge Hotel 9 Neville Cres,
Central Promenade ☎(0492) 77713 Plan
29 *D3*
Apr–Oct

Single-fronted Victorian mid-terrace on Central Promenade within a short walk of shops.

12hc (8⇄4卿) (7fb) ✖ ® ✳B&b£10–
£11.15 Bdi£14–£15.15 W£98–£106.05 ½
LDO5pm

Lic 卿 CTV 12P nc4yrs

GH Rosaire Private Hotel
2 St Seiriol's Rd ☎(0492) 77677
Plan **31** *B2*
Mar–Oct

Edwardian house in quiet corner position of residential area.

12hc (4fb) ✖ LDO5pm

Lic CTV 6P nc4yrs

GH Rose-Tor Mostyn St ☎(0492) 70433
Plan **31A** *B4*

Well-run family guesthouse with good facilities.

8hc (1⇄7卿) (4fb) CTV in all bedrooms
✳B&b£10 Bdi£14.30 W£100 ½ LDO7pm

Lic 卿 ✗

GH St Davids 32 Clifton Rd ☎(0492)
79216 Plan **31B** *B3*

Semi-detached building in central position just off sea front.

6hc (3fb) ✖ ✳B&b£9–£9.50 Bdi£11.50–
£12 W£79.50–£84 ½ LDO3pm

Lic 卿 CTV ✗

GH St Hilary Hotel 16 Promenade, Craig-
y-Don ☎(0492) 75551 Plan **32** *E3*
Mar–Nov

Single-fronted Victorian terraced house ⅜ mile from main shopping area.

11hc (4卿) (8fb) CTV in all bedrooms ®
✳B&b£8–£10 Bdi£11.50–£14 W£80.50–
£91 ½ LDO5pm

卿 CTV ✗

ⓥ

GH Sandilands Private Hotel Dale Rd,
West Shore ☎(0492) 75555 Plan **33** *A2*
Apr–Sep rs Oct–Mar

Detached hotel 50 yards from West Parade Beach.

11hc (5fb) ® LDO6pm

Lic 卿 CTV 9P

GH Stratford Hotel Promenade, Craig-y-
Don ☎(0492) 77962 Plan **34** *E3*

10hc (6卿) (3fb) ✖ ®

Lic 卿 CTV ✗

GH Tan-y-Marian Private Hotel 87 Abbey Rd, West Shore ☎(0492) 77727 Plan **35** A3
Etr–Oct

Family-run private hotel near the town's West Shore.

8hc (2🚿) (2fb) ® ✱B&b£8.50–£10.50 Bdi£12.50–£15.50 W£80–£100 ⅃ LDO7pm
Lic ▦ CTV 4P 2🏂 nc2yrs
Ⓥ

GH Tilstone Private Hotel Carmen Sylva Rd, Craig-y-Don ☎(0492) 75588 Plan **36** E3

On corner position in quiet secondary shopping area; short walk to beach.

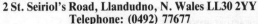

Llandudno

8hc ✕ ✱B&b£8–£8.50 Bdi£13–£13.50 W£91–£94 ⅃
Lic ▦ CTV 🅿 nc

GH Warwick Hotel 56 Church Walks ☎(0492) 76823 Plan **37** B4
May–Oct

Semi-detached Victorian house with good views over the town.

17hc (6🚿) (9fb) CTV in all bedrooms ® ✱B&b£9.50–£11 Bdi£13.50–£15 W£90–£98 ⅃ LDO6pm
Lic ▦ CTV 🅿 🐕
Ⓥ

See advertisement on page 238

GH Wilton Hotel South Parade ☎(0492) 76086 Plan **38** C4
Mar–Oct

15hc (4🚿 3🚿) (7fb) CTV in all bedrooms ® ✱B&b£12 Bdi£17 W£98 ⅃ LDO4.30pm
Lic 🅿
Ⓥ

LLANFAIR CLYDOGAU
Dyfed
Map **2**   SN65

─────── *Recommended* ───────

FH Mrs M Eleri-Davies **Pentre**
(*SN625506*) ☎Llangybi (057045) 313
Apr–Oct

Hospitable and comfortable stone-built farmhouse overlooking the Vale of Teifi. Spacious lounge with oak beams and inglenook fireplace. Fishing available. Ideal for country walks.

3hc (1⇨ 1🛏) (2fb) ✗ ® ✱B&b£9–£9.50 Bdi£14–£15 W£98–£100 ⱡ
LDO6pm

🍴CTV 4P ⚬ ↗

300acres dairy sheep

Ⓥ

LLANFAIR DYFFRYN CLWYD
Clwyd
Map **6**   SJ15

GH Eyarth Station ☎(08242) 3643

3hc (1🛏) (1fb) ✱B&b£10 W£120 M
LDO4pm

CTV 6P ⚬ ⌂(heated)

FH Mrs E Jones **Llanbenwch** (*SJ137533*)
☎Ruthin (08242) 2340
Feb–Nov

┌─────────────────────────┐
│ **Llanfair Clydogau** │
│   —   │
│   **Llanfyllin**   │
└─────────────────────────┘

17th-century farmhouse, 3 miles S of Ruthin on A525.

3hc (2fb) TV in all bedrooms ✗ ®
✱B&bfr£7.50 Bdifr£10.50 Wfr£66.50 ⱡ
LDO5pm

🍴CTV P 40acres mixed

Ⓥ

LLANFAIRFECHAN
Gwynedd
Map **6**   SH67

↠**GH Myrtlewood** Penmaenmawr Rd
☎(0248) 680735

This hotel, standing in its own gardens, has lovely views of Puffin Island and the Menai Straits.

10hc (5fb) B&b£7–£8 Bdifr£11.50 Wfr£49
M LDO7pm

Lic 🍴 CTV 15P

See advertisement on page 131

LLANFAIR WATERDINE
Shropshire
Map **7**   SO27

INN *Red Lion* ☎Knighton (0547) 528214
Closed Xmas Day

3hc (1⇨) ✗ LDO9pm

🍴 2CP ⇘ nc14yrs

LLANFIHANGEL-YNG-NGWYNFA
Powys
Map **6**   SJ01

FH Mrs E Jenkins *Cyfie* (*SJ085147*)
☎Llanfyllin (069184) 451

17th-century beamed farmhouse set in peaceful undulating countryside. 2m S on unclass rd off B4382.

2hc (1fb) CTV in 1 bedroom ✗ ®

🍴 CTV 6P 178acres beef sheep mixed

LLANFIHANGEL-Y-PENNANT
Gwynedd
Map **6**   SH60

FH Mrs M Jones **Tynybryn** (*SH659080*)
☎Abergynolwyn (065477) 277

1½m SW unclass rd.

3hc (1⇨ 1🛏) (1fb) ✗ ® ✱B&b£7.50–£11
Bdi£11–£14 W£77–£90 ⱡ LDO6pm

CTV P 300acres mixed

Ⓥ

See advertisement on page 394

LLANFYLLIN
Powys
Map **6**   SJ11

GH Challenge Adventure Centre
Y Dollyd (½m E) ☎(069184) 703

Accommodation is separate from, although a part of, the adventure centre which is available to guests if desired.

5hc Annexe: 1🛁🚿 (1fb) 🚭 in 2 bedrooms 🐕 [R] ✱B&b£10–£16 Bdi£13–£19 W£91–£133 Ł LDO10.15pm

Lic ♨ CTV 25P snooker sauna bath solarium

[V]

LLANGATTOCK
Powys
Map **3** SO21

GH Parc Place The Legar ☎Crickhowell (0873) 810562

Small and friendly rural guesthouse with modest bedrooms and cosy public areas.

10hc (4fb) 🐕 [R] ✱B&b£9–£10 Bdifr£13.50 Wfr£90 Ł LDOam

Lic ♨ CTV 10P

Credit cards [1] [2] [3] [V]

LLANGOLLEN
Clwyd
Map **7** SJ24

FH Mrs A Kenrick **Rhydonnen Ucha Rhewl** *(SJ174429)* ☎(0978) 860153
Etr–Nov

Large, stone-built, three-storey farmhouse, pleasantly situated with shooting on farm and trout fishing on River Dee (permit).

4hc (2fb) ✱B&b£8.50–£9 Bdi£13–£13.50 W£88–£91.50 Ł LDO5pm

♨ CTV 6P 125acres dairy

LLANGRANOG
Dyfed
Map **2** SN35

FH Mrs B Williams **Hendre** *(SN344538)*
Hendre (3m E B4321) ☎(023978) 342
May–Oct

Conveniently positioned 2 miles from the sandy beach, offering good home cooking.

3hc (1fb) 🚭 in 2 bedrooms 🐕 ✱B&b£9–£10 Bdi£13–£14 W£90–£97 Ł LDOnoon

♨ CTV 6P

100acres beef mixed

[V]

INN Pentre Arms Hotel ☎(023978) 229

Simply-appointed inn situated in friendly seaside town.

7hc (2fb) ✱B&bfr£12 Bdifr£17 Lunch £1–£2.25 Dinner 9.30pm fr£5

♨ CTV 6P snooker

LLANGURIG
Powys
Map **6** SN98

INN *Blue Bell* ☎(05515) 254

10hc (1🛁)

♨ CTV 40P 🚗

LLANGYNOG
Dyfed
Map **2** SN31

Recommended

FH Mrs M Thomas **Plas** *(SN332176)*
☎Bancyfelin (026782) 492
Mar–Nov

Set in Dylan Thomas country. Plas Farm offers a very high standard of modern farmhouse accommodation, with friendly family attention. Within easy reach of south and west coast and Pembrokeshire National Park.

3hc (2fb) 🐕 [R] ✱B&b£7.50

♨ CTV 4P nc2½yrs 136acres dairy sheep

Credit cards [1] [2] [3] [4] [5] [V]

LLANRHAEADR
Clwyd
Map **6** SJ06

FH Mrs S Evans **Tan-yr-Accar** *(SJ078614)* ☎Llanynys (074578) 232
Mar–Oct

Good family accommodation in 18th century farmhouse within the lovely Vale of Clwyd.

2rm (1fb) 🐕 ✱B&b£7.50–£8 Bdi£10–£12.50 Wfr£45 M̸ LDO previous day

♨ CTV 4P 🏠 85acres dairy sheep

[V]

LLANRUG
Gwynedd
Map **6** SH56

FH Mr & Mrs D Mackinnon **Plás Tirion** *(SH524628)* ☎Caernarfon (0286) 3190
Whit–Oct

100-year-old farmhouse set in open position with traditional farm buildings and gardens.

5hc (2fb) 🐕 [R] ✱B&b£10 W£70 M̸

Lic ♨ CTV 🏠 450acres mixed

LLANRWST
Gwynedd
Map **6** SH86

FH Mrs M Owen **Bodrach** *(SH852629)*
Carmel ☎(0492) 640326
May–Oct

Situated in peaceful setting approximately 5 miles from Llanwrst.

2rm (1fb) 🐕 ✱B&b£8 Bdi£11 Wfr£77 Ł LDO5pm

♨ CTV 6P 185acres sheep mixed

Credit cards [1] [2] [3] [V]

LLANSANTFFRAID-YM-MECHAIN
Powys
Map **7** SJ22

FH Mrs M E Jones **Glanvyrnwy** *(SJ229202)* ☎Llansantffraid (069181) 258

200-year-old stone-built farmhouse, set back from main road, with pleasant lawns and orchard.

3rm (2hc) (1fb) 🐕 ✱B&b£8–£9 Bdi£11–£12.50 W£65–£80 Ł LDO6pm

CTV 3P nc3yrs 42acres dairy

LLANTRITHYD
South Glamorgan
Map **3**   ST07

FH Mrs T Lougher **Treguff** *(SS032711)*
☎St Athan (0446) 750210
Closed Xmas wk

Traditionally furnished Elizabethan
farmhouse amid 525 acres.

3rm ✹ B&b£8.50–£10 Bdi£13.50–£15
W£51–£60 Ⓜ LDOnoon

CTV 6P 2🐑 no babies

525acres beef sheep mixed

LLANUWCHLLYN
Gwynedd
Map **6**   SH83

FH Mrs D Bugby **Bryncaled** *(SH866314)*
☎(06784) 270
Closed Xmas

Small farmhouse with oak-beamed dining
room, overlooking Aran mountains. A
fishing river runs through the grounds.
Approximately 6 miles from Bala.

3rm (2hc) ✹ Ⓡ ✱B&b£8.50 Bdi£13
Wfr£84 ⅃

Lic 🏵 CTV 8P 500acres beef sheep
mixed

LLANVAIR-DISCOED
Gwent
Map **3**   ST49

FH Mrs A Barnfather **Cribau** *(ST454941)*
The Cwm ☎Shirenewton (02917) 528
Closed Xmas

16th-century farmhouse at the head of the
"cwm". (Off unclass road joining Llanvair-
Discoed & Shirenewton).

2🏠 ✹ Ⓡ ✱B&b£9 W£63 Ⓜ

🏵 4P nc12yrs 33acres smallholding

FH Mr & Mrs S Price **Great Llanmellyn**
(SO456923) ☎Shirenewton (02917) 210
Apr–Oct

Family farmhouse full of character with
flag-stone floors and cosy
accommodation.

2hc (2fb) ✹ Ⓡ B&b£9 W£54 Ⓜ

🏵 CTV 3P 250acres dairy mixed

Ⓥ

Llantrithyd
—
Lochinver

LLANWARNE
Hereford & Worcester
Map **3**   SO52

FH Mrs I E Williams **Llanwarne Court**
(SO503275) ☎Golden Valley (0981)
540385
Mar–Oct

Farmhouse, set away from the main road
with large walled garden.

3hc (1🏠) ✹ Ⓡ

🏵 CTV P ⚗ 260acres mixed

LLANWDDYN
Powys
Map **6**   SJ01

FH R B & H A Parry **Tynymaes**
(SJ048183) ☎(069173) 216
May–Oct

The farmhouse is situated on the edge of
the nature reserve at Lake Vyrnwy.

2hc (1fb) ✹ ✱B&b£8.50–£9 Bdi£12.50–
£13 W£85–£87.50 ⅃ LDO5pm

🏵 CTV 4P 420acres mixed

Ⓥ

LLANWRIN
Powys
Map **6**   SH70

FH Mrs R J Hughes **Mathafarn**
(SN812055) Cemmaes Rd ☎Cemmaes
Road (06502) 226
Apr–Oct

Comfortable, ivy-clad farmhouse dating
back to 1628 in the beautiful Dovey
Valley.

2hc (1🏠) ✹ ✱B&b£8.50–£9.50
Bdi£13.50–£14.50

CTV 3P 600acres sheep mixed

LLANWRTYD WELLS
Powys
Map **3**   SN84

GH Carlton Court Hotel Dolecoed Rd
☎(05913) 248

9hc (1🏠) CTV in 8 bedrooms TV in 1
bedroom Ⓡ ✱B&b£9.95–£12.95
Bdi£14.95–£17.95 W£95–£113 ⅃
LDO9.30pm

Lic 🏵 sauna bath

Ⓥ

━ Recommended ━
GH Lasswade House
(Guestaccom) ☎(05913) 515

Handsome Edwardian house with
high quality rooms, very enjoyable
meals, and charming country house
atmosphere. Outdoor swimming
pool.

8hc (2🏠 4🏠) CTV in 2 bedrooms TV
in 6 bedrooms Ⓡ ✱B&b£13–£15
Bdi£21–£24 W£130–£150 ⅃ LDO9pm

Lic 🏵 12P ⌂(heated) sauna bath

Credit cards ① ③ Ⓥ

LOCHEYNORT' (NORTH)
Isle of South Uist, Western Isles *Inverness-*
shire
See **Uist (South), Isle of**

LOCHGOILHEAD
Strathclyde *Argyllshire*
Map **10**   NN10

FH Mrs J H Jackson **Pole** *(NN192044)*
☎(03013) 221
Etr–Sep

Pleasant well-kept farmhouse, 2 miles
from Lochgoilhead.

3rm (1🏠) (1fb) ✗ in 2 bedrooms
✱B&b£7.50–£8.50 Bdi£12–£13 W£77–£82
⅃ LDO7.45pm

🏵 CTV 3P 7,550acres sheep mixed

LOCHINVER
Highland *Sutherland*
Map **14**   NC02

GH Ardglas ☎(05714) 257
Closed Dec

Modern villa on elevated site overlooking
the village.

8hc (3fb) ✱B&b£9 Wfr£63 Ⓜ

🏵 CTV 20P

Llanwarne Court
B&B FARMHOUSE ACCOMMODATION
Tel: (0981) 540 385 **AA Reccommended**

★ Set in its own 262 acres of Beautiful Herefordshire Farm Land.
★ Central Heating, with H&C and Shaver Points.
★ Full English Breakfast.
★ Colour TV in Residents' Lounge plus Tea Making Facilities.
★ Walled Garden, Tree Swings, Lawn Games.
★ Ground floor bedrooms with en suite facilities.
★ Bridal Room with Jacobean Four Poster Bed.
★ In the centre of the Herefordshie — Ross — Monmouth Triangle
   Triangle between A466 & A49.
We only close between 15th December-15th January whether you want
a winter or a summer farm break, you will be warmly welcomed here.

For further details SAE to the proprietor, Mrs I.E.WILLIAMS.
LLANWARNE COURT, LLANWARNE, HEREFORDSHIRE HR2 8JE

GH Hillcrest Badnaban ☎(05714) 391
Apr–Oct

*Modern bungalow set in unspoilt
environment, 2 miles S of the village on
unclass rd.*

4hc ✱B&b£10 Bdi£15 W£105 ⫽ LDO5pm
🎦 CTV 7P

LOCHRANZA
Isle of Arran, Strathclyde *Buteshire*
See **Arran, Isle of**

LOCHWINNOCH
Strathclyde *Renfrewshire*
Map **10**   NS35

FH Mrs A Mackie **High Belltrees**
(NS377584) ☎(0505) 842376

*Situated 1m off the A737, Paisley to Largs
road. Overlooks Castle Semple Loch
which has an R.S.P.B. Bird Sanctuary and
yachting facilities.*

4rm (3hc) (2fb) CTV in 1 bedroom TV in 1
bedroom ✖ ® ✱B&b£9–£10 W£60–£65 M
🎦 CTV 6P 220acres dairy mixed.

Lochinver
–
Loddon

LOCKERBIE
Dumfries & Galloway *Dumfriesshire*
Map **11**   NY18

GH Rosehill Carlisle Rd ☎(05762) 2378

*Victorian, two-storey, sandstone house
with attractive garden.*

5hc (3fb) ✱B&b£8.50
🎦 CTV 6P

LODDISWELL
Devon
Map **3**   SX74

FH Mrs A Pethybridge **Reads** *(SX727489)*
☎Kingsbridge (0548) 550317
Jun–Aug

*Two-storey stone-built farmhouse in
secluded position with fine views.*

2rm (1hc) (1fb) ® ✱B&b£7.50–£8.50
W£56 M
CTV 2P ≋(heated) 100acres mixed

LODDON
Norfolk
Map **5**   TM39

FH Mrs J Rackham **Stubbs House**
(TM358977) ☎(0508) 20231
Mar–Oct

*Fine, old Georgian farmhouse with
excellent kitchen producing delicious,
professional meals.*

9hc (3🛁) (1fb) ✖ ✱B&bfr£14 Bdifr£21
Wfr£95 ⫽
Lic 🎦 CTV 20P nc8yrs 180acres arable
ⓥ

LONDON
Greater London
Map **4** & **5**
See plans 1–4 pages 243–247
A map of the London postal area appears on pages 248–249
Places within the London postal area are listed below in postal district order commencing East then North, South and West, with a brief indication of the area covered. Detailed plans **1–3** show the locations of AA-listed hotels within the Central London postal districts which are indicated by a number. Plan **4** highlights the districts covered within the outer area keyed by a grid reference eg A5
Other places within the county of London are listed under their respective placenames and are also keyed to this plan or the main map section.

E18
South Woodford
London plan **4** F5

Grove Hill Hotel 38 Grove Hill, South Woodford ☎01-989 3344
Comfortably appointed small hotel offering good standard of service.
21hc (5🛁) (2fb) CTV in all bedrooms [R] *B&b£16.10–£21.85 W£112.70–£152.95 M̸
Lic 🛋 CTV 8P 4🚗 (charge)
Credit cards [1] [2] [3] [V]

N8
Hornsey
London plan **4** D5

Aber Hotel 89 Crouch Hill ☎01-3402847
Converted private house offering simple accommodation and informal atmosphere.
8hc (4fb) ✖
🛋 CTV P̸

NW2
Cricklewood
London plan **4** C4

Clearview House 161 Fordwych Rd, Cricklewood ☎01-452 9773

London E18 — London SE9

6hc (1fb) TV in 4 bedrooms ✖ *B&b£9 W£59.50 M̸
🛋 CTV nc5yrs
[V]

Garth Hotel 70–76 Hendon Way, Cricklewood ☎01-455 4742
Well appointed hotel with well-furnished bedrooms.
54hc (20🛁 19🚿) (10fb) CTV in all bedrooms ✖ LDO9pm
Lic 🛋 CTV 36P
Credit cards [1] [2] [3] [4] [5]

NW3
Hampstead and Swiss Cottage
London plan **4** D4

Frognal Lodge Hotel 14 Frognal Gdns, off Church Row, Hampstead ☎01-435 8238 Telex no 8812714
Comfortable informal hotel.
17hc (7🛁) (5fb) CTV in 10 bedrooms *B&b£15–£24
Lic lift 🛋 CTV P̸ ⌂
Credit cards [1] [2] [3] [5] [V]

NW4
Hendon
London plan **4** C5

Peacehaven Hotel 94 Audley Rd, Hendon ☎01-202 9758
Modern, bright bedrooms, all with colour TV. Bathroom facilities well above average.
12hc (1🛁) (2fb) CTV in all bedrooms ✖ B&bfr£17
🛋 CTV 2P
Credit cards [1] [3]

NW11
Golders Green
London plan **4** C5

Central Hotel 35 Hoop Ln, Golders Green ☎01-458 5636 Telex No 922488
Two modern buildings with well-equipped bedrooms.
18🛁 Annexe: 18hc (3fb) CTV in 18 bedrooms TV in 18 bedrooms ✖ *B&b£25–£35
🛋 CTV 10P
Credit cards [1] [2] [3] [5]
See advertisement on page 250

Croft Court Hotel 44–46 Ravenscourt Av, Golders Green ☎01-458 3331 Telex no 8950511
Modest but comfortable accommodation.
15hc (7🛁) (7fb) TV in all bedrooms LDO6pm
🛋 CTV 4P

SE3
Blackheath
London Plan **4** E3

Recommended

Bardon Lodge Hotel 15 Stratheden Rd, Blackheath ☎01-853 4051
Warm, friendly private hotel, tastefully decorated and offering good standard of accommodation.
42hc (26🚿) (5fb) CTV in all bedrooms ✖ [R] *B&b£25–£44 LDO8.30pm
Lic 🛋 CTV 16P
Credit cards [1] [3]

Stonehall House 35–37 Westcombe Park Rd, Blackheath ☎01-858 8706
Old fashioned and comfortable guesthouse with pleasant TV lounge and garden.
23hc (1🚿) (9fb) CTV in all bedrooms B&b£14–£18 W£84–£108 M̸
🛋 CTV P̸

SE9
Eltham
London plan **4** F2
See entry on page 249 for Yardley Court

London Plan 1

Details of the establishments shown on this map can be found under the *London Postal District* which follows the establishment name

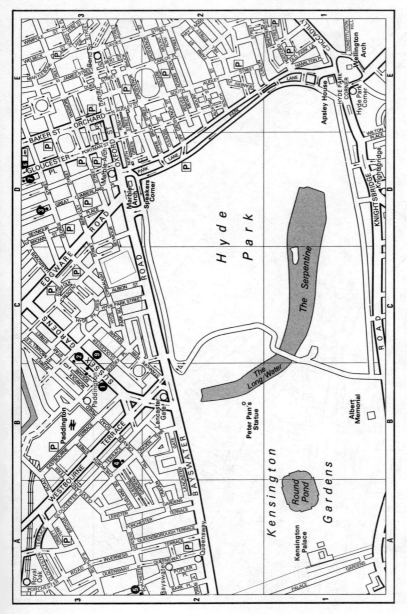

London Plan 1

1 Ashley Hotel (W2)
2 Camelot Hotel (W2)
3 Hotel Concorde (W1)
4 Dylan Hotel (W2)

5 Garden Court Hotel (W2)
6 Georgian House Hotel (W1)
7 Hart House Hotel (W1)
9 Nayland Hotel (W2)

Details of the establishments shown on this map can be found under the *London Postal District* which follows the establishment name

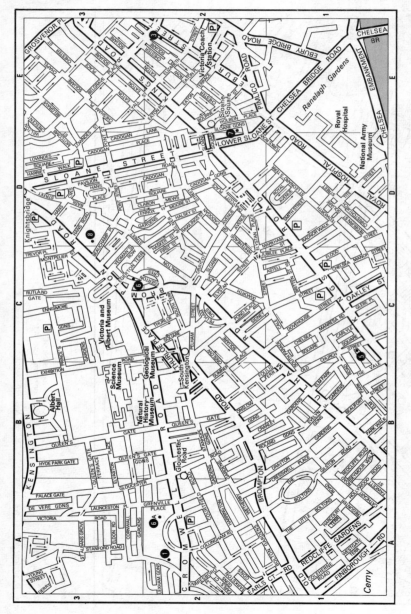

London Plan 2

1 Atlas Hotel *(W8)*
3 Chesham House *(SW1)*
5 Eden House Hotel *(SW3)*

6 Garden House Hotel *(SW3)*
6A Number Eight Hotel *(SW7)*
7 Willett Hotel *(SW1)*
8 Knightsbridge Hotel *(SW3)*

Details of the establishments shown on this map can be found under the *London Postal District* which follows the establishment name

London Plan 3

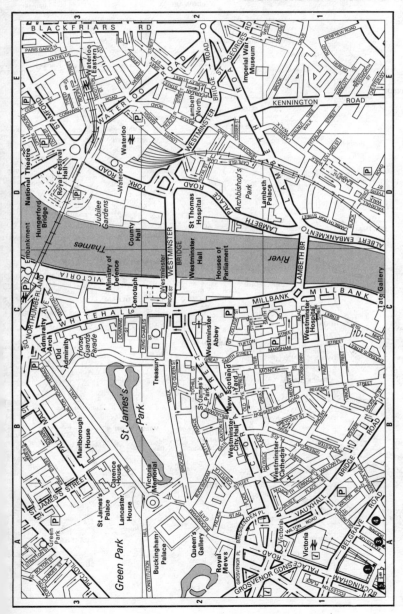

London Plan 3

1 Arden House *(SW1)*
3 Elizabeth Hotel *(SW1)*
4 Windermere Hotel *(SW1)*
5 Hanover Hotel *(SW1)*

London Plan 4

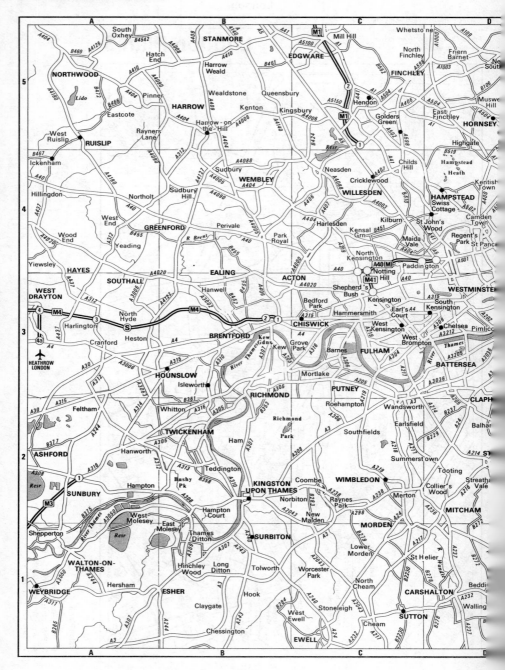

London Plan 4

The placenames highlighted by a **dot** are locations of AA listed establishments outside the Central London Plan area (Plans 1–3). Some of these fall within the London Postal District area and can therefore be found in the gazetteer under **London** in postal district order (see London Postal District map on following page). Others outside the London Postal District area can therefore be found under their respective placenames in the main gazetteer.

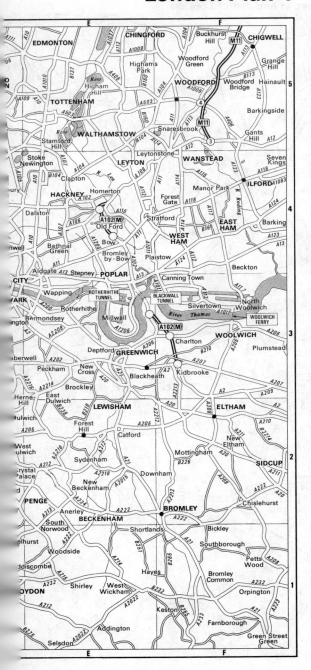

London Postal Districts and ways in and out of London

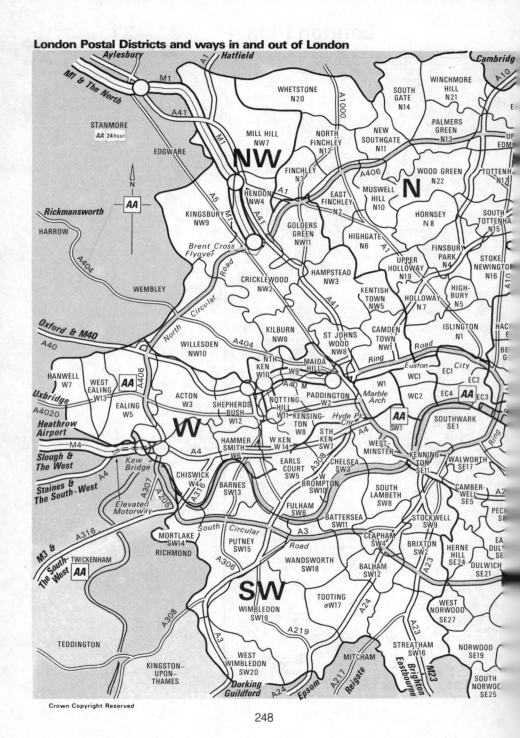

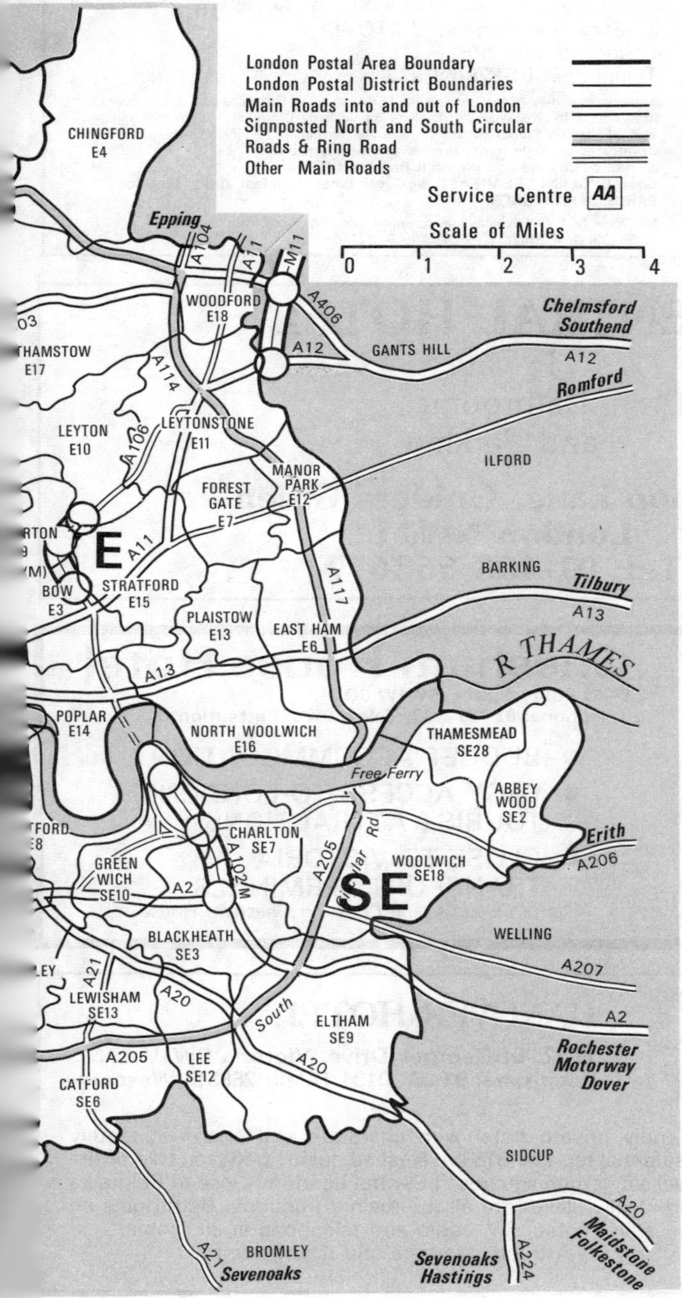

Recommended

Yardley Court Private Hotel 18 Court Rd, Eltham ☎01-850 1850

Closed Xmas wk

Small private hotel with very comfortable and generous accommodation. Extensive service is available.

8hc (1🛁 4🚿) (2fb) CTV in all bedrooms 🐕 B&b£20–£26 Bdi£24–£30 (inc High Tea) LDO9pm

🍽 CTV 8P nc3yrs [V]

SE19

Norwood

London plan **4** D2

Crystal Palace Tower Hotel 114 Church Rd ☎01-653 0176

Large Victorian house with large, comfortable bedrooms.

11hc (2🛁 2🚿) (5fb) TV in all bedrooms ✱B&b£10.50–£12

🍽 CTV 10P [V]

SE23

Forest Hill

London plan **4** E2

Rutz 16 Vancouver Rd, Forest Hill ☎01-699 3071

Closed Xmas–New Year

6hc (1🛁 2🚿) (1fb) 🚭 in 2 bedrooms 🐕 [R] B&b£13–£16 Bdi£19–£22 W£129.50–£140 V LDO2pm

🍽 CTV 🅿 [V]

SW1

West End–Westminster, St James's Park, Victoria Station

London plan **4** D3

Arden House 12 St Georges Dr ☎01-834 2988 Telex no 22650 Plan 3:**1** *A1*

Simply furnished hotel with easy access to Victoria Station.

35hc (10🛁 4🚿) (10fb) CTV in all bedrooms 🐕 B&b£12.50–£20 W£75–£95 M

🍽 CTV 🅿 [V]

Chesham House 64–66 Ebury St, Belgravia ☎01-730 8513 Telex no 912881 (ESP) Plan 2:**3** *E2*

23hc (3fb) CTV in all bedrooms 🐕 ✱B&b£16–£20

🍽 🅿 nc5yrs

Credit cards [2] [3] [5]

See advertisement on page 250

Elizabeth Hotel 37 Eccleston Sq, Victoria ☎01-828 6812 Plan 3:**3** *A1*

Simply furnished hotel situated near Victoria Station.

24hc (1🛁 2🚿) (6fb) CTV in 4 bedrooms 🐕 ✱B&b£12.50–£25 W£78.75–£175 M

🍽 CTV 🎾(hard)

See advertisement on page 250

GH Hanover Hotel 30 St Georges Dr
☎01-834 0134 Plan 3:**5** *A1*

An early 19th-century terrace house with comfortable accommodation.

34hc (8🛁 18🚿) (4fb) CTV in all bedrooms
B&b£19–£25 (W only Nov–Feb)

♨ CTV 🅿̸

Credit cards [1] [2] [3]

Willett Hotel 32 Sloane Gdns, Sloane Sq
☎01-824 8415 Plan 2:**7** *E2*

Terraced house with spacious comfortably furnished bedrooms.

17hc (14🛁) (10fb) CTV in all bedrooms [R]
✱B&b£19.55–£26.45

♨ 🅿̸

Windermere Hotel 142 Warwick Way, Victoria ☎01-834 5163 Plan 3:**4** *A1*

Well-maintained, small guesthouse, with comfortable bedrooms.

8hc (4🚿) (5fb) CTV in all bedrooms ⋈
✱B&b£20–£30

♨ 🅿̸

SW3
Chelsea
London plan **4** D3

Eden House Hotel 111 Old Church St
☎01-352 3403 Plan 2:**5** *C1*

Homely Edwardian house with a comprehensive room service but lacking any public rooms.

London SW1 — London SW19

14hc (4🛁 5🚿) (3fb) CTV in all bedrooms
✱B&b£16–£25 W£112–£175 M

♨ CTV 🅿̸

Credit cards [1] [2] [3] [4] [5] [V]

Garden House Hotel 44–46 Egerton Gdns ☎01-584 2990 Plan 2:**6** *C3*
Closed Xmas

Friendly establishment with spacious, cheerful bedrooms.

30hc (7🛁 7🚿) (4fb) CTV in 14 bedrooms
✱B&b£10–£34

lift ♨ P

Knightsbridge Hotel 10 Beaufort Gdns
☎01-589 9271 Plan 2:**8** *D3*

Comfortable, well-equipped bedrooms, limited lounge accommodation and small basement dining room. Ideally located close to Harrods.

20rm 7hc (4🛁 5🚿) (2fb) CTV in 4 bedrooms ⋈ B&b£25.75–£35.75 W£148.05–£204.75 M (W only Dec, Jan & Feb) LDO10.30pm

Lic ♨ CTV 🅿̸

Credit cards [2] [3] [V]

SW7
South Kensington
London plan **4** D3

Number Eight Hotel 8 Emperors Gate, South Kensington ☎01-370 7516

Small, friendly hotel where bedrooms are attractively decorated and have many modern facilities.

14hc (10🛁 2🚿) (2fb) CTV in all bedrooms
⋈ [R] ✱B&b£25–£37.95

♨ 🅿̸

Credit cards [1] [2] [3] [5] [V]

SW19
Wimbledon
London plan **4** C2

GH Trochee Hotel 21 Malcolm Rd, Wimbledon ☎01-946 1579 & 3924

17hc (2fb) CTV in all bedrooms
✱B&bfr£19

♨ CTV 3P

[V]

See advertisement on page 252

Wimbledon Hotel 78 Worple Rd, Wimbledon ☎01-946 9265

Hotel has modernised compact bedrooms, with limited comfortable lounge facilities and easy car parking.

14hc (4🛁 4🚿) (4fb) 🚭 in 2 bedrooms ⋈
[R] ✱B&b£19

♨ CTV 10P

Credit cards [1] [3] [V]

Worcester House 38 Alwyne Rd ☎01-946 1300

Hotel has compact, well-fitted bedrooms limited dining facilities and breakfast room service.

9🚿 (1fb) CTV in all bedrooms ✖ [R] ✱B&b£21.85–£33.35 LDO11am

♨ P̸

Credit cards [1] [2] [3] [5] [V]

W1

West End; Piccadilly Circus, St Marylebone and Mayfair
London plan **4** D3/4

Hotel Concorde 50 Great Cumberland Pl ☎01-402 6169 Plan 1:**3** *D3*

Tastefully decorated and comfortable accommodation with good lounge. Well situated in the centre of London.

28hc (5🛁 23🚿) CTV in all bedrooms ✖ LDO10.30pm

Lic lift ♨ CTV P̸

Credit cards [1] [2] [3] [4] [5]

Georgian House Hotel 87 Gloucester Pl, Baker St ☎01-935 2211 Plan 1:**6** *D3*

A terraced house in busy road just off Marble Arch.

19hc (14🛁 5🚿) (3fb) CTV in all bedrooms ✖ B&b£18–£21 W£70–£120 M̸ (W only Nov–Feb)

London SW19 — London W2

Lic lift ♨ CTV P̸ nc5yrs

Credit card [3] [V]

Hart House Hotel 51 Gloucester Pl, Portman Sq ☎01-935 2288 Plan 1:**7** *D3*

Imposing, five-storey terrace house with well-appointed bedrooms.

15hc (7🛁) (4fb) CTV in all bedrooms ✖ [R] ✱B&b£15–£25

♨ CTV P̸

Credit cards [1] [2] [3] [V]

Montagu House 3 Montagu Pl ☎01-935 4632

18hc (1🚿) (3fb) CTV in all bedrooms ✖ [R]

♨ CTV nc2yrs

W2

Bayswater, Paddington
London plan **4** C/D3/4

Ashley Hotel 15 Norfolk Sq, Hyde Park ☎01-723 3375 Plan 1:**1** *B3*
Closed 1wk Xmas

Situated in a quiet square close to Paddington Station.

16hc (4🚿) (1fb) CTV in all bedrooms ✖ B&b£12

♨ CTV P̸

Camelot Hotel 45 Norfolk Sq ☎01-723 9118 Plan 1:**2** *C3*

Friendly hotel providing modern facilities in a range of accommodation.

34hc (13🛁 1🚿) (10fb) CTV in all bedrooms ✖ [R] ✱B&b£23

♨ CTV P̸

Credit cards [1] [3] [V]

Dylan Hotel 14 Devonshire Ter Lancaster Gate ☎01-723 3280 Plan 1:**4** *B3*

Traditional style guesthouse, homely and comfortable.

18hc (2🛁 6🚿) (3fb) ✖ [R] ✱B&b£15–£28 (W only Nov–Feb)

♨ CTV P̸

Credit cards [2] [3] [5]

Garden Court Hotel 30–31 Kensington Gardens Sq ☎01-727 8304 Plan 1:**5** *A3*

Friendly, family-run, quietly situated hotel.

37hc (8🛁 4🚿) (6fb) ✱B&b£17–£21

Lic ♨ CTV P̸

Nayland Hotel 134 Sussex Gdns ☎01-723 3380 Plan 1:**9** *B3*

Small, friendly hotel with modern facilities in bedrooms including videos.

14hc (2fb) CTV in all bedrooms ✖ [R]

♨ CTV 2P

Credit cards [1] [2] [3] [5]

30hc (5🛁 10🚿) (7fb) CTV in all bedrooms ✱B&b£19.25–£29.50 Bdi£26.75–£34.25 W£168.53–£215.78 Ⱡ LDO8.30pm

Lic ♨ CTV 15P sauna bath solarium

Credit cards [1] [2] [3] [5]

W8
Kensington
London plan **4** C3

Apollo Hotel 18–22 Lexham Gdns, Kensington ☎01-373 3236 Telex no 264189

Sister to Atlas Hotel, has many modern facilities and modest prices.

59hc (40🛁 10🚿) ✱B&b£14.50–£19.50 Bdi£20.50–£25.50 LDO7.30pm

Lic lift ♨ CTV P̸

Credit cards [1] [2] [3] [4] [5]

Atlas Hotel 24–30 Lexham Gdns, Kensington ☎01-373 7873 Telex no 264189 Plan 2: **1** *A2*

Modestly priced accommodation with many modern facilities.

70hc (19🛁 30🚿) (1fb) B&b£14.50–£19.50 Bdi£20.50–£25.50 LDO7.30pm

Lic lift ♨ CTV P̸

Credit cards [1] [2] [3] [4] [5]

W14
West Kensington
London plan **4** C3

Recommended

Avonmore Hotel 66 Avonmore Rd ☎01-603 4296 Telex no 945922 (Gladdex G)

Very comfortable accommodation offered by friendly proprietors.

9hc (2fb) CTV in all bedrooms ✱B&b£17.50–£23 W£80–£150 M̸ (W only Sep–Dec)

Lic ♨ CTV P̸

Ⓥ

WC1
Bloomsbury, Holborn
London plan **4** D4

Mentone Hotel 54–55 Cartwright Gdns, Bloomsbury ☎01-387 3927

London W4 — Looe

Comfortable family accommodation, with public shower facilities and friendly service.

27hc (4🚿) (10fb) ✗ ✱B&b£15–£20 W£112–£150 M̸ (W only Dec–Feb)

♨ CTV P̸ ℛ

LONGFRAMLINGTON
Northumberland
Map **12** NU10

Recommended

INN Granby ☎(066570) 228
Closed Xmas Day

The ideal village inn, the Granby has justifiably earned an excellent reputation for good food, hospitality and comfortable accommodation. Bedrooms, both in the inn and the modern chalets adjacent, are equally comfortable and well-furnished.

3hc (1🛁) CTV in all bedrooms ✗ Ⓡ ✱B&b£15.50–£16.50 Bdi£25.25 Lunch £4.50–£15&alc Dinner 9.30pm £9.75&alc

Lic ♨ 30P ✗ nc8yrs

Credit cards [1] [2] [3]

LONGLEAT
Wiltshire
Map **3** ST84

FH Mrs J Crossman **Stalls** *(ST806439)* ☎Maiden Bradley (09853) 323
Closed Xmas

Detached house built of Bath stone, originally the home farm for Longleat House. Sun terrace with trim lawns and garden to stream. Access off A362 at Corsley Lane End.

3hc (1fb) ✗ ✱B&b£10–£12 Wfr£70 M̸

♨ CTV 6P 281acres dairy

LONGRIDGE
Lancashire
Map **7** SD63

FH Mr F K Johnson **Falicon** *(SD629361)* Fleet Street Ln, Hothersall ☎Ribchester (025484) 583

A delightful sandstone farmhouse over 200 years old in pleasant rural surrounds with comfortably furnished bedrooms. Situated off B6245 Longridge to Ribchester road.

3🛁 (1fb) CTV in 2 bedrooms ✗ B&b£16–£20 Bdi£26–£30 W£170–£196 Ⱡ LDO5pm

♨ 6P nc10yrs 13 acres beef sheep

Ⓥ

LONGSDON
Staffordshire
Map **7** SJ95

FH Mr & Mrs M M Robinson ***Bank End*** *(SJ953541)* Old Leek Rd (½m SW off A53) ☎Leek (0538) 383638

Good modern farmhouse in pleasant rural area, 2m SW of Leek.

6🛁 (2fb) CTV in all bedrooms Ⓡ LDO9.30pm

Lic lift ♨ CTV 20P 2🚗 ⛺ ⛱heated ⚓ 62acres beef

See advertisement on page 227

LOOE
Cornwall
Map **3** SX25
See plan on page 256

GH 'Kantara' 7 Trelawney Ter ☎(05036) 2093 Plan **3** *A4*
Closed Dec

6hc (3fb) TV in 2 bedrooms ✱B&b£7.50–£8.50 W£52.50–£56 M̸

CTV 1🚗

Ⓥ

GH *Ogunquit* Portuan Rd, Hannafore ☎(05036) 3105 Plan **4** *C1*

Personally-run guesthouse in an elevated position in West Looe which affords superb views.

6hc (1🚿) (2fb) LDO4.30pm

♨ CTV P

GH *Panorama Hotel* Hannafore Rd,
Hannafore ☎(05036) 2123 Plan **5** *B2*
Apr–Oct

12hc (11⇄ 1🚿) (4fb) CTV in 5 bedrooms
TV in 1 bedroom LDO7pm

Lic 🏨 CTV 8P ⌂

Credit cards ① ③

GH **St Aubyns** Marine Dr, Hannafore,
West Looe ☎(05036) 4351 Plan **7** *C1*
Etr–mid Oct

8hc (2⇄) (5fb) ✗ Ⓡ ✱B&b£10–£15
W£67–£100 ᴹ

CTV 4P

Looe
—
Lostwithiel

FH Mr & Mrs Hembrow **Tregoed**
(SX272560) St Martins ☎(05036) 2718
Etr–Oct

*Georgian-style manor house on high
ground with sea view.*

6hc (4fb) ✁ in 3 bedrooms CTV in all
bedrooms Ⓡ ✱B&b£9–£12 Bdi£14–£17
W£98–£119 ⅃ LDO4pm

Lic CTV 10P ✔ 60acres dairy

LOSTWITHIEL
Cornwall
Map **2**   SX15

FH Mrs H Dunn *Pelyn Barn* (SX091588)
Pelyn Cross ☎Bodmin (0208) 872451
Closed Xmas

*Large farmhouse, formerly an old toll
house, with large sun lounge affording
scenic views. There is a well-kept lawn
enclosure at rear.*

3hc (1fb) ✗ LDOnoon

CTV 6P ⚘ 142acres dairy sheep potatoes
corn   →

The Granby

Inn & Restaurant
Longframlington, Morpeth NE65 8DP
Tel: Longframlington (066570) 228
Proprietors: Mr & Mrs G Hall and family

Formerly a coaching stop, the Granby is around 200 years old, and has retained much of its character. The restaurant caters for up to 26 diners, offering thoughtfully prepared and carefully cooked meals using fresh local produce plus an extensive wine list. The cosy bar makes an excellent meeting place where you can enjoy a refreshing drink and a bar meal. The bedrooms have colour television, central heating and complimentary tea and coffee making facilities. The Inn is centrally placed in the country on the A697 north of Morpeth and within easy reach of many places of interest.

Falicon Farm

**Fleet Street Lane, Hothersall, Longbridge,
Preston PR3 3XE. Tel: Ribchester (025484) 583.**
Welcome to our delightful countryside and well-furnished, luxurious farmhouse. Fully centrally heated, providing all bedrooms with private bathroom.
Our freshly prepared food is for the discerning and particular. Alternative diet on request. Offering high standards of personal, attentive service, providing the best food available in our superb, quiet, country atmosphere. 15 mins from M6 exits 31 & 32.

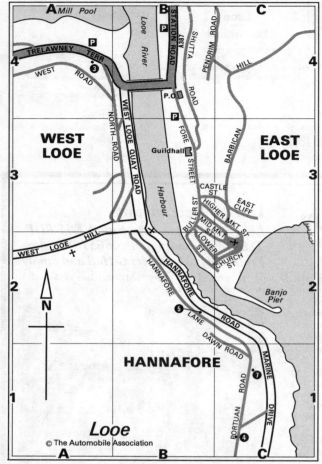

A Mill Pool

TRELAWNEY TERR

WEST ROAD

Looe River

STATION ROAD

SHUTTA ROAD

PENDRIM ROAD

HILL

WEST LOOE

NORTH-ROAD

WEST LOOE QUAY ROAD

P.O

FORE STREET

Guildhall

Harbour

CASTLE ST

HIGHER MKT ST

BARBICAN

BULLER ST

MID MKT

LOWER ST

CHURCH ST

EAST CLIFF

EAST LOOE

WEST LOOE HILL

HANNAFORE

HANNAFORE ROAD

LANE

DAWN ROAD

MARINE ROAD

BORTUAN ROAD

MARINE DRIVE

HANNAFORE

Banjo Pier

Looe

© The Automobile Association

N

A   **B**   **C**

Looe

3	'Kantara'	**5**	Panorama Hotel
4	Ogunquit	**7**	St Aubyns

FH Mrs R C Dunn *Pelyn Barn Farm Bungalow* (SX091588) Pelyn Cross ☎Bodmin (0208) 873062

250 yds off A390 St Austell–Lostwithiel rd.

3hc (1🍴) (1fb) ✖

🏠 CTV 12P 1🐕 ⚘ 380acres mixed

GH De Montfort Hotel 88 Leicester Rd ☎(0509) 216061

9hc (1fb) CTV in all bedrooms ✱B&bfr£13.50 Bdifr£18 Wfr£108 ⅃ LDO4pm

Lic 🏠 CTV ✗

Credit cards 1 3 Ⓥ

GH Sunnyside Hotel The Coneries ☎(0509) 216217
Closed 24 Dec–2 Jan

11hc B&b£12.50–£13 Bdi£18–£19 W£117.25–£123.90 ⅃ LDO4pm

🏠 CTV 8P 3🐕 nc5yrs

Credit cards 1 3

FH Mr J Christian **Brookfield Farm Hotel** (TQ212282) Winterpit Ln, Plummers Plain ☎(040376) 568

An efficiently managed farmhouse with compact bedrooms, comfortable lounge and a popular lake and lawn to the rear.

14hc (3⇨ 9🍴) (3fb) CTV in all bedrooms ✱B&b£12.50–£17.50 Bdi£20–£25 W£126–£157.50 ⅃ LDO9pm

Lic 🏠 CTV 100P ⚘ ✈ 300acres mixed

Credit cards 1 3 Ⓥ

GH Amity 396 London Road South ☎(0502) 2586

12hc (4🍴) (6fb) CTV in all bedrooms Ⓡ ✱B&b£10.50–£11.50 Bdi£15.50–£16.50 W£100–£110 ⅃ LDO4pm

Lic 🏠 CTV 4P solarium

Credit cards 1 3

GH Belmont 270 London Road South ☎(0502) 3867

Friendly family-run guesthouse within walking distance of sandy beach.

6hc (3fb) Ⓡ ✱B&b£8–£8.50 Bdi£11 W£65–£69 ⅃ (W only in season) LDO1pm

🏠 CTV ✗

Ⓥ

GH Clarendon Hotel 46 Kirkley Cliff ☎(0502) 87061

Private hotel facing seafront and close to Kensington Gardens.

10hc (2⇨ 3🍴) (3fb) ✗ in 2 bedrooms CTV in all bedrooms Ⓡ ✱B&b£10–£12 Bdi£14–£16 W£85–£95 ⅃ LDO7.30pm

Lic 🏠 CTV 7P 1🐕 (charge) ⚘ snooker

Credit cards 1 2 3 Ⓥ

GH Hotel Katherine Kirkley Cliff Rd ☎(0502) 67858
Closed Xmas

Family-run hotel on south side of town overlooking Kensington Gardens.

10hc (3⇨) (6fb) CTV in all bedrooms Ⓡ ✱B&bfr£13.50 Bdi£19–£25.50 W£126.35–£169.58 ⅃ LDO8.30pm

Lic 5P solarium

Credit cards 1 3 Ⓥ

GH Kingsleigh 44 Marine Pde ☎(0502) 2513
Closed Xmas

6hc (2fb) CTV in all bedrooms Ⓡ

🏠 CTV 6P 1🐕 nc3yrs

Ⓥ

GH Lodge Private Hotel London Rd South, Pakefield ☎(0502) 69805
Closed Xmas & New Year

This family managed hotel offers modern, comfortable accommodation in a friendly relaxed atmosphere.

7hc (2⇨ 3⋔) (1fb) CTV in all bedrooms ✱
® ✱B&b£14.25–£21 Bdi£20.25–£27
W£116–£150 ⅟ LDO6.30pm
Lic ⁽ᵐ⁾ CTV 15P
Credit cards ① ② ③

GH Rockville House 6 Pakefield Rd
☎(0502) 81011

*Small, family-managed establishment with
good bedrooms and public lounge.*

8hc (2⇨ 1⋔) (1fb) CTV in all bedrooms ✱
® B&b£9 Bdi£12.75 W£75 ⅟ LDO6pm
Lic
Credit cards ① ③

GH Seavilla Hotel 43 Kirkley Cliff Rd
☎(0502) 4657

*Close to Kensington Gardens on A12.
Good home cooking.*

9hc (2⋔) CTV in all bedrooms ®
✱B&b£15 Bdi£20 W£133 ⅟ LDO8pm
Lic CTV 4P 2🐾 ♨
Credit cards ① ② ③

LUDDENDEN FOOT
West Yorkshire
Map **7**   SE02

FH Mrs P Hitchin **Crib** *(SE026245)*
☎Halifax (0422) 883285
Closed Dec

*16th-century Pennine Farmhouse, with
low beams and mullioned windows. In the
hills overlooking the Calder Valley.*

Lowestoft
—
Lulworth

4rm (2hc) (1⇨) CTV in 1 bedroom ✱
✱B&b£8–£9.50 Bdi£14–£15.50 W£94.50–
£101.50 ⅟
⁽ᵐ⁾ CTV 6P 2🐾 200acres dairy
ⓥ

LUDFORD
Lincolnshire
Map **8**   TF28

INN White Hart Magna Mile ☎Burgh-on-
Bain (050781) 664
4⋔ ✱B&b£13.50–£15.50 Bdi£18.50–
£20.50 Bar lunch £2.25 alc Dinner 9.30pm
£5 alc
⁽ᵐ⁾ CTV 40P
Credit card ①

LUDLOW
Shropshire
Map **7**   SO57

GH Cecil Private Hotel Sheet Rd
☎(0584) 2442

*Large modern house providing
comfortable accommodation on edge of
town.*

11hc (1fb) ✱B&b£11 Bdi£17 W£119 ⅟
LDO8pm

Lic ⁽ᵐ⁾ CTV 10P 1🐾
ⓥ
See advertisement on page 258

LULWORTH
Dorset
Map **3**   SY88

GH Gatton House Hotel ☎West
Lulworth (092941) 252
Mar–Oct

*Elevated position nestling into hillside
with panoramic views.*

9hc (3⇨ 2⋔) (2fb) TV in 1 bedroom ®
LDO9.30pm
Lic ⁽ᵐ⁾ CTV 12P 1🐾
See advertisement on page 258

GH Shirley Hotel ☎West Lulworth
(092941) 358
Mar–Oct

*Comfortable family-owned hotel with
swimming pool and patio.*   →

17hc (10🛁 7🚿) (2fb) CTV in all bedrooms [R] ✱B&b£13–£15 Bdi£18–£20.50 W£126–£143.50 Ⱡ LDO9pm

Lic 🚗 20P ⛲ 🏊(heated)

Credit cards [1] [3] [V]

LUSTLEIGH
Devon
Map **3** SX78

GH Eastwrey Barton Hotel
Moretonhampstead Rd ☎(06477) 338

Granite-built farmhouse standing in 3 acres of gardens; comfortable bedrooms and friendly service.

8hc (2🛁) B&bfr£13.10 Bdifr£22 Wfr£140 Ⱡ LDO6pm

Lic CTV 10P nc8yrs

LUTON
Bedfordshire
Map **4** TL02

GH Ambassador Hotel 31 Lansdowne Rd ☎(0582) 31411
Closed Xmas & Boxing Day

Friendly and comfortable house run by young proprietors.

14hc (10🚿) (1fb) CTV in all bedrooms [R] ✱B&b£17–£36.80 Bdi£20–£43.75 LDO9pm

Lic 🚗 CTV 20P

[V]

Lulworth — Lyme Regis

GH Arlington Hotel 137 New Bedford Rd ☎(0582) 419614

Well-managed and comfortable commercial guesthouse.

17hc (1🛁 2🚿) (2fb) CTV in all bedrooms ⋈ ✱B&b£15–£32 Bdi£21.75–£38.75 LDO7.30pm

Lic 🚗 25P

Credit cards [2] [5]

GH Humberstone Hotel 616–618 Dunstable Rd ☎(0582) 574399

Very comfortable and clean hotel where the welcome is warm and friendly.

10hc (2🚿) (3fb) 🚭 in 4 bedrooms CTV in all bedrooms ⋈ [R] ✱B&b£20–£28 LDO9pm

Lic 🚗 18P nc7yrs

Credit cards [1] [3]

GH *Stoneygate Hotel* 696 Dunstable Rd ☎(0582) 582045

Small comfortable guesthouse.

11hc (5🚿) (2fb) CTV in 8 bedrooms TV in 3 bedrooms ⋈ [R] LDO9.30pm

Lic 🚗 CTV 25P

Credit card [1]

LUTTERWORTH
Leicestershire
See **Shearsby**

LYDFORD
Devon
Map **2** SX58

INN Castle ☎(082282) 242
Closed Xmas Day

7hc (2fb) CTV in all bedrooms [R] ✱B&b£12.50–£15 LDO9.45pm

🚗 40P

INN Dartmoor ☎(082282) 221
Closed Xmas Day

Friendly inn with comfortable rooms and large menu. Situated on A386 between Tavistock and Okehampton.

6hc (4🛁) (1fb) CTV in 5 bedrooms TV in 1 bedroom [R] ✱B&b£10–£14.50 W£60–£87.50 M̸ LDO9.50pm

Lic 🚗 50P

Credit cards [1] [2] [3] [5] [V]

LYME REGIS
Dorset
Map **3** SY39

GH Coverdale Woodmead Rd ☎(02974) 2882
Apr–Oct

Quiet location near to shops and sea. →

9hc (3fb) B&b£8.25–£9.75 Bdi£12.65–£14.15 W£77–£89.50 ⊬ LDO5pm
🍴 CTV 12P ⚓

GH Kersbrook Hotel & Restaurant
Pound Rd ☎(02974) 2596
Feb–Nov

Thatched 18th-century building in extensive picturesque gardens, overlooking Lyme Bay, at the top of the town, a few minutes walk from the centre.

14hc (4⇆10🏚) (1fb) ⓇⒷ ✶B&b£15.50–£19.50 Bdi£24.50–£28.50 Wfr£159.50 ⊬ LDO8.15pm

Lic 🍴 CTV 16P nc10yrs in dining room
Credit cards ① ② ③

GH Old Monmouth Hotel Church St
☎(02974) 2456
Mar–Oct

16th-century building opposite the parish church, a few minutes walk from the harbour.

6hc (1⇆2🏚) (1fb) ✶ ✶B&b£9.50–£13.50 W£63–£91 ⋈
Lic 🍴 CTV 6P nc3yrs
Ⓥ

GH Rotherfield View Rd ☎(02974) 2811
Mar–Sep

Situated in quiet residential area with coastal and country views.

7hc (3fb) ✶B&b£8.50–£9.50 Bdi£13–£14 W£83.75–£92.25 ⊬ LDO4.30pm

---

Lyme Regis
—
Lynmouth

Lic 🍴 CTV 7P
Ⓥ

GH White House 47 Silver St ☎(02974) 3420
Apr–Oct

18th-century listed building close to beach, gardens and shops.

7hc (3🏚) (2fb) CTV in all bedrooms Ⓡ
LDO10am
Lic 🍴 6P nc3yrs

LYNDHURST
Hampshire
Map **4**   SU30

GH Bench View Southampton Rd
☎(042128) 2502
Closed Xmas–Jan

A small house, close to the main road, with modest, compact bedrooms.

8hc (5fb) CTV in all bedrooms ✶ B&b£10–£15 W£66.50–£70 ⋈
CTV 10P

GH Ormonde House Hotel Southampton Rd ☎(042128) 2806
Closed first 2 wks Jan

Smart, private hotel with new restaurant and bar.

15hc (2⇆4🏚) (4fb) CTV in all bedrooms
✶ Ⓡ LDO3pm
Lic 🍴 CTV 15P ⚓
Credit cards ① ② ③

GH Whitemoor House Hotel
Southampton Rd ☎(042128) 2186

A very pleasant guesthouse indeed, with good sized well-maintained rooms. Close to main road.

5hc (2fb) LDO9.30pm
Lic 🍴 CTV 8P ⚓

LYNMOUTH
Devon
Map **3**   SS74
See plan. See also **Lynton**

GH Countisbury Lodge Hotel
Countisbury Hill ☎Lynton (0598) 52388
Plan **3** *D2*
Mar–Oct

8hc (2⇆) (3fb) LDOnoon
Lic 🍴 CTV 8P

GH East Lyn 17 Watersmeet Rd
☎Lynton (0598) 52540 Plan **5** *D2*
Mar–Oct

8hc (3fb) ✶ LDOnoon
Lic 🍴 CTV 5P 5�car

GH Glenville Hotel 2 Tors Rd ☎Lynton (0598) 52202 Plan **7** *D2*

7hc (2fb) ✶ Ⓡ ✶B&b£9 Bdi£14 Wfr£90 ⊬ LDO5pm
Lic CTV

ORMONDE HOUSE HOTEL

SOUTHAMPTON ROAD, LYNDHURST, HANTS Tel: Lyndhurst 2806

is a comfortable and friendly hotel under the personal supervision of Derek & Maureen Birch, facing south overlooking the New Forest. 15 bedrooms including doubles with en suite facilities. All with 2 channel radio, intercom, Colour television and tea making facilities. Lounge bar. Colour TV lounge. Good English fare our speciality. For weekly and daily rates for dinner, bed and breakfast SAE for colour brochure.

The Heatherville

Tors Park, Lynmouth, Devon.
Telephone: (0598) 52327

★ Beautiful House, situated in sunny, quiet, secluded position.
★ Overlooking the River Lyn.
★ Excellent home cooking of Traditional English Cuisine.
★ Full central heating.
★ Comfortable colour TV lounge.
★ Separate charming bar lounge.
★ 4 minutes from village and harbour.
★ Private car park.
★ Some rooms with private shower and toilet.
★ Brochure, sample menu and tariff on request from resident proprietors Frank and Sylvia Bilney.

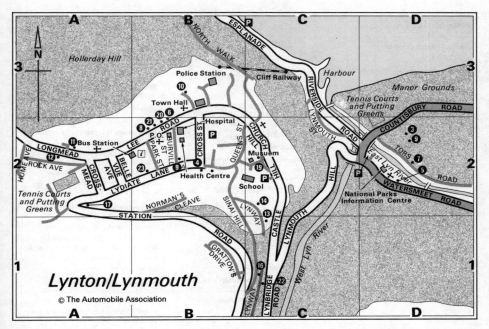

© The Automobile Association

Lynton/Lynmouth

Lynmouth & Lynton

3 Countisbury Lodge Hotel *(see under Lynmouth)*
4 Croft *(see under Lynton)*
5 East Lyn *(see under Lynmouth)*
6 Gable Lodge *(see under Lynton)*
7 Glenville Hotel *(see under Lynmouth)*
8 Hazeldene *(see under Lynton)*
9 Heatherville *(see under Lynmouth)*
9A Horwood House *(see under Lynton)*
10 Ingleside Hotel *(see under Lynton)*
11 Kingford House Private Hotel *(see under Lynton)*
12 Longmead House *(see under Lynton)*
13 Lyndhurst Hotel *(see under Lynton)*
14 Mayfair Hotel *(see under Lynton)*
16 Pine Lodge *(see under Lynton)*
17 Retreat *(see under Lynton)*
19 St Vincent *(see under Lynton)*
20 Southcliffe *(see under Lynton)*
21 Turret *(see under Lynton)*
22 Valley House Hotel *(see under Lynton)*
23 Waterloo House Hotel *(see under Lynton)*

GH Heatherville Tors Park (Guestaccom) ☎Lynton (0598) 52327 Plan **9** *D2*
Etr–Oct

Enthusiastically run Victorian guesthouse in elevated position, with nice warm atmosphere.

8hc (4🛏) (2fb) ✖ ✱B&b£12 Bdi£18 W£115 ⅃ LDO5.30pm

Lic 🅿 CTV 8P nc5yrs

LYNTON
Devon
Map **3**   SS74
See also **Lynmouth**

GH The Croft Lydiate Ln ☎(0598) 52391
Plan **4** *B2*

10hc (2fb) ✖ ✱B&b£8–£9 Bdi£12.50–£13.50 W£76–£85 ⅃ LDO5.30pm

Lic CTV ₽
ⓥ

GH Gable Lodge Lee Rd ☎(0598) 52367
Plan **6** *B2*
Closed Nov–Jan

9hc (2🛏4🛏) (2fb) CTV in 4 bedrooms ✖ ✱B&b£9.45–£11.25 Bdi£14.95–£16.75 W£98.85–£111.40 ⅃ LDO5pm

Lic 🅿 CTV 9P nc5yrs

GH Hazeldene 27–28 Lee Rd ☎(0598) 52364 Plan **8** *B2*
Closed mid–end Dec

9hc (3🛏) (3fb) CTV in all bedrooms ℝ B&b£10.50–£14 Bdi£16.50–£20.50 W£99–£125 ⅃ LDO5pm

Lic 🅿 CTV 8P nc5yrs

Credit cards ① ② ③ ⓥ

See advertisement on page 262

GH Horwood House Lydiate Ln ☎(0598) 52334 Plan **9A** *B2*
Apr–Oct

5hc (1fb) ℝ ✱B&b£8–£9 Bdi£14–£15 W£90–£96 ⅃ LDOnoon

Lic CTV 6P ⚭
ⓥ

GH Ingleside Hotel Lee Rd ☎(0598) 52223 Plan **10** *B3*
mid Mar–mid Oct

7hc (4🛏3🛏) (2fb) CTV in all bedrooms ✖ ℝ B&b£13–£17 Bdi£21–£25 W£147–£175 ⅃ LDO6pm

Lic 🅿 10P nc5yrs
ⓥ

GH Kingford House Private Hotel
Longmead ☎(0598) 52361 Plan **11** *A2*
Apr–Oct

8hc (4🛏) (1fb) ✖ ✱B&b£8.50–£10 Bdi£13.75–£15.25 W£90.75–£100.75 ⅃ LDO4.30pm

Lic CTV 8P nc5yrs
ⓥ

GH Longmead House 9 Longmead ☎(0598) 52523 Plan **12** *A2*

Attractively decorated and well-furnished accommodation in quiet residential area.

8hc (1fb) ✖ B&b£9–£10 Bdi£14–£15 W£94–£100 ⅃ LDO4.30pm

Lic 🅿 CTV 8P nc5yrs
ⓥ

GH Lyndhurst Hotel Lynway ☎(0598) 52241 Plan **13** *C1*
Mar–Oct

7hc (5🛏) (1fb) TV in all bedrooms ✱B&b£11–£12 Bdi£12–£14 W£78 ⅃ LDO4pm

Lic CTV ₽ nc5yrs

261

GH *Mayfair Hotel* Lynway ☎(0598) 53227 Plan **14** *C2*
12hc (2⇌) (4fb) LDO6pm
Lic 🍽 CTV 12P

GH Pine Lodge Lynway ☎(0598) 53230 Plan **16** *C1*
Etr–Sep
8hc (1⇌ 2🚿) [R] ✱B&b£11–£12.50 Bdi£15.50–£17 W£103.25–£113.75ⱡ
CTV 8P nc12yrs
[V]

⊢⊣**GH Retreat** 1 Park Gdns ☎(0598) 53526 Plan **17** *A2*
Mar–Oct
6hc (2fb) ✈ [R] B&b£7.50 Bdi£12 W£75ⱡ LDOnoon
🍽 CTV 3P
[V]

GH St Vincent Castle Hill ☎(0598) 52244 Plan **19** *C2*
Apr–Oct
Comfortable house offering good home-cooking.
Apr–Oct
6hc (2fb) ✈ [R] B&b£8.50–£9.50 Bdi£13.50–£14.50 W£92–£99ⱡ LDO5pm
Lic CTV 4P
[V]

Lynton — Lytham St Annes

GH Southcliffe Lee Rd ☎(0598) 53328 Plan **20** *B2*
Mar–Oct rs Nov & Dec
8hc (2⇌ 6🚿) CTV in all bedrooms [R] ✱B&b£11–£14 Bdi£18–£21 W£118–£130 LDO6.30pm
Lic 🍽 8P nc5yrs
Credit cards [1] [3]

GH Turret Lee Rd ☎(0598) 53284 Plan **21** *B2*
Feb–Nov
6hc (2⇌) ✈ ✱B&b£8–£9.50 W£52.50–£63M
CTV 5🚗 nc5yrs

GH *Valley House Hotel* Lynbridge Rd ☎(0598) 52285 Plan **22** *C1*
8hc (2fb) [R] LDO6pm
Lic CTV 8P
Credit cards [4] [5]

GH *Waterloo House Hotel* Lydiate Ln ☎(0598) 53391 Plan **23** *B2*
12rm (10hc) (4fb) LDO9.30pm
Lic CTV 2P

LYTHAM ST ANNES
Lancashire
Map **7** SD32

GH *Beaumont Private Hotel*
11 All Saints Road ☎(0253) 723958
Closed first 2 wks Nov
Pleasant, well-furnished, family-run guesthouse in quiet side road.
9hc (3fb) LDO6pm
Lic CTV ⌂

GH Cullerne's Hotel 55 Lightburne Av ☎(0253) 721753
Small, friendly house situated just off the promenade.
6hc TV in all bedrooms [R] ✱B&b£11 Bdi£13 Wfr£91ⱡ LDOnoon
Lic 🍽 CTV P nc5yrs

GH Endsleigh Private Hotel 315 Clifton Drive South ☎(0253) 725622
Family run hotel close to sea front.
14hc (9🚿) (3fb) CTV in 9 bedrooms ✈ [R] ✱B&b£11.50–£13 Bdi£15.50–£17 W£88–£108.50ⱡ LDO4pm
Lic 🍽 CTV 8P

GH *Ennes Court* 107 South Prom ☎(0253) 723731
Apr–Oct
A well-furnished and comfortable sea front hotel.

10hc (7🛁 3🚿) (1fb) CTV in all bedrooms 🐕 [R] LDO6.45pm

Lic ♨ CTV nc2½yrs solarium

GH Harcourt Hotel 21 Richmond Rd ☎(0253) 722299
Closed Xmas & New Year

Small, personally-run, well-furnished guesthouse in quiet side road.

10hc (4fb) [R] B&b£9.20–£9.77 Bdi£12.07–£13.22 W£84.52–£92.57 Ł LDO6pm

Lic ♨ CTV 6P nc3yrs

[V]

GH *Lyndhurst Private Hotel*
338 Clifton Drive North ☎(0253) 724343

A family-owned and run house close to town centre and sea.

12hc (1🛁) (4fb) CTV in 4 bedrooms 🐕 [R]

♨ CTV 11P

MABELTHORPE
Lincolnshire
Map **9** TF58

GH Auralee ☎(0521) 77660
Closed Xmas & Boxing Day

Friendly, comfortable, family-run seaside house for holiday and commercial trade.

10hc (2fb) TV in all bedrooms 🐕 *B&b£8.50 Bdi£11.15 W£70 Ł LDO9pm

Lic CTV 9P nc3yrs

[V]

MACHRIHANISH
Strathclyde *Argyllshire*
Map **10** NR62

Recommended

GH Ardell House ☎(058681) 235
Closed Xmas & New Year

Detached house standing opposite golf course. Attractive bedrooms and friendly proprietors. Annexe rooms are in picturesque converted stables. ***Winner for Scotland of the 1986–7 AA Guesthouse of the Year Award.***

8hc (1🚿) Annexe: 3🚿 (1fb) CTV in 8 bedrooms TV in 1 bedroom [R] *B&b£14.50–£18 Bdi£21–£25.50 W£140–£145 Ł

Lic ♨ CTV 12P

[V]

MAIDSTONE
Kent
Map **5** TQ75

GH Carval Hotel 56–58 London Rd ☎(0622) 62100

Comfortable homely accommodation located alongside a busy road, with basement dining room.

10hc (2🚿) CTV in all bedrooms 🐕 [R] B&b£12–£12.50

Lic ♨ CTV 9P

Credit cards [1] [2] [3] [5]

Lytham St Annes — Man, Isle of

GH Howard Hotel 22–24 London Rd ☎(0622) 58778

Pleasant and comfortable hotel with brightly decorated and well-equipped bedrooms.

16hc (4fb) CTV in 3 bedrooms [R] *B&b£13 W£91 M̸

Lic ♨ CTV 15P nc1½yrs

GH Kingsgate Hotel 85 London Rd ☎(0622) 53956

Comfortable, modern accommodation in appealing, late 19th-century house with modern extension.

16hc (4🚿) (3fb) CTV in 12 bedrooms *B&b£13–£16 Bdi£18.50–£21.50 W£112–£130 Ł LDO8pm

Lic CTV 12P 5🚗

Credit card [3]

GH Rock House Hotel 102 Tonbridge Rd ☎(0622) 51616
Closed 24 Dec–1 Jan

Small modern guesthouse with cheerful bedrooms and limited lounge facilities.

10hc (2fb) CTV in 4 bedrooms 🐕 [R] B&b£11.50–£15.50 W£73.50–£101.50 M̸

♨ CTV 7P nc1yr

Credit cards [1] [3] [V]

MALDON
Essex
Map **5** TL80

INN Swan Hotel Maldon High St ☎(0621) 53170

Small pub and restaurant with modestly furnished bedrooms.

6hc (2fb) TV in all bedrooms 🐕 B&b£16.10 Bdifr£19.10 Wfr£128 Ł Lunch £3–£6&alc Dinner9pm£4–£7.50&alc LDO8.30pm

♨ CTV 25P 2🚗 🚗

Credit cards [1] [2] [3] [5] [V]

MALHAM
North Yorkshire
Map **7** SD96

GH Sparth House Hotel ☎Airton (07293) 315

Agreeable family run guesthouse in centre of this lovely Dales village.

10hc (1🚿) (3fb) 🐕 *B&b£11.50–£13.50 Bdi£17.45–£19.45 W£115–£130 Ł LDO5pm

Lic ♨ CTV 10P 🅿(grass)

[V]

MALVERN
Hereford & Worcester
Map **3** SO74

GH *Bredon Hotel* 34 Worcester Rd ☎(06845) 66990
Closed 25 Dec–1 Jan

Georgian-style hotel near town centre. Relaxing lounge has good views of Severn Valley.

9hc (3🛁 3🚿) (2fb) CTV in all bedrooms [R] LDO9.30pm

Lic ♨ CTV 10P

Credit cards [1] [2] [3]

GH Sidney House Hotel 40 Worcester Rd ☎(06845) 4994
Closed Xmas

Listed Georgian building, fully restored to offer pleasant accommodation and attentive service.

7hc (4🚿) (1fb) TV in all bedrooms [R] B&b£13–£20 Bdi£21–£30 W£138–£154.50 Ł LDO6pm

Lic ♨ CTV 8P

Credit cards [1] [2] [3] [5] [V]

MAN, ISLE OF
Map **6**

BALLAUGH
Map **6** SC39

INN Ravensdale Castle Glen Rd ☎Sulby (0624 89) 7330

A Georgian/Victorian country inn, featuring a clock tower. Set in own grounds, it offers comfortable accommodation.

11hc (7🛁) (3fb) CTV in 2 bedrooms TV in 3 bedrooms [R] *B&b£12.50–£17.50 Wfr£87.50 M̸ Lunch£5–£7&alc Dinner9.30pm£7–£10&alc

♨ CTV P ⌂

Credit cards [1] [3] [V]

DOUGLAS
Map **6** SC37

GH Ainsdale 2 Empire Ter, Central Prom ☎(0624) 76695
Apr–Sep

Pleasantly furnished and personally-run guesthouse.

19hc (6fb) [R] *B&b£7.25–£8 Bdi£9.25–£10.25 LDO8pm

CTV P̸ ⌂

GH Ascot Private Hotel 7 Empire Ter ☎(0624) 75081
May–Sep

Large, central private hotel providing good family entertainment.

32hc (14🛁) (6fb) CTV in 14 bedrooms 🐕 *B&b£12 Bdi£14 W£96 Ł

Lic lift ♨ CTV P̸

GH Gladwyn Private Hotel Queen's Prom ☎(0624) 75406
May–Sep

Modern well-furnished hotel overlooking Douglas Bay.

38hc (4🚿) (16fb) *B&b£10.50 Bdi£14.75–£16.75 W£103.25–£117.25 Ł LDO6.15pm

Lic CTV Ᵽ snooker

Credit card [3] [V]

GH *Holyrood Hotel* 51 Loch Promenade ☎(0624) 73790

Personally supervised private hotel offering comfortable accommodation.

19hc (2🚿) (9fb) ✖ LDOam

Lic CTV Ᵽ

GH Hydro Hotel Queen's Prom ☎(0624) 76870
May–Sep rs Etr

Large, well-furnished house on the sea front.

71hc (8🛁 2🚿) (27fb) ✖ [R] ✱B&b£9.50–£11.40 Bdi£11.40–£14.50 W£79.80–£101.50 Ⱡ LDO7pm

Lic lift 🍸 CTV Ᵽ

Credit cards [1] [3] [V]

GH Rosslyn 3 Empire Ter, Central Prom ☎(0624) 76056

Near promenade, this guesthouse is personally run by owners.

16hc (4🛁 4🚿) (3fb) ✖ [R] B&b£9.50–£12.50 Bdi£10.50–£15.50 W£73.50–£108.50 Ⱡ

Lic CTV 2🚗

[V]

GH *Rutland Hotel* Queen's Prom ☎(0624) 21218
Etr–Oct

Large seafront hotel supervised by resident owners

107hc (12🛁 13🚿) (17fb) ✖ LDO7.30pm

Lic lift CTV Ᵽ 🏠

Credit cards [1] [3]

GH Welbeck Private Hotel Mona Dr ☎(0624) 75663
Apr–Oct

Well-furnished private hotel near promenade.

26hc (1🛁 10🚿) (13fb) ✖ B&b£11.50–£14.40 Bdi£13.80–£16.70 W£96.60–£116.90 Ⱡ LDO6.30pm

Lic 🍸 CTV Ᵽ

[V]

Man, Isle of — Mappowder

GH Rothesay Private Hotel 15–16 Loch Prom ☎(0624) 75274
Closed Xmas & New Year

Well-furnished, family-run hotel with good bedrooms.

30hc (10🚿) (3fb) CTV in all bedrooms B&b£13–£15 Bdi£15.50–£17.50 W£108.50–£122.50 Ⱡ LDO7.30pm

Lic lift 🍸 CTV Ᵽ

Credit cards [1] [3] [5]

PORT ST MARY
Map **6** SC26

GH *Mallmore Private Hotel* The Promenade ☎(0624) 833179
Etr–Sep

Delightfully situated hotel overlooking the bay.

43hc (10fb) [R]

CTV P billiards

MANATON
Devon
Map **3** SX78

FH Mrs M Hugo ***Langstone*** *(SX747823)* ☎(064722) 266
Mar–Oct

Long, low, granite farmhouse in traditional Dartmoor-style, with own garden and glorious views.

3hc ✖

CTV 3P nc6yrs 132acres beef

FH Mrs B Y Hunt ***Neadon*** *(SX754815)* ☎(064722) 310

Large and comfortable Devon farmhouse with beautiful views.

3rm ✖

🍸 CTV 3P nc10yrs 110acres arable beef sheep

MANCHESTER
Gt Manchester
Map **7** SJ89

GH *Horizon Hotel* 69 Palatine Rd, West Didsbury ☎061–445 4705

Modern hotel with well-equipped bedrooms in pleasant residential area.

13hc (5🛁 7🚿) (1fb) CTV in all bedrooms ✖ [R] LDOnoon

Lic 🍸 CTV 25P

Credit cards [1] [2] [3] [5]

GH Kempton House Hotel 400 Wilbraham Rd, Chorlton-Cum-Hardy ☎061–881 8766
Closed Xmas & Boxing Day

Large semi-detached house with nice décor and furnishings.

14hc (1fb) CTV in 5 bedrooms ✖ [R] B&b£11.25–£13.50 Bdi£14.25–£16.50 LDO5pm

Lic 🍸 CTV 9P

[V]

GH New Central Hotel 144–146 Heywood St (Guestaccom) ☎061–205 2169
Closed Xmas–New Year

Double-fronted hotel in a residential area, yet convenient for city centre.

10hc ✖ [R] B&b£14–£19 W£93–£126 M LDO7.30pm

Lic 🍸 CTV 10P nc5yrs

[V]

GH *Hotel Tara* 10–12 Oswald Rd, Chorlton-Cum-Hardy ☎061–861 0385

Victorian houses converted to large, modern hotel in quiet area.

18hc (2fb) ✖ [R] LDO4pm

Lic 🍸 CTV 30P

MAPPOWDER
Dorset
Map **3** ST70

FH Mrs A K Williamson-Jones **Boywood** *(ST733078)* ☎Hazelbury Bryan (02586) 416

1½m N unclass rd towards Hazelbury Bryan →

3rm ✗ *B&b£9 Bdi£14

🛋 CTV P 🏠 🏊(heated) 🎾(hard) 17acres beef poultry

MARGARET RODING (nr Dunmow)
Essex
Map **5** TL51

FH Mr & Mrs J Mathews **Greys** *(TQ604112)* Ongar Rd ☎ Good Easter (024531) 509
Apr–Oct

Small, comfortable farmhouse of some quality set away from main farm buildings.

3rm (2hc) ✗ *B&b£8.50–£9 Wfr£60 M̸

🛋 CTV 3P nc10yrs 340 acres arable sheep

MARGATE
Kent
Map **5** TR37

GH Alice Springs Hotel 6–8 Garfield Rd ☎Thanet (0843) 223543

Situated in residential cul-de-sac, near the sea with compact well-equipped bedrooms.

15hc (1fb) CTV in 11 bedrooms TV in 4 bedrooms ✗ [R] *B&b£8–£8.50 Bdi£11–£11.50 W£60–£65 Ł LDO6pm

Lic 🛋 CTV P̸ nc6yrs

[V]

GH Beachcomber Hotel 2–3 Royal Esplanade, Westbrook ☎Thanet (0843) 221616
Apr–Sep rs Oct

15hc (3fb) ✗ *B&b£9.77 Bdi£14.37 W£74.75–£86.25 Ł LDOnoon

Lic CTV P̸ nc3yrs

↔ **GH Charnwood Private Hotel** 20–22 Canterbury Rd ☎Thanet (0843) 224158

Old-fashioned, traditional accommodation under new and friendly management.

9hc (4fb) ✗ B&b£7.50–£8.50 Bdi£11–£12.50 W£65–£75 Ł LDO4pm

Lic 🛋 CTV P̸

Credit card [3] [V]

GH Galleon Lights Hotel 12–14 Fort Cres, Cliftonville ☎Thanet (0843) 291703

Mappowder — Marstow

Comfortable modernised accommodation, with a basement dining room and bar, facing the Winter Gardens.

20hc (5🛁 3🚿) (2fb) CTV in 11 bedrooms *B&b£9–£12.50 Bdi£11–£17.50 W£72–£95 Ł LDO5pm

Lic 🛋 CTV P̸ nc10yrs

Credit cards [1] [3]

GH Greswolde 20 Surrey Rd, Cliftonville ☎ Thanet (0843) 223956
Mar–Oct

10hc (4fb) *B&b£8 Bdi£13 W£53 M̸ LDOnoon

Lic 🛋 CTV P̸

[V]

GH Tyrella Private Hotel 19 Canterbury Rd ☎Thanet (0843) 292746
Closed Xmas & New Year

Small, family-run house, close to the sea with modern, well-decorated bedrooms.

7hc (4fb) ✗ [R] *B&b£8–£9 Bdi£11.50–£12.50 W£58–£72 Ł LDO1pm

Lic 🛋 CTV P̸ nc6yrs

GH Westbrook Bay House 12 Royal Esp, Westbrook ☎Thanet (0843) 292700

Well-maintained bedrooms, some with excellent sea views, and tastefully furnished public rooms.

12hc (3🚿) (4fb) ✗ B&b£9–£10 Bdi£12–£13 W£80 Ł LDO4.30pm

Lic 🛋 CTV P̸

[V]

MARK CAUSEWAY
Somerset
Map **3** ST34

FH Mrs E Puddy **Croft** *(ST355475)* ☎Mark Moor (027864) 206
Etr–Xmas

Comfortable and well-decorated farmhouse with traditional furnishings throughout.

4hc ✗ *B&bfr£9.50 Bdifr£11.50 Wfr£70 Ł LDO5pm

CTV P nc14yrs 130acres dairy

MARLOW
Buckinghamshire
Map **4** SU88

GH Glade Nook 75 Glade Rd ☎(06284) 4677

Small, modern house, family-run to a very high standard.

7hc (1🚿) (1fb) *B&b£20–£23.50

🛋 CTV 5P nc5yrs

MARPLE
Cheshire
Map **7** SJ98

FH Mrs M G Sidebottom **Shire Cottage Ernocroft** *(SJ982910)* Marple Bridge ☎Glossop (04574) 66536 or 061-427 2377
Closed Xmas Day

Modern bungalow with good furnishings overlooking delightful farming country.

3hc (1🚿) (1fb) 🚭 in 2 bedrooms CTV in all bedrooms ✗ [R] *B&b£9–£13 Bdi£13–£17 W£85–£110 Ł LDO1pm

🛋 CTV 6P 1🚗 🏠 180acres mixed

MARSHGATE
Cornwall
Map **2** SX19

FH Mrs P Bolt **Carleton** *(SX153918)* ☎Otterham Station (08406) 252
Etr–Oct

Farmhouse is situated adjacent to the Boscastle road in Marshgate with views over the surrounding farmlands.

3rm (1fb) ✗ *B&b£9.20 Bdi£12.65 W£74.75 Ł

CTV 3P 120acres dairy

[V]

MARSTOW
Hereford & Worcester
Map **3** SO51

FH Mrs S C Watson **Trebandy** *(SO544203)* ☎Llangarron (098984) 230
Apr–Oct

Large, Georgian farmhouse situated in the remote Garron Valley, well off the A4137, 1m NW unclass rd. Ideal for peaceful stay.

2hc (2fb) 🚫 [R] B&b£8.50–£9 W£59.50 M

🛋 CTV 6P 🎲 🎣 287acres arable beef

[V]

MARTIN HUSSINGTREE
Hereford & Worcester
Map **3** SO86

FH Mr & Mrs J J Lane **Harlington** *(SO884598)* Pershore Ln ☎Worcester (0905) 52354

Welcoming smallholding with a variety of animals.

2rm 🚫 ✱B&b£8.50–£9

🛋 CTV 4P 3acres smallholding

[V]

MARTON
Warwickshire
Map **4** SP46

FH Mrs P M Dronfield **Marton Fields** *(SP402680)* ☎(0926) 632410
Closed Xmas

A large farmhouse on edge of quiet village. Proprietor Mrs Dronfield is an accomplished amateur artist and hopes to run specialised painting holidays.

4hc 🚫 [R] ✱B&b£10–£12 Bdifr£17 Wfr£119Ł

🛋 CTV P 🎲 🎣 U snooker 240 acres arable mixed

Marstow — Matlock

MARYBANK
Highland *Ross & Cromarty*
Map **14** NH45

FH Mrs R Macleod **Easter Balloan** *(NH484535)* ☎Urray (09973) 211
Etr–Oct

Roadside farmhouse standing in its own garden on edge of village.

5rm (4hc) (2fb) 🚫 ✱B&b£7.50–£8 Bdi£13.50–£14 W£91–£98Ł LDO8pm

🛋 CTV 10P 143acres mixed

Credit card [3]

MARY TAVY
Devon
Map **2** SX57

FH Mrs B Anning **Wringworthy** *(SX500773)* ☎(082281) 434
Apr–Sep

2m S A386.

3rm (1fb) 🚫 ✱B&b£9.50–£10 Bdi£15–£15.50 LDO10am

🛋 CTV 3P nc3yrs 80acres beef dairy

MASHAM
North Yorkshire
Map **8** SE28

GH Bank Villa (Guestaccom) ☎Ripon (0765) 89605
Mar–Oct

Good home-cooking in comfortable, personally-run guesthouse.

7hc ✱B&b£11–£13.50 Bdi£19.50–£22 Wfr£125–£140Ł LDOnoon

Lic 🛋 CTV 7P nc5yrs

[V]

MATHON
Hereford & Worcester
Map **3** SO74

FH Mrs S Williams **Moorend Court** *(SO726454)* (Guestaccom) ☎Ridgway Cross (088684) 205

Beautiful 15th-century farmhouse in secluded position with panoramic views towards Malvern. Trout fishing on farm.

7hc (1🛁) (3fb) TV in all bedrooms [R] ✱B&b£10–£12.50 Bdi£15.50–£18.50 LDOnoon

🛋 40P 🎾(grass) 🎣 120acres mixed

[V]

MATLOCK
Derbyshire
Map **8** SK36

FH Mrs M Brailsford **Farley** *(SK294622)* ☎(0629) 2533
Closed Xmas & New Year →

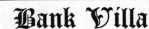

Stone-built farmhouse, parts of which
date back to 1610, set high in the
Derbyshire hills. 1½m NNW unclass rd.
3hc (1fb) ® ✱B&b£9 Bdi£15 Wfr£105 ⚊
LDO7pm
🍴 CTV 8P 225acres arable dairy mixed
Ⓥ

FH Mrs R A Groom **Manor** *(SK327580)*
Dethick ☎Dethick (062984) 246
Closed Dec

*Large, beautifully preserved mid 16th-
century Manor house, once home of Sir
Anthony Babbington.*

4hc (1⇆ 1🛏) (1fb) CTV in 1 bedroom ✄
✱B&b£10–£12 Bdi£14.50–£19 Wfr£96.50
⚊ LDO10am
🍴 CTV 4P 200acres beef sheep

FH M Haynes **Packhorse** *(SK323617)*
Tansley ☎(0629) 2781

*Former inn on much travelled Chesterfield
to Manchester packhorse route. Tastefully
furnished. Lawns and putting greens. 2m
NE of Matlock off A632 at Tansley
signpost.*

5hc (3fb) ✄ ✱B&b£8–£8.50 Wfr£56 Ⓜ
🍴 CTV 20P nc3yrs 40acres mixed

FH Mrs J Hole **Wayside** *(SK324630)*
Matlock Moor ☎(0629) 2967
Closed Xmas Day & New Years Day

Matlock
–
Melksham

---

*Pleasant, modernised, stone-built
farmhouse, adjacent to A632 Matlock–
Chesterfield road.*

6hc (2fb) ✄ ✱B&b£8
🍴 CTV 6P 60acres dairy

MATTISHALL
Norfolk
Map **9**   TG01

FH Mrs M Faircloth **Moat** *(TG049111)*
☎Dereham (0362) 850288
May–Oct

*Simple but most comfortable
accommodation in welcoming small, red-
brick and pantiled farmhouse.*

2hc (1fb) ✄ LDO1am
CTV 2P nc8yrs 100acres mixed

MAWGAN PORTH
Cornwall
Map **2**   SW86

GH White Lodge Hotel ☎St Mawgan
(0637) 860512
Mar–Oct

*Large building in commanding position
overlooking sea and countryside.*

15hc (10⇆) (6fb) CTV in all bedrooms
B&b£11.75–£15.50 Bdi£14.50–£19.50
W£104–£129 ⚊ LDO7.45pm
Lic 🍴 CTV 18P ♿
Ⓥ

MAYFIELD
Staffordshire
Map **7**   SK14

INN Queen's Arms ☎Ashbourne (0335)
42271

*Cosy and relaxed accommodation in this
main road inn.*

7hc (3fb) CTV in 6 bedrooms
CTV 20P

MELKSHAM
Wiltshire
Map **3**   ST96

GH Longhope 9 Beanacre Rd ☎(0225)
706737
Closed Xmas

8hc (2fb) (3fb) CTV in 6 bedrooms
LDO4pm
🍴 CTV 12P

GH Regency Hotel 10–12 Spa Rd
☎(0225) 702971

*A terraced Regency house in town centre
with attentive, friendly owners.*

11hc (4🛏) (1fb) CTV in all bedrooms
✱B&b£10–£13 Bdi£14.95–£17.95 W£100–
£120 ⚊ LDO8.30pm

Lic 🍴 CTV ⚑
Credit cards ① ③ ⓥ

Recommended

GH Shaw Farm Shaw ☎(0225) 702836
Closed 24–26 Dec
1¼ NW off A365.

Delightful, 400-year-old farmhouse, covered in creepers, on outskirts of town. Its two lounges, breakfast room and bar are comfortably furnished.

11hc (1⇄5🛁) (2fb) ✗ ® LDO8pm
Lic 🍴 CTV 20P ⊃(heated)

GH York Church Walk ☎(0225) 702063
10hc (3fb) ✷B&b£9.50 Bdi£15 Wfr£90 ⅃ LDO8pm
🍴 CTV P

MELMERBY
Cumbria
Map **12**   NY63

FH Mrs M Morton **Meadow Bank** (NY615375) ☎Langwathby (076881) 652

Comfortable bungalow adjacent to main farm building.

2rm (1fb) ✗ ✷B&b£7.50–£8 W£50–£52 ℳ
🍴 CTV 3P 185acres sheep mixed

MELTON MOWBRAY
Leicestershire
Map **8**   SK71

GH Westbourne House Hotel 11A–15 Nottingham Rd ☎(0664) 69456
Closed Xmas wk

16hc (2fb) CTV in all bedrooms B&b£14 Bdi£16–£21 LDO7.15pm
Lic 🍴 CTV 16P ⊞

MENDHAM
Suffolk
Map **5**   TM28

FH Mrs J E Holden **Weston House** (TM292828) ☎St Cross (098682) 206 Apr–Oct

Fine old house approximately 300 years old, in 1 acre of garden with fishing nearby.

4hc (1fb) LDOnoon
🍴 CTV 6P 330acres arable dairy mixed

MENHENIOT
Cornwall
Map **2**   SX26

FH Mrs S Rowe **Tregondale** (SX294643) ☎Liskeard (0579) 42407

Farm offering friendly atmosphere and attractive rooms. E of Liskeard, 1½m N of A38.

3rm (2hc) (1fb) ✗ ✷B&b£8.50–£9 Bdi£12–£12.50 W£80–£84 ⅃ LDO7pm
CTV 3P ♨ 180acres arable beef sheep mixed

MERE
Wiltshire
Map **3**   ST83

INN Talbot Hotel The Square ☎(0747) 860427

Oak timbers abound both outside and inside this 16th-century village hostelry.

8hc (4⇄2🛁) (1fb) CTV in all bedrooms ✷B&b£14–£20 Bdi£22–£28 W£120 ⅃ Lunch £5–£6&alc Dinner 9pm £8–£9&alc
🍴 25P

Credit card ①

MERIDEN
West Midlands
Map **4**   SP28

GH Meriden Hotel Main Rd ☎(0676) 22005

Small friendly hotel offering good accommodation at competitive prices.

8hc (2fb) ✷B&b£13.50–£25 Bdi£18.50–£30 W£130–£180 ⅃ LDOnoon
Lic 🍴 CTV 20P

MEVAGISSEY
Cornwall
Map **2**   SX04

GH Headlands Hotel Polkirt Hill ☎(0726)
843453
Mar–Oct & Xmas

*Large detached house, standing above
road with magnificient sea views.*

14hc (6🎁) (3fb) B&b£10.50–£12.50
Bdi£16.50–£18.50 W£115.50–£129.50⊬
LDO6pm
Lic ໝ CTV 11P

GH Mevagissey House Vicarage Hill
☎(0726) 842427
Mar–Oct

*Large, detached former rectory in
elevated position with views over harbour.*

6hc (2🎁) (2fb) CTV in all bedrooms ✠ ®
B&b£10–£14 Bdi£16.50–£20.50 W£107–
£135⊬ LDOnoon
Lic ໝ 12P nc7yrs

GH Valley Park Private Hotel Tregoney
Hill ☎(0726) 842347

*Detached residence in own gardens a few
minutes walk from the harbour. Good
facilities and friendly service.*

8hc (3🎁) (4fb) ✠ LDOnoon
Lic CTV 11P ⅍

FH Mrs A Hannah **Treleaven** *(SW008454)*
☎(0726) 842413
Closed 15 Dec–7 Jan

Mevagissey
—
Middletown

*Large detached farmhouse on a hill with
lawned garden and swimming pool.*

6hc (1fb) ✠ ✱B&b£9–£10.50 Bdi£14–£17
W£90–£110⊬ LDO8pm
Lic ໝ CTV 6P ⌇heated 200acres mixed
Credit cards ① ③ Ⓥ

INN Ship Fore St ☎(0726) 843324

5hc (1fb) ✠ B&bfr£9 W£54–£63 M
Dinner8.30pm£2.20–£6.80
CTV ✗ ⇶

MIDDLESBROUGH
Cleveland
Map **8**   NZ42

GH Chadwick Private Hotel 27 Clairville
Rd ☎(0642) 245340

*Spacious Edwardian style house with
comfortable bedrooms.*

6hc (1fb) ✠ LDO4pm
CTV ✗

GH Grey House Hotel 79 Cambridge Rd
☎(0642) 817485
Closed 2 weeks Xmas & New Year

*Sizeable rooms of charm and character,
enhanced by proprietor's own paintings
and drawings.*

10hc (4🎁) (1fb) CTV in 4 bedrooms
✱B&b£12–£20 Bdi£17–£25 W£107–£155⊬
LDO7pm
Lic ໝ CTV 10P

GH Longlands Hotel 295 Marton Rd
☎(0642) 244900

*Converted end terrace house, well-suited
to business people, with spacious and
colourful rooms.*

7hc (1fb) ✠ ✱B&bfr£13.80 Bdifr£17.80
W£124.60⊬ LDO5pm
Lic ໝ CTV 2P 6🛁

MIDDLETON-ON-SEA
West Sussex
Map **4**   SU90

GH Ancton House Hotel Ancton Ln
☎(024369) 2482

*Cosy 16th-century guesthouse set in rural
surroundings.*

9hc (2⇉ 3🎁) (2fb) ® ✱B&b£13.50–
£15.50 Bdi£17.50–£19.50 W£105–£119⊬
Lic ໝ CTV 6P 5🛁 ⅍
Credit card ③ Ⓥ

MIDDLETOWN
Powys
Map **7**   SJ21

FH Mrs E J Bebb **Bank** *(SJ325137)*
☎Trewern (093874) 260
Mar–Oct

MEVAGISSEY HOUSE
Vicarage Hill, Mevagissey, Cornwall PL26 6SZ
Telephone: (0726) 842427

Georgian country house in 4 acres, hillside and
woodland setting, views to sea. A quiet,
friendly, relaxing atmosphere, elegant spacious
rooms with CH and log fires. 6 bedrooms
H & C, colour TV, tea/coffee making
facilities, and en suite. Lounge, sun lounge,
licensed bar, candle lit dining room, home
cooking, à la carte highly praised. Car parking
easy access to numerous attractions. Brochure
on request from Mrs Diana Owens.

Valley Park Private Hotel
Valley Park, Mevagissey, Cornwall PL26 6RS Tel: (0726) 842347

The Valley Park Hotel is an eight-bedroomed family run hotel. We offer
a full English Breakfast and Table d'hôte dinner menu plus Coffee.
Early morning tea and Evening Beverages available on request at
reasonable prices.
There are numerous tourist attractions and sporting facilities available
in Cornwall. Fishing and Boat Trips may be arranged. Each day of your
holiday you may be fully occupied. There are Sandy Beaches within
walking distance and many other delightful Coves wihin easy reach also
National Trust property nearby.
Car Park for the free use of Guests and there are ample Public Rooms:
Dining Room, Television Lounge, Bar Lounge and Sun Lounge.
Proprietors: Barbara & Bryan Wildgoose.

Situated on the A458 Shrewsbury–Welshpool road at the foot of the Breidden Hills with good views.

3rm (2hc) (1fb) ✈ ✱B&bfr£8.50

🛋 CTV 3P nc3yrs 30acres sheep

MIDHURST
West Sussex
Map **4** SU82
See **Bepton** and **Rogate**

MILBORNE PORT
Somerset
Map **3** ST61

FH Mrs M J Tizzard **Venn** *(ST684183)* ☎(0963) 250208

Attractive accommodation in a modern house, set back off main road on Shaftesbury side of village.

3rm (2hc) (2fb) TV in all bedrooms ✈ [R] ✱B&b£9 Wfr£56 M

🛋 CTV P ⌂ 375acres dairy

MILFORD-ON-SEA
Hampshire
Map **4** SZ29

Recommended

GH Seaspray 8 Hurst Rd ☎Lymington (0590) 42627

A small, delightful guesthouse facing the sea. Pretty, bright bedrooms, TV lounge and separate bar.

6hc (2🚿) (1fb) CTV in 1 bedroom TV in 5 bedrooms ✱B&b£11–£15 Bdi£17.50–£21.50 W£120–£140 Ł LDO9am

Lic 🛋 8P nc3yrs

MILLPOOL
Cornwall
Map **2** SW53

GH *Chyraise Lodge Hotel* ☎Penzance (0736) 763485

Tastefully furnished guesthouse in large, attractive gardens.

10hc (1🛁 3🚿) (3fb) ✈ [R] LDO9pm

Lic CTV 12P ⌂

Credit card [3]

Middletown — Minsterworth

MILNGAVIE
Strathclyde *Dunbartonshire*
Map **11** NS57

FH Mrs L Fisken **High Craigton** *(NS525766)* ☎041-956 1384

Off A809, two-storey painted stone-built farmhouse on hill-top with views over fields towards Glasgow.

2hc (2fb) ✱B&b£8 W£56 M

🛋 CTV 4P 1100acres sheep

MILTON KEYNES
Buckinghamshire
Map **4** SP83
See **Brickhill (Great), Gayhurst** and **Salford**

GH The Different Drummer 94 High St, Stony Stratford ☎(0908) 564733 Telex no 946240
Closed 24 Dec–2 Jan

A popular family-run residential hotel and restaurant with cosy bedrooms.

17hc (3🛁 9🚿) (2fb) CTV in all bedrooms ✈ [R] ✱B&b£22.50–£33 Bdifr£26.70 LDO8.30pm

Lic 6P

Credit cards [1] [3]

MINEHEAD
Somerset
Map **3** SS94
See plan on page 272

GH Carbery Hotel Western Ln, The Parks ☎(0643) 2941 Plan **1** *A3*
Mar–Nov

7hc (1🛁 2🚿) (2fb) CTV in all bedrooms ✈ [R] B&b£10 Bdi£16 W£98 Ł LDO7.30pm

Lic 🛋 CTV 8P 1🚗 nc10yrs

GH Dorchester Hotel 38 The Avenue ☎(0643) 2052 Plan **2** *C3*

13hc (4fb) CTV in all bedrooms ✈ [R] ✱B&b£9.75–£10.50 Bdi£14.75–£15.50 W£83–£90 Ł LDO7pm

Lic 🛋 CTV 10P nc7yrs

Credit cards [1] [3] Ⓥ

GH Gascony Hotel The Avenue ☎(0643) 5939 Plan **3** *C3*
Mar–Oct

Friendly and efficient guesthouse in a prime position.

14hc (2🛁 7🚿) (5fb) CTV in 5 bedrooms [R] ✱B&b£11–£12 Bdi£17–£18 Wfr£86 Ł LDO6.30pm

Lic CTV 12P

Credit cards [3] [5] Ⓥ

See advertisement on page 273

GH *Glen Rock Hotel* 23 The Avenue ☎(0643) 2245 Plan **4** *C3*
Mar–Nov

12hc (2fb) LDO7pm

Lic CTV 10P 1🚗 nc3yrs

GH Mayfair Hotel 25 The Avenue ☎(0643) 2719 Plan **5** *C3*
Etr–Oct

18hc (1🛁 7🚿) (7fb) CTV in all bedrooms [R] B&b£11.50–£14 Bdi£17–£20 W£90–£106 Ł LDO7.15pm

Lic 🛋 14P

MINSTER LOVELL
Oxfordshire
Map **4** SP31

FH Mrs K Brown **Hill Grove** *(SP334110)* ☎Witney (0993) 3120
Closed Xmas

A Cotswold stone-built farmhouse with extensive views over the Windrush Valley, with river running through. Off B4047 1½ m E of village towards Crawley village.

2rm ✈ [R] ✱B&b£10–£11

🛋 CTV 4P 90acres arable beef mixed Ⓥ

MINSTERWORTH
Gloucestershire
Map **3** SO71

GH Severn Bank ☎(045275) 357
Closed Xmas

Pleasant and spacious guesthouse in six acres beside the river. →

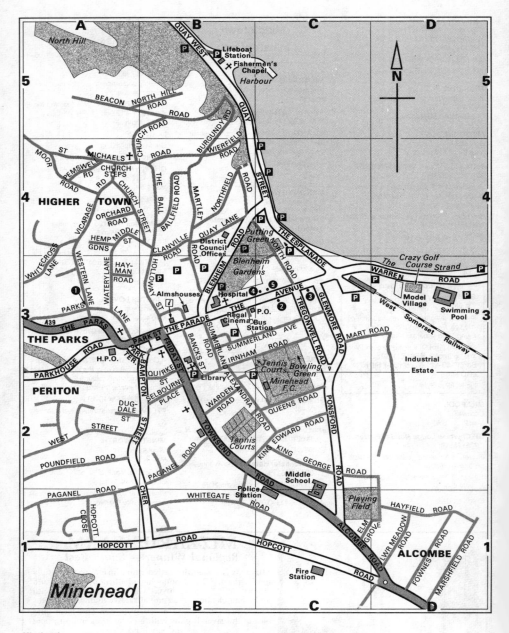

Minehead

1 Carbery Hotel
2 Dorchester Hotel
3 Gascony Hotel
4 Glen Rock Hotel
5 Mayfair Hotel

6hc (4fb) CTV in all bedrooms ✕ ®
B&b£12 W£84 ⅟
Lic ♨ CTV 12P nc5yrs ⏀
Ⓥ

MOFFAT
Dumfries & Galloway *Dumfriesshire*
Map **11**   NT00

GH Arden House High St (Guestaccom)
☎(0683) 20220
Apr–Sep

*Converted sandstone bank building,
attractively decorated and furnished,
dating from 1738, in town centre.*

7hc (4⋔) (2fb) ® ✱B&b£8.50–£10
Bdi£13.50–£15.50 W£94.50–£108.50 ⅟
LDO6pm
♨ CTV 9P

GH Barnhill Springs Country ☎(0683)
20580

*Quiet and friendly small country-house
offering plain but good food.*

6hc (1fb) B&b£10 Bdi£16 W£105 ⅟
LDO6pm
Lic ♨ CTV 10P

GH *Buchan* 13 Beechgrove ☎(0683)
20378
Apr–Oct

*An attractively decorated and furnished
house.*

8hc (2fb) LDO7.30pm
♨ CTV 6P

GH Hartfell House Hartfell Cres ☎(0683)
20153
Mar–Nov   →

Converted Victorian house to rear of the town with two acres of gardens.

9hc (3fb) ✱B&b£9.50 Bdi£16.50 W£108 ⨏ LDO6.45pm

Lic ㎖ CTV 10P

Ⓥ

GH Del-Robin (formerly Robin Hill) Beechgrove ☎(0683) 20050
Apr–Oct

Tastefully decorated, Victorian house in a quiet residential road.

6hc (2⇆) (2fb) ⚬ in 4 bedrooms Ⓡ ✱B&b£9.50–£12 Bdi£14.50–£17 W£96–£110 ⨏ LDO5.30pm

㎖ CTV 7P 1🐾

Ⓥ

GH *Rockhill* 14 Beechgrove ☎(0683) 20283
Mar–Oct

Attractive house close to a park with bowling green and tennis courts.

10hc (4fb) LDO5pm

㎖ CTV 6P

GH *St Olaf* Eastgate, Off Dickson St
☎(0683) 20001
Apr–Oct

Converted two-storey house dating from 1880 situated just off the main shopping centre.

7hc (3fb) ✱B&b£8 Bdi£12 W£84 ⨏ LDO6.30pm

㎖ 4🐾

─── **Recommended** ───

GH Well View Hotel Ballplay Rd
☎(0683) 20184

Nicely re-decorated interior, with good pine furnishings are to be found in this attractive house situated on outskirts of town. Well-kept gardens and adjoining woollen craft workshop.

8rm (6hc) (1⇆3㎖) (1fb) ✱B&b£9.50–£11 Bdi£15.50–£17.50 Wfr£105 ⨏

Lic ㎖ CTV 10P ⚙

Moffat — Montrose

INN Black Bull Hotel Churchgate
☎(0683) 20206

A small, historic hotel, full of character, serving real ale and excellent pub food.

3hc CTV in all bedrooms Ⓡ ✱B&b£12.50 LDO8.30pm

㎖ 6P 🚗

Ⓥ

MOLESWORTH
Cambridgeshire
Map **4**   TL07

INN Cross Keys ☎Bythorn (08014) 283

Village pub built in early 1900's, in quiet country location, offering fresh home-cooking.

3hc (1⇆ 1㎖) Ⓡ ✱B&b£10–£12 W£70–£84 M Lunch £3.50alc Dinner 10.30pm £5alc

㎖ 30P

MOLLAND
Devon
Map **3**   SS82

FH Mrs P England ***Yeo*** *(SS785266)*
☎Bishop's Nympton (07697) 312
Mar–Oct

Well-maintained farmhouse with good furnishings and décor, set in large garden.

4hc LDO6pm

㎖ CTV P ⚓ 200acres mixed sheep

MONEYDIE
Tayside *Perthshire*
Map **11**   NO02

FH Mrs S Walker **Moneydie Roger** *(NO054290)* ☎Almondbank (073883) 239
Apr–end Sep

A substantial, two-storey farmhouse situated on unclassified road signed Methven, off the B8063, 2½m W of the A9.

1rm (1fb) ✗ B&b£7.25–£7.50

2P 143acres arable sheep cattle mixed

MONKSILVER
Somerset
Map **3**   ST03

FH Mrs S J Watts **Rowdon** *(ST082381)*
☎Stogumber (0984) 56280

Modern farmhouse with bright comfortable accommodation overlooking Quantock Hills. Ideal touring centre for Exmoor and West Somerset coast.

4hc (2fb) CTV in 1 bedroom ✱B&b£8–£10 Bdi£10–£15 W£76–£90 ⨏ LDO5pm

㎖ CTV 10P 300acres mixed

Ⓥ

MONK SOHAM
Suffolk
Map **5**   TM26

FH Mrs S E Bagnall **Abbey House**
(TM216656) ☎Earl Soham (072882) 225

Former Victorian rectory in ten acres, including an open-air swimming pool.

3⇆ (2fb) ✱B&b£12–£14 Bdi£18–£21 W£112–£126 ⨏ LDOnoon

㎖ CTV 6P 🏊 10acres mixed

Ⓥ

MONMOUTH
Gwent
Map **3**   SO51

INN Queen's Head St James Street
☎(0600) 2767

Attractive small inn with bar of character and pretty bedrooms. Situated by Haberdashers school.

3hc (1⇆ 2㎖) (3fb) CTV in all bedrooms Ⓡ ✱B&b£12 Bdi£19 Wfr£119 ⨏ Lunch £2.50alc Dinner 10pm £7alc

㎖ CTV 6P

Credit cards ① ③ Ⓥ

MONTROSE
Tayside *Angus*
Map **15**   NO75

GH Linksgate 11 Dorward Rd ☎(0674) 72273

Small, family run guesthouse in substantial stone villa close to the sea front.

9hc (2🛁) (3fb) CTV in 2 bedrooms
✱B&b£9.50–£11 Bdi£14.50–£16.50
LDO6pm

♨ CTV 9P

FH Mrs A Ruxton **Muirshade of Gallery**
(NO671634) ☎Northwaterbridge (067484) 209
Apr–Oct
Situated in beautiful countryside facing the Grampian mountain range, only 5m from the sea.
2hc (1fb) ✱B&bfr£7.50 Bdifr£12 LDO4pm

CTV 2P 175acres arable

[V]

MORCHARD BISHOP
Devon
Map **3** SS70

FH Mr & Mrs S Chilcott **Wigham**
(SS757087) ☎(03637) 350
Very attractive thatched farmhouse of 16th century date. Carefully restored to provide stylish accommodation.
4hc (3🛁 1🚿) (3fb) CTV in all bedrooms ⋈
[R] ✱Bdi£21–£27
Lic ♨ CTV 9P 🏊heated U 11acres mixed

MORDIFORD
Hereford & Worcester
Map **3** SO53

FH Mrs M J Barrell **Orchard** *(SO575384)*
☎Holme Lacy (043273) 253
Peaceful and relaxing stone-built farmhouse overlooking the River Lugg.
3hc (1fb) [R] ✱B&b£9–£10 Bdifr£14.50
W£90 Ł

Lic CTV P 🏠 ♩ 60acres mixed

MORECAMBE
Lancashire
Map **7** SD46

GH *Ashley Private Hotel* 371 Marine Road East ☎(0524) 412034
Small family-run sea front guesthouse.
14hc (4fb) ⋈ LDO4pm
Lic ♨ CTV 4P

GH Beach Mount 395 Marine Road East
☎(0524) 420753
Mar–Nov
Modern family-run hotel overlooking the bay.
26hc (22🛁) (3fb) CTV in 22 bedrooms
✱B&b£13–£14.50 Bdi£18–£19.50
W£110.50–£121 Ł LDO7pm
Lic ♨ CTV 6P
Credit cards [1] [3] [5]

GH Ellesmere Private Hotel
44 Westminster Rd ☎(0524) 411881
May–Oct
Small, friendly guesthouse with good home-made food.
5hc (2fb) ⋈ ✱B&b£7–£7.50 Bdi£8.50–£9
W£57–£59 Ł
♨ CTV 🚫P

[V]

GH *New Hazelmere Hotel* 391 Marine Road East ☎(0524) 417876
Apr–Nov rs Dec–Mar
Private hotel occupying a corner site on the promenade.
22hc (2🛁 6🚿) (5fb) TV in 3 bedrooms [R]
LDO5pm
Lic CTV 1P

See advertisement on page 276

GH Hotel Prospect 363 Marine Road East ☎(0524) 417819
Etr–Oct
Modern well-furnished hotel overlooking the bay.
14hc (11🛁) (5fb) CTV in 8 bedrooms [R]
✱B&b£9–£10 Bdi£12–£13 W£82–£92 Ł
LDO4pm
Lic ♨ CTV 6P

GH Rydal Mount Private Hotel
361 Marine Road East ☎(0524) 411858
Etr–Oct

Nicely furnished sea front guesthouse.

14hc (3🚿) (4fb) TV in 1 bedroom [R]
✱B&b£11–£12.50 Bdi£12.50–£13.50
Wfr£83 Ł LDO4pm

Lic CTV 12P nc3yrs

GH Hotel Warwick 394 Marine Road East
☎(0524) 418151

Pleasantly furnished modern sea front hotel.

23hc (2🛁 9🚿) (3fb) CTV in 14 bedrooms
TV in 3 bedrooms [R] ✱B&b£10–£12
Bdi£14–£18 LDO6pm

Lic lift 🍴 CTV ₱

Credit cards [1] [2] [3] [5] [V]

GH Wimslow Private Hotel 374 Marine Rd East ☎(0524) 417804
Feb–Oct

A pleasant family-run hotel on the promenade overlooking the bay.

15hc (3🚿) (4fb) CTV in all bedrooms 🐕 [R]
✱B&bfr£12.50 Bdifr£17 Wfr£98 Ł
LDO4.30pm

Lic 🍴 CTV 4P 6🚗

Credit cards [1] [3]

INN *York Hotel* Lancaster Rd ☎(0524) 418226

Main road pub near town centre offering spacious bedrooms.

Morecambe — Mortehoe

12hc (10fb) LDO6pm
🍴 CTV 6P 2🚗

MORETONHAMPSTEAD
Devon
Map **3** SX78

GH Cookshayes 33 Court St ☎(0647) 40374
mid Mar–Oct

Large Victorian house set in well-kept gardens.

8hc (1🛁 4🚿) (1fb) [R] ✱B&b£10–£12
Bdi£16–£18.50 W£108.50–£120 Ł
LDO5.30pm

Lic 🍴 CTV 15P nc8yrs

Credit cards [1] [3] [V]

GH Elmfield Station Rd ☎(0647) 40327
Etr–Oct

Large detached house at the foot of Dartmoor, with some lovely views.

6hc (3🚿) (2fb) ✱B&b£8.50–£9.50
Bdi£14.25–£15.25 W£88–£95 Ł LDO7pm

Lic 🍴 CTV 8P

MORETON-IN-MARSH
Gloucestershire
Map **4** SP13

GH Moreton House High St ☎(0608) 50747

Small personally-run house in the centre of town. Good home cooking.

12hc (1🛁 3🚿) (1fb) CTV in 5 bedrooms
TV in 7 bedrooms [R] B&b£11–£12.50
Bdi£16–17.50 W£112–£122.50 Ł LDO8pm

Lic 🍴 CTV 5P

Credit card [1]

FH Mr & Mrs Righton **Old Farm** *(SP205340)* Dorn (1m N off A429)
☎(0608) 50394
Apr–Oct

3hc (2fb) [R] ✱B&b£8–£9 W£50–£52 M

CTV 10P 🚜 250acres mixed

MORFA NEFYN
Gwynedd
Map **6** SH23

GH Erw Goch Hotel ☎Nefyn (0758) 720539

Georgian house with good leisure facilities including snooker (¾ size table) and table tennis.

15hc (5fb) ✱B&bfr£11.50 Bdifr£16.50
Wfr£99.50 Ł

Lic 🍴 CTV 25P table tennis

[V]

MORTEHOE
Devon
Map **2** SS44

GH Baycliffe Hotel Chapel Hill
☎Woolacombe (0271) 870393

Standing on high ground overlooking sea and countryside, Baycliffe offers good English fare.

10hc (3⇄5fl) ⊁ ® ✳B&b£8–£15
Bdi£14.50–£21.50 W£95–£140 ⊬ LDO6pm

Lic 🞧 CTV 9P nc11yrs

Ⓥ

See advertisement on page 424

GH Haven ☎Woolacombe (0271) 870426
Apr–Oct rs Mar

17rm (4hc 13⇄) (6fb) ® B&b£10–£12
Bdi£15–£17 W£100–£117 ⊬ LDO8pm

Lic 🞧 CTV 20P 1🐾 ♨

See advertisement on page 424

─── *Recommended* ───

GH Sunnycliffe Hotel (Guestaccom)
☎Woolacombe (0271) 870597
Closed Dec & Jan

All bedrooms in this attractive, well-furnished hotel have fine sea views. Public rooms and bar are comfortable, and the set menu offers good, well-cooked food.

8hc (4⇄4fl) ⊱ in 4 bedrooms CTV in all bedrooms ⊁ ® ✳B&b£16–£18
Bdi£22–£24 W£136–£160 LDO6pm

Lic 🞧 10P nc12yrs

MORTIMER'S CROSS
Hereford & Worcester
Map **3**   SO46

INN Mortimers Cross ☎Kingsland
(056881) 238

An imposing roadside inn with an aviary and barbecue area in the rear gardens.

5hc (2fb) ✳B&b£9.50 Bdi£14.50 W£94.50
⊬ Lunch £3.75alc Dinner 10.30pm £5alc

🞧 20P 1🐾

MORVAH
Cornwall
Map **2**   SW33

FH Mrs J Mann **Merthyr** (SW403355)
☎Penzance (0736) 788464
Apr–Oct

─────────────────

┌─────────────────┐
│   **Mortehoe**   │
│   ─   │
│ **Muir of Ord** │
└─────────────────┘

Well-appointed farmhouse with sun lounge and sea views, on B3306 NW of Penzance.

5hc (2fb) ⊁ ✳B&b£8–£9 W£49–£56 ᴍ

CTV 6P nc8yrs 100acres mixed

MOUNT
Cornwall
Map **2**   SX16

⊢─**FH** Mr & Mrs J T Capper **Mount Pleasant** (SX152680) ☎Cardinham
(020882) 342
Mar–Oct rs Nov & Feb

Farmhouse situated 6m E of Bodmin in open country on the edge of Bodmin Moor. Own transport essential.

8hc (1⇄) ⊁ ® ✳B&b£7.50–£10
Bdi£11.50–£14.50 W£75–£95 ⊬
LDO5.30pm

Lic 🞧 CTV 15P 6acres non-working

Ⓥ

MOUSEHOLE
Cornwall
Map **2**   SW42

GH Tavis Vor ☎Penzance (0736) 731306
mid Mar–mid Oct

Delightful country house-style residence, in own grounds running to the edge of the sea.

7hc (3fl) (2fb) ® ✳B&b£11.50–£14.50
Bdi£16–£19.50 W£112–£133 ⊬ LDO6pm

Lic 🞧 CTV 7P nc5yrs

MOY
Highland *Inverness-shire*
Map **14**   NH73

GH Invermoy House ☎Tomatin (08082) 271
Closed Nov

Formerly the local railway station, the main line still runs close by. 1½m off A9.

7hc (1fl) ® B&b£9.25–£11 Bdi£15.50–
£17.25 W£100–£112.25 ⊬ LDO6pm

Lic 🞧 CTV 10P

Ⓥ

MOYLEGROVE
Dyfed
Map **2**   SN14

FH Mrs J I Young **Cwm Connell**
(SN119461) ☎(023986) 220

Charming 200-year-old farmhouse in picturesque location with lovely views of sea and coastline. Comfortable bedrooms each with its own sitting/dining room and TV. There is a walled garden at the rear available to guests.

3rm (1hc) CTV in all bedrooms ⊁
✳B&b£7–£9 Bdi£10–£12 W£70–£77 ⊬ (W only Jul & Aug)

🞧 3P 1🐾 nc7yrs 5acres mixed

Ⓥ

FH Mrs A D Fletcher **Penrallt Ceibwr**
(SN116454) ☎(023986) 217

True Welsh hospitality, comfortable accommodation and delicious meals using home-grown produce at this farmhouse on the St Dogmaels/Newport coast road. Views of village and Cibwr Bay, where seals may sometimes be seen.

6hc (2fb) ✳B&b£9–£10 Bdi£16–£17
W£100–£110 ⊬

Lic 🞧 CTV 30P ♨ 300acres arable dairy

Ⓥ

See advertisement on page 112

MUIR OF ORD
Highland *Ross & Cromarty*
Map **14**   NH55

FH Mrs Fraser **Gilchrist** (NH538493)
☎(0463) 870243
Apr–Sep

Compact but comfortable house just outside the town.

2rm ® ✳B&b£7.50–£8.50 Bdi£12.50–£14
W£80–£90 ⊬ LDO5pm

CTV 6P 160acres arable mixed

Ⓥ

MULL, ISLE OF
Strathclyde *Argyllshire*
Maps **10** & **13**

SALEN
Map **10** NM54

GH Craig Hotel ☎ Aros (06803) 347
Mar–Oct rs Nov–Feb
Painted roadside hotel offering comfortable accommodation and friendly atmosphere.
7hc *B&b£13–£15 Bdi£19–£22 W£120–£150 ⱠLDO7.15pm
Lic ⚱ 7P

TOBERMORY
Map **13** NM55

GH Harbour Hotel (formerly Suidhe Hotel) 59 Main St ☎(0688) 2209
Mar–Nov
A friendly family-run licensed guesthouse situated on the front overlooking Tobermory Bay.
9hc (1⇌) (2fb) Ⓡ *B&b£13 Bdi£20 LDO7.45pm
Lic CTV 9P

MULLION
Cornwall
Map **2** SW61

GH Belle Vue ☎(0326) 240483
Apr–Sep
Small family residence, close to golf course and beaches.
8hc (1fb) ✗ *B&b£8–£10 Bdi£14–£16 W£90–£100 ⱠLDO4pm
CTV 10P
Ⓥ

GH Henscath House Mullion Cove ☎(0326) 240537
Closed Xmas–New Year
All public rooms and front bedrooms have magnificient views, and there is a good atmosphere and good food.
6hc (3⇌ 2⋔) (1fb) ✗ Ⓡ B&b£10–£12 Bdi£17.50–£19.50 W£118–£132 Ⱡ LDO6.30pm
Lic ⚱ CTV 8P

GH Trenowyth House Private Hotel Mullion Cove ☎(0326) 240486
Mar–Oct
Family hotel well-positioned offering good views.
6hc (1⇌ 2⋔) (2fb) CTV in 4 bedrooms TV in 1 bedroom Ⓡ *£B&b£10.50–£13.50 Bdi£15–£17.50 W£105–£122.50 Ⱡ LDO7pm
Lic ⚱ CTV 11P ⌂
Credit card [1] Ⓥ

INN *Old Inn* Church Town ☎(0326) 240240
Closed 25 Dec–1 Jan
Character inn with attractive bar, comfortable rooms and good food.
5hc (3⇌) TV in all bedrooms ✗ Ⓡ LDO9pm
⚱ 10P nc14yrs
Credit card [3]

MUMBLES
West Glamorgan
Map **2** SS68
See also **Bishopston & Langland Bay**

GH *Carlton Hotel* 654–656 Mumbles Rd, Southend ☎Swansea (0792) 60450
Closed Xmas
Seafront hotel with modestly appointed bedrooms.
19hc (1⇌ 7⋔) (1fb) CTV in 12 bedrooms ✗ Ⓡ LDO10.15pm
Lic ⚱ CTV nc7yrs

GH Harbour Winds Private Hotel Overland Rd, Langland ☎Swansea (0792) 69298
Apr–Sep
Well-maintained comfortable detached house in own grounds.
8hc (1⇌ 1⋔) (3fb) Ⓡ *B&b£12–£14 Bdi£18–£20 W£115–£125 ⱠLDOnoon
⚱ CTV 14P nc5yrs
Ⓥ

GH *Shoreline* 648 Mumbles Rd, Southend ☎Swansea (0792) 66322
Modestly appointed yet friendly guesthouse overlooking Swansea Bay.
13hc (1⇌ 5⋔) (3fb) CTV in 6 bedrooms LDO5.30pm
Lic ⚱ CTV ⚲
Credit cards [1] [3]

GH *Southend Hotel & Restaurant* 724 Mumbles Rd ☎Swansea (0792) 66329
A modestly appointed establishment.
11hc (4fb) CTV in 6 bedrooms Ⓡ LDO9.30pm
Lic ⚱ CTV ⚲
Credit cards [1] [2] [3]

MUNGRISDALE
Cumbria
Map **11** NY33

GH The Mill ☎Threlkeld (059683) 659
Mar–Oct
17th-century mill, restored and converted to highest standards. Good fresh food.
8hc (2⇌) (1fb) CTV in 2 bedrooms Ⓡ *B&b£14–£23.50 Bdi£19.75–£29 W£122.50–£145.25 ⱠLDO7pm
Lic ⚱ CTV 12P ⌂ ⚲ billiards

FH Mr & Mrs G Wightman **Near Howe** *(NY286373)* ☎Threlkeld (059683) 678
Apr–Nov
Set in well-tended gardens at the end of a quiet lane 1½ miles from the A66. Comfortable accommodation in pleasant surroundings.
7hc (5⋔) (3fb) *B&b£7.50–£9 Bdi£11.50–£13 W£76.50–£86 Ⱡ
Lic ⚱ CTV 12P ⌂ 380acres mixed

FH Mrs J M Tiffin **Wham Head** *(NY373342)* Hutton Roof ☎Skelton (08534) 289
Mar–Sep
Traditional old farmhouse offering homely accommodation in quiet surroundings.
4rm (3hc) (2fb) *B&bfr£7.50 Bdifr£11.50 Wfr£75 ⱠLDO4pm
CTV 8P ⌂ 126acres mixed

INN Mill ☎Threlkeld (059683) 632
Closed Xmas day
A friendly little inn in delightful countryside offering home-cooked food.
8hc (1🛁 1🚿) Ⓡ B&b£12–£14.50 Bdi£18–£20.50 W£115–£130 Ɏ Bar lunch 75p–£4.50&alc LDO4pm
🛋 CTV 25P 🎣
Ⓥ

NAILSWORTH
Gloucestershire
Map **3** ST89

GH Gables Private Hotel Tiltups End, Bath Rd (Guestaccom) ☎(045383) 2265
Closed Dec & Jan
A modestly appointed establishment.
6rm (5hc) (2fb) ✱B&b£11–£12 Bdi£17–£18 W£126 Ɏ LDO9pm
Lic CTV 8P

GH Orchard Close Springhill ☎(045383) 2503
In a quiet position yet near to town centre, with spacious, tasteful and comfortable rooms.
3hc (2🛁 1🚿) (1fb) CTV in all bedrooms 🐕 Ⓡ ✱B&b£11–£14.50 Bdi£15.50–£19.00 W£107.50–£121.50 Ɏ LDO9pm
🛋 3P 1🚗 🏠
Credit cards [1] [2] [3] [4] [5] Ⓥ

NAIRN
Highland *Nairnshire*
Map **14** NH85

GH Bruach House 35 Seabank Rd ☎(0667) 54194
Closed Xmas & New Year
A well-appointed house with attractive lounge and some nice family bedrooms.
8hc (3🛁) (3fb) Ⓡ B&b£10–£13.50 Bdi£16.50–£20 W£110–£133 Ɏ LDO5.15pm
🛋 CTV 8P 🏠
Ⓥ

GH *Greenlaws Private Hotel* 13 Seafield St ☎(0667) 52738
Detached house with tasteful extension in residential area. Neat, well-equipped bedrooms in varying sizes and styles.
8hc (2🛁 2🚿) (1fb) CTV in all bedrooms Ⓡ LDO6pm
Lic 🛋 CTV 7P snooker

GH Sandown Farmhouse Sandown Farm Ln ☎(0667) 54745
Former farmhouse with homely atmosphere and small covered swimming pool.
6hc (2fb) 🐕 ✱B&b£9 Bdi£13 W£91 Ɏ LDO5pm
🛋 CTV 10P 🏊(heated)

Mungrisdale — Needham Market

Recommended

GH Sunny Brae Marine Rd ☎(0667) 52309
4 Apr–Oct
Modern villa, purpose-built as a guesthouse in 1970. Standing in its own gardens with views across Nairn Links and Moray Firth, offering high standards throughout.
10hc (1fb) CTV in all bedrooms Ⓡ B&b£13–£15 Bdi£19.50–£21.50 W£126–£140 Ɏ LDO5.30pm
Lic 🛋 CTV 14P
Ⓥ

NANTGAREDIG
Dyfed
Map **2** SN42

FH Mrs J Willmott **Cwmtwrch** *(SN497220)* ☎(026788) 238
Early 19th-century Welsh-stone farmhouse, carefully modernised and furnished.
3🚿 🐕 Ⓡ ✱B&b£10–£15 Bdi£16–£21 W£100–£150 Ɏ LDO9pm
Lic Lift 🛋 CTV 16P 🏠 30acres dairy sheep mixed
Credit cards [1] [3] Ⓥ

NANTWICH
Cheshire
Map **7** SJ65

FH Mrs S Allwood **Burland** *(SJ604534)* Wrexham Rd, Burland (3m W A534) ☎Faddiley (027074) 210
Spacious, comfortable accommodation on 200 acre dairy farm.
3hc (2🚿) TV in all bedrooms ✱B&b£10–£15 Bdi£16–£21 Wfr£63 M̸
🛋 6P 200acres arable dairy

NARBERTH
Dyfed
Map **2** SN11

GH Blaenmarlais ☎(0834) 860326
Closed Dec
Attractive country hotel in own grounds.
11hc (1🛁 5🚿) (4fb) Ⓡ ✱B&b£10–£11.50 Bdi£15–£16.50 W£79–£82 Ɏ LDO6.30pm
Lic 🛋 CTV 20P 6🚗 🏊 🎾(hard)
Ⓥ

FH Mrs I M Bevan **Jacob's Park** *(SN103158)* ☎(0834) 860525
Closed Xmas wk
A comfortable well-furnished farmhouse on A40.
3hc (1fb) 🐕 ✱B&b£8.50–£9 Bdi£12.50–£13 W£77–£80 Ɏ LDO7pm
🛋 CTV P 🏠 28acres beef sheep
Ⓥ

NARBOROUGH
Norfolk
Map **9** TF71

INN Ship Swaffham Rd ☎(0760) 337307
17th-century coaching inn, formerly a barge station, which aims to be a sporting hostelry. Shooting parties, coarse and trout fishing can be arranged.
6🛁🚿 CTV in all bedrooms ✱ B&b£12.50–£16.50 Bdi£18.45–£22.45 Lunch £4.50&alc Dinner £5.95&alc
50P 3🚗 🎣

NEAR SAWREY
Cumbria
Map **7** SD39

GH Garth ☎Hawkshead (09666) 373
6hc (1🚿) (1fb) CTV in 1 bedroom Ⓡ B&b£11.50 Bdi£18.50 LDO5pm
Lic 🛋 CTV 12P 🏠

GH *High Green Gate* ☎Hawkshead (09666) 296
Mar–Oct rs Xmas–New Year
A small yet pleasant guesthouse with attractive gardens, in the heart of Beatrix Potter country.
7hc (1🚿) (2fb) LDO6pm
🛋 CTV 7P 🏠

GH Sawrey House Country Hotel ☎Hawkshead (09666) 387
Feb–Nov
Delightful house offering warm comfortable accommodation and good home-cooking.
11hc (4🛁 3🚿) (3fb) Ⓡ ✱B&b£11.50–£14.25 Bdi£18.25–£21 W£122.50–£142 Ɏ LDO4pm
Lic 🛋 CTV 20P
Ⓥ

NEATISHEAD
Norfolk
Map **9** TG32

GH Barton Angler Lodge Hotel Irstead Rd ☎Horning (0692) 630740
Secluded country house with relaxed atmosphere and quality restaurant offering 'country cuisine'.
7hc (1🛁 4🚿) (1fb) CTV in all bedrooms Ⓡ ✱B&b£16.50–£20 W£101.50–£129.50 M̸ LDO9.30pm
Lic 🛋 CTV 40P 2🚗 nc12yrs 🎣
Credit cards [1] [2] [3] [5]

NEEDHAM MARKET
Suffolk
Map **5** TM05

FH Mrs R M Hackett-Jones ***Pipps Ford*** *(TM108537)* (Guestaccom) ☎Coddenham (044979) 208
Closed Xmas & New Year
16th-century farmhouse close to the River Gipping, with delightful old-fashioned garden, surrounded by farmland and meadows. Entrance off roundabout junction A45/A140.
→

3🛁 (1fb) [R] LDO noon
♨ CTV 8P 🏊 🎾(hard) 🎣 8acres smallholding

NESSCLIFF
Shropshire
Map **7** SJ31

INN ***Nesscliff Hotel*** ☎(074381) 253
5hc (2fb) [R] LDO10pm
CTV 20P 3🚗

NETHER LANGWITH
Nottinghamshire
Map **8** SK57

FH Mrs J M Ibbotson ***Blue Barn*** *(SK539713)* ☎Mansfield (0623) 742248
Closed Xmas
Roomy and relaxing Victorian farmhouse in the heart of Robin Hood country. 2¼m NW of Cuckney, 2nd lane on the left off A616 to Creswell.
4rm (1hc) (1fb) 🐕 [R]
♨ CTV 8P 2🚗 250acres arable mixed

NETLEY
Hampshire
Map **4** SU40

GH White House 48 Victoria Rd ☎Southampton (0703) 453718
3 miles from Southampton a cosy, friendly guesthouse well-situated for all the local attractions including Netley Abbey.
7hc (1fb) CTV in all bedrooms 🐕 [R] ✱B&b£12–£13.50 Bdi£17–£18.50 Wfr£100 Ł LDO6pm
♨ 2P 1🚗
[V]

NETTLECOMBE
Dorset
Map **3** SY59

INN ***Marquis of Lorne*** ☎Powerstock (030885) 236
Closed Xmas
8hc (4🚿) (3fb) 🐕 [R] LDO10pm
CTV 80P
See advertisement on page 89

NEWARK-ON-TRENT
Nottinghamshire
Map **8** SK75

GH Edgefield Hotel & Restaurant Vicarage Ln, North Muskham ☎(0636) 700313
A former mid-Victorian vicarage situated ½m west of North Muskham and adjacent to junction of A1 with A6065, 4m north of Newark.
8hc (2🛁) (2fb) CTV in all bedrooms [R] ✱B&b£18–£22.50 Bdi£26.50–£32.50 Wfr£140 Ł LDO10pm
Lic ♨ CTV 40P 3🚗
Credit cards [1] [2] [3]

NEWBOLD-ON-STOUR
Warwickshire
Map **4** SP24

FH Mrs J M Everett **Newbold Nurseries** *(SP253455)* ☎Alderminster (078987) 285
Mar–Oct
Modern farmhouse with large rooms and a quiet situation.
2rm (1hc) (1fb) ✱B&bfr£8.50
♨ CTV 2P 25acres arable
[V]

NEWBOROUGH
Staffordshire
Map **7** SK12

FH Mrs B Skipper ***Chan Try View*** Moat Hill *(SK135247)* ☎Hoar Cross (028375) 200
This modern farmhouse, 1 mile S of the village on the slope of Moat Hill, offers friendly service and comfortable accommodation.
2rm (1fb) [R] B&b£7.50
♨ CTV 6P 55acres beef sheep
[V]

NEWBRIDGE
Lothian *Midlothian*
Map **11** NT17

FH Mr & Mrs W Pollock ***Easter Norton*** *(NT157721)* ☎031-333 1279
Apr–Sep
Small homely farmhouse in excellent position for motorway and Edinburgh Airport.
2rm (1fb) 🐕 B&b£8.50
♨ CTV P 5acres poultry

NEWBURY
Berkshire
Map **4** SU46

INN Hare & Hounds Hotel Speen (1m W A4) ☎(0635) 47215 Telex no 847662
Annexe contains modern accommodation with well-equipped bedrooms.
7🛁 Annexe: 15🚿 (1fb) TV in all bedrooms 🐕 [R] ✱B&b£30–£35 LDO9.30pm
♨ 20P
Credit cards [1] [2] [3] [5]

NEWBY BRIDGE
Cumbria
Map **7** SD38

GH Furness Fells ☎(0448) 31260
Mar–Oct
Attractive house with annexe overlooking large well-tended garden.
4hc Annexe: 2hc (2fb) 🐕 [R] ✱B&b£9–£9.50 Bdi£14.50–£15 Wfr£94 Ł LDO5.30pm
Lic ♨ CTV 10P nc3yrs
[V]

NEWCASTLE ON CLUN
Shropshire
Map **7** SO28

FH Mr & Mrs Davies **Lower Duffryn** *(SO229822)* ☎ Clun (05884) 239
Etr–Nov
Pleasant, old farmhouse providing simple but well-maintained accommodation.
2hc 🐕 ✱B&bfr£8 Bdifr£12 Wfr£80 Ł LDO5pm
♨ CTV 2P 130acres cattle sheep mixed

Newcastle-under-Lyme — Newport

NEWCASTLE-UNDER-LYME
Staffordshire
Map **7** SJ84

GH Grove Court Hotel 100 Lancaster Rd
☎(0782) 614406
Simple but comfortable well-equipped accommodation in a large Victorian house.
9rm (1🛁 6🚿) Annexe: 2🛁 (1fb) CTV in all bedrooms ✱B&b£14–£17.50 Bdi£19.50–£23 LDO5pm
Lic ♨ CTV 12P
Credit cards [1] [3]

FH Mrs M J Heath ***Home*** *(SJ823454)*
Keele ☎(0782) 627227
Apr–Oct
1¾m W along A5525.
2rm (1fb) TV in 1 bedroom 🚫🐕 [R]
LDO4.30pm
CTV 6P nc2yrs 🎣 250acres dairy sheep

NEWCASTLE UPON TYNE
Tyne & Wear
Map **12** NZ26

GH Avenue Hotel 2 Manor House Rd, Jesmond ☎091-281 1396
Closed Xmas Day & New Year's Day
Small commercial hotel close to town centre, overlooking county cricket ground.
9hc (1fb) 🚫🐕 ✱B&b£14.50–£17.82 Bdi£19.96–£23.28 LDO6.15pm
Lic ♨ CTV P̸
Credit cards [1] [2] [5] [V]

GH Chirton House Hotel 46 Clifton Rd
☎091-273 0407
Comfortable and welcoming hotel offering good value home cooked dinners.
11hc (1🛁 3🚿) (3fb) CTV in 4 bedrooms ✱B&b£17.25–£23 Bdi£24.15–£29.90 W£140–£160 ℔ LDO6pm
Lic ♨ CTV 12P
Credit card [1] [V]

GH Clifton Cottage Dunholme Rd
☎091-273 7347
Simple but comfortable accommodation and helpful proprietors.
6hc (2fb) TV in all bedrooms [R]
✱B&b£10–£11
♨ CTV 6P
[V]

GH *Western House Hotel* 1 West Av, Gosforth ☎091-285 6812
Family run guesthouse offering modest accommodation in a convenient location.
14hc (3fb) LDO8pm
Lic ♨ CTV P̸
Credit card [3]

NEW MILTON
Hampshire
Map **4** SZ29

GH Ashley Court Hotel 105 Ashley Rd
☎(0425) 619256
Family-run guesthouse with warm atmosphere and good home-cooking.
8hc (4🛁 2🚿) (1fb) 🚫🐕 [R] ✱B&b£15 Bdi£19.50 W£135 ℔ LDOnoon
Lic ♨ CTV 10P 🏊
Credit cards [1] [3]

NEWNHAM BRIDGE
Hereford & Worcester
Map **7** SO66

FH Mrs E J Adams **Lower Doddenhill** *(SO661698)* ☎(058479) 223
Etr–Oct
17th century farmhouse with beams and panoramic views. Small antique shop in oast house.
3hc (1🚿) (1fb) ✱B&b£9–£10.50 Bdi£15–£16.50 W£100 ℔ LDOnoon
♨ CTV 4P 230acres mixed
[V]

INN *Talbot Hotel* ☎(058479) 355
Georgian inn in a prominent roadside position, but overlooking Teme Valley meadowland.
3hc (1fb) 🚫🐕 [R] LDO10pm
CTV 25P 🎣 snooker

NEWPORT
Dyfed
Map **2** SN03

GH Cnapan Country House East St
☎(0239) 820575
Closed Feb
A delightful village guesthouse with comfortable accommodation and good food, including specially wholefood lunches.
5hc (3🚿) (1fb) TV in all bedrooms [R] ✱B&b£10.50–£12.50 Bdi£17–£19 W£66.15–£78.75 M̸ LDO9pm
Lic ♨ 6P
Credit cards [1] [3]

INN Golden Lion East St ☎(0239) 820321
Cosy inn of character with bright, well-equipped bedrooms.
10rm (9hc 5🛁 4🚿) (1fb) CTV in 9 bedrooms 🚫🐕 [R] ✱B&b£10–£14 Wfr£75 M̸ Lunch £3alc High tea £4alc Dinner 9.30pm £6alc
♨ CTV 10P 🏊 sauna bath solarium
Credit cards [1] [3] [V]

NEWPORT
Gwent
Map **3** ST38

GH Caerleon House Hotel Caerau Rd
☎(0633) 64869
Conveniently positioned for the town centre and M4 Link roads this comfortable guesthouse offers friendly, hospitable service.
8hc (1fb) CTV in all bedrooms [R] B&b£14–£18 LDO9pm
Lic ♨ 8P
[V]

NEWPORT
Isle of Wight
See **Wight, Isle of**

NEWQUAY
Cornwall
Map **2** SW86

GH Arundell Hotel Mount Wise ☎(0637) 872481 Plan **1** *B1*
Etr–Sep
Large seasonal family hotel, comfortable and recently renovated.

37hc (10🛁 9🚿) (12fb) CTV in 30 bedrooms [R] *B&b£5.25–£10.30 Bdi£7.25–£12.30 W£56.52–£91.30 Ł LDO6pm

Lic CTV 31P 9🚗 snooker sauna bath solarium

Credit cards [1] [2] [3] [4] [5] [V]

GH Barrowcliff Hotel Henver Rd ☎(0637) 873492 Plan **1A** *E3*
May–Sep

23hc (1🛁 4🚿) (6fb) CTV in all bedrooms [R] *B&b£8–£12 Bdi£9.50–£14.50 W£66.50–£101.50 Ł LDO6.30pm

Lic CTV 20P nc3yrs

Credit cards [1] [3]

GH *Cherington Hotel* 7 Pentire Av ☎(0637) 873363 Plan **3** *A2*
Apr–Sep
Family hotel close to Pentire beach.

22hc (2🛁 4🚿) (3fb)

Lic CTV 14P 2🚗

GH Copper Beech Hotel 70 Edgcumbe Av ☎(0637) 873376 Plan **4** *D2*
Etr–mid Oct
Well-appointed family hotel in peaceful area, adjoining Trenance Gardens.

15hc (2🛁 5🚿) (3fb) 🐕 *B&b£9.78–£11.50 Bdi£12.65–£16.10 W£86.25–£100 Ł (W only Jun, Jul & Aug) LDO6.15pm

Lic 🍽 CTV 15P

Credit card [3]

GH Fairlands 107 Tower Rd ☎(0637) 872917 Plan **5** *B2*
Closed Dec rs Oct, Nov, Jan & Feb
Comfortable small terraced hotel, overlooking Fistral Beach.

8hc (4fb) 🐕 *B&b£6–£9 Bdi£9–£12 W£63–£84 Ł LDO2pm

🍽 CTV 8P

Newquay

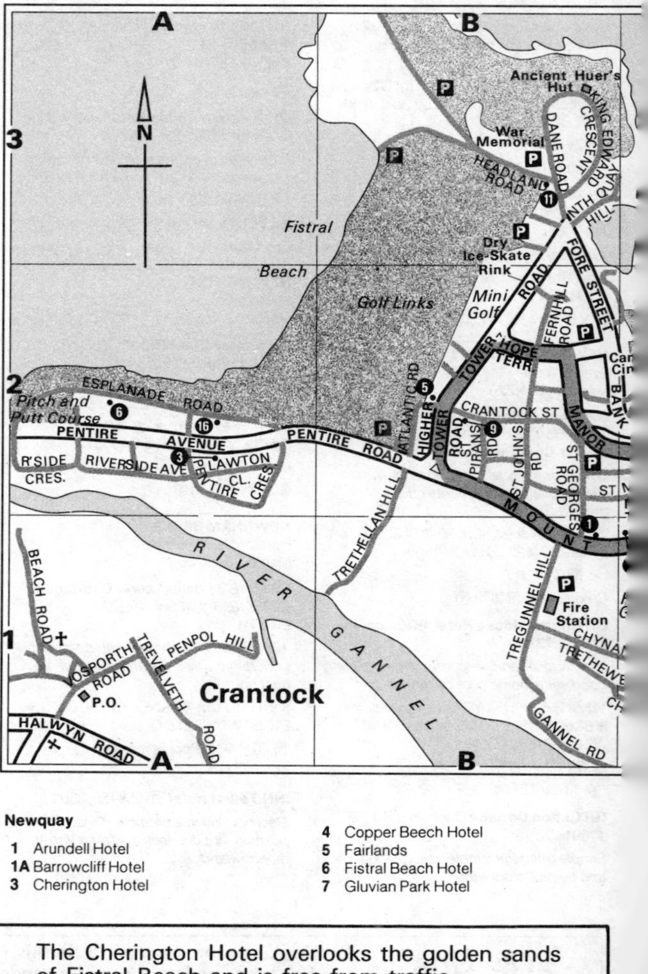

Newquay

1 Arundell Hotel
1A Barrowcliff Hotel
3 Cherington Hotel
4 Copper Beech Hotel
5 Fairlands
6 Fistral Beach Hotel
7 Gluvian Park Hotel

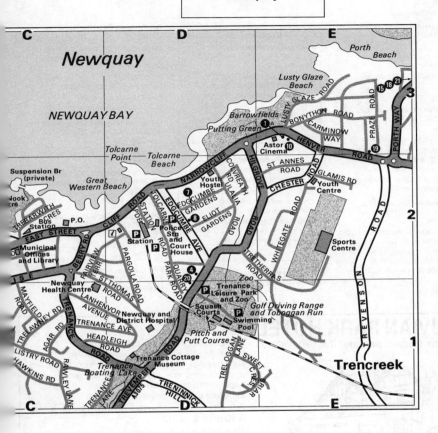

Newquay

8	Hepworth Hotel	
9	Jonel	
10	Kellsboro Hotel	
11	Links Hotel	
14	Mount Wise Hotel	
15	Pendeen Hotel	
16	Porth Endoc	
17	Priory Lodge Hotel	
18	Rolling Waves	
19	Rumours Hotel	
20	Wheal Treasure	
21	Windward Hotel	

GH Fistral Beach Hotel Esplanade Rd, Pentire ☎(0637) 873993 Plan **6** *A2*
Mar–Oct

Modern small very comfortable family hotel, adjacent to beach.

15hc (7🛁) (3fb) ✱B&b£11–£17.50 Bdi£13.50–£20 W£84.75–£129.50 ⅃ (W only mid Jul–mid Aug) LDO6.45pm

Lic 🅿 CTV 12P

Credit card 🛈 Ⓥ

GH Gluvian Park Hotel 12 Edgcumbe Gdns ☎(0637) 873133 Plan **7** *D2*
Apr–Oct

Comfortable modern family hotel close to sea front and Tolcarne beach.

23hc (2🛁 16🛁) (7fb) CTV in all bedrooms ✈ ® B&b£10.50–£15.50 Bdi£15–£19.50 W£94–£126 ⅃ LDO6.30pm

Lic 🅿 CTV 10P

Credit cards 🛈 ③

See advertisement on page 284

GH Hepworth Hotel 27 Edgcumbe Av ☎(0637) 873686 Plan **8** *D2*
Etr–Sep

Modern comfortable family hotel, recently refurbished to high standards.

13rm (9hc 4🛁) (4fb) ✈ ✱B&b£9.20–£13.50 Bdi£14–£18.10 W£79–£114 ⅃ (W only 11 Jul–30 Aug) LDO6.30pm

Lic 🅿 CTV 12P

GH Jonel 88–90 Crantock St ☎(0637) 875084 Plan **9** *B2*

Small comfortable well-appointed terraced hotel, close to town.

12hc (2fb) ✈ ® ✱B&b£7–£11 Bdi£9–£14.50 W£55–£95 ⅃

Lic CTV 7P

Ⓥ

GH Kellsboro Hotel 12 Henver Rd ☎(0637) 874620 Plan **10** *E3*
Apr–Oct

Well-appointed family hotel, close to beaches.

→

14hc (6🛁 1🚿) (7fb) CTV in all bedrooms ✱B&b£12.75–£14 Bdi£15–£18 W£80.50–£115 Ł LDO7pm

Lic 🍽 CTV 14P [🏊](heated)

GH *Links Hotel* Headland Rd ☎(0637) 873211 Plan **11** *B3*
Mar–Oct

Personally-run private hotel with well-equipped bedrooms.

15hc (9🚿) (3fb) CTV in all bedrooms LDO4.30pm

Lic 🍽 CTV P

GH Mount Wise Hotel Mount Wise ☎(0637) 873080 Plan **14** *C1*
Closed Xmas

Modern comfortable high rise property.

34hc (8🛁 14🚿) Annexe: 2hc (17fb) CTV in all bedrooms [R] ✱B&b£10–£16 Bdi£13–£19 W£83–£132 Ł LDO7pm

Lic Lift 🍽 CTV 20P 6🚗 ⛺ 🏊(heated) sauna bath gymnasium [V]

GH Porth Enodoc 4 Esplanade Rd, Pentire ☎(0637) 872372 Plan **16** *A2*
Etr–Oct & Xmas

Large detached house standing in its own gardens overlooking the sea.

10🚿 (4fb) CTV in all bedrooms 🚫 ✱B&b£10–£12.50 Bdi£15–£17.50 W£87.50–£110 Ł (W only Jun–Aug) LDO5.30pm

Lic 🍽 CTV 12P [V]

Newquay

Recommended

GH *Pendeen Hotel* Alexandra Rd, Porth ☎(0637) 873521 Plan **15** *E3*
Mar–mid Oct

A modern private hotel only 200 yards from Porth Beach. Rooms are pleasant, and equipped with metred TV.

15hc (6🛁 4🚿) (5fb) CTV in 10 bedrooms 🚫 LDO5pm

Lic 🍽 CTV 15P

Recommended

GH *Priory Lodge Hotel* Mount Wise ☎(0637) 874111 Plan **17** *C1*

Hotel of character set in its own grounds with attractive and comfortable rooms.

21hc (5🛁 11🚿) Annexe: 2🚿 (13fb) CTV in all bedrooms 🚫 [R] LDO7pm

Lic 🍽 CTV 25P 🏊(heated)

[V]

GH Rolling Waves Alexandra Rd, Porth ☎(0637) 873236 Plan **18** *E3*
Etr–Oct

9hc (3🚿) (3fb) 🚫 ✱B&b£8.25–£9.25 Bdi£9.75–£10.75 W£68–£78 Ł (W only Jul & Aug) LDO5pm

Lic CTV 10P

GH *Rumours Hotel* 89 Henver Rd ☎(0637) 872170 Plan **19** *E3*

Large modern guesthouse with pleasant public rooms and nicely appointed bedrooms.

14rm (9hc 6🛁 1🚿) (2fb) CTV in all bedrooms 🚫 [R] LDO10.30pm

Lic 🍽 18P ⛺ 🏊(heated)

Credit cards [1] [2] [3] [5]

GH Wheal Treasure 72 Edgcumbe Av ☎(0637) 874136 Plan **20** *D1/2*
May–Sep

Comfortable hotel, close to Trenance Gardens.

9hc (2🚿) 🚫 ✱B&b£8.50–£10 Bdi£11.50–£15 W£85–£95 Ł (W only late Jul–Aug) LDO5.30pm

Lic 🍽 CTV 9P nc5yrs

GH *Windward Hotel* Alexandra Rd, Porth ☎(0637) 873185 Plan **21** *E3*
Etr–Sep

7hc (1🛁 1🚿) (2fb) CTV in 2 bedrooms

Lic 🍽 CTV 10P

FH J C Wilson ***Manuels*** *(SW839601)* Lane ☎(0637) 873572
Closed Xmas–New Year

17th-century farmhouse in sheltered, wooded valley, 2m from Newquay. Take the west road off the A392 at Quintrill Downs.

5rm (2hc) (2fb) ✠ LDO4.30pm

CTV 6P ⚓ 44acres mixed

NEW QUAY
Dyfed
Map **2**   SN35

⊢•┤**FH** Mr & Mrs White **Nanternis**
Nanternis *(SN374567)* (2m SW off A486)
☎(0545) 560181
Etr–Oct

Farmhouse of great character tucked away in a snug little village. Organic garden produce.

2hc (1fb) ✠ ⓡ B&b£8–£9.50 Bdi£11.50–£13 W£80.50–£87.50 ⱳ LDOnoon

🍴 CTV 3P 8acres sheep mixed

ⓥ

FH Mr H Kelly **Ty Hen** *(SN365553)*
Llwyndafydd (S of Cross Inn, A486)
☎(0545) 560346
Feb–Nov

A high quality of accommodation and excellent food are offered in two adjacent but separate buildings.

5🛏 Annexe: 2🛏 ⱳ in 5 bedrooms CTV in all bedrooms ⓡ ✱B&b£10–£12 Bdi£16–£18 W£105–£119 ⱳ LDOnoon

Lic 🍴 CTV 20P ⚓ 15acres sheep

ⓥ

NEW ROMNEY
Kent
Map **5**   TR02

GH Blue Dolphins Hotel & Restaurant
Dymchurch Rd ☎(0679) 63224

8hc (1🛏) (2fb) ✠ ✱B&b£10–£17 Bdi£22.95–£29.95 Wfr£147.70 ⱳ LDO9.15pm

Lic 🍴 CTV 15P ⚓

Credit cards ① ③ ⓥ

NEWTON (nr Vowchurch)
Hereford & Worcester
Map **3**   SO33

Newquay
Newton Stewart

FH Mrs J C Powell **Little Green**
(SO335337) ☎Michaelchurch (098123) 205
Closed Xmas

Modernised farmhouse, once an inn, with friendly atmosphere.

3hc (2fb) ✱B&b£7–£8.50 Bdi£12–£13 W£84–£90 ⱳ

CTV 5P 50acres beef sheep

ⓥ

NEWTON ABBOT
Devon
Map **3**   SX87

GH Lamorna Exeter Rd, Coombe Cross, Sandygate (3m N A380) ☎(0626) 65627

7hc (2fb) TV in all bedrooms ✠ ⓡ ✱B&b£9.50–£13 Bdi£15–£18.50 W£105–£129 ⱳ

Lic 🍴 CTV 20P 1⛵ ▨(heated)

ⓥ

NEWTONMORE
Highland *Inverness-shire*
Map **14**   NN79

GH Alvey House Hotel Golf Course Rd ☎(05403) 260
Jan–Oct

Detached house in 1½ acres of garden 50 yards from golf course.

7hc (4🛏) (2fb) ✱B&b£12–£14 Bdi£20–£22 W£133–£147 ⱳ LDO7.30pm

Lic 🍴 CTV 10P

ⓥ

GH Coig Na Shee Fort William Rd ☎(05403) 216
Feb–Nov

Large family house, with comfortable bedrooms, set in its own tree-studded grounds.

6hc (1fb) ⓡ ✱B&b£10.50–£11.50 Bdi£16.50–£18.50 W£105–£119 ⱳ LDO5pm

🍴 CTV 8P

GH Glenquoich Glen Rd ☎(05403) 461
Closed Xmas

6rm (5hc) (3fb) ✱B&b£8.50–£9.90 Bdi£14.50–£16.90 W£95–£115 ⱳ LDO5pm

CTV 6P

GH Pines Hotel Station Rd ☎(05403) 271
Apr–Oct

6hc (1⇆5🛏) (1fb) ✠ ⓡ B&b£13.50–£14 Bdi£20–£21 W£133–£140 ⱳ LDO6pm

Lic 🍴 CTV 7P

ⓥ

NEWTON REGIS
Staffordshire
Map **4**   SK20

FH Mrs M Lane **Newton House**
(SK278075) ☎Tamworth (0827) 830632

Extensive Georgian-style farmhouse in elevated village position.

3hc (1fb) ✠ ✱B&b£8.50 Bdi£14 W£90 ⱳ LDO2pm

🍴 CTV 5P 1⛵(charge) nc7yrs ♪(grass) 6acres mixed beef

NEWTON STEWART
Dumfries & Galloway *Wigtownshire*
Map **10**   NX46

GH Duncree House Hotel King St ☎(0671) 2001

Simple, inexpensive accommodation in a country lodge on outskirts of town.

7hc (6fb) ✱B&b£9 Bdi£12 W£84 ⱳ LDO5.50pm

Lic CTV 30P ⚓

FH Mrs Hewitson **Auchenleck**
(NX450709) Minnigaff ☎(0671) 2035
Etr–mid Oct

Large turreted farmhouse in an isolated position bordering Kiroughtree Forest and Glentrool National Park.

3hc ✠ ⓡ B&b£9 Bdi£14 LDOnoon

🍴 CTV 6P 103acres beef sheep

NEWTOWN
Powys
Map **6**   SO19

FH L M & G T Whitticase *Highgate*
(SO111953) ☎(0686) 25981
Mar–Oct

*15th-century black and white timbered
farmhouse, in elevated position with
commanding views over valley and hills.
Rough shooting, fishing and ponies
available.*

3hc (1🚿) � LDO5pm
Lic 🅿 CTV P ✿ ♪ ↺ 250acres beef
sheep mixed

FH Mrs I Jarman *Lower Gwestydd*
(SO126934) Llanllwchaiarn ☎(0686)
26718
Mar–Nov

*17th-century farmhouse with historical
features both inside and out. 2m E off
B4568.*

3hc (2fb) ✠ Ⓡ ✱B&b£9–£9.50 Bdi£13.50–
£14 W£88–£92 ⊬ LDO4pm
🅿 CTV 4P ✿ 200acres arable beef sheep
mixed

NITON
Isle of Wight
See **Wight, Isle of**

NORMANBY
North Yorkshire
Map **8**   NZ90

FH D I Smith *Heather View (NZ928062)*
☎Whitby (0947) 880451
Mar–Oct

*Attractive modern farmhouse, well-
appointed and comfortable. Conveniently
situated for coastal visits.*

5hc (3fb) Ⓡ ✱B&b£8.50 Bdi£10.50–
£11.50 W£70 ⊬ LDO2.30pm
🅿 CTV 5P nc5yrs 40acres cattle sheep
mixed

NORTHALLERTON
North Yorkshire
Map **8**   SE39

GH *Windsor* 56 South Pde ☎(0609)
774100
Closed first 2 wks Oct & 24 Dec–2 Jan

Newtown
—
Northwood

*Friendly proprietors offer hospitality and
comfortable accommodation in this well
managed guesthouse.*
6hc Annexe: 2rm (3fb) Ⓡ
🅿 CTV ✏

NORTHAMPTON
Northamptonshire
Map **4**   SP76

GH Poplars Hotel Cross St, Moulton
☎(0604) 43983
Closed Xmas wk

21hc (2↩ 3🚿) (5fb) TV in 20 bedrooms
CTV in 1 bedroom ✱B&b£13.50–£22
Bdi£20–£28.50 Wfr£136 ⊬ LDO5pm
Lic 🅿 CTV 21P ✿
Credit card ① Ⓥ

NORTH BERWICK
Lothian *East Lothian*
Map **12**   NT58

GH Cragside Private Hotel 16 Marine
Pde ☎(0620) 2879

*Neatly appointed guesthouse on sea front
in East Bay.*

6hc (2fb) ✠ Ⓡ ✱B&bfr£10.50 Bdifr£14.75
Wfr£94.50 ⊬ LDO4pm
🅿 CTV ✏
Ⓥ

NORTH CADBURY
Somerset
Map **3**   ST62

FH E J Keen *Hill (ST634279)* ☎(0963)
40257
Etr–Sep

*Attractive, small, period farmhouse with
pretty garden on edge of peaceful village.*

3rm (1hc) (1fb) ✠
🅿 TV P 100acres mixed

NORTH COWTON
North Yorkshire
See **East Cowton**

NORTH NIBLEY
Gloucestershire
Map **3**   ST79

GH Burrows Court Nibley Gn, Dursley
☎Dursley (0453) 46230

*Recently converted 18th-century weaving
mill set in 1 acre of gardens with good
views.*

8hc (3↩ 2🚿) CTV in 5 bedrooms ✠ Ⓡ
✱B&b£12–£18 Bdi£19.50–£25.50 W£105–
£150.50 ⊬ LDO8.45pm
Lic 🅿 CTV 10P nc10yrs ⌇
Credit cards ① ③ Ⓥ

NORTHOWRAM
West Yorkshire
Map **7**   SE12

FH Mr W Longbottom *Royd (SE107268)*
Hall Ln ☎Halifax (0422) 206718
Apr–Sep (rs Oct–Mar prior bookings only)

*Converted 19th-century farmhouse with
spacious bedrooms. Farm has a stud of
Arabian stallions, riding stables and guest
stabling.*

4rm (3fb) TV in all bedrooms Ⓡ ✱B&bfr£9
Bdifr£14 Wfr£98 ⊬ LDO4pm
CTV 5P ✿ ↺ 22acres Arab horse stud
beef poultry

NORTH WALSHAM
Norfolk
Map **9**   TG23

GH Beechwood Private Hotel
20 Cromer Rd ☎(0692) 403231
Closed Xmas–7 Jan

11hc (3↩ 4🚿) (5fb) ✱B&b£13.50 Bdi£18–
£23 W£106–£118 ⊬ LDO7pm
Lic 🅿 CTV 12P nc5yrs
Ⓥ

NORTHWOOD
Shropshire
Map **7**   SJ43

GH Woodlands Wolverley ☎Wem (0939)
33268

*Set in spacious grounds, this large
Georgian house is off the B5063 1 mile S
of the village.*

8hc (1↩ 2🚿) (2fb) ✠
Lic 🅿 CTV 15P

NORTH WOOTTON
Somerset
Map **3** ST54

FH Mrs M White **Barrow** *(ST553416)* ☎Pilton (074989) 245
Mar–Nov
15th-century stone-built farmhouse on edge of village, situated between Wells, Glastonbury and Shepton Mallet.
3hc (1fb) 🚫 [R] *B&bfr£9 Bdifr£13 Wfr£85 L
CTV 3P 150acres dairy
[V]

NORTON
Nottinghamshire
Map **8** SK57

FH Mrs J Palmer **Norton Grange** *(SK572733)* ☎Mansfield (0623) 842666
Etr–Oct
A 200-year-old stone-built farmhouse fronted by small gardens, at edge of village.
3rm (2hc) (1fb) 🚭 in 3 bedrooms 🚫 *B&b£8–£9 W£49–£54 M
CTV 4P 172acres arable beef
[V]

NORWICH
Norfolk
Map **5** TG20

North Wootton — Nottingham

GH Grange Hotel 230 Thorpe Rd ☎(0603) 34734
Closed Xmas wk
39hc (4🛁 35🚿) (1fb) CTV in 38 bedrooms TV in 1 bedroom 🚫 [R] *B&b£16–£23.50 Bdi£22–£29.50 LDO8.30pm
Lic 🛋 CTV 40P sauna bath solarium
Credit cards [1] [2] [3] [5] [V]

GH *Marlborough House Hotel* 22 Stracey Rd, Thorpe Rd ☎(0603) 628005
12hc (3🚿) (2fb) CTV in 4 bedrooms LDO4.30pm
Lic 🛋 CTV 5P 2🚗
Credit card [3]

GH Wedgewood 42 St Stephens Rd ☎(0603) 625730
Closed Xmas & New Year
Situated on a busy main road close to the town centre and coach station.
11hc (3🛁) (3fb) CTV in all bedrooms 🚫 [R] B&b£9.50–£15 W£63–£101.50 M
🛋 CTV 9P
Credit cards [1] [3] [V]

NOTTINGHAM
Nottinghamshire
Map **8** SK53

GH Balmoral Hotel 55–57 Loughborough Rd, West Bridgford ☎(0602) 818588
Warm and welcoming hotel one mile south of city centre with modern well-equipped rooms.
24hc CTV in all bedrooms 🚫 *B&b£16.10–£18.40 Bdi£23–£25.40
Lic 🛋 CTV 36P
Credit cards [1] [3] [V]

GH *Bridgford Lodge* 88/90 Radcliffe Rd, West Bridgford ☎(0602) 814042
Pair of semi-detached houses, converted to provide tasteful accommodation.
12hc (6🚿) (3fb) CTV in all bedrooms 🚫 [R] LDO7pm
Lic 🛋 14P
Credit cards [1] [3]

GH Crantock Hotel 480 Mansfield Rd ☎(0602) 623294
10hc (1🛁) (1fb) CTV in all bedrooms [R] *B&b£12.50–£14.75 Bdi£18.50–£20.75 W£129.50–£145.25 L LDO9pm
Lic 🛋 15P 8🚗

GH Grantham Commercial Hotel 24–26 Radcliffe Road, West Bridgford ☎(0602) 811373
Simple and businesslike accommodation close to Trent Bridge. →

24hc (2fb) CTV in all bedrooms B&b£9.50–£11.50 Bdi£12.75–£14.75 W£60–£68 Ł LDO 6pm

♨ CTV 8P 2🚗

GH *Waverley* 107 Portland Rd, Waverley St ☎(0602) 786707
Closed 2 wks Xmas

17hc (2fb) LDOnoon

♨ CTV 1🚗

GH Windsor Lodge Hotel 116 Radcliffe Rd, West Bridgford ☎(0602) 813773

Popular and impeccably maintained hotel one mile south of city centre on A6011.

43hc (5🛁 35🚿) (6fb) CTV in all bedrooms ✗ [R] ✱B&b£18.70–£23 Bdi£25.60–£29.90 LDO7.45pm

Lic ♨ CTV 48P snooker solarium

Credit cards [1] [2] [3]

NUNEATON
Warwickshire
Map **4** SP39

GH *Abbey Grange Hotel* 100 Manor Court Rd ☎(0203) 385535

9hc CTV in all bedrooms ✗ [R] LDO9.30pm

Lic ♨ CTV 30P

Credit cards [1] [2] [3] [5]

GH Drachenfels Hotel 25 Attleborough Rd ☎(0203) 383030

8hc (2🚿) (2fb) CTV in all bedrooms [R] ✱B&b£10.50–£14.50 LDO8pm

Lic ♨ 8P

Credit card [1] [V]

NUNNEY
Somerset
Map **3** ST74

INN *George* Church St ☎(037384) 458

Attractive inn near Nunney Castle, with good restaurant and separate residents' lounge.

12rm (5🛁 4🚿) CTV in 5 bedrooms [R] LDO10pm

CTV 20P

Credit cards [1] [2] [3] [5]

NUTHURST
West Sussex
Map **5** TQ12

FH Mrs S E Martin **Saxtons** *(TQ199275)* ☎ Lower Beeding (040376) 231

There is a warm and friendly atmosphere and comfortable, homely accommodation at this Georgian farmhouse.

4hc (1fb) ✗ [R] ✱B&b£11–£13 Bdi£18–£20 W£126–£140 Ł LDO3pm

♨ CTV 6P 2🚗 97acres sheep

OAKAMOOR
Staffordshire
Map **7** SK04

INN Admiral Jervis Inn & Restaurant Mill Rd ☎(0538) 702187

18th-century inn with lots of character, providing comfortable accommodation. Conveniently situated for Alton Towers.

5hc (1🚿) (4fb) [R] ✱B&bfr£14.50 Dinner 9.30pm alc

10P

Credit cards [1] [2] [3] [5]

OAKFORD
Devon
Map **3** SS92

FH A Boldry **Newhouse** *(SS892228)* ☎(03985) 347
Closed Xmas

Comfortable 17th-century farmhouse with oak beams and inglenook fireplace.

3hc (1fb) [R] ✱B&b£9.50 Bdi£14 W£88 Ł

♨ CTV 3P 🎣 42acres beef

[V]

See advertisement on page 144

FH Mr J R Pearce **Westcott** *(SS910214)* ☎(03985) 265

200-year-old farmhouse in secluded setting on the edge of Exmoor. Bedrooms have four poster beds. High standard of cooking. Horse riding and fishing are available.

4hc (3🛁 1🚿) CTV in all bedrooms [R] ✱B&b£18.50 Bdi£30 W£192.50 Ł LDO10pm

Lic ♨ CTV 30P nc10yrs 🎣 U sauna bath solarium 350acres beef dairy horses sheep mixed

---

OBAN
Strathclyde *Argyllshire*
Map **10** NM83
See plan

⊢⊣**GH Ardblair** Dalriach Rd ☎(0631) 62668 Plan **1** *C4*
5 Apr–29 Nov

Behind town centre, convenient to swimming pool, bowling green and tennis courts.

16hc (5fb) B&b£6.50–£8 Bdi £11.50–£13 LDO5pm

CTV 10P

GH *Crathie* Duncraggen Rd ☎(0631) 62619 Plan **3** *C3*
Etr–Oct

Modern house on a hill behind town centre, adjacent to McCaig's tower.

9hc (2fb) ✗ [R] LDO5pm

Lic CTV 12P nc 2yrs

GH *Foxholes Hotel* Cologin (along unclass rd from junc with A816) ☎(0631) 64982
Plan **4** *B1*
Apr–Oct

Peacefully situated in a quiet glen 3 miles south of Oban. Bedrooms are tastefully furnished and well-equipped, the lounge opens onto a patio and gardens, with a small dining room adjacent, where appetising 'Taste of Scotland' dishes are served.

7hc (2🛁 🚿) (1fb) CTV in all bedrooms [R] LDO8.30pm

Lic ♨ P ⛺

GH Glenburnie Private Hotel The Esplanade ☎(0631) 62089 Plan **5** *A5*
Apr–Oct

Grey stone-built hotel on sea front with private parking to front of hotel.

15hc (8🚿) (3fb) CTV in all bedrooms ✱B&b£10.50–£17.50

♨ CTV 12P 1🚗 nc4yrs

Credit card [3]

GH Heatherfield Private Hotel Albert Rd ☎(0631) 62681 Plan **6** *C3*

Pleasant house situated on hill behind town with ¾ acre of garden.

10hc (4fb) CTV in all bedrooms [R] ✱B&bfr£11 Bdifr£16 Wfr£108 LDO7pm

10P

GH Kenmore Soroba Rd ☎(0631) 63592 Plan **7** *C1*

White-painted stone house situated on A816 with small modern extension.

6hc (2fb) ✗ ✱B&b£8.50–£9

CTV 12P

[V]

⊢⊣**GH Roseneath** Dalriach Rd ☎(0631) 62929 Plan **8** *C4*
Closed Dec

Attractive sandstone house in terrace on hillside offering views across bay to Kerrera.

10hc (1🚿) (1fb) CTV in 2 bedrooms B&b£8–£10 Bdi£12–£14 W£78–£92 Ł LDO6.30pm

♨ CTV 8P

GH *Sgeir Mhaol* Soroba Rd ☎(0631) 62650 Plan **9** *C1*

Small friendly guesthouse on the A816 just outside town centre.

7hc (3fb) ✗ LDO6pm

♨ CTV 10P

GH *Thornloe* Albert Rd ☎(0631) 62879 Plan **9A** *C4*
Apr–Nov

Large semi-detached house in high position, convenient to many leisure facilities.

9hc (2fb) LDO5pm

♨ CTV 7P

GH Wellpark Hotel Esplanade ☎(0631) 62948 Plan **10** *A5*
Apr–Sep

Semi-detached hotel built in granite and sandstone, offering good standard of accommodation in a seafront location.

17fil CTV in all bedrooms ®
✱B&b£13.30–£15.25 Bdi£19.30–£21.25
W£123.27–£136.20 ½ LDO6pm
🅿 14P
Ⓥ

ODDINGTON
Gloucestershire
Map **4**   SP22

INN Horse & Groom ☎Cotswold (0451)
30584
Closed Xmas

5rm (1🚪3 4fil) (1fb) CTV in 2 bedrooms ✘
® B&b£14.50–£17.50 Bdi £22.50–£25.50
Bar lunch £1.50–£3.50 Dinner 9.45pm £8
alc
🅿 40P

OKEHAMPTON
Devon
Map **2**   SX59

FH Mrs K C Heard **Hughslade**
(SX561932) ☎(0837) 2883
Closed Xmas

Pleasant farmhouse on the edge of the
town. Ideal base for exploring Dartmoor
and the north and south Devon coasts.

4hc (3fb) ✱B&b£9–£11.50 Bdi£14–£17
Wfr£95 ½

CTV P ∪ snooker 600acres beef sheep
mixed

Credit cards ② ③ Ⓥ

See advertisement on page 290

OKEOVER
Staffordshire
Map **7**   SK14

FH Mrs E J Harrison **Little Park**
(SK160490) ☎Thorpe Cloud (033529) 341
Apr–Oct

200-year-old stone and brick farmhouse
with oak beams in most rooms.
Outstanding views from all windows.

3hc (1fb) ✘ ✱B&b£8–£9 Bdi£12–£14

CTV 3P nc3yrs 123acres dairy
Ⓥ

OLD DALBY
Leicestershire
Map **8**   SK62

FH Mrs V Anderson **Home Farm**
(SK673236) Church Ln ☎Melton
Mowbray (0664) 822622

19th-century farmhouse, on edge of
peaceful village in lovely Vale of Belvoir.

3hc (1fb) ✘ B&b£8–£12

🅿 CTV 5P ¾acre non-working

OLD SODBURY
Avon
Map **3**   ST78

GH Dornden Church Ln ☎Chipping
Sodbury (0454) 313325
Closed Xmas & New Year rs last 2 wks
Oct

Charming house, once a vicarage, set in
lovely grounds.   →

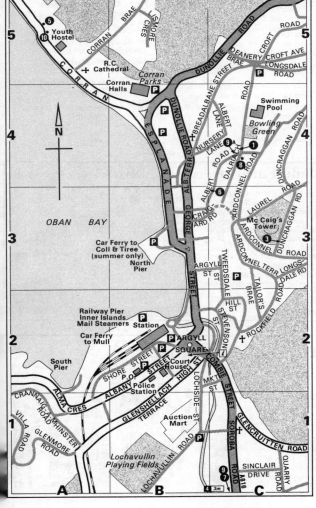

Oban

1   Ardblair
3   Crathie
4   Foxholes Hotel
5   Glenburnie Private Hotel
6   Heatherfield Private Hotel
7   Kenmore
9   Roseneath
9   Sgeir Mhaol
9A Thornloe
10 Wellpark Hotel

9hc (2⇨) (5fb) CTV in 2 bedrooms
✳B&b£13.50–£20 Bdi£19–£25 Wfr£73.50
M LDO3pm
🍴 CTV 15P ₽(grass)
Ⓥ

See advertisement on page 96

ONICH
Highland *Inverness-shire*
Map 14   NN06

GH *Glenmorven House* ☎(08553) 247
Mar–Oct

Nicely appointed guesthouse situated on the shores of Loch Linnhe with superb outlook.

7hc (2fb) ® LDO7pm
Lic 🍴 20P

GH *Tigh-A-Righ* ☎(08553) 255
Closed 22 Dec–7 Jan

5hc (3fb) ✳B&b£7.50–£8.50 Bdi£13.80–£14 W£96.60 ⥮ LDO9pm
Lic 🍴 CTV 15P ♿

FH Mr & Mrs A Dewar **Cuilcheanna House** *(NN019617)*(Guestaccom)
☎(08553) 226
Etr–early Oct

Large Victorian house with gardens set in sloping fields leading to Loch Linnhe. Excellent views over lochs and mountains.

Old Sodbury
—
Otterburn

8⇨ (2fb) ® ✳B&b£12–£14 Bdi£19–£21
W£125–£135 ⥮ LDO5pm
🍴 CTV 10P ♨ 120acres beef

ORFORD
Suffolk
Map 5   TM44

INN King's Head Front St
☎(0394) 450271
Closed Jan

5hc (1fb) ✕ ® ✳B&b£13.75–£16 Lunch £12alc Dinner 9pm £12alc

100P 1🐎

Credit card 5 Ⓥ

ORTON
Cumbria
Map 12   NY60

↦FH Mr P Hinkley **Dawns** *(NY617090)*
☎(05874) 622

Good, wholesome vegetarian cooking at this casual, friendly smallholding.

3rm (1fb) ® B&b£8 Bdi£13.50 W£88 ⥮ LDOnoon
🍴 3P

5acres smallholding

OSWESTRY
Shropshire
Map 7   SJ22

GH Ashfield Country House Llwyn-y-Maen, Trefonen Rd ☎(0691) 655200

Modern, purpose-built establishment 1½ miles south-west of town.

12⇨ (2fb) CTV in all bedrooms ⊙
✳B&b£20–£30 Bdi£27–£37 Wfr£130 ⥮
LDO5.30pm
Lic 🍴 30P

OTTERBURN
Northumberland
Map 12   NY89
See also **Elsdon** and **Rochester (Northumberland)**

FH Mrs A Anderson **Blakehope Burnhaugh** *(NT783002)* Byrness ☎(0830) 20267
Mar–Oct

Farmhouse in the Redesdale forest offering comfort and tranquility.

3hc (1fb) ✳B&b£8 Bdi£12.50 W£85 ⥮
LDO4pm
🍴 CTV 5P 3🐎 ♨ 150acres beef

Credit cards 1 2 3 4 5 Ⓥ

FH GF & MA Stephenson **Monkridge** *(NY913917)* ☎(0830) 20639
Feb–Nov

Hughslade Farm Okehampton, Devon

The farm is ideally situated for touring Devon, Cornwall. Dartmoor and Exmoor. Hughslade is a large working farm with plenty of animals around. The farmhouse is comfortably furnished. Lounge with colour TV and central heating on the ground floor. Meals served in the dining room, are minly made from home-produced vegetables and meat. Bed, breakfast and evening meal or bed and breakfast daily. Okehampton is just 2 miles from the farm and has a superb golf course, tennis courts and covered swimming pool. Horse riding available at the farm. Happy holiday assured. Our farmhouse has been offering holiday accommodation for the last 30 years. SAE please for terms to Mrs K C Heard, Hughslade Farm, Okehampton, Devon. Tel: Okehampton 2883.

Week Farm   Bridestowe, Okehampton, Devon EX20 4HZ
Telephone: Bridestowe (083 786) 221

Homely farmhouse accommodation with its friendly atmosphere set in peaceful surroundings ¾ mile from the main A30.
Ideal touring centre for both the north and south Coasts and Dartmoor with its beautiful walks and scenery.
Special Attractions: Lydford Gorge, Brentnor Church and Meldon Lake.
Local Activities: fishing, pony trekking, golf, tennis, also there is a heated swimming pool at Okehampton. Good home cooking is assured. Dining room with separate tables. Lounge with colour television. Washbasins in bedrooms. Fire Certificate held.
Proprietress: Mrs. Margaret Hockridge.

Well-cared for, comfortable farmhouse in the attractive environment of the Northumberland Moors.

2rm (1fb) ✖ LDO2pm
CTV 2P 1400acres arable beef sheep mixed

OTTERY ST MARY
Devon
Map **3**   SY19

FH Mrs S Hansford **Pitt Farm** *(SY089966)*
☎(040481) 2439
Closed Xmas

5rm (1hc) (2fb) ✖ ® ✲B&b£8.50–£10
Bdi£12.50–£14 W£87.50–£98 ⅄ LDO5pm
CTV 6P 190acres arable beef mixed
Ⓥ

OXENHOPE
West Yorkshire
Map **7**   SE03

FH Mrs A Scholes **Lily Hall** *(SE023362)*
Uppermarsh Ln ☎Haworth (0535) 43999
Closed Xmas

Stone built smallholding rearing cattle and geese, overlooking the moors near Haworth.

4hc ✖ ✲B&b£8–£9 Bdi£13–£14 W£80–£85 ⅄

Otterburn
—
Oxford

〽 CTV 12P nc5yrs 9acres mixed smallholding
Credit card ②

OXFORD
Oxfordshire
Map **4**   SP50

GH Bravalla 242 Iffley Rd ☎(0865) 241326
Small and homely guesthouse.

6hc (2fb) CTV in all bedrooms ®
✲B&b£10–£12 W£65–£84 Ⓜ
〽 CTV 6P
Ⓥ

GH Brown's 281 Iffley Rd ☎(0865) 246822
Homely family guesthouse, well-decorated and clean accommodation. 1m from city.

6hc (3fb) CTV in 4 bedrooms TV in 2 bedrooms ® ✲B&b£10–£13
〽 CTV 3P

GH Burren 374 Banbury Rd ☎(0865) 513513
Clean, well-decorated family house with spacious accommodation.

7hc (2🏠) (3fb) TV in all bedrooms ✖
✲B&b£10–£12
〽 CTV 5P nc3yrs
Ⓥ

GH Combermere 11 Polstead Rd
☎(0865) 56971
Apr–Oct
Small, friendly place, close to city centre, in residential area.

6hc (2fb) TV in all bedrooms ✖ ®
3P nc8yrs

GH Conifer 116 The Slade, Headington
☎(0865) 63055
Small, family-run establishment providing clean, comfortable bedrooms.

8hc (1⇄2🏠) (1fb) CTV in all bedrooms ✖
® ✲B&b£12–£22
〽 8P ⌲(heated)

GH Courtfield Private Hotel 367 Iffley Rd
☎(0865) 242991
Small, family-run house with modern, well-decorated bedrooms.

6hc (1⇄3🏠) (1fb) ✖ ✲B&b£16–£18
〽 CTV 6P 1🕿 nc3yrs
Ⓥ

See advertisement on page 292

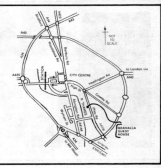

GH Dial House 25 London Rd, Headington (2m E) ☎(0865) 69944 Closed Xmas & New Year

7hc (1⇄ 2🏠) (3fb) CTV in all bedrooms Ⓡ ✱B&b£13–£15 W£91 Ⓜ

🍴 7P nc6yrs

Ⓥ

GH Earlmont 322–324 Cowley Rd ☎(0865) 240236

Friendly guesthouse with modern standards.

5hc Annexe: 7hc (5fb) ✂ in 1 bedroom CTV in 7 bedrooms TV in 1 bedroom ✗ ✱B&b£10.50–£13

🍴 CTV 11P 1🐾 nc5yrs

GH *Falcon* 88–90 Abingdon Rd ☎(0865) 722995 Closed 15 Dec–15 Jan

Accommodation here is above average and the lounge is comfortable.

10hc (2fb) ✗

🍴 CTV 10P

GH Galaxie Private Hotel 180 Banbury Rd ☎(0865) 515688

33hc (6⇄ 9🏠) (3fb) CTV in all bedrooms ✱B&b£14–£28

lift 🍴 CTV 26P

Ⓥ

GH Green Gables 326 Abingdon Rd ☎(0865) 725870 Closed 20 Dec–7 Jan

Detached family house about a mile south of the city centre.

8hc (3🏠) (3fb) CTV in all bedrooms ✗ Ⓡ ✱B&b£11–£15

🍴 8P

Ⓥ

COURTFIELD
PRIVATE HOTEL

367 IFFLEY ROAD
OXFORD OX4 4DP
Tel. Oxford (0865) 242991

Individually designed house, situated in tree lined road. Modern spacious bedrooms, majority 'en suite'. Close to the picturesque village of Iffley and River Thames yet easy access to City centre. Own private car park.

Galaxie Private Hotel
180 BANBURY ROAD, OXFORD
Reception: (0865) 515688 Guests: (0865) 53663

This is a small, select, family hotel, run under the personal supervision of the resident proprietors. Situated 1 mile from the city centre, and the colleges. All 30 bedrooms are fully equipped, have full central heating, colour TV, majority with private facilities. Lift. There is ample car parking. Terms include full English breakfast.

The hotel is open all year round and enjoys international patronage.

GreenGables

326 Abingdon Road, Oxford.
Telephone: Oxford (0865) 725870

Green Gables is an original Edwardian house, set in mature gardens, offering friendly, spacious accommodation.
Situated one mile south of Oxford city centre on the main Abingdon Road (A4144), Green Gables is convenient for visiting historic Oxford, Blenheim Palace, the Cotswolds and also Stratford upon Avon. All bedrooms have TV, tea and coffee making facilities and many of the rooms also have en-suite bathrooms. There is also a ground floor bedroom.

GH Micklewood 331 Cowley Rd ☎(0865) 247328

Simple and homely accommodation.

6hc (3fb) TV in all bedrooms 🚫🐕 ✱B&b£10–£11

♨ CTV 6P

[V]

GH Pickwicks 17 London Rd, Headington ☎(0865) 750487

Comfortable, detached corner house with good bedrooms.

8hc (3🛁 3🚿) (2fb) 🚭 in 2 bedrooms CTV in all bedrooms [R] ✱B&b£12–£18 Bdi£16–£23 Wfr£98 🚫🍴 LDO1pm

♨ CTV 12P 1🚗

GH Pine Castle 290 Iffley Rd ☎(0865) 241497

Homely guesthouse with comfortable, well-furnished rooms.

6hc (2fb) CTV in 4 bedrooms TV in 2 bedrooms [R] ✱B&b£10–£14 Bdi£14–£19 W£93–£126.50 🚫🍴 LDO8pm

♨ CTV 3P

[V]

GH *Red Mullions* 23 London Rd, Headington ☎(0865) 64727 Closed 1 wk Xmas

Spacious detached house with own garden offering comfortable, modern bedrooms.

Oxford — Oxhill

9rm (6hc 2🛁 4🚿) (4fb) CTV in 8 bedrooms 🚫🐕 [R]

♨ CTV 9P nc3yrs

GH Tilbury Lodge 5 Tilbury Ln, Botley ☎(0865) 862138

Spotlessly kept modern accommodation in quiet almost rural area away from city centre.

7hc (3🛁 3🚿) (3fb) 🚫🐕 B&b£12–£13

♨ CTV 7P 2🚗

[V]

GH Westgate Hotel 1 Botley Rd ☎(0865) 726721

Small, friendly family run hotel with simple accommodation.

13hc (1fb) CTV in all bedrooms 🚫🐕 [R] ✱B&b£16.50–£22 Bdi£21.50–£27 LDO8pm

Lic ♨ 12P

Credit card [3]

Recommended

GH Westwood Country Hotel
Hinksey Hill Top ☎(0865) 735408
Telex no 295141

Small hotel in lovely woodland setting on outskirts of the city.

26hc (17🛁 9🚿) (6fb) CTV in all bedrooms 🚫🐕 [R] ✱B&b£21–£35 Bdi£30–£45 LDO8pm

Lic ♨ CTV 25P ♿ gymnasium

Credit cards [1] [2] [3] [V]

See advertisement on page 241

GH Willow Reaches Private Hotel
1 Wytham St ☎(0865) 721545
rs 16 Dec–Jan

Small, homely guesthouse in a quiet residential area.

9hc (2🛁 2🚿) (2fb) CTV in all bedrooms 🚫🐕 [R] B&b£12.50–£29 Bdi£20–£36.50 LDO6.30pm

Lic ♨ CTV 4P 4🚗

Credit cards [2] [3] [5] [V]

See advertisement on page 294

OXHILL
Warwickshire
Map **4** SP34

FH Mrs S Hutsby **Nolands** *(SP312470)*
☎Kineton(0926) 640309
Closed Xmas
1m E Pillaton Priors on A422. →

Annexe: 6hc (4🛏) (4fb) CTV in 4 bedrooms ✗ ℝ ✱B&b£6.50–£10 Bdi£14 ㎝ CTV 8P 4🐾 nc3yrs ✦ ᘁ 300acres arable
ⓥ

OXWICH
West Glamorgan
Map **2**   SS58

GH Oxwich Bay Hotel Gower
☎Swansea (0792) 390329
Closed 25–28 Dec
Family holiday hotel, close to the beach.

Oxhill
—
Padstow

14hc (2fb) ✗ ℝ B&b£11.93–£14.85 Bdi£17.93–£21.85 W£125.50–£135.50 ⅃ LDO4.30pm
Lic ㎝ CTV 60P
Credit cards ① ② ③ ⑤ ⓥ

PADOG
Gwynedd
Map **6**   SH85

FH Mrs E A Jones **Pant Glas** *(SH846513)* Pentrefoelas Rd ☎Pentrefoelas (06905) 248
Etr–Oct
3m W of Betws-y-Coed, S of A5
3hc (1🛏) (1fb) ✗ ✱B&b£7.50–£8 Bdi£12–£12.50 LDO3.30pm
CTV 6P 1🐾 181acres beef sheep

PADSTOW
Cornwall
Map **2**   SW97

GH Alexandra 30 Dennis Rd ☎(0841) 532503
Mar–Oct

Willow Reaches Hotel
1 Wytham St., Oxford
Telephone: Oxford (0865) 721545 and 243767

A private hotel with a high standard of comfort, in a quiet location just a mile south of Oxford city centre.

The hotel is near a fishing lake and a public park with swimming pools and children's boating lake.

All bedrooms have service telephone, radio, colour television and tea/coffee-making facilities, some bathrooms en suite.

Central heating throughout. Residents' lounge with teletext TV, bar, restaurant, garden. Children welcome. Parking facilities.

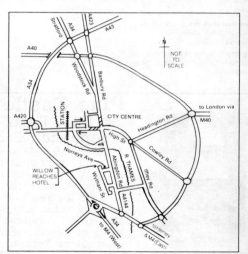

Oxwich Bay Hotel

Oxwich, Gower, West Glamorgan, South Wales SA3 1LS
Tel: (0792) 390329 (2 lines)
Terry, Margaret and Ian Williams

The hotel is situated just 60 yards from a beautiful three mile stretch of beach which is ideal for families. Safe bathing, yachting, water ski-ing and board saling with tuition can be enjoyed on the bay. Pony trekking and golf are nearby. Fully centrally heated, all 14 bedrooms are well appointed with tea and coffee making facilities, razor points and radio. Cots and high chairs provided.
The comfortable lounge has colour TV and there are facilities for various indoor games.
Bed and breakfast. Optional evening meal or restaurant à la carte menu. Sorry no pets.
The hotel also has a secluded caravan park offering serviced space for touring caravans, and self-catering caravan for hire.
Please write or phone Ian Williams (Dept 4) for free colour brochure.

6hc (2fb) CTV in all bedrooms ✗ ®
B&b£9.50–£10.50 Bdi£14.50–£15.50
W£90–£95 ⅃ LDO4pm
5P

GH *Dower House Private Hotel*
Fentonluna Ln ☎(0841) 532317
Etr–Oct

*A house of character with comfortable
bedrooms and friendly service.*

10hc (4fb) ® LDOnoon
Lic ♨ CTV 10P

GH *Tregea Hotel* High St ☎(0841)
532455

8hc (2fb) B&b£12–£16 Bdi£16.75–£20.85
Wfr£106.75 ⅃

Lic ♨ CTV 8P ♨

GH *Woodlands Hotel* Treator ☎(0841)
532426

At Treator 1m W B3276.

9fⅢ (3fb) ✻B&b£12.75–£13.50 Bdi£18.75–
£19.50 W£105.25–£112 ⅃ LDO4.30pm

Lic ♨ CTV 20P ♨

Ⓥ

PAIGNTON
Devon
Map **3** SX86
See plan on page 296

GH *Bayview Hotel* 6 Cleveland Rd
☎(0803) 557400 Plan **1** *C1*

Padstow
–
Paignton

*A bright, friendly, modern establishment
within walking distance of the sea front.*

10hc (3fb) ✗ ® ✻B&b£7.50–£9.50
Bdi£11.50–£13.50 W£70–£92 ⅃

Lic ♨ CTV 10P

Ⓥ

GH *Beresford* 1 Adelphi Rd ☎(0803)
551560 Plan **1A** *C2*

Closed Oct, Xmas & New Year

8hc (4fⅢ) (1fb) ✗ ® ✻B&b£8–£12 Bdi£12–
£16 W£72.50–£90 ⅃ (W only Jul–Aug)
LDO10am

Lic ♨ CTV 3P

Ⓥ

GH *Brackencroft* 3 St Andrews Rd
☎(0803) 556773 Plan **1B** *B2*

*Pleasantly-furnished villa within walking
distance of sea-front lawns.*

10hc (5fb) LDO6pm

♨ CTV 5P

GH *Cambria Hotel* Esplanade Rd, Sea
Front ☎(0803) 559256 Plan **2** *C3*

25hc (1fⅢ) ® ✻B&b£12–£14 Bdi£15–£18
W£80–£102 ⅃ LDO6pm

Lic ♨ CTV ⏣ ♨

GH *Channel View Hotel* 8 Marine Pde
☎(0803) 522432 Plan **3** *C4*

12hc (8fⅢ) (3fb) CTV in all bedrooms ®
✻B&bfr£8 Bdifr£10 Wfr£55 ⅃ LDOnoon

Lic ♨ CTV 12P

See advertisement on page 297

GH *Cherra Hotel* 15 Roundham Rd
☎(0803) 550723 Plan **4** *B1*
Mar–Oct

*Friendly, family-run private hotel close to
harbour. Good garden with putting green.*

14hc (3fⅢ) (7fb) CTV in all bedrooms ®
✻B&b£9–£12 Bdi£12–£15 W£80–£95 ⅃
LDO5pm

Lic ♨ CTV 14P

Ⓥ

See advertisement on page 297

GH *Clennon Valley Hotel* 1 Clennon Rise
☎(0803) 550304 Plan **5** *B1*
Closed Xmas

12hc (1☒ 9fⅢ) (3fb) CTV in 10 bedrooms
✻B&b£10–£13.50 Bdi£15–£17 W£85–
£115 ⅃ LDO5pm

Lic ♨ CTV 12P

GH *Commodore Hotel* 14 Esplanade Rd
☎(0803) 553107 Plan **6** *C2*
Etr–Oct

15hc (1fⅢ) (6fb) CTV in all bedrooms ®
B&b£9.14–£13.74 Bdi£11.78–£16.04
W£80.50–£114 ⅃

→

Lic CTV 7P nc2yrs
Ⓥ

GH Danethorpe Hotel 23 St Andrews Rd
☎(0803) 551251 Plan **7** *B1* ·
Apr–Oct

*Bright, spotlessly clean private hotel with
spacious public rooms.*

11hc (3🛏) (1fb) ✠ ✱B&b£9–£10 Bdi£13–
£15 W£90–£100 ⑀ LDO6pm
Lic ㎖ CTV 9P
Credit card ③ Ⓥ

GH *Orange Tubs Hotel* 14 Manor Rd
☎(0803) 551541 Plan **9** *C4*
Apr–Oct

11hc (6🛏) (2fb) ✠ Ⓡ LDO6.30pm
Lic ㎖ CTV 7P nc2yrs
Credit card ①
See advertisement on page 298

GH Preston Sands Hotel 12 Marine Pde,
Preston ☎(0803) 558718 Plan **10** *C4*
16hc (11🛏) (4fb) CTV in 6 bedrooms
✱B&b£8.50–£12 Bdi£12.50–£16.50
W£84–£108.50 ⑀ LDO4.30pm

Paignton

Lic ㎖ CTV 12P nc5yrs
Ⓥ

GH Radford Hotel 28–30 Youngs Park
Rd ☎(0803) 559671 Plan **11** *B1*
14hc (5fb) ✱B&b£6.50–£10.50 Bdi£9.75–
£13 W£56–£90 ⑀ LDO4pm
Lic ㎖ CTV 4P

GH *Redcliffe Lodge Hotel* 1 Marine Dr
☎(0803) 551394 Plan **12** *C4*
Mar–Nov

19 rm (13hc 7🛏6🛏) (3fb) CTV in 13
bedrooms ✠ Ⓡ LDO7pm
Lic ㎖ CTV 20P ᏹ
Credit card ③
See advertisement on page 298

GH Hotel Retreat 43 Marine Dr ☎(0803)
550596 Plan **12A** *C4*
Etr–Sep

---

*Comfortable, family-owned private hotel in
spacious gardens on the sea front.*

15hc (3🛏) (2fb) CTV in all bedrooms
✱B&b£10–£12 Bdi£14.50–£18 W£95–
£115 ⑀ LDO6pm
Lic CTV 14P
Credit cards ① ③ Ⓥ

GH St Weonard's Private Hotel
12 Kernou Rd ☎(0803) 558842 Plan **13** *B2*
Apr–Oct

9hc (4fb) ✠ Ⓡ ✱B&b£7.50–£11
Bdi£10.50–£13.50 W£68–£80 ⑀ LDO4pm
Lic CTV 2P
Ⓥ

GH Sattva Hotel 29 Esplanade Rd
☎(0803) 557820 Plan **15** *C3*
Etr–Oct

*Friendly, private hotel with comfortable,
modern bedrooms. Adjacent to seafront.*

24hc (3🛏9🛏) (6fb) ✠ Ⓡ ✱B&b£13–£17
Bdi£16.50–£20.50 W£99–£135 ⑀
LDO5.30pm

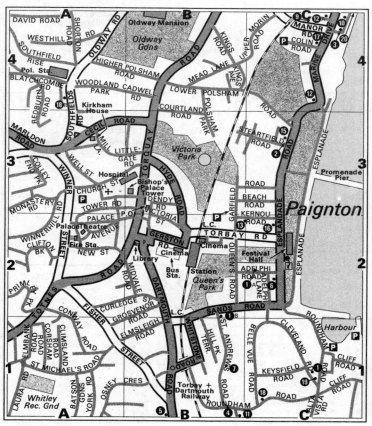

Paignton

298

Lic 🏨 CTV 10P
Credit card 1

GH Sealawn Hotel Sea Front ☎(0803)
559031 Plan **16** *C2*
*Semi-detached Victorian holiday hotel
opposite sea front.*
14hc (6⇄5🏠) (3fb) ⚥ in 3 bedrooms ®
CTV in all bedrooms B&b£14–£17 Bdi£18–
£21 W£84–£114 ⅃ LDO6pm
Lic 🏨 CTV 13P ⚓
Ⓥ

GH Sea Verge Hotel Marine Dr, Preston
☎(0803) 557795 Plan **17** *C4*
Closed Xmas
12hc (5🏠) (1fb) CTV in all bedrooms ✂
✳B&b£9–£12.50 Bdi£15–£18.50 W£105–
£129.50 ⅃ LDO4pm
Lic 🏨 CTV 12P nc5yrs
Credit cards 1 2 3 5

GH *Shorton House Hotel* 17 Roundham
Rd ☎(0803) 557722 Plan **18** *C1*
Mar–Nov
*Modern friendly hotel in an elevated
position with views of Goodrington beach.*
21hc (3🏠) Annexe: 2hc (9fb) ® LDO4pm
Lic 🏨 CTV 10P ⅋ snooker
Credit card 1

GH Singmore House Hotel Five Lanes
Rd, Marldon ☎(0803) 525547 Not on plan

Paignton
Parbold

*Small comfortable hotel situated just
outside Paignton in a semi-rural setting.*
10rm (8hc 1🏠) (4fb) TV in 3 bedrooms ®
✳B&b£8–£9 Bdi£12.50–£13.50 W£81.50–
£91.50 ⅃ LDO6pm
Lic 🏨 CTV 16P 3⚓ solarium
Credit card 3 Ⓥ

GH South Mount Hotel 7 Southfield Rd
☎(0803) 557643 Plan **18A** *A4*
Apr–Oct rs Jan–Mar & Nov
9hc (2🏠) (2fb) ✳B&b£8.50–£10
Bdi£11.50–£13.75 W£75–£85 ⅃ LDO10am
Lic CTV 7P
Ⓥ

See advertisement on page 300

GH Sunnybank Private Hotel
2 Cleveland Rd ☎(0803) 525540
Plan **19** *C1*
rs Nov–Feb
*Friendly, personal service at comfortable
private hotel.*
12hc (2🏠) (4fb) ✳B&b£8.50–£10 Bdi£12–
£14 W£62–£92 ⅃ LDO6pm
Lic 🏨 CTV 7P ⚓
Credit card 1 Ⓥ

GH Torbay Sands Hotel Sea Front, 16
Marine Pde, Preston ☎(0803) 525568
Plan **20** *C4*
12hc (3fb) ✳B&b£9.50–£12.50 Bdi£13.50–
£16.50 W£75–£99 ⅃ (W only Jul & Aug)
LDO1pm
Lic 🏨 CTV 7P
Ⓥ

PAISLEY
Strathclyde *Renfrewshire*
Map **11**   NS46
For accommodation details see **Glasgow
Airport**

PANTYGELLI (nr Abergavenny)
Gwent
Map **3**   SO31

FH Mrs M E Smith **Lower House**
(SO314159) Old Hereford Rd
☎Abergavenny (0873) 3432
Etr–Oct
*Isolated stone-built farmhouse with
mountain views, 3m from Abergavenny.*
3hc (1fb) ✳B&b£8–£8.50
CTV 6P 200acres beef sheep

PARBOLD
Lancashire
Map **7**   SD41

INN Wayfarer Alder Ln ☎(02576) 2542
*Attractive cottage-style building (C1668)
with well furnished bedrooms and
extensive a la carte menu.*   →

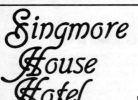

3hc (2⇌ 1fl) CTV in all bedrooms ®
✱B&b£10–£13 Bdi£14–£18 W£98–£130 ⅃
Lunch£4.95–£10.95&alc Dinner10pm
£4.95–£15&alc
🍴 26🐾
Credit card ① Ⓥ

PARKMILL (nr Swansea)
West Glamorgan
Map **2**   SS58

FH Mrs D Edwards *Parc-le-Breos House*
(SS529896) ☎Penmaen (044125) 636
1½m NW off A4118.

4hc (4fb) ✖
🍴 CTV P ♌ snooker 45acres mixed

PARRACOMBE
Devon
Map **3**   SS64

FH Mr H Bearryman *Lower Dean*
Trentishoe ☎(05983) 215
Mar–Sep

3m W unclass rd and ½m N off A399.

9hc (2⇌) (6fb) ✖
Lic 🍴 CTV 10P ♌ snooker 13acres mixed

PATELEY BRIDGE
North Yorkshire
Map **7**   SE16

───── *Recommended* ─────

**GH Grassfields Country House
Hotel** ☎Harrogate (0423) 711412
Mar–Oct

*An elegant Georgian country house
of listed architectural interest,
standing in 4 acres of gardens and
woodlands. The spacious and
comfortable bedrooms are equipped
with modern facilities whilst the well-
proportioned public areas are stylish
with an atmosphere of relaxed
charm.*

9hc (4⇌5fl) (3fb) ® B&b£16.50–
£17.50 Bdi£24.50–£25.50 LDO7pm
Lic 🍴 CTV 20P

┌─────────────────┐
│   **Parbold**   │
│   **–**   │
│   **Pencarreg**   │
└─────────────────┘

───── *Recommended* ─────

GH Roslyn 9 King St ☎Harrogate
(0423) 711374
Feb–Nov

*Ideally placed in a delightful Dales
town on the river Nidd, Roslyn House
offers good food and hospitality in
pleasant surroundings. The
bedrooms are full of charm and
character yet well-equipped with
modern facilities. There is also a cosy
lounge and a friendly bar.*

6hc (1⇌5fl) ✖ ® ✱B&b£10.50–
£13.50 Bdi£17.45–£20.45 W£112–
£120 ⅃ LDO4pm
Lic 🍴 CTV 3P nc

PEEBLES
Borders *Peeblesshire*
Map **11**   NT24

GH Lindores Old Town ☎(0721) 20441
Closed some wks Nov

*Neat house with combined lounge and
dining room.*

5hc (3fb) ✖ ✱B&b£8.50–£9 W£59.50–£63
M
🍴 CTV 3P
Ⓥ

GH Whitestone House Innerleithen Rd
☎(0721) 20337

*Neat, well-maintained guesthouse to E of
town.*

5hc (2fb) ✖ ✱B&b£8.50–£9
🍴 CTV 5P
Ⓥ

FH Mrs J M Haydock *Winkston*
(NT244433) Edinburgh Rd ☎(0721) 21264
Apr–Oct

*Nicely decorated farmhouse 1½ miles
north of town off Edinburgh road. Shower
room only, no bath.*

3hc ✖ ✱B&b£8.50–£9.25

15acres smallholding

PELYNT
Cornwall
Map **2**   SX25

FH Mrs L Tuckett **Trenderway**
(SX214533) ☎Polperro (0503) 72214
Etr–Oct

*Friendly accommodation and stylish
bedrooms at this 16th-century farmhouse
situated off the beaten track yet just 2
miles from Polperro and Looe.*

3hc ✖ ✱B&b£9–£10

🍴 CTV 3P 1🐾 nc8yrs 600acres arable
sheep

PEMBROKE
Dyfed
Map **2**   SM90

GH High Noon Lower Lamphey Rd
☎(0646) 683736

*Modern family-run guesthouse offering
relaxed accommodation and attentive
service.*

8hc (1fb) ✱B&b£8.50 Bdi£12 W£80 ⅃
Lic 🍴 CTV 8P
Ⓥ

PENARTH
South Glamorgan
Map **3**   ST17

GH Albany Hotel 14 Victoria Rd
☎Cardiff (0222) 701598

*Stone-built house in quiet road with
residents' bar.*

14hc (1⇌4fl) (4fb) CTV in all bedrooms
✖ B&bfr£15.50
Lic 🍴 CTV 3P
Credit card ①

PENCARREG
Dyfed
Map **2**   SN54

INN Red Lion ☎Llanybyther (0570)
480018

*Good, homely food and comfortable
bedrooms at cosy inn.*

3hc (2fl) ® ✱B&b£10–£12 Bdi£14.50–
£16.50 Lunch £4.50&alc Dinner9pm
£4.50&alc

CTV 20P

Credit cards ① ③

PENMACHNO
Gwynedd
Map **6**   SH75

FH M Jones **Tyddyn Gethin** (SH799514)
☎(06903) 392
Feb–Nov

Farm situated high on mountainside with panoramic views of the surrounding country.

3hc ✕ ✳B&b£7.50–£8 Bdi£12 W£84 ∦
CTV P nc2yrs 80acres mixed
Ⓥ

PENNANT
Dyfed
Map **2**   SN56

GH Bikerehyd Farm (Guestaccom)
☎Nebo (09746) 365
Feb–Nov

Accommodation is in three carefully restored 14th-century cottages adjacent to main building. Full of character.

3hc Annexe: 3🛏 CTV in 3 bedrooms Ⓡ
✳B&b£13–£16 Bdifr£21–£24 W£125–£140 ∦ LDO6pm

Lic ⑭ CTV P nc8yrs
Ⓥ

PENRHYNDEUDRAETH
Gwynedd
Map **6**   SH63

FH Mrs P Bayley **Y Wern** (SH620421)
Llanfrothen (2m N off B4410) ☎(0766) 770556

Large 17th-century house with good family bedrooms. Ideal location for touring Southern Snowdonia.

4hc (3fb) ✕ Ⓡ ✳B&bfr£7 Bdifr£11.50 Wfr£70 ∦ LDO6.30pm

⑭ CTV P

110acres beef sheep

PENRITH
Cumbria
Map **12**   NY53

GH Brandelhow 1 Portland Pl ☎(0768) 64470

Town centre house offering neat, comfortable accommodation.

6hc (3fb) CTV in 5 bedrooms Ⓡ
✳B&b£7.50–£8.50 Bdi£11.50–£12.50
W£77–£84 ∦ LDO5pm
⑭ CTV 1P
Ⓥ

GH Limes Country Hotel Redhills
Stainton (2m W A66) ☎(0768) 63343
Mar–Oct

Clean accommodation in a large house near junction 40 of the M6.

8hc (2fb) ✕
⑭ CTV 12P

GH Pategill Villas Carleton Rd ☎(0768) 63153
Closed Xmas rs Jan–Mar

Spacious guesthouse in its own attractive gardens.

12hc Annexe: 1hc (6fb) ✳B&b£9–£10.50
W£63–£73.50 Ṁ
Lic ⑭ CTV 13P
Ⓥ

GH Woodland House Hotel Wordsworth
St ☎(0768) 64177

Red-sandstone house with attractive public rooms.

8hc (2🛏) (2fb) ⚡ in 2 bedrooms CTV in 2 bedrooms ✕ ✳B&b£10.50–£12.50
Bdi£15.50–£17.50 W£99–£113 ∦ LDO4pm
Lic ⑭ CTV 10P 1🛇
Ⓥ

PENRUDDOCK
Cumbria
Map **12**   NY42

FH Mrs S M Smith **Highgate** (NY444275)
☎Greystoke (08533) 339
Feb–Nov

250-year old stone-built farmhouse with beamed ceilings; tastefully modernised. Good base for touring and recreational facilities. Situated on the A66 Penrith to Keswick road 1m E of village and 4m W of M6 junc 40.

4rm (3hc) (1fb) ⚡ in 2 bedrooms CTV in all bedrooms ✕ Ⓡ ✳B&b£10–£11
Bdi£15–£16 W£86–£90 ∦ LDO6pm
⑭ 4P nc10yrs 400acres beef dairy sheep mixed

PENYBONT
Powys
Map **3**   SO16

GH Ffaldau Country House Llandegley
(2m E A44) ☎(059787) 421

Good home-cooking is a speciality at this authentic 16th-century crook-frames farmhouse.

3hc (1🛏) ✕ ✳B&b£10.50–£12.50
LDO9pm
Lic ⑭ CTV 25P

PENZANCE
Cornwall
Map **2**   SW43
See plan on page 302

GH Beachfield Hotel The Promenade
☎(0736) 62067 Plan **3** B1
Mar–Nov

32hc (12🛏) (2fb) Ⓡ
Lic ⑭ CTV ⚡

GH Bella-Vista Private Hotel
7 Alexandra Ter, Lariggan ☎(0736) 62409
Plan **4** A1
Feb–Nov

Simple, homely guesthouse with views over Mounts Bay.

10hc (5fb) ✕ Ⓡ ✳B&b£9–£14 Bdi£14–£19
W£98–£133 ∦ LDO4pm
Lic ⑭ CTV 8P nc3yrs
Credit cards ① ③ Ⓥ

See advertisement on page 303

GH Blue Seas Hotel (formerly Killindini
Private Hotel) 13 Regent Ter ☎(0736)
64744 Plan **12** D2

Regency terraced house, comfortably appointed offering friendly service.

12hc (1🛇 4🛏) (5fb) CTV in all bedrooms
✕ B&b£9–£13 Bdi£14–£18 W£98–£125 ∦
LDO5.30pm
Lic ⑭ P nc5yrs

See advertisement on page 303

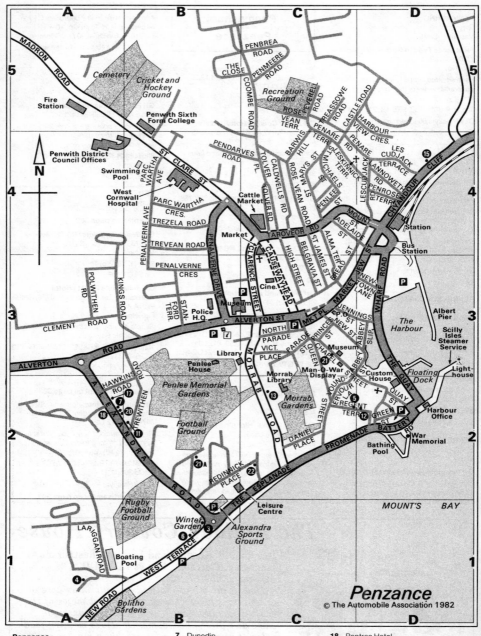

Penzance

© The Automobile Association 1982

Penzance

3 Beachfield Hotel
4 Bella-Vista Private Hotel
5 Camilla Hotel
6 Carlton Private Hotel

7 Dunedin
11 Holbein House Hotel
12 Blue Seas Hotel
13 Kimberley House
15 Mount Royal Hotel
17 Penmorvah Hotel

18 Pentrea Hotel
20 Trenant Private Hotel
21 Trevelyan Hotel
21A Trewella
22 Willows

GH Camilla Hotel Regent Ter ☎(0736) 63771 Plan **5** *C2*

Character Regency residence with comfortable friendly family atmosphere, positioned close to promenade.

10hc (1⇌ 2fl) (2fb) ✱B&b£8.50–£11 Bdi£13–£15.50 W£88–£97.50 ⱡ LDO6pm

Lic ♨ CTV 6P

ⓥ

GH Carlton Private Hotel ☎(0736) 62081 Plan **6** *B1*
Mar–Oct

Small modest family hotel, personally-run, and positioned on sea front offering commanding views.

12hc (5fl) CTV in all bedrooms ✈ Ⓡ ✱B&b£10–£14 Bdi£15.50–£19.50 W£90–£100 ⱡ LDO4pm

Lic CTV P̸ nc12yrs

ⓥ

GH Dunedin Alexandra Rd ☎(0736) 62652 Plan **7** *A2*
Closed Jan

Very comfortable, small, personally-run guesthouse positioned close to sea front.

9hc (1fl) (4fb) CTV in all bedrooms Ⓡ ✱B&b£8.50–£9.50 Bdi£13.50–£14.50 W£80–£95 ⱡ LDO4.30pm

Lic ♨ CTV P̸

GH Holbein House Hotel Alexandra Rd ☎(0736) 65008 Plan **11** *B2*

Penzance

Small comfortable family hotel, personally-run and positioned in quiet area leading to sea front.

10⇌fl (7fb) CTV in all bedrooms Ⓡ B&b£9–£15 Bdi£14.50–£20.50 W£90–£134 ⱡ LDO8.30pm

Lic ♨ CTV P̸

Credit card ③

GH Kimberley House 10 Morrab Rd (Guestaccom) ☎(0736) 62727 Plan **13** *C2*
Closed Nov

Small tastefully furnished residence offering warm and friendly welcome from resident proprietors.

9hc (2fb) CTV in 6 bedrooms ✈ Ⓡ ✱B&b£9–£10 Bdi£14.25–£15.25 W£92–£96 ⱡ LDO5pm

Lic ♨ CTV 4P nc5yrs

Credit cards ① ③

See advertisement on page 304

GH Mount Royal Hotel Chyandour Cliff ☎(0736) 62233 Plan **15** *D4*
Mar–Oct

Small family hotel facing sea and harbour.

8hc (3⇌) (1fb) B&b£12–£14 W£80.50–£94.50 M

♨ CTV 8P 4🚗

ⓥ

GH Penmorvah Hotel Alexandra Rd ☎(0736) 63711 Plan **17** *A2*
Closed Xmas

Personally-run private hotel with comfortable accommodation.

10hc (5⇌ 5fl) (4fb) CTV in all bedrooms Ⓡ ✱B&b£13–£14 Bdi£20–£22 W£115–£130 ⱡ LDO6pm

Lic ♨ P̸

Credit cards ① ② ③

See advertisement on page 304

GH Pentrea Hotel Alexandra Rd ☎(0736) 69576 Plan **18** *A2*

9hc (2fl) (2fb) CTV in all bedrooms Ⓡ ✱B&b£9–£11 Bdi£14–£15.50 W£87–£98 ⱡ LDO6pm

Lic ♨ CTV 1🚗(charge)

Credit cards ① ③

GH Trenant Private Hotel Alexandra Rd ☎(0736) 62005 Plan **20** *A2*
Jan–Oct

A personally-run guesthouse, with interesting antiques, close to local amenities.

10hc (1fl) (5fb) CTV in 1 bedroom Ⓡ ✱B&b£8.50–£12.50 Bdi£13–£18 W£84–£115 ⱡ LDO4pm

♨ CTV P̸ nc4yrs

ⓥ

GH *Trevelyan Hotel* 16 Chapel St
☎(0736) 62494 Plan **21** *C3*
Closed Xmas

17th-century property offering comfortable accommodation within town centre.

8hc (1⍾) (4fb) ⌘ LDOnoon

Lic ☗ CTV 8P

⊢**GH Trewella** 18 Mennaye Rd
☎(0736) 63818 Plan **21A** *B2*
Etr–Oct

Cosy little guesthouse with good home-cooking about two minutes from sea front.

8hc (3fb) B&b£7.50–£8.50 Bdi£11–£12 W£72–£80 Ɫ LDO4.30pm

Lic CTV ⌀ nc3yrs

Ⓥ

GH Willows Cornwall Ter ☎(0736) 63744 Plan **22** *C2*

Victorian corner house with attractive gardens.

7hc (1fb) Ⓡ B&b£9.50–£10.50 Bdi£15.50–£16.50 W£103–£110 Ɫ LDO5pm

☗ CTV 6P nc5yrs

Ⓥ

PERRANPORTH
Cornwall
Map **2** SW75

GH Cellar Cove Hotel Droskyn Way
☎Truro (0872) 572110

Penzance — Perth

14hc (4fb) CTV in all bedrooms Ⓡ
✱B&b£10.50–£12.50 Bdi£16.50–£18.50 W£95–£120 Ɫ (W only mid Jul–Aug)

Lic CTV 20P ⌂

Credit cards 1 3 Ⓥ

GH Fairview Hotel Tywarnhayle Rd
☎Truro (0872) 572278
Mar–Sep

Good views from this comfortable family hotel.

15hc (6fb) Ⓡ ✱B&b£10–£11 Bdi£14–£15.50 W£87.50–£103.50 Ɫ LDO5pm

Lic ☗ CTV 6P

GH *Lamorna Private Hotel* Tywarnhayle Rd ☎Truro(0872) 573398
Closed Xmas

Comfortable personally-run small family hotel.

10hc (4fb) Ⓡ ✱B&b£10–£12 Bdi£14–£17 W£85–£98 Ɫ LDO5pm

Lic CTV ⌀

GH Villa Margarita Private Hotel
Bolingey ☎Truro (0872) 572063

Exceptionally well-appointed colonial-style villa. Turn off A3075 at Perranzabuloe Church, Bolingey approx 1m NW of this junction.

5hc (3⍾) Annexe: 2⍾ (1fb) ⌘ Ⓡ
✱B&b£11.35–£12.50 Bdi£18.85–£20 W£114–£122 Ɫ LDO6pm

Lic CTV 8P nc8yrs ♨ solarium

PERTH
Tayside *Perthshire*
Map **11** NO12

⊢**GH Clark Kimberley** 57–59 Dunkeld Rd ☎(0738) 37406

Pleasant family-type bedrooms available on a bed-and-breakfast basis.

8hc (5fb) B&b£8–£9 W£56–£63 M

☗ CTV 12P

Ⓥ

GH Clunie 12 Pitcullen Cres ☎(0738) 23625
Closed Xmas & New Year

7hc (1⇌ 4⍾) (3fb) CTV in all bedrooms ⌘ Ⓡ B&b£10 Bdi£15.50 Wfr£108.50 Ɫ

☗ 7P

Ⓥ

GH Darroch 9 Pitcullen Cres ☎(0738) 36893

A very pleasant guesthouse set on the northern outskirts of the city.

6hc (3🚿) (3fb) CTV in all bedrooms 🐕 [R]
*B&b£9–£11 Bdi£14–£16 W£94.50–£105
L LDO5pm

♨ CTV 10P

[V]

GH Gables 24–26 Dunkeld Rd ☎(0738) 24717

Two adjoining houses on a busy junction N of the town.

8hc (3fb) CTV in 5 bedrooms *B&b£8.50–£10 Bdi£11.50–£15 W£56–£70 M
LDO4pm

♨ CTV 6P

Credit cards [1] [3] [V]

GH Iona 2 Pitcullen Cres ☎(0738) 27261

Small well-appointed house with modern bedrooms and pleasant public rooms.

6hc (1fb) [R] *B&b£9.50–£12 Wfr£60 M

♨ CTV 6P

GH Pitcullen 17 Pitcullen Cres ☎(0738) 26506
Mar–Oct rs Feb

A stone-built guesthouse providing comfortable bedrooms on a bed-and-breakfast basis.

6hc (2fb) [R] B&bfr£9 Bdifr£14 Wfr£95 L
5.30pm

♨ CTV 6P

[V]

PETERSFIELD
Hampshire
Map **4** SU72

GH *Concorde Hotel* 1 Weston Rd ☎(0730) 63442

8hc (2fb) TV in 2 bedrooms 🐕 [R] LDO5pm

Lic ♨ CTV 12P

Credit cards [1] [3]

PETWORTH
West Sussex
Map **4** SU92

GH Almshouses Tillington ☎(0798) 43432
Closed Xmas

2hc (1🚿) (1fb) CTV in all bedrooms [R]
*B&b£12–£16 W£77–£105 M

♨ CTV 6P nc6yrs

See advertisement on page 306

PEVENSEY BAY
East Sussex
Map **5** TQ60

GH Napier The Promenade ☎Eastbourne (0323) 768875

6hc (2fb) TV in 2 bedrooms *B&b£9–£12 Bdi£12.50–£15.50 Wfr£70 L LDO4.30pm

Lic ♨ CTV 6P 🎣

[V]

PICKERING
North Yorkshire
Map **8** SE88

GH Cottage Leas Country Middleton ☎(0751) 72129

Converted 18th-century farmhouse with antique bric-a-brac.

12hc (1🛁 4🚿) (2fb) CTV in 6 bedrooms TV in 6 bedrooms [R] *B&b£12.50–£15 Bdi£19.50–£22 LDO9pm

Lic ♨ 30P 🎾(hard) solarium

Credit card [5] [V]

See advertisement on page 306

PILSDON
Dorset
Map **3** SY49

FH K B Brooks ***Monkwood*** *(SY429986)* ☎Broadwindsor (0308) 68723

Thatched farmhouse with pleasant views. Charmouth 6m, Bridport 5m.

2rm (1fb) 🐕

CTV P 160acres beef dairy sheep mixed

PILTON
Somerset
Map **3** ST54

GH Long House ☎(074989) 701
mid Feb–mid Dec

Delightful little hotel in 17th-century building set in charming historic village.

7hc (3🛁 3🚿) (1fb) *B&b£16.25–£23 Bdi£24.50–£31 W£134.75–£180.25 L
LDO6.30pm

Lic ♨ 8P nc6yrs

Credit cards [1] [2] [3] [5] [V]

PITLOCHRY
Tayside *Perthshire*
Map **14** NN95

See plan on page 307

GH *Adderley Private Hotel* 23, Toberargan Rd ☎(0796) 2433
Plan **1** *C3*
Etr–mid Oct

Small family-run hotel, close to town centre.

10hc (1fb) [R] *B&b£9.60–£10.50 Bdi£14.70–£15.70 W£67.40–£70.40 M
LDO5pm

♨ CTV 9P nc6yrs

[V]

Recommended

GH Balrobin Hotel Higher Oakfield ☎(0796) 2901 Plan **2** *D3*
Apr–Oct

Neatly appointed guest house.

8hc (1🛁 4🚿) (1fb) CTV in all bedrooms [R] B&b£11–£12 Bdi£16–£19.50 W£114–£131 L LDO6.40pm

Lic ♨ 10P nc12yrs

[V]

GH Craigmore 27 West Moulin Rd ☎(0796) 2123 Not on plan
Mar–Oct

A secluded location for this stone built house with cottage annexe. Comfortable, well-maintained accommodation.

7hc (2🛁 1🚿) Annexe: 8hc (4fb) *B&bfr£10 Bdifr£16.50 LDO6.30pm

Lic CTV 13P

Recommended

GH Dundarave House Strathview Ter ☎(0796) 3109 Plan **2A** *B3*
Apr–Oct

A charming and well-appointed late Victorian house set in formal, terraced gardens with views over the town. A hearty Scottish breakfast is served in the dining room. The owners aim to provide personal and friendly attention in relaxing surroundings.

7hc (5🛁) (1fb) CTV in all bedrooms [R] *B&b£16

8P

See advertisement on page 308

The Almshouses

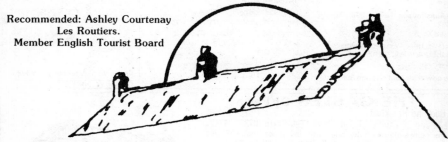

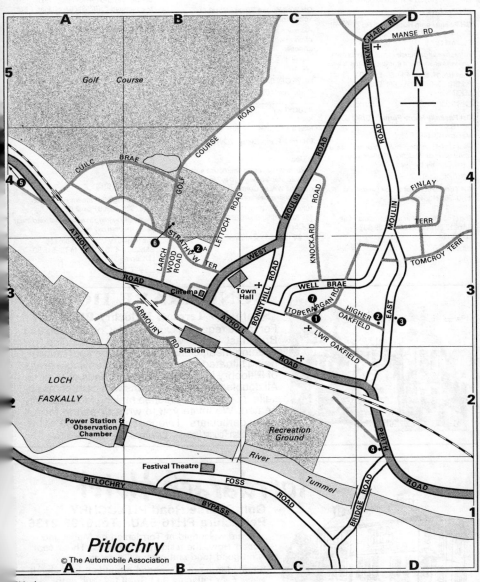

Pitlochry

1 Adderley Private Hotel
2 Balrobin Hotel
2A Dundarave
3 Duntrune
4 Fasganeoin Hotel
5 Faskally Home Farm
6 Torrdarach Hotel
7 Well House Private Hotel

GH Duntrune 22 East Moulin Rd ☎(0796)
2172 Plan **3** *D3*
Etr–Oct

Pleasantly furnished house.

7hc (3▥) (1fb) CTV in all bedrooms ✱ ®
▥ 8P nc5yrs

GH Fasganeoin Hotel Perth Rd ☎(0796)
2387 Plan **4** *D2*
Etr–mid Oct

*Attractive large house standing in its own
grounds at southern entrance to the town.*

9hc (4fb) ✱ ✲B&b£11.50–£12.50
Bdi£18.50–£19.50 W£124–£131.50½
LDO7.30pm

Lic ▥ 20P

GH Faskally Home Farm ☎(0796) 2007
Plan **5** *A4*
Mar–mid Oct

*Pleasant 'U-shaped' building on west side
of A9 north of Pitlochry. Sheltered from
Loch Faskally by trees.*

8rm (6hc) (2fb)

GH Torrdarach Hotel Golf Course Rd
☎(0796) 2136 Plan **6** *B4*
Etr–mid Oct

7hc (1⇄ 2▥) CTV in all bedrooms ✱ ®
B&b£12.50 Bdi£18.50 W£139.50½
LDO6pm

Lic ▥ 8P ♨
Ⓥ

Pitlochry
—
Plymouth

GH Well House Private Hotel 11
Toberargan Rd ☎(0796) 2239 Plan **7** *C3*

*Pleasant, small, family-run, private hotel
offering wholesome dinners and personal
attention.*

7hc ✱ ® B&b£10–£11 Bdi£16–£17
W£110–£117½LDO7.15pm

Lic ▥ CTV 8P

Credit cards ① ③

PLUCKLEY
Kent
Map **5**   TQ94

FH Mrs F Harris **Elvey** *(TQ916457)*
☎(023384) 442
rs Dec

*Detached converted oasthouse and
modern stableblock with extensive views
over the Weald. Comfortable bedrooms.
Traditional meals served in farmhouse.*

10hc (7⇄ 3▥) (6fb) CTV in all bedrooms
® B&bfr£15.50 Bdifr£25.50 W£165½
LDO5pm

Lic ▥ 12P ♨ 75acres mixed Ⓥ

PLYMOUTH
Devon
Map **2**   SX45
See plan on pages 310–311

GH Benvenuto 69 Hermitage Rd,
Mannamead ☎(0752) 667030 Plan **1** *E8*
rs Xmas

*End of terrace Victorian property 1 mile
from the city centre.*

8hc (2fb) ® ✱B&b£9–£9.50 Bdi£13–
£13.50 Wfr£87.50½LDO4pm

Lic ▥ CTV ⚲
Ⓥ

GH Bowling Green Hotel 9–10 Osborne
Pl, Lochyer St, The Hoe ☎(0752) 667485
Plan **1A** *C2*

*Double-fronted Georgian hotel
overlooking Drake's famous bowling
green.*

12hc (4fb) CTV in all bedrooms ®
B&b£17.50–£25

▥ CTV ⚲

Credit cards ① ③

GH Cadleigh 36 Queens Rd, Lipson
☎(0752) 665909 Plan **2** *F8*

*Redbrick building in residential road, near
park, 1m from city centre.*

8hc (4fb) CTV in all bedrooms ®
B&b£9.75–£10.90 Bdi£14.75–£15.90
LDO6pm

Lic ▥ CTV ⚲

Plymouth

GH Carnegie Hotel 172 Citadel Rd, The Hoe ☎(0752) 225158 Plan **2A** *B3*
Closed Xmas wk

9hc (2fb) 🐕 Ⓡ B&b£11.50–£15 Bdi£18–£23 W£117–£138 K LDO7.30pm

Lic 🍽 CTV P̸

Credit cards [1] [2] [3] [5] [V]

GH Chester 54 Stuart Rd, Pennycomequick ☎ (0752) 663706 Plan **3** *A7*

Detached house in large, walled garden, 1m from city centre; walking distance to shops and Hoe.

9hc (2🚿) (2fb) CTV in all bedrooms *B&b£10 Bdi£15 LDOnoon

Lic 🍽 CTV 7P

GH Cranbourne Hotel 282 Citadel Rd, The Hoe ☎(0752) 263858 Plan **3A** *C3*
Closed last 2 wks Dec

Modern comforts are provided in this end of terrace Georgian hotel.

10hc (3fb) CTV in all bedrooms *B&b£9–£12 W£63–£84 M

Lic 🍽 CTV P̸

[V]

GH Drakes View Hotel 33 Grande Pde, West Hoe ☎(0752) 221500 Plan **3B** *B1*
Closed Xmas wk

Listed building facing Drake's Island with glorious views over the Sound. Comfortable bedrooms.

6hc (3fb) CTV in all bedrooms Ⓡ *B&b£10–£12.50

Lic 🍽 CTV ⌂

Credit cards [1] [3] [V]

See advertisement on page 312

Elvey Farm

Pluckley, Nr Ashford, Kent
Tel: Pluckley (023384) 442

Together with Elvey Farm Oast House featured in the 1984 edition as one of the most interesting and unusual places to stay we now offer accommodation in the converted stables and old Kent barn, giving traditional charm and comfort with modern luxury and convenience. Double and family bedrooms, all with private bath/shower rooms and colour TV.
Children and pets are welcome on our family working farm for a happy homely holiday.

BOWLING GREEN HOTEL

Overlooking the Famous Green itself and very close to City Centre and Sea-Front. In all rooms we have provided:
• Showers • Radio • Intercom • Colour T.V. • Tea/Coffee making facilities
An elegant Breakfast Room on the ground floor where full English Breakfast is served and Continental Breakfast for the very early risers.
Contact Resident Proprietor Arend J. van der Marel.

BOWLING GREEN HOTEL

9-10 Osborne Place, Lockyer Street, Plymouth PL1 2PU
Telephone: (0752) 667485

Carnegie Hotel

Licensed

172 CITADEL ROAD, THE HOE, PLYMOUTH, PL1 3BD

Telephone: Plymouth (0752) 25158.

Resident Proprietors Mr. and Mrs. Richard C. Pither
If you like a warm friendly atmosphere and a high standard of service, then Richard & Jo will be pleased to welcome you at their licensed Hotel at the Hoe. All bedrooms have shaver points, tea/coffee making facilities, radio alarm clocks & some have showers. Close Brittany Ferries Terminal. Unrestricted street parking & large car park within 100 yards.

Plymouth

- **1** Benvenuto
- **1A** Bowling Green Hotel
- **2** Cadleigh
- **2A** Carnegie Hotel
- **3** Chester
- **3A** Cranbourne Hotel
- **3B** Drakes View Hotel
- **4** Dudley
- **5** Gables End Hotel
- **6** Georgian House Hotel
- **7** Headland Hotel
- **8** Kildare
- **9** Lockyer House Hotel
- **10** Merville Hotel
- **10A** Olivers Hotel
- **11** Riviera Hotel
- **11A** Russell Lodge Hotel
- **12** St James Hotel
- **12A** Smeaton's Tower
- **14** Trillium

GH Dudley 42 Sutherland Rd, Mutley ☎(0752) 668322 Plan **4** *D8*
rs Xmas

Double-fronted house in quiet residential street.

6hc (3fb) CTV in all bedrooms [R] ✱B&bfr£10 Bdifr£16 Wfr£101.50 ⱡ LDO9am

♨ CTV P

Credit cards [1] [3]

GH *Gables End Hotel* 29 Sutherland Rd, Mutley ☎(0752) 20803 Plan **5** *D7*

7hc (3fb) 🚫🐕 LDO6pm

♨ CTV 3🚗(charged)

Recommended

GH Georgian House Hotel 51 Citadel Rd, The Hoe ☎(0752) 663237 Plan **6** *B3*

Tastefully converted Georgian town house providing good food and friendly service.

10hc (4🛁 6🚿) (1fb) CTV in all bedrooms [R] ✱B&b£19.95–£21 LDO9.30pm

Lic ♨ CTV 2P

Credit cards [1] [2] [3] [5] [V]

See advertisement on page 312

GH Headland Hotel Radford Rd, West Hoe ☎(0752) 660866 Plan **7** *B2*

Lounge corner hotel with easy access to Plymouth Hoe and the Barbican.

Annexe: 28rm 15hc (7🛁 6🚿) (5fb) [R]

♨ CTV

GH *Kildare* 82 North Road East ☎(0752) 29375 Plan **8** *D7*

8hc (1🛁) (3fb) 🚫🐕 [R]

♨ CTV P̸

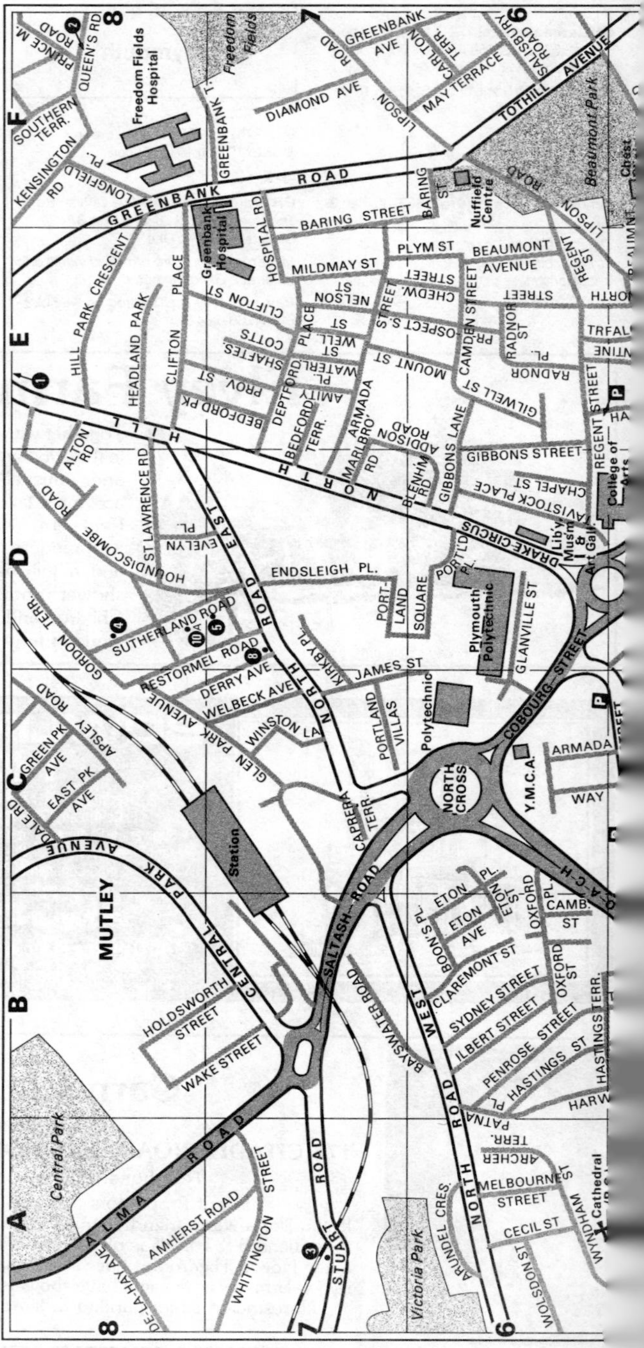

Plymouth

COXSIDE

MILLBAY

GH Lockyer House Hotel 2 Alfred St, The Hoe ☎ (0752) 665755 Plan **9** *C3*

An end of terrace Georgian house situated in quiet side street, although close to city centre.

6hc (1fb) ✱B&b£9.90–£11 Bdi£17.05–£18.15 W£119.35–£127.05 Ⱡ

Ⓥ

GH Merville Hotel 73 Citadel Rd, The Hoe ☎(0752) 667595 Plan **10** *B3*

10hc (3fb) Ⓡ ✱B&b£9–£10 Bdi£13.95–£14.95 W£90–£97 Ⱡ LDO3pm

Lic 🍴 CTV 2P

Plymouth

GH Olivers Hotel 33 Sutherland Rd, The Hoe ☎(0752) 663923 Plan **10A** *D8*

Victorian building with friendly atmosphere and excellent food.

6hc (2fb) TV in all bedrooms 🚫 Ⓡ ✱B&b£11.50–£12 Bdi£17–£17.50 W£110–£113 Ⱡ LDO9.30pm

Lic 🍴 CTV 3P nc8yrs

Credit cards [1] [2] [3] [5] Ⓥ

GH Riviera Hotel 8 Elliott St, The Hoe ☎(0752) 667379 Plan **11** *C2*
Closed Xmas

Personally run hotel on Plymouth Hoe with very well equipped bedrooms.

11hc (6🛁) (3fb) CTV in all bedrooms Ⓡ ✱B&b£13–£20 Bdi£19–£26 W£128–£141 Ⱡ LDO4pm

Lic 🍴 Ᵽ

Credit cards [1] [2] [3] [5] Ⓥ

GH Russell Lodge Hotel 9 Holyrood Pl, The Hoe ☎(0752) 667774 Plan **11A** *C2*

Terraced Georgian residence just 5 minutes walk from city centre.

Georgian House Hotel
and Fourposter Restaurant

51 Citadel Road, The Hoe, Plymouth
Telephone: management 663237
visitors 667166

Licensed hotel near famous Plymouth Hoe, the ferry port, shopping centre and theatres. All rooms with private shower and toilet, colour TV, radio and tea making facilities.

Drake's View Hotel

33, Grand Parade, West Hoe, Plymouth, Devon.
Telephone: (0752) 221500 Proprietress: Mrs. Jill Russell

Sample the delights of this popular hotel, favoured by world-wide yachtsmen, business people, actors from nearby Theatre Royal, honeymooners, families who just want to relax.

The welcoming, caring atmosphere in this beautiful listed historical building with breath taking views is unrivalled in the West.

Sun patio, garden, with the sea only feet away. Pause and watch the ships, yachts and ferry pass by.

Tea and coffee making facilities, colour TV in all rooms, licensed bar, sun loungers provided, drinks served by your friendly proprietress. Central heating, pets welcome.
Highest Standards maintained.
Two minutes drive Brittany Ferry and Theatre Royal.

10hc (2fb) 🚭 in 2 bedrooms CTV in 6 bedrooms [R] *B&b£10–£11.50 Wfr£67.50 M̸

♨ CTV 3P

Credit cards [1] [2] [3] [5]

GH St James Hotel 49 Citadel Rd, The Hoe ☎(0752) 661950 Plan **12** *B3*
Closed Xmas

10🛁🚿 (1fb) CTV in all bedrooms [R] *B&b£15–£18 Bdi£20.95–£23.95 LDO6pm

Lic ♨ P̸ nc6yrs

Credit cards [1] [3] [V]

GH *Smeaton's Tower* 44 Grand Pde ☎(0752) 21007 Plan **12A** *B1*

18hc (6fb) CTV in all bedrooms 🚫🐕 [R] LDO9pm

Lic CTV P̸

GH Trillium 4 Alfred St, The Hoe (Guestaccom) ☎ (0752) 670452 Plan **14** *C3*
Closed 2 wks Xmas

5hc (1fb) 🚫🐕 [R] *B&b£10–£12 Bdi£15–£17 W£98–£112 Ⱡ LDO4pm

Lic ♨ CTV 3P nc5yrs

Credit cards [1] [2] [3]

Plymouth — Polzeath

POLBATHIC
Cornwall
Map **2** SX35

GH Old Mill ☎St Germans (0503) 30596

8hc (2fb) B&b£9 Bdi£14.50–£17 W£95–£110 LDO7.30pm

Lic CTV 12P 1🚗 🐴

[V]

POLMASSICK
Cornwall
Map **2** SW94

GH Kilbol House ☎Mevagissey (0726) 842481

7hc (3🛁 1🚿) (1fb) *B&b£13.80–£16.10 Bdi£19.55–£21.85 W£133.40–£149.50 Ⱡ LDO5pm

Lic ♨ CTV 12P ⛱

Credit cards [1] [2] [3] [5] [V]

POLPERRO
Cornwall
Map **2** SX25

GH Landaviddy Manor Landaviddy Ln ☎(0503) 72210
Mar–Oct

Charming country house of Cornish stone, furnished in keeping with its style and character.

10hc (4🚿) 🚫🐕 [R] *B&b£10.50–£13.50 Bdi£18.50–£21.50 W£119.50–£140 Ⱡ LDO9am

Lic ♨ CTV 12P 1🚗 nc5yrs

GH Lanhael House ☎(0503) 72428
Mar–Oct

6hc (1🚿) 🚫🐕 *B&b£11.50–£13

♨ CTV 7P nc⛱

GH Penryn House Hotel The Coombes ☎(0503) 72157
Etr–Oct rs Nov–Etr

14hc (6🛁) (3fb) TV in all bedrooms [R] *B&b£9.50–£12 Bdi£13–£17 W£90–£119 Ⱡ (W only Jul & Aug) LDO6pm

Lic ♨ CTV 15P

[V]

See advertisement on page 314

POLZEATH
Cornwall
Map **2** SW97

GH White Lodge Old Polzeath ☎Trebetherick (020886) 2370

10hc (2fb) *B&b£10–£11.50 Bdi£14.50–£16 W£80.50–£112

Lic ♨ CTV 10P

PONSWORTHY
Devon
Map **3**　SX77

FH Mr & Mrs Fursdon **Old Walls**
(SX697745) ☎Poundsgate (03643) 222
Apr–Oct

Farmhouse standing in its own small
estate in isolated position, on Dartmoor.
Pleasant atmosphere.

3rm ✗ ✱B&b£11.82–£13.82
🍴 CTV 4P ♨ 36acres beef

PONTARDULAIS
West Glamorgan
Map **2**　SN50

FH Mr & Mrs G Davies **Croft** (SN612015)
Heol-y-Barna ☎(0792) 883654
Closed Xmas & New Year

Situated in elevated position with open
aspect to the Gower Peninsula and the
Loughor Estuary. Approx ½m from A48.

3hc (1fb) ✱B&b£8–£10 Bdi£12–£14
W£80–£95 Ł LDOnoon

🍴 CTV 3P nc5yrs 5 acres beef small
holding

PONTFAEN
Dyfed
Map **2**　SN03

FH Mrs S Heard **Tregynon** (SN054345)
☎Newport(0239) 820531
Closed 2 wks Jan/Feb

A comfortable, beamed 16th-century
farmhouse in the foothills of the Preseli
mountains. Vegetarian and wholefood
meals are a speciality. 3m E of village, off
unclass road joining B4313 and Newport.
5m from Newport sands.

5hc (3fb) ✗ ⓡ ✱B&b£10 Bdi£16 W£98–
£107 Ł LDO6pm

Lic 🍴 CTV P ♨ 60acres sheep mixed
ⓥ

PONTLLYFNI
Gwynedd
Map **6**　SH45

GH Bron Dirion Hotel ☎Clynnogfawr
(028686) 346
Mar–Sep

Detached country house in quiet rural
situation.
9hc (4fb) LDO6.30pm
Lic 🍴 CTV 10P

PONTYPRIDD
Mid Glamorgan
Map **3**　ST09

INN White Hart Hotel 1 High St ☎(0443)
405922

Central location amidst shops. Traditional,
popular hosteiry with disco bar and pool.
Well-fitted bedrooms.

4hc (1fb) CTV in all bedrooms ✗ ⓡ
✱B&bfr£16 Wfr£102 ⋈
🍴 CTV 15P

POOLE
Dorset
Map **4**　SZ09
For locations and additional guesthouses
see **Bournemouth**

GH Avoncourt Private Hotel 245
Bournemouth Rd, Parkstone ☎(0202)
732025 Branksome & Westbourne plan **83**
A3

Simple guesthouse with comfortable
bedrooms and lounge.

6hc (3fb) ✗ ✱B&b£7–£10.50 Bdi£10–
£13.50 W£59–£95 Ł
🍴 CTV 5P 1🅰 ♨

GH Blue Shutters Hotel 109 North Rd,
Parkstone ☎(0202) 748129

Neat and comfortable accommodation on
the edge of Poole.

12hc ⓡ ✱B&b£14–£18 W£88.20–
£113.40 ⋈ LDO8pm
Lic 🍴 CTV 10P nc5yrs

GH Ebdon House Hotel 21 St Clair Rd
☎(0202) 707286

8hc (1🔾 2🚽) (2fb) TV in 4 bedrooms ✗
✱B&b£9.50–£12.50 Bdi£15–£19 W£102–
£129 Ł LDO4pm

Lic 🍴 CTV 5P
ⓥ

GH Grovefield Hotel 18 South Pinewood
Rd, Branksome Park ☎(0202) 766798
Branksome & Westbourne plan **89A** A1
Mar–Oct

An attractive, quietly situated small hotel.

12hc (7🔾) (2fb) CTV in 8 bedrooms ⓡ
✱B&b£13.40–£18.40 Bdi£18.70–£23
W£90–£124 Ł LDO5pm
Lic 🍴 CTV 12P nc5yrs

GH Redcroft Hotel
20 Pinewood Rd, Branksome Park
☎(0202) 763959 Branksome &
Westbourne plan **95** B1

Situated in a quiet residential area
opposite entrance to Branksome Dene
Chire. Comfortable, well-furnished rooms.

10hc (4🔾 1🚽) (3fb) CTV in all bedrooms
✗ ⓡ B&b£15.40–£16.90 Bdi£22.40–
£23.90 W£107.14–£116.14 Ł LDO4.30pm
Lic 🍴 CTV 12P nc5yrs

GH Sheldon Lodge 22 Forest Rd,
Branksome Park ☎(0202) 761186
Branksome & Westbourne plan **97** A2
Closed Xmas & New Year

Detached guesthouse in quiet area with
attractive public rooms and good
bedrooms.

14🔾🚽 (4fb) ⓡ ✱B&b£14–£17.50
Bdi£18.50–£22.50 W£113–£140 Ł
LDO7pm
Lic 🍴 CTV 14P snooker solarium
ⓥ

GH Twin Cedars Hotel 2 Pinewood Rd,
Branksome Park ☎(0202) 761339
Branksome & Westbourne plan **100** A2
Closed Nov

Set in own grounds in quiet area near
Branksome beach.

13hc (4🔾 4🚽) (7fb) CTV in all bedrooms
ⓡ ✱B&b£12–£14 Bdi£16–£18 W£110 Ł
Lic 🍴 CTV 15P nc14yrs

GH Westminster Cottage Hotel
3 Westminster Road East, Branksome
Park ☎(0202) 765265 Branksome &
Westbourne Plan **102** A2

Red-brick gabled house in pleasant gardens with neat, simple rooms.

10hc (8⇄ 2🛁) (3fb) CTV in all bedrooms ® B&b£20 Bdi£25 W£150 ⫽ (W only Jul–Aug) LDO7.30pm

Lic 🗝 12P nc5yrs

Credit cards ① ③ Ⓥ

POOLEY BRIDGE
Cumbria
Map **12**   NY42

FH Mrs A Strong **Barton Hall** *(NY478251)* ☎(08536) 275
Etr–Oct

Attractive farmhouse, well-furnished and decorated; large garden.

2hc ✖ ✱B&b£9

P nc8yrs 72acres dairy

Credit card ③

PORLOCK
Somerset
Map **3**   SS84

GH *Gables Hotel* ☎(0643) 862552
Mar–Nov rs Dec

7hc (1⇄) LDO10am

Lic 🗝 CTV 🅿 nc12yrs

GH Lorna Doone Hotel High St ☎(0643) 862404

A comfortable guesthouse offering good home-cooking.

11hc (1⇄ 1🛁) (2fb) ✖ ® ✱B&b£11.50–£13.50 Bdi£16.50–£18.50 W£108–£124 ⫽ LDO6pm

Lic 🗝 CTV 9P

Credit cards ① ③

GH Overstream Parson St ☎(0643) 862421
Closed Xmas

8hc (2🛁) (3fb) ✖ ✱B&b£9.50–£13 Bdi£14–£18 W£92–£120 ⫽ LDO5pm

Lic lift 15P nc3yrs

PORTESHAM
Dorset
Map **3**   SY68

GH Millmead Country Goose Hill ☎Abbotsbury (0305) 871432
Feb–Nov

Poole
—
Porthmadog

The friendly proprietors offer good facilities, comfortable bedrooms and wholesome food.

8hc (2🛁) (1fb) CTV in all bedrooms ✱B&b£13–£16.50 Bdi£20.50–£24 W£132–£154 ⫽ LDO6pm

Lic 🗝 CTV 12P nc10yrs

Credit cards ① ③ Ⓥ

PORTHALLOW
Cornwall
Map **2**   SW72

GH Gallen Treath ☎St Keverne (0326) 280400
Closed Dec

Offering comfort and good food in attractive surroundings.

6hc (2🛁) (2fb) CTV in all bedrooms ® ✱B&b£8.50–£9.50 Bdi£12.50–£13.50 W£84–£90 ⫽ LDO6.30pm

Lic 🗝 CTV 5P ♨

Ⓥ

PORTHCAWL
Mid Glamorgan
Map **3**   SS87

GH Collingwood Hotel 40 Mary St ☎(065671) 2899

Modestly appointed establishment.

8hc (4fb) ✱B&b£8.50 Bdi£12.50 W£77 ⫽ LDO5pm

Lic 🗝 CTV 🅿

⊢↔**GH Minerva Private Hotel** 52 Esplanade Av (Guestaccom) ☎(065671) 2428

8hc (2⇄) (3fb) ® B&b£8.50 Bdi£13 W£86.50 ⫽ LDO6pm

Lic 🗝 CTV 🅿 ♨

PORTHCOTHAN BAY
Cornwall
Map **2**   SW87

GH Bay House ☎Padstow (0841) 520472
28 Mar–3 Oct

17hc (1fb) ✱B&b£10–£12 Bdi£13–£17 W£80–£108 ⫽

Lic CTV 17P

PORTHCURNO
Cornwall
Map **2**   SW32

FH Mr M B Silcox **Corniché Trebehor** *(SW376244)* ☎Sennen (073687) 685
Mar–Oct & Xmas rs Nov & Dec

Well appointed, modern farmhouse. Situated 2m from village, 2m from Lands End and 8m from Penzance. Ideal for touring.

6hc (1fb) ✖ ✱B&b£8.50–£9.25 Bdi£12.50–£13.25 W£82–£89 ⫽ (W only Jul & Aug) LDO6pm

Lic 🗝 CTV 8P nc6yrs 200acres dairy mixed

Ⓥ

PORTHMADOG
Gwynedd
Map **6**   SH53

GH Oakleys The Harbour ☎(0766) 2482
Mar–Nov

Detached Victorian house in quiet town position.

8hc (1⇄) (2fb) ✖ ✱B&b£8.50–£9.50 Bdi£13.50–£15 W£90–£100 ⫽ LDO5pm

Lic CTV 12P

Credit card ③ Ⓥ

See advertisement on page 316

GH *Owen's Hotel* High St ☎(0766) 2098
Mar–Oct

A guesthouse attached to cafe/bakers in centre of town.

12rm (8hc 1🛁) CTV in 6 bedrooms ® LDO6.45pm

Lic 🗝 CTV 4P 5🚗

PORTHTOWAN
Cornwall
Map **2**   SW64

GH Porthtowan Beach Hotel ☎(0209) 890228

16hc (1⇌6⋒) (6fb) ⚓ in 3 bedrooms B&b£12.08 Bdi£15.53 W£100.05 ⫽ LDO8pm

Lic ⍱ CTV 16P

Credit cards ① ③ Ⓥ

FH Mrs M R Honey **Torvean** *(SW704483)* Coast Rd ☎(0209) 890536
Mar–Oct

Nicely furnished detached house in well-kept gardens. Views over countryside to the sea.

3hc (1fb) CTV in all bedrooms ⋈ ® ✱B&b£8–£9 Bdi£12–£13 Wfr£84 ⫽

CTV P 250acres arable beef sheep mixed

PORT ISAAC
Cornwall
Map **2**   SW98

GH Archer Farm Hotel Trewetha ☎Bodmin (0208) 880522
Mar–Dec

Attractive, detached converted farmhouse set in own grounds. 1m E B3267.

8hc (1⇌3⋒) (1fb) CTV in 1 bedroom B&b£12.50–£14 Bdi£20.50–£22 Wfr£140 ⫽ LDO8pm

---

Porthtowan
–
Portnancon

Lic ⍱ CTV 10P

Ⓥ

GH Bay Hotel 1 The Terrace ☎Bodmin (0208) 880380
Etr–Oct

Double-fronted building in elevated position overlooking sea.

11hc (5fb) B&b£10.50–£13.50 Bdi£15–£18 W£90–£110 ⫽ LDO7pm

Lic CTV 10P

GH Fairholme 30 Trewetha Ln ☎Bodmin (0208) 880397
rs Xmas

Detached double-fronted building on main road leading to Port Isaac.

7hc (3fb) ⋈ ✱B&b£7.50–£8.50 Bdi£12.50–£13.50 W£80.50–£84 ⫽ LDO10am

⍱ CTV 8P

GH St Andrews Hotel The Terrace ☎Bodmin (0208) 880240
Mar–Nov

Personally-run guesthouse with lovely views of sea and countryside.

13hc (2⇌4⋒) (5fb) ® ✱B&b£11.50–£14 Bdi£17.50–£20 W£105–£120 ⫽ LDO9pm

Lic ⍱ CTV 14P

GH Trethoway Hotel 98 Fore St ☎Bodmin (0208) 880214
Mar–Nov

9hc (3fb) ✱B&b£10.50–£12.50 Bdi£16.50–£18.50 W£95–£115 ⫽ LDO3pm

Lic CTV 6P ⚿

Ⓥ

PORTLOE
Cornwall
Map **2**   SW93

INN Ship ☎Truro (0872) 501356
Feb–Oct

6hc LDO9pm

⍱ CTV 25P 🚗

Credit card ③

PORTNANCON
Highland *Sutherland*
Map **14**   NC46

GH Port-na-Con House Loch Eriboll ☎Durness (097181) 367
Feb–Nov

Beautifully located on W shore of Loch Eriboll by the old pier. A former harbour store converted to provide compact, comfortable accommodation.

4hc (2fb) ✱B&b£8.50–£10.50 Bdi£15–£17
W£100–£110 ⁄ LDO7pm
Lic ▥ 8P
Ⓥ

PORT OF MENTEITH
Central *Perthshire*
Map **11**   NN50

FH Mrs J Fotheringham **Collymoon**
(NN593966) ☎Buchlyvie (036085) 268
May–Sep
*Clean, simple farmhouse peacefully
situated well off the B8034.*
2rm (1▥) LDO6pm
▥ CTV 2P ✇ 500acres mixed
Credit cards ① ③

PORTPATRICK
Dumfries & Galloway *Wigtownshire*
Map **10**   NX05

GH Blinkbonnie School Brae ☎(077681)
282
Mar–Oct
*Pleasantly appointed bungalow in
elevated position with fine views seaward
from dining room and lounge.*
5hc (1fb) Ⓡ B&b£8.50 Bdi£14 LDO5.30pm
▥ CTV 6P

PORTREATH
Cornwall
Map **2**   SW64

Portnancon
—
Portsmouth & Southsea

INN Portreath Arms The Square
☎(0209) 842534
7hc (5▥) CTV in all bedrooms ✹ Ⓡ
✱B&b£12–£16 W£84–£112 ▯ Lunch
£3alc Dinner9pm£6alc
50P ⚗ nc14yrs
Credit card ③

PORTREE
Isle of Skye, Highland *Inverness-shire*
See **Skye, Isle of**

PORT ST MARY
Isle of Man
See **Man, Isle of**

PORTSMOUTH & SOUTHSEA
Hants
Map **4**   SZ69
See plan on pages 318–319

GH Abbeville Hotel 26 Nettlecomb Av,
Southsea ☎(0705) 826209 Plan **1** *F2*
11hc (2fb) ✱B&bfr£10 Bdifr£14.50 Wfr£90
⁄
▥ CTV P
Ⓥ

GH Amberley Court 97 Waverley Rd,
Southsea ☎(0705) 735419 Plan **1A** *F3*
*Pleasant family-run guesthouse of some
quality.*
9hc (3fb) Ⓡ LDO5.30pm
▥ CTV 🅿

GH Astor House 4 St Andrew's Rd,
Southsea ☎(0705) 755171 Plan **2** *E4*
*Very comfortable and homely
establishment with antique furniture.*
6hc (3fb) CTV in 1 bedroom TV in 5
bedrooms Ⓡ ✱B&b£9–£9.50 W£58.50–
£63 ▯
▥ CTV 🅿
Ⓥ

GH Beaufort Hotel 71 Festing Rd,
Southsea ☎(0705) 823707 Plan **4** *F3*
Closed Xmas
*Smart, homely, comfortable hotel close to
gardens and seafront.*
16hc (2⇆) (5fb) ✂ in 2 bedrooms ✹
✱B&b£12.50–£15 W£87.50–£100 ▯ (W
only Nov–Apr)
▥ CTV 8P nc3yrs
Credit Cards ① ③ ④ Ⓥ

GH Birchwood 44 Waverley Rd,
Southsea ☎(0705) 811337 Plan **5** *F3*
*Simple yet comfortable and homely house
in city centre.*   →

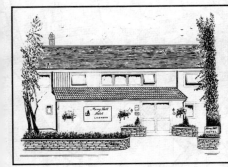

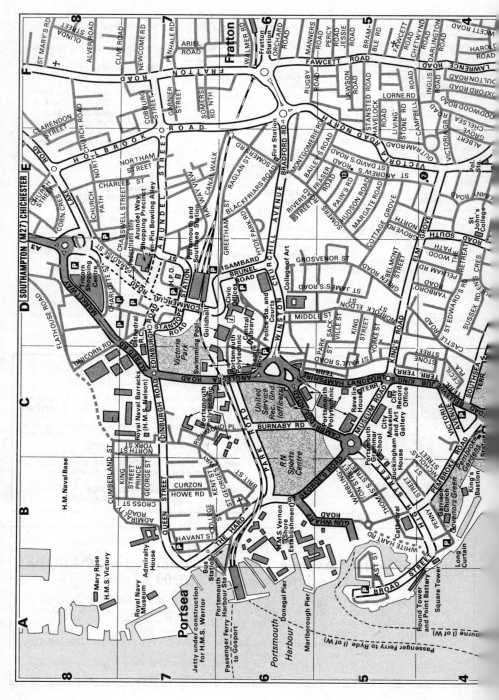

318

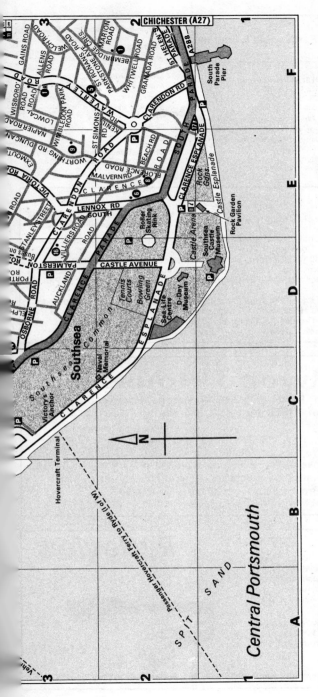

CHICHESTER (A27)

Central Portsmouth

Portsmouth

1   Abbeville Hotel
1A Amberley Court
2   Astor House
4   Beaufort Hotel
5   Birchwood
6   Bristol Hotel
7   Chequers Hotel
8   Gainsborough House
9   Goodwood House
11 Lyndhurst
12 Ryde View
13 St Andrews Lodge
14 Somerset Private Hotel
16 Upper Mount House Hotel
17 White House Hotel

6hc (4fb) ⚥ in 2 bedrooms 🛏
✱B&b£9.50–£10 Bdi£12.50–£14 W£75–
£80 ⫶ LDO5.30pm
🏠 CTV ⫶

GH Bristol Hotel 55 Clarence Pde,
Southsea ☎(0705) 821815 Plan **6** *E2*

*Four-storey Victorian house overlooking
seafront, gardens and Southsea
Common.*

14hc (9🍴) (7fb) CTV in 9 bedrooms TV in 5
bedrooms 🛏 ℝ ✱B&b£13.50–£18
Bdi£18–£22 W£98–£120 ⫶ LDO4pm
Lic 🏠 CTV 7P
Ⓥ

See advertisement on page 320

GH Chequers Hotel Salisbury Rd,
Southsea ☎(0705) 735277 Plan **7** *F3*

*Comfortable hotel in quiet residential area
with simple accommodation and good
public areas.*

14hc (3fb) TV in 2 bedrooms
✱B&b£13.80–£15 Bdi£20–£22 W£88–
£110 ⫶ LDO6pm
Lic 🏠 CTV 12P ⚓
Credit cards ① ③ Ⓥ

GH Gainsborough House 9 Malvern Rd,
Southsea ☎(0705) 822604 Plan **8** *E2*
Closed Xmas

*Well-established guesthouse, 2 minutes
from the sea front, with a warm,
welcoming atmosphere.*

7hc (1fb) 🛏 ℝ B&b£9–£10
🏠 CTV ⫶ nc3yrs

GH Goodwood House 1 Taswell Rd,
Southsea ☎(0705) 824734 Plan **9** *E3*

*Comfortable accommodation in a friendly
informal atmosphere, within easy reach of
shopping centre and promenade.*

8hc (1fb) TV in 8 bedrooms 🛏 ℝ
✱B&b£11–£13.50
🏠 CTV ⫶ nc2yrs

See advertisement on page 320

GH Lyndhurst 8 Festing Gv, Southsea
☎(0705) 735239 Plan **11** *F3*
Closed Xmas

*A homely house set in quiet residential
area.* →

7hc (2fb) ® ✱B&bfr£10 Bdifr£13.50
Wfr£77 ≵ LDOnoon
🕮 CTV ⅌
Credit cards ② ③

GH Ryde View 9 Western Pde, Southsea
☎(0705) 820865 Plan **12** C4
Closed Xmas
Comfortable establishment overlooking the common with excellent sea views.
14hc (3flm) (7fb) CTV in all bedrooms
✱B&b£11.50–£15 Bdi£16–£21
Lic 🕮 CTV
Credit cards ① ③ ⓥ

GH St Andrews Lodge
65 St Andrews Rd, Southsea ☎(0705) 827079 Plan **13** E5
Closed 23 Dec–6 Jan
Bright, modern bedrooms and friendly service at this comfortable guesthouse.
10rm (9hc) (5fb) ✖ ® ✱B&b£9–£11
W£60–£70 M
🕮 CTV
ⓥ

GH Somerset Private Hotel 16 Western Pde, Southsea ☎(0705) 822495
Plan **14** C3
Well-maintained and efficiently managed with a friendly atmosphere. Some bedrooms on the top floors have extensive views of the harbour.
19hc (5flm) (3fb) CTV in all bedrooms ®
✱B&b£12–£14 Bdi£17–£19 W£110–£126 ≵
LDO7pm
Lic 🕮 CTV ⅌
Credit cards ① ③

GH Upper Mount House Hotel The Vale, Clarendon Rd, Southsea ☎(0705) 820456
Plan **16** D3

Listed three-storey building set to the rear of a main road in a quiet lane.

9hc (2🛁 4🚿) (2fb) CTV in all bedrooms [R] ✱B&b£14.50–£17.50 Bdi£20.45–£23.45 W£95–£125 ⱡ LDO6pm

Lic ♨ CTV 8P

Credit cards [1] [3] [V]

GH White House Hotel 26 South Parade, Southsea ☎(0705) 823709 Plan **17** *F2*

17hc (6🚿) (1fb) CTV in all bedrooms [R] ✱B&b£11–£16 Bdi£16.50–£22.50 W£95–£140 ⱡ LDO7pm

Lic ♨ CTV Ᵽ

Credit cards [1] [2] [3] [5]

POUNDSGATE
Devon
Map **3** SX77

GH Leusdon Lodge (Guestaccom) ☎(03643) 304

150-year-old granite-built house on edge of Dartmoor, offering traditional English fare.

8hc (2🛁 2🚿) (2fb) CTV in all bedrooms ✱B&b£14.15–£18.15 Bdi£22.60–£26.60 W£146.30 ⱡ LDO9pm

Lic ♨ CTV 20P

Credit cards [1] [2] [3] [5]

PRAA SANDS
Cornwall
Map **2** SW52

Portsmouth & Southsea — Preston

GH La Connings ☎Germoe (0736) 762380
Jun–Oct

Chalet-style guesthouse surrounded by farmland and adjacent coast.

6hc (3fb) ✱B&b£8–£10 Bdi£13–£15 W£91–£105 ⱡ LDO6.30pm

Lic ♨ CTV 8P nc5yrs 🏊(heated)

GH White House Castle Dr ☎Penzance (0736) 762100
Etr–Oct

Friendly, relaxed guesthouse, with an easy, level walk to the beach.

16hc [R] ✱B&b£9.50–£11 Bdi£14–£15.50 LDO6.30pm

Lic CTV 10P 🐴

Credit cards [1] [3]

See advertisement on page 322

PRESTATYN
Clwyd
Map **6** SJ08

GH Bryn Gwalia Inn 17 Gronant Rd ☎(07456) 2442
rs Xmas

Edwardian house in residential area, short walk to shops.

9hc (1🛁 4🚿) (1fb) CTV in all bedrooms ✗ [R] ✱B&b£16–£19 Bdi£21–£29 W£125–£155 ⱡ LDO9pm

Lic ♨ 20P

See advertisement on page 322

GH Hawarden House 13 Victoria Rd ☎(07456) 4226

6hc (2fb) CTV in 5 bedrooms TV in 1 bedroom ✗ ✱B&b£7–£8.50 Bdi£10.50–£12 Wfr£75 ⱡ LDO5pm

Lic ♨ CTV P

PRESTEIGNE
Powys
Map **3** SO36

FH Mrs K Owens **Broadheath** *(SO339633)* ☎(0544) 267416
Apr–Oct

Charming character farmhouse in secluded position.

3rm (2hc) (1fb) ✗ [R] ✱B&b£9–£10 W£60–£67 Ṁ

CTV 3P 300acres mixed

[V]

PRESTON
Lancashire
Map **7** SD52

GH Fulwood Park Hotel 49 Watling Street Rd ☎(0772) 718067
rs Xmas

Extensively modernised family-run hotel. →

21hc (7🛁 8🚿) Annexe: 4hc (1🚿) (2fb) ✗ [R] B&b£15–£24.75 Bdi£21–£31 LDO7.15pm

Lic 🍴 CTV 24P 1🚗 ♿

Credit cards [1] [2] [3] [5] [V]

GH Tulketh Hotel 209 Tulketh Rd, Ashton ☎(0772) 728096

Comfortable modern accommodation is provided in this Victorian-style hotel.

7hc (1🚿) (1fb) CTV in 3 bedrooms TV in 4 bedrooms [R] ✱B&b£20.07–£25.87 Bdi£28.17–£33.34 W£197.19–£233.38ⱡ LDO8pm

Lic 🍴 CTV 15P

[V]

GH Withy Trees 175 Garstang Rd, Fullwood ☎(0772) 717693
Closed Xmas

Mainly commercial, simple-style guesthouse offering bed-and-breakfast only. 2m N on A6.

10hc (2fb) ✗ ✱B&b£11–£12 W£77–£84 M

🍴 CTV 30P

[V]

PRESTWICK
Strathclyde *Ayrshire*
Map **10** NS32

GH Fairways (formerly Villa Marina Hotel), 19 Links Rd ☎(0292) 70396

Preston — Pwllheli

Nicely appointed with bright cheerful bedrooms. Overlooking the golf course.

6hc (1fb) ✱B&b£11–£12 Bdi£15–£17 W£95–£105ⱡ

Lic 🍴 CTV 8P ⛳

[V]

Recommended

GH Fernbank 213 Main St ☎(0292) 75027

A very comfortable and well-appointed guesthouse with tastefully furnished and decorated lounges and attractive bedrooms – four of which have en-suite facilities.

7hc (4🚿) ✗ ✱B&b£11–£13 Bdi£17–£19 W£114–£128ⱡ

🍴 CTV 7P nc5yrs

[V]

GH Kincraig Private Hotel 39 Ayr Rd ☎(0292) 79480

Attractive red-sandstone villa on main road with neatly appointed good-sized rooms.

6hc (1fb) ✗ [R] ✱B&b£9.50 Bdi£14.50 LDO5pm

Lic 🍴 CTV 8P nc3yrs

PWLLHELI
Gwynedd
Map **6** SH33

GH Sea Haven Hotel West End Pde ☎(0758) 612572
Apr–Nov

Friendly holiday hotel facing a lovely sandy beach.

10hc (4🚿) (8fb) CTV in 8 bedrooms [R] ✱B&b£8–£12 Bdi£12–£15 W£86–£115 (W only Jul & Aug) LDO10pm

Lic CTV P

Credit cards [1] [2] [3]

FH Mrs M Hughes **Bryn Crin** *(SH379358)* ☎(0758) 612494
Apr–Sep

Large spacious farmhouse situated on hillside with panoramic views of Cardigan Bay and Snowdonia. Situated off unclass road.

3rm (2hc) (2fb) ✗ ✱B&b£7.50–£8.50 W£50–£58 M

CTV 3P 80acres beef

[V]

FH Mrs J E Ellis **Gwynfryn** *(SH364357)* ☎(0758) 612536
Closed Xmas

Large granite-built farmhouse, surrounded by 2 acres of gardens and woodland, bordered to the south by a stream. 1m NW.

3hc ✗ ✱B&b£7.50–£10 Bdi£12.50–£15 Wfr£49.50 Ⓜ

🍴 CTV 3P nc7yrs 90acres dairy

QUEEN CAMEL
Somerset
Map **3**   ST52

INN *Mildmay Arms* ☎Yeovil (0935) 850456

6hc (2🖾) LDO10pm

🍴 25P

Credit card ③

RAGLAN
Gwent
Map **3**   SO40

GH Grange Old Abergavenny Rd ☎(0291) 690260
rs 1 wk Xmas

A well-run, attractive house in 1½ acres, approximately ½m outside Raglan.

4hc (1🖾) (1fb) ✗ in 1 bedroom ✱B&bfr£11.50 Bdifr£18.50 Wfr£129.50 Ⓛ LDO9pm

Lic 🍴 CTV 10P ⚙
Ⓥ

INN Cripple Creek Bryngwyn (2m W off A40) ☎(0291) 690256

Pwllheli
—
Raskelf

Off old Abergavenny rd, ¾ mile from Raglan. Modern Accommodation combined with old-world charm.

3hc ✱B&bfr£12 Bdifr£17.50 Wfr£95 Ⓛ LDO10.30pm

🍴 CTV 40P

RAMSGATE
Kent
Map **5**   TR36

GH Jalna Hotel 49 Vale Sq ☎Thanet (0843) 593848
Closed Xmas

Located in a quiet residential part of the town, with well-maintained bedrooms and a basement dining room.

9hc (5🖾) (5fb) ✗ ✱B&b£8–£11 Bdi£12–£15 W£65–£84.50 Ⓛ LDO2pm

Lic 🍴 CTV 3P nc2yrs
Ⓥ

GH *Piper Lodge Hotel* 26 Victoria Rd, East Cliff ☎Thanet (0843) 591661

12hc (3🖾) (5fb) TV in all bedrooms ✗ Ⓡ LDO7pm

Lic 🍴 CTV 15P ⊶(heated)

GH St Hilary Private Hotel 21 Crescent Rd ☎Thanet (0843) 591427
Closed Xmas

Cheerful compact bedrooms, basement dining room, situated in residential area.

7hc (4fb) ✗ ✱B&b£8–£9.50 Bdi£11.50–£12.50 W£63–£72 Ⓛ (W only Jul & Aug) LDO3.30pm

Lic CTV ⚑ nc4yrs

Credit card ① Ⓥ

RASKELF
North Yorkshire
Map **8**   SE47

— *Recommended* —

GH Old Farmhouse (Guestaccom) ☎Easingwold (0347) 21971
16 Jan–20 Dec

This former farm building has been converted into a charming and friendly guesthouse. The accommodation includes comfortable bedrooms, a quaint lounge with an enormous log fire and a pleasant dining room. The friendly proprietors are justifiably proud of their excellent home cooking which includes bread, marmalade and jams.

10hc (5⇄5🖾) (2fb) B&b£13.50–£17.50 Bdi£20.50–£24.50 W£143.50–£161 Ⓛ LDO5.30pm

Lic 🍴 CTV 15P
Ⓥ

RAVENGLASS
Cumbria
Map **6** SD09

GH St Michael's Country House
Muncaster ☎(06577) 362

Old schoolhouse of sandstone and granite, converted to provide comfortable accommodation.

10hc (1⇨ 1⋔) (1fb) ⍚ ® ✱B&bfr£11
Bdifr£17 LDO5pm
Lic CTV 20P ⚓

RAVENSCAR
North Yorkshire
Map **8** NZ90

GH Smugglers Rock Country
☎Scarborough (0723) 870044
Mar–Dec

Converted and restored farmhouse, close to moors and sea.

9hc (3⇨ 4⋔) (2fb) ✱B&b£10–£12
Bdi£14.50–£16 W£95–£105 ⊬ LDO4pm
Lic ⌘ CTV 10P nc2yrs snooker
ⓥ

RAVENSTONEDALE
Cumbria
Map **12** NY70

FH Mrs M Wildman **Ellergill** *(NY737015)*
☎Newbiggin-on-Lune (05873) 240
Mar–Nov

3rm (1hc) (1fb) ⍚ ® ✱B&bfr£8
Bdifr£13.50 Wfr£82 ⊬
CTV 6P 300acres dairy sheep
ⓥ

INN Fat Lamb Country Cross Bank
(Guestaccom) ☎Newbiggin-on-Lune
(05873) 242

17th-century farmhouse, now an inn, has comfortable accommodation and well appointed restaurant.

9hc (5⇨) (3fb) CTV in 2 bedrooms ®
✱B&b£14–£17 Bdi£23–£26 W£144.90–
£163.80 ⊬ Lunch£9&alc Dinner9.30pm
£9&alc
⌘ CTV 50P ⓰
ⓥ

READING
Berkshire
Map **4** SU77

GH Aeron 191 Kentwood Hill, Tilehurst
☎(0734) 424119
Closed Xmas rs 27 Dec–1 Jan

Professionally-run clean and friendly establishment. 3m W off A329.

9hc Annexe: 10hc (1fb) CTV in all
bedrooms ® ✱B&b£16.50–£18.50
Bdi£22.75–£24.75
Lic ⌘
Credit cards ① ③

GH Private House Hotel 98 Kendrick Rd
☎(0734) 874142
Closed Xmas

Comfortable and cheerful establishment offering good accommodation, run by friendly proprietors.

7hc ⍚ ✱B&b£16–£17 Bdi£23–£25
W£161–£175 ⊬ LDOnoon
Lic ⌘ CTV 7P nc12yrs

REDCAR
Cleveland
Map **8** NZ62

GH Claxton House Private Hotel
196 High St ☎(0642) 486745
Closed 24 Dec–2 Jan

Accommodation here is clean and comfortable and there is an interesting lounge dining room.

17rm (16hc) (6⋔) (2fb) ✱B&b£10–£11.50
Bdi£14–£15.50 W£98–£108.50 ⊬
LDO5.30pm
Lic ⌘ CTV 10P

REDDITCH
Hereford & Worcester
Map **7** SP06

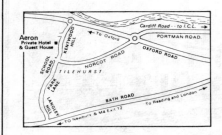

GH Old Rectory Ipsley Ln ☎(0527) 23000

A very hospitable hotel set in a new town, within peaceful surroundings.

10hc (5🛁 5🚿) ✖ B&b£20–£25 Bdi£29–£34 LDOnoon

Lic ♨ CTV 15P 2🚗 ⌂

Credit card [1] [V]

REDHILL (nr Bristol)
Avon
Map **3** ST46

FH Mrs M J Hawkings **Hailstones** *(SS502638)* ☎Wrington (0934) 862209
Closed Dec

Farmhouse in quiet, yet convenient position with pleasant dining room and croquet lawn.

3hc (1🚿) ✖ *B&bfr£10 Wfr£59.50 M/

♨ CTV 4P 150acres dairy sheep mixed

[V]

REDHILL
Surrey
Map **4** TQ25

Recommended

GH Ashleigh House Hotel 39 Redstone Hill ☎(0737) 64763
Closed Xmas

Very comfortable homely accommodation with outstanding hospitality.

9hc (1🚿) (1fb) ✖ *B&b£14–£16.50

♨ CTV 9P 🏊(heated)

REDMILE
Leicestershire
Map **8** SK73

FH Mr & Mrs P Need ***Peacock*** *(SK791359)* (Guestaccom) ☎Bottesford (0949) 42475

Modernised 280-year-old farmhouse situated in the Vale of Belvoir, close to Castle. Small licensed restaurant.

6hc (1🚿) (2fb) ✖

Lic ♨ CTV 20P ⌂ 🎱 U solarium gymnasium 5acres non-working

Redditch — Rhos-on-Sea

REDRUTH
Cornwall
Map **2** SW64

GH Aviary Court Marys Well, Illogan (2m NW unclass) ☎Portreath (0209) 842256

Charming country house set in 2½ acres of grounds, offering a high standard of accommodation.

6hc (1🛁 2🚿) (1fb) CTV in all bedrooms ✖ [R] *B&b£13.75–£22 Bdi£21–£29.25 W£138.25–£163.25 ⊬ LDO9pm

Lic ♨ 25P nc3yrs

Credit cards [2] [5] [V]

REIGATE
Surrey
Map **4** TQ25

Recommended

GH Cranleigh Hotel 41 West St ☎(07372) 40600
Closed 24–26 Dec

An efficient, well-managed hotel, with well-equipped modern bedrooms, an outdoor heated swimming pool and rear garden.

10hc (4🛁) (2fb) CTV in all bedrooms [R] *B&b£18–£30 Bdi£26–£38 LDO7.30pm

Lic ♨ CTV 6P 🏊(heated)

Credit cards [1] [2] [3] [4] [5] [V]

See advertisement on page 326

GH Priors Mead Blanford Rd ☎(07372) 48776

Comfortable family-run hotel with good size bedrooms. Quietly located.

9hc (1🛁) (3fb) *B&b£12.50–£15

♨ CTV 6P nc5yrs

[V]

REYNOLDSTON
West Glamorgan
Map **2** SS48

Recommended

GH Fairyhill Country House Hotel & Restaurant Fairyhill ☎Gower (0792) 390139
Closed 2 wks Xmas

Good hospitality and a high standard of cuisine will be found at this luxurious restored manor house standing in 24 acres of parkland.

12🛁🚿 (12fb) CTV in all bedrooms [R] *B&bfr£24.50 Bdifr£39.45 LDO9.30pm

Lic ♨ 60P ⌂ 🎣 sauna bath solarium

Credit cards [1] [2] [3] [5]

RHANDIRMWYN
Dyfed
Map **3** SN74

INN Royal Oak ☎(05506) 201

Small, inn of character with panoramic views. Spotless bedrooms, modern restaurant and cosy bars.

5hc (2🛁 1🚿) (1fb) CTV in 3 bedrooms ✖ [R] *B&b£10.50–£12 Bdi£12.50–£20 Bar lunch£2.75–£4.50 Dinner9.30pm£8alc

20P

RHES-Y-CAE
Clwyd
Map **7** SJ17

INN *Miners Arms* ☎Halkyn (0352) 780567

Part 16th-century village inn in quiet rural situation.

8hc (1fb) CTV in 3 bedrooms TV in 5 bedrooms ✖ LDO10pm

♨ CTV 150P

RHOS-ON-SEA
Clwyd
Map **6** SH88

See **Colwyn Bay**

Rhuallt — Ripley

RHUALLT
Clwyd
Map **6** SJ07

INN White House ☎St Asaph (0745) 582155
Large inn on main A55 offering accommodation, restaurant and party nights at weekends.
5hc TV in all bedrooms B&b£10 Lunch fr£4 Dinner 9.30pm £3–£7
CTV P
Credit cards [1] [3]

RHYD
Gwynedd
Map **6** SH64

FH Mrs N Griffiths **Bodlondeb** *(SH637420)* ☎Penrhyndeudraeth (0766) 770640
Bright, modern accommodation in farmhouse on the B4410. Ideal base for touring Southern Snowdonia.
3hc (1fb) ✖ *B&b£7.50 Bdi£11.50 W£75 Ł LDO6pm
🐕 CTV 4P 420acres beef sheep mixed

RHYL
Clwyd
Map **6** SJ08

GH Pier Hotel 23 East Pde ☎(0745) 50280
Closed Xmas
Mid-terrace, on seafront, short walk to shops.
11hc (1🛁 1🚿) (3fb) *B&b£9–£10 Bdi£12.50–£13.50 W£65–£82 Ł LDO3pm
Lic 🐕 CTV 2P solarium
[V]

GH *Toomargoed Private Hotel* 31–33 John St ☎(0745) 4103
Double-fronted mid-terrace in residential area off Marine Parade.
15hc (8fb) ✖
Lic CTV

RICHMOND
North Yorkshire
Map **7** NZ10

GH Pottergate 4 Pottergate ☎(0748) 3826
Small, cosy house on fringe of town centre.
6hc (2fb) TV in all bedrooms [R] *B&bfr£9 Bdifr£13
Lic 🐕 CTV 2P 2🚗

Recommended

FH Mrs M F Turnbull **Whashton Springs** *(NZ149046)* (3m W on unclass rd) (Guestaccom) ☎(0748) 2884
Feb–Nov
This charming Georgian farmhouse is situated in the heart of 'Herriot' country. A Yorkshire farmhouse breakfast is served in the attractive dining room and in the evening local and home-produced meat, fruit and vegetables feature on the menu. The bedrooms, both in the main house and the stable courtyard, are comfortable and well-equipped.
3hc CTV in all bedrooms ✖ [R] *B&b£9–£12 Bdi£15–£18 W£96–£117 Ł LDOam
Lic 🐕 600acres arable beef sheep mixed
[V]

RICKINGHALL
Suffolk
Map **5** TM07

INN Hamblyn House The Street ☎Diss (0379) 898292
4hc (1fb) CTV in all bedrooms [R] B&b£14–£18 Bdi£18–£22 Wfr£90 M̸ Lunch£7alc Dinner10pm£10alc
🐕 CTV 15P solarium
Credit cards [2] [3] [5] [V]

RIEVAULX
North Yorkshire
Map **8** SE58

FH Mrs M E Skilbeck **Middle Heads** *(SE584869)* ☎Bilsdale (04396) 251
Mar–Nov
Old stone-farmhouse of character, comfortably furnished and with a homely atmosphere, 1m E of B1257 and 3m NW of Helmsley.
3rm (1fb) ✖ *B&b£8–£9 Wfr£56 M̸
🐕 CTV 6P 170acres arable beef sheep mixed

RINGWOOD
Hampshire
Map **4** SU10

GH Little Forest Lodge Poulner Hill ☎(0425) 478848
An elegant country-style house with particularly attractive bedrooms. Situated off the A31 eastbound.
5hc (2🛁 3🚿) (2fb) 🚭 in 2 bedrooms CTV in all bedrooms ✖ [R] B&b£16.50–£19 Bdi£22–£25 W£150–£175 Ł LDO5pm
Lic 🐕 CTV 10P 2🚗
[V]

GH *Little Moortown House Hotel* 244 Christchurch Rd ☎(04254) 3325
Georgian house with comfortable accommodation and an attractively furnished dining room.
6hc (4🚿) (1fb) CTV in all bedrooms [R] LDO9pm
Lic 🐕 CTV 8P
Credit cards [1] [3]

RIPLEY
Derbyshire
Map **8** SK45

GH Britannia 243 Church St, Waingroves ☎(0773) 43708
Modern detached house, $1\frac{1}{2}$ miles south of Ripley.
6hc (1🚿) (1fb) ✖ [R] *B&b£13 Bdi£18.50 LDOnoon
🐕 CTV 10P

RIPON
North Yorkshire
Map **8** SE37

GH Crescent Lodge 42 North St
☎(0765) 2331
Closed Xmas & New Year

Early 18th-century town house retaining lovely period rooms and fine Georgian staircase.

12hc (3fb) CTV in all bedrooms ✟ ®
✱B&b£9–£11 Bdi£15–£17 W£105 ⌇
Lic ⑭ CTV ⬝ ₽

GH Nordale 1 & 2 North Pde ☎(0765) 3557

Accommodation here is simple, but clean and the lounge is comfortable.

12hc (4fb) ® ✱B&b£9.50–£12.50 Bdi£15–£17.50 W£105–£119 ⌇ LDO5pm
Lic CTV 14P

GH Old Country 1 The Crescent ☎(0765) 2162

A graceful old Victorian house of character with spacious bedrooms and interesting public rooms.

7hc (6fb) ⌇ in 3 bedrooms TV in 2 bedrooms ✟ ✱B&bfr£8 Wfr£98 ⌇
⑭ CTV 10P
Ⓥ

ROBIN HOOD'S BAY
North Yorkshire
Map **8** NZ90

FH Mrs P Featherstone **Croft** *(NZ941051)* Fylingthorpe ☎Whitby (0947) 880231
May–Oct

Comfortable accommodation on edge of village with good views of moors and sea.

2rm (1hc) (1fb) ✟ B&b£8.50–£9.50 W£56–£63 M
CTV 3P nc5yrs 45acres dairy

ROCHE
Cornwall
Map **2** SW96

GH Greystones Mount Pleasant ☎(0726) 890863

Although a new building, tasteful furnishing, including many antiques, has created an olde-worlde atmosphere.

Ripon
Romsey

7hc (2⇆ 5⚅) (2fb) LDO7.30pm
⑭ CTV 10P 1⚘ Ʊ
See advertisement on page 74

ROCHESTER
Northumberland
Map **12** NY89

FH Mrs J M Chapman **Woolaw** *(NY821984)* ☎Otterburn (0830) 20686

Comfortable farmhouse in a tranquil setting with lovely views over surrounding countryside.

2rm (1fb) ✟ ✱B&bfr£9 Bdifr£12 W£77 ⌇ LDO8.30pm
⑭ CTV P ✔ Ʊ 740acres beef sheep horses
Ⓥ

ROCK
Cornwall
Map **2** SW97

GH Roskarnon House Hotel ☎Trebetherick (020886) 2785
Mar–Oct

16hc (4⇆ 1⚅) (5fb) CTV in 4 bedrooms TV in 1 bedroom ✟ ✱B&b£12.50–£16 Bdi£17.50–£25 W£110–£150 ⌇ LDO8.30pm
Lic CTV 14P 2⚘
Ⓥ

RODBOURNE (nr Malmesbury)
Wiltshire
Map **3** ST98

FH Mrs C M Parfitt **Angrove** *(ST949842)* ☎Malmesbury (06662) 2982
May–Sep

A typical Cotswold-style farmhouse backed by woodland and bordered by the River Avon where trout and coarse fishing is available. 1m NW unclass.

3hc ✟ ® B&b£10 W£57 M
⑭ CTV P ✔ 204acres beef

ROGART
Highland *Sutherland*
Map **14** NC70

FH Mrs J S R Moodie **Rovie** *(NC716023)* ☎(04084) 209
Mar–Oct

Lodge-style farmhouse in lovely surroundings with river flowing through. Rabbit shooting on farm and fishing locally in River Fleet. 4m from sea and S off A839.

6hc (1fb) ✱B&b£7.50–£8 Bdi£14–£14.50 Wfr£98 ⌇ LDO6.30pm
CTV 6P 120acres arable beef sheep
Ⓥ

ROGATE
West Sussex
Map **4** SU82

FH Mrs J C Francis **Mizzards** *(SU803227)* ☎(073080) 656
Closed Xmas Day

A beautiful old farmhouse, skilfully modernised in a peaceful setting by a small river. Off A272 between Petersfield and Midhurst.

3⇆ (1fb) CTV in all bedrooms ✟ ✱B&b£12.50–£16.50
⑭ CTV 10P nc4yrs ⌐(heated) 13½acres sheep
Ⓥ

See advertisement on page 271

ROMFORD
Gt London
Map **5** TQ58

GH Repton Private Hotel 18 Repton Dr, Gidea Park ☎(0708) 45253

8hc ✟ ✱B&b£12.65–£17.25 LDOam
⑭ CTV
Ⓥ

ROMSEY
Hampshire
Map **4** SU32

GH Adelaide House 45 Winchester Rd ☎(0794) 512322

Small homely house on the edge of the town. →

5hc ✻ ✳B&b£8.75–£9.75 W£55–£60 M
🏠 CTV 5P
Ⓥ

GH Chalet Botley Rd, Whitenap ☎(0794)
514909
*Comfortable house set in quiet residential
area.*
3hc Annexe: 2⇆ (2fb) CTV in 4 bedrooms
✻ ✳B&b£9–£10 W£60–£70 M
🏠 CTV 6P

ROSLIN
Lothian *Mid Lothian*
Map **11**   NT26

INN Olde Original Rosslyn 4 Main St
☎031-440 2384
*Early 18th-century inn, full of character,
providing a good standard of modern
accommodation. Pleasant, popular bars.*
6hc (5⇆ 1🚿) (1fb) CTV in all bedrooms Ⓡ
✳B&b£17.50 Bdi£22.50 Lunch£5
Dinner9.30pm£11&alc
14P
Credit cards ① ② ③

ROSS-ON-WYE
Hereford & Worcester
Map **3**   SO52
For details of farmhouse accommodation
in the vicinity, see **Marstow** and **St
Owen's Cross**

GH Arches Country House Walford Rd
☎(0989) 63348
Closed Xmas & New Year
6hc (1⇆) (2fb) ⚡ in 1 bedroom CTV in all
bedrooms Ⓡ ✳B&b£9.25–£12 Bdi£15.50–
£18.50 W£91–£104 ⫶ LDO6pm
Lic 🏠 CTV 8P ♨
Ⓥ

GH Bridge House Hotel Wilton ☎(0989)
62655
Closed Xmas
*Cosy little hotel on edge of town with
garden sloping to banks of the River Wye.*
9hc (1⇆ 1🚿) (1fb) CTV in 4 bedrooms ✻
✳B&b£10.50–£14.50 Bdi£16.50–£20.50
W£115–£134 ⫶
Lic CTV 14P

GH Brookfield House Ledbury Rd
☎(0989) 62188
rs Nov, Dec & Jan
*Comfortable rooms and pleasant
welcoming proprietors at main road
guesthouse.*
8hc (1⇆ 2🚿) (1fb) Ⓡ ✳B&b£11–£18
W£70–£120 M
Lic CTV 10P 1🏇
Credit cards ① ③

GH Ryefield House Gloucester Rd
☎(0989) 63030
Jan–Oct
7hc (1⇆ 1🚿) (3fb) Ⓡ B&b£9.25–£11.25
Bdi£15–£17.20 W£89–£103 ⫶ LDO4.30pm
Lic 🏠 CTV 10P
Ⓥ

GH Sunnymount Hotel Ryefield Rd
(Guestaccom) ☎(0989) 63880
Closed Xmas
*Personally-run house in quiet area of town
offering friendly attentive service.*
6hc ✻ B&b£11.50–£13 Bdi£18.50–£20
W£119–£129.50 ⫶ LDO6pm
Lic 🏠 CTV 7P nc6yrs
Credit card ③ Ⓥ

ROSTON
Derbyshire
Map **7**   SK14

FH Mrs E K Prince **Roston Hall**
(SK133409) ☎Ellastone (033524) 287
May–Sep
*Former manor house, part Elizabethan
and part Georgian, in centre of quiet
village. Ideal for touring the Peak District.*
2rm (1hc) (1fb) ✻ ✳B&b£8.50–£9.50
Bdi£12.50–£13.50 W£80–£90 ⫶ LDO10am
TV 4P nc13yrs 90acres arable beef
Ⓥ

ROTHBURY
Northumberland
Map **12**   NU00

GH Orchard High St ☎(0669) 20684
Closed Xmas
*Delightful house in town centre, tastefully
fitted throughout.*
6hc (1🚿) (1fb) CTV in all bedrooms ✻ Ⓡ
B&b£11–£12 Bdi£18–£19 W£120.75–
£127.75 ⫶ LDO7pm
Lic 🏠 ⚡
Ⓥ

ROTHLEY
Leicestershire
Map **9**   SK51

GH Limes Hotel 35 Mountsorrel Ln
☎Leicester (0533) 302531
Closed Xmas
*Friendly, effeciently run hotel with
comfortable bedrooms and pleasant bar..*
11hc (3🚿) CTV in all bedrooms Ⓡ
✳B&b£17.25 Bdi£24.20 LDO9pm
Lic P ♨

ROTTINGDEAN
East Sussex
Map **5**   TQ30

GH Braemar House Steyning Rd
☎Brighton (0273) 34263
*Family-run comfortable and homely
accommodation, near the Downs.*
16hc (2fb) ✳B&b£9–£10 Wfr£63 M
🏠 CTV ⚡
Ⓥ

GH Corner House Steyning Rd
☎Brighton (0273) 34533
*In a beautiful village, this small
guesthouse offers comfortable
accommodation.*
6hc (1fb) CTV in 3 bedrooms TV in 3
bedrooms ✳B&b£9.50–£10.50 Wfr£66.50
M
🏠 ⚡ nc4yrs
Ⓥ

ROWLEY REGIS
West Midlands
Map **7**   SO98

GH Highfield House Hotel Holly Rd
☎021-559 1066
*Busy private hotel in heart of the Black
Country having predominance of single
rooms.*
12hc ✻ ✳B&b£13 Bdi£18 W£126 ⫶
LDO2pm
Lic 🏠 CTV 12P
Ⓥ

ROWTON
Shropshire
Map **7**   SJ61

FH Mrs V I Evans **Church** *(SJ614198)*
☎High Ercall (0952) 770381
*300-year-old farmhouse providing simple
but comfortable accommodation.*
4rm (2hc) (1fb) ✳B&b£8–£10 Bdi£15–£17
W£100–£115 ⫶ LDO6pm
🏠 CTV 6P ♨ 30acres dairy pig sheep
mixed

ROXTON
Bedfordshire
Map **4**   TL15

FH Mrs J Must **Church** *(TL153545)*
☎(0234) 870234
*Fully modernised farmhouse in a quiet
village. Close to river.*
2hc ✳B&b£12.50
Lic CTV P 66acres arable

RUDYARD
Staffordshire
Map **7**   SJ95

⊶**FH** Mrs E J Lowe **Fairboroughs**
(SJ957609) ☎Rushton Spencer (02606)
341
Apr–Nov
*4½m NW of Leek off A523 then off unclass
rd.*
3hc (1fb) B&b£7.50–£8.50 LDO2pm
🏠 CTV 4P ♨ 140acres beef sheep
Ⓥ

RUFFORTH
North Yorkshire
Map **8**   SE55

GH Wellgarth House Wetherby Rd
☎(090483) 592
Closed 25 & 26 Dec

328

A large well appointed modern house on the edge of the village.

7hc (2🚿) (1fb) CTV in all bedrooms ✖ Ⓡ
B&b£9.50–£14 Bdi£14–£18.50 LDO4pm
🍴 CTV 7P
Ⓥ

RUGBY
Warwickshire
Map **4**   SP57

GH *Mound Hotel* 17–19 Lawford Rd
☎(0788) 3486
Closed Xmas wk

18hc (4🚿) (4fb) CTV in 17 bedrooms TV in
1 bedroom ✖ LDO3pm

Lic 🍴 CTV 14P

RUISLIP
Gt London
London plan **4**   A5
(pages 246–247)

GH 17th-Century Barn Hotel West End
Rd ☎(08956) 36057
Closed 24 Dec–1 Jan

17th-century house with relaxed friendly atmosphere offering comfortable period or modern bedrooms.

58🚿🚿 (6fb) CTV in all bedrooms Ⓡ
✱B&b£34.80–£44.80 Bdi£42.80–£52.80
W£280–£350 ᴷ LDO9.30pm

Lic 🍴 CTV 60P 🏊(heated) sauna bath
gymnasium

Credit cards ①②③ Ⓥ

RUSHTON SPENCER
Staffordshire
Map **7**   SJ96

FH Mrs J Brown **Barnswood** *(SJ945606)*
☎(02606) 261
Closed 2 wks Xmas

Large stone-built farmhouse with grounds stretching to the edge of Rudyard Lake, with splendid views to distant hills.

4rm (2hc) (2fb) ✖ ✱B&b£8–£9 W£52.50 ᴹ
🍴 CTV 5P 100acres dairy

RUSKIE
Central *Perthshire*
Map **11**   NN60

Rufforth
—
Rye

FH Mrs S F Bain **Lower Tarr** *(NN624008)*
☎Thornhill (078685) 202
Etr–Xmas

Large, well-maintained 200-year-old farmhouse, fully modernised and with good views over rolling hill land.

2rm (1hc) (1fb) ✖ Ⓡ ✱B&b£8–£8.50
Bdi£13 LDO5pm

CTV P 2🚗 🐴 ✦ 210acres arable beef
sheep
Ⓥ

RUSTINGTON
West Sussex
Map **4**   TQ00

GH Kenmore Claigmar Rd ☎(0903)
784634

Close to shops and sea front with modern well-appointed rooms.

5hc (1🚿🚿 3🚿) (3fb) CTV in all bedrooms Ⓡ
B&b£10–£12.50 W£62.50–£77.50 ᴹ
🍴 CTV 5P
Ⓥ

GH Mayday Hotel 12 Broadmark Ln
☎(0903) 771198
Closed Oct

A delightful large detached building close to sea front offering good, honest English cooking.

10hc (6🚿) (1fb) CTV in 9 bedrooms ✖ Ⓡ
✱B&b£18–£22 Bdi£24–£27.50 W£135–
£160 ᴷ LDO7pm

Lic 🍴 CTV 12P nc6yrs

RUTHIN
Clwyd
Map **6**   SJ15

FH Mrs B J Jones **Bryn Awel** *(SJ087579)*
Bontuchel (1½m W of Ruthin unclass rd)
☎(08242) 2481

Fishing and other country pursuits are available at this cosy farmhouse.

3rm ✖ ✱B&b£7–£8.50 Bdi£12–£13.50
W£49–£59 ᴹ LDO6pm

CTV 4P ✦ 35acres arable beef sheep

FH Margaret E Jones **Pencoed**
*(SJ107538)*Pwllglas ☎Clawdd Newydd
(08245) 251
Closed Xmas

Stone-built farmhouse with timbered ceilings overlooking the Vale of Clwyd.

3hc (2fb) ✱B&bfr£7.50 Bdifr£10.50
Wfr£72 ᴷ

🍴 CTV P 160acres mixed

FH Mrs T Francis **Plas-Y-Ward**
(SJ118604) Rhewl ☎(08242) 3822
May–Sep

Period farmhouse, dating back to 14th century, set beside River Clwyd and looking towards the Clwydian range. 1½m from Ruthin.

2rm (1hc) ✖ ✱B&b£9–£9.25 Wfr£63 ᴹ

TV 6P nc5yrs ✦ 215acres arable dairy
sheep mixed

RYDAL
Cumbria
Map **11**   NY30
See **Ambleside**

RYDE
Isle of Wight
See **Wight, Isle of**

RYE
East Sussex
Map **5**   TQ92

GH Little Saltcote 22 Military Rd
☎(0797) 223210
Closed Xmas wk

Attractive, Victorian family house providing comfortable accommodation.

5hc (1🚿🚿) (2fb) TV in all bedrooms ✖ Ⓡ
✱B&b£10–£11 W£63–£70 ᴹ
🍴 4P

GH *Mariner's Hotel* 15 High St ☎(0797)
223480

17th-century house retaining some of its old-world charm including original beams. Comfortable rooms.   →

14hc (13🛁) CTV in all bedrooms [R]
LDO10.30pm
Lic ♨ CTV ℙ
Credit cards [1] [2] [3] [4] [5]

GH Old Borough Arms The Strand
☎(0797) 222128
Closed Feb
Skilfully modernised house built in 1720 into the original medieval town walls.
9🚿 (3fb) CTV in all bedrooms [R] ✱B&b£14
Wfr£98 M
Lic ♨ CTV 2P
Credit cards [1] [3] [V]

GH Playden Oasts Hotel Playden
☎(0797) 223502
Mar–Oct
200-year-old oasthouse with considerable character and charm.
5🛁 (2fb) CTV in all bedrooms [R]
✱B&b£18–£23 Bdi£28–£33 Wfr£196 ℓ
LDO9.30pm
Lic ♨ CTV 20P
Credit cards [1] [2] [3] [V]
See advertisement on page 329

FH Mrs P Sullivin **Cliff** *(TQ933237)* Iden Lock ☎Iden (07978) 331
Mar–Oct

Rye — St Albans

Elevated farmhouse run by charming young couple. Extensive views of Romney Marsh; also free coarse fishing on River Rother. Comfortable bedrooms served by a shower room. 2m NE on Military road.
3hc (1fb) [R] ✱B&b£8.50–£9.50 Wfr£56 M
♨ CTV P 6acres small holding

ST AGNES
Cornwall
Map **2** SW75

GH Penkerris Penwinnick Rd ☎(087255) 2262
Peaceful, detached house in lovely garden on the edge of the village.
6hc (3fb) TV in all bedrooms [R]
✱B&b£7.50–£9 Bdi£12–£14 W£70–£85 ℓ
(W only 15 Jul–23 Aug)
CTV 8P

GH Porthvean Hotel Churchtown
☎(087255) 2581
Apr–Nov
Comfortable village-centre guesthouse with friendly owners, also Frin's Restaurant with some vegetarian dishes.
7hc (5🚿) (3fb) ✱B&bfr£11.50 LDO9pm
Lic CTV 7P ⌂
Credit cards [1] [3]

ST ALBANS
Hertfordshire
Map **4** TL10

GH Ardmore House 54 Lemsford Rd
☎(0727) 59313
Comfortable, modern accommodation large detached house with pleasant garden.
14hc (5🚿) (3fb) CTV in all bedrooms ✈ [R]
✱B&b£14.38–£31.05
♨ 16P

GH *Glenmore House Hotel*
16 Woodstock Road North ☎(0727) 53794
Detached family house with large well-kept secluded garden. Sited in quiet residential area.
8hc (2fb) [R]
♨ CTV 5P

GH Melford 24 Woodstock Road North
☎(0727) 53642
Converted house tastefully furnished with pleasant, relaxing décor

12hc (4💧) Ⓡ ✱B&b£19.55–£33.35
W£117.30–£200.10 ⋈ (W only Nov–Mar)
Lic ⌷ CTV 12P
Ⓥ

ST ANDREWS
Fife
Map **12**   NO51

GH Albany 56 North St ☎(0334) 77737
Closed Jan

Neat and compact terraced house.

10hc (3💧) (2fb) ⋎ in 2 bedrooms CTV in 7
bedrooms Ⓡ ✱B&b£8–£12 Bdi£13.50–
£17.50 W£90–£110 ⅄ LDO5.30pm
⌷ CTV ⋟
Ⓥ

GH Argyle 127 North St ☎(0334) 73387
Apr–Oct

*Large private hotel on prominent corner
site, with spacious bedrooms and good
lounge accommodation.*

19💧 (6fb) CTV in 18 bedrooms TV in 1
bedroom Ⓡ ✱B&b£12.50–£17.50 Bdi£18–
£23 W£120–£145 ⅄ LDO6pm
Lic ⌷ CTV ⋟ nc2yrs
Credit cards ① ③ Ⓥ

GH Arran House 5 Murray Park ☎(0334)
74724

*Family-run guesthouse offering good
standard of accommodation near sea
front and golf course.*

6hc (3💧) (4fb) Ⓡ ✱B&b£8–£11 Wfr£65 ⋈
⌷ CTV ⋟
Ⓥ

GH Beachway House 4–6 Murray Pk
☎(0334) 73319
Jan–Nov

*Conversion of three adjoining houses in
between town centres and sea.*

9hc (2💧) (3fb) Ⓡ ✱B&b£8–£15 Bdi£14–
£21 W£95–£135 ⅄ LDO4pm
⌷ CTV ⋟
Ⓥ

GH Bell Craig 8 Murray Pk ☎(0334)
72962

*A neat house with combined lounge/
dining room.*

6hc (3fb) CTV in all bedrooms Ⓡ
B&b£9.50–£13 Wfr£60.70 ⋈
⌷ CTV ⋟
Ⓥ

GH Cleveden House 3 Murray Pl
☎(0334) 74212

*Nicely decorated house in side street
between town centre and sea.*

6hc (2fb) ⋈ ✱B&b£10–£12 W£65–£78 ⋈
⌷ CTV ⋟
Ⓥ

GH Craigmore 3 Murray Pk ☎(0334)
72142
Closed Dec–2 Jan

*Nicely-appointed guesthouse having a
combined lounge and dining room.*

6hc (1↩ 1💧) (4fb) CTV in 2 bedrooms Ⓡ
B&b£8.50–£13 W£56–£87.50 ⋈
⌷ CTV ⋟
Ⓥ

GH Number Ten 10 Hope St ☎(0334)
74601
Feb–Oct

*Attractively decorated house in terraced
row off town centre.*

10hc (4fb) Ⓡ B&b£9.50–£11.50 Bdi£16–
£18 W£108.50–£119 ⅄ LDO4.30pm
⌷ CTV ⋟
Ⓥ

GH West Park House 5 St Mary's Pl
☎(0334) 75933
Closed Dec

*Small but stylish detached Georgian
house close to town centre. Attractive
dining room also open to non-residents,
including à la carte dinners.*

5hc (3💧) (1fb) ⋈ Ⓡ B&b£10.50–£16.50
Bdi£18.50–£24.50 LDO5pm
Lic ⌷ CTV ⋟
Ⓥ

GH Yorkston Hotel 68 & 70 Argyle St
☎(0334) 72019
rs Xmas Day, Boxing Day & New Years
Day

*Neatly appointed house on roadside
leading into town from west.*

11hc (1↩ 1💧) (4fb) Ⓡ ✱B&b£11–
£12.50 Bdi£17.50–£19 W£118–£128 ⅄
LDO6.30pm
Lic ⌷ CTV ⋟
Ⓥ

FH Mrs A Duncan **East Balrymouth**
(NO537142) ☎(0334) 73475
Apr–Oct

*Spacious and well-furnished Victorian
farmhouse overlooking St Andrews Bay.*

3rm (2hc) ⋈ ✱B&b£8.50–£10 Bdi£13.50–
£15
CTV 3P 400acres arable beef sheep

ST AUBIN
Jersey
See **Channel Islands**

ST AUSTELL
Cornwall
Map **2**   SX05

GH Alexandra Hotel 52–54 Alexandra Rd
☎(0726) 74242
Closed 2 wks Xmas

14hc (4💧) (6fb) CTV in all bedrooms
✱B&b£9.50–£10.50 Bdi£13.50–£14.50
W£85.95–£92 ⅄ LDO5pm
Lic ⌷ CTV 16P
Credit cards ① ③

GH *Cornerways* Penwinnick Rd ☎(0726)
61579

6hc (2fb) CTV in 1 bedroom LDO4pm
Lic ⌷ CTV 15P

GH Selwood House Hotel 60 Alexandra
Rd ☎(0726) 65707
Closed 24–28 Dec

12hc (3fb) Ⓡ ✱B&b£10–£11 Bdi£14.50–
£15.50 W£100–£105 ⅄ LDO5pm
Lic ⌷ CTV 10P
Credit cards ① ② ③ Ⓥ

GH Wimereux 1 Trevanion Rd ☎(0726) 72187

Large guesthouse with good facilities and many ensuite bedrooms. Ample car parking.

12hc (5🛁) (4fb) CTV in 4 bedrooms TV in 5 bedrooms ✱B&b£12–£18 Bdi£17–£25 W£126–£140 Ł LDO8pm

Lic ♨ CTV 20P ⌂

Credit cards [1] [2] [3] [5]

ST BLAZEY
Cornwall
Map **2** SX05

GH Moorshill House Hotel Rosehill ☎Par (072681) 2368
Closed Xmas

17th-century house situated along private drive.

5hc (2fb) 🐕 ✱B&b£7.50 Bdi£11 W£70–£75 Ł

♨ CTV 8P

[V]

ST BRIAVELS
Gloucestershire
Map **3** SO50

GH Stowe Court ☎Dean (0594) 530214
Closed Xmas & New Year

17th-century country house in rural location, furnished with antiques and offering friendly atmosphere and good food.

3hc (1🛁) (1fb) LDO10am

6P 1🚗 ⌂

ST BURYAN
Cornwall
Map **2** SW42

GH Higher Trevorian Hotel ☎(073672) 348

Friendly family hotel offering relaxed happy atmosphere and home-cooking.

9hc (2🛁) (2fb) [R] ✱B&b£8.50–£9.50 Bdi£14–£15 W£95–£100 Ł

Lic ♨ CTV 10P ⌂

[V]

St Austell — St Erme

⊢⊣**FH** Mr & Mrs W Hosking **Boskenna Home** *(SW423237)* ☎(073672) 250
Etr–Sep

Farmhouse with pleasant spacious rooms and traditional furniture. In a convenient position with beaches a few miles away.

3rm (1hc) (1fb) 🐕 B&b£7.50 Bdi£12 Wfr£84 Ł

CTV P ⌂ 73acres arable dairy

⊢⊣**FH** Mrs M R Pengelly **Burnewhall** *(SW407236)* ☎(073672) 200
mid May–Oct rs Wed

Spacious former 'gentleman's residence' with all bedrooms having sea views. A footpath from the farmhouse leads to the beach affording safe bathing.

3hc (1fb) TV in 1 bedroom 🐕 B&b£6.50–£7.50 Bdi£11.50–£12.50 W£72–£79 Ł LDO4.30pm

CTV 3P 150acres dairy

Credit cards [1] [2] [3] [V]

ST CATHERINE'S
Strathclyde *Argyllshire*
Map **10** NN10

GH Thistle House ☎Inveraray (0499) 2209
May–mid Oct

Spacious detached Victorian house on Loch Fyne with attractive rooms and loch views.

6hc (2🛁) (1fb) 🐕 [R] ✱B&bfr£12.50 Bdifr£21.50 Wfr£150.50 Ł

♨ 12P nc10yrs

[V]

ST CLEARS
Dyfed
Map **2** SN21

INN *Black Lion Hotel* ☎(0994) 230700

Modestly appointed village inn.

11hc (3fb) CTV in 4 bedrooms TV in 1 bedroom [R] in 4 bedrooms LDO9pm

♨ CTV 25P snooker

ST CLEMENT
Jersey
See **Channel Islands**

ST DAVIDS
Dyfed
Map **2** SM72

GH *Alandale* 43 Nun St ☎(0437) 720333
Closed Dec

6hc (1fb) LDO6pm

♨ CTV nc9yrs

Credit cards [1] [2]

GH Pen-y-Daith 12 Millard Pk ☎(0437) 720720
Apr–Dec

Comfortable modern house, neat and well-maintained.

8hc (2fb) ✱B&bfr£10 Bdifr£16 Wfr£103 Ł

Lic ♨ CTV P

GH The Ramsey Lower Moor ☎(0437) 720321

7hc (1fb) [R] ✱B&b£9 Bdi£14 W£90 Ł
Lic CTV 10P

GH Redcliffe House 17 New St ☎(0437) 720389
Apr–Oct

A small family-run guesthouse near the town centre.

6hc (2fb) 🐕 [R] ✱B&b£9–£10 Bdi£14–£15 Wfr£93 Ł

♨ CTV 2P nc6yrs

GH Y Glennydd 51 Nun St ☎(0437) 720576

Traditional proprietor run guesthouse.

10hc (4fb) 🐕 [R] ✱B&b£8–£9.50 Bdi£12.95–£14.25 W£75–£90 Ł

Lic ♨ CTV

ST ERME
Cornwall
Map **2** SW85

FH Mrs F Hicks **Pengelly** *(SW856513)* Trispen ☎Mitchell (087251) 245
rs Etr–Sep

Attractive, well-built farmhouse. Good central base for touring Cornwall.

3hc (1fb) 🐕 ✱B&b£7–£8 Wfr£49 Ḿ

CTV 4P nc10yrs 230acres mixed

FH Mrs B Dymond **Trevispian Vean** *(SW850502)* Trispen ☎Truro (0872) 79514
Apr–Oct

Extensively modernised farmhouse, clean and well-maintained. Large sun lounge at the front.

7rm (6hc) (3fb) ✗ ✱B&b£7.50–£8.50 Bdi£11.50–£12.50 W£70–£75 Ł LDO4.30pm

CTV P 400acres arable beef sheep mixed

ⓥ

ST HELIER
Jersey
See **Channel Islands**

ST IVES
Cambridgeshire
Map **4** TL37

GH Olivers Lodge Hotel 50 Needingworth Rd ☎(0480) 63252

7hc (1fb) CTV in 1 bedroom TV in 6 bedrooms ✗ Ⓡ ✱B&b£18.50–£27.50 Bdi£24.50–£33.50 W£145.77–£199.33 Ł

Lic 🍴 15P

Credit cards [1] [3] ⓥ

ST IVES
Cornwall
Map **2** SW54
See plan on page 334

GH Bay View Headland Rd, Carbis Bay ☎Penzance (0736) 796469
Plan **1** *B1*

9hc (2⇌ 2‡) (3fb) ✗ ✱B&b£9.25–£12.25 Bdi£12.25–£15.50 W£85.75–£108.50 Ł (W only Jul–Aug) LDO7pm

Lic 🍴 CTV 9P U

GH Blue Mist The Warren ☎Penzance (0736) 795209 Plan **2** *B4*
Etr–Oct

A comfortable and relaxed guesthouse, with well-appointed bedrooms, in centre of town. Seaviews from most bedrooms.

9hc (4‡) (3fb) CTV in all bedrooms Ⓡ ✱B&bfr£9.77 Bdifr£13.80 W£60–£96 Ł LDO5.30pm

4P(charge) nc3yrs

ⓥ

GH Chy-an-Creet Private Hotel Higher Stennack ☎Penzance (0736) 796559
Plan **3** *A5*
mid Mar–mid Oct

Soundly appointed, personally-run residence with grounds and gardens. Close to town centre.

13hc (1⇌1‡) (4fb) CTV in 2 bedrooms Ⓡ ✱B&b£7.95–£11.95 Bdi£10.95–£17.95 Wfr£80 Ł LDO4.30pm

Lic CTV 17P ⌂

Credit cards [1] [3] ⓥ

GH Cottage Hotel Carbis Bay ☎Penzance (0736) 796351 Plan **5** *B2*
May–Oct

Modern hotel in four acres of wooded grounds, overlooking St Ives Bay.

59⇌ (51fb) CTV in all bedrooms ✗ Ⓡ ✱B&b£15–£20 Bdi£15.50–£25 W£129.50–£175 Ł LDO7.30pm

Lic lift 🍴 CTV 100P ⌂ ≈(heated) squash snooker sauna bath

Credit cards [1] [3]

Recommended

GH Dean Court Hotel Trelyon Av ☎Penzance (0736) 796023 Plan **6** *B4*
Apr–Oct

Charming small hotel overlooking bay with particularly well-equipped bedrooms.

12hc (6⇌ 6‡) CTV in all bedrooms ✗ Ⓡ B&b£18–£24 Bdi£22–£28 W£131–£144 Ł (W only Jun–Aug) LDO4pm

Lic 🍴 12P

ⓥ

GH Hollies Hotel Talland Rd ☎Penzance (0736) 796605 Plan **7** *B4*

A very friendly family guesthouse offering good home cooking, well furnished bedrooms, bar and lounge. →

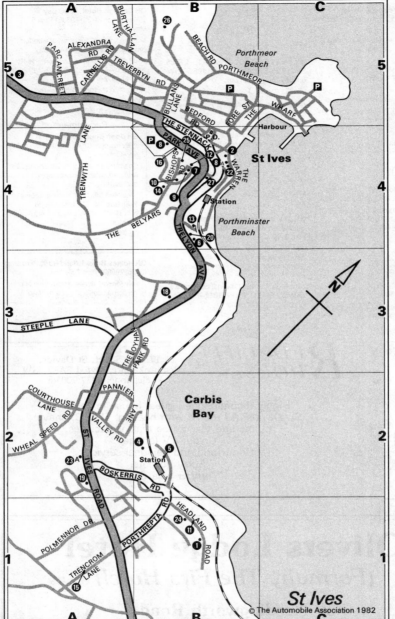

St Ives

1 Bay View
2 Blue Mist
3 Chy-an-Creet
  Private Hotel
4 White House
  Hotel
5 Cottage Hotel
6 Dean Court
  Hotel
7 Hollies Hotel
8 Island View
8A Kandahar &
  Cortina
10 Lyonesse Hotel
11 Monowai
  Private Hotel
12 Pondarosa
13 Primrose Valley
  Hotel
14 Rosemorran
  Private Hotel
15 Hotel Rotorua
18 St Merryn Hotel
19 Sherwell
20 Shun Lee
  Private Hotel
22 Sunrise
23A Thurleston
24 Tregorran Hotel
25 Trelissick Hotel
26 Verbena
27 Windsor

St Ives
© The Automobile Association 1982

10hc (2⇌ 8🛏) (4fb) CTV in all bedrooms
✱ ℝ B&b£10.50–£16 Bdi£15.50–£21
W£98–£139 ⏀ LDO6pm
Lic ▦ CTV 12P ⊶
Ⓥ

GH Island View 2 Park Ave ☎Penzance
(0736) 795111 Plan **8** *B4*
Mar–Oct

*Victorian terraced house, overlooking
harbour.*

10hc (4fb) CTV in all bedrooms ℝ
✱B&b£7.50–£8.50 Bdi£10.50–£12
LDO6.30pm
P

GH Kandahar & Cortina
The Warren ☎Penzance (0736)
796183 Plan **8A** *B4*
Closed Xmas & New Year
*Two delightful character cottages in the
heart of old St Ives at the waters edge.*
11hc (2🛏) (1fb) CTV in 5 bedrooms
B&b£8.50–£15 W£59.50–£100 Ⓜ
▦ CTV 6P(charge)
Ⓥ

GH Lyonesse Hotel 5 Talland Rd
☎Penzance (0736) 796315 Plan **10** *B4*
*Comfortable family hotel in good position
with views of bay.*
16hc (8🛏) (7fb) ✱ B&b£9.50–£13.50
Bdi£13.50–£17.50 W£80–£115 ⏀ LDO6pm
Lic ▦ CTV 8P
Ⓥ

GH Monowal Private Hotel Headland
Rd, Carbis Bay ☎Penzance (0736)
795733 Plan **11** *B1*
May–Sep

*Family hotel, friendly and comfortable,
with pleasant gardens and unrestricted
views of St Ives Bay.*

9hc (4🛏) (2fb) ✱B&b£7.50–£9 Bdi£10–£15
W£70–£105 ⏀ (W only end Jul & Aug)
LDO6.30pm
Lic ▦ CTV 7P nc5yrs ⌁(heated)
Ⓥ

GH Pondarosa 10 Porthminster Ter
☎Penzance (0736) 795875 Plan **12** *B4*
Apr–Oct

St Ives

*Conveniently positioned close to town
and beaches, friendly relaxed atmosphere
and interesting gardens.*

10hc (1🛏) (2fb) ✱ ✱B&b£8–£14
Bdi£13.50–£20 W£91–£133 ⏀ LDO6.30pm
▦ CTV 8P nc5yrs
Ⓥ

GH Primrose Valley Hotel Primrose
Valley ☎Penzance (0736) 794939 Plan **13**
B4
Mar–Oct rs Nov–Feb

*Pleasant, small family hotel ideally
positioned about 100yds from
Porthminster beach.*
11hc (5⇌ 1🛏) (6fb) ✱B&b£9.75–£18.08
Bdi£14.75–£23.08 W£94.70–£145.70 ⏀ (W
only Jul–Aug) LDO6pm
Lic lift CTV 15P ⌁
Ⓥ

GH *Rosemorran Private Hotel*
The Belyars ☎Penzance (0736) 796359
Plan **14** *B4*
Mar–Oct

*Small, comfortably furnished, family hotel
set in own grounds, close to beaches and
town.*

14hc (2⇌ 10🛏) (4fb) ✱ LDOnoon
Lic ▦ CTV 14P
Credit card ①

GH Hotel Rotorua Trencrom Ln, Carbis
Bay ☎Penzance (0736) 795419 Plan **15**
A1
Etr–Oct rs Nov–Etr

*Purpose-built in quiet lane just off St Ives
rd, close to Carbis Bay.*

13⇌🛏 (10fb) ✔ in 2 bedrooms CTV in 1
bedroom TV in 1 bedroom ℝ ✱B&b£9–
£14 Bdi£14–£19 Wfr£112 ⏀ LDO5pm
Lic ▦ CTV 10P ⊶ ⌁
Ⓥ

GH St Merryn Hotel Trelyon ☎Penzance
(0736) 795767 Plan **18** *B3*
Mar–Nov

16hc (11🛏) (8fb) ✱ ✱B&b£8.80–£10.90
Bdi£12.40–£15.10 W£69–£105 ⏀ LDO6pm
Lic ▦ CTV 20P

GH Shun Lee Private Hotel Trelyon Av
☎Penzance (0736) 796284 Plan **20** *B4*
15 Mar–Oct

*Family-owned hotel in superb location
overlooking bay and harbour.*

11hc (3⇌ 8🛏) (1fb) ✱ ✱B&b£12.50–
£15.50 Bdi£17–£21 W£98–£137 ⏀
LDO6pm
Lic ▦ CTV 10P nc5yrs
Ⓥ

See advertisement on page 336

GH Sunrise 22 The Warren ☎Penzance
(0736) 795407 Plan **22** *B4*
Closed Nov

*Picturesque and welcoming cottage
guesthouse close to the sea in old part of
town.*

8hc (1⇌ 1🛏) TV in all bedrooms ℝ
✱B&b£8–£11 W£56–£77 Ⓜ

CTV 4P(charge)
Credit cards ① ③ Ⓥ

See advertisement on page 336

GH Thurleston St Ives Rd, Carbis Bay
☎Penzance (0736) 796369 Plan **23A** *A2*
Mar–Oct

*Attractive detached granite house with
friendly service and public rooms of
character.*

9hc (1⇌ 2🛏) (3fb) ✱ ✱B&b£8–£10
Bdi£12–£14 W£80–£95 ⏀ (W only Jul–Aug)
LDO6pm
Lic ▦ CTV 6P 1🚗
Ⓥ

GH *Tregorran Hotel* Headland Rd,
Carbis Bay ☎Penzance (0736) 795889
Plan **24** *B1*
Apr–Oct   →

Small, well-appointed family-run hotel with good sports facilities.

15hc (7🖾) (3fb) Ⓡ LDO5pm
Lic 🏵 CTV 20P ⚓ ⇘(heated)

GH Trelissick Hotel Bishop's Rd
🕾Penzance (0736) 795035 Plan **25** *B4*

Comfortable family hotel set in own grounds overlooking harbour and St Ives Bay.

15hc (3⇨ 1 🖾) (6fb) CTV in all bedrooms
✱B&b£10–£13.50 Bdi£12.50–£16.50
W£80–£115 ½ LDO6.30pm
Lic CTV 12P ⚶
Credit cards ① ③ Ⓥ

GH Verbena Orange Ln 🕾Penzance
(0736) 796396 Plan **26** *B5*
Closed Dec

Comfortable personally-run guesthouse in elevated position with good views over Porthmeor Beach.

9hc (2fb) ✖ Ⓡ ✱B&b£9.25–£9.75
Bdi£12.50–£13 W£86–£89 ½ LDO4.30pm
lift 🏵 CTV 9P

GH Westaway Farm Hotel Old Coach
Rd, Trink (3m S off unclass rd between
B3311 and Lelant) 🕾Penzance (0736)
797571 Not on plan

Tastefully modernised building on 3 acres of farmland, with trout stream and extensive gardens. Well-equipped bedrooms and a high standard of cooking.

11hc (4fb) CTV in all bedrooms ✖ Ⓡ
✱Wfr£105 ½ LDO8pm
Lic 20P ⚶
Credit card ①

GH White House Hotel The Valley,
Carbis Bay 🕾Penzance (0736) 797405
Plan **4** *B2*
May–Oct

Situated at the foot of a wooded valley a few yards from Carbis Bay beach.

10hc (4⇨ 1🖾) (3fb) ✖ Ⓡ ✱B&b£8–£11
Bdi£12–£15 W£84–£105 ½ LDO4.30pm
Lic 🏵 CTV 10P
Ⓥ

St Ives
St Keyne

GH *Windsor Hotel* The Terrace
🕾Penzance (0736) 798174 Plan **27** *B4*

Pleasant small family hotel with good views, offering friendly warm atmosphere.

9hc (4fb) LDO10pm (previous night)
Lic CTV 3⚓

ST JOHN'S IN THE VALE
Cumbria
Map **11**   NY32

FH Mrs M E Harrison **Shundraw**
(NY308236) 🕾Threlkeld (059683) 227
Etr–Oct

Large, well-maintained, stone-built farmhouse, parts of which date from 1712. In elevated position with views across valley.

3rm (1fb) ✖ ✱B&bfr£7.50 Wfr£49 M̶
TV 4P 52acres mixed

ST JUST
Cornwall
Map **2**   SW33

GH Boscean Country Hotel
🕾Penzance (0736) 788748
Mar–Nov

Well-appointed charming country house. Peaceful location, just a short walk from sea.

9hc (7⇨ 2🖾) (4fb) Ⓡ B&b£12.50–£13.50
Bdi£19–£20 W£118–£126 ½ LDO7pm
Lic 🏵 CTV 12P ⚶

GH Boswedden House Cape Cornwall
🕾Penzance (0736) 788733

Comfortable Georgian family house in peaceful surrounding.

7hc (3🖾) (2fb) B&b£9.50–£11.50
Bdi£13.50–£16.50 W£90–£111 ½ LDOnoon
Lic 🏵 CTV 6P ⚶
Ⓥ

GH Kenython 🕾Penzance (0736) 788607

Friendly welcome and good honest food. Situated at end of a ½m farm track.

4hc (2⇨1🖾) ✱B&b£8.50–£12 Bdi£13.50–
£17 LDO7pm
CTV 6P ⚓ ⚶

ST JUST-IN-ROSELAND
Cornwall
Map **2**   SW83

Recommended

GH Rose-Da-Mar Hotel 🕾'St
Mawes (0326) 270450
Apr–Oct

An attractive detached building, offering good food and friendly service, with views over River Fal.

8hc (4⇨ 1🖾) (1fb) B&b£13.30–£17.40
Bdi£22.80–£26.90 W£155.61–£183.59
½ LDO7.15pm
Lic 🏵 CTV 8P nc11yrs

FH Mrs W Symons **Commerrans**
(SW842375) 🕾Portscatho (087258) 270
Etr–Oct

Pleasant modernised farmhouse, attractively decorated throughout, and situated in a large garden.

4rm (3hc) (1fb) ✱B&b£8–£8.50
Bdi£11.50–£12.50 W£80–£85 ½ LDO9am
CTV 6P nc1yr 61acres arable beef sheep
Ⓥ

ST KEYNE
Cornwall
Map **2**   SX26

GH *Old Rectory Country House Hotel*
(Guestaccom) 🕾Liskeard (0579) 42617

Secluded former Rectory dating from the 16th century. Some four-poster beds.

9rm (5hc 3⇨ 2🖾) (1fb) Ⓡ
Lic 🏵 CTV 10P
Credit cards ① ③

FH Mr & Mrs P Cummins **Badham**
(SX249590) 🕾Liskeard (0579) 43572
Mar–Dec

Traditional Cornish farmhouse, carefully modernised to retain some original features. Set in lovely wooded valley.

5hc (2fb) ✖ Ⓡ B&b£11.50–£12.50
Bdi£18.50–£19.50 W£118–£124 ½
LDO6pm   →

Lic 🏴 CTV 20P ♪(grass) ✔ 4acres small holding
Ⓥ

FH Mr V R Arthur **Killigorrick** *(SX228614)*
☎Liskeard (0579) 20559
Pleasant farmhouse in peaceful surroundings. 3¼m from Liskeard, 500yds W off Duloe–Dobwalls Rd.
4hc (2fb) TV in 1 bedroom ✖
CTV 6P nc5yrs 21acres mixed

ST LAWRENCE
Isle of Wight
See **Wight, Isle of**

ST MARTIN
Guernsey
See **Channel Islands**

ST MARTIN
Jersey
See **Channel Islands**

ST MARYS
Isles of Scilly
No Map
See **Scilly, Isles of**

ST MARY'S LOCH
Borders *Selkirkshire*
Map **11** NT22

INN Tibbie Shiels ☎Cappercleuch (0750) 42231
Closed Xmas Day rs Nov–Mar
Historic little inn standing in a picturesque loch-side position.
6hc (1fb) ✖ B&b£11–£12 Bdi£16–£18 W£112–£126 ⱡ Bar lunch £3.25–£4 Dinner9pm£3.25–£4&alc
🏴 CTV 50P ✔
Credit cards ①③

ST OWEN'S CROSS
Hereford & Worcester
Map **3** SO52

FH Mrs F Davies **Aberhall** *(SO529242)*
☎Harewood End (098987) 256
Mar–Oct

St Keyne — Salcombe

Cosy little farmhouse with basement games room and hard tennis court in grounds.
3hc ✖ Ⓡ ✳B&b£9–£10 Bdi£13.50–£15 W£87.50–£94.50 ⱡ LDO5pm
🏴 CTV 3P nc ♪(hard) snooker table tennis 132acres arable beef

ST PETER PORT
Guernsey
See **Channel Islands**

ST PETER'S VALLEY
Jersey
See **Channel Islands**

ST SAMPSON'S
Guernsey
See **Channel Islands**

ST SAVIOUR
Guernsey
See **Channel Islands**

ST TEATH
Cornwall
Map **2** SX08

FH Mrs S M Mewton **Hillcrest** *(SX056809)*
☎Bodmin (0208) 850258
Closed Xmas wk
A detached farmhouse situated on the edge of the village.
3rm (2hc) ✳B&b£7–£7.50 Bdi£12–£12.50 Wfr£84 ⱡ
🏴 CTV 3P ♨ 19acres smallholding
Credit card ③
See advertisement on page 109

SALCOMBE
Devon
Map **3** SX73

GH Bay View Hotel Bennett Rd
☎(054884) 2238
Mar–Oct

Cosy, spotless property in a commanding position with unrestricted views of estuary and coastline.
10hc (1⇄ 1📺) (2fb) ✖ ✳B&b£15–£20 W£105–£140 M
Lic 🏴 CTV 8P nc6yrs
Credit cards ①③

GH Charborough House Hotel Devon Rd ☎(054884) 2260
mid Jan–mid Oct
9hc (1⇄ 5📺) (2fb) CTV in all bedrooms ✖ Ⓡ B&b£13.50–£18 Bdi£21–£26 W£115–£165 ⱡ LDO8.15pm
Lic 🏴 9P
Credit cards ①③ Ⓥ

GH Devon Tor Private Hotel Devon Rd ☎(054884) 3106
Etr–mid Oct
Small, non-smoking private hotel offering a high standard of accommodation.
6hc (1fb) ✖ ✳B&b£11–£13 Bdi£15–£16.50 W£108–£116 ⱡ LDOnoon
CTV 6P nc6yrs

GH Lodge Higher Town, Marlborough ☎Kingsbridge (0548) 561405
6hc (1⇄ 3📺) Ⓡ ✳B&b£11.50–£16.10 Bdi£19.25–£32 W£140–£220 ⱡ LDO9pm
Lic 🏴 CTV 8P nc9yrs
Ⓥ

GH Lyndhurst Hotel Bonaventure Rd ☎(054884) 2481
Closed Xmas & New Year rs Nov–Feb
6hc (5📺) (1fb) ⚲ in all bedrooms CTV in all bedrooms ✖ Ⓡ B&b£11–£11.50 Bdi£17–£17.50 W£112 ⱡ LDO7pm
Lic 🏴 CTV 8P nc7yrs
Credit cards ①③ Ⓥ

GH Trennels Private Hotel Herbert Rd ☎(054884) 2500
Apr–Oct
Good views of Salcombe, the estuary and the countryside from this friendly, personally-run hotel.
11hc ⚲ in 4 bedrooms ✖ ✳B&b£10–£11 Bdi£14–£15 W£88–£92 ⱡ LDO10am
🏴 CTV 8P 1🏠(charge) nc12yrs

GH Woodgrange Private Hotel Devon Rd ☎(054884) 2439
Apr–Oct
10hc (6🛁 2🚿) (2fb) CTV in all bedrooms [R] B&b£12–£14 Bdi£19.50–£21.50 W£112–£133 M LDO10.30am
Lic 🛋 10P 🏠
Credit cards [1] [2] [3]

SALEN
Isle of Mull, Strathclyde *Argyllshire*
See **Mull, Isle of**

SALFORD
Bedfordshire
Map **4** SP93

INN Red Lion Country Hotel Wavendon Rd ☎Milton Keynes (0908) 583117
11hc (6🛁) CTV in all bedrooms [R] ✱B&b£16.50–£33 Bar lunch 80p–£2.20 Dinner 9pm £8alc
🛋 34P 🚘 nc4yrs
Credit cards [1] [2] [3] [5]

SALFORD
Gt Manchester
Map **7** SJ89

GH Hazeldean Hotel 467 Bury New Rd ☎061-792 6667
rs Xmas Day & Boxing Day
Large and well-equipped family-run house with good restaurant.

21hc (12🛁 5🚿) (2fb) CTV in all bedrooms [R] B&b£27.83–£34.15 W£196.02–£201.60 M LDO8.30pm
Lic 🛋 CTV 21P 🏠
Credit cards [1] [2] [3] [5]

SALISBURY
Wiltshire
Map **4** SU12

GH Byways House 31 Fowlers Rd ☎(0722) 28364
17hc (10🚿) (3fb) CTV in all bedrooms 🐕 ✱B&b£11–£13 W£77–£91 M
🛋 12P 1🚘

GH Glen Lyn 6 Bellamy Ln, Milford Hill ☎(0722) 27880
Quietly but conveniently situated guesthouse with comfortable bedrooms.
5hc (1🛁 1🚿) (1fb) CTV in all bedrooms 🐕 [R] ✱B&b£18–£23
5P nc12yrs

GH Hayburn Wyke 72 Castle Rd ☎(0722) 24141
Handsome gabled corner house beside public park.
6hc (1🚿) (2fb) 🐕 ✱B&bfr£9.50
🛋 CTV 5P 1🚘 nc8yrs
See advertisement on page 340

GH Holmhurst Downton Rd ☎(0722) 23164
Detached brick-built villa situated on main A338 adjacent to Cathedral.
8hc (5🚿) (1fb) 🚭 in 1 bedroom 🐕 ✱B&b£9–£10
🛋 CTV 8P nc5yrs
See advertisement on page 340

INN Old Bell 2 St Ann Street ☎(0722) 27958
Small, personally-run inn dating from the 14th century, with comfortable bedrooms. Parking arranged on request.
7hc (1🛁 4🚿) 🐕 [R] ✱B&b£38
Lic CTV 🅿 🚘 nc14yrs
Credit cards [1] [2] [3] [5]

INN *White Horse Hotel* Castle St ☎(0722) 27844
Red brick, corner-sited property in town centre with good bedrooms and neat restaurant.
12hc (4🛁) (1fb) CTV in all bedrooms [R]
🛋 CTV 6P 6🚘
Credit cards [1] [3] [5]
See advertisement on page 340

Hayburn Wyke

72 Castle Road, Salisbury, Wilts. SP1 3RC
Tel: (0722) 24141

A spacious, well appointed family run guest house with six bedrooms, all with hot and cold water. Full central heating. TV lounge. Car parking. Adjacent to Victoria Park. Convenient for City Centre and historical sites which abound in the area. Open all year.

HOLMHURST GUEST HOUSE

Downton Road, Salisbury, Wiltshire   Tel: (0722) 23164

A well-appointed guest house a few minutes walk from Salisbury Cathedral, city centre and pleasant riverside and country walks. All rooms centrally heated, hot and cold, some have showers and toilets en-suite. Colour TV and free parking in grounds. Reasonable rates.

10 minutes drive from Salisbury.
Come to the quiet, unspoilt village of Downton for a comfortable bed and delicious breakfast at

THE WARREN

HIGH STREET, DOWNTON, SALISBURY, WILTS.

A modernised Georgian house of great antiquity and character offering pleasant English fare and homely high-class accommodation.
Tel: Downton (0725) 20263
2 MILES FROM THE NEW FOREST.

THE WHITE HORSE HOTEL
Castle Street, Salisbury, Wiltshire
Telephone: Salisbury 27844
Proprietors: George & Jan Maidment

A modernised Victorian building tastefully decorated and situated about two minutes walk from the centre of the city with its open air market. The hotel is family run. All the bedrooms have hot & cold, colour TV, radio, tea & coffee facilities, baby listening service and intercom. Residents' lounge with colour television, two large bars and a dining room. The hotel is a free house and has a fine selection of beers, wines and spirits. Garaging and parking available for residents' cars. The hotel is ideally situated for visiting places of interest like Salisbury Cathedral, Wilton House, Stonehenge, Old Sarum and the New Forest. Market days Tuesday and Saturday.

SALTDEAN
East Sussex
Map **5**   TQ30
See also **Brighton & Hove**

— Recommended —

GH Linbrook Lodge 74 Lenham Av
(Guestaccom) ☎Brighton (0273)
33775
Closed Nov

*House built on a slope in quiet
residential area, all rooms have bright
and colourful décor.*

8hc (4🛏) (3fb) CTV in 5 bedrooms TV
in 1 bedroom ® B&b£10–£12.50
Bdi£14–£17.50 W£80.50–£101.50 ⊮
LDO4pm

Lic ⬛ CTV 8P

See advertisement on page 93

SANDOWN
Isle of Wight
See **Wight, Isle of**

SANDPLACE
Cornwall
Map **2**   SX25

GH *Polraen Country House Hotel*
☎Looe (05036) 3956
Closed 15 Dec–Jan

*An attractive and comfortable country
house built of Cornish stone in the early
1700s. Reputed to have once been a
coaching inn.*

6hc (1🛏5🛏) (3fb) ® LDO6pm
Lic ⬛ CTV 12P ⌀
Credit cards 1 3

SANDWICH
Kent
Map **5**   TR35

INN Fleur De Lis Delf St ☎(0304) 611131

4hc (1fb) TV in all bedrooms ®
✳B&bfr£15 Bdifr£21 Lunch £4.50alc
Dinner 9.30pm £6alc
CTV
Credit cards 1 2 3 5

SANNOX
Isle of Arran, Strathclyde *Buteshire*
See **Arran, Isle of**

SANQUHAR
Dumfries & Galloway *Dumfriesshire*
Map **11**   NS71

GH Drumbringan 53 Castle St ☎(06592)
409

*Tidy, comfortable house with open-plan
lounge/dining room standing on the
town's main street.*

5hc (2fb) ✳B&b£8.50–£9 Bdi£12.50–
£13.50 W£85–£92 ⊮ LDO7pm
Lic ⬛ CTV 6P ⌀
Ⓥ

INN *Blackaddie House Hotel*
Blackaddie Rd ☎(06592) 270

*Detached country house, near River Nith,
popular with businessmen.*

7hc (1🛏4🛏) (2fb) CTV in all bedrooms ®
LDO8.30pm
⬛ 25P 2🚗

SANTON BRIDGE
Cumbria
Map **6**   NY10

INN *Bridge* ☎Wasdale (09406) 221
19hc (14🛏5🛏) (3fb) ® LDO9pm
⬛ CTV

SARISBURY GREEN
Hampshire
Map **4**   SU50

GH Dormy ☎Locks Heath (04895) 2626
*Small, homely guesthouse with friendly,
family service.*

7hc (1🛏2🛏) (1fb) CTV in 2 bedrooms TV
in 5 bedrooms ✈ ® ✳B&b£9–£14
Bdi£13–£18 W£91–£112 ⊮ LDO5pm
⬛ CTV 14P

SAUNDERSFOOT
Dyfed
Map **2**   SN10

GH Claremont Hotel St Brides Hill
☎(0834) 813231
Apr–Oct

*Modest family residence in an elevated
position close to beaches and town.*

20hc (6🛏) (5fb) CTV in all bedrooms ✈ ®
✳B&b£12–£14.50 Bdi£15.50–£17 W£85–
£103 ⊮ (W only Jul–Aug) LDO7.30pm
Lic ⬛ CTV 30P 🏊(heated) ⌀ pool table
Credit cards 1 3

GH Harbour Light Private Hotel 2 High
St ☎(0834) 813496
Closed Dec

*Cheerful, small hotel with residents bar. A
few minutes from harbour and beach.*

11hc (5fb) ✈ ® ✳B&b£9.50–£11.75
Bdi£14.50–£15.75 W£98–£109 ⊮ LDO4pm
Lic ⬛ CTV 9P
Credit cards 1 3

GH Jalna Hotel Stammers Rd ☎(0834)
812282
Mar–Oct

*Purpose-built, well-maintained hotel. Few
minutes walk to beach and harbour.*

14hc (8🛏6🛏) (8fb) CTV in all bedrooms
✈ ® ✳B&b£12–£14 Bdi£17–£19 W£106–
£125 ⊮ LDO6pm
Lic ⬛ CTV 16P solarium
Credit cards 1 3 Ⓥ

GH Malin House Hotel St Brides Hill
☎(0834) 812344
Apr–Oct

*Family hotel standing in its own grounds
in elevated position. Bar for residents.*

11hc (4🛏7🛏) (4fb) CTV in all bedrooms
✈ ® ✳B&b£12–£14 Bdi£17–£19 W£115–
£125 ⊮ (W only Jul & Aug) LDO7pm
Lic ⬛ CTV 15P ⌀ 🏊
Credit card 3 Ⓥ

See advertisement on page 342

GH Merlewood Hotel St Brides Hill
☎(0834) 812421
Etr–Nov

*Modern family-run hotel standing in
elevated position overlooking the bay.*

30hc (17🛏11🛏) (24fb) CTV in all
bedrooms ✈ ® ✳B&b£14–£17 Bdi£17–
£20 W£106–£130 ⊮ (W only Jul & Aug)
LDO7pm   →

Lic ♨ CTV 30P 🌳 ≈(heated) pool table

Credit card [3]

GH Rhodewood House Hotel St Brides Hill ☎(0834) 812200

Comfortable, friendly hotel in quiet road overlooking Carmarthen Bay.

33hc (17🛁 4🚿) (7fb) CTV in all bedrooms Ⓡ B&b£15–£22 Bdi£21.50–£28.50 W£135–£179Ł LDO10pm

Lic ♨ CTV 50P 🌳 snooker solarium

Credit cards [1] [2] [3] [5] Ⓥ

GH Sandy Hill Sandy Hill Rd ☎(0834) 813165

Mar–Oct

Well-converted farmhouse in a rural setting offering good home-cooking.

5hc (3fb) CTV in all bedrooms Ⓡ ✱B&b£9–£10 Bdi£12–£14 W£84–£98Ł(W only Jul & Aug)

Lic ♨ 7P nc3yrs ≈(heated)

Ⓥ

SAWLEY
Lancashire
Map **7** SD74

GH Spread Eagle Hotel ☎Clitheroe (0200) 41202

Superbly furnished bedrooms, with lots of extra facilities, are in converted store barn.

10hc (7🛁 3🚿) (2fb) CTV in all bedrooms ✗ Ⓡ ✱B&b£22–£36 Bdi£33–£47 LDO9pm (9.30pm Sat)

Lic ♨ 80P

Credit cards [1] [2] [3] [5] Ⓥ

SAXELBY
Leicestershire
Map **8** SK62

FH Mrs M A Morris **Manor House** *(SK701208)* ☎Melton Mowbray (0664) 812269

Etr–Oct

The manor house, parts of which date back to the 12th- and 15th-centuries, is situated on the edge of the village. 5m from Melton Mowbray.

3hc (2fb) ✗ Ⓡ ✱B&bfr£9 Bdifr£14.75 Wfr£95Ł LDOnoon

♨ CTV 6P 🌳 125acres dairy sheep

SCARBOROUGH
North Yorkshire
Map **8** TA08
See plan

GH *Avoncroft Hotel* Crown Ter ☎(0723) 372737 Plan **1** *C2*

Mar–Oct rs Nov–Feb

Modest, tidy accommodation in a Victorian terraced house.

31hc (1🛁) (13fb) CTV in all bedrooms Ⓡ

Lic CTV

GH Bay Hotel 67 Esplanade, South Cliff ☎(0723) 373926 Plan **2** *D1*

Mar–Dec

Stone-built house overlooking sea, with comfortable public rooms and smart basement dining area.

18hc (2🛁 16🚿) (2fb) CTV in all bedrooms Ⓡ ✱B&b£19–£22 Bdi£24–£27 W£154Ł LDO6pm

Lic ♨ 8P

See advertisement on page 344

GH Burghcliffe Hotel 28 Esplanade, South Cliff ☎(0723) 361524 Plan **3** *C2*

14hc (2🛁 4🚿) (5fb) CTV in all bedrooms ✗ Ⓡ ✱B&b£14–£15 Bdi£19–£22 W£121–£140Ł LDO4pm

Lic CTV ₱

Credit card [3] Ⓥ

GH *Church Hills Private Hotel* St Martins Av, South Cliff ☎(0723) 363148 Plan **4** *C2*

Sturdy Victorian building with comfortable lounge and bar, and cosy basement dining room.

MALIN HOUSE HOTEL
St. Brides Hill, Saundersfoot
Telephone Saundersfoot (0834) 812344

Malin House is a small family hotel, situated in its own grounds, 400 yards from the beach and shops. We offer our patrons, many who return the following year, a relaxing and enjoyable holiday. Residential licensed, with a high standard of accommodation, food and wine. All bedrooms have private facilities, colour TV's and tea makers. Full central heating. Heated swimming pool, children's playground, badminton and croquet lawns. Ample parking. Free courtesy coach to Tenby and surrounding areas in low season.
Reduced rates for senior citizens. Fire certificate.
Telephone or send stamp for colour brochure to:
Janet & Christopher Coleman.

Rhodewood House HOTEL

St Brides Hill, Saundersfoot, Pembrokeshire, Dyfed SA69 9NU Tel: 812200

Rhodewood House is situated in 1½ acres of woodland and gardens, overlooking Carmarthen Bay and only two minutes from Glen Beach. This hotel of charm and character offers a warm welcome to all ages. There is a friendly atmosphere and excellent food together with solarium, launderette, snooker room, à la carte restaurant, lounge bar, Ballroom, car park, children's play park and entertainment during the season, to ensure you our customer a most memorable holiday.

FULLY LICENSED Open all year round
Proprietors: Cynthia & Tony Dowler.

16hc (1fb)

Lic ♨ CTV 🚫 nc9yrs

GH Geldenhuls Hotel 145–147 Queens Pde ☎(0723) 361677 Plan **5** *B4*

Terraced houses on sea front overlooking North Bay with comfortable lounge and separate bar lounge.

Scarborough

35hc (5fb) [R] LDO6pm

Lic ♨ CTV 26P

GH *Park Hotel* 21–23 Victoria Park, Peasholm ☎(0723) 375580 Plan **6** *B4*

Large detached house on the outskirts of the town.

16hc (1🛁 7🚿) (3fb) LDO6pm

Lic ♨ CTV 🚫

Credit cards [1] [2] [3] [4] [5]

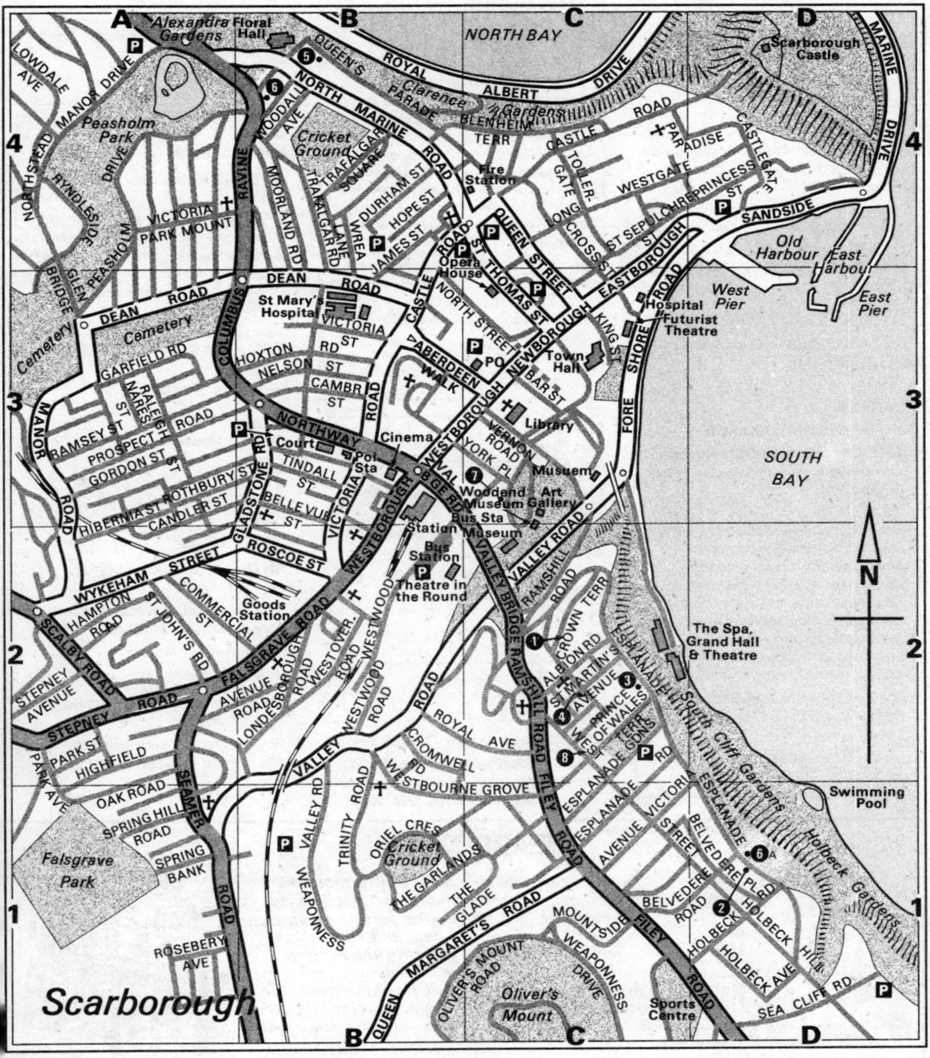

Scarborough

1 Avoncroft Hotel
2 Bay Hotel
3 Burghcliffe Hotel
4 Church Hills Private Hotel
5 Geldenhuis Hotel
6 Park Hotel
6A Premier Hotel
7 Ridbech Private Hotel
8 Sefton Hotel

GH Premier Hotel 66 Esplanade ☎(0723) 361484 Plan **6A** *D1*

Comfortable, family-run hotel overlooking the bay. Dinners are good value.

20hc (16⇌ 4fl) (5fb) CTV in all bedrooms Ⓡ B&b£19–£22 Bdi£24–£27 W£154–£175 ⱢLDO5.30pm

Lic lift ⚐ 6P

GH *Ridbech Private Hotel* 8 The Crescent ☎(0723) 361683 Plan **7** *C3*
May–Oct

In Georgian terrace, hotel has charming, spacious lounge and character dining room.

27hc (3fb) LDO5.45pm

CTV Ᵽ

GH Sefton Hotel 18 Prince of Wales Ter ☎(0723) 372310 Plan **8** *C2*
Apr–Sep

Victorian town house with spacious public rooms and some charming bedrooms.

16hc (2⇌) (2fb) ✗ Ⓡ ✱B&b£11–£11.50 Bdi£12.50–£12.80 W£87.50–£94.60Ⱡ LDO6pm

Lic lift ⚐ CTV Ᵽ nc4yrs

Ⓥ

SCILLY, ISLES OF

No map

ST MARY'S

Recommended

GH Carnwethers Country House
Carnwethers, Pelistry Bay ☎Scillonia (0720) 22415
Apr–Oct

Perched above the secluded bay of Pelistry, in a beautiful part of St Mary's, stands this very friendly country-house retreat. Tastefully furnished bedrooms, a cosy lounge and fresh home-cooking are among the attractions along with a swimming pool discreetly tucked away in the gardens.

5hc (1⇌ 2fl) (1fb) ✗ Ⓡ B&b£12–£17 Bdi£19–£24 W£133–£168Ⱡ LDO6.30pm

Lic ⚐ CTV P ⩧(heated) sauna bath

Ⓥ

Scarborough — Seaton

SCOTCH CORNER

North Yorkshire
Map **8** NZ20

Recommended

INN Vintage Hotel ☎Richmond (0748) 4424
rs Sun Closed Xmas & New Year

A charming inn situated just a few yards from the A1 on the A66, yet still offering attractive views of the surrounding countryside. The cosy bedrooms are modern and equipped with CTV and a hot beverage tray. The rustic-style lounge and bars feature a wealth of chunky stone and wood, whilst excellent-value meals are served in the dining room and bars.

8hc (4⇌ 1fl) CTV in all bedrooms ✗ Ⓡ ✱B&b£16.25–£25 Bdi£25–£35 W£155–£185Ⱡ Lunch £6.25–£7.50&alc Dinner9.15pm £8.75–£9.50&alc

⚐ 50P nc3yrs

Credit cards 1 3 Ⓥ

SEAFORD

East Sussex
Map **5** TV49

GH Avondale Hotel 5 Avondale Rd ☎(0323) 890008

Small, family-run house with friendly atmosphere.

12hc (4fb) ✗ ✱B&b£9–£11 Bdi£14–£16 W£98–£105ⱢLDOnoon

⚐ CTV P

Ⓥ

SEASCALE

Cumbria
Map **6** NY00

GH Cottage Black How ☎(0940) 28416

Delightful guesthouse at edge of Seascale with high standard of accommodation and lovely fells views.

8hc (7⇌ 1fl) (1fb) CTV in all bedrooms ✗ Ⓡ ✱B&bfr£12.50 Bdifr£18 LDO2pm

⚐ CTV 10P

SEATON (nr Looe; 7m)

Cornwall
Map **2** SX35

GH Blue Haven Hotel Looe Hill ☎Downderry (05035) 310
Apr–Sep & Xmas

6hc (3fl) (2fb) ✱B&b£9–£10.50 Bdi£14–£15.50 W£90–£97ⱢLDO8pm

Lic CTV 6P

Ⓥ

SEATON

Devon
Map **3** SY29

GH Check House Beer Rd ☎(0297) 21858
Apr–Sep rs Mar

Victorian-Gothic, listed building in pretty 2-acre woodland garden with gate to beach. Superb location overlooking Lyme Bay. Quiet, comfortable family-run guesthouse.

10hc (2⇌ 3fl) (1fb) ✗ Ⓡ ✱B&b£9.50–£14 Bdi£15–£19.50 W£100–£131.50Ⱡ LDOnoon

Lic ⚐ CTV 12P 1🚘 nc8yrs

Ⓥ

GH Eyre House Queen St ☎(0297) 21455

9hc (4fb) CTV in 3 bedrooms Ⓡ ✱B&b£8.50–£9.50 Bdi£12–£13 W£97Ⱡ

Lic CTV 11P ⩧

GH *Glendare* 46 Fore St ☎(0297) 20542
Apr–Oct

Snug town centre guesthouse with easy access to beach and shops.

6hc (3fb) ✗ LDO4.50pm

Lic ⚐ CTV nc5yrs

GH *Harbourside* 2 Trevelyan Rd ☎(0297) 20085

Personally-run guesthouse with pleasant atmosphere, adjacent to seafront.

7hc (3fb) TV/CTV available in bedrooms [R] LDO5pm

🛋 CTV 10P

GH *Mariners Homestead* Esplanade ☎(0297) 20560
Mar–Oct & Xmas

Neat, clean accommodation on seafront offering good, well-prepared English and Continental dishes.

11hc (1🛁 3🚿) (1fb) CTV in 1 bedroom TV in 1 bedroom [R] LDO4.30pm

Lic 🛋 CTV 9P nc3yrs

Credit card [3]

GH St Margarets 5 Seafield Rd ☎(0297) 20462
Mar–Nov

Large double-fronted house overlooking playing fields. Close to town centre.

9hc (6🚿) (5fb) CTV in all bedrooms [R] *B&b£8.25–£9.25 Bdi£13.75–£14.75 W£83–£96.25 Ⱡ LDO8.30pm

Lic 🛋 6P 🏠 solarium

[V]

GH Thornfield 87 Scalwell Ln (Guestaccom) ☎(0297) 20039

9hc (6🚿) (2fb) 🚭 in 1 bedroom CTV in 7 bedrooms TV in 2 bedrooms [R] B&b£12–£14.50 Bdi£18–£20.50 W£116–£126.50 Ⱡ LDO5pm

Lic 🛋 CTV 10P 🏠 🏊(heated) solarium

[V]

SEAVIEW
Isle of Wight
See **Wight, Isle of**

SEBERGHAM
Cumbria
Map **11** NY34

FH Mrs E M Johnston **Bustabeck** *(NY373419)* ☎Raughton Head (06996) 339
May–Sep

Stone-built farmhouse dating from 1684. Extensively modernised.

3rm (1fb) 🚫 *B&bfr£8 Bdifr£11 Wfr£70 Ⱡ LDOnoon

TV 5P 72acres dairy mixed

Seaton — Sevenoaks

SEDGEFIELD
Co Durham
Map **8** NZ32

Recommended

INN Dun Cow High St ☎(0740) 20894

A quaint village inn recently modernised to offer comfortable and inviting accommodation yet still retaining its original character. All bedrooms have CTV and thoughtful extras such as fresh fruit and a hot drinks tray. Meals are served in the attractive dining room and the cosy bar.

6hc (6fb) CTV in all bedrooms [R] *B&b£16–£27 Lunch£4.50alc Dinner£6.50alc

🛋 P

Credit cards [1] [2] [3] [5]

SELBY
North Yorkshire
Map **8** SE63

GH Hazeldene 34 Brook St (A19) ☎(0757) 704809
Closed Xmas wk

Friendly guesthouse near the town centre with homely accommodation. Comfortable TV lounge and separate breakfast room.

7hc (2fb) 🚭 in 2 bedrooms 🚫 *B&b£10–£11

CTV 5P

SELKIRK
Borders *Selkirkshire*
Map **12** NT42

GH Hillholm 36 Hillside Ter ☎(0750) 21293
Mar–Nov

A spotlessly maintained, well-decorated and furnished house on the south side of town.

3hc 🚫 *B&bfr£10 Wfr£70 M

🛋 CTV 🚫P nc10yrs

SEMLEY
Wiltshire
Map **3** ST82

INN Benett Arms ☎East Knoyle (07483) 221 Telex no 41671

Delightful setting on village green opposite church.

2rm Annexe: 3🚿 CTV in all bedrooms [R] *B&b£15–£18 Bdi£20–£28 W£140–£206 Ⱡ Lunch £8alc Dinner10pm £10alc

🛋 40P

Credit cards [1] [2] [3] [5] [V]

SENNEN
Cornwall
Map **2** SW32

GH Old Manor ☎(073687) 280

8rm (7hc) (3fb) 🚫 [R] *B&b£8–£9 Bdi£13–£14 W£91–£98 Ⱡ LDO9pm

Lic 🛋 CTV 50P 🏠

GH Sunny Bank Hotel Sea View Hill ☎(073687) 278
Feb–Nov

11hc (2fb) *B&b£8.50–£9.50 Bdi£13.50–£14.50 W£89–£95 Ⱡ LDO9pm

Lic 🛋 CTV 20P nc5yrs

SETTLE
North Yorkshire
Map **7** SD86

GH Liverpool House Chapel Sq ☎(07292) 2247

Charming 200-year-old house of great character, in quiet part of town.

8hc (1fb) 🚫 [R] B&b£11–£13 Bdi£17–£19 W£111.30–£117.60 Ⱡ LDO11am

Lic CTV 8P

[V]

SEVENOAKS
Kent
Map **5** TQ55

GH Moorings Hotel 97 Hitchin Hatch Ln ☎(0732) 452589

Cosy homely hotel run by friendly proprietor.

→

9rm (4hc 1呼) Annexe: 2呼 (1fb) CTV in all
bedrooms ✗ ® ✱B&b£24.15 (max)
Lic 🍴 15P
Credit cards ① ③

SHALDON
Devon
See **Teignmouth**

SHANKLIN
Isle of Wight
See **Wight, Isle of**

SHAP
Cumbria
Map **12**   NY51

GH *Brookfield* ☎(09316) 397
Closed Jan

*A friendly, welcoming house with a
comfortable lounge and good meals
served in the attractive restaurant.*

6hc (3fb) ✗ LDO7.30pm
Lic 🍴 CTV 25P 6🚗

↦FH E & S Hodgson **Green Farm**
(NY551121) ☎(09316) 619
Etr–Sep

*Large farmhouse dating from 1705.
Countryside suitable for walking holidays.
Set back off A6.*

3rm (2hc) (2fb) ✗ B&b£8–£8.50
CTV 3P 167acres beef dairy sheep mixed

FH S J Thompson **Southfield** *(NY561184)*
☎(09316) 282
Etr–Sep

*Farmhouse set in pleasant area with good
views. Guests are welcome to interest
themselves in farm work.*

2rm (1hc) ✗ ✱B&b£8–£9 W£63 Ḿ
CTV 2P nc 110acres mixed

SHAWBURY
Shropshire
Map **7**   SJ52

FH Mrs S J Clarkson **Longley** *(SJ602228)*
Stanton Heath ☎(0939) 250289
Closed Xmas

*Originally dating back to 1710, this
attractive brick and tile cottage is
associated with Paul C Bragg, the world
authority on Natural Farming. ½m NE off
A53.*

2rm (1fb) Annexe: 1↩呼 ✱B&b£8–£10
Bdi£12 Wfr£56 Ḿ
🍴 CTV 6P 1🚗 15acres sheep mixed

FH G C Evans **New** *(SJ586215)*
Muckleton ☎(0939) 250358

*Modern farmhouse with large, newly
furnished and extremely comfortable
rooms. 2m NE of Shawbury off A53 on
unclass rd.*

4hc (1呼) (1fb) ® ✱B&b£8–£10 Bdi£14–
£16 W£90–£100 Ⱡ

𝄫 CTV 10P nc3yrs 70acres arable beef
Ⓥ

FH Mr P E Griffiths **Sowbath** *(SJ576230)*
☎(0939) 250417

*Large Victorian farmhouse on A53, 1½m
north of Shawbury and midway between
Shrewsbury and Market Drayton.*

3rm (2hc) (2fb) ✗

𝄫 CTV 8P 1🐾 ♟(grass) ⚓ 200acres
arable dairy

SHEARSBY
Leicestershire
Map **4**   SP69

FH Mrs A M Knight **Knaptoft House**
(SP619894) Brungtingthorpe Rd
☎Peatling Magna (053758) 388

3hc (4fb) Ⓡ ✻B&b£9–£10 Bdi£14–£15.50
W£98–£105 ⅃ LDO2pm

𝄫 CTV 10P ⚙ 145acres mixed

Credit card ①

See advertisement on page 258

FH Mrs S E Timms **Wheathill** *(SP622911)*
Church Ln ☎Peatling Magna (053758)
663
Closed Xmas

*Old brick-built farmhouse retaining
original beams and inglenook fireplaces.*

3rm (1hc) (1🖾) ✗ Ⓡ ✻B&b£8.50–£9.50
Bdi£13–£14 W£85–£95 ⅃ LDOam

𝄫 CTV 3P 133acres dairy
Ⓥ

SHEFFIELD
South Yorkshire
Map **8**   SK38

GH Lindum Hotel 91 Montgomery Rd
☎(0742) 552356
Closed Xmas

*Victorian town house with well-equipped
bedrooms and cosy public areas.*

10hc (1fb) TV in 2 bedrooms Ⓡ
✻B&bfr£15.50 Bdifr£20 Wfr£140 ⅃
LDO7pm

Lic 𝄫 CTV 5P ⚙

GH Millingtons 70 Broomgrove Rd (off
A625 Eccleshall Rd) ☎(0742) 669549

Shawbury
—
Sheriff Hutton

*A smartly fitted and furnished terraced
guesthouse.*

5hc CTV in all bedrooms ✗ Ⓡ B&b£11–
£13 W£77–£87.50 Ɱ

𝄫 CTV 4P nc12yrs

SHELFANGER
Norfolk
Map **5**   TM18

FH Mrs D A Butler **Shelfanger Hall**
(TM109832) (S of village off B1077) ☎Diss
(0379) 2094
Apr–Oct

*A pink-washed, brick-built 16th-century
farmhouse encircled by a moat.*

3hc (1fb) ✗ ✻B&b£8–£10 W£56–£63 Ɱ

𝄫 CTV 10P nc8yrs 400acres dairy

SHELSLEY BEAUCHAMP
Hereford & Worcester
Map **3**   SO76

FH Mr & Mrs Moore **Church House**
(SO729627) ☎(08865) 393
Mar–Oct

*Imposing 18th-century farmhouse on the
banks of the River Teme, offering good
English cooking.*

2hc (1⇆) Ⓡ ✻B&b£9–£9.50 Bdi£14–
£14.50 W£98–£101.50 ⅃ LDO10am

𝄫 CTV 10P

200acres arable beef poultry sheep
Ⓥ

SHENNINGTON
Oxfordshire
Map **4**   SP34

FH Mrs R Nunneley **Sugarswell**
(SP361441) ☎Tysoe (029588) 512

*Modern farmhouse with colourful
bedrooms. Public areas tastefully
furnished with antiques.*

3hc (2⇆) CTV in 2 bedrooms TV in 1
bedroom ✗ Ⓡ ✻B&b£12–£14 Bdi£22–
£25 W£145–£165 ⅃

𝄫 10P nc5yrs
300acres dairy

SHEPTON MALLET
Somerset
Map **3**   ST64

INN Kings Arms Leg Sq ☎(0749) 3781
Closed Xmas

*17th-century inn of charm and character
with pretty bedrooms and good fresh
food.*

3hc TV in all bedrooms Ⓡ B&b£12–£14.50
Bar lunch £2.25–£6.50

𝄫 CTV 40P nc10yrs
Ⓥ

SHERBOURNE
Warwickshire
Map **4**   SP26
See **Warwick**

SHERFIELD ON LODDON
Hampshire
Map **4**   SU65

GH Wessex House Hotel
☎Basingstoke (0256) 882243
Closed 10 days Xmas

*Attractive, smart well-equipped hotel in
neat grounds.*

8⇆ CTV in all bedrooms ✗ Ⓡ ✻B&b£15–
£25 LDO9.30pm

Lic 𝄫 nc5yrs

Credit cards ① ③

See advertisement on page 51

SHERIFF HUTTON
North Yorkshire
Map **8**   SE66

GH Rangers House Sheriff Hutton Park
(Guestaccom) ☎(03477) 397

*Interesting and unusual building with
minstrel's gallery and ornate marble
fireplace, as well as attractive garden.*

6hc (2⇆ 2🖾) (1fb) ✗ ✻B&b£19–£24
Bdi£25–£35 W£175–£220 ⅃ LDO10.30pm

Lic 𝄫 CTV 20P ⚙

SHERINGHAM
Norfolk
Map **9** TG14

GH Beacon Hotel Nelson Rd ☎(0263) 822019
Apr–Oct

8hc ⋈ [R] ✱B&bfr£12.50 Bdifr£17 Wfr£100 ⱡLDO7pm

Lic ♨ CTV 8P nc12yrs

Credit cards [1] [3] [V]

GH Beeston Hills Lodge 64 Cliff Rd ☎(0263) 822615
Etr–Oct

7hc (2🛁) (1fb) ⋈ [R] ✱B&bfr£9 Bdifr£12.50 Wfr£85 ⱡ

♨ CTV 7P nc8yrs

GH Camberley House Hotel 62 Cliff Rd ☎(0263) 823101
May–Sep

7hc (6🚿) (4fb) [R] B&b£9–£12 Bdi£13.50–£16.50 W£89–£109 ⱡ LDOnoon

Lic ♨ CTV 9P ⌂

[V]

GH Melrose Hotel 9 Holway Rd ☎(0263) 823299
Mar–Dec

Family-owned and run hotel near town centre.

10hc (2fb) [R] ✱B&b£10–£11 Bdi£15–£16 W£79–£89 ⱡ LDO2pm

Lic ♨ CTV 10P

Credit card [1] [3]

SHETLAND
Map **16**

LERWICK
Map **16** HU44

GH Glen Orchy 20 Knab Rd ☎(0595) 2031

Large house on top of hill overlooking Lerwick Harbour.

6hc (2🚿) (1fb) ⋈ ✱B&b£10–£13.50 Bdi£15–£18.50 W£105–£129.50 ⱡ

♨ CTV P̸ ⌂

[V]

SHIPDHAM
Norfolk
Map **8** TF90

GH Pound Green Hotel & Restaurant Pound Green Ln ☎Dereham (0362) 820165

Large modern house in residential area, with an acre of grounds and heated outdoor swimming pool.

14hc (7🚿) (3fb) ✱B&b£12.35–£16.95 Bdi£18.85–£23.45 W£131.95–£164 ⱡ LDO9.30pm

Lic ♨ CTV 45P 2🚗 🏊(heated) snooker

SHIPSTON-ON-STOUR
Warwickshire
Map **4** SP24

FH Mr & Mrs Boyes **Portobello** *(SP234399)* ☎(0608) 61618

Good value for money is offered at this small 17th-century farmhouse. 1½m W at B4035/A429 junction.

4hc (1🛁) (1fb) ⋈ ✱B&b£8.50–£9 Bdi£13.50–£14 W£90–£95 ⱡ LDO3pm

♨ CTV 10P 2🚗 6acres non-working

INN Bell Sheep St ☎(0608) 61443

7hc (2🛁) (1fb) [R] CTV in all bedrooms ✱ B&b£20–£30 Bdi£25–£35 W£170–£230 ⱡ LDO9.30pm

Lic ♨ CTV 24P

Credit cards [1] [2] [3] [4] [5]

INN *White Bear* High St (Guestaccom) ☎(0608) 61558

Friendly town centre inn with comfortable attractive bedrooms.

9hc (3🛁 6🚿) (2fb) [R] CTV in all bedrooms LDO9.30pm

♨ 20P

Credit cards [1] [2] [3] [5]

SHIRWELL
Devon
Map **2**   SS53

FH Mrs G Huxtable **Woolcott** *(SS600388)*
☎(027182) 216
Apr–Nov

*Situated in a quiet picturesque area on
the foothills of Exmoor. The bedrooms
overlook the unspoilt Devon countryside
1½ NE off A39.*

3rm (2fb) ✱B&b£6.50 Bdi£9.50 W£65.50 ⊬
LDO4pm
🍴 CTV 4P ⚭ 83acres beef sheep
ⓥ

SHOREHAM-BY-SEA
West Sussex
Map **4**   TQ20

GH *Pende-Shore Hotel* 416 Upper
Shoreham Rd ☎(07917) 2905
Closed 24 Dec–1 Jan

*Very smart private hotel with added
personal touches. There is a bistro-style
restaurant and a bar.*

14hc (1⇄) (2fb) TV in 6 bedrooms ✖ ⓡ
LDO7pm
Lic 🍴 CTV 8P

SHOTTLE
Derbyshire
Map **8**   SK34

GH Shottle Hall Farm ☎Cowers Lane
(077389) 276
Closed Xmas

9hc (3fb) ⓡ ✱B&b£14–£16 Bdi£21–£23
W£143.50–£157.50 ⊬ LDO7.30pm
Lic 🍴 CTV 20P
ⓥ

See advertisement on page 139

SHREWSBURY
Shropshire
Map **7**   SJ41
See also **Bomere Heath** and **Uffington**

GH *Cannock House Private Hotel*
182 Abbey Foregate ☎(0743) 56043
Closed Xmas

Shirwell
—
Skegness

7hc (2fb) ✖
🍴 CTV 7P

GH Fieldside Hotel 38 London Rd
☎(0743) 53143

*Situated on A5112, 1½m SE of town
centre. Comfortable accommodation for
both tourists and commercial guests.*

7hc (3🛏) (1fb) CTV in all bedrooms ✖
✱B&b£12–£15 Bdi£17–£20 LDO8pm
Lic 8P 2⚭ nc11yrs

GH Sandford House Hotel St Julians
Friars ☎(0743) 3829
Closed 2 wks Dec–Jan

*Listed building close to town centre and
river walks.*

7hc (1⇄) (1fb) CTV in all bedrooms ⓡ
✱B&b£11–£14 W£77–£98 M
Lic 🍴 CTV ⨯ ⚭
Credit cards ① ③ ⓥ

GH Sydney House Hotel Coton Cres,
Coton Hill ☎(0743) 54681

*Edwardian house, north of town centre,
offering modern, well-maintained
accommodation.*

8hc (1🛏) (3fb) CTV in all bedrooms ✖
✱B&bfr£9 Bdifr£14.50 W£100–£112.50 ⊬
LDO8pm
Lic 🍴 7P 1⚑
ⓥ

SIDMOUTH
Devon
Map **3**   SY18

GH Canterbury Salcombe Rd ☎(03955)
3373
Mar–Oct

7hc (1⇄ 4🛏) (3fb) ⓡ ✱B&b£10.50–£12
Bdi£14.50–£16 W£96–£108 ⊬ LDO5pm
Lic CTV 6P

GH Ryton House 52–54 Winslade Rd
☎(03955) 3981

*Victorian converted semis in residential
road. Well-situated for town centre and
seafront.*

9hc (2fb) ✱B&b£7–£8 Bdi£10–£12 W£69–
£84 ⊬ (W only 1–19 Aug) LDO4pm
🍴 CTV 8P
ⓥ

SILLOTH
Cumbria
Map **11**   NY15

GH Nith View 1 Pine Ter ☎(0965) 31542

*A lovely guesthouse overlooking the
Solway Firth with attractive and
comfortable bedrooms.*

8hc (4🛏) ✚ in 1 bedroom CTV in 1
bedroom TV in 4 bedrooms ⓡ ✱B&b£11
Bdi£15.50 W£103–£103.50 ⊬ LDO3pm
Lic 🍴 CTV 10P
Credit cards ① ③ ⓥ

SKEGNESS
Lincolnshire
Map **9**   TF56

GH Chatsworth Hotel North Pde
☎(0754) 4177
May–Oct rs Mar, Apr & Nov

22hc (8⇄ 5🛏) (5fb) ⓡ B&b£13.25–£15.50
Bdi£17.50–£19.75 W£106–£122 ⊬
LDO7.30pm
→

Lic 🍴 CTV 8P 4🛥
Credit cards ① ③ Ⓥ

SKIPTON
North Yorkshire
Map **7**   SD95

GH Craven House 56 Keighley Rd
☎(0756) 4657

*Family-run house with good all round
facilities.*

7hc (2⇔) (1fb) ⑧ ✳B&b£9–£10.50
Bdi£15–£15.50 W£105–£112 ⫽ LDO5pm
🍴 CTV P

GH Fairleigh 24 Bell Vue Ter, Broughton
Rd ☎(0756) 4153

*A small, family-run house with a homely
atmosphere, close to town centre.*

5hc (2fb) ✳B&bfr£9 Bdifr£14 LDO3pm
CTV 6P

GH Highfield Hotel 58 Keighley Rd
☎(0756) 3182

*Pleasant stone-house in Victorian-style,
close to town centre.*

9hc (2⇔) (1fb) CTV in 5 bedrooms TV in 4
bedrooms ⑧ B&b£11.25–£20 W£74–£135
Ⓜ LDO7pm
Lic CTV 🅿

Skegness
─
Skye, Isle of

GH Unicorn Keighley Rd ☎(0756) 4146
*Well-furnished town centre hotel.
Continental breakfast only is available,
served in bedrooms.*

10⇔🛏 (6fb) CTV in all bedrooms ⑧
✳B&b£16–£22 W£100.80–£140 Ⓜ
🍴 CTV 🅿
Credit cards ② ③ Ⓥ

INN *Red Lion Hotel* High St ☎(0756)
60718

*Cosy well-furnished inn (the oldest
building in Skipton).*

4hc (2⇔) (1fb) CTV in all bedrooms ⑧
🍴 CTV 6P

SKIPTON-ON-SWALE
North Yorkshire
Map **8**   SE37

GH Skipton Hall ☎Thirsk (0845) 567457
*Stone-built Georgian farmhouse with
comfortable spacious rooms of character;
standing in own grounds by the village
centre.*

7hc (2⇔ 2🛏) ⑧ ✳B&b£15–£19 Bdi£21–
£27 W£139–£181 ⫽ LDO7pm
Lic 🍴 CTV 12P 🏌(grass)
Credit cards ① ② ③ Ⓥ

SKYE, ISLE OF
Highland *Inverness-shire*

BROADFORD
Map **13**   NG62

GH *Hilton* ☎(04712) 322
Apr–Oct

Two-storey bungalow with sea views.

8hc (2fb) ✈ LDO6pm
Lic 🍴 CTV 16P

DUNVEGAN
Map **13**   NG24

GH Roskhill Roskhill (3m S A863)
☎(047022) 317
Mar–Nov

*A comfortable and friendly guesthouse
situated about 3 miles from Dunvegan
(A863).*

5hc (2fb) ⑧ ✳B&bfr£9 Bdifr£15 W£100–
£110 ⫽ LDO6pm
Lic 🍴 CTV 6P
Ⓥ

ISLE ORNSAY
Map **13**   NG71

GH Old Post Office House ☎(04713)
201
Mar–Oct

*Tidy garden with pleasant hill and sea
views.*

4rm (3hc) Annexe: 2hc (3fb) ✳B&b£9
W£63 Ⓜ
CTV 10P
Ⓥ

PORTREE
Map **13**   NG44

GH Bosville Bosville Ter ☎(0478) 2846
End Apr–Sep

*Well-maintained rough-cast building
overlooking harbour and Raasay.*

14hc (7🛏) (2fb) ⑧ ✳B&b£13.50–£16.50
Bdi£19.50–£23 Wfr£129 ⫽ LDO8pm
Lic 🍴 CTV 10P
Credit card ①

GH Craiglockhart Beaumont Cres
☎(0478) 2233
Closed Dec

*Comfortable house in pleasant seafront
location overlooking the harbour and
Raasay.*

4hc (2🛏) Annexe: 6hc (2fb) ⑧
✳B&b£11.50–12.50 Bdi£16.80–£17.80
W£110–£117 ⫽ LDO7pm
🍴 CTV 4P

FH Mrs M Bruce **Cruachanlea**
(NG513373) Braes ☎Sligachan (047852)
233

Situated 5m SE of Portree on B883, overlooking sea to the Isle of Raasay. Hill views all around.

4hc (2fb) [R] ✱B&b£7.50–£8.50 Bdi£11.50–£12.50 LDO5pm

♨ CTV 6P 15acres sheep

FH Sylvia P MacDonald **Upper Ollach** *(NG518362)* Braes ☎Sligachan (047852) 225

May–Sep

Grey, stone crofting farm in hilly farmland with gardens and trees screening the house. Close to coastline, 6½m SE of Portree on B883.

2rm (1fb) 🐕 ✱B&bfr£7.50 Bdifr£11.50 LDO5pm

CTV 3P 8acres arable poultry sheep

WATERLOO
Map **13** NG62

GH Ceol-na-Mara ☎Broadford (04712) 323

Etr–Sep

6hc (1fb) 🚭 in 3 bedrooms 🐕 [R] ✱B&b£8–£8.50 Bdi£15–£15.50 Wfr£98 Ł LDO9pm

CTV 6P

SLAIDBURN
Lancashire
Map **7** SD75

Recommended

FH Mrs P M Holt **Parrock Head** *(SD697527)* Woodhouse Ln ☎(02006) 614

Feb–Dec

A charmingly modernised, 17th-century farmhouse set in lovely countryside. The comfortable lounge has an open-fire and there is also a library and small bar. Bedrooms are very well furnished with lots of thoughtful extras. Excellent home-cooking is provided by Mrs Holt.

3🛁 Annexe: 6🛁 CTV in all bedrooms [R] ✱B&b£18 Bdi£24–£27 LDO7.45pm

Lic ♨ 14P 200acres beef sheep mixed

Credit card [2] [V]

SLEAFORD
Lincolnshire
Map **8** TF04

GH The Mallards 6–8 Eastgate ☎(0529) 303062

12rm (11hc 2🛁 4🚿) (2fb) CTV in all bedrooms [R] ✱B&b£15–£20 Bdi£22.50–£29.50 LDO8.30pm

Lic ♨ CTV 4P

Credit cards [1] [2] [3] [5] [V]

SLEDMERE
Humberside
Map **8** SE96

INN Triton ☎Driffield (0377) 86644

Good value accommodation in a period inn in this attractive estate village.

6rm (5hc 1🛁) (1fb) CTV in 4 bedrooms TV in 2 bedrooms [R] ✱B&b£10.50 Bdi£15 W£94.50 Ł Lunch£4–£6&alc High tea£3–£4.50 Dinner10pmfr£5&alc

♨ CTV 30P

[V]

SLINFOLD
West Sussex
Map **4** TQ13

GH Park Stane St ☎(0403) 790723

7hc (4🚿) (1fb) CTV in all bedrooms 🐕 [R] B&b£17.50–£20 W£122.50–£140 M

♨ CTV 12P

Credit cards [1] [3] [V]

SLOUGH
Berkshire
Map **4** SU97

GH Colnbrook Lodge Bath Rd, Colnbrook(3m E A4) (Guestaccom) ☎(0753) 685958

Closed 24–26 Dec

A cosy house with a friendly, informal atmosphere within easy reach of Heathrow Airport.

8hc (1🚿) (2fb) 🐕 [R] ✱B&b£15–£20 W£70–£110 M

Lic ♨ CTV 12P ⌂

Credit cards [1] [3] [V]

See advertisement on page 352

SLYNE
Lancashire
Map **7** SD46

INN Slyne Lodge ☎Hestbank (0524) 823389

Pleasant inn with some excellent bedrooms in adjacent converted barn.

13🛁 🚿 (4fb) CTV in all bedrooms [R] ✱B&b£15–£20 W£95–£126 M Bar lunch £2–£7 Dinner10pm£5–£8.50

♨ 100P

Credit card [1] [V]

SMEATON, GREAT
North Yorkshire
Map **8** NZ30

FH Mrs N Hall **Smeaton** *(NZ349044)* ☎(060981) 336

May–Sep rs Oct–Apr Closed Xmas & New Year

A 17th-century working farm on the edge of the village. Spacious rooms of period character, clean, well-furnished and comfortable. Situated in rural surroundings.

3hc 🐕 ✱B&b£9–£10 Bdi£15.25–£16.25 Wfr£100 Ł LDO10am

♨ CTV 4P nc7yrs 120acres dairy mixed

[V]

SNAPE
Suffolk
Map **5** TM35

INN Crown ☎(072888) 324

Closed Xmas Day

4hc CTV in all bedrooms ✱B&bfr£14.30 Lunch £5–£20 Dinner8.30pm £6–£25

♨ 200P

Credit cards [1] [2] [3] [5]

See advertisement on page 352

SOLVA
Dyfed
See **Llandeloy**

SOMERTON
Somerset
Map **3**   ST42

GH Church Farm School Ln, Compton
Dundon ☎(0458) 72927

4hc Annexe: 2⇆᷈ (2fb) CTV in all
bedrooms ® B&b£12.50 Bdi£20 W£120 ⚹
LDO6pm
Lic ♔ 6P

SOPWORTH
Wiltshire
Map **3**   ST88

FH Mrs D M Barker **Manor** *(ST826865)*
☎Didmarton (045423) 676
Apr–Oct

3rm (1fb) ✻ ✻B&b£8–£10 Wfr£50 ⓜ
TV 4P 300acres mixed

SOUTHAMPTON
Hampshire
Map **4**   SU41
See plan

GH Banister House Hotel 11 Brighton
Rd, off Banister Rd ☎(0703) 221279
Plan **1** *B4*
Closed Xmas wk

*Private hotel with warm and friendly
atmosphere. Popular bar meals and
dining room.*

23hc (1⇆ 2᷈) (3fb) CTV in all bedrooms
✻B&b£13–£21 Bdi£17.50–£25.50
W£122.50–£178.50 ⚹ LDO8.15pm
Lic ♔ 14P
Credit card ① ⓥ

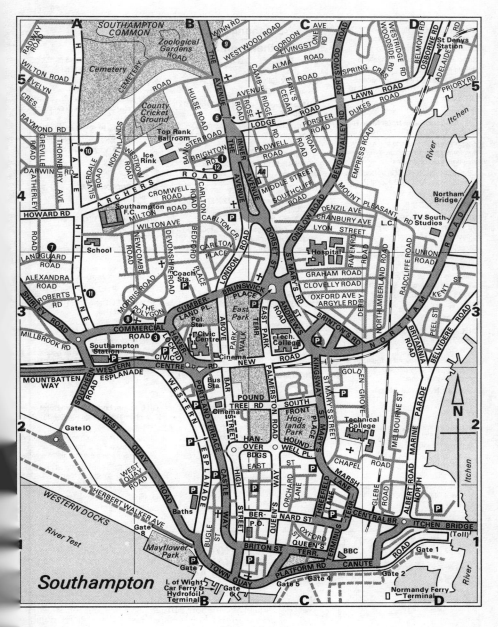

Southampton

1	Banister House Hotel	**9**	Lodge
3	Claremont	**10**	Madison
6	Elizabeth House Hotel	**11**	Rosida Garden Hotel
7	Hunters Lodge Hotel	**12**	St Regulus Hotel
8	Linden		

GH Claremont 33 The Polygon ☎(0703) 223112 Plan **3** *B3*
Closed 2 wks Xmas

Small, homely house within walking distance of city centre.

14hc (2🚿) (4fb) CTV in all bedrooms
*B&b£9.20–£11.50 Bdi£12.65–£16.10
LDO8.30pm

Lic ♨ CTV 10P

GH *Elizabeth House Hotel* 43/44 The Avenue ☎(0703) 224327 Plan **6** *B5*

Friendly, efficient service and modern, comfortable accommodation with some well-equipped bedrooms.

25hc (5🛁 9🚿) (3fb) CTV in all bedrooms
[R] in 14 bedrooms LDO8.45pm

Lic ♨ CTV 22P

Credit cards [1] [2] [3] [5]

GH Hunters Lodge Hotel 25 Landguard Rd, Shirley ☎(0703) 227919 Plan **7** *A3*
Closed 18 Dec–7 Jan

Quietly situated, this proprietor-run hotel combines modern and traditional standards.

18hc (3🛁 3🚿) (3fb) 🚭 in 12 bedrooms CTV in all bedrooms [R] *B&b£12.50–£20 Bdi£18.50–£26 Wfr£126 Ⱡ LDO7.15pm

Lic ♨ 🚗

Credit card [3] [V]

GH Linden 51 The Polygon ☎(0703) 225653 Plan **8** *A3*
Closed Xmas wk

Two terraced houses set in the heart of the city centre. Well-decorated and comfortably furnished.

13hc (4fb) ✗ *B&b£9–£10.50

♨ CTV 7P

[V]

GH Lodge 1 Winn Rd, The Avenue ☎(0703) 557537 Plan **9** *B5*
Closed Xmas wk

Comfortable well-managed accommodation with spacious lounge amenities.

13hc (2🛁 3🚿) (5fb) CTV in 10 bedrooms
[R] *B&b£14 Bdi£20 W£126–£163.80 Ⱡ
LDO9pm

Southampton — Southend-on-Sea

Lic ♨ CTV 10P

Credit cards [1] [3] [V]

GH Madison 137 Hill Ln ☎(0703) 333374 Plan **10** *A4*

Well-maintained, small but comfortable guesthouse with lounge. Friendly and efficient service.

8hc (4fb) TV in all bedrooms ✗ [R]
*B&b£9 Bdi£13 W£91 Ⱡ LDOnoon

♨ CTV 6P

[V]

GH *Rosida Garden Hotel* 25–27 Hill Ln ☎(0703) 228501 Plan **11** *A3*
rs 22 Dec–2 Jan

Friendly, family hotel with well-equipped modern bedrooms and public facilities.

29hc (27🛁 🚿) (4fb) CTV in all bedrooms
[R] LDO9pm

Lic lift ♨ CTV 30P 🏊(heated)

Credit cards [1] [3]

GH St Regulus Hotel 5 Archers Rd ☎(0703) 224243 Plan **12** *B4*

Large Victorian hotel set in quiet residential area.

27🛁🚿 (3fb) CTV in all bedrooms
B&b£14.75 W£103.25 M̸ LDO6.30pm

Lic ♨ CTV P

SOUTH BRENT
Devon
Map **3** SX66

FH M E Slade **Great Aish** *(SX689603)*
☎(03647) 2238
Closed Dec

Situated near Dartmoor National Park. Extensive views of countryside from farmhouse.

5hc (3fb) ✗ *B&b£8–£9

CTV 6P 60acres dairy mixed

SOUTH BREWHAM
Somerset
Map **3** ST73

FH Mrs D Dabinett **Holland** *(ST732357)*
☎Upton Noble (074985) 263
Etr–mid Sep

Quietly situated with fine views of open countryside. A former dairyhouse with comfortable bedrooms and excellent bathrooms.

4rm (3hc) (1fb) ✗ [R] B&b£8.50–£9.50
Bdi£14–£16 W£90–£110 Ⱡ LDOnoon

♨ CTV P 2🚗 nc5yrs 250acres dairy sheep

[V]

SOUTHEND-ON-SEA
Essex
Map **5** TQ88

GH Argyle Hotel 12 Clifftown Pde
☎(0702) 339483
Closed 2–3 wks Xmas

Small, comfortable hotel overlooking sea and public gardens.

11hc (2fb) CTV in all bedrooms
*B&b£10–£13 W£70–£91 M̸

Lic ♨ CTV P̸ nc7yrs

GH Bay 187 Eastern Esp, Thorpe Bay
☎(0702) 588415
Closed Xmas

Small, comfortable sea-front hotel with some modern bedroom facilities.

9hc (1🛁 1🚿) (1fb) CTV in all bedrooms [R]
B&b£10–£13 Bdi£14–£17 W£90–£110 Ⱡ
LDOnoon

♨ CTV 3P

[V]

GH Cobham Lodge Private Hotel
2 Cobham Rd, Westcliff-on-Sea ☎(0702) 346438

Larger hotel with much to offer, attractive modern bedrooms, smart dining room, two lounges and a full size snooker table.

30hc (6🛁 10🚿) (4fb) CTV in all bedrooms
✗ *B&b£14.50–£17.50 Bdi£20.50–£23.50
W£97.50–£115 Ⱡ LDO6.30pm

Lic ♨ CTV ⛳ P̸ ⛳ snooker

Credit cards [1] [3] [5] [V]

GH *Gladstone Hotel* 40 Hartington Rd ☎(0702) 62776

A comfortable hotel providing modern accommodation.

7hc (2fb) CTV in all bedrooms 🐕

Lic 🛋 CTV P̸ nc3yrs

GH *Maple Leaf Private Hotel*
9–11 Trinity Av, Westcliff-on-Sea ☎(0702) 346904

Friendly guesthouse offering compact, old-fashioned accommodation with well-equipped bedrooms.

16hc (2fb) 🐕 [R] LDO8.30pm

Lic 🛋 CTV 4P

Credit cards [1] [2] [3] [5]

GH Marine View 4 Trinity Av, Westcliff-on-Sea ☎(0702) 344104

6hc (1fb) 🚭 in 4 bedrooms CTV in all bedrooms 🐕 [R] ✱B&b£8.50–£9 W£58.50–£63 M̸

Lic 🛋 CTV P̸

GH Mayfair 52 Crowstone Av, Westcliff-on-Sea ☎(0702) 340693
Closed Xmas

6hc (1fb) 🐕 ✱B&b£8.50–£9 Bdi£12–£12.50 W£66–£69 K̸ LDO4pm

🛋 CTV 4P nc5yrs

[V]

GH Mayflower Hotel 5–6 Royal Ter ☎(0702) 340489

Grade II listed Regency building overlooking the sea.

24hc (3🚿) (3fb) CTV in 23 bedrooms TV in 1 bedroom ✱B&b£11.50–£17.25 W£80.50–£120.75 M̸

🛋 CTV 2P 2🚗

[V]

GH Regency Hotel 18 Royal Ter ☎(0702) 340747

12hc (5fb) CTV in all bedrooms [R] ✱B&b£15–£17 LDO7pm

Lic 🛋 CTV 1P

[V]

GH Terrace Hotel 8 Royal Ter ☎(0702) 348143
Closed mid Dec–mid Jan

Southend-on-Sea — Southport

Small, homely, clifftop guesthouse with excellent sea views.

9hc (3fb) [R] B&b£11–£12 W£66–£72 M̸

Lic 🛋 CTV P̸ nc10yrs

[V]

GH *Tower Hotel* 146 Alexandra Rd ☎(0702) 348635

Large hotel situated in a quiet residential area offering well-equipped bedrooms.

15hc (2🚿) (2fb) CTV in all bedrooms [R] LDO11pm

Lic 🛋 CTV P̸

Credit cards [1] [2] [3] [5]

GH West Park Private Hotel 11 Park Rd, Westcliff-on-Sea ☎(0702) 330729

Larger hotel with many modern bedroom facilities and welcoming service.

12hc (5🛁 2🚿) (3fb) CTV in all bedrooms ✱B&b£17.50–£20 Bdi£23.75–£26.25 LDO6.30pm

Lic 🛋 CTV 16P 🏠

Credit cards [1] [3] [V]

SOUTH HARTING
West Sussex
Map **4** SU71

FH Mrs H S Wroe ***Foxcombe House*** *(SU771187)* ☎Harting (073085) 357

Fine country house in quiet downland with elegant and spacious accommodation.

3hc (1🛁) (1fb) CTV in 1 bedroom TV in 1 bedroom

🛋 CTV 8P 🎾(hard) 🐎 snooker 1,000acres arable dairy

SOUTH LUFFENHAM
Leicestershire
Map **4** SK90

INN Boot & Shoe ☎Stamford (0780) 720177
rs Mon

Typical English stone-built inn, with lots of character, near Rutland Water.

4hc CTV in all bedrooms [R] ✱B&b£10 W£70 M̸ Bar lunch 80p–£5 Dinner9.30pm£8.50alc

🛋 20P

SOUTH PETHERTON
Somerset
Map **3** ST41

FH Mrs M E H Vaux **Rydon** *(ST427173)* Compton Durville ☎(0460) 40468
Apr–Sep rs Oct

Attractive, mellow, stone farmhouse in a quiet location. Well-appointed throughout.

4hc (1fb) 🚭 in 2 bedrooms 🐕 [R] B&b£10–£10.50 Bdi£15–£15.50 W£100–£105 K̸ LDO4.30pm

🛋 CTV 6P 150acres arable horticulture sheep mixed

[V]

SOUTHPORT
Merseyside
Map **7** SD31
See plan on pages 356–357

GH Ambassador Private Hotel 13 Bath St ☎(0704) 43998 Plan **1** *A2*
Closed 2 wks Mar & New Year

A well-furnished and comfortable small hotel, set in a quiet side road just off Lord St.

8hc (6🚿) (3fb) CTV in all bedrooms [R] ✱B&b£12.50–£15 Bdi£18.50–£20 W£100–£115 K̸ LDO6pm

Lic 🛋 CTV 6P

Credit cards [1] [3] [V]

See advertisement on page 356

GH Brentwood 16 Duke St ☎(0704) 41185 Plan **2** *C3*
Closed Xmas & New Year

8hc (1🚿) (2fb) [R] ✱ B&b£7.50–£9 Bdi£10–£11.50 W£65–£70 K̸ LDO4pm

CTV 5P

[V]

GH Crimond Hotel 28 Knowsley Rd (Guestaccom) ☎(0704) 36456 Plan **3** *D3*

Comfortable and well-equipped hotel in quiet side road. Heated indoor swimming pool.

→

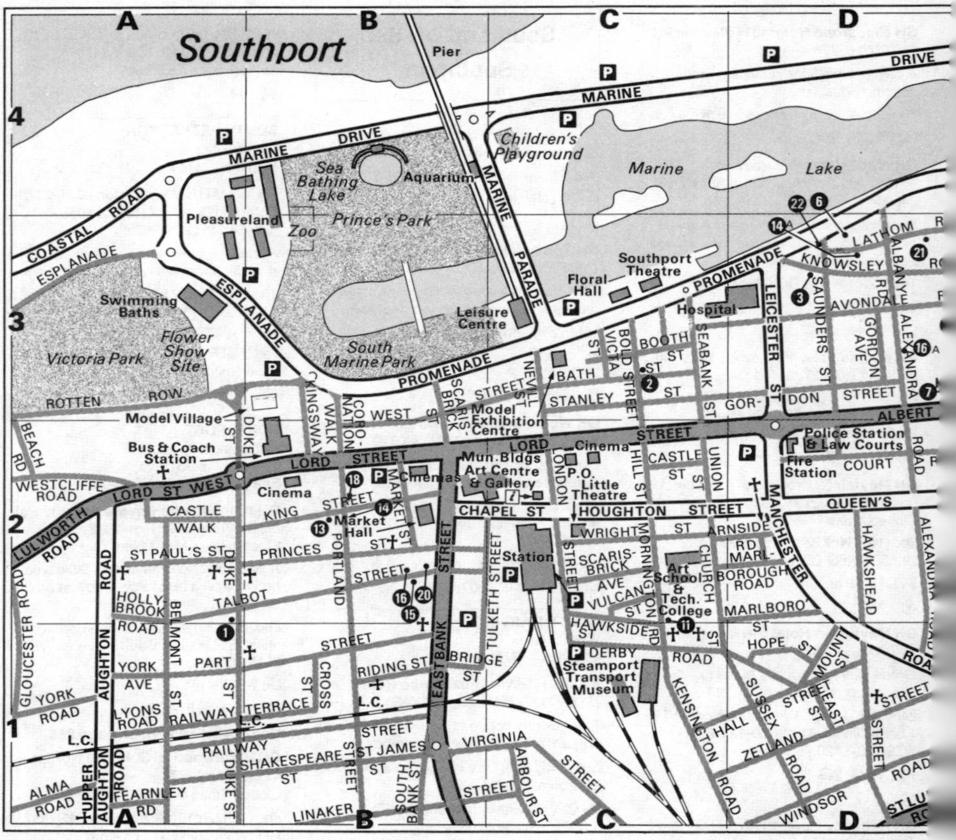

Southport
A
B
C
D
1
2
3
4
Pier
MARINE DRIVE
MARINE
DRIVE
COASTAL ROAD
ESPLANADE
Sea Bathing Lake
Aquarium
Pleasureland
Zoo
Prince's Park
Children's Playground
Marine Lake
MARINE PARADE
Swimming Baths
Victoria Park
Flower Show Site
South Marine Park
Leisure Centre
Floral Hall
Southport Theatre
PROMENADE
Hospital
LATHOM
KNOWSLEY
SAUNDERS ST
ALBANY RD
AVONDALE
GORDON AVE
ALEXANDRA
DON STREET
ALBERT
ROTTEN ROW
Model Village
Bus & Coach Station
KINGSWAY
WALK
CORONATION
WEST ST
SCARISBRICK
STREET
NEVILL ST
BATH
VICTA
BOLD STREET
BOOTH ST
ST
SEABANK ST
LEICESTER ST
STANLEY
GOR-
Model Exhibition Centre
Police Station & Law Courts
Fire Station
COURT
ROAD
QUEEN'S
LORD STREET
LORD ST WEST
WESTCLIFFE ROAD
BEACH RD
DUKE ST
Cinema
Cinemas
Mun. Bldgs Art Centre & Gallery
LONDON ST
P.O.
Little Theatre
HILL ST
CASTLE ST
UNION ST
MANCHESTER
CHAPEL ST
HOUGHTON STREET
KING STREET
MARKET ST
Market Hall
CASTLE WALK
LULWORTH ROAD
ST PAUL'S ST
PRINCES
PORTLAND
STREET
EAST BANK STREET
Station
WRIGHT ST
MORNINGTON RD
CHURCH ST
ARNSIDE RD
SCARISBRICK AVE
Art School & Tech. College
MARLBOROUGH ROAD
HAWKSHEAD
VULCAN ST
TALBOT
HOLLYBROOK ROAD
BELMONT ST
TULKETH STREET
HAWKSIDE ST
MARLBORO'
HOPE ST
MOUNT ST
GLOUCESTER ROAD
AUGHTON ROAD
YORK AVE
PART STREET
CROSS ST
RIDING ST
BRIDGE ST
DERBY ROAD
Steamport Transport Museum
KENSINGTON ROAD
SUSSEX ROAD
EAST ST
YORK ROAD
LYONS ROAD
RAILWAY TERRACE
L.C.
HALL STREET
ZETLAND
STREET
L.C.
RAILWAY
STREET
ST JAMES ST
VIRGINIA STREET
SHAKESPEARE ST
ALMA ROAD
UPPER AUGHTON ROAD
FEARNLEY RD
LINAKER
SOUTH BANK ST
ARBOUR ST
WINDSOR
ST LU

10hc (5🛁 5🚿) (2fb) CTV in all bedrooms [R] ✱B&b£20–£22 Bdi£27–£30 W£179–£200 ℒ LDO7pm

Lic 🍴 15P 🏊(heated) sauna bath

Credit cards [1] [2] [3] [5] [V]

GH Fairway Private Hotel 106 Leyland Rd ☎(0704) 42069 Plan **4** *D3*

Mar–Oct

Large, well-furnished house in quiet area.

9hc (4🚿) (4fb) CTV in 8 bedrooms 🐕 [R] ✱B&b£10–£11 Bdi£13–£14 W£80–£87 ℒ LDO5pm

Lic CTV 14P nc1yr

GH *Franklyn Hotel* 65 The Promenade ☎(0704) 40290 Plan **6** *D3*

Large, well-appointed hotel facing the sea and offering good value.

28hc (6fb) [R] LDO7pm

Lic 🍴 CTV 20P

Credit card [3]

Southport

1 Ambassador Private Hotel
2 Brentwood
3 Crimond Hotel
4 Fairway Private Hotel
6 Franklyn Hotel
7 Fulwood Private Hotel
8 Garden Hotel
11 Hollies Hotel
13 Newholme
14 Oakwood Private Hotel
14A Orleans Christian Hotel
15 Rosedale Hotel
16 Sidbrook Hotel
16A Stutelea Hotel
17 Sunningdale Hotel
18 Talbot Hotel
20 White Lodge Private Hotel
21 Whitworth Falls Hotel
22 Windsor Lodge Hotel

Lic 🎂 CTV P
Ⓥ

See advertisement on page 358

GH *Hollies Hotel* 7 Mornington Rd
☎(0704) 30054 Plan **11** *C2*

*Family-run town centre hotel some
distance from sea.*

15hc (4⇆ 4fl) (3fb) CTV in all bedrooms
✖ Ⓡ LDOnoon
🎂 15P

GH Newholme 51 King St ☎(0704)
30425 Plan **13** *B2*
Closed Xmas

*Small, well-furnished house personally-run
by resident family.*

6hc (3fb) ✖ Ⓡ ✳B&b£7.50–£8 Bdi£10.50–
£11.50 W£78 ⅟ LDO3pm
🎂 CTV 3P
Ⓥ

GH Oakwood Private Hotel 7 Portland
St ☎(0704) 31858 Plan **14** *B2*
Etr–Nov

*Family-run guesthouse, small but well-
furnished and with good facilities.*

6hc (3fl) (2fb) CTV in all bedrooms ✖ Ⓡ
B&b£12–£16 Bdi£17–£21 LDO3pm
🎂 CTV 8P nc4yrs

GH Orleans Christian Hotel 6–8 Lathom
Rd ☎(0704) 38430 Plan **14A** *D3*

*Family-run hotel which 'encourages
Christian fellowship, friendliness and
happiness'. No smoking in house.*

35hc (8fb) ⅟ in all bedrooms ✳B&b£10–
£12 Bdi£14–£16 W£90–£100 ⅟ LDO6pm
🎂 CTV 12P ♿

GH Rosedale Hotel 11 Talbot St
☎(0704) 30604 Plan **15** *B2*

*Small family-run guesthouse in a quiet
side road.*

11hc (5fb) ⅟ in 5 bedrooms ✖ ✳B&b£10
Bdi£13 W£65–£79 ⅟ LDO4pm
Lic CTV 8P

GH *Sidbrook Hotel* 14 Talbot St ☎(0704)
30608 Plan **16** *B2*
Closed Xmas →

GH Fulwood Private Hotel 82 Leyland
Rd ☎(0704) 30993 Plan **7** *E3*

*Large detached family house situated in a
quiet side road.*

11hc (1fb) B&bfr£10.50 Bdifr£14.75
Wfr£89 ⅟ LDOnoon
Lic 🎂 CTV 9P

GH Garden Hotel 19 Latham Rd
☎(0704) 30244 Plan **8** *E3*

Friendly guesthouse in quiet side road.

9hc (3fb) CTV in 6 bedrooms TV in 3
bedrooms Ⓡ ✳B&b£8–£10 Bdi£13.50–
£15 W£90–£100 ⅟ LDO5pm

Nice little hotel in quiet side road close to town centre.

9hc (4fb) ® LDO6pm

Lic CTV 10P sauna bath

GH *Stutelea Hotel* Alexandra Rd
☎(0704) 44220 Plan **16A** *D3*

Detached house set in a quiet side road, offering inexpensive yet quality accommodation supervised by owner.

12hc (6⇨ 6🛏) (3fb) CTV in all bedrooms
✕ ® LDO7pm

Lic 🍴 10P 🏊(heated) sauna bath

Credit cards ① ② ③

GH Sunningdale Hotel 85 Leyland Rd
☎(0704) 38673 Plan **17** *D3*

Pleasant detached hotel in quiet side road with large garden to rear.

15hc (5🛏) (5fb) CTV in 14 bedrooms ®
✳B&b£12.08–£13.23 Bdi£16.68–£17.83
W£110.40–£119.60 ⅟ LDO4.30pm

Lic 🍴 CTV 10P

Ⓥ

GH Talbot Hotel Portland St ☎(0704)
33975 Plan **18** *B2*
Closed Xmas & New Year

Attractive large hotel on corner site.

24hc (7⇨ 11🛏) (2fb) CTV in all bedrooms
® ✳B&b£12.25–£20.50 Bdi£16.85–£25
W£115–£160 ⅟

Lic 🍴 CTV 30P

Credit cards ① ③ Ⓥ

GH White Lodge Private Hotel 12 Talbot
St ☎(0704) 36320 Plan **20** *B2*

Homely guesthouse in peaceful location not far from town centre.

10hc (3fb) ✕ ✳B&b£9.50–£11 Bdi£11.50–
£13 W£70–£85 ⅟ LDO6pm

Lic CTV 6P ♨

Ⓥ

GH Whitworth Falls Hotel 16 Lathom Rd
☎(0704) 30074 Plan **21** *D3*

Comfortable, homely, small hotel in quiet area.

14hc B&b£11.50 Bdi£15.81 W£94.86 ⅟

Lic CTV 14P

Ⓥ

GH Windsor Lodge Hotel 37 Saunders
St ☎(0704) 30070 Plan **22** *D3*

Well-furnished hotel with bar and games room adjacent to promenade and marine lake.

12hc (1⇨) (2fb) ✕ ✳B&b£10.25–£12.25
Bdi£14.25–£16.25 W£89–£103 ⅟ LDO6pm

Lic 🍴 CTV 10P

Ⓥ

SOUTHSEA
Hampshire
See **Portsmouth & Southsea**

SOUTH SHIELDS
Tyne & Wear
Map **12**   NZ36

GH Sir William Fox Private Hotel
5 Westoe Village ☎Tyneside 091–456
4554

An elegant Georgian house situated in a sedate terrace and offering comfortable accommodation and friendly service.

14hc (1⇨ 13🛏) (2fb) CTV in all bedrooms
✳B&b£21.85 Bdi£29.25 LDO6.30pm

Lic 🍴 CTV 15P

Credit card ③ Ⓥ

SOUTHWOLD
Suffolk
Map **5**   TM57

GH Mount North Pde ☎(0502) 722292

7hc (5fb) ✕ ®

🍴 CTV ✏

INN Kings Head Hotel 23/25 High St
☎(0502) 723829

Etr–Oct rs Nov–Etr

Small, old fashioned inn in the centre of this quiet resort town.

3hc (1fb) CTV in all bedrooms ®
✳B&b£14–£18 Lunch £7.50alc Dinner
9.30pm £8.50alc
🍴 ✍ nc5yrs
Credit cards 1 3 4 5 Ⓥ

SOUTH ZEAL
Devon
Map **3** SX69

GH Poltimore 🕿Okehampton (0837)
840209

7hc (2⇆ 2🛏) ® B&b£12.50–£15
Bdi£18.50–£21.50 W£121–£136 ⫽
LDO10am
Lic 🍴 CTV 20P nc12yrs
Ⓥ

SOWERBY BRIDGE
West Yorkshire
Map **7** SE02

INN The Hobbit Hob Ln, Norland
🕿Halifax (0422) 832202

Extended and converted row of stone
moorside cottages overlooking the Calder
Valley.

4🛏 CTV in all bedrooms 🧹 ® ✳B&b£13–
£20 Bdi£18–£25 W£122–£160 ⫽
Lunch£4.45alc Dinner10.45pm£7.50alc
🍴 90P nc4yrs
Credit cards 1 2 3 Ⓥ

SPALDWICK
Cambridgeshire
Map **4** TL17

INN George High St 🕿Huntingdon
(0480) 890293

An old coaching inn, with exposed
beams, dating from 1545.

5rm (3hc) (1fb) CTV in 4 bedrooms 🧹 ®
B&b£13.75–£16.50 W£82.50–£99 ᴹ Bar
lunch £3–£5 Dinner 9.30pm fr£5
🍴 50P

SPARROWPIT
Derbyshire
Map **7** SK08

Southwold
—
Stamford Bridge

FH Mrs E Vernon **Whitelee** (SK099814)
🕿Chapel-en-le-Frith (0298) 812928
Etr–Oct

Modernised farmhouse, part-built in 1600,
in pleasant hillside setting. Good centre
for hill walking or touring.

3hc ® B&b£8.50–£9.50 Bdi£13–£14
W£87.50 ⫽ LDO4pm
🍴 TV 6P 42acres beef

SPAXTON
Somerset
Map **3** ST23

FH Mrs D M Porter **Headford** (ST208345)
Higher Merridge 🕿(027867) 250

3½m SW unclass.

2rm (1fb) 🧹 LDO2pm
🍴 CTV 10P 3🐄 104acres mixed
Credit cards 1 3

SPEAN BRIDGE
Highland Inverness-shire
Map **14** NN28

➤⊷**GH Coire Glas** 🕿(039781) 272
15 Apr–15 Oct

Well-appointed modern bungalow with
small private garden situated 50yds back
from A86.

14hc (5🛏) (2fb) ® B&b£8–£10 Bdi£14.50–
£16.50 Wfr£98 ⫽ LDO7pm
Lic CTV 25P
Ⓥ

GH 'Lesanne' 🕿(039781) 231
Feb–Oct

A bungalow-style house standing in an
elevated position in its own grounds
overlooking the village, adjacent to A82.

5hc (1fb) 🧹 ✳B&b£8–£9 W£56–£63 ᴹ
CTV 5P nc5yrs
Ⓥ

SPITTAL
Dyfed
Map **2** SM92

FH Mrs N M Thomas **Lower Haythog**
(SM996214) 🕿Clarbeston (043782) 279
Closed Xmas

2m SE off B4329.

2hc (1fb) 🧹
🍴 CTV P ✍ 250 acres arable dairy sheep

STAFFORD
Staffordshire
Map **7** SJ92

GH Bailey Hotel 63 Lichfield Rd 🕿(0785)
214133

Small friendly establishment on the A34
1m S of town centre.

9hc (2fb) CTV in all bedrooms
✳B&b£11.50–£12.50 Bdi£13.95–£17.50
W£97.65–£122.50 ⫽ LDO7pm
Lic 🍴 CTV 10P
Credit cards 1 3 Ⓥ
See advertisement on page 360

GH Leonards Croft Hotel 80 Lichfield Rd
🕿(0785) 3676
Closed Xmas

12hc Annexe: 6hc (2fb) ® ✳B&b£8–£8.75
Bdi£11.50–£12.25 LDOnoon
🍴 CTV 16P

STAMFORD
Lincolnshire
Map **4** TF00

INN Bull & Swan St Martins 🕿(0780)
63558

14th-century inn of great charm and
character offering simple
accommodation. ½m S on B1081.

6rm CTV in all bedrooms 🧹 ®
LDO9.30pm
🍴 CTV 25P 🚗
Credit card 3

STAMFORD BRIDGE
Humberside
See **High Catton**

STANDLAKE
Oxfordshire
Map **4**   SP30

FH Mr & Mrs W J Burton **Church Mill**
(SP396038) Downs Rd ☎(086731) 524
Mar–Oct

A grade II listed 17th-century Mill House with adjoining water mill, on mixed farm on the River Windrush. Well-situated for fishing and water sports in the area. Off Downs Rd between A415 and B4449, N of Standlake.

2hc ✗ ✱B&b£10–£12
4P nc12yrs 70acres mixed

FH Mrs S R Pickering **Hawthorn**
(SP373048) ☎(086731) 211

Recently modernised ground-floor accommodation on a working farm where you can try spinning, bottle-feeding the lambs and milking the cows.

2hc ✗
♨ CTV 3P nc5yrs 25acres dairy sheep

STANFORD-LE-HOPE
Essex
Map **5**   TQ68

GH *Homesteads* 216 Southend Rd
☎(0375) 672372
rs Xmas Day

Small, homely guesthouse with neat accommodation.

15hc (3fb) LDO2pm
Lic ♨ CTV 8P 2☎

STAPLE FITZPAINE
Somerset
Map **3**   ST21

FH Mrs D M Jee **Ruttersleigh** (ST261164)
☎Buckland St Mary (046034) 392

Small, very pleasant farmhouse off A303.

2rm (1fb) ✗ ✱B&b£7–£8.50 Bdi£11.50–£12.50
CTV 3P 69acres dairy

STAUNTON
Gloucestershire
Map **3**   SO51

FH Mrs S Fairhead **Upper Beaulieu**
(SO530118) ☎Monmouth (0600) 5025

Situated on the Gloucester/Gwent border, near the Forest of Dean off A4136 SW of village.

3hc (1fb) ✱B&b£8.50 Bdi£14 W£89.50 ⚡
LDO3pm
♨ CTV 8P 1☎ 60acres mixed
ⓥ

STEEPLE ASTON
Oxfordshire
Map **4**   SP42

GH *Westfield Farm Motel* The Fenway
☎(0869) 40591 (Guestaccom)

Clean, well-kept motel style accommodation grouped around a farm yard.

6⌁ ♒ (2fb) CTV in all bedrooms ®
LDO9pm
Lic ♨ CTV 20P

STEPASIDE
Dyfed
Map **2**   SN10

GH Bay View Hotel Pleasant Valley
☎Saundersfoot (0834) 813417
Apr–Oct

Modern proprietor-run hotel catering for family holidays.

12hc (4fb) ✗ ✱B&b£11–£13 Bdi£13.20–£16 W£92–£112 ⚡ (W only Jul–Aug)
LDO5pm
Lic ♨ CTV 14P ♨ ⌂(heated)
ⓥ

STEVENAGE
Hertfordshire
Map **4**   TL22

GH Archways Hotel 11 Hitchin Rd
☎(0438) 316640

Friendly and comfortable detached Victorian residence with tastefully furnished, spacious accommodation.

15⇔ Annexe: 16⇔ (8fb) CTV in all bedrooms ✗ ® ✳B&b£15–£25 Bdi£21–£31 LDO9pm

Lic ♨ CTV 60P ◑

Credit cards ① ② ③ ⑤ ⓥ

STEYNING
West Sussex
Map **4**   TQ11

GH Down House King's Barn Villas
☎(0903) 812319
Closed Nov–Xmas

A large family-run Edwardian house set in large well-tended gardens, overlooking the South Downs.

7hc (2fb) ® B&b£11–£14 W£71.50–£91 ⊬
♨ CTV 8P nc2yrs

ⓥ

GH Nash Hotel Horsham Rd ☎(0903) 814988

Remotely situated and skilfully extended country house, surrounded by a vineyard and a pond.

7hc (1⇔) (2fb) CTV in 3 bedrooms TV in 3 bedrooms ® ✳B&b£17–£19 Bdi£24–£26 W£168 ⊬

Lic ♨ CTV 16P ⚭ ⏢ ♟(hard)

ⓥ

GH Springwells 9 High St ☎(0903) 812446

Comfortable, pretty bedrooms in a charming ivy-clad house with swimming pool.

10hc (6⇔) (1fb) CTV in all bedrooms ®
✳B&b£20–£30

Lic ♨ CTV 6P ⏢(heated)

Credit cards ① ② ③ ⑤ ⓥ

STIPERSTONES
Shropshire
Map **7**   SJ30

GH Tankerville ☎ Shrewsbury (0743) 791401

4hc ® ✳B&b£10–£12 Bdifr£16
♨ CTV 4P

ⓥ

STIRLING
Central Stirlingshire
See **Denny**

STOCKBRIDGE
Hampshire
Map **4**   SU33

GH Carbery Salisbury Hill ☎Andover (0264) 810771
Closed 2 wks Xmas

Comfortable house with many facilities including pool, badminton, and swimming pool.

12hc (2fb) ✗ ✳B&bfr£12.65 Bdifr£19.55 Wfr£134.30 ⊬ LDO6pm

♨ CTV 14P ⏢(heated)

GH Old Three Cups Private Hotel
☎Andover (0264) 810527
Closed Xmas & Jan rs Sun & Mon night

15th-century coaching inn with comfortable bedrooms and popular well-managed restaurant.

8hc (3⇔) (2fb) CTV in 3 bedrooms TV in 1 bedroom ✗ ✳B&b£12.50–£28 Bdi£17–£40 LDO9.30pm

Lic ♨ 12P

Credit cards ① ③

STOCKPORT
Greater Manchester
Map **7**   SJ98

GH Ascot House Hotel 195 Wellington Rd North, Heaton Norris ☎061-432 2380
Closed 2 wks Xmas

A large family-run house situated on the A6 north of Stockport.

14hc (6⇔) CTV in all bedrooms ✗ ®
✳B&b£15–£22 Bdi£20.50–£27.50 LDO7.15pm   →

The Castle Hotel

The Street, Bramber, West Sussex
Telephone: (0903) 812102

Situated in the delightful historical village of Bramber in West Sussex, ten miles from Brighton, four from Shoreham and seven miles from Worthing. A village Inn where the accommodation has been converted to a high standard, the restaurant has a full á la carte menu and a wide variety of bar snacks, ample car parking and conveniently situated for a multitude of outdoor activities and picturesque walks.
For further information see gazetteer entry under Bramber.

Springwells Hotel

STEYNING · WEST SUSSEX (Nr. Brighton)
Telephone: 0903-812446

Once a Georgian merchant's town house now an elegant ten-bedroomed bed & breakfast hotel. All rooms have telephones & colour TV and most have private facilities.
Tea/coffee making facilities if required. Some four-poster beds. Lovely walled gardens, outdoor pool. Victorian style conservatory. ½ hour from Gatwick/Newhaven. £20 - £50 per room.

361

Lic 🏮 CTV 15P nc11yrs sauna bath
Credit cards ① ②

STOCKTON
Warwickshire
Map **4**   SP46

FH Mrs J Bankes-Price **New Zealand**
(SP453628) 🏠Southam (092681) 4604
Apr–Sep

1½m SE unclass rd.

3rm (1hc) ✖ ✱B&b£9–£12 W£63–£84
🏮 CTV 6P ⚲ 45acres arable

STOCKTON-ON-TEES
Cleveland
Map **9**   NZ41

GH Court Private Hotel 49 Yarm Rd
🏠(0642) 604483

Three-storey, mid-terrace property near
the town centre with small dining room
and comfortable sitting room.

7hc (3fb) CTV in all bedrooms ✖ ®
✱B&b£11.50–£13 Bdi£16.50–£18
W£115.50–£126 ⅃ LDO6pm

Lic 🏮 ⚲ nc2yrs

GH *Grange Hotel* 91 Yarm Rd 🏠(0642)
65908

A comfortable and friendly establishment
near town centre.

15hc
Lic 🏮 CTV 20P

STOKE FLEMING
Devon
Map **3**   SX84

GH Endsleigh Hotel 🏠(0803) 770381

Very pretty village-centre hotel.

8hc (2fl) (2fb) ® ✱B&b£11.50–£15
Bdi£17–£20.50 W£112–£136.50 ⅃
LDO9pm

Lic lift 🏮 CTV 20P

See advertisement on page 138

STOKE HOLY CROSS
Norfolk
Map **5**   TG20

FH Mr & Mrs Harrold *Salamanca*
(TG235022) 🏠Framingham Earl (05086)
2322
Closed Xmas & Etr

Comfortable Victorian farmhouse, with
comfortable rooms and large garden, 4
miles south of Norwich.

3hc Annexe: 1⇄ (1fb) ✖ LDO24hrs prior
🏮 CTV 7P nc6yrs 168acres dairy mixed

STOKEINTEIGNHEAD
Devon
Map **3**   SX97

GH Bailey's Farm 🏠Shaldon (062687)
3361
May–Oct

10hc (2fb) ✱B&b£8–£10 Bdi£12–£15
W£78–£100 ⅃ LDO7pm

CTV 10P

Stockport
Stow-on-the-Wold

GH Rocombe Country House Lower
Rocombe 🏠Shaldon (0626) 873367
Mar–Nov

Large, converted farmhouse in 2½ acres of
gardens with swimming pool. Simply
furnished bedrooms with good facilities.
Relaxed house-party atmosphere.

14⇄ CTV in all bedrooms ®
✱B&b£14.50–£16.50 Bdi£25–£27
W£158.50–£174 ⅃ LDO8.30pm

Lic 🏮 26P nc12yrs ⌣

Credit card ③

STOKE-ON-TRENT
Staffordshire
Map **7**   SJ84

GH The White House Stone Rd, Trent
Vale (Guestaccom) 🏠(0782) 642460
Closed last wk Dec–first wk Jan

Comfortable, modern accommodation is
offered at this guesthouse, 2 miles SW of
city.

8hc (2fb) CTV in 4 bedrooms ✖ ®
B&b£13–£30 Bdi£19.50–£36.50
W£136.50–£255.50 ⅃ LDO7pm

Lic 🏮 CTV 10P
ⓥ

STOKE ST GREGORY
Somerset
Map **3**   ST32

GH Jays Nest 🏠North Curry (0823)
490250

6hc (1fb) ⚲ in 4 bedrooms ✖ ®
✱B&b£9.50–£11 Bdi£13.50–£16 Wfr£90 ⅃
LDO9pm

Lic 🏮 CTV 10P 3🐾 nc8yrs
ⓥ

STONE (nr Berkeley)
Gloucestershire
Map **3**   ST69

GH The Elms 🏠Falfield (0454) 260279

A well-appointed small hotel set in
garden, alongside the A38.

10hc (2fb) ✱B&b£12

Lic 🏮 CTV 15P

STONE (in Oxney)
Kent
Map **5**   TQ92

FH Mrs E I Hodson **Tighe** *(TQ937268)*
Tighe 🏠Appledore (023383) 251
May–Oct

Late 16th-century farmhouse with
panoramic views of Romney Marsh,
situated in spacious gardens with a pond.
The rooms have antique furniture, with
residents lounge having an inglenook
fireplace and historic dining room with
exposed beams.

3hc (1fb) ✖ ✱B&b£9.50–£10 W£58 M
🏮 CTV 4P nc8yrs ⬋ 100acres sheep

STON EASTON
Somerset
Map **3**   ST65

FH Mrs J Doman **Manor** *(ST626533)*
🏠Chewton Mendip (076121) 266
Closed Dec

Large stonebuilt listed Somerset
farmhouse with nice atmosphere and
home-grown produce served at meals.

2rm (1hc) (1fb) ✖ ✱B&bfr£9 Bdifr£14
Wfr£84 ⅃

🏮 CTV P 1🐾 ⚲ 350acres dairy mixed
ⓥ

STONEHOUSE
Gloucestershire
Map **3**   SO80

FH Mrs D A Hodge **Welches** *(SO813065)*
Standish 🏠(045382) 2018
Closed Xmas

3rm (1hc) (2fb) ✖ ✱B&b£9
🏮 CTV P 101acres dairy
ⓥ

STORNOWAY
Isle of Lewis, Western Isles *Ross &*
Cromarty
See **Lewis, Isle of**

STOURBRIDGE
West Midlands
Map **7**   SO98

GH Limes 260 Hagley Rd, Pedmore
🏠Hagley (0562) 882689
Closed Xmas

10hc B&b£12–£14.50 Bdi£18–£20.50
LDO7.30pm

🏮 CTV 12P ♿

STOW-ON-THE-WOLD
Gloucestershire
Map **4**   SP12

GH Limes Evesham Rd 🏠Cotswold
(0451) 30034

Large gabled house within walking
distance from town centre offering
friendly family service.

5hc Annexe: 1hc (1fb) CTV in 3 bedrooms
B&b£9.50–£10 W£63–£65 M
🏮 CTV 6P

FH Mrs D S Smith **Corsham Field**
(SP217249) Bledington Rd 🏠Cotswold
(0451) 31750
rs Xmas

Newly constructed, Cotswold-stone
farmhouse incorporating many traditional
features.

3hc (1⇄) (1fb) ⚲ in 2 bedrooms CTV in 1
bedroom TV in 2 bedrooms ® ✱B&b£10–
£13.50 Bdi£13.50–£17 W£94.50–£119 ⅃
LDO6pm

🏮 8P 100acres arable beef sheep

STRAITON
Lothian *Midlothian*
Map **11** NT26

FH Mrs A M Milne **Straiton** *(NJ273667)*
Straiton Rd ☎031-440 0298
Mar–Nov

*Modest, homely farmhouse on southern
outskirts of Edinburgh off A701. Pets,
swings and chute for the children. Dogs
welcome.*

4hc (3fb) ® ✱B&b£10

CTV 10P ♫ 200acres arable beef horse
pig mixed
Ⓥ

STRATFORD-UPON-AVON
Warwickshire
Map **4** SP25
See plan on page 365

GH Ambleside 41 Grove Rd ☎(0789)
297239 Plan **1** *A2*

6hc (1🏠) (3fb) CTV in all bedrooms ®
✱B&b£9–£12 Wfr£63 M (W only Nov–Mar)
🍴 CTV 10P 1🏠 ♫ 🏊
Credit cards ① ③

GH Avon House 8 Evesham Pl ☎(0789)
293328 Plan **2** *A2*
Closed Xmas

*Friendly guesthouse with comfortable
well-equipped bedrooms.*

**Straiton
—
Stratford-upon-Avon**

10hc (2fb) ✱B&b£8.50–£10 W£59.50–£70
M
🍴 CTV 2P

GH Avon View Hotel 121 Shipston Rd
☎(0789) 297542 Plan **3** *C1*

10rm (7hc 1🛏 6🏠) (5fb) CTV in 9
bedrooms ® LDO7.45pm
Lic 🍴 20P
Credit cards ① ② ③

┠─┄**GH Brook Lodge** 192 Alcester Rd
☎(0789) 295988 Plan **4** *A3*

18hc (2🏠) (3fb) CTV in all bedrooms ®
B&b£8–£16 Bdi£12–£20 W£84–£140 M
LDO8.30pm
🍴 CTV 15P
Ⓥ

See advertisement on page 364

GH Coach House 17 Warwick Rd
(Guestaccom) ☎(0789) 204109 Plan **5** *C3*
Closed Xmas

12hc (3🛏 4🏠) (2fb) CTV in all bedrooms
✖ ® ✱B&b£12–£15 Bdi£18.50–£22.50
Wfr£126.50 M LDO4pm
Lic 🍴 10P
Credit cards ① ③

GH Eastnor House Hotel Shipston Rd
☎(0789) 68115 Plan **5A** *C1*

*Attentive, friendly service at this
comfortable Victorian house close to
centre.*

8hc (2🛏) (6fb) CTV in 4 bedrooms ®
✱B&b£10–£16 W£60–£96 M
Lic 🍴 CTV 8P
Credit cards ① ② ③ Ⓥ

See advertisement on page 364

GH Glenavon Chestnut Walk ☎(0789)
292588 Plan **6** *A2*
Closed Xmas

11hc (3fb) B&b£10–£11.50
🍴 CTV ♫

GH Hardwick House 1 Avenue Rd
☎(0789) 204307 Plan **7** *C4*
Closed Xmas

12hc (2🛏 2🏠) (4fb) CTV in all bedrooms
✖ ® ✱B&b£11–£17 W£77–£105 M
🍴 10P
Ⓥ

See advertisement on page 366

GH Hollies 16 Evesham Pl ☎(0789)
66857 Plan **7A** *A2*

*Friendly guesthouse on corner-site with
own car park. Handy for town centre and
theatre.*

6hc (1🏠) (3fb) ✖ ® ✱B&b£15
CTV P ♫

Sequoia HOUSE

51 Shipston Road Stratford-upon-Avon CV37 7LN
Telephone (0789) 68852

Superbly situated across the River Avon opposite the Theatre — recently restored and modernized to a high standard — offers charmingly appointed private hotel accommodation with friendly personal attention of resident proprietors — Most bedrooms have private bathrooms/showers/wc — All bedrooms have colour television; tea/coffee facilities, H & C, shaver points and central heating.

Large private car park and beautifully mature gardens in which stands the "Sequoia" tree that gives the house its name — a delightful garden walk leads to the theatre, Riverside gardens, Shakespeare Properties, Shops and Leisure complex.

- ● Bed and Breakfast ● Licensed Mini-Bar
- ● Pre Theatre Suppers ● Private Car Park
- ● Bargain Breaks ● House Parties.

'Brook Lodge'

192, Alcester Rd., Stratford-upon-Avon, Warwickshire CV37 9DR. Tel. 0789-295988

As well as being situated near to Anne Hathaway's, about a mile from Stratford's town centre and its many attractions, Brook Lodge is in easy reach of many other places of interest such as the castles of Warwick and Kenilworth, the stately homes of Ragley, Blenheim and Coughton, the university city of Oxford, the spa towns of Cheltenham and Leamington, the agricultural centre of Stoneleigh and the Birmingham National Exhibition Centre.

Brook Lodge offers a wide variety of accommodation. Single, twin, double and family rooms are available, all with central heating, hot and cold water and hot drink making facilities. If required there are rooms with private showers, toilets and televisions. There is a television lounge and large car park. All prices are inclusive of a full English breakfast. Evening meal if required. Well behaved dogs are welcome.

EASTNOR HOUSE HOTEL

Licensed

Shipston Road, Stratford-upon-Avon, Warwickshire CV37 7LD
Telephone: Stratford-upon-Avon (0789) 68115
Good service, a comfortable friendly atmosphere in a fine Victorian House with oak panelling, central open staircase, antique furniture and spacious rooms. A short stroll across the River Avon from the Theatre.

THE HEART
OF ENGLAND
TOURIST
BOARD

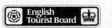

Resident Proprietors: Margaret Everitt and Graham Everitt

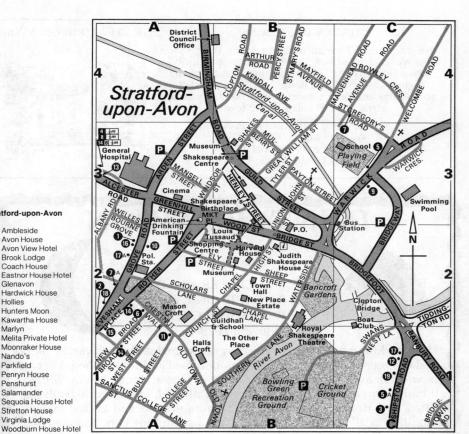

Stratford-upon-Avon

GH Hunters Moon 150 Alcester Rd
☎(0789) 292888 Plan **8** A3

7hc (5🛏) (5fb) CTV in all bedrooms ®
B&b£10–£15 W£60–£95 ₥

🍴 CTV 6P

Credit cards 1 3 Ⓥ

See advertisement on page 366

GH Kawartha House 39 Grove Rd
☎(0789) 204469 Plan **10** A2
Closed Xmas

*Semi-detached house on busy road just
out of town centre in area of hotels,
opposite a small park. Family atmosphere.*

6hc (3fb) ✘ ✱B&b£10–£12 W£70–£84 ₥

🍴 CTV ₽

GH *Marlyn* 3 Chestnut Walk ☎(0789)
293752 Plan **11** A1
Closed Xmas

8hc (2fb) ✘ ®

🍴 CTV ₽

GH Melita Private Hotel 37 Shipston Rd
☎(0789) 292432 Plan **12** C1
Closed Xmas & New Year

12hc (8🛏 4🛏) (3fb) CTV in all bedrooms
✘ ® ✱B&b£16–£21 W£100.80–£132.30 ₥
Lic 🍴 CTV 12P 2🚗

See advertisement on page 366

GH Moonraker House 40 Alcester Rd
☎(0789) 67115 Plan **13** A3

6🛏 Annexe: 9rm (2🛏 7🛏) (4fb) CTV in all
bedrooms ® B&b£9.50–£13 W£66.50–£91
₥

🍴 12P 3🚗

See advertisement on page 367

GH Nando's 18–19 Evesham Pl ☎(0789)
204907 Plan **14** A2

20rm 15hc (1🛏 4🛏) (6fb) TV in 5
bedrooms ✱B&b£9–£14 Bdi£13–£18
W£91–£126 ⅃ LDO6pm

🍴 CTV 8P

GH Parkfield 3 Broad Wlk ☎(0789)
293313 Plan **14A** A1
Closed Xmas

*Attractive Victorian house in quiet setting.
Superb breakfasts provided by friendly
proprietor.*

6hc (1fb) CTV in all bedrooms ✘ ®
✱B&b£9–£12.50 W£60–£80 ₥

CTV P ⚬⚬

Credit card 3

See advertisement on page 368

GH Penryn House 126 Alcester Rd
☎(0789) 293718 Plan **14B** A3

*Detached corner house where most
rooms have en-suite facilities.*

6hc (1🛏 1🛏) (4fb) CTV in all bedrooms ®
✱B&b£10–£12.50

🍴 9P

Credit cards 1 2 3

GH Penshurst 34 Evesham Pl ☎(0789) 205259 Plan **15** *A1*

Comfortable, friendly guesthouse close to the town's attractions.

8hc (2🏠) (3fb) ⚓ in 2 bedrooms CTV in 6 bedrooms TV in 2 bedrooms ✗
✱B&b£8.50–£11 W£54–£75 M LDO24hrs prior

Lic ▥ 2P 1🏠 nc3yrs

See advertisement on page 368

GH Salamander 40 Grove Rd ☎(0789) 205728 Plan **16** *A2*

6hc (1fb) ✱B&b£8.50–£10.50 Bdi£12.50–£14.50 W£84–£91 ⚮ LDO7pm

▥ CTV 2🏠

Ⓥ

See advertisement on page 368

GH Sequoia House Hotel 51 Shipston Rd ☎(0789) 68852 Plan **17** *C1*

17hc (1⇆4🏠) (6fb) CTV in all bedrooms ✗ Ⓡ B&b£10.50–£20 Bdi£16–£25.50 W£110–£160 ⚮ LDO4pm

Lic ▥ 20P nc5yrs

Credit cards ①③Ⓥ

See advertisement on page 364

GH Stretton House 38 Grove Rd ☎(0789) 68647 Plan **17A** *A2*

Victorian town house close to town centre.

Stratford-upon-Avon — Strathpeffer

5hc (3fb) CTV in all bedrooms Ⓡ B&b£8.50–£12.50 W£59.50–£87.50 M

▥ CTV ⚲

GH Virginia Lodge 12 Evesham Pl ☎(0789) 292157 Plan **18** *A2*

Closed Xmas & New Year

8hc (3fb) CTV in all bedrooms ✱B&b£8–£10 W£55–£75 M

Lic ▥ 8P

See advertisement on page 368

GH Woodburn House Hotel 89 Shipston Rd ☎(0789) 204453 Plan **19** *C1*

Closed Xmas

7hc (3🏠) (3fb) CTV in all bedrooms ✗ Ⓡ B&b£14–£20

▥ 10P nc5yrs

FH Mrs M K Meadows **Monk's Barn** *(SP206516)* Shipston Rd ☎(0789) 293714 Closed Xmas Day & Boxing Day

Warm and welcoming small farm, just two miles from centre of Stratford-upon-Avon.

4hc (1🏠) (1fb) ✗ ✱B&b£7.50–£8

▥ CTV 5P 75acres arable beef sheep mixed

STRATHAVEN
Strathclyde *Lanarkshire*
Map **11** NS74

GH Springvale Hotel 18 Letham Rd ☎(0357) 21131
Closed 25, 26 Dec & 1 & 2 Jan

Grey-stone detached house with painted annexe on opposite side of road, situated approximately 150 yards from the village.

13hc (1⇆8🏠) (3fb) CTV in 11 bedrooms ✱B&b£10–£12 Bdi£15–£17 LDO6.45pm

Lic ▥ CTV 8P

Ⓥ

FH Mrs E Warnock **Laigh Bent** *(NS701413)* ☎(0357) 20103 Jun–Sep

Attractive stone-built farmhouse with outbuildings surrounding the courtyard. 1½m SW of Strathaven on the A71.

2rm ✗

TV P nc8yrs 100acres beef

STRATHPEFFER
Highland *Ross & Cromarty*
Map **14** NH45

GH Kilvannie Manor Fodderty ☎(0997) 21389

Country manor house situated 1 mile east of A834. Dinners served to non-residents.

7hc (2fb) ✱B&b£10–£11.50 Bdi£16–£18.50 W£105–£120 ⚮ LDO6.30pm

Lic CTV 20P ♨

FH Mrs M Tait **Beechwood House**
(NH497594) Fodderty ☎(0997) 21387
May–Sep

Spacious and comfortable two-storey
house, approx 1m NE of the village on
A834.

3hc (1fb) ✠ ® ✱B&b£7.50–£8 Bdi£11.50–
£12 Wfr£80.50 ⅄ LDO4pm

ᴴᵖᵖ CTV 6P 18acres mixed

ⓥ

STRATHYRE
Central *Perthshire*
Map **11**   NN51

GH *Rosebank House Hotel* Main St
☎(08774) 208
Closed Dec

Roadside guesthouse in attractive village,
personally-run by young owners.

6hc (1fb) LDO6pm

Lic ᴴᵖᵖ CTV 3P

STRENSHAM
Hereford & Worcester
Map **3**   SO94

FH Mr & Mrs Hott **Strensham** *(SO901395)*
☎Tewkesbury (0684) 295295

Victorian farmhouse standing in a large
garden with extensive views of the Severn
Valley.

3hc ✱B&b£10.50 Bdi£15.50 W£70 Ⓜ

CTV 10P

260acres arable

STRETE
Devon
Map **3**   SX84

GH *Tallis Rock Private Hotel* ☎Stoke
Fleming (0803) 770370
Apr–Oct

9hc (4fb)

CTV 10P

STRETTON
Leicestershire
Map **8**   SK91

INN **Shires Hotel** ☎Castle Bytham
(078081) 332

200-year-old Georgian inn situated next to
the A1 (southbound) offering spacious
facilities and fresh home-cooked food.

5hc (2fb) CTV in all bedrooms ®
✱B&b£15–£17 Bdi£22–£25 Wfr£105 ⅄
Lunch £7.50alc Dinner 10.30pm£8.50alc

ᴴᵖᵖ 100P ⚖

Credit cards ① ③ ⓥ

STROUD
Gloucestershire
Map **3**   SO80

GH **Downfield Hotel** Cainscross Rd
☎(04536) 4496
Closed 1 wk Xmas

Pleasant, personally-run hotel situated on
the A419 on the western edge of town.

Strathpeffer
—
Sutton

22hc (3⇄) (2fb) ✱B&b£13–£16 Bdi£18–
£21 W£115–£133 ⅄ LDO8pm

Lic ᴴᵖᵖ CTV 20P 2☎

STURMINSTER NEWTON
Dorset
Map **3**   ST71

FH Mrs S Wingate-Saul **Holbrook**
(ST743117) Lydlinch ☎Hazelbury Bryan
(02586) 348
Closed Xmas Day

Attractive 'stable' bedroom-suites at this
farm which also offers simply fly fishing,
clay-pigeon shoot and a small outdoor
pool. 3m W off A357 Stalbridge Rd.

2rm (1hc) Annexe: 4rm (3fl) CTV in 3
bedrooms ✠ ✱B&b£9–£13.50 Bdi£14–
£18.50 W£95–£129.50 ⅄ LDO6pm

ᴴᵖᵖ CTV 7P ⚖ ⚓ ⚓ 125acres mixed

ⓥ

STURTON BY STOW
Lincolnshire
Map **8**   SK88

FH Mrs S Bradshaw **Village** *(SK889807)*
☎Gainsborough (0427) 788309
Mar–Oct

Good quality, well maintained
accommodation in early Victorian village-
centre farmhouse. W off B1241.

4hc ✠ ® ✱B&b£10–£12 Bdi£15–£17
W£98–£110 ⅄ LDO2 days prior

ᴴᵖᵖ CTV 6P nc10yrs ♪(hard) ⚓

400acres arable beef sheep mixed

ⓥ

SUDBURY
Suffolk
Map **5**   TL84

GH *Hill Lodge Private Hotel* 8 Newton
Rd ☎(0787) 77568
Closed Xmas wk

16hc (5fl) CTV in all bedrooms ✠
LDOnoon

ᴴᵖᵖ CTV 20P 2☎

INN *Black Boy Hotel* Market Hill
☎(0787) 79046

5hc (1fb) ✠ LDO9pm

ᴴᵖᵖ CTV 10P

Credit card ②

SUMMERCOURT
Cornwall
Map **2**   SW85

FH Mr & Mrs J A Mingo **Burthy**
(SW911565) ☎St Austell (0726) 860018
Apr–Oct

3hc (1fb) ✠ ✱B&b£10 Bdi£12.50 W£70 ⅄
(W only Jun–Sep) LDO5pm

CTV P 1☎ ⚖ 200acres beef pig sheep
mixed

FH Mrs R J B Richard **Goonhoskyn**
(SW871573) ☎Mitchell (087251) 226
Mar–Oct

Friendly proprietors run this farmhouse of
character with well-decorated bedrooms
and public areas.

3hc (1fb) CTV in all bedrooms ✠
✱B&b£7.50–£9.50 Bdi£12.50–£14.50
W£87.50–£101.50 ⅄

ᴴᵖᵖ CTV 3P nc6yrs

50acres arable sheep

ⓥ

FH Mrs W E Lutey **Trenithon** *(SW895553)*
☎St Austell (0726) 860253
Closed Dec

Modern farmhouse situated in quiet
location in open countryside a few miles
from the coast.

4hc (1fb) ✠ ✱B&b£7–£7.50 Bdi£10–
£10.50 W£65–£70 ⅄ LDO3.30pm

ᴴᵖᵖ CTV 6P 150acres arable beef sheep
mixed

Credit cards ② ③ ⓥ

SURBITON
Gt London
London plan **4**   B1
(Pages 246–247)

GH **Holmdene** 23 Cranes Dr ☎01-399
9992
Closed Etr & Dec

Attractive two-storey house in residential
area, peaceful and comfortable, near to
town centre.

6hc (1fb) CTV in 1 bedroom TV in 1
bedroom ® ✱B&b£13–£15 Wfr£77 Ⓜ

ᴴᵖᵖ CTV 🅿 nc5yrs

GH **Warwick** 321 Ewell Rd ☎01-399 5837

9hc (1⇄) (2fb) CTV in 7 bedrooms ✠ ®
✱B&b£13.50–£19.50 Bdi£18.50–£24.50
W£115.50–£157.50 ⅄ LDO2pm

ᴴᵖᵖ CTV 8P

ⓥ

See advertisement on page 370

SUTTON
Gt London
London plan **4**   C1
(Pages 246–247)

GH **Dene Hotel** 39 Cheam Rd ☎01-642
3170

Set in peaceful surroundings, this hotel
offers good service in an informal and
friendly atmosphere.

19hc (5⇄ 2fl) (2fb) CTV in 10 bedrooms
TV in 9 bedrooms ✠ ® B&b£14.95–
£34.50

ᴴᵖᵖ 8P nc5yrs

ⓥ

See advertisement on page 370

GH **Eaton Court Hotel** 49 Eaton Rd ☎01-
643 6766
Closed Xmas

Charming Victorian house, well-positioned
in quiet residential area.   →

14hc (2🛏) (3fb) CTV in 5 bedrooms
✳B&b£17–£24 W£107–£151 M
Lic ♨ CTV 6P
Credit cards ① ② Ⓥ

GH Tara House 50 Rosehill ☎01-641 6142

Converted private house with warm homely atmosphere in residential area.

8hc (2🛏) (2fb) CTV in all bedrooms ✶
✳B&b£16.10–£17.75 Bdi£22 W£154 ⅃
LDOnoon
♨ 10P nc7yrs

SUTTON COLDFIELD
West Midlands
Map **7**   SP19

GH *Standbridge Hotel* 138 Birmingham Rd ☎021-354 3007 Birmingham plan **12**

9🗧 CTV in 1 bedroom TV in 1 bedroom Ⓡ LDO4pm
Lic ♨ CTV 11P nc5yrs jacuzzi
See advertisement on page 67

SWANAGE
Dorset
Map **4**   SZ07

GH Bella Vista Hotel 14 Burlington Rd
☎(0929) 422873
May–Sep rs Mar Apr & Oct

Neat, pleasant accommodation in a cottage-style property within easy reach of beach and town centre.

6hc (5🗧) (4fb) ✶ ✳B&b£9.50–£12 Bdi£14.50–£16 W£79–£105 ⅃ (W only Jun Jul & Aug) LDO2pm
Lic CTV 6P nc4yrs

GH Burlington House Hotel 7 Highcliffe Rd ☎(0929) 422422
Mar–23 Oct

Views of Swanage Bay and located in quiet cul de sac.

9hc (2🛏 3🛏) (4fb) CTV in 3 bedrooms TV in 5 bedrooms B&b£9.50–£12.25 Bdi£14.50–£17.25 W£96.50–£114.75 LDO5pm

Lic ⊞ CTV 9P

ⓥ

GH *Byways* 5 Ulwell Rd ☎(0929) 422322
mid May–mid Sep

Well-appointed and comfortable guesthouse a short distance from the beach.

11hc (4fb) LDO6.30pm

CTV 3P nc5yrs

GH *Castleton Private Hotel* Highcliffe Rd ☎(0929) 423972
Feb–Oct

Corner-sited guesthouse just 100yds from beach.

12hc (2🛏 2🛏) (4fb) ✗ ® LDO5pm

Lic ⊞ CTV 10P nc3yrs

GH Chines Hotel 9 Burlington Rd ☎(0929) 422457
Apr–Oct

Neat two-storey house in quiet road near beach and town.

12hc (5🛏) (5fb) ✗ in 4 bedrooms ✗ ® ✱B&b£10.95–£13.80 Bdi£16.68–£19.55 W£96–£106 LDO6pm

Lic ⊞ CTV ✗

GH Clive Court Hotel Cranborne Rd ☎(0929) 425299
Mar–Oct

Small, private hotel in residential area, with car park behind.

13hc (5🛏) (4fb) ® ✱B&b£11.50–£13.50 Bdi£17.50–£19.50 W£112–£125 LDO5.30pm

Lic ⊞ CTV 12P

GH Eversden Private Hotel Victoria Rd ☎(0929) 423276

Private hotel with good views, a few minutes walk from the beach.

12hc (2🛏 3🛏) (3fb) ✗ in 2 bedrooms ✗ ✱B&b£9.78–£11.50 Bdi£14.95–£17.25 Wfr£87.40 LDO6pm

Lic ⊞ CTV 12P

ⓥ

GH Firswood Hotel 29 Kings Rd ☎(0929) 422306
rs Oct–Apr (closed Dec)

6hc (4fb) ✗ ® ✱B&bfr£10 Bdifr£14 Wfr£86 (W only Jul–Aug)

⊞ CTV 7P nc5yrs

Credit cards ① ③

GH Havenhurst Hotel 3 Cranbourne Rd ☎(0929) 424224
Mar–Oct

Pleasant guesthouse in quiet area with neat bedrooms.

17🛏 🛏 (4fb) ✗ ® ✱Bdi£19.50 W£120–£130 (W only Jun & Aug) LDO6.30pm

Lic ⊞ CTV 17P

ⓥ

GH Ingleston Private Hotel 2 Victoria Rd ☎(0929) 422391
Feb–Nov

Corner sited villa in quiet position 250yds from the beach.

9hc (4fb) ✗ ✱B&b£8–£10 Bdi£11.25–£13.80 W£78.75–£95.45 LDO5.30pm

Lic CTV 8P nc6mths

GH *Kingsley Hall Hotel* 8 Ulwell Rd ☎(0929) 422872
rs Dec–Feb

Situated a short distance from the beach with uninterrupted views across bay.

13hc (3🛏 4🛏) (4fb) CTV in all bedrooms ® LDO6.15pm

Lic ⊞ CTV 20P

GH Nethway Hotel Gilberts Rd ☎(0929) 423909
Whit–21 Oct

Near to shops and sea front.

12hc (4🛏) (4fb) ✗ ® ✱B&b£10–£11.50 Bdi£15–£16.50 W£91–£104 LDO6.30pm

Lic ⊞ CTV 10P nc5yrs

GH Oxford Hotel 3/5 Park Rd ☎(0929) 422247

Located on the rise of hill leading from town centre and sea front.

14hc (5fb) ✗ B&b£8.50–£10 Bdi£13.50–£15 W£94.50–£105 LDO3pm

Lic ⊞ CTV ✗

ⓥ

GH St Michael Hotel 31 Kings Rd ☎(0929) 422064
Mar–Nov

Neat town centre guesthouse with attractive bedrooms and attentive service.

6hc (3🛏) (4fb) CTV in all bedrooms ® ✱B&b£10–£13 Bdi£14–£17 W£89–£99 LDO2pm

Lic ⊞ 5P nc5yrs

ⓥ

GH Sandringham Hotel 20 Durlston Rd ☎(0929) 423076
Mar–Oct

Detached house in quiet residential area 10 minutes walk from beach.

10hc (4🛏) (4fb) ✗ ® ✱B&b£10–£13 Bdi£15–£18 W£66–£76 M LDO6.30pm

CTV P

GH Seychelles Private Hotel 7 Burlington Rd ☎(0929) 422794
Apr–Oct

Attractive, comfortable property with own private beach and beach hut, 1½ minutes walk.

9hc (6🛏) (4fb) ✗ ® ✱B&b£11.50–£13.50 Bdi£17.30–£19.50 W£90.50–£102.35 (W only Jul–Aug) LDO7pm

⊞ CTV 9P

SWANSEA
West Glamorgan
Map **3**   SS69
See also **Bishopston, Langland Bay** and **Mumbles**

GH Alexander Hotel 3 Sketty Rd, Sketty ☎(0792) 470045
Closed Xmas wk   →

Proprietor-run commercial guesthouse in city.

7hc (4🛁 2🚿) (3fb) CTV in all bedrooms 🚫 [R] ✱B&b£16–£20 Bdi£22.50–£26.50 W£125–£150Ł

Lic 🛋 CTV P̸ nc2yrs

Credit cards [1] [2] [3] [5] [V]

GH Cefn Bryn 6 Upland Cres ☎(0792) 466687)
Closed Xmas

Tastefully and comfortably appointed with interesting objects d'art and paintings.

7hc (3🚿) (2fb) TV in all bedrooms 🚫 [R] ✱B&b£12–£15 Bdi£18.50–£21.50 W£129.50–£150.50Ł LDOnoon

CTV P̸

GH Channel View 17 Bryn Rd, Brynmill ☎(0792) 466834

Stone-built house overlooking St Helens cricket and rugby ground.

6hc (1fb) ✱B&b£8 Wfr£56 M̸

🛋 CTV P̸

[V]

GH Crescent 132 Eaton Cres, Uplands ☎(0792) 466814
Closed Xmas & New Year

Family-run guesthouse.

7hc (1🚿) (2fb) TV in 1 bedroom [R] ✱B&b£10–£11 Bdi£15–£16 W£93–£100Ł LDO4pm

Swansea

🛋 CTV 4P

Credit cards [1] [3]

GH The Guesthouse 4 Bryn Rd ☎(0792) 466947

Small friendly guesthouse opposite St Helen's County Cricket Ground. Small bar for residents.

7hc 🚫 [R] ✱B&b£8–£8.50 Bdi£13–£13.50 W£90Ł LDO1pm

Lic 🛋 CTV P̸ nc12yrs

[V]

GH Parkway Hotel 253 Gower Rd, Sketty ☎(0792) 201632

A warm welcome awaits at this small private hotel in lovely mature grounds.

17hc (12🚿) (1fb) [R] ✱B&b£12.50–£21 Bdi£19.50–£28 W£119–£171Ł LDO6.30pm

Lic 🛋 CTV 17P pool table

Credit cards [1] [2] [3] [5] [V]

See advertisement on page 374

GH St Davids Private Hotel 15 Sketty Rd, Uplands ☎(0792) 473814

Commercial city guesthouse with cosy bar for residents.

11hc (2🛁 2🚿) (3fb) CTV in 2 bedrooms TV in 9 bedrooms ✱B&b£9–£12.50 Bdi£14.50–£18 W£85–£95Ł LDO4pm

Lic 🛋 CTV 2P

Credit cards [1] [3] [V]

GH *St Helens House* St Helens Cres ☎(0792) 460065
Closed Xmas

A proprietor-run guesthouse near the Civic Buildings with modestly appointed bedrooms.

6hc (2fb) [R]

🛋 CTV 2P

Credit card [3]

GH Tregare Hotel 9 Sketty Rd, Uplands ☎(0792) 470608

Small hotel.

10hc (3🛁 6🚿) (3fb) CTV in all bedrooms TV in 1 bedroom 🚫 [R] ✱B&b£12–£16 Bdi£17.50–£21.50 W£105–£129Ł LDO6pm

Lic 🛋 CTV 5P nc5yrs snooker

Credit cards [1] [3]

GH Uplands Court 134 Eaton Cres ☎(0792) 473046

Property of character in an elevated position with views over city and coast.

8hc (2fb) TV in all bedrooms 🚫 [R] B&b£10–£15 Bdi£15–£20 LDO1pm

Lic 🛋 CTV P̸

GH *Westlands* 34 Bryn Rd, Brynmill
☎(0792) 466689
*Family guesthouse within walking
distance of the city centre.*
6hc (2fb) CTV in all bedrooms ✗ ®
LDO10.30am
🍴 CTV ₧

SWINESHEAD
Bedfordshire
Map **4**   TL06

─── *Recommended* ───

FH D Marlow **The Manor** *(TL057659)*
☎Riseley (023063) 8126 (due to
change to Bedford (0234) 708126)
Closed Xmas

*Beautiful farmhouse, recently
renovated and comfortably
furnished.*

3rm (1fb) ✗ ✳B&b£10–£12 W£70–
£84 M
🍴 CTV 6P nc10yrs 3acres mixed
small holding

SYMONDS YAT, EAST
Hereford & Worcester
Map **3**   SO51

GH *Garth Cottage Hotel* ☎(0600)
890364
Mar–mid Nov
*Small, modernised hotel on the banks of
the River Wye, run on informal lines.*

Swansea
─
Taplow

7hc (1⇄2🏠) ✗ LDO6pm
Lic 🍴 CTV 9P nc7yrs
Credit card ①

INN Saracens Head ☎(0600) 890435
*Well-restored inn on banks of River Wye
with good accommodation.*
10hc (4🏠) ✗ ® ✳B&b£13–£16.50
Bdi£21–£24.50 W£146–£171 ⱡ
Dinner10pm£8&alc
CTV P ♩ solarium
Credit cards ① ② ③ ⊽

See advertisement on page 373

SYMONDS YAT, WEST (nr Ross-on-
Wye)
Hereford & Worcester
Map **3**   SO51

GH Woodlea ☎(0600) 890206
Feb–Nov & Xmas
10hc (3🏠) (2fb) B&b£11.75–£12.95
Bdi£17.95–£19.15 W£118–£126 ⱡ
Lic 🍴 CTV 8P nc2yrs ⌫
⊽

See advertisement on page 373

TADCASTER
North Yorkshire
Map **8**   SE44

GH Shann House 47 Kirkgate ☎(0937)
833931

*Charming, well-restored Georgian house
with spacious, well-fitted bedrooms and
attractive lounge.*
8hc (6⇄2🏠) (1fb) CTV in all bedrooms ®
✳B&b£13–£17.50
Lic 🍴 8P
Credit cards ① ③ ⊽

TALGARTH
Powys
Map **3**   SO13

FH Mrs B Prosser **Upper Genffordd**
(SO171304) ☎(0874) 711360

*Cheerful and welcoming family farmhouse
of character with good food and mountain
views. 3m S by A479.*

2hc (1fb) ✳B&b£8–£9 Bdi£12–£12.50
W£84–£87.50 ⱡ LDO5pm
🍴 CTV 4P ⚗ 200acres arable dairy sheep
mixed
⊽

TAPLOW
Buckinghamshire
Map **4**   SU98

GH *Norfolk House* Bath Rd
☎Maidenhead (0628) 23687   →

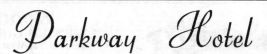

Parkway Hotel

AT THE GATEWAY TO THE GOWER

A small, well-appointed house with comfortable rooms and a friendly atmosphere.

6hc CTV in bedrooms 🚫 [R]

CTV 10P

TARPORLEY
Cheshire
Map **7** SJ56

GH Perth Hotel High St ☎(08293) 2514
Closed Jan

8hc (1🛁 1🚿) (2fb) TV in all bedrooms [R] ✱B&b£15–£18.50 Bdi£21–£27 W£137–£176 Ƚ LDO9.30pm

Lic 🍴 12P

Credit cards [1] [3] [5]

TAUNTON
Somerset
Map **3** ST22

GH Brookfield 16 Wellington Rd ☎(0823) 72786

7hc (2fb) CTV in 1 bedroom ✱B&bfr£15 Bdifr£19.50 Wfr£136.50 Ƚ LDO3pm

Lic 🍴 CTV 10P

Credit cards [1] [3]

GH Meryan House Hotel Bishop's Hull Rd ☎(0823) 87445

Georgian house in own grounds, personally-run with friendly relaxed atmosphere and comfortable, attractive public rooms, situated outside Taunton, off A38.

8hc (3🛁) (1fb) CTV in all bedrooms 🚫 ✱B&b£14.95–£19.95 Bdi£21.70–£26.70 W£136.71–£168.20 LDO7pm

Lic 🍴 CTV 12P

GH Ruishton Lodge Ruishton ☎Henlade (0823) 442298

Large detached house in own grounds, personally-run with country house atmosphere and sound cooking. Situated a short distance from M5 junction, on A358.

6hc (2fb) TV in 4 bedrooms [R] ✱B&b£10–£12 Bdi£14–£16 W£98–£112 Ƚ LDO8pm

Lic 🍴 CTV 10P

[V]

GH *Rumwell Hall* Rumwell ☎(0823) 75268
Closed Xmas Day

Elegant and spacious Georgian mansion set in 10 acres of gardens with swimming pool. The large, comfortable bedrooms and attractive public rooms are complemented by the warm friendly atmosphere.

10hc (4🛁) (7fb) CTV in 4 bedrooms [R] LDO7pm

Lic 🍴 CTV 100P 🏊(heated) ⛳

GH White Lodge Hotel 81 Bridgwater Rd ☎(0823) 73287

10🚿 (3fb) CTV in all bedrooms 🚫 [R] ✱B&b£18.50–£27 Bdi£26.50–£35 W£218 Ƚ LDO8pm

Lic 🍴 12P nc5yrs

Credit cards [1] [2] [3]

TAVISTOCK
Devon
Map **2** SX47

FH Mrs E C Blatchford **Parswell Farm Bungalow** *(SX464731)* Parswell ☎(0822) 2789
Etr–Oct

Well-situated bungalow on the Callington road, commanding good views of surrounding countryside.

3rm (1hc) (1fb) ✱B&b£7.50–£8 Wfr£49 M

TV 3P 106acres mixed

TEIGNMOUTH
Devon
Map **3** SX97

GH Baveno Hotel 40 Higher Brimley Rd ☎(06267) 3102

14hc (5🚿) (7fb) CTV in 12 bedrooms [R] ✱B&b£8–£10 Bdi£10.50–£12.50 W£69–£82 Ƚ LDO6.30pm

Lic CTV 12P 🏠

GH *Bay Cottage Hotel* 7 Marine Pde, Shaldon ☎Shaldon (062687) 2394
Mar–Nov

8hc 🚫 LDO4.30pm

Lic 🍴 CTV 3P

⊢⊣**GH Glen Devon** 3 Carlton Pl ☎(06267) 2895

7hc (2🛁 2🚿) (4fb) 🚫 [R] B&b£8–£10 Bdi£12–£15 W£84–£105 Ƚ LDO5pm

Lic 🍴 CTV 6P

[V]

GH Hillrise Winterbourne Rd ☎(06267) 3108

Comfortable house with good-sized, bright bedrooms, a separate lounge and bar.

8hc (1🚿) (3fb) [R] ✱B&b£7.50–£11.50 Bdi£10.50–£14.50 W£70–£95 Ƚ LDO6pm

Lic 🍴 CTV 4P 1🚗

⊢⊣**GH Hillsley** Upper Hermosa Rd ☎(06267) 3878

Semi-detached house with new extension in quiet residential area.

8rm (7hc) (4fb) B&b£7.50–£11 Bdi£10.50–£15.50 Wfr£69 Ƚ LDOnoon

Lic CTV 10P nc3yrs

Credit cards [2] [3] [V]

GH *Knoll Hotel* 5 Winterbourne Rd ☎(06267) 4241

19hc (4fb) [R] LDO7pm

Lic 🍴 CTV P 🏠

GH Lyme Bay House Hotel Den Promenade ☎(06267) 2953

12hc (4🚿) (1fb) CTV in 3 bedrooms [R] B&b£11.25–£15 Bdi£16.75–£20.75 W£93–£116.50 Ƚ LDO4pm

Lic lift 🍴 CTV

[V]

GH *Rathlin House Hotel* Upper Hermosa Rd ☎(06267) 4473
Mar–Oct

10hc (5fb) 🚫 [R] LDO5.30pm

Lic 🍴 CTV 12P

Hill Rise Hotel

LICENSED

Winterbourne Road, Teignmouth. Tel: 06267-3108

★ Quiet location but close to town centre & promenade
★ Residents' bar lounge/separate lounge with colour TV
★ Pleasant garden and sea views
★ Centrally heated for off season holidays
★ Some bedrooms with en suite shower rooms — all with tea/coffee making facilities
★ Good food and personal service
★ Private parking on the premises

GH Ravensbourne Hotel Higher Woodway Rd ☎(06267) 3415

13hc (4🅵) (7fb) ✱B&b£9.50–£14 Bdi£13–£18 W£78–£108 ⚡ (W only Jul & Aug) LDO6pm

Lic 🅿 CTV 20P ⌂(heated) sauna bath solarium

Ⓥ

GH Teign Holiday Inn Hotel Teign St ☎(06267) 2976

Apr–Oct

11hc (2🅵) (4fb) ✱B&b£8.50–£12.50 Bdi£13–£18 W£89–£126 ⚡ (W only Jul & Aug) LDO5pm

Lic 🅿 CTV 11P

Ⓥ

TELFORD
Shropshire
Map **7**   SJ60

INN Cock Hotel 148 Holyhead Rd, Wellington ☎(0952) 44954

Former coaching inn with comfortable, well-equipped bedrooms. Located at junction of A442 with B5061

6hc (1fb) CTV in all bedrooms ✖ Ⓡ LDO9.30pm

🅿 30P 3🐾 🚲

Credit cards 🯱 🯲

INN Swan Hotel Watling St, Wellington ☎(0952) 3781

Teignmouth
—
Tenby

10hc (4fb) CTV in all bedrooms Ⓡ LDO10pm

🅿 CTV 150P snooker

Credit card 🯱

TEMPLE CLOUD
Avon
Map **3**   ST65

FH Mr J Harris **Cameley Lodge** *(ST609575)* Cameley ☎(0761) 52790

Farmhouse barn newly-converted into small country residence, attractively designed in keeping with the area. Overlooking 13th-century church and trout lakes. 1m W unclass rd.

4hc (2🅵) TV in 4 bedrooms ✖ Ⓡ LDO9.30pm

Lic 🅿 30P 🏊 60acres non-working

See advertisement on page 54

FH Mr & Mrs Wyatt **Temple Bridge** *(ST627575)* ☎(0761) 52377

Etr–Oct

Comfortable small listed farm offering good accommodation and friendly atmosphere.

2hc (2fb) ✖ Ⓡ ✱B&b£9.50–£10.50

🅿 CTV 2P nc2yrs 250acres arable beef

Ⓥ

TENBURY WELLS
Hereford & Worcester
Map **7**   SO56

INN Crow Hotel Teme St ☎(0584) 810503

4hc CTV in all bedrooms ✖ Ⓡ LDO10pm

🅿 50P 2🐾

TENBY
Dyfed
Map **2**   SN10

GH Clareston House Warren St ☎(0834) 4148

Family-run guesthouse a few minutes from sea and town centre.

6hc (5fb) ✖ ✱B&b£7–£8.50 Bdi£10.50–£12 W£73.50–£84 ⚡ LDO1pm

Lic CTV 4P

Ⓥ

GH Hotel Doneva The Norton ☎(0834) 2460

Mar–Oct

Attractive house situated a few minutes walk from town and harbour.

14hc (3🅵) (7fb) Ⓡ ✱B&b£10.50–£12 Bdi£14.50–£16 W£85–£110 ⚡ (W only Jul & Aug) LDO6.30pm

---

Lic ♨ CTV 14P

Credit card [3] [V]

GH Gumfreston Private Hotel Culver Park ☎(0834) 2871
Closed Nov

A few minutes from town centre and the South Beach with comfortable bedrooms and friendly owners.

11hc (1🛁 10🚿) (5fb) 🚫🐕 [R] *B&b£11–£13 Bdi£14–£18 W£107–£122 Ł LDO4pm

Lic ♨ CTV P̸

Credit card [3] [V]

GH Heywood Lodge Heywood Ln ☎(0834) 2684

Attractive house in own grounds, proprietor-run and well-appointed throughout.

13hc (4🛁 1🚿) (4fb) [R] *B&b£12.50–£15 Bdi£19–£21.50 W£120.75–£138.25 Ł LDO8pm

Lic ♨ CTV 20P ⌂

GH Hildebrand Hotel Victoria St ☎(0834) 2403
Closed Dec & Jan rs Feb–Apr & Nov

Cosy modern bedrooms and popular refreshments bar in attractive Victorian property.

11hc (2🛁 5🚿) (7fb) CTV in all bedrooms [R] B&b£8.50–£13 Bdi£12–£17.75 W£84–£118 Ł (W only 18 Jul–29 Aug)

Lic ♨ P̸

Credit cards [1] [2] [3] [5] [V]

Tenby

GH Myrtle House Hotel St Mary's Street ☎(0834) 2508
Mar–Nov

A well-maintained and enthusiastically run small hotel with bright, airy bedrooms and restaurant of character.

9hc (2🚿) (4fb) 🚫🐕 [R] *B&b£10.50–£12.50 Bdi£13.50–£16 W£90–£100 Ł LDO4pm

Lic ♨ CTV P̸

Credit cards [1] [3]

GH Penally Manor Hotel Pennally ☎(0834) 2668
Etr–Oct

16hc (2🛁 8🚿) (8fb) CTV in all bedrooms [R] *B&b£8.50–£14 Bdi£13–£18.50 W£90–£128 Ł LDO7.45pm

Lic ♨ CTV 30P ⌂ 🏊(heated) solarium

Credit card [3] [V]

GH *Red House Hotel* Heywood Ln ☎(0834) 2770
Apr–Oct

Well-maintained house in own grounds.

29hc (17🛁 3🚿) (10fb) 🚫🐕 LDO7pm

Lic ♨ CTV 30P nc3yrs 🏊(heated) 🎾

GH Redlands 2 St Florence Pde ☎(0834) 2097
Feb–Oct

Conveniently positioned for sea front and town centre, a recently renovated comfortable Victorian property.

9hc (2🚿) (3fb) [R] *B&b£9–£10 Bdi£12.50–£13.50 W£84–£91 Ł LDO5.30pm

Lic CTV P̸

[V]

GH Richmond Hotel The Croft, North Beach ☎(0834) 2533
Apr–Oct

18hc (3🛁 2🚿) (12fb) CTV in 10 bedrooms 🚫🐕 [R] *B&b£10.50–£15.50 Bdi£14.50–£19.50 W£90–£127 Ł LDO6.30pm

Lic CTV P̸ nc3yrs

Credit cards [1] [2] [3] [V]

GH Ripley St Marys Hotel St Mary's Street ☎(0834) 2837
Etr–Oct

14hc (6🛁 🚿) (6fb) CTV in all bedrooms [R] B&b£10–£15 Bdi£15–£20 W£100–£130 Ł LDO5.30pm

Lic CTV P̸

Credit cards [1] [3] [V]

GH Sea Breezes Hotel 18 The Norton ☎(0834) 2753
Mar–Nov
Guesthouse with popular residents' bar, near harbour town and North Beach. Friendly, hospitable, family service.
26hc (10⇨ 1🚿) (5fb) CTV in 10 bedrooms TV in 16 bedrooms ⊗ [R] ✱B&b£10–£16 Bdi£14–£20 W£82–£110 L̸ LDO4.30pm
Lic ♨ CTV snooker
[V]

TEWKESBURY
Gloucestershire
Map **3** SO83

GH Abbey Hotel 67 Church St ☎(0684) 294247
Comfortable town house with walled garden to the rear.
16rm (15hc 6⇨ 2🚿) (5fb) CTV in all bedrooms ✱B&b£16–£23 Bdi£19–£25 W£114–£150 L̸ LDO8.30pm
Lic ♨ 11P ⌂
Credit cards [1] [2] [3]

THAME
Oxfordshire
Map **4** SP70

FH Mrs M Aitken **Upper Green** *(SU736053)* Manor Rd, Towersey (1½m E unclass rd) ☎(084421) 2496
Closed Xmas & New Year
Homely, friendly atmosphere at this 15th-century thatched farmhouse in lovely countryside. Non-smokers only.
3rm (1hc) 🚭 in all bedrooms TV in all bedrooms ⊗ ✱B&b£10–£14
♨ CTV 7P nc16yrs
7 acres poultry sheep

THIRKLEBY
North Yorkshire
Map **8** SE47

FH Mr & Mrs J Knowles **Manor** *(SE478787)* Little Thirkleby ☎(0845) 401216
Closed Xmas
Comfortable Georgian farmhouse in peaceful setting facing the Hambleton Hills.
3rm (2fb) ⊗ [R] ✱B&b£8–£9 W£54–£56 M̸
♨ CTV P ⌂ 176acres arable stock
[V]

THIRLMERE
Cumbria
Map **11** NY31

FH Mr & Mrs J Hodgson **Stybeck** *(NY319188)* ☎Keswick (0596) 73232
Closed Xmas day
Quiet farmhouse at northern end of the lake, within attractive fell country.
3hc (1fb) ⊗ [R] ✱B&b£9–£10 Bdi£14–£15 LDO6pm
♨ CTV 3P nc4yrs 165acres dairy sheep mixed

THORGANBY
North Yorkshire
Map **8** SE64

INN Jefferson Arms Main St ☎Wheldrake (090489) 316
rs Mon
300-year-old inn fitted and furnished in 'cottage'-style with beamed bars and comfortable bedrooms. Local fresh produce used in restaurant.
3🚿 Annexe: 3rm 2🚿 (2fb) 🚭 in 3 bedrooms CTV in all bedrooms [R] ✱B&b£17.50–£28.75 Bdi£26.45–£37.70 W£185.15–£140.85 L̸ Lunch £5.25–£7.50&alc High tea £4.50 Dinner 9.30pm £8.95&alc
40P ⌂ solarium
Credit cards [1] [2] [3] [5] [V]

THORNHILL
Dumfries & Galloway *Dumfriesshire*
Map **11** NX89

FH Mrs J Mackie **Waterside Mains** *(NS870971)* ☎(0848) 30405
Mar–Nov
Farmhouse with nice bedrooms, set on banks of River Nith, catering for fishing parties. 1m off A76.
3hc (1fb) [R] ✱B&b£8.50–£9 Bdi£12.50–£13 LDO4pm
♨ CTV 4P nc 🎣 170acres arable dairy

THORNTHWAITE (nr Keswick)
Cumbria
Map **11** NY22

GH Ladstock Country House Hotel ☎Braithwaite (059682) 210
Mar–Nov
Attractive country house, filled with period furnishings.
23hc (11⇨ 2🚿) (1fb) CTV in 15 bedrooms TV in 1 bedroom [R] ✱B&b£13–£18 Bdi£20.50–£25.50 W£127–£164 L̸
Lic ♨ CTV 30P

GH Thornthwaite Grange ☎Braithwaite (059682) 205
6hc (2🚿) (3fb) CTV in 1 bedroom [R] ✱B&b£10–£12.50 Bdi£15.50–£18.50 W£100–£125 L̸ LDO5pm
Lic ♨ CTV 10P ⌂

THORNTON HEATH
Gt London London plan **4** D1 (pages 246–247)

GH Dunheved Hotel 639–641 London Rd ☎01-684 2009
Closed Xmas
Family-run hotel situated on A233, close to Croydon town centre. Central London easily accessible.
17hc (2🚿) (4fb) CTV in 1 bedroom TV in 1 bedroom ⊗ ✱B&b£14–£30 W£98–£210 M̸
Lic ♨ CTV 8P
Credit cards [1] [3]

THORPE (Dovedale)
Derbyshire
Map **7** SK15

GH Hillcrest House ☎Thorpe Cloud (033529) 436
Mar–Oct
Large house in picturesque situation close to Dovedale.
7hc (2fb) [R] B&b£13 Bdi£20.50 LDO3pm
Lic ♨ CTV 12P

THORPE BAY
Essex
See **Southend-on-Sea**

THRAPSTON
Northamptonshire
Map **4** SP97

INN Court House Hotel ☎(08012) 3618

7hc (2⇿) TV in all bedrooms ✱ ®
✱B&b£13–£16 Bdi£18–£26 W£126–£182 ⫽
Lunch £3.50–£5.50&alc Dinner9.30pm
£3.50–£5.50

🅿 5P

Credit cards ① ③ ⓥ

THREE COCKS
Powys
Map **3** SO13

GH Old Gwernyfed Country Manor
Felindre (2m SE) ☎Glasbury (04974) 376
mid Mar–mid Dec

*A unique Elizabethan manor house in
peaceful surroundings offering modern
comforts and good home-cooking.*

8hc (6⇿) (2fb) B&b£21–£26 Bdi£31–£36
LDO8pm

Lic 20P croquet

THRESHFIELD
North Yorkshire
Map **7** SD96

Thorpe Bay
—
Thursby

GH Greenways Wharfeside Av
(Guestaccom) ☎Skipton (0756) 752598
Apr–Oct

*Delightfully furnished house in own
grounds with superb views across the
River Wharfe.*

5hc (1fb) ® B&b£13.50 Bdi£20 W£142.50
⫽ LDO5pm

Lic 🅿 CTV 8P nc7yrs ⏎

THRINGSTONE
Leicestershire
Map **8** SK41

FH Mr F E White **Talbot House**
(SK423173) ☎Coalville (0530) 222233

*Large old farmhouse and former coaching
inn on B587 between Whitwick and
Swanington, 2¾ miles from Coalville and 4½
miles W M1 junction 23.*

4rm (2fb) ✱ ✱B&b£9 Bdi£16 Wfr£104 ⫽
LDO11am

🅿 CTV 6P 150acres dairy

THROWLEIGH
Devon
Map **3** SX69

FH Mr & Mrs C R Mosse **East Ash Manor**
(SX680911) ☎Whiddon Down (064723)
244

*17th-century thatched farmhouse with
oak beams. Situated in Dartmoor National
Park. 1m E on Whiddon Down road.*

3rm (2hc) (1fb) ✱ ® ✱B&b£9
🅿 CTV 4P ♧ 160acres dairy

ⓥ

THURNING
Norfolk
Map **9** TG02

FH Mrs A M Fisher **Rookery** (TG078307)
☎Melton Constable (0263) 860357
Mar–Nov

*Off B1235 onto unclassified road at
Briston.*

3rm (1⏟) (1fb) ✱ ✱B&b£8.50 Bdifr£12
CTV 400acres arable

ⓥ

THURSBY
Cumbria
Map **11** NY35

FH Mrs M G Swainson **How End**
(NY316497) ☎Wigton (0965) 42487
Apr–Oct

*A conveniently situated farmhouse on
A595 between Carlisle and Wigton.* →

3rm (2fb) TV in 1 bedroom ✈
✱B&b£7.50–£8 Bdi£12 W£80–£87 Ⱡ
LDOnoon

🛋 CTV 4P 200acres dairy mixed

THWAITE
North Yorkshire
Map **7** SD89

GH Kearton ☎Richmond (North Yorks) (0748) 86277
Closed Jan & Feb

Pleasant Swaledale cottage, extended to provide particularly spacious dining facilities.

13hc (2fb) ✈ [R] ✱B&b£9.50 Bdi£15.50 W£101.50 Ⱡ LDO6.30pm

Lic 🛋 25P

[V]

TICEHURST
East Sussex
Map **5** TQ63

INN *Bell Hotel* The Square ☎(0580) 200234

Well-kept old inn with beamed accommodation.

3hc (1fb) ✈ LDO Dinner9.30pm

🛋 20P 🚌 nc3yrs

TIDEFORD
Cornwall
Map **2** SX35

Thursby — Tintagel

FH Mrs B A Turner **Kilna House** *(SX353600)* ☎Landrake (075538) 236
Mar–Oct

Stone-built house set in a large pleasant garden on A38, ¼ mile outside village. Overlooking the River Tiddy Valley.

6hc (3fb) ✱B&b£8.50–£9.50 W£56–£59.50 M

🛋 CTV 6P 10acres arable beef

[V]

TIMSBURY
Avon
Map **3** ST65

GH Old Malt House Hotel & Licensed Restaurant Radford ☎(0761) 70106
Closed Xmas

Quietly situated family-run hotel offering a welcoming atmosphere with personal service.

10hc (4⇌ 6🚿) (2fb) CTV in all bedrooms ✈ B&bfr£18 Bdifr£26.50 Wfr£168 Ⱡ LDO8.30pm

Lic 🛋 23P nc3yrs

Credit cards [1] [2] [3] [5] [V]

TINTAGEL
Cornwall
Map **2** SX08

GH Belvoir House Tregatta ☎Camelford (0840) 770265
Closed Xmas

7hc (2🚿) (1fb) TV in 1 bedroom [R]
✱B&b£8–£10 Bdi£12.25–£14.25 W£77.75–£91.75 Ⱡ LDO6pm

Lic CTV 12P nc1yr

[V]

GH *Penallick Hotel* Treknow ☎Camelford (0840) 770296

10rm (4hc 1🚿) (3fb) [R] LDO6.30pm

Lic 🛋 CTV 12P ⌂

Credit cards [1] [3]

Recommended

GH Trebrea Lodge Trenale ☎Camelford (0840) 770410
Etr–Oct

A fine 12th-century, stone-built country house in rural surroundings overlooking village and coastline. The interior is tastefully furnished and includes a comfortable 1st-floor drawing room with excellent views and a Victorian-style smoking room. Good home-cooked dinners are served.

7hc (3⇌ 4🚿) (2fb) CTV in all bedrooms B&b£15 Bdi£20 W£133 Ⱡ LDO7pm

Lic 🛋 7P

GH Trevervan Hotel Trewarmett
☎Camelford (0840) 770486

Fine country views at personally-run guesthouse in village of Trewarmett, 2m S B3263.

6hc (4fb) *B&b£10.50–£11.50 Bdi£15.50–£16.50 W£95–£102 ⧸ LDO7.30pm

Lic 🍷 CTV 12P

Credit cards [1] [3] [V]

GH Trewarmett Lodge ☎Camelford (0840) 770460
Apr–Oct rs Nov–Mar

Small stone-built hotel with good restaurant.

Tintagel — Tintern

6hc (1🛁 1🚿) (2fb) 🚭 in 2 bedrooms [R] B&b£12.50–£14.50 Bdi£18.50–£21 W£110–£118 ⧸ LDO9pm

Lic 🍷 CTV 10P

Credit cards [1] [3] [5] [V]

GH Willapark Manor Hotel Bossiney
☎Camelford (0840) 770782

8hc (7🛁 1🚿) (2fb) CTV in 2 bedrooms B&bfr£14.50 Bdifr£19.50 Wfr£129 ⧸ LDO8.30pm

Lic CTV 20P ⌂

[V]

See advertisement on page 382

TINTERN
Gwent
Map **3** SO50

GH Parva Farmhouse ☎(02918) 411

A comfortable 17-century house just 50yds from the banks of the River Wye with beamed sitting room and pretty bedrooms.

5hc Annexe; 1🛁 (3fb) [R] *B&b£11–£15 Bdi£17–£21 W£105–£141 ⧸ LDO7pm →

Trebrea Lodge
Trenale, Nr. Tintagel, North Cornwall.

This grand old Cornish house dates from 1300 AD and is now a small family-run hotel in its own rural setting on the magnificent north coast. Our bedrooms, all with colour TV and all with private bathrooms, look out across fields to the sea as does the first floor drawing room. The bar and Victorian smoking room are for those comfortable cosy evenings. Our reputation, for really good home-made food and a friendly atmosphere, is borne out by previous guests' written comments which we'll send you with our brochure. We offer reductions for children, there's a games room in the grounds, and dogs are welcome too.

Phone or write for brochure pack to Ann & Guy Murray. Tel. 0840 (STD) 770410.

Hotel and Licensed Restaurant
Trewarmett • Tintagel • Cornwall
Tel. Camelford 0840 770460

Trewarmett Lodge

Small family run hotel with magnificent sea and country views. Offering modest comfort coupled with friendly personal service. In quiet surroundings yet close to all amenities, it makes an ideal base for touring or a completely relaxing holiday. Known locally for our excellent restaurant offering Table D'hôte and A La Carte Menus. Small well behaved pets and children catered for, Varied Tariff consessions for children sharing. 2/3/5 day breaks.
Open all the year for bookings. Access/Visa welcome.

Lic ᵐ CTV 10P 2🚗
Ⓥ

INN *Fountain* Trellech Grange ☎(02918) 303
rs Mon Closed Dec–Feb
Attractive rural inn with restaurant providing à la carte menu.
5hc CTV in 1 bedroom TV in 4 bedrooms Ⓡ LDO9.30pm
ᵐ 60P

TISSINGTON
Derbyshire
Map **7** SK15

FH Mrs B Herridge **Bent** *(SK187523)*
☎Parwich (033525) 214
mid Mar–mid Nov
Traditional stone-built farmhouse situated in the Peak District National Park.
4hc (2fb) ✻ Ⓡ ✳B&bfr£8 Bdifr£12 Wfr£85 ⫽ LDO5pm
ᵐ CTV 10P nc5yrs 280acres dairy sheep

TIVERTON
Devon
Map **3** SS91

GH *Bridge* 23 Angel Hill ☎(0884) 252804
11hc (2⇆) (2fb) TV in 6 bedrooms LDO6.30pm
Lic ᵐ CTV 6P 1🚗 ♨ ♪

┌─────────────────────┐
│   **Tintern**   │
│   **—**   │
│   **Torcross**   │
└─────────────────────┘

FH Mr L Fullilove **Lodge Hill** *(ST945112)*
Ashley ☎(0884) 252907
Large rendered farmhouse on hillside in the Exe Valley, situated 1 mile S of town, Off A396.
7hc (1fb) Ⓡ B&b£8.75–£9.50 Bdi£12.50– £14 W£84.25–£93 ⫽ LDO6pm
Lic ᵐ CTV 12P 8acres beef sheep
Ⓥ

FH Mrs I R Olive **Lower Collipriest** *(SS953117)* ☎(0884) 252321
Apr–Oct
Lovely thatched farmhouse with attractive courtyard offering speciality traditional cooking.
3⇆🍽 ✻ Ⓡ B&b£13–£14 Bdi£16–£18 W£105–£112 ⫽ LDOnoon
ᵐ CTV 3P 3🚗 nc12yrs ♪ 220acres beef dairy

TOBERMORY
Isle of Mull, Strathclyde *Argyllshire*
See **Mull, Isle of**

TODMORDEN
West Yorkshire
Map **7** SD92

FH Mrs R Bayley **Todmorden Edge South** *(SD924246)* Parkin Ln, Sourhall Rd ☎(070681) 3459
Converted 17th-century farmhouse on hillside. Clean, comfortable rooms and a cosy residents lounge 1m from town centre.
3hc (1fb) ✻ Ⓡ B&b£9.50–£13.25 Bdi£15.50–£21 W£105–£140 ⫽ LDO7.30pm
ᵐ CTV 10P nc8yrs ♨ 1acre non-working
Ⓥ

TOMDOUN
Highland *Inverness-shire*
Map **14** NH10

FH Mrs H Fraser **No 3 Greenfield** *(NH201006)* ☎(08092) 221
mid May–Sep
Small modern bungalow set in isolated position in rugged, hilly countryside. 2m E on S side of Loch Garry.
3rm (1fb) ✳B&b£7.50 Bdi£11.50 W£77 ⫽
CTV 6P 172acres mixed
Ⓥ

TORBAY
Devon
See **Brixham, Paignton** and **Torquay**

TORCROSS
Devon
Map **3** SX84

GH Cove House ☎Kingsbridge (0548) 580448

Mar–Nov

12hc (2⇆2🚿) (1fb) CTV in all bedrooms ✻ ✱B&b£11–£13 Bdi£18.50–£21 W£135–£145 ⅃ (W only Jul & Aug) LDO5pm

Lic 10P nc10yrs

Ⓥ

TORQUAY
Devon

Map **3**　　SX96

See Central & District plans on pages 384–385 & 388

GH Abbey Court Hotel Falkland Rd ☎(0803) 27316 Central plan **1** *B3*

Etr–Oct

25hc (4⇆1🚿) (4fb) ✻ B&bfr£12 Bdifr£15.50 Wfr£78 M

Lic CTV 20P ⊇(heated)

GH Allandene Seapoint Hotel
5 Clifton Gv, Old Torwood Rd ☎(0803) 211808 Central plan **30** *F3*

Etr–Nov

10hc (3fb) ✻ ✱B&b£6.50–£8.50 Bdi£8.50–£11 W£56–£77 ⅃ (W only Jul & Aug) LDO4pm

Lic 🍴 CTV 4P 1🛏 ⚙

Ⓥ

GH Ambergate Hotel Solsbro Rd, Chelston ☎(0803) 605146 Central plan **1A** *A2*

Torcross
—
Torquay

Bright friendly residence overlooking town.

12hc (9⇆3🚿) (3fb) Ⓡ ✱B&b£7–£11 Bdi£10–£14 W£70–£98 ⅃ (W only 5 Jul–Aug) LDO4pm

Lic 🍴 CTV 8P

GH Ambleside Hotel Avenue Rd ☎(0803) 28669 Central plan **1B** *A3*

Etr–Nov & Xmas

Conveniently located small, friendly hotel, part of the larger Bancourt Hotel.

12hc (2⇆2🚿) (6fb) CTV in all bedrooms ✻ Ⓡ ✱B&b£10–£12 Bdi£16.50–£18.50 W£88–£123 ⅃ LDO7.30pm

Lic 🍴 12P ⊇(heated)

Credit cards 1 3

See advertisement on page 384

GH Ashwood Hotel 2 St Margarets Rd, St Marychurch ☎(0803) 38173 District plan **45**

Etr–Oct

9hc (2fb) CTV in 1 bedroom

Lic CTV 10P ⅊

Ⓥ

GH *Avon Hotel* Torbay Rd, Livermead ☎(0803) 23946 District plan **45A**

rs Oct–Etr

Bright, modern hotel with lawned frontage, near Livermead beach.

18hc (5fb) LDO6pm

Lic 🍴 CTV 17P 1🛏

Credit cards 1 3

GH Avron Hotel 70 Windsor Rd ☎(0803) 24182 District plan **46**

end May–mid Sep

14hc (6🚿) (2fb) TV in all bedrooms Ⓡ W£75–£81 ⅃ LDO6.30pm

CTV 8P nc2yrs

GH Aylwood House Hotel 24 Newton Rd ☎(0803) 23501 Central Plan **1C** *A4*

Etr–Oct

10hc (2⇆1🚿) (2fb) CTV in all bedrooms ✱B&b£7.50–£9 Bdi£10.50–£13 Wfr£73.50 ⅃ LDO5pm

🍴 CTV 10P ⚙

GH *Beechmoor Hotel* 10/12 Vansittart Rd ☎(0803) 22471 Central plan **2** *B3*

Mar–Oct rs Nov–Feb

Quiet, residential location near shops and seafront. Bright, pleasant atmosphere.

16hc (2⇆1🚿) (2fb) ✻ LDO6.30pm

Lic 🍴 CTV 26P 1🛏

Knowstone Court
LICENSED COUNTRY HOUSE

**Knowstone North Devon EX36 4RW
NW of Tiverton via V3221 on
North Devon Link Road**

This elegant Victorian rectory has been carefully re-designed by Baron Stefan von Kaltenborn and his young wife to offer luxury to your person and pleasure to your palate. Whether on holiday or business, dining room, cellar and bar add comfort to the bracing effect of Exmoor Country. French and German spoken. *See gazetteer under Knowstone*
Write or telephone for brochure STD (03984) 457

GUIDE TO GOLF COURSES
— *in Britain* —
1987

Full details of more than 1500 golf courses where visitors are welcome to test their handicap. The many

course plans are a useful extra feature. All entries are cross referenced to clear location maps.

GH Blue Waters Hotel 58 Bampfylde Rd
☎(0803) 26410 Central plan **2A** *B2*
Etr–Oct

8hc (1🛁) (1fb) ✗ ✱B&b£7.50–£12.50
Bdi£12.50–£17.50 W£80–£115 ⌿ LDO6pm

Lic CTV 8P nc8yrs
ⓥ

GH Braddon Hall Hotel Braddons Hill
Road East ☎(0803) 23908 Central plan **3**
F3
Jan–Oct & Xmas

13hc (1⇄2🛁) (5fb) ® B&b£8.50–£11
Bdi£11.50–£15 W£75–£100 ⌿ LDO6.30pm

Lic 🍴 CTV 10P
ⓥ

GH Burley Court Hotel Wheatridge Ln,
Livermead ☎(0803) 607879 District plan
47
Etr–Oct

21hc (1⇄20🛁) (7fb) CTV in all bedrooms
✗ ® ✱B&b£12–£16 Bdi£16–£20 W£90–
£128 ⌿ (W only Jul & Aug) LDO6.30pm

Lic 🍴 CTV 25P ⇌(heated) solarium
gymnasium
ⓥ

GH Carn Brea 21 Avenue Rd ☎(0803)
22002 Central plan **5** *B3*
Closed Xmas

20hc (14fb) (4fb) ✗ ✱B&b£10–£12
Bdi£15–£17 Wfr£105 ⌿ LDO4pm

Lic 🍴 CTV 20P ⇌(heated)
ⓥ

GH *Cary Park Hotel* Palermo Rd,
Babbacombe ☎(0803) 37843 District plan
47A
Etr–Oct

*Pleasant, family-run hotel backing onto
Cary Park.*

12hc (2fb) ✗ ✱B&b£6–£9 Bdi£10–£13
W£65–£85 ⌿ LDO7.30pm

CTV 10P ⏺

GH *Castleton Private Hotel* Castle Rd
☎(0803) 24976 Central plan **7** *D3*

15hc ✗ LDO4pm

Lic 🍴 CTV 8P nc4yrs

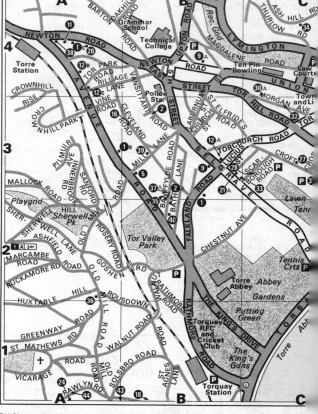

GH Chesterfield Private Hotel
62 Belgrave Rd ☎(0803) 22318 Central
plan **9** *B3*

10hc (4🛁) (3fb) CTV in all bedrooms ®
✱B&b£8–£11 Bdi£11.50–£14.50 W£75–
£100 ⌿ LDO4pm

🍴 CTV 3P

Credit card ③ ⓥ

GH Clairville 1 Teignmouth Rd,
Brunswick Square, Torre ☎(0803) 24540
Central plan **9A** *B4*
Closed 2 wks Xmas

10hc (3fb) ✱B&b£6.50–£8.50 Bdi£9–£11
W£63–£77 ⌿ LDO9pm

🍴 CTV 🐾
ⓥ

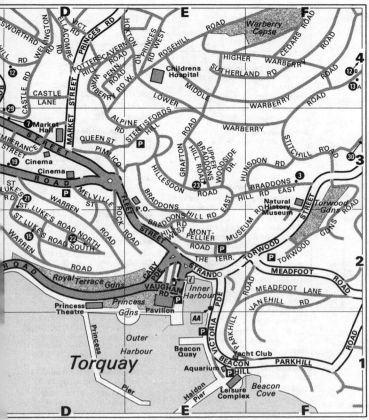

GH Hotel Concorde 26 Newton Rd
☎(0803) 22330 Central plan **11** *A4*
Etr–Oct

22hc (6⇨5▥) CTV in all bedrooms ✖ ®
✳B&b£10.35–£13.80 Bdi£15.35–£18.80
W£80–£110 (W only Jul & Aug)
Lic ♨ CTV 12P ⌷(heated)

GH Craig Court Hotel 10 Ash Hill Rd,
Castle Circus ☎(0803) 24400 Central plan
12 *D4*
Etr–Oct

10hc (4▥) (2fb) ✖ ✳B&b£10–£12
Bdi£11.50–£15 W£84–£105 ⅃ LDO5.30pm
Lic CTV 10P
Ⓥ

GH Cranborne Hotel 58 Belgrave Rd
☎(0803) 28046 Central plan **12A** *B3*
Closed Dec

14hc (6⇨) (5fb) CTV in all bedrooms ✷ ⓡ
B&b£8.50–£10.50 Bdi£12.50–£14.50
W£74–£94 ⅃ LDO3pm

CTV 3P

Credit cards ① ③ ⓥ

GH Cranmore 89 Avenue Rd ☎(0803)
28488 Central plan **12B** *A4*

*Modest semi-detached guesthouse on
main road into town.*

8hc (2fb) ✷ ✻B&b£6–£8.50 Bdi£9.50–£12
W£66.50–£84 ⅃ (W only 19 Jul–8 Aug)
LDO5pm

❰ CTV 4P

ⓥ

GH *Crewe Lodge* 83 Avenue Rd
☎(0803) 28772 Central plan **12C** *A4*

*Semi-detached villa on main road into
Torquay with bright, modern fittings.*

7hc (1⍟) (3fb) ✷ ⓡ LDO4pm

❰ CTV P

GH *Daphne Court Hotel* Lower Warberry
Rd ☎(0803) 212011 Central plan **12D** *F4*

15hc (10⍟) (12fb) ⓡ LDO6pm

Lic ❰ CTV 14P ⇲(heated)

GH *Devon Court Hotel* Croft Rd ☎(0803)
23603 Central plan **13** *C3*
Feb–Nov

*Friendly hotel with well-maintained
gardens, bright bedrooms and
comfortable public rooms*

14hc (1⍟) (2fb) ✷ ⓡ

Lic ❰ CTV 15P ⇲(heated)

Credit cards ① ③

GH El Marino Hotel Lower Warberry Rd
☎(0803) 26882 Central plan **13A** *F4*
Etr–Oct

21hc (3⇨ 15⍟) (6fb) ⓡ ✻B&b£8–£12
Bdi£10–£15 W£70–£99 ⅃ (W only High
Season)

Lic ❰ CTV 21P ⅗ ⇲(heated)

Torquay

GH *Exmouth View Hotel* St Albans Rd,
Babbacombe Downs ☎(0803) 37307
District plan **51**
Etr–Oct & Xmas

36rm (33hc 6⍟) (7fb)

Lic ❰ CTV 25P

GH *Fretherne Hotel* St Lukes Road
South ☎(0803) 22594 Central plan **15** *D2*
Etr–Oct

24hc LDO5pm

Lic CTV 20P

Recommended

GH Glenorleigh Hotel 26 Cleveland
Rd ☎(0803) 22135 Central plan **16** *B3*

*This attractive hotel was a worthy
winner of the AA 'Best in Britain'
Family Hotel in 1984. Situated in its
own delightful grounds, Glenorleigh
offers very comfortable, modern
bedrooms and elegant, public rooms.
You can also count on a personal
welcome and warm hospitality.*

16hc (7⍟) (5fb) ✷ ⓡ ✻B&b£13.80–
£15 Bdi£15–£20 W£85–£130 ⅃ (W
only Jun Jul & Aug) LDO6pm

Lic ❰ CTV 10P ⇲(heated) sauna
bath solarium gymnasium games
room

GH *Glenwood Hotel* Rowdens Rd
☎(0803) 26318 Central plan **16A** *B3*

10hc (5fb) ✷ LDOnoon

Lic ❰ CTV 9P

GH *Hart-Lea* 81 St Marychurch Rd
☎(0803) 312527 District plan **54**
Closed Xmas

*A comfortable house offering a very good
standard of accommodation and an
interesting menu.*

6hc (2fb) ✷ ⓡ ✻B&b£6–£8 Bdi£8–£11
W£56–£74 ⅃ (W only Jul & Aug)
LDO6.30pm

❰ CTV ⅌

ⓥ

GH Ingoldsby Hotel 1 Chelston Rd
☎(0803) 607497 Central plan **18** *B1*

*Informal, friendly hotel standing in own
grounds.*

16hc (5⍟) (5fb) ✷ ⓡ ✻B&b£9–£14.50
Bdi£11.50–£18 W£75–£115 ⅃ LDO7pm

Lic ❰ CTV 15P

Credit cards ① ③

⊢•GH Jesmond Dene Private Hotel
85 Abbey Rd ☎(0803) 23062 Central plan
19 *D3*

May–Sep rs Oct–Apr (closed Xmas)

11hc (3fb) ⓡ B&b£8–£10 Bdi£11–£13
W£67–£75

❰ CTV 3P

ⓥ

GH Kilworthy 157 Westhill Rd,
Babbacombe ☎(0803) 36452 District plan
55
4 Apr–Oct

13hc (2⇨) (6fb) ✻B&b£8–£11 Bdi£11–
£14 W£70–£91 ⅃ (W only 20 Jul–6 Sep)

Lic CTV 12P

GH Lindum Hotel Abbey Rd ☎(0803)
22795 Central plan **20** *C3*
Apr–Nov

21hc (10⍟) (2fb) CTV in 6 bedrooms
✻B&b£9.50–£12.50 Bdi£11.50–£14.50
W£77–£105 ⅃

Lic ❰ CTV 14P

ⓥ

GH Mapleton Hotel St Lukes Rd North
☎(0803) 22389 Central plan **21** *D3*

*Select, elegant family hotel in attractive
grounds offering a high standard of
accommodation and good food.*

10hc (1⇨ 6⍟) (3fb) CTV in all bedrooms
✷ ⓡ ✻B&b£11–£14.50 Bdi£13–£16.50
W£72.50–£123.50 ⅃ LDO5pm

Lic ❰ CTV 9P ⅗

GH Marlow Hotel 23 Belgrave Rd
☎(0803) 22833 Central plan **21A** *B3*

13hc (3fb) ⓡ B&b£9–£11 Bdi£13–£15
W£91–£105 ⅃ LDO4pm

Lic CTV 2P
Ⓥ

GH *Mount Nessing Hotel* St Lukes Rd
North ☎(0803) 22970 Central plan **22** *D2*
Etr–Oct & Xmas
13hc (5fb) LDO4pm
Lic ▥ CTV 10P

GH Olivia Court Braddons Hill Rd
☎(0803) 22595 Central plan **23** *E3*
Mar–Oct (also Xmas)
*Very attractive, personally-run property in
own secluded gardens overlooking
Torbay.*
16hc (2▥) (3fb) Ⓡ ✱B&b£10–£12.50
Bdi£14–£16.50 W£90–£112 ⅃ LDO5pm
Lic ▥ CTV 5P nc3yrs

GH Pencarrow Hotel 64 Windsor Rd
☎(0803) 23080 District plan **57**
Mar–Oct & 4 days Xmas
13hc (8▥) (3fb) CTV in all bedrooms Ⓡ
✱B&b£11–£12.50 Bdi£14–£16 Wfr£88 ⅃
(W only Jul–Aug) LDO2pm
Lic ▥ CTV 6P

GH Pines Hotel St Marychurch Rd
☎(0803) 38384 District plan **58**
22hc (2⇆) (7fb) ✖ Ⓡ B&b£7.50–£10.50
Bdi£10.50–£14.50 W£63.25–£92.50 ⅃
LDO5pm
Lic ▥ CTV 20P solarium

Torquay

GH *Porthcressa Hotel* 28 Perinville Rd,
Babbcombe ☎(0803) 37268 District plan
58A
12hc (3fb) ✱B&b£8.50–£10.50 Bdi£12–
£14.30 W£75–£94 ⅃
Lic ▥ CTV 6P
Ⓥ

GH Rawlyn House Hotel Rawlyn Rd,
Chelston ☎(0803) 605208 Central plan
24 *A1*
Mar–Oct & Xmas
17hc (8▥) (4fb) ✖ Ⓡ B&b£9.50–£14
Bdi£11.75–£16.50 W£80–£113.50 ⅃
LDO7.15pm
Lic ▥ CTV 15P ⌀ ⌂(heated)

GH *Richwood Hotel* 20 Newton Rd
☎(0803) 23729 Central plan **26** *A4*
Etr–Oct
23hc (11▥) (8fb) CTV in all bedrooms
Lic CTV 12P ⌂(heated) solarium

GH Riva Lodge Croft Rd ☎(0803) 22614
Central plan **27** *C3*
Apr–Oct

20hc (3⇆ 8▥) (4fb) CTV in all bedrooms
Ⓡ ✱B&b£10.50–£13.65 Bdi£15.75–£18.38
W£85.05–£119.18 ⅃ LDO3pm
Lic ▥ CTV 20P ⌂(heated) snooker
Credit cards ① ③ Ⓥ

GH *Rosewood* Teignmouth Rd,
Maidencombe ☎(0803) 38178 District
plan **59**
Mar–Sep rs Oct–Feb
8hc (4▥) (4fb) ✖ LDO4.30pm
▥ CTV 14P nc2yrs ⌀

GH *Rothesay Hotel* Scarborough Rd
☎(0803) 23161 Central plan **28** *C3*
35rm (33hc 9⇆▥) (10fb) CTV in 21
bedrooms Ⓡ LDO5.30pm
Lic ▥ CTV 30P ⌀
Credit cards ① ③

⊢⊷**GH St Bernards Private Hotel** Castle
Rd ☎(0803) 22508 Central plan **29** *B3*
Closed Xmas
14rm (11hc 3▥) (4fb) ✖ B&b£8–£12.25
Bdi£11–£15.25 W£70–£112 ⅃ (W only Jul &
Aug) LDO10am
Lic ▥ CTV 8P

GH Sevens Hotel 27 Morgan Av ☎(0803)
23523 Central plan **30A** *C4*
13hc (3▥) (3fb) ✖ ✱B&b£7–£9.75
Bdi£11.50–£14.50 W£74–£100 ⅃ LDO4pm
Lic ▥ CTV 10P
Ⓥ

See advertisement on page 389

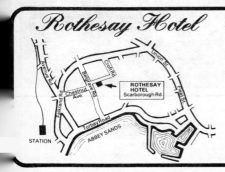

⊢•⊷GH Skerries Private Hotel
25 Morgan Av ☎(0803) 23618 Central
plan **32** *C3*

12hc (3fb) Ⓡ B&b£7–£10 Bdi£10–£13
W£66–£83 ⅃ LDO10.30am
⛤ CTV 7P
Ⓥ

GH *Southbank Hotel* 15/17 Belgrave Rd
☎(0803) 26701 Central plan **33** *B3*
Closed Jan & Feb

20hc (7fb) ✖ Ⓡ LDO5pm
Lic CTV 14P

Torquay

GH Stephen House Hotel 50 Ash Hill Rd
☎(0803) 25796 Central plan **34** *C4*
Mar–Nov & Xmas

*Friendly, detached house with
comfortable lounges and modest
bedrooms.*

15hc (1⇌3 4⿴) (4fb) Ⓡ B&b£8–£16
Bdi£12–£20 W£69–£109 ⅃ (W only Jul–
Aug) LDO5.30pm
Lic CTV 12P ⚓ ⊃(heated)
Ⓥ

GH Sun Court Hotel Rowdens Rd
☎(0803) 27242 Central plan **35** *B3*

12hc (2⇌3) (2fb) ✖ Ⓡ ✳B&b£6.75–£11.25
Bdi£10–£15.25 W£71–£104.50 ⅃
LDO6.30pm
Lic ⛤ CTV 15P
Credit cards ① ③ Ⓥ

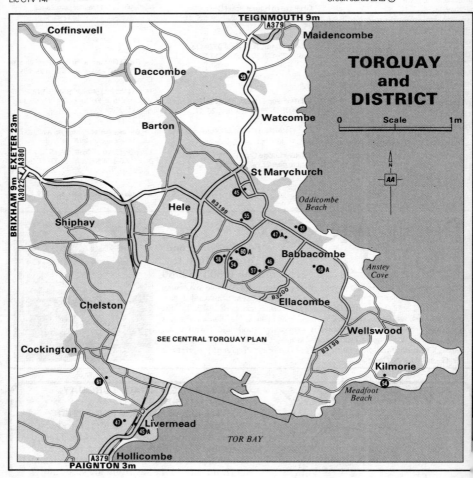

TEIGNMOUTH 9m A379

Coffinswell

Daccombe

Maidencombe

**TORQUAY
and
DISTRICT**

0   Scale   1m

Barton

Watcombe

N
AA

St Marychurch

Oddicombe
Beach

Hele
B3199

Shiphay

Babbacombe

Anstey
Cove

Ellacombe
B3200

SEE CENTRAL TORQUAY PLAN

Chelston

Wellswood
B3199

Cockington

Kilmorie

Meadfoot
Beach

Livermead

TOR BAY

A379 Hollicombe
PAIGNTON 3m

BRIXHAM 9m EXETER 23m A3022 A380

Torquay District

45	Ashwood	**51**	Exmouth View Hotel	**58A**	Porthcressa Hotel
45A	Avon Hotel	**54**	Hart-Lea	**59**	Rosewood
46	Avron Hotel	**55**	Kilworthy	**60A**	Ventnor
47	Burley Court Hotel	**57**	Pencarrow Hotel	**61**	Villa Marina Hotel
47A	Cary Park Hotel	**58**	Pines Hotel		

388

GH Torbay Rise Old Mill Rd ☎(0803) 605541 Central plan **36** *A2*
Apr–Oct

15hc (8⇄) (2fb) ✖ B&b£10.50–£16 Bdi£15–£20.50 W£86–£130 ⅃ LDO6pm

Lic CTV 12P ⊇(heated)

Credit cards ① ③

➤GH **Torcroft Hotel** Croft Rd ☎(0803) 28292 Central plan **37** *C3*
Mar–Oct

Friendly private hotel conveniently positioned for sea and town centre. Compact modern accommodation.

21hc (6ﬁ) (6fb) ✖ B&b£8–£11 Bdi£10.50–£14.50 W£70–£98 ⅃ LDO5pm

Lic CTV 18P ♨

GH Tor Dean Hotel 27 Bampfylde Rd ☎(0803) 24669 Central plan **37A** *B2/3*
mid Apr–mid Oct

Bright, compact bedrooms in friendly private hotel close to beach and Abbey gardens.

14hc (1fb) ✖ Ⓡ ✱B&b£10.35–£12.65 Bdi£14.95–£17.25 W£73–£89 ⅃ (W only Jul & Aug)

Lic CTV 10P nc2yrs

GH Tormohun Hotel 28 Newton Rd ☎(0803) 23681 Central plan **38** *A4*

23rm (18hc 4⇄ 4ﬁ) (2fb) CTV in all bedrooms LDO7.30pm

Torquay

Lic 🕮 23P ⊇(heated)

Credit cards ① ②

GH Trafalgar House Hotel 30 Bridge Rd ☎(0803) 22486 Central plan **39** *B3*

12hc (2ﬁ) (2fb) ✖ ✱B&bfr£7 Bdifr£10 Wfr£68 ⅃ LDO6pm

Lic CTV 8P nc5yrs

Ⓥ

GH Tregantle Hotel 64 Bampfylde Rd ☎(0803) 27494 Central plan **40** *B2*
Apr–Oct rs Nov–Mar

Spotlessly clean hotel with friendly service.

11hc (2fb) ✖ ✱B&b£8.50–£10 Bdi£12–£15 W£84–£105 ⅃ LDOnoon

Lic 🕮 CTV 10P

Credit card ③ Ⓥ

GH Ventnor 85 St Marychurch Rd ☎(0803) 39132 District plan **60A**
Mar–Oct

Small, friendly guesthouse offering comfortable accommodation in a residential area.

6hc (2fb) CTV in all bedrooms ✖ Ⓡ ✱B&b£6.90–£8 Bdi£11.90–£12.50 W£78.80–£84 ⅃ (W only Jul & Aug) LDO11am

🕮 nc5yrs

GH Villa Marina Hotel Cockington Ln, Livermead ☎(0803) 605440 District plan **61**
Apr–Sep

26hc (18⇄ 2ﬁ) (5fb) LDO6.45pm

🕮 CTV 25P

GH Westowe Hotel Chelston Rd ☎(0803) 605207 Central plan **43** B1
Apr–Oct

Attractively positioned hotel with comfortable, modern bedrooms. For non-smokers only.

10hc (1⇄) ✂ in all bedrooms CTV in 3 bedrooms ✖ Bdi£12.50–£18 W£91–£126 ⅃

Lic 🕮 CTV 8P nc5yrs

Ⓥ

GH White Gables Private Hotel Rawlyn Rd ☎(0803) 605233 Central plan **44** *A1*

10hc (1ﬁ) (7fb) ✖ Ⓡ B&b£11–£14 Bdi£14–£17 W£89–£115 ⅃ (W only Jul & Aug) LDO5pm

Lic 🕮 CTV 10P

TORTHORWALD
Dumfries & Galloway *Dumfriesshire*
Map **11** NY07

INN *Torr House Hotel* ☎Collin (038775) 214

Small village hotel, a converted manse, which looks across farmland to Dumfries and the Solway coast.

6hc (3fb) [R] LDO9.45pm

Lic 🍽 CTV 120P 🎣

TOTLAND BAY
Isle of Wight
See **Wight, Isle of**

TOTNES
Devon
Map **3** SX86

GH Four Seasons 13 Bridgetown ☎(0803) 862091

7hc (4fb) CTV in 1 bedroom [R] *B&b£8.50–£9.50 Wfr£57 Ł

Lic CTV 6P

GH Old Forge Seymour Pl, Bridgetown ☎(0803) 862174
Closed Xmas wk

Converted 600 year old smithy still incorporating village prison cell. Now charming and hospitable with pretty, modern bedrooms.

6hc (2🚿) (2fb) CTV in all bedrooms ✖ [R] *B&b£12.50–£14.50 Bdi£18–£20 W£108–£120 Ł LDO10am

🍽 CTV 8P ⌂

Recommended

GH *Ridgemark Hotel* Bridgetown Hill ☎(0803) 862011

A tasteful and comfortably furnished establishment with friendly owners. The hotel stands in half an acre of secluded grounds on the main road into Totnes.

7hc (2🚿) (1fb) CTV in all bedrooms ✖ [R]

Lic 🍽 CTV 10P 1🚘 nc9yrs

FH Mrs G J Veale **Broomborough House** *(SX793601)* Broomborough Dr ☎(0803) 863134
Mar–Nov

Spacious, country-manor style house in hilly parkland with views of Dartmoor and the surrounding countryside. Games room and local game fishing.

3hc (1fb) ✖ [R] *B&b£12.50 Bdi£19.50 W£131 Ł LDO10.30am

Lic 🍽 CTV P ⌂ 🎣 squash 🎾 sauna bath solarium gymnasium 600acres arable, beef dairy

[V]

TOTTENHILL
Norfolk
Map **9** TF61

GH Oakwood House Private Hotel ☎Kings Lynn (0553) 810256
Closed 24–28 Dec

5hc (1🛁 1🚿) Annexe: 7🛁 CTV in all bedrooms ✖ [R] B&b£15–£22 Bdi£23–£30

Lic 🍽 20P

Credit cards [1] [2] [3] [5] [V]

See advertisement on page 220

TOWCESTER
Northamptonshire
Map **4** SP64

INN *Brave Old Oak* Watling St ☎(0327) 50533

12hc (1🛁) (2fb) CTV in all bedrooms [R] LDO9.30pm

🍽 15P 🚌

Credit cards [1] [2] [3] [5]

TRAWSFYNYDD
Gwynedd
Map **6** SH73

FH Mrs A Swann **Fronoleu** *(SS711350)* ☎(076687) 397
Closed Xmas

A real farmhouse atmosphere, complete with pets and pony rides.

7hc (4🛁 3🚿) (3fb) 🚭 in 1 bedroom CTV in all bedrooms [R] *B&b£9.50–£11.50 Bdi£14–£16 LDO6pm

🍽 CTV 7P ⌂ 5acres small holding

[V]

TREARDDUR BAY
Gwynedd
Map **6** SH27

GH Highground Hotel off Ravenspoint Rd ☎(0407) 860078

Large personally-run house, with sun veranda, set in landscaped gardens. Close to beaches and sporting amenities.

7hc (3fb) 🚭 in 3 bedrooms CTV in all bedrooms ✖ [R] *B&b£11 Bdi£17 W£115.50 Ł LDO4pm

Lic 🍽 CTV 7P

Credit cards [1] [3] [V]

GH Moranedd ☎(0407) 860324

6hc (1fb) [R] B&b£9 Bdi£13 W£85 Ł LDO5pm

Lic 🍽 CTV 8P

TREBARWITH
Cornwall
Map **2** SX08

INN *Mill House* ☎Camelford (0840) 770200
Closed 24–28 Dec

Imaginatively converted corn mill offering a high standard of accommodation.

9hc (1🛁 5🚿) (1fb) CTV in all bedrooms [R] LDO10pm

🍽 50P 🚌 nc10yrs

Credit cards [1] [3]

TRECASTLE
Powys
Map **3** SN82

INN Castle Hotel ☎Sennybridge (087482) 354
Closed Jan

Charming and thoughtfully furnished Georgian building offering good food and excellent modern bedrooms.

8hc (3⫟) (1fb) CTV in all bedrooms ®
✱B&b£15–£17.50 W£87.50–£105 M Bar
lunch £4alc Dinner9.45pm £9alc
🍴 40P 🚭
Credit cards ① ③ ⓥ

TREFIN (TREVINE)
Dyfed
Map **2**   SM83

FH Mrs B C Morgan *Binchurn*
(SM843313) ☎Croesgoch (03483) 264
Apr–Nov

*Modestly appointed family farmhouse
close to the coast.*

6hc ✗ ® LDO6pm
🍴 CTV P beef dairy sheep mixed

TREFRIW
Gwynedd
Map **6**   SH76

FH Mr & Mrs D E Roberts *Cae-Coch*
(SH779646) ☎Llanrwst (0492) 640380
Etr–Sep rs Oct–Etr

*Pleasant farmhouse in elevated position
on side of Conwy Valley.*

3rm B&b£8.50 W£55 M
CTV 4P 1🐾 nc3yrs 50acres mixed

TREGARON
Dyfed
Map **3**   SN65

Trecastle
—
Treveighan

FH M E Davies *Aberdwr* *(SN687597)*
Abergwesyn Rd ☎(09744) 255
Apr–Oct

Situated 1 mile from the village.

3hc ✗ ✱B&b£9–£10 Bdi£15–£16 Wfr£100
⚡LDO5pm

CTV 6P ⛵ 14acres smallholding
ⓥ

FH Mrs M J Cutter *Neuadd Las*
(SN663620) ☎(09744) 380

5hc (1⫟) (2fb) ✗
🍴 CTV 10P ♨ ⛵ 25acres mixed

TRENEAR (nr Helston)
Cornwall
Map **2**   SW63

FH Mrs G Lawrence *Longstone*
(SW662319) ☎Helston (0326) 572483
Feb–Nov

*Well-appointed farmhouse set in beautiful
countryside. Facilities include a playroom
and sun lounge. From the Helston–
Redruth road, B3297, take unclass road to
Coverack Bridges–Helston 1½m; Trenear
1m, turn right & follow road for 2m.*

5hc (2fb) ✱B&b£7.50–£8.50 Bdi£10.50–
£11.50 Wfr£75 ⚡LDO3pm
🍴 CTV 6P 62acres dairy ⓥ

TRETOWER
Powys
Map **3**   SO12

INN Tretower Court ☎Bwlch (0874)
730204

*Family-run character inn with good bars
and modestly appointed bedrooms.*

4hc (1fb) ✱B&b£10–£10.50 Bar lunch
£3.20–£7.35&alc Dinner10pm £3.20–
£7.35&alc
🍴 CTV 100P
Credit card ③

TREVEIGHAN
Cornwall
Map **2**   SX07

FH Mrs M Jory *Treveighan*
(SX075795) ☎Bodmin (0208) 850286
Mar–Oct

*Two-storey, stone-built farmhouse with
farm buildings attached. Situated in
isolated village with views over valley.*

2hc (1fb) CTV in 1 bedroom TV in 1
bedroom ✗ ® ✱B&b£8 Bdi£12–£14
W£84–£98 ⚡ (W only May–Jun) LDO4pm
CTV 3P ♨ 175acres beef dairy
ⓥ

TREVONE
Cornwall
Map **2** SW87

GH Coimbatore Hotel West View
☎Padstow (0841) 520390
Apr–Sep

Detached house in quiet situation with some sea views. Comfortable accommodation and friendly proprietors.

11hc (3fb) ⅍ ✱B&b£10–£12 Bdi£12.50–£16 W£80–£95 ⊭ (W only mid Jul & Aug) LDOnoon
Lic CTV 6P 5🏖

GH Green Waves Private Hotel
☎Padstow (0841) 520114

Large detached house with some superb sea views.

15rm (9hc 8🛏) (5fb) ⅍ LDO7pm
Lic CTV 12P 6🏖 nc4yrs
See advertisement on page 295

TRINITY
Jersey
See **Channel Islands**

TROON
Cornwall
Map **2** SW63

FH Mrs H Tyack **Sea View** *(SW671370)*
☎Praze (0209) 831260

Trevone
—
Truro

Farmhouse has been modernised, yet still retains atmosphere of family-run farm. Tastefully furnished with extensive pinewood décor.

8rm (7hc) (3fb) ✱B&b£6.50 Bdi£10 Wfr£69.50 ⊭
🍴 CTV 10P ⚒ ≋(heated) 10acres mixed
Credit card ③ Ⓥ

TROUTBECK (nr Penrith)
Cumbria
Map **11** NY32

FH Mrs R Bird **Askew Rigg** *(NY371280)*
☎Threlkeld (059683) 638

17th-century stone-built farmhouse, attractively modernised to retain original character. Entrance to drive is situated only a few yards from the A66.

3rm (2hc) (2fb) Ⓡ ✱B&bfr£8 Bdifr£12
Lic 🍴 CTV 5P ⚒ 200acres mixed
Ⓥ

Recommended

FH Mr P Fellows **Lane Head**
(NY375271) ☎Threlkeld (059683) 220
Mar–Oct

Oak beams and gleaming brasses are a feature of this pleasant 18th-century farmhouse. It has two cosy lounges and a most attractive dining room where you can enjoy a really good 5-course dinner. Each bedroom is individually decorated and furnished to a very high standard including one with a lovely four-poster bed.

9hc (1🛏 2🛏) (3fb) ⅍ ✱B&b£10–£15 Bdi£17.50–£22.50 W£116.50–£157 ⊭ LDO5.30pm
Lic 🍴 CTV 10P 110acres mixed
Ⓥ

TRURO
Cornwall
Map **2** SW84

GH Colthrop Tregolls Rd ☎(0872) 72920

Small, friendly guesthouse convenient to city, and good base for touring.

7hc (3fb) ⅍ ✱B&b£9–£11 Bdi£14–£16 W£98–£110 ⊭ LDO5pm
🍴 CTV 8P nc8yrs

Lane Head Farm

Troubeck, Penrith, Cumbria   Threlkeld (059 683) 220

A charming 17th century farmhouse, set in beautiful gardens overlooking undisturbed views of Lakeland Fells. Midway between Keswick and Penrith. The house has been tastefully decorated throughout with many rooms featuring beams. Three bedrooms have en suite bathrooms, one has a four poster bed, and the others have washbasins and shaver points. A pretty lounge with colour TV and separate sitting room, all add to the comfort of our guests. Our main attraction is the high standard of food, a large breakfast with five-course dinner, prepared from local home-fed produce, bring our guests back time after time. Separate dining tables, selected wine list and small well-stocked bar complete our package for relaxation.
We will be happy to supply further details. SAE.

GUESTACCOM   # THE DRIFFOLD HOTEL   WEST COUNTRY TOURIST BOARD

DEVORAN LANE, DEVORAN, Nr. TRURO,
CORNWALL, TR3 6PA.
Telephone: (0872) 863314

Small family run hotel, midway Truro/Falmouth, overlooking quiet creek of the Fal Estuary. Licensed, friendly atmosphere, excellent food. A comfortable base for touring all parts of The Duchy. Some rooms en-suite. Full central heating. Special winter rates.

Ring or write for brochure.

GH *Farley Hotel* Falmouth Rd ☎(0872) 70712
Closed Xmas
Comfortable, well-positioned hotel for both business and tourist clientèle.
20hc (4fb) B&b£12.65–£14 Bdi£17.25–£19 W£108.05–£119.70 Ł LDO7.30pm
Lic 🛋 CTV 18P 2🚗 nc12yrs
Credit cards [1] [3]

GH Manor Cottage Tresillian (3m NW at Tresillian) ☎Tresillian (087252) 212
mid Mar–mid Oct
Large cottage-type building on main road, attracting large cream tea trade.
5hc (1fb) *B&b£9–£9.50 Wfr£59 M
Lic 🛋 CTV 7P

GH Marcorrie Hotel 20 Falmouth Rd ☎(0872) 77374
Privately owned guesthouse with modern bedrooms all equipped with colour TVs.
10hc (2🚿) (3fb) CTV in all bedrooms Ⓡ
*B&b£12.50–£20 Bdi£17.75–£25.25 W£126–£163 Ł
Lic 🛋 CTV 16P
Ⓥ

TUNBRIDGE WELLS (ROYAL)
Kent
Map **5** TQ53

GH *Firwood* 89 Frant Rd ☎(0892) 25596
Closed 20 Dec–5 Jan
10hc (6🛁 4🚿) (2fb) CTV in all bedrooms
🍴 LDO5.30pm
🛋 CTV 12P
Credit cards [1] [2] [3] [5]

The Manor Cottage Guest House
Tresillian, Near Truro, Cornwall Tel: Tresillian 212

6 bedrooms, 17th-Century charm, modern comfort and a warm welcome from Margery and John Nicholls. Open March to October, an ideal touring base, three miles east of Truro (A390), residential licence, colour TV, central heating, double glazing, ample parking. Fire Certificate held.
Bed and breakfast terms from £9.00 inclusive per person nightly.

MARCORRIE HOTEL
20 FALMOUTH ROAD, TRURO TR1 2HX
RESERVATIONS: (0872) 77374
Centrally situated for touring Cornwall, whether on business or leisure.
Close to city centre. Ample parking.
All rooms with colour TV, radio, kettle and central heating. Most rooms with shower, some en suite. Open all year. Licensed.

FIRWOOD GUEST HOUSE HOTEL
89 Frant Road, Royal Tunbridge Wells, Kent TN2 5LP,
Telephone Tunbridge Wells (0892) 25596
AA

Small comfortable hotel. All rooms with bathroom en suite, radio intercom and television. Tea room with snacks available all day. Conference facilities maximum 18 also other functions on request. Special 3 day rate.
Bargain breaks. Convenient to historic Pantiles and central for touring South East England.
Good parking.

TWEEDSMUIR
Borders *Lanarkshire*
Map **11**   NT02

─── *Recommended* ───

GH Menzion Farmhouse ☎(08997) 247

A well-furnished and decorated country guesthouse retaining much of the character of the original farmhouse. Mr and Mrs Brett offer excellent hospitality and first class country house cordon bleu cooking, they serve a superb 5-course set dinner in house-party style.

4hc (1fb) CTV in 2 bedrooms ⓇB&b£12–£14 Bdi£18–£20 LDO2pm

Lic ⊞ 12P

TWO BRIDGES
Devon
Map **2**   SX67

GH Cherrybrook Hotel ☎Tavistock (0822) 88260
Closed Xmas & New Year

Large detached house in pleasant grounds in the middle of Dartmoor.

7⊞ (2fb) CTV in all bedrooms Ⓡ B&b£15 Bdi£22.50 W£145 ⊬ LDO7.15pm

Lic ⊞ 12P
Ⓥ

TYWARDREATH
Cornwall
Map **2**   SX05

GH Elmswood Tehidy Rd, Tywardreath Park ☎Par (072681) 4221

7hc (3fb)

Lic CTV 7P

TYWYN
Gwynedd
Map **6**   SH50

GH Min-y-Mor Private Hotel 7 Marine Pde ☎(0654) 710139

8hc (4⊞) (4fb) ✕ LDO5pm

Lic ⊞ CTV 2P
Ⓥ

Tweedsmuir
—
Ullingswick

GH Monfa Pier Rd ☎(0654) 710858
Feb–Nov

Semi detached Victorian house adjacent to the beach, a short walk from the shops.

8hc (3⊞) (3fb) ✕ B&b£10–£11 Bdi£14.50–£15.50 Wfr£95 ⊬

⊞ CTV 2P
Ⓥ

UFFCULME
Devon
Map **3**   ST01

FH Mrs M D Farley **Houndaller** *(ST058138)* ☎Craddock (0884) 40246

Very old attractive farmhouse standing in beautiful garden. Quiet, though only 800 yards from A38 at Waterloo Cross, close to M5 junction 27.

3hc (2fb) Ⓡ B&b£8.50–£10 Bdi£12.50–£16 W£87.50–£112 ⊬

CTV 4P 2🡢 176acres mixed
Ⓥ

FH Mr & Mrs A F Baker **Woodrow** *(ST054107)* ☎Craddock (0884) 40362
Closed Xmas

Farmhouse set in pleasant lawns and gardens with meadowland stretching to River Culm. Trout fishing available.

2hc (2fb) ✕ ✱B&b£9 Bdi£14 Wfr£98 ⊬ LDO7pm

CTV 6P 🡢 200acres mixed

UFFINGTON
Shropshire
Map **7**   SJ51

FH Mr & Mrs D Timmis **Preston Boats** *(SJ530118)* Preston on Severn ☎Upton Magna (074377) 240
Closed Xmas

17th-century farmhouse with beams and inglenook fireplace. 1¼m S on unclass road joining B5062 and A5.

3rm (1hc) (2fb) TV in 1 bedroom
✱B&b£8.50–£9 W£58–£60 M
⊞ CTV 12P 2🡢 ⋏(grass) 150acres arable mixed

UIST (SOUTH), ISLE OF
Western Isles *Iverness-shire*
Map **13**   NF

LOCHEYNORT' (NORTH)
Map **13**   NF72

FH Mrs A MacDonald **Arinabane** *(NF787283)* 8 North Locheynort ☎Bornish (08785) 379
Apr–Oct

A modern house and croft in peaceful location on north side of a sea loch. 1¼m ESE unlass road.

2hc LDO9pm

⊞ 3P 30acres fish sheep mixed

ULEY
Gloucestershire
Map **3**   ST79

FH Sam & Kay Trump **Hodgecombe** *(ST783994)* ☎(0453) 860365
Apr–Oct

Small cottage farm dedicated to rare breeds of sheep. Simple accommodation and good hospitality.

3rm (2fb) ✕ LDOam

⊞ CTV P 13acres non-working

ULLINGSWICK
Hereford & Worcester
Map **3**   SO54

FH Mrs P A Howland **The Steppes** *(SO586490)* ☎Hereford (0432) 820424
Closed 2 wks before Xmas

17th-century listed building, being noted for its many points of historical and architectural interest and although it retains its original features, including a wealth of exposed beams throughout, it has been sympathetically modernised.

3⊞ (1fb) CTV in all bedrooms Ⓡ ✱B&b£14.50–£15.50 Bdi£25–£33 W£175–£195 ⊬ LDO7pm

Lic ⊞ 6P nc12yrs
Ⓥ

UPLYME
Devon
Map **3**   SY39

INN *Black Dog Hotel* Lyme Rd ☎Lyme
Regis (02974) 2634
Mar–Oct

*Roadside inn with garden offering simply
appointed comfortable accommodation.*

5hc ® LDO9.30pm CTV P 2🖕

UPOTTERY
Devon
Map **3**   ST20

FH Mrs M M Reed **Yarde** *(ST193045)*
☎(040486) 318

*17th-century farmhouse with interesting
oak panelling and beams, overlooking the
Otter Valley. Near Monkton on the A30.*

(3hc) (1fb) ✗ ✳B&b£7.50–£8.50 Bdi£11–
£12 W£70–£75 LDO6pm

CTV 3P 1🖕 ♩ snooker 94acres mixed

UPPER HULME
Staffordshire
Map **7**   SK06

FH Mrs J Lomas **Keekorok Lodge**
(SK005616) ☎Blackshaw (053834) 218
Etr–Sep

*Modernised stone-built house with views
over Tittesworth Reservoir, well known
locally for fishing, situated 1m NW of
village towards The Roaches (Landmark).*

3rm (2hc) (1fb) ✗ LDO10am

🍴 CTV 10P nc2yrs 15acres arable

UPTON PYNE
Devon
Map **3**   SX99

⊢✗**FH** Mrs Y M Taverner **Pierce's**
(SX910977) ☎Stoke Canon (039284) 252
Etr–Sep

*Large farmhouse about 1 mile north of
A377 Exeter–Barnstaple road.*

1hc (1fb) ✗ B&b£8 W£54 M̶

🍴 CTV 2P 300acres mixed

Uplyme
Vowchurch

UPTON UPON SEVERN
Hereford & Worcester
Map **3**   SO84

GH *Pool House* ☎(06846) 2151
Closed Xmas (rs Oct–Apr)

*Homely country house on banks of River
Severn with charming garden.*

9hc (2⇄ 3🛏) (3fb) ✗ ✳B&b£11–£21.50
Bdi£16–£26 LDO6.30pm

Lic ♩

Credit cards ① ② ③

USK
Gwent
Map **3**   SO30

FH J Arnett **Ty Gwyn** *(SO391045)*
☎(02913) 2878
Closed Xmas day

*Large modernised farmhouse situated
between Raglan and Usk at Gwehelog,
2½m NE of Usk.*

3hc (1fb) ✂ in 2 bedrooms TV in 1
bedroom ✗ ® ✳B&b£8.50–£9.50
Bdi£13.50–£14 Wfr£98 ⁄ LDO2pm

🍴 CTV P nc8yrs snooker 26acres beef
chickens horses

Ⓥ

UTTOXETER
Staffordshire
Map **7**   SK03

GH *Hillcrest* 3 Leighton Rd ☎(08893)
4627
Closed Xmas Day

*Large Victorian house in a residential area
close to town centre.*

8hc (3fb) ® B&b£9.50–£10.50 Bdi£13.50–
£14.50 W£85.05–£91.35 ⁄ LDO2.30pm

🍴 CTV 8P ⚿

Ⓥ

FH Mrs B L Noakes **Holly Grange**
(SU063333) Bramshall (2m W of B5027)
☎(08893) 2405

*Large, attractive farmhouse with pleasant
garden and modest accommodation.*

2rm (1fb) ® LDO previous day

🍴 CTV 3P 162acres dairy

FH R J & K P Stockton **Popinjay**
(SK074322) Stafford Rd ☎(08893) 66082

1m SW off A518.

2rm (1fb) ✗ ✳B&b£8–£9 Bdi£13–£14
W£84 ⁄

CTV 4P 2🖕 10acres beef ⚿

Ⓥ

VENN OTTERY
Devon
Map **3**   SY09

GH Venn Ottery Barton Country Hotel
☎Ottery St Mary (040481) 2733

*Guesthouse in rural position, having good
facilities and a high standard of cuisine.*

13hc (4⇄ 4🛏) (3fb) ® B&b£13–£21
Bdi£16.50–£29.50 W£115.50–£171.50 ⁄
LDO7.30pm

Lic 🍴 CTV 20P

Credit cards ① ③ Ⓥ

VENTNOR
Isle of Wight
See **Wight, Isle of**

VOWCHURCH
Hereford & Worcester
Map **3**   SO33

FH Mrs A Spencer **The Croft** *(SO368366)*
☎Peterchurch (09816) 226

*A warm welcome and appealing
accommodation are offered in a restful
situation.*

3⇄ CTV in all bedrooms ✗ ® B&b£13–
£16 Bdi£18.50–£22 W£126–£139 ⁄
LDO5.30pm

Lic 🍴 CTV 8P nc10yrs ♞(grass) 7acres
livestock

Ⓥ

See advertisement on page 194

WADHURST
East Sussex
Map **5**   TQ63

INN *Fourkeys* Station Rd ☎(089288) 2252

Small, old house with friendly proprietor and comfortable bedrooms, most with modern facilities.

8hc (2fb) CTV in 2 bedrooms TV in 6 bedrooms ® LDO10.30pm

💷 25P

Credit cards ① ③

WALLASEY
Merseyside
Map **7**   SJ29

GH *Divonne Hotel* 71 Wellington Rd, New Brighton ☎051–639 4727

A popular commercial hotel set on rising ground overlooking the Mersey Estuary.

15hc (5🏠) TV in all bedrooms ® LDO7.55pm

Lic 💷 CTV 6P

GH Sandpiper Private Hotel 22 Dudley Rd, New Brighton ☎051-639 7870

Simple-style guesthouse in a quiet side road.

7hc (2fb) ⚱ in 1 bedroom CTV in all bedrooms ✖ ® ✱B&b£10.50 Bdi£14.75 W£62.50 M LDO4.30pm

💷 4P

Ⓥ

WANSFORD
Cambridgeshire
Map **4**   TL09

INN *Cross Keys* ☎Stamford (0780) 782266

3hc Annexe: 3hc TV in all bedrooms ® LDO9.30pm

💷

Credit cards ① ③

WAREHAM
Dorset
Map **3**   SY98

Wadhurst
—
Washford

FH L S Barnes **Luckford Wood** *(SY873865)* East Stoke ☎Bindon Abbey (0929) 463098
Closed Xmas

3hc (1🏠) (2fb) ⚱ in 1 bedroom CTV in 1 bedroom TV in 1 bedroom ® ✱B&b£10–£12 Bdi£16–£18 W£101.50–£115.50 ⱡ (W only end Jul & Aug)

💷 CTV 6P 167acres dairy

Ⓥ

─── *Recommended* ───

FH Mrs J Barnes **Redcliffe** *(SY932866)* ☎(09295) 2225

Modern farmhouse in quiet, rural surroundings. Pleasant location adjacent to River Frome and overlooking hills and fields. ½ mile from Wareham.

5hc (1⇆) (1fb) ✖

💷 CTV 5P 2🚗 ➷ 250acres dairy

WARREN STREET (nr Lenham)
Kent
Map **5**   TQ95

INN Harrow ☎Maidstone (0622) 858727
Closed Xmas

7hc (1⇆ 2🏠) (1fb) ✱B&bfr£14 W£184.50–£204.50 ⱡ Bar lunch £1–£7.50 Dinner9pm £8.50&alc

💷 CTV 30P

Credit cards ① ③ Ⓥ

WARSASH
Hampshire
Map **4**   SU40

─── *Recommended* ───

GH *Solent View Private Hotel* 33–35 Newton Road ☎Locks Heath (04895) 2300

6hc (1⇆ 5🏠) CTV in all bedrooms LDOam

Lic 💷 CTV 10P

WARWICK
Warwickshire
Map **4**   SP26

GH Austin House 96 Emscote Rd ☎(0926) 493583

Large, personally-run Victorian house on the busy Warwick–Leamington Rd. Rear garden.

7hc (1🏠) (3fb) ✱B&b£10–£11 Bdi£15–£16 W£98–£105 ⱡ

💷 CTV 7P 2➷

GH Avon 7 Emscote Rd ☎(0926) 491367

Small, well-run private hotel on Warwick–Leamington Rd. Close to tourist amenities.

7hc (4fb) ✖ ® B&b£9.50 Bdi£14.50 W£101.50 ⱡ LDO4.30pm

💷 CTV 6P 1➷

GH Cambridge Villa Private Hotel 20A Emscote Rd ☎(0926) 491169
Closed Xmas Day

16hc (4🏠) (3fb) CTV in all bedrooms ® ✱B&b£13.80–£14.50 LDO9pm

Lic 💷 CTV 18P

Credit card ③

GH Old Rectory Sherbourne (off A46 2m SW) ☎Barford (Warwicks) (0926) 624562
Closed 23 Dec–1 Jan

Tastefully restored house offering very comfortable accommodation and home-cooked food.

7hc (1⇆ 5🏠) (1fb) TV in 1 bedroom ® ✱B&b£10–£17 Bdi£15–£18 W£100–£140 ⱡ LDO4pm

Lic 💷 CTV 9P ♿

Ⓥ

WASHFORD
Somerset
Map **3**   ST04

GH Washford House ☎(0984) 40484
Closed Xmas

Comfortable, detached Victorian residence in 3 acres, set well back on A39. Fine views of Quantock Hills and only 6 miles from Minehead.

This small exclusive guest house offers something special in style and comfort. The beautiful rooms each have a private bathroom with shower, colour TV, radio, use of telephone and coffee/tea/chocolate making faclities. There is the warm elegant sitting room or charming garden in which to relax. No rigid times for the super breakfasts.

Set in peaceful countryside, Northleigh House is handy for Midlands motorways, Exhibition Centres and historic towns. Terms from £14. Please telephone Sylvia Fishwick for brochures.

Northleigh House
Five Ways Road, Hatton, Warwick CV35 7HZ
Telephone Haseley Knob (0926 87) 203

6hc (1fb) ✗ ✱B&b£10–£12 Bdi£15–£17
W£98–£112∥ LDO5pm
Lic ♨ CTV 14P

WATERHOUSES
Staffordshire
Map **7** SK05

GH Croft House Farm Waterfall (1m NW
unclass) ☎(05386) 553

*Former farmhouse dating back to the 17th
century, recently extended to provide
good well-equipped accommodation.*

6hc (2fb) CTV in all bedrooms ®
✱B&bfr£7.50 Bdifr£12.50 LDO9pm
Lic CTV 12P

FH Mrs K Watson **Weaver** *(SK102467)*
☎Oakamore (0538) 702271

*Solid stone-built 19-century farm in a
hollow of the Weaver hills.*

6hc (4fb) ✗ ® ✱B&b£8–£9 Bdi£12–£14
♨ CTV 4P 320acres mixed
Ⓥ

INN Ye Olde Crown ☎(05386) 204

*A warm and friendly atmosphere awaits
you at this 17th-century village inn on the
A523.*

8hc (3🍴) (2fb) CTV in all bedrooms ✗ ®
B&b£10.50–£15.50 Lunch£2–£8 Dinner
10pm £2–£8
♨ 50P

WATERLOO
Isle of Skye, Highland *Inverness-shire*
See **Skye, Isle of**

WATERLOOVILLE
Hampshire
Map **4** SU60

GH Far End Private Hotel 31 Queens Rd
☎(0705) 263242
Closed 23 Dec–1 Jan

*Peaceful detached house with spacious
beamed-lounge and good 'home grown'
cooking.*

10hc (1🛁 1🍴) (2fb) ✱B&b£16–£22
Bdi£23–£29 W£130–£160 ∥ (W only Nov–
Apr) LDO4pm
Lic ♨ CTV 20P 3🚗
Ⓥ

WATERPERRY
Oxfordshire
Map **4** SP60

FH Mrs S Fonge **Manor** *(SP628064)*
☎Ickford (08447) 263

*Stone farmhouse standing in large
garden, in centre of village. Coarse fishing
available.*

3rm (2hc) (1fb) ✱B&b£9–£10.50 Bdi£16–
£18 W£108.50–£122.50∥ LDOam
♨ TV 4P ⚙ ♪ 160acres arable beef
poultry sheep mixed
Ⓥ

WATERROW
Somerset
Map **3** ST02

FH Mr J Bone **Hurstone Farmhouse
Hotel** *(ST056252)* ☎Wiveliscombe (0984)
23441

*17th-century farmhouse, furnished in
keeping, in 65 acres. Much of food served
is produced on the farm.*

4rm (3hc 1🛁) (1fb) ✗ ®
Lic CTV 8P ⚙ ♪ 65acres dairy

INN Rock ☎Wiveliscombe (0984) 23293

6rm (5hc 4🛁) ⚡ in 1 bedroom CTV in all
bedrooms ✱B&b£11.50–£14.50 W£76.50–
£96.50 Ⓜ Lunch £2.50alc Dinner11pm
£5alc
♨ CTV 20P
Ⓥ

See advertisement on page 398

WATFORD
Hertfordshire
Map **4**　TQ19

GH White House Hotel 26–29 Upton Rd
☎(0923) 37316 Telex no 8955439

Close to town centre, offers well-equipped bedrooms. Ideal for business people.

37hc (15⇦ 22🛁) Annexe: 26hc (17⇦ 7🛁)
(6fb) CTV in all bedrooms ® B&b£24.50–
£43 Bdi£34.10–£52.60 W£287.70 ⫽
LDO9.45pm

Lic 🍴 40P

Credit cards ① ② ③

WEEDONLOIS
Northamptonshire
Map **4**　SP64

FH Mrs C Raven **Croft** *(SP600465)*
Milthorpe ☎Blakesley (0327) 860475
Feb–Nov

New detached house, built of Cotswold stone, in rural surroundings on edge of delightful Northamptonshire village.

2rm ⋈ ✳B&b£11.50 Bdi£15.50 W£108.50
⫽ LDO5.30pm

🍴 CTV 4P 25acres pigs turkeys

WEETON
Lancashire
Map **7**　SD33

FH Mrs E Colligan **High Moor** *(SD388365)*
☎(039136) 273
Closed Xmas & New Year

Compact, homely farmhouse, clean and tidy. Much farm produce used in cooking.

2rm (1fb) TV in 1 bedroom CTV in 1
bedroom ⋈ ® ✳B&b£8 W£48 Ⓜ

🍴 CTV 10P 1🐎 7acres non-working

WELLINGBOROUGH
Northamptonshire
Map **4**　SP86

GH Oak House Private Hotel 9 Broad
Green ☎(0933) 71133
Closed Xmas

10hc (9🛁) CTV in all bedrooms ®
✳B&b£14.50–£19 Bdi£20–£24.50 W£140–
£171.50 ⫽ LDOnoon

Watford
–
Welshpool

🍴 CTV 10P
Credit cards ① ③ Ⓥ

WELLINGTON
Shropshire
Map **7**　SJ61
See **Telford**

WELLINGTON
Somerset
Map **3**　ST12

FH Mrs N K Ash **Pinksmoor Mill House**
(ST109198) (3m W off A38 at Beam Bridge
Hotel) ☎Greenham (0823) 672361

Part 13th-century property, 3m W of Wellington, with neat comfortable accommodation. Original mill house on site.

3hc (1🛁) (1fb) ® ✳B&b£8.50–£9.50
Bdi£13.50–£14.50 W£56–£63 Ⓜ LDO5pm

🍴 CTV P 98acres dairy

WELLS
Somerset
Map **3**　ST54

GH Bekynton House 7 St Thomas Street
☎(0749) 72222

9hc (2🛁) (2fb) ⋈ ® ✳B&b£10–£14.50
Bdi£15.50–£21.50 LDO11am

🍴 CTV 7P Ⓥ

Recommended

GH Coach House Stoberry Pk
☎(0749) 76535

A delightful converted coach house, standing in 6 acres of attractive parkland, with excellent furnishings and décor. Unique views of the city of Wells with the majestic Cathedral taking prominence.

3⇦ ✳B&b£12–£18 Bdi£18–£27
W£119–£175 ⫽ LDO8.30am

Lic 🍴 CTV 6P

Ⓥ

GH Tors 20 Tor St ☎(0749) 72322
9hc (7fb) LDO5pm
CTV 10P

FH Mrs P Higgs **Home** *(ST538442)*
Stoppers Ln, Upper Coxley ☎(0749)
72434
Closed Xmas rs Oct–Apr

2m SW off A39.

7hc (3fb) ✳B&b£8.50–£9.50 Bdi£14.50–
£15.50 W£85–£90 ⫽ LDO previous day

Lic 🍴 CTV 10P 10acres pig, market garden

FH Mrs J Gould **Manor** *(ST546474)* Old
Bristol Rd, Upper Milton (1m W A39
towards Bristol, 200 yds beyond
roundabout) ☎(0749) 73394
Closed Xmas

Attractive stone-built farmhouse on the edge of the City. Simple, clean standard of furnishings and appointments.

3hc (1fb) ⋈ ® ✳B&b£8–£11 W£53–£70 Ⓜ

🍴 CTV 6P ⚓ 130acres beef

WELSHPOOL
Powys
Map **7**　SJ20

FH Mrs K Owens **Coed-y-Brenin**
(SJ248025) Kingswood Ln (3m S off A490
at Kingswood) ☎Forden (093876) 510

Modern farmhouse in lovely Border countryside, signposted Kingswood from B4388. ⅓m E off B4388 on unclass rd.

2hc 🛏 in 1 bedroom ⋈ ® ✳B&b£8.50–
£9.50 W£59.50–£66.50 Ⓜ

🍴 CTV 6P nc2yrs 320acres beef dairy
sheep mixed

Ⓥ

FH Mrs E Jones **Gungrog House**
(SJ235089) Rhallt ☎(0938) 3381
Apr–Oct

300-year-old farmhouse in quiet situation high on hillside, commanding superb views of the Severn Valley 1m NE off A458.

3hc (2🛁) (1fb) ⋈ ® ✳B&b£9.50–£10 Bdi£15
Wfr£95 ⫽ LDO5.30pm

🍴 CTV 6P ⚓ 21acres mixed

THE ROCK INN

WATERROW
TAUNTON, SOMERSET
Tel: Wiveliscombe 23293
(STD code 0984)

Situated on the A361, 14 miles west of Taunton in the Brendon foothills making places like Exmoor, Clatworthy Reservoir and the north and south coasts very accessible. Fully centrally heated, with comfortable residents' lounge. All bedrooms have private bath, wc & colour TV. Breakfast, luncheon & dinner are served in addition to food at the bar, all year round.

FH Mr & Mrs M C Payne **Heath Cottage** *(SJ239023)* Kingswood (3m S off A490)
☎ Forden (093876) 453
Apr–Oct

Former country pub within yards of Offa's Dyke. Clean, modest accommodation.

3rm (2hc 1⇨ 1fl) ✈ Ⓡ ✱B&b£9 Bdi£14 W£92Ł

♨ CTV 4P 6acres poultry sheep

ⓥ

FH Mr & Mrs W Jones **Moat** *(SJ214042)*
☎(0938) 3179
Apr–Oct

16th-century farmhouse with timbered dining room and canopied stone fireplace. The gardens have a tennis lawn, and lead down to the river. Situated in the Severn Valley.

3hc (1fb) TV in 1 bedroom ✈ Ⓡ ✱B&b£9.50–£10.50 Bdi£14.50–£15.50 W£96.50–£103.50Ł LDO2pm

♨ CTV 3P ⌂ 𝒫(grass) 260acres dairy

ⓥ

FH Mr & Mrs J Emberton **Tynllwyn** *(SJ215085)* ☎(0938) 3175
Closed Xmas

Peaceful 19th-century farmhouse offering good, modern accommodation. On A490 N of Welshpool.

6hc (3fb) CTV in all bedrooms ✱B&b£10–£10.50 Bdi£15–£15.50 Wfr£98Ł LDO6.30pm

Lic ♨ CTV P 150acres dairy mixed

ⓥ

WEST BAGBOROUGH
Somerset
Map **3** ST13

GH Higher House ☎Bishops Lydeard (0823) 432996
Closed Xmas wk rs Dec–Mar

7hc (1fl) ✱B&b£10–£12.50 Bdi£17–£21 W£110–£130Ł LDO4.30pm

Lic ♨ CTV 10P ⌂ ⌒(heated)

ⓥ

WEST CHILTINGTON
West Sussex
Map **4** TQ01

FH A M Steele **New House** *(TQ091186)*
☎(07983) 2215
Closed Dec

Listed 15th-century farmhouse with oak-beamed rooms and inglenook fireplace, surrounded by beautifully kept grounds.

4hc (1⇨ 1fl) (1fb) CTV in all bedrooms ✈ Ⓡ ✱B&b£11–£15 W£70–£98M̸

♨ CTV 4P 2🚗 nc10yrs 50acres mixed

ⓥ

WESTCLIFF-ON-SEA
Essex
See **Southend-on-Sea**

WEST COKER
Somerset
Map **3** ST51

GH Old Rectory Church St ☎(093586) 2048

A detached, stone-built Victorian rectory off the A30 offering sound accommodation.

4hc ✈ Ⓡ B&b£10 W£56M̸

CTV 6P ⌂

See advertisement on page 427

WEST DOWN
Devon
Map **2** SS54

GH Sunnymeade Country House Hotel Dean Cross (1m W on A361) ☎Ilfracombe (0271) 63668 Plan **31** *B1*

10hc (3fl) (3fb) ✈ Ⓡ B&b£8.50–£11 Bdi£14–£18 W£77–£115Ł LDO6pm

Lic ♨ CTV 14P ⌂

Credit cards 1 2

WEST KIRBY
Merseyside
Map **7** SJ28

GH *Park Hotel* Westbourne Rd ☎051-625 9319

29hc (1fl) (3fb) CTV in 3 bedrooms Ⓡ LDO9pm

Lic ♨ CTV P

WEST LAYTON
North Yorkshire
Map **12** NZ10

Recommended

GH West Layton Manor Hotel
☎Darlington (0325) 718633

A beautifully converted Victorian manor house standing in extensive, landscaped grounds not far from the A66. High standard of comfort and food, and very pleasant, welcoming atmosphere.

North Country Winner of the AA 1987 Guesthouse of the Year Award

6⇨ (3fb) CTV in all bedrooms Ⓡ ✱B&b£18.50–£21.50 Bdi£25.50–£26.50 W£154Ł LDO8pm

Lic ♨ CTV 20P snooker

ⓥ

WEST LINTON
Borders *Peeblesshire*
Map **11** NT15

GH Medwyn House Medwyn Rd
☎(0968) 60542

Nice, spacious bedrooms in country mansion close to village golf course.

3⇨ B&b£16.50 Bdi£25 W£168Ł LDOnoon

♨ CTV 12P 2🚗 sauna bath solarium

ⓥ

WEST LULWORTH
Dorset
See **Lulworth**

WESTON-SUPER-MARE
Avon
Map **3** ST36
See plan on page 402

GH Baymead Hotel Longton Grove Rd
☎(0934) 22951 Plan **1** *C4*

32hc (5⇨) (10fb) Ⓡ ✱B&b£12–£15 Bdi£15–£18 W£85–£110Ł LDO6.30pm

Lic lift ♨ CTV P̸

GH Fourways 2 Ashcombe Rd ☎(0934) 23827 Plan **3** C3
Apr–Oct
6hc Annexe: 3hc ✗ ✳B&b£7–£8.50
🏠 CTV 6P nc10yrs

⊷**GH Lydia** 78 Locking Rd ☎(0934) 25962 Plan **7** C3
Closed Xmas
6hc (2fb) CTV in all bedrooms ✗ ®
B&b£7–£9 Bdi£11–£13 W£72–£85 K
LDOnoon
Lic 🏠 CTV 5P
ⓥ

GH Milton Lodge 15 Milton Rd ☎(0934) 23161 Plan **8** C4
Apr–Oct
Recent guesthouse created with painstaking care to provide a good standard of accommodation.
6hc (3⇄ 3🚿) CTV in all bedrooms ✗ ®
B&b£10–£11 Bdi£15–£16 W£89–£99 K (W only 23 May–29 Aug) LDO4pm
🏠 5P nc15yrs

GH Moorlands Hutton (3m E unclass between A368 and A370) ☎Bleadon (0934) 812283 Not on plan
8hc (1⇄ 2🚿) (5fb) ✗ ✳B&b£10.35–£11.50 Bdi£16.10–£17.25 W£82.80–£87.40 K LDO5pm
Lic 🏠 CTV 7P 🐾
ⓥ

GH Newton House 79 Locking Rd ☎(0934) 29331 Plan **9** C3
Small, comfortable and friendly guesthouse.
8hc (2🚿) (4fb) ® ✳B&b£10–£11 Bdi£14.50–£15.50 W£85–£96.50 K LDO2pm →

 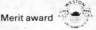

Lic 🍴 CTV 9P
ⓥ

GH *Scottsdale Hotel* 3 Ellenborough
Park North ☎(0934) 26489 Plan **11** *B2*
Mar–Oct

13hc ✠ ⓡ LDO4pm
🍴 CTV 13P nc

Weston-super-Mare

GH *Shire Elms* 71 Locking Rd ☎(0934)
28605 Plan **12** *C3*
Closed 23 Dec–2 Jan

11hc (1⇨) Annexe: 2hc (3fb) CTV in all
bedrooms ✠ LDO3pm
Lic 🍴 CTV 10P

GH Southmead 435 Locking Rd ☎(0934)
29351 Plan **13** *C3*

*Bright, clean semi-detached house on
approach road to town. Modest
bedrooms.*

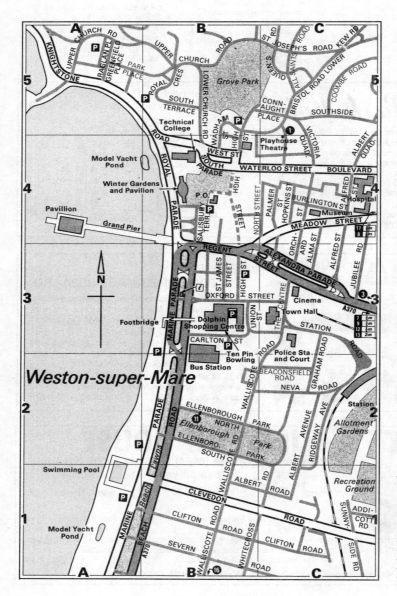

Weston-super-Mare

1	Baymead Hotel
3	Fourways
7	Lydia
8	Milton Lodge
9	Newton House
11	Scottsdale Hotel
12	Shire Elms
13	Southmead
16	Willow
17	Wychwood Hotel

6hc (2fb) TV in 1 bedroom ✱B&b£7–£9 Bdi£11.50–£13.50 W£69–£76 ⒦ LDO4pm ⦅⦆ CTV 6P ♠♦
Ⓥ

GH Willow 3 Clarence Road East
☎(0934) 413736 Plan **16** B1
Etr–Oct

8hc (2⇨ 1⏃) (4fb) ✕ Ⓡ B&b£9–£13 Bdi£12–£16 W£70–£96 ⒦ LDO9pm ⦅⦆ CTV 8P ▣(heated)

GH Wychwood Hotel 148 Milton Rd
☎(0934) 27793 Plan **17** C4

10hc (3fb) CTV in all bedrooms LDO5pm
Lic ⦅⦆ 12P ⌫(heated)

WEST PENNARD
Somerset
Not on map

INN Red Lion Newtown ☎Glastonbury (0458) 32941

Attractive 17th-century inn with former barn converted to a comfortable, bedroom annexe. All rooms have en-suite bathrooms. Friendly staff serve a wide range of food.

Annexe: 7⇨ (1fb) CTV in all bedrooms ✕ Ⓡ B&b£25 Bdi£27.50–£31 W£150 ⓜ Lunch£2.50–£6 Dinner 10.30pm£2.50–£6

P ⊯ ♠♦
Credit cards ① ③

Weston-super-Mare
—
Weymouth

WEST SCRAFTON
North Yorkshire
Map **7**   SE08

GH Coverdale Country Hotel Great Swinside ☎Wensleydale (0969) 40601

A converted farmhouse situated in an unspoilt, rural area of the dales. Friendly atmosphere.

7⏃ (1fb) ✕ Ⓡ ✱B&b£13.50–£18.50 Bdi£20–£26

Lic ⦅⦆ CTV 15P ♠♦
Credit cards ① ③ Ⓥ

WESTWARD HO!
Devon
Map **2**   SS42

GH Buckleigh Lodge 135 Bayview Rd ☎Bideford (02372) 75988
Mar–Oct rs Nov–Feb

6hc (1⇨) (2fb) CTV in 1 bedroom ✕ ✱B&b£9.50–£11.50 Bdi£14–£16 W£92–£104 ⒦ LDO8pm
Lic ⦅⦆ CTV 7P

WETHERBY
West Yorkshire
Map **8**   SE44

GH Prospect House 8 Caxton St
☎(0937) 62428

Bright and cheerful guesthouse with comfortable, clean accommodation.

6hc (1fb) ✱B&b£10–£10.50 W£70–£75 ⓜ ⦅⦆ CTV 6P

WEYBRIDGE
Surrey
London plan **4**   A1
(pages 246–247)

GH Warbeck House Hotel 46 Queens Rd ☎(0932) 48764
Closed 22 Dec–2 Jan

Fine Edwardian house with comfortable, modernised bedrooms and relaxing atmosphere.

10hc (1⇨) (1fb) CTV in all bedrooms ✕ Ⓡ ✱B&b£21.85–£27.02
Lic ⦅⦆ CTV 16P nc4yrs

WEYMOUTH
Dorset
Map **3**   SY67

GH Beechcroft Private Hotel 128–129 The Esplanade ☎(0305) 786608
Apr–Sep

Located on sea front with continental awnings.   →

29hc (2🛁 11🚿) (10fb) CTV in all bedrooms [R] ✱B&b£13.11–£16.10 Bdi£17.94–£20.93 W£101.20–£118.40 LDO4.30pm

Lic 3P(charge) 10🚗(charge)

Credit cards [1] [3]

GH Hotel Concorde 131 The Esplanade ☎(0305) 776900
Feb–Nov

End of Georgian terrace on sea front.

17hc (2🚿) (7fb) ✱B&bfr£11.50 Bdifr£16.50 Wfr£80 Ⱡ

Lic CTV 4P

Credit card [1] [V]

GH Hazeldene 16 Abbotsbury Rd, Westham ☎(0305) 782579

Comfortably furnished guesthouse, a short distance from the town centre and harbour, situated on the Bridport road.

7hc (4fb) ✗ [R] ✱B&b£8–£9 Bdi£10 W£55–£70 Ⱡ LDO2pm

Lic 🍴 CTV 7P 1🚗 nc5yrs

[V]

GH Kenora 5 Stavordale Rd ☎(0305) 771215
May–Oct

In quiet cul-de-sac a short distance from the harbour.

17hc (1🛁 8🚿) (5fb) ✗ [R] ✱B&b£10–£13 Bdi£14.50–£17.50 W£77–£110 Ⱡ (W only Jun Jul & Aug) LDO4.30pm

Lic 🍴 CTV 20P

GH Kings Acre Hotel 140 The Esplanade ☎(0305) 782534
Mar–Sep (rs Feb & Oct)

Terraced Georgian hotel on sea front.

14hc (4fb) CTV in all bedrooms ✗ [R] ✱B&b£12–£16 Bdi£16–£20 W£87.50–£98 Ⱡ (W only Jul–Aug) LDO4.30pm

Lic 🍴 9P

Credit cards [1] [3] [V]

GH Leam Hotel 103 The Esplanade ☎(0305) 784127
Mar–Nov

Sea front hotel with wrought iron balcony situated opposite the Jubilee clock.

Weymouth — Whaplode

19hc (9fb) CTV in all bedrooms [R] ✱B&b£12.50 Bdi£16.50 W£86–£92.50 Ⱡ LDO4.30pm

Lic 🚭

Credit cards [1] [3]

GH Richmoor Hotel 146 The Esplanade ☎(0305) 773435
Mar–Nov

Georgian terraced hotel opposite the pier and bandstand.

22hc (2🛁 1🚿) (10fb) ✗ [R] ✱B&b£9–£13 Bdi£14–£18 W£82–£105 Ⱡ (W only mid Jul–Aug) LDO4.30pm

Lic lift CTV 8P

Credit cards [1] [3]

GH Sou'west Lodge Hotel Rodwell Rd ☎(0305) 783749
May–Sep rs Oct–Apr

Modern building on Portland road a short distance from the harbour and town centre.

9hc (2🛁 4🚿) (2fb) CTV in 4 bedrooms TV in 2 bedrooms [R] ✱B&b£10–£13 Bdi£14.50–£17.50 W£86.50–£106.50 Ⱡ LDO9am

Lic 🍴 CTV 14P nc3yrs

Credit card [1] [V]

GH Sunningdale Private Hotel 52 Preston Rd, Overcombe ☎(0305) 832179
Etr–mid Oct

Guesthouse set back off main Preston road enjoying elevated position.

21hc (5🛁 2🚿) (8fb) CTV in 5 bedrooms TV in 2 bedrooms [R] B&b£12.60–£14.40 Bdi£16.80–£20.40 W£105–£128 Ⱡ LDO6pm

Lic CTV 25P 🏊(heated) putting

[V]

GH Tamarisk Hotel 12 Stavordale Rd, Westham ☎(0305) 786514
Mar–Oct

Situated in a quiet cul-de-sac a short walk from the town centre and harbour.

16hc (4🛁 8🚿) (5fb) ✗ [R] ✱B&b£8.50–£11.50 Bdi£11–£14 W£74–£88 Ⱡ (W only Jul & Aug) LDO4pm

Lic 🍴 CTV 19P

[V]

GH Westway House 62 Abbotsbury Rd ☎(0305) 784564

Family run guesthouse 10 minutes walk from town centre and sea front.

11hc (1🛁 4🚿) CTV in all bedrooms [R] B&b£10.50–£12.50 Bdi£15.50–£17.50 W£65–£90.75 M̸ LDO6.30pm

Lic CTV 8P

INN *Golden Lion Hotel* St Edmonds Street ☎(0305) 786778
Closed winter

19hc (1🛁) ✗

🍴 CTV ⌗ nc5yrs

INN Turks Head 6–8 East St (3m NW B3157) ☎(0305) 783093
(For full entry see **Chickerell**)

WHADDON

Buckinghamshire
Map **4** SP83

INN Lowndes Arms & Motel 4 High St ☎Milton Keynes (0908) 501706

11🚿 Annexe: 11🚿 CTV in all bedrooms ✗ [R] ✱B&b£23–£33.35 Bdi£27.80–£43.35 W£256.35 Ⱡ Lunch £6.30–£11.50 Dinner 9.30pm£6.30–£11.50

🍴 30P ⌗ nc16yrs

Credit cards [1] [3] [5] [V]

WHAPLODE

Lincolnshire
Map **8** TF32

FH Mrs A Thompson **Guy Wells** *(TF337241)* ☎Holbeach (0406) 22239
Mar–Oct

Beautifully preserved Queen Anne farmhouse with a wealth of charm and character.

3rm (1hc) (2fb) ✗ [R] B&b£10–£12 Bdi£16–£18 Wfr£100 Ⱡ LDO4pm

（CTV 6P 80acres arable flowers
Ⓥ

WHEDDON CROSS
Somerset
Map **3**　SS93

GH Higherley ☎Timberscombe (064384)
582

6hc (1fb) ✔ in 3 bedrooms CTV in 2
bedrooms ✳B&b£10.25–£14.25
Bdi£16.75–£18 Wfr£116 ⱡ LDO9pm

Lic （CTV 50P 4🐾

Credit cards ① ③ Ⓥ

FH Mrs J C Norman **Gupworthy**
(SS969353) ☎Brompton Regis (03987)
267
Jun–Nov

*Comfortable, clean farmhouse in the
Exmoor National Park. Good-sized
bedrooms.*

4hc (1fb) ✔ ✳B&b£6.50–£9 Bdi£12.50–
£15 W£87.50–£105 ⱡ LDO8.30pm

（CTV 12P 1🐾 ♨

654acres beef sheep

WHIDDON DOWN
Devon
Map **3**　SX69

FH Mrs J S Robinson **South Nethercott**
(SX688947) ☎(064723) 276
Mar–Nov

*A warm welcome awaits you at this 16th-
century farmhouse with its oak beams
and open fireplaces.*

2hc (1⇄) ✔ ✳B&b£9.50–£10.50 Bdi£16–
£17 LDO7.30pm

CTV 4P nc12yrs 170acres arable dairy
Ⓥ

WHIMPLE
Devon
Map **3**　SY09

GH Down House ☎(0404) 822860
Closed Xmas & New Year

*Attentive, friendly owners provide sound
accommodation at this attractive, gabled
house. Fine views of surrounding
countryside.*

5hc (1fb) ✘ Ⓡ ✳B&b£7.50–£9.50
Bdi£11.50–£13.50 Wfr£80.50 ⱡ LDO4pm

CTV 8P ♨

5acres mixed small holding
Ⓥ

WHITBY
North Yorkshire
Map **8**　NZ81

GH Beach Cliff Hotel North Prom, West
Cliff ☎(0947) 602886

*Comfortable private house with spacious
public areas.*

10hc (1⇄4㊍) (2fb) ✘ Ⓡ ✳B&b£10.50–
£12 Bdi£15–£16.50 W£100–£110 ⱡ
LDO6pm

Lic （CTV 6P

Credit cards ① ② ③ Ⓥ

GH Esklet 22 Crescent Av ☎(0947)
605663
Closed Nov & Jan

*Small, friendly guesthouse in residential
area.*

7hc (3fb) ✔ in 1 bedroom Ⓡ ✳B&b£8–
£9.50 Bdi£12–£13.50 W£79–£86 ⱡ
LDO5.30pm

（CTV 1P
Ⓥ

GH Europa Private Hotel 20 Hudson St
☎(0947) 602251
Mar–Oct

*Pleasant small guesthouse near harbour,
well-furnished and with good, comfortable
accommodation.*

8hc (1㊍) (1fb) ✘ ✳B&b£7.75–£8.25
Bdi£11.50–£12 W£75 ⱡ LDO4.30pm

（CTV ✔ nc2yrs
Ⓥ

GH Glendale 16 Crescent Ave ☎(0947)
604242
Mar–Oct

---

*Cosy and cheerful establishment offering
neat, well-maintained rooms.*

6hc (4fb) CTV in 2 bedrooms TV in 4
bedrooms Ⓡ ✳B&b£9.50 Bdi£13 Wfr£84 ⱡ
LDO4.15pm

Lic CTV 6P

GH Old Hall Hotel Ruswarp ☎(0947)
602801
Mar–Oct

*A rambling 17th-century hotel full of
character and standing in its own
grounds. 1½m SW B1416.*

20hc (3⇄4㊍) (2fb) ✘ ✳B&b£12.50–
£14.50 Bdi£19 W£80.50–£94.50 M
LDO6pm

Lic （CTV 18P ♨
Ⓥ

GH Oxford Hotel West Cliff ☎(0947)
603349

*Well-run family hotel on the sea front. The
restaurant is open all day serving coffee,
lunch and teas.*

20hc (1⇄) (6fb) CTV in all bedrooms ✘ Ⓡ
B&b£13–£18 Bdi£18.25–£23.25
W£127.75–£162.75 ⱡ

Lic lift 4P solarium

Credit cards ① ② ③

GH Prospect Villa 13 Prospect Hill
☎(0947) 603118
Feb–Nov

*Although dinner is not served here
substantial home-made snacks are
available during the evening.*

6hc (1⇄) (2fb) TV in 1 bedroom Ⓡ
B&b£9.50–£12 W£60–£79 M LDO4.30pm

Lic （CTV 4P
Ⓥ

GH Sandbeck Hotel Crescent Ter, West
Cliff ☎(0947) 604012
Apr–4 Oct

*A high standard of accommodation and a
warm welcome are assured at this
charming hotel.*

19hc (3fb) Ⓡ ✳B&b£10.50–£11.50
Bdi£15.50–£17 Wfr£105 ⱡ LDO5pm

Lic CTV

GH Seacliffe Hotel North Prom, West Cliff ☎(0947) 603139

With views of sea, harbour and abbey the hotel has a good lounge and bar.

19hc (2⇌ 9fl) (3fb) CTV in 14 bedrooms *B&b£12.42–£14.95 W£74.75–£94.30 M LDO8.45pm

Lic CTV 8P solarium gymnasium

Credit cards [1] [2] [3] [V]

FH Mrs E Moreley **Cross Butts** *(NZ881101)* (1½m W A171) ☎(0947) 602519

May–Oct

Near to the beaches and the moors, a 17th-century farmhouse W of the town off the A171.

3rm (1hc) *B&b£8.50–£10 W£56–£65 M

CTV 4P nc5yrs

240acres dairy mixed

WHITCHURCH
Hereford & Worcester
Map **3** SO51

GH Portland ☎Symonds Yat (0600) 890757

Closed Jan

Genial village centre guesthouse.

8hc (2fb) TV in all bedrooms [R] *B&b£11–£12 Bdi£15.50–£16 W£102–£105 L

Lic CTV 7P

[V]

INN *Crown Hotel* ☎Symonds Yat (0600) 890234

Closed Xmas Day & Boxing Day

5hc (3fb) LDO9.30pm

CTV 40P

Credit cards [1] [2] [3] [5]

WHITCHURCH
Shropshire
Map **7** SJ54

FH Mrs M H Mulliner **Bradeley Green** *(SJ537449)* (Waterfowl Sanctuary) Tarporley Rd ☎(0948) 3442

Whitby — Whitney-on-Wye

Nature trails, water gardens and wild fowl number among the attractions of this comfortable Georgian farmhouse on the A49.

3hc (1⇌ 2fl) (2fb) *B&b£8.50–£10 Bdi£12–£15 W£84–£105 L LDO10am

CTV 6P

180acres dairy waterfowl sanctuary

WHITECROSS (nr Wadebridge)
Cornwall
Map **2** SW97

FH Mrs E L D Nicholls ***Torview*** *(SW966722)* ☎Wadebridge (020881) 2261

Modern farmhouse on main A39. Wadebridge 1½ miles.

4hc

CTV 6P 22acres mixed

WHITESTONE
Devon
Map **3** SX89

FH Mrs S K Lee **Rowhorne House** *(SX880948)* ☎Exeter (0392) 74675

Farmhouse set in attractive gardens and lawns.

3hc (2fb) *B&b£8 Bdi£12 W£84 L

CTV 4P 103acres dairy

Credit cards [1] [2] [3] [4] [5] [V]

WHITEWELL
Lancashire
Map **7** SD64

INN The Inn at Whitewell ☎Dunsop Bridge (02008) 222

Old stone-inn in the lovely Bowland Forest. Good range of food.

11hc (6⇌) (5fb) *B&b£21.50–£32 W£135.45–£201.60 M Bar lunch £6alc Dinner9.30pm £12alc

CTV 40P

Credit cards [1] [2] [3] [5] [V]

WHITHORN
Dumfries & Galloway *Wigtownshire*
Map **10** NX44

FH Mrs E C Forsyth **Baltier** *(NX466429)* ☎Garlieston (09886) 241

Mar–Nov

Modernised, stone-built farmhouse situated 2m NW on B7004.

2hc (1fb) [R] *B&b£8.50 Bdi£13.50 W£94.50 L LDO1pm

CTV 4P 220acres dairy sheep

WHITLAND
Dyfed
Map **2** SN21

FH C M & I A Lewis ***Cilpost*** *(SN191184)* ☎(0994) 240280

Apr–Sep

Well-appointed 300 year old farmhouse offering good meals and a warm welcome. 1½ miles south of the village.

7hc (3⇌ 3fl) (3fb)

Lic 12P snooker 160acres dairy

WHITLEY BAY
Tyne & Wear
Map **12** NZ37

GH Lindisfarne Hotel 11 Holly Av ☎091–251 3954

9hc (2fb) CTV in 3 bedrooms [R] *B&b£8–£9.50 Bdi£11–£12.50 W£77–£87.50 L LDO4pm

Lic CTV

[V]

GH York House Hotel 30 Park Pde ☎091–252 8313

A family-run guesthouse offering comfort, good home-cooking and a friendly atmosphere.

8hc (1⇌ 6fl) (2fb) CTV in all bedrooms [R] B&b£12.50 Bdi£16.50 W£108.50 L LDO7pm

Lic CTV 2P

Credit cards [1] [3] [V]

WHITNEY-ON-WYE
Hereford & Worcester
Map **3** SO24

INN Rhydspence (2m W A438) ☎Clifford (04973) 262

Lovely old timber-framed inn offering high quality accommodation and food.

6hc (4🛁 2🚿) CTV in 3 bedrooms TV in 3 bedrooms 🐕 [R] ✱B&b£18–£20 Bdifr£25.50 Wfr£178.50 Ł Lunch £7.50alc Dinner9.45pm £7.50alc

♨ 75P 🚌

Credit cards [1] [2] [3]

WHITTINGTON
Shropshire
Map **7** SJ33

FH Mrs H M Ward **Perry** *(SJ348303)* ☎Oswestry (0691) 662330
Etr–Oct

Comfortable accommodation in a large, early 19th century farmhouse 1m E of A5, approx 2m from village.

2hc (1fb) 🐕 [R] ✱B&b£9–£10 Bdi£13–£15

♨ CTV P 850acres arable beef dairy

[V]

WHITTLESFORD
Cambridgeshire
Map **5** TL44

INN Red Lion Hotel Station Rd ☎Cambridge (0223) 832047
Closed Xmas

A rambling, flint-faced and timber inn, 750 years old. Modern, fitted-bedrooms.

18hc (4🛁 14🚿) (3fb) CTV in all bedrooms 🐕 [R] B&b£25 Bdi£31.95 Lunch £6.95&alc Dinner 9.30pm£6.95&alc

175P

Credit cards [2] [3] [5]

WICKFORD
Essex
Map **5** TQ79

GH Wickford Lodge 26 Ethelred Gdns ☎(03744) 62663 due to change to (0268) 762663

Tudor-style detached house in quiet residential area, offering modern, comfortable accommodation.

6hc (2fb) ✱B&b£15.50–£16

♨ CTV 6P

WICKHAM
Berkshire
Map **4** SU47

INN *Five Bells* ☎Boxford (048838) 242

4hc CTV in all bedrooms [R] LDO10pm

♨ CTV 50P 🏊

WIDDINGTON
Essex
Map **5** TL53

FH Mrs L Vernon **Thistley Hall** *(TL556311)* ☎Saffron Walden (0799) 0388
Feb–Nov (closed 3rd wk Sep)

The historic farmhouse is pleasantly surrounded by gardens and pastureland with beautiful views of the countryside.

3rm (2hc) (1fb) 🐕 ✱B&b£9.50–£15 Wfr£64 Ḿ (W only Mar–May)

♨ CTV 6P nc5yrs 30acres mixed

WIDEGATES
Cornwall
Map **2** SX25

GH Coombe Farm ☎(05034) 223
Mar–Oct

Attractive 1920's detached house affording superb views.

8hc (3fb) 🐕 B&b£10–£15 Bdi£18–£23 W£120–£150 Ł LDO7pm

Lic ♨ CTV 12P nc5yrs 🏊(heated)

[V]

See advertisement on page 257

WIDEMOUTH BAY
Cornwall
Map **3** SS20

GH Beach House Hotel ☎(028885) 256
Apr–Sep

13hc (5🚿) (5fb) 🐕 [R] ✱B&bfr£11 Bdifr£14.50 Wfr£93 Ł

Lic CTV 20P

[V]

FH Mr J C Soar **Kennacott** *(SS215017)* ☎(028885) 683

3rm (1fb) 🐕 [R] ✱B&b£8.50–£12 Bdi£13–£16.50 W£86.50 Ł LDO10am

Lic ♨ CTV 6P 11½acres sheep small holding

WIGAN
Gt Manchester
Map **7** SD50

GH Aalton Court 23 Upper Dicconson St (Guestaccom) ☎(0942) 322220

Small, family-run guesthouse close to the town centre, museums and Wigan pier.

6hc (2🛁 4🚿) (1fb) CTV in all bedrooms 🐕 ✱B&b£19 Bdi£26 Wfr£182 Ł LDO2pm

Lic ♨ CTV 8P

[V]

INN Th'old Hall 240A Warrington Rd, Lower Ince, Ince in Makerfield ☎(0942) 866330

A typical Lancashire pub with modern bedrooms.

4hc (2🛁) CTV in all bedrooms 🐕 [R] ✱B&bfr£10.92 Bdifr£12.92 Wfr£90.44 Ł Lunch £5.50alc

♨ 30P snooker

Credit card [2] [V]

WIGHT, ISLE OF
Map **4**

ARRETON
Map **4** SZ58

GH *Stickworth Hall* ☎(098377) 233
May–Sep

Lovely 18th-century home in extensive grounds with lake for fishing.

25hc (2🛁 14🚿) (6fb) 🐕 [R] LDO7pm

Lic ♨ CTV 50P nc5yrs

CHALE
Map **4** SZ47

INN Clarendon Hotel & Wight Mouse (Guestaccom) ☎(0983) 730431

Delightful antique furnished bedrooms.

13hc (2🛁 6🚿) (8fb) CTV in all bedrooms [R] ✱B&b£14.95–£17.25 Bdi£23–£25.30 W£132–£149 Ł Lunch£4–£9&alc Dinner10pm £3–£6&alc

♨ CTV 100P 🏠 boule

FRESHWATER
Map **4** SZ38

GH Blenheim House Gate Ln ☎(0983) 752858
May–Sep

Small guesthouse with relaxing atmosphere. Outdoor swimming pool.

8hc (6🚿) (5fb) CTV in all bedrooms 🐕 ✱B&b£11.50–£14 Bdi£17–£20 W£112–£129.50 Ł LDOam

Lic ♨ CTV 6P 1🚗 nc3yrs 🏊(heated)

NEWPORT
Map **4** SZ48

INN Shute Clatterford Shute, Carisbrooke ☎(0983) 523393
Feb–Nov

Georgian country residence on hillside nesting below the famous Carisbrooke Castle, with a lovely restaurant/bar. 1m W B3323.

3hc (1🚿) CTV in all bedrooms 🐕 [R] ✱B&b£10.95–£11.95 LDO9.30pm

♨ 25P nc10yrs

Credit cards [1] [3] [V]

See advertisement on page 408

NITON
Map **4** SZ57

GH Pine Ridge Niton Undercliff ☎(0983) 730802

A comfortable house with a homely atmosphere and good views.

8hc (1🛁 2🚿) (4fb) CTV in all bedrooms [R] ✱B&b£10–£15.50 Bdi£15–£22 W£95–£139 Ł LDO7pm

♨ CTV 8P

[V]

RYDE
Map **4** SZ59

GH Dorset Hotel 33 Dover St ☎(0983) 64327
May–Sep
Friendly hotel with good lounge facilities and simple, adequately furnished bedrooms.
26hc (1🛁 6🚿) (2fb) ✗ ✱B&b£10.50–£15.50 Bdi£15–£19.50 W£100–£130 Ⱡ (W only Jul & Aug) LDO6pm
Lic CTV P nc6yrs 🏊(heated)

GH Teneriffe 36 The Strand ☎(0983) 63841
Mar–Dec
Large house close to the sea, with large bar and dance floor, two lounges and basement restaurant.
31hc (20🛁 2🚿) (6fb) CTV in all bedrooms ✗ [R] ✱B&b£11–£12 Bdi£14–£16 W£97 Ⱡ
Lic 🛋 CTV 9P
[V]

FH Mrs S Swan **Aldermoor** *(SZ582906)* Upton Rd ☎(0983) 64743
Apr–Oct
Modernised old stone and brick farmhouse.
3hc ✗ ✱B&b£8–£10 W£56–£70 M
🛋 CTV 20P 2🚗 nc7yrs 27acres beef
[V]

Wight, Isle of

ST LAWRENCE
Map **4** SZ57

GH Woody Bank Hotel Undercliff Dr ☎Ventnor (0983) 852610
Mar–Oct
Personally supervised by the owners, this small hotel has a warm, informal atmosphere and comfortable lounges.
8hc (4🛁 4🚿) ✱B&b£14–£16 Bdi£19.50–£22.50 W£132–£150 Ⱡ LDO7.30pm
Lic 🛋 CTV 8P nc5yrs
[V]
See advertisement on page 412

SANDOWN
Map **4** SZ58

GH Braemar Hotel 5 Broadway ☎(0983) 403358
Small family-run hotel with relaxing atmosphere.
16hc (4🚿) (5fb) CTV in all bedrooms ✗ [R] ✱B&b£11.50–£13.50 Bdi£15–£17 W£86–£99 Ⱡ LDO10am
Lic 🛋 CTV 12P nc3mths
[V]

GH Chester Lodge Hotel Beachfield Rd ☎(0983) 402773
Closed mid Dec–mid Jan
Small, comfortable, family-run guesthouse near to beach, five minutes walk to town centre.
19hc (1🛁 2🚿) (6fb) CTV in 5 bedrooms [R] ✱B&b£11.50–£12.65 Bdi£12.65–£16.10 Wfr£103.50 Ⱡ LDO6pm
Lic 🛋 CTV 15P
[V]

GH *Cliff House Hotel* Cliff Rd ☎(0983) 403656
Etr–mid Oct
Nicely appointed, comfortable house, overlooking the sea.
16hc (3🛁 5🚿) (5fb) [R] LDO6.30pm
Lic 🛋 CTV 20P
Credit card [3]

GH *Culver Lodge* Albert Rd ☎(0983) 403819
Apr–Oct
Small and friendly private hotel with good public rooms and relaxing atmosphere.
24hc (2🛁 11🚿) (3fb) ✗ [R] B&b£10–£15.25 Bdi£13.50–£17 W£89–£118 Ⱡ LDO7.30pm
Lic 🛋 CTV 20P nc3yrs

GH St Catherine's Hotel 1 Winchester Park Rd ☎(0983) 402392
Closed Xmas & New Year

Excellent accommodation, with all bedrooms en-suite, at this smart private hotel.

17hc (7⇄10🛏) (3fb) CTV in all bedrooms ✠ ® ✱B&b£13.25–£17 Bdi£19.25–£23 W£115.50–£138 Ⅼ LDO7pm

Lic 🍺 CTV 9P

Credit cards ① ③ Ⓥ

SEAVIEW
Map **4** SZ69

GH Northbank Hotel Circular Rd
☎(098371) 2227
Etr–Sep

Large traditional family house with excellent sea views.

18hc (6fb) CTV in 3 bedrooms ® ✱B&b£15–£20 Bdi£23.50–£30 W£118–£150 Ⅼ LDO8pm

Lic 🍺 CTV 8P 4🏊 ♗ snooker

SHANKLIN
Map **4** SZ58
See plan

GH *Afton Hotel* Clarence Gdns ☎(0983) 863075 Plan **1** *B4*
Feb–Nov

Luxurious guesthouse with period furniture and colourful accommodation.

9hc (6🛏) (2fb) CTV in all bedrooms ✠ ®

Lic 🍺 P nc5yrs

GH *Aqua Hotel* The Esplanade ☎(0983) 863024 Plan **2** *C2*
Etr–Oct

Modern hotel in an elevated position overlooking the beach and seafront.

24hc (3⇄) (8fb) ✠ LDO6pm

Lic CTV 2P

Credit card ③

GH Apse Manor Country House Apse
Manor Rd ☎(0983) 866651 Plan **3** *A1*

Good bedrooms and a warm and friendly atmosphere at this charming 16th-century manor house.

6⇄ (2fb) CTV in all bedrooms ® ✱B&b£13–£14 Bdi£19–£21 W£130–£140 Ⅼ LDO7pm

Lic 🍺 8P

GH *Bay House Hotel* 8 Chine Av, off Keats Green ☎(0983) 863180
Plan **4** *C2*
Closed Xmas

Overlooks the chine with lovely sea views.

20hc (13⇄3🛏) (3fb) CTV in 5 bedrooms LDO6.30pm

Lic 🍺 CTV 25P 2🏊 &

Credit card ③

GH Culham Private Hotel 31 Landguard
Manor Rd ☎(0983) 862880 Plan **7** *A3*
Apr–Oct →

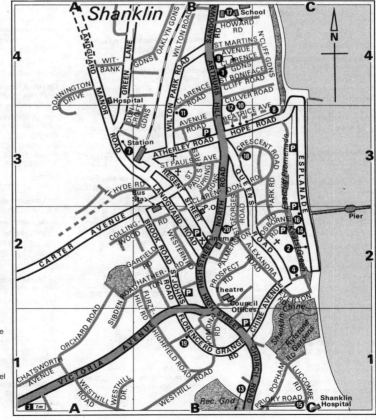

Shanklin

Attractive small hotel in tree-lined road with heated swimming pool in secluded garden.

10hc (1⇆6🚿) ✠ ® ✳B&b£10.50–£11.50 Bdi£14.50–£15.50 W£89–£97 🗶 LDO4pm 🍴 CTV 8P nc12yrs ♨(heated) solarium ⓥ

GH Curraghmore Hotel 22 Hope Rd ☎(0983) 862605 Plan **8** *B3* Mar–Oct

Small private hotel close to sea front. Nicely appointed with the emphasis on entertainment.

24hc (10⇆6🚿) (9fb) ✳B&b£11–£14.50 Bdi£14–£17.50 W£102–£115 🗶 LDO6pm Lic CTV 20P putting Credit cards ① ③ ⓥ

GH Edgecliffe Hotel Clarence Gdns ☎(0983) 866199 Plan **9** *B4* Telex no 89441 Closed Dec

A warm friendly atmosphere exists in this converted private house situated in quiet residential area.

10hc (2⇆4🚿) (2fb) CTV in all bedrooms ✠ ® ✳B&b£10.50–£14 Bdi£14.50–£18 W£93–£119 🗶 LDO9.30am Lic 🍴 CTV 3P nc3yrs ♨ Credit cards ① ② ③ ⓥ

GH Fawley Hotel 12 Hope Rd ☎(0983) 862190 Plan **10** *B3* 23 Apr–2 Oct

A small tastefully appointed hotel with a friendly atmosphere.

9hc (1⇆2🚿) (2fb) ✠ ® ✳B&b£10.50–£11.50 Bdi£13.50–£14.50 W£85–£95 🗶 LDO4.30pm Lic CTV 12P nc5yrs

GH Kenbury Private Hotel Clarence Rd ☎(0983) 862085 Plan **11** *B3* Apr–Oct

Comfortable accommodation in a small family hotel.

17hc (4⇆7🚿) (3fb) 🚭 in 3 bedrooms ✠ ® ✳B&b£10.50–£12.50 Bdi£13.50–£17.50 W£94.50–£115 🗶 LDO7.30pm Lic 🍴 CTV 6P ♨ snooker Credit card ③ ⓥ

GH Leslie House Hotel 10 Hope Rd ☎(0983) 862798 Plan **12** *B3* Closed Dec

Well-decorated and furnished detached house with a homely informal atmosphere.

10hc (2fb) ✠ ✳B&b£8.50–£11 Bdi£11.50–£14 W£74–£94 🗶 Lic 🍴 CTV 10P

GH Luccombe Chine House Country Hotel ☎(0983) 862037 Plan **13** *B1* Closed Xmas

An old manor house in a secluded setting. All bedrooms are en-suite and have four-poster beds.

6🚿 CTV in all bedrooms ✠ ® B&b£14–£18 Bdi£23–£27 W£161–£189 🗶 LDO8pm Lic 🍴 16P nc16yrs Credit cards ① ③

GH Meyrick Cliffs The Esplanade ☎(0983) 862691 Plan **14** *C2* May–Oct

Nicely appointed seafront house with Victorian atmosphere.

20hc (1⇆1🚿) (7fb) ✠ LDO6.30pm Lic CTV 5P nc5yrs

GH Monteagle Hotel Priory Rd ☎(0983) 862854 Plan **15** *C1* Mar–Oct & Xmas

Large hotel with many facilities including snooker table and outdoor swimming pool.

40hc (24⇆6🚿) (3fb) ✠ ✳B&b£14–£22 Bdi£18–£25 W£110–£135 🗶 Lic 🍴 CTV 35P nc5yrs ♨(heated) snooker ⓥ

GH Ocean View Hotel 38 The Esplanade ☎(0983) 862602 Plan **16** *C2* Mar–Nov

Seafront hotel with excellent sun lounge and attractive wood-panelled dining room.

36hc (4⇆17🚿) (12fb) ® LDO7.30pm Lic 🍴 CTV 25P Credit cards ① ② ③

GH Overstrand Private Hotel Howard Rd ☎(0983) 862100 Plan **17** *B4* Etr–Oct

Stone-built house in attractive gardens. Rooms have character and comfort.

15hc (4⇆7🚿) (8fb) CTV in all bedrooms ✠ ® ✳B&b£13.50–£18 Bdi£16.50–£21 W£116–£147 🗶 LDO6.30pm Lic 🍴 CTV 20P ♨ ♇(grass) Credit card ① ⓥ

GH Perran Lodge Private Hotel 2 Crescent Rd ☎(0983) 862816 Plan **18** *B3* Etr–Oct

Red-brick two-storey south-facing house with lawn and verandah.

20hc (5⇆5🚿) (7fb) ✳B&b£9–£12 Bdi£12–£15 W£72–£94 🗶 Lic 🍴 CTV 10P nc3yrs ⓥ

GH Soraba 2 Paddock Rd ☎(0983) 862367 Plan **19** *B1* rs Xmas

Quiet location near the chine within a few minutes walk of sea and shops. Personal attention and home-cooking.

6hc (2fb) B&b£8.50–£10.50 Bdi£13–£15 W£72–£89 🗶 LDO3pm Lic 🍴 CTV 4P ⓥ

GH Swiss Cottage Hotel 10 St Georges Rd ☎(0983) 862333 Plan **20** *B2* Apr–Oct

Attractive compact house with friendly proprietors.

12hc (3🚿) (2fb) ✠ ® ✳B&b£12.65–£14.95 Bdi£17.25–£20.13 W£89.70–£101.78 🗶 Lic 🍴 CTV 10P nc5yrs ⓥ

TOTLAND BAY
Map **4** SZ38

GH Garrow Hotel Church Hill ☎(0983) 753174 May–Sep

15hc (1⇆8🚿) (7fb) ® ✳B&b£11–£14 Bdi£16–£19 LDO7pm Lic 🍴 CTV 18P nc3yrs

GH Hermitage Hotel Cliff Rd ☎(0983) 752518 Mar–Nov

Small, family-run hotel with comfortable lounges and nicely appointed bedrooms.

12hc (2⇆2🚿) (4fb) ✳B&b£11.50–£18 Bdi£18–£25 W£108–£157 🗶 LDO7pm Lic 🍴 CTV 12P 1♨(charge) ♨ ♨ Credit cards ① ③ ⓥ

GH Hilton House Private Hotel Granville Rd ☎(0983) 754768 Mar–Oct rs Nov–Feb

A small, well-appointed guesthouse with a warm, informal atmosphere. Good, honest cooking.

6hc (1🚿) (2fb) CTV in all bedrooms ✠ ® ✳B&b£11–£12 Bdi£16.50–£17.50 W£108.50–£115.50 🗶 Lic 🍴 CTV Credit cards ① ③ ⓥ

GH Lismore Private Hotel 23 The Avenue ☎(0983) 752025

Small, friendly, well-kept accommodation.

7hc (5🚿) (3fb) ✠ ✳B&b£11–£12 Bdi£16–£17 W£99–£105 🗶 LDO3pm Lic 🍴 CTV 8P nc5yrs ⓥ

GH Nodes Country Hotel Alum Bay Old Rd ☎(0983) 752859

A country house set in 2¼ acres of downland countryside, with modern compact well-appointed bedrooms.

11hc (2⇆6🚿) (6fb) CTV in 4 bedrooms ® B&b£12–£15 Bdi£17–£22 W£110–£140 🗶 LDO7pm Lic 🍴 CTV 16P ♨ ⓥ

GH Sandford Lodge Private Hotel 61 The Avenue ☎(0983) 753478 Apr–Nov

A well-appointed house with comfortable bedrooms and a relaxing atmosphere.

6hc (1⇄) (1fb) ⚬ in 1 bedroom ®
✳B&b£10.50–£12.50 Bdi£15.50–£17.50
W£99–£109 ⫽ LDO4.30pm

Lic ♨ CTV 7P

Ⓥ

GH Westgrange Country Hotel Alum Bay Old Rd ☎(0983) 752227
Mar–Oct

Small, friendly country hotel with comfortable bedrooms and good cooking.

13hc (2⇄7🛁) (7fb) CTV in all bedrooms ® ✳B&b£12.50–£17.50 Bdi£17–£21.50
W£103–£142 ⫽ LDO7pm

Lic ♨ CTV 14P ⛵

Ⓥ

VENTNOR
Map **4**   SZ57

GH Channel View Hotel Hambrough Rd
☎(0983) 852230
Mar–Oct

Set on a cliff between the sea and town.

14hc (2🛁) (5fb) ⚬ ® B&b£11–£13
Bdi£14–£16 W£90–£105 ⫽ LDO10pm

Lic CTV 🅿

Credit card ③ Ⓥ

GH Hillside Private Hotel Mitchell Av
☎(0983) 852271
Mar–Oct

Wight, Isle of

11hc (3⇄3🛁) (6fb) CTV in all bedrooms
®
Lic ♨ CTV 16P

GH Horseshoe Bay Hotel Shore Rd,
Bonchurch ☎(0983) 852487
Etr–mid Oct

Small private hotel where a warm welcome is assured. Overlooks Bonchurch Bay.

7hc (4⇄1🛁) CTV in all bedrooms ®
B&b£10–£13.75 Bdi£14.25–£18 W£99.75–£126 ⫽ LDO6pm

Lic ♨ 7P nc8yrs

Credit card ① Ⓥ

GH Lake Hotel Shore Rd, Bonchurch
☎(0983) 852613
Apr–Oct

Set in 2¼ acres of gardens close to beach and countryside.

11hc (1⇄8🛁) Annexe: 10hc (8🛁) (7fb) ®
B&b£10–£13 Bdi£13.50–£17.50 W£94.50–£122.50 ⫽ LDO6.30pm

Lic ♨ CTV 20P nc2yrs

Ⓥ

See advertisement on page 412

GH Macrocarpa Mitchell Av ☎(0983) 852428
Etr–mid Oct

Large house in own grounds with good sea views.

20hc (6⇄5🛁) (7fb) ® LDO7.15pm

Lic CTV 20P

GH Picardie Hotel Esplanade ☎(0983) 852647
Apr–Oct

Small, comfortable house, close to the beach.

15hc (5fb) ® LDO5.30pm

Lic CTV 🅿

GH Richmond Private Hotel The Esplanade ☎(0983) 852496
Etr–Oct

Friendly and comfortable accommodation, well-situated on the edge of the Esplanade.

12hc (6🛁) (2fb) ® ✳B&b£9.50–£10.50 Bdi£13–£15 W£90–£105 ⫽ LDO6pm

Lic CTV 6P

Credit card ③

GH St Maur Hotel Castle Rd ☎(0983) 852570
Mar–Nov
Well-kept house run by friendly family, in quiet residential area.
15hc (11🛁 2🚿) (4fb) 🐾 Ⓡ ✱B&b£10.50–£14 Bdi£16–£19 LDO7pm
Lic ♨ CTV 12P nc4yrs
Credit cards [1] [3]

GH Under Rock Hotel Shore Rd, Bonchurch (1m E) ☎(0983) 852714
Mar–Oct
A secluded comfortable small hotel, personally supervised by the proprietors who offer a warm welcome together with good, honest home-cooking. Delightful gardens.
7hc CTV in all bedrooms 🐾 ✱B&b£15 Bdi£19 W£126 Ⓛ
Lic ♨ 12P nc10yrs
Ⓥ

WIGMORE
Hereford & Worcester
Map **7** SO46

INN Compasses Hotel ☎(056886) 203
A stone-built inn in rural village close to the Welsh Marches, offering pleasant accommodation and good food.
3hc (1fb) CTV in all bedrooms Ⓡ ✱B&b£10–£12 Bdi£15–£17 W£90–£107 Ⓛ Lunch £2–£5&alc Dinner10pm £2–£5&alc
♨ 70P
Credit cards [1] [2] [3] [5] Ⓥ

WILBERFOSS
Humberside
Map **8** SE75

FH Mrs J M Liversidge **Cuckoo Nest** *(SE717510)* ☎(07595) 365
Closed Xmas
Traditional Yorkshire farmhouse with bright and homely rooms. 1m W of village on south side of A1079.
2hc (1fb) 🐾 ✱B&b£8–£10
♨ TV P nc2yrs 150acres arable beef dairy sheep mixed

WILLAND
Devon
Map **3** ST01

FH Mrs J M Granger ***Doctors*** *(ST015117)* Halberton Rd ☎Tiverton (0884) 820525
rs Xmas
Farmhouse situated in garden and farmland. Tiverton and Cullompton 4 miles.
2rm (1fb) 🐾 LDO3pm
CTV P 🎣 95acres dairy

WILLERSEY
Gloucestershire
Map **4** SP13

— *Recommended* —

GH Old Rectory Church St ☎Evesham (0386) 853729
Closed Xmas
Outstanding 18th-century house with relaxing bedrooms and a secluded walled garden.
6hc (3🛁 3🚿) (2fb) CTV in all bedrooms 🐾 Ⓡ ✱B&b£17–£37 W£98–£250 Ⓜ
♨ CTV 10P 2🚗 nc10yrs ♞18 U
Credit cards [1] [3]
See advertisement on page 99

WILMINGTON
East Sussex
Map **5** TQ50

GH Crossways Hotel ☎Polegate (03212) 2455
Set in 2 acres of garden with pond. Colourful rooms and log fires in lounge, 7 miles from Eastbourne.
8hc (1🛁 1🚿) (2fb) CTV in 7 bedrooms TV in 1 bedroom Ⓡ ✱B&b£15–£17
Lic ♨ CTV 10P 2🚗
Ⓥ

WIMBORNE MINSTER
Dorset
Map **4** SZ09

GH Riversdale 33 Poole Rd ☎(0202) 884528
Mar–Oct closed Xmas wk rs Nov Jan & Feb
Detached guesthouse with sound, neat accommodation on the edge of town centre.
8hc (2fb) 🚭 in 4 bedrooms CTV in 4 bedrooms TV in 4 bedrooms Ⓡ ✱B&b£10.50–£14.50 Bdi£16–£20 W£98–£136
LDO9am
♨ CTV 5P 2🚗 nc3yrs
Ⓥ

GH Stour Lodge 21 Julian's Rd ☎(0202) 888003
Small, comfortable well-appointed house with sufficient parking, a pleasant garden and friendly hosts. On A31 Dorchester Rd.
3hc (1🛁) (2fb) CTV in all bedrooms 🐾 Ⓡ ✱B&b£17.50–£20 Bdi£24–£27.50 W£144–£165 Ⓛ LDO8pm
Lic ♨ CTV 6P 🏠
Ⓥ

WIMPSTONE
Warwickshire
Map **4** SP24

FH Mrs J E James **Whitchurch Farm** *(SP222485)* ☎Alderminster (078987) 275
Lovely Georgian farmhouse built 1750, set in park-like surroundings on edge of Cotswolds, 4½ miles from Stratford-upon-Avon.
3hc (2fb) 🐾 ✱B&b£8–£10 Bdifr£12
♨ CTV 3P 208acres arable beef sheep
Ⓥ

WINCANTON
Somerset
Map **3** ST72

FH Mrs J Brunt **Hatherleigh** *(ST707276)* ☎(0963) 32142
Mar–Oct
Small cottage farm with simple bedrooms, charming living room and friendly welcome.
2hc (1fb) ✱B&b£8–£9 W£56–£60 Ⓜ
CTV 6P nc3yrs 40acres beef mixed
Ⓥ

WINCLE
Cheshire
Map **7** SJ96

GH Four Ways Diner Motel Cleulow Cross (1m N of A54) ☎(02607) 228
Small, family-run motel in Peak District National Park.
6hc (1🛁 5🚿) (2fb) CTV in all bedrooms Ⓡ ✱B&b£15–£20 Bdi£22–£28 LDO7.30pm
Lic ♨ 50P
Credit cards [1] [3] Ⓥ

WINDERMERE
Cumbria
Map **7** SD49
See plan on page 414

GH Archway College Rd ☎(09662) 5613
Plan **1** *B5*
Neat and cosy guesthouse on quiet side street near town centre.
6hc (1fb) B&b£8.50–£9.50 Bdi£13.50–£15 W£90–£98 Ⓛ LDO4pm
♨ CTV 3P
Ⓥ

GH Biskey Howe Villa Hotel Craig Walk, Bowness ☎(09662) 3988
Plan **2** *B2*
An extensive private hotel in an elevated position overlooking the lake.
11hc (1🛁 6🚿) (5fb) CTV in all bedrooms 🐾 Ⓡ ✱B&b£13–£20 Bdi£19–£26 W£120–£163 Ⓛ LDO8.30pm
Lic CTV 11P 🏊(heated)
Credit cards [1] [3]
See advertisement on page 415

GH Brooklands Ferry View, Bowness ☎(09662) 2344 Plan **3** *B1*
Feb–mid Nov
Good food and a warm welcome are offered at this charming guesthouse. →

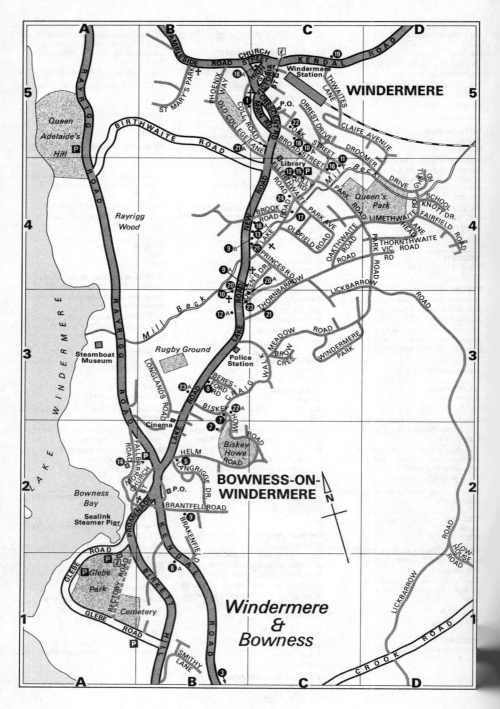

414

Windermere

1 Archway
2 Biskey Howe Villa Hotel
3 Brooklands
5 Crag Brow Cottage Private Hotel
6A Cranleigh Hotel
7 Eastbourne Hotel
8 Elim Bank Hotel
9 Fairfield Country House Hotel
9A Fir Trees
9B Glenburn
10 Glenville Hotel
10A Green Gables
11 Greenriggs
12 Halsthorpe
12A Hawksmoor
13 Hilton House Hotel
14 Holly Cottages
15 Kenilworth
16 Lynwood
16A Meadfoot
17 Mylne Bridge Private Hotel
18 Oakfield
18A Oakthorpe Hotel
19 Orrest Head House
20 Rosemount
20A St Johns Lodge
21 Thornleigh
21A Tudor
22 Westbeck House
22A Westbourne Hotel
23 Westlake
23A White Lodge Hotel
24 Winbrook
25 Woodlands

Windermere

6hc (3🚿) (1fb) [R] Bdi£21–£23 W£142–£155 Ⱡ LDO5.30pm

Lic 🍴 CTV 6P

[V]

See advertisement on page 416

GH Crag Brow Cottage Private Hotel Helm Rd, Bowness ☎(09662) 4080 Plan **5** *B2*

Attractive Georgian house in its own grounds. Comfortable and well-decorated throughout.

5hc (4🛁 1🚿) (2fb) CTV in all bedrooms 🚫 [R] ✱B&bfr£17.50 Bdifr£22.50

Lic 🍴 20P

Credit cards [1] [2] [3] [V]

See advertisement on page 416

GH Cranleigh Hotel Kendal Rd, Bowness ☎(09662) 3293 Plan **6A** *B2*
Mar–Nov

Attractive Victorian house. Well-equipped bedrooms include remote control colour TVs and hairdryers.

9hc (8🛁 1🚿) (1fb) CTV in all bedrooms 🚫 [R] ✱B&b£14–£17 Bdi£21–£26 W£140–£170 Ⱡ LDO9pm

Lic 🍴 CTV 9P

See advertisement on page 416

GH Eastbourne Hotel Biskey Howe Rd ☎(09662) 3525 Plan **7** *B3*

Cheery, friendly proprietors run this large end-terrace house.

9hc (2fb) [R] ✱B&b£9.50–£11.50 Bdi£16–£18

Lic 🍴 CTV 3P

Credit cards [1] [3] [5] [V]

See advertisement on page 416

GH *Elim Bank Hotel* Lake Rd, Bowness ☎(09662) 4810 Plan **8** *B3*
Mar–Dec

This large, detached house is built of traditional Lakeland slate. The à la carte restaurant is also open to non-residents.

7hc (3fb) CTV in 2 bedrooms 🚫 LDO9pm

Lic 🍴 CTV 6P

Credit cards [1] [2] [3]

See advertisement on page 417

GH Fairfield Country House Hotel Brantfell Rd, Bowness ☎(09662) 6565 Plan **9** *B2*

Peaceful hotel in secluded gardens above the lake. →

10hc (3⇌ 7🚿) (4fb) CTV in all bedrooms [R] ✱B&b£12.25–£17.50 Bdi£18–£25.25 W£111–£145 ⅄ LDO5pm

Lic 🍽 10P 🚗

Credit cards [1] [2] [3] [5] [V]

GH Fir Trees Lake Rd ☎(09662) 2272 Plan **9A** *B4*

A very comfortable and spacious house with a friendly atmosphere. All bedrooms are en-suite.

7hc (1⇌ 6🚿) (3fb) CTV in all bedrooms B&b£11.50–£13.50 W£75–£90 M̸

🍽 9P 1🚗

Credit cards [1] [3] [V]

Windermere

GH Glenburn New Rd ☎(09662) 2649 Plan **9B** *C4*

Pleasant and comfortable guesthouse with tasteful décor.

10hc (3⇌) (2fb) CTV in 8 bedrooms TV in 2 bedrooms B&b£9.50–£12.50 Bdi£17–£20 W£103–£133 ⅄ LDO4.30pm

Lic 🍽 CTV 14P

[V]

See advertisement on page 418

GH Glenville Hotel Lake Rd ☎(09662) 3371 Plan **10** *B3*

Feb–Nov

Elegant house with comfortable lounges, attractive dining room and neat bedrooms.

9hc (1🚿) (1fb) ✗ [R] ✱B&b£10.50–£13 Bdi£18.50–£21 W£125–£142 ⅄ LDO2pm

Lic 🍽 CTV 12P

[V]

See advertisement on page 418

GH Green Gables 37 Broad St ☎(09662) 3886 Plan **10A** *C5*

Closed Xmas & New Year →

Small friendly guesthouse with very pretty bedrooms.

5hc (3fb) ✻ B&b£7.50–£9 Bdi£13–£14.50 W£80–£98 ⚬ LDO4pm

🅿 CTV 2P

GH Greenriggs 8 Upper Oak St
☎(09662) 2265 Plan **11** *C4*
Mar–Oct

Friendly, conveniently situated hotel offering simple, clean accommodation.

6hc (2fb) ⓡ B&b£8.50 W£55 Ṁ

🅿 CTV 3P

Ⓥ

GH *Haisthorpe* Holly Rd ☎(09662) 3445
Plan **12** *C4*
Mar–Oct

Cosy and welcoming guesthouse in a quiet part of the town.

6hc (3fb) ✻ LDO4.30pm

🅿 CTV

GH Hawksmoor Lake Rd ☎(09662) 2110
Plan **12A** *B3*
Feb–Nov

An attractive house offering a cosy atmosphere. It stands in its own grounds, backed by woodland, half-way between Bowness and Windermere.

10hc (6⇨ 4🚿) (3fb) ⚬ in 3 bedrooms CTV in all bedrooms ✻ ⓡ ✻B&b£12.50–£19.50 Bdi£19–£26 W£125–£160 ⚬ LDO5pm

Lic 🅿 11P

Ⓥ

GH Hilton House Hotel New Rd
☎(09662) 3934 Plan **13** *C4*

Detached Edwardian house in elevated position within easy reach of shops and lake.

7hc (3🚿) (2fb) CTV in 6 bedrooms ⓡ ✻B&b£10.95–£14.95 Bdi£18.90–£22.90 W£130–£144 ⚬ LDO6pm

Lic 🅿 CTV 12P

Credit card ③ Ⓥ

GH Holly Cottages Rayrigg Rd
☎(09662) 4250 Plan **14** *B2*
mid Feb–mid Nov

Windermere

Small, attractive bedrooms in a family-run establishment close to town centre.

7hc (1🚿) (1fb) ✻ B&b£10.50–£16 W£70–£105 Ṁ

🅿 CTV 4P

Ⓥ

GH Kenilworth Holly Rd ☎(09662) 4004
Plan **15** *C4*
Mar–Oct

A comfortable guesthouse with a spacious lounge and a friendly atmosphere.

7hc (1fb) ✻ ✻B&b£8.50–£9 Bdi£13.50–£14 W£87–£92 ⚬ LDO2pm

🅿 CTV

Ⓥ

GH Lynwood Broad St ☎(09662) 2550
Plan **16** *C4*
Closed Jan

Six-bedroomed Lakeland stone house, built in 1865, situated in a quiet residential area.

6hc (2fb) ⓡ ✻B&b£8–£9 W£56–£63 Ṁ

🅿 CTV ⚬

Ⓥ

GH Meadfoot New Rd ☎(09662) 2610
Plan **16A** *C4*
Etr–Oct

A very nice detached house with attractive gardens and comfortable bedrooms.

8hc (5🚿) (1fb) ⓡ ✻B&b£8–£12.50

Lic CTV 8P

GH Mylne Bridge House Brookside,
Lake Rd ☎(09662) 3314 Plan **17** *C4*
Mar–Oct

Very comfortable, friendly house with good choice of dishes at dinner.

13hc (4🚿) (1fb) CTV in all bedrooms ⓡ ✻B&b£10–£12 Bdi£17.50–£19.50 W£65–£70 Ṁ LDO10am

---

Lic 🅿 CTV 12P

Ⓥ

GH Oakfield 46 Oak St ☎(09662) 5692
Plan **18** *C5*

Comfortable little guesthouse in good central position.

5hc (3fb) CTV in all bedrooms ⓡ ✻B&b£8.50–£10 Bdi£11–£15 Wfr£87 ⚬ LDO5pm

Lic 🅿 CTV 🅿

Ⓥ

GH Oakthorpe Hotel High St ☎(09662) 3547 Plan **18A** *C5*
Closed 24 Dec–24 Jan

Personally supervised, comfortable hotel with Continental and English dishes served at dinner.

20hc (2⇨ 2🚿) (3fb) ⓡ ✻B&b£12.50–£18 Bdi£20.50–£28.50 W£133–£190 ⚬ LDO8.30pm

Lic CTV 16P

Credit cards ① ③ Ⓥ

See advertisement on page 420

GH Orrest Head House Kendal Rd
☎(09662) 4315 Plan **19** *C5*
Apr–Oct

Large detached house in extensive gardens in a peaceful location outside town.

7hc ✻B&b£9–£9.50 W£60 Ṁ

Lic CTV 12P nc5yrs

GH Rosemount Lake Rd ☎(09662) 3739
Plan **20** *B4*
Closed 2 wks Dec

Bright and cheerful guesthouse with a nice warm atmosphere.

8hc (5🚿) (1fb) ✻ ✻B&b£10.50–£12.50 Bdi£18.50–£21 W£122–£140 ⚬ LDO6pm

Lic 🅿 CTV 6P 3🚗

Credit cards ① ③

See advertisement on page 420

GH St Johns Lodge Lake Rd ☎(09662) 3078 Plan **20A** *B3*
Feb–Nov

A charming private hotel with comfortable accommodation.
→

11hc (1⇄8🛏) (4fb) CTV in 1 bedroom TV in 10 bedrooms ® ✶B&b£10–£12.50 Bdi£17–£19 W£115–£125 ⊬ LDO6pm

Lic 🍴 11P nc2yrs

GH Thornleigh Thornbarrow Rd, Bowness ☎(09662) 4203 Plan **21** *C3*
Mar–Nov

A small family-run house with pretty window boxes, friendly atmosphere and a warm welcome.

6hc (4fb) CTV in all bedrooms ✼ ®
✶B&b£9–£10.50 Bdi£14–£16 W£95–£100 ⊬ LDO10am

Lic 🍴 CTV 6P nc2yrs

ⓥ

GH Tudor 60 Main St ☎(09662) 2363 Plan **21A** *C5*
Mar–Oct

A roadside Tudor-style house in town centre. Restaurant open to non-residents.

6hc (2🛏) (1fb) CTV in all bedrooms ®
✶B&b£8.50–£15 Bdi£14–£19.50 LDO9pm

Lic 🍴 CTV nc12yrs

GH Westbeck House 11 Oak St ☎(09662) 4763 Plan **22** *C5*
Closed Xmas

Simple, neat, clean bed-and-breakfast accommodation in small guesthouse.

5hc (1🛏) (2fb) TV in all bedrooms ✼ ®
✶B&b£9–£10 W£63–£70 ⊬

🍴 CTV 2P

Windermere

GH Westbourne Hotel Biskey Howe Rd ☎(09662) 3625 Plan **22A** *B3*
Closed Jan

A spacious detached house with an attractive and comfortable lounge bar.

9hc (2fb) ✼ ® ✶B&b£10.95 Bdi£17.45 W£115 ⊬ LDO4pm

Lic CTV 7P

Credit cards ① ③

GH Westlake Lake Rd ☎(09662) 3020 Plan **23** *B3*

Comfortable private hotel with attractive bedrooms and good home cooking.

7hc (2⇄5🛏) (2fb) CTV in all bedrooms ®
B&b£10.50–£12.50 Bdi£17–£20 W£112–£128 ⊬ LDO5pm

Lic 🍴 7P

GH White Lodge Hotel Lake Rd, Bowness ☎(09662) 3624 Plan **23A** *B3*
Mar–Nov

Relaxed, high standard of accommodation and an interesting menu.

12hc (4⇄8🛏) (3fb) CTV in all bedrooms ✼ ® ✶B&b£15–£19 Bdi£20–£25 W£140–£150 ⊬ LDO6.30pm

Lic 🍴 CTV 20P ♿
Credit cards ① ③

See advertisement on page 422

GH Winbrook 30 Ellerthwaite Rd ☎(09662) 4932 Plan **24** *C4*

Traditional family-run guesthouse with warm welcome and good home-cooking.

6hc (1⇄2🛏) CTV in all bedrooms ®
✶B&b£8.75–£10.50 Bdi£15.70–£17.45 W£106.40–£118.65 ⊬ LDO3pm

🍴 CTV 7P nc5yrs

ⓥ

GH Woodlands New Rd ☎(09662) 3915 Plan **25** *C4*
Closed Dec

One of a pair of houses built in local stone offering comfortable and spacious bedrooms, two small lounges and dining room.

10hc (8🛏) (1fb) CTV in all bedrooms ✼ ✶B&b£13.50–£16.50 Bdi£22–£25 W£126–£147 ⊬ LDO4pm

Lic 🍴 CTV 10P 2🚗 nc5yrs

ⓥ

See advertisement on page 422

Windsor — Witheridge

WINDSOR
Berkshire
Map **4** SU97

GH Christopher Hotel High St ☎(07535) 52359
(For full entry see **Eton**)

GH Clarence Hotel Clarence Rd ☎(0753) 864436
Comfortable and nicely appointed rooms with good public areas run by friendly management.
21hc (18🛁) (6fb) CTV in 20 bedrooms B&b£14.75–£17.50 W£103.25–£122.50 M
Lic 🍴 CTV 2P
Credit cards [1] [2] [3] [5]

WINTERBOURNE ABBAS
Dorset
Map **3** SY69

GH Church View ☎Martinstown (030588) 296
10hc (2fb) [R] *B&b£9–£10 Bdi£14–£15 W£90–£100 L
Lic 🍴 CTV 7P 1🚗
[V]

WISBECH
Cambridgeshire
Map **5** TF40

GH *Glendon* Sutton Rd ☎(0945) 584812
Mar–Oct
18hc (2fb)
Lic CTV 60P 🏠

WITHERIDGE
Devon
Map **3** SS81

FH Mr & Mrs Sankey **Coombe Barn Cottage** *(SS791141)* ☎Tiverton (0884) 860646

Detached farmhouse offering comfortable accommodation and good food. Just outside village.
4hc (1🛁 1🚿) (2fb) TV in all bedrooms ✖ [R] ✱B&b£11 Bdi£16.50 W£85–£100 Ł LDO8pm
Lic 🍴 CTV 6P 4🚗 ⌂ sauna bath
3acres smallholding
[V]

WIVELISCOMBE
Somerset
Map **3** ST02

GH Mount Country Ford ☎(0984) 23992
A detached country cottage of character, offering pleasant accommodation in a rural setting.
5hc ✱B&b£11–£12 Bdi£16.50–£17.50 W£101.50–£108.50 Ł LDO4pm
🍴 CTV 6P 1🚗
[V]

FH Mr & Mrs L Featherstone **Deepleigh Farm Hotel** *(ST079294)* Langley Marsh (1m N unclass) ☎(0984) 23379
16th-century farmhouse converted into small hotel having comfortable lounge with original beams, panelling and log fire. 1m N unclass rd.
7🚿 (4fb) CTV in all bedrooms ✖ [R] B&bfr£15 Bdifr£24 Wfr£140 Ł
Lic 🍴 8P ⌂ U 15acres mixed

FH Mrs E M Wyatt ***Hillacre*** *(ST104275)* Crowford ☎(0984) 23355
Traditional farmhouse set back about 200 yds to the north of A361.
2rm (1hc) CTV in 1 bedroom
CTV 4P 1🚗 850acres mixed

INN *Bear* 10 North St ☎(0984) 23537
17th-century coaching inn with pleasant rooms and friendly personal service.
4hc (1fb) [R] LDO9.30pm
CTV 6P 1🚗

WIX
Essex
Map **5** TM12

Witheridge — Woolfardisworthy

FH Mrs H P Mitchell **New Farmhouse** *(TM165289)* ☎(025587) 365
A modern farmhouse with open views and self-contained well-equipped kitchen. ½m N on right off Wix/Bradfield rd.
5hc (2fb) 🚭 in 2 bedrooms CTV in all bedrooms ✖ B&b£10–£11 Bdi£16.50–£17.50 W£99–£105 Ł
🍴 CTV 8P ⌂ 110acres arable
[V]

WOLSINGHAM
Co Durham
Map **12** NZ03

FH Mr & Mrs T Allen **Chatterley** *(NY075359)* ☎Weardale (0388) 527385
May–Sep
A cosy farmhouse on a dairy farm in an attractive setting. 1m out of town on the Homsterly Rd.
2rm (1fb) ✖ [R] ✱B&bfr£8
CTV 3P nc3yrs
120acres dairy mixed

WOODHALL SPA
Lincolnshire
Map **8** TF16

GH Dunns The Broadway ☎(0526) 52969
Closed 24 Dec–5 Jan
Large semi-detached house opposite the golf club.
6hc (2fb) ✱B&b£9 Bdi£13 Wfr£84 Ł LDO5pm
🍴 CTV 10P
[V]

WOODY BAY
Devon
Map **3** SS64

GH The Red House ☎Parracombe (05983) 255
Apr–Oct
6hc (3🛁 1🚿) (1fb) B&b£11.50–£13 Bdi£17.50–£19 W£112–£122.50 Ł LDO5pm
Lic 🍴 CTV 8P nc4yrs
[V]

WOOLACOMBE
Devon
Map **2** SS44

GH Barton House Hotel Barton Rd ☎(0271) 870548
May–Sep
12rm (4hc) (6🛁 2🚿) (5fb) [R] ✱B&b£11–£13.50 Bdi£16–£18.50 W£109–£120 Ł
Lic 🍴 CTV 12P

GH *Castle* The Esplanade ☎(0271) 870788
Etr–Oct
9hc (2🚿) (2fb) LDO5pm
Lic 🍴 CTV 9P

GH Combe Ridge Hotel The Esplanade ☎(0271) 870321
Closed early Nov
9hc (3fb) [R] ✱B&b£8.50–£13.50 Bdi£12.50–£16 W£88–£104 Ł (W only Jul & Aug) LDO4pm
Lic CTV 8P
[V]

GH *Holmesdale Hotel* Bay View Rd ☎(0271) 870335
15🚿 (12fb) ✖ LDO10.30pm
Lic CTV 10P ⌂
Credit cards [1] [2] [3] [5]

GH *Springside Country Hotel* Mullacott Rd ☎(0271) 870452
Mar–Oct
7hc (2🛁) (4fb) ✖ LDO5pm
Lic 🍴 CTV 10P

WOOLFARDISWORTHY
Devon
Map **2** SS32

FH R C & C M Beck **Stroxworthy** *(SS341198)* ☎Clovelly (02373) 333
Apr–Oct →

Tastefully decorated and set in beautiful countryside offering a variety of farm produce on menu. Herd of Guernsey cows.

10rm (9hc) (3fb) ✱B&b£7–£8.50 Bdi£12–£13.50 W£75–£85 Ł (W only mid-Jul & Aug) LDO6.30pm

Lic ♨ CTV 20P ♩ 90acres dairy

[V]

FH Mrs P I Westaway **Westvilla** *(SS329215)* ☎Clovelly (02373) 309
Etr–Oct

3hc (1fb) 🚫 [R] ✱B&b£8–£10 Bdi£12–£14 W£80–£83 Ł

CTV 4P 22acres non working

WOOLHOPE
Hereford & Worcester
Map **3** SO63

INN Butchers Arms ☎Fownhope (043277) 281

3hc TV in all bedrooms 🚫 [R] B&b£14.50 W£87.50 M Bar lunch £5alc Dinner8pm £8.75alc

♨ 80P nc14yrs

[V]

WOOTTON BASSETT
Wiltshire
Map **4** SU08

INN Angel Hotel 47 High St ☎Swindon (0793) 852314

Standing in High St this semi-detached inn is built of red brick and has a good bar and restaurant menu.

6hc CTV in all bedrooms 🚫 [R] ✱B&b£13.50–£18.50 Lunch £5alc Dinner9.30pm £5–£7alc

♨ CTV 8P nc12yrs

Credit cards [1] [2] [3] [5]

WORCESTER
Hereford & Worcester
Map **3** SO85

GH Barbourne 42 Barbourne Rd ☎(0905) 27507
Closed Xmas

Comfortable Victorian house on busy main road.

7hc (3fb) CTV in all bedrooms ✱B&b£8.50–£12 Bdi£12–£15.50 Wfr£100 Ł LDO6pm

Lic ♨ CTV 5P 5🚗

Credit cards [1] [2] [3] [V]

GH Loch Ryan Hotel 119 Sidbury ☎(0905) 351143

Deceptively large hotel on busy road, but with quiet garden at rear.

14hc (1🛁) Annexe: 5hc (1🛁) (2fb) 🚫 B&b£15 LDO8.45pm

Lic ♨ CTV P̸ 🐎

[V]

WORKINGTON
Cumbria
Map **11** NY02

INN Morven Hotel Siddick ☎(0900) 2118

Busy little inn with lots of oak beams and polished brasses.

8hc (4fb) TV in 4 bedrooms ✱B&bfr£10 Bdifr£14 Bar lunch fr£1.50 LDO4pm

♨ CTV 20P 🚗

[V]

WORMBRIDGE
Hereford & Worcester
Map **3** SO43

FH J T Davies **Duffryn** *(SO415319)* ☎(098121) 217

Very hospitable farmhouse where guests are welcome to take an interest in the farm. Traditional farmyard, complete with duck pond.

4hc (2fb) [R] ✱B&bfr£10 Bdifr£15 Wfr£100 Ł LDO5pm

♨ CTV 8P 🐎 184acres mixed

[V]

WORTHING
West Sussex
Map **4** TQ10

GH Blair House 11 St Georges Rd ☎(0903) 34071

Three-storey Victorian house close to sea front in quiet residential area.

7hc (2🚿 4🛁) (1fb) [R] ✱B&b£10.50–£14 Bdi£15.50–£19.50 W£108–£129 Ł

Lic ♨ CTV 4P 1🚗(charge)

[V]

GH Camelot House 20 Gannon Rd ☎(0903) 204334
Closed Xmas & New Year

7hc (1🚿 1🛁) (1fb) CTV in 5 bedrooms TV in 2 bedrooms 🚫 [R] ✱B&b£9.50–£10.50 Bdi£14.50–£15.50 W£98–£105 Ł

Lic ♨ CTV 3P

[V]

GH Meldrum House 8 Windsor Rd ☎(0903) 33808
Closed Dec

Small terraced house with friendly atmosphere offering simple yet comfortable accommodation.

6hc (2fb) TV in all bedrooms 🚫 [R] ✱B&b£8.50–£11 Bdi£13.50–£16 W£85–£98 Ł LDO5.30pm

♨ CTV P̸ nc3yrs

GH Moorings Private Hotel 4 Selden Rd ☎(0903) 208882

Comfortably modernised Victorian house close to the sea front.

7rm (2🚿 1🛁) (2fb) CTV in all bedrooms 🚫 [R] ✱B&b£10.50–£13.50 Bdi£15–£18 W£95–£113 Ł

Lic ♨ 3P

Credit cards [1] [3] [V]

GH Osborne 175 Brighton Rd ☎(0903) 35771

Two-storey Georgian house facing the sea, run by friendly, helpful proprietors.

7hc (1🛁) (3fb) CTV in all bedrooms [R] ✱B&b£9–£11.50 Bdi£14–£16.50 W£95–£110 Ł LDO5pm

Lic ♨ CTV P̸

Credit cards [1] [3]

GH St George's Lodge Hotel 46 Chesswood Rd ☎(0903) 208926

19hc (6🛁 7🚿) (13fb) CTV in all bedrooms Ⓡ ✱B&b£13.50–£16.25 Bdi£18.75–£21.50 W£100–£125 ⱡ LDO9.30pm

Lic lift 18P sauna bath solarium gymnasium

Credit cards [1] [2] [3]

GH Southdene 41 Warwick Gdns ☎(0903) 32909

Quiet three-storey Victorian house close to the sea.

6hc (1🚿) (1fb) CTV in 3 bedrooms 🚫 Ⓡ ✱B&b£10–£13 Bdi£14–£17 W£93–£96 ⱡ LDO3pm

Lic 🛋 CTV 🚫P nc5yrs

GH Wansfell Hotel 49 Chesswood Rd (Guestaccom) ☎(0903) 30612

Town house close to sea front.

12hc (2🛁 4🚿) (2fb) CTV in all bedrooms 🚫 Ⓡ ✱B&b£12–£14 Bdi£18.50–£20.50 W£108.50–£134.50 ⱡ LDO7.15pm

Lic 🛋 10P nc4yrs

Credit card [1]

GH Windsor House Hotel 14–20 Windsor Rd ☎(0903) 39655

Large house in quiet residential area.

29hc (5🛁 12🚿) (6fb) CTV in all bedrooms Ⓡ ✱B&b£11.50–£19.50 Bdi£17–£25.50 W£99–£123 ⱡ LDO6.30pm

Lic 🛋 CTV 18P

Ⓥ

GH *Windsor Lodge Hotel* 3 Windsor Rd ☎(0903) 200056
Closed Xmas

Family-run house close to sea front with comfortable lounge and pleasant dining room.

6hc Ⓡ LDO2pm

🛋 CTV 🚫P nc2yrs

GH Wolsey Hotel 179–181 Brighton Rd ☎(0903) 36149
Closed Xmas

Two terraced houses on the sea front simply but prettily furnished.

14hc (3fb) CTV in all bedrooms Ⓡ B&b£13.50–£15 Bdi£19.50–£21 W£135–£142.50 ⱡ LDO6.30pm

Lic 🛋 CTV 🚫P

Credit cards [1] [3] Ⓥ

WREXHAM
Clywd
See **Hanmer**

WYE
Kent
Map **5** TR04

INN New Flying Horse Upper Bridge St ☎(0233) 812297

Comfortable and well-managed inn with well-equipped bedrooms, an à la carte dining room and a rear patio garden.

6hc Annexe: 4🛁 (1fb) CTV in all bedrooms Ⓡ ✱B&b£18.75–£27.50 Bdi£28.75–£37.50 W£150–£190 ⱡ Lunch £5.50–£7.50 Dinner9.50pm £10–£12

🛋 100P

Credit cards [1] [2] [3] [5] Ⓥ

YARMOUTH, GREAT
Norfolk
Map **5** TG50

⟼**GH Avalon** 4 Avondale Rd, Gorleston-on-Sea (2m S off A12) ☎(0493) 661521

A small guesthouse in a quiet residential road where the proprietors aim to provide a personal service.

6hc (2fb) 🚫 Ⓡ B&b£7.50 Bdi£10.50 W£63 ⱡ LDO6.30pm

Lic CTV 🚫P 🏠

GH Frandor 120 Lowestoft Rd, Gorleston-on-Sea (2m S A12) ☎(0493) 662112

8hc (3fb) 🚭 in 4 bedrooms CTV in 2 bedrooms 🚫 Ⓡ ✱B&b£8–£9 Bdi£10–£12 W£55–£70 ⱡ LDO7.30pm

Lic 🍴 CTV 12P
Credit cards [1] [3] [V]

GH Georgian House Private Hotel 16–17 North Dr ☎(0493) 842623
rs winter (closed Xmas)

25hc (10🛁 5🚿) (1fb) CTV in all bedrooms 🚫 B&b£12.50–£20 W£75–£105 M̸ (W only Jun–Sep)

Lic 🍴 CTV 24P nc5yrs

GH Gladstone House 92 St Peters Rd ☎(0493) 843181

A neat, modern guesthouse offering fresh home cooking.

11hc (4fb) CTV in all bedrooms B&b£10.50 W£73.50 M̸ LDO6.30pm

Lic CTV 4P

GH Hazelwood House 57 Clarence Rd, Gorleston-on-Sea ☎(0493) 662830

9hc (3fb) TV in all bedrooms 🚫 [R] ✱B&b£7.50–£8.50 Bdi£9–£11 Wfr£80 Ł LDO4pm

Lic 🍴 CTV P̸

[V]

GH Jennis Lodge 63 Avondale Rd, Gorleston-on-Sea (2m S off A12) ☎(0493) 662840

Situated in a quiet residential road 100 yards from Marine Parade and steps to the promenade and beach.

11hc (4fb) [R] B&b£8.50 Bdi£10.50 W£66.50 Ł LDO6pm

Lic CTV 🏠

GH Palm Court Hotel 10 North Dr ☎(0493) 844568
Mar–Oct

47hc (12🛁 19🚿) (8fb) CTV in all bedrooms [R] B&b£15–£32 Bdi£19–£36 W£105–£160 Ł LDO8pm

Lic lift 🍴 CTV 47P 🏊(heated) sauna bath solarium

Credit cards [1] [3] [V]

YEALAND CONYERS
Lancashire
Map **7** SD57

Yarmouth, Great — York

GH Holmere Hall Hotel ☎Carnforth (0524) 735353
Closed mid Jan–mid Feb

A small, comfortable country hotel in a garden setting. Building dates from the 17th century.

6hc (1🛁) (1fb) CTV in all bedrooms [R] ✱B&b£15–£18.50 Bdi£23–£27.50 W£153–£174 Ł LDO9pm

Lic 🍴 12P

Credit cards [1] [3]

YEALMPTON
Devon
Map **2** SX55

Recommended

FH Mrs A German **Broadmoor** *(SX574498)* ☎Plymouth (0752) 880407

Stone-built farmhouse and outbuildings, situated in open countryside enjoying distant views of Dartmoor.

3hc 🚫 ✱B&b£8–£8.50 Wfr£56 M̸

CTV P nc7yrs 200acres mixed

YELVERTON
Devon
Map **2** SX56

GH Harrabeer Country House Hotel Harrowbeer Ln ☎(0822) 853302

Country house hotel on the edge of Dartmoor offering friendly services and large garden with swimming pool.

7hc (2🛁 3🚿) (1fb) CTV in all bedrooms 🚫 [R] B&bfr£14.75 Bdifr£22.25 Wfr£145.75 Ł LDO7.30pm

Lic 🍴 CTV 10P 🏠 🏊

Credit cards [1] [2] [3] [5] [V]

See advertisement on page 313

GH Waverley 5 Greenbank Ter ☎(0822) 854617

Small terraced guesthouse situated in the centre of village. Ideal base for touring Dartmoor.

5hc (3fb) CTV in all bedrooms ✱B&bfr£9 Bdifr£12 Wfr£84 Ł

🍴 CTV 4P 🏠

[V]

YEOVIL
Somerset
Map **3** ST51

FH Mrs M Tucker **Carents** *(ST546188)* Yeovil Marsh ☎(0935) 76622
Feb–Nov

Clean, pleasant traditional additional-style farmhouse on outskirts of Yeovil 2m N of A37.

3rm (1hc) 🚫 [R] ✱B&bfr£9 Bdifr£15 LDOnoon

CTV P 350acres arable beef

YORK
North Yorkshire
Map **8** SE65
See also **Acaster Malbis** and **Copmanthorpe**

GH Aberford Hotel 35–36 East Mount Rd ☎(0904) 22694

Three-storey Edwardian town house with basement lounge bar and snug-lounge. Well equipped bedrooms.

13hc (2🚿) (2fb) CTV in all bedrooms 🚫 [R] ✱B&b£9.50–£15 Bdi£15–£21 W£101–£130 Ł LDO2pm

Lic 🍴 9P 2🚗

Credit cards [1] [2] [3]

See advertisement on page 428

GH Abingdon 60 Bootham Cres, Bootham ☎(0904) 21761
Closed Xmas

Nicely furnished Victorian terraced house.

7hc (4🚿) CTV in 4 bedrooms 🚫 [R] ✱B&b£9–£11 W£59.50–£70 M̸

🍴 CTV P̸

[V]

See advertisement on page 428

GH Acomb Rd 128 Acomb Rd ☎(0904) 792321

Three-storey, end-of-terrace house about a mile from city centre.

14hc (4fb) CTV in all bedrooms [R] *B&b£10–£12 Bdi£14–£16 W£98–£112 K LDO7.30pm

Lic CTV 20P

GH Adams House Hotel 5 Main St, Fulford ☎(0904) 55413
Closed Xmas

Guesthouse of great charm and elegance about a mile from city centre.

7hc (2🛁 4🚿) (2fb) CTV in all bedrooms B&b£12.50–£15 W£80–£95 M

Lic 🍴 CTV 8P

[V]

GH Albert Hotel The Mount ☎(0904) 32525

An impressive period building 1m W of city centre near race course. Comfortable bedrooms.

10hc (1🛁 6🚿) (3fb) CTV in 9 bedrooms TV in 1 bedroom 🐕 [R] *B&b£13.50–£17.50 Bdi£20–£24 W£120–£144 K LDOnoon

Lic 🍴 CTV 6P

Credit cards [1] [2] [3] [5]

GH *Alcuin Lodge* 15 Sycamore Pl, Bootham ☎(0904) 32222
Feb–Nov

York

Three-storey, brick-built Edwardian mid-terraced property in quiet residential area a short distance from city centre.

6hc (2fb) TV in all bedrooms 🐕 [R] LDO9am

Lic 🍴 CTV 3P nc3yrs

GH Alhambra Court Hotel 31 St Marys, Bootham ☎(0904) 28474

Two stylishly converted and restored Victorian townhouses with an excellent restaurant.

26hc (24🛁 2🚿) (3fb) CTV in all bedrooms 🐕 [R] *B&b£14.50–£21 Bdi£21–£28.50 W£147–£199.50 K LDO10pm

Lic lift 🍴 CTV 26P

Credit cards [1] [3]

See advertisement on page 430

GH *Amblesyde* 62 Bootham Crescent ☎(0904) 37165
2nd wk Jan–end Nov

Hospitable guesthouse in residential area offering clean, comfortable accommodation.

7hc (1fb) CTV in all bedrooms [R] LDOam

CTV

GH Arndale Hotel (formerly the Voltgeur Hotel) 290 Tadcaster Rd ☎(0904) 702424
Closed Xmas

Spacious, well-fitted bedrooms and an especially beautiful lounge in Victorian building retaining many original features.

10hc (5🛁 4🚿) (2fb) CTV in all bedrooms [R] B&b£12.50–£16 Bdi£19–£22.50 W£120–£140 K LDOnoon

Lic 🍴 15P

[V]

GH Ascot House 80 East Pde ☎(0904) 426826

Attractive Victorian house with unusual oriel staircase window. Bedrooms have modern fittings.

9🚿 (2fb) TV in all bedrooms [R] *B&b£10–£13 Bdi£18.50–£21.50 Wfr£149.50 K LDO6pm

🍴 CTV 10P 3🚗 sauna bath solarium

[V]

GH Avenue 6 The Avenue, Clifton ☎(0904) 20575
Feb–Nov

Three-storey, late Victorian house with attractive small forecourt garden, in quiet tree-lined street, near city centre.

6hc (2fb) TV in all bedrooms 🐕 *B&b£8–£10 Bdi£14–£16 W£98–£108 K LDOnoon

🍴 CTV 6P

[V]

See advertisement on page 430

York

GH Beckett 58 Bootham Cres ☎(0904) 644728

Situated on the northern side of town offering clean bright bedrooms with good matching fabrics and furnishings.

7hc (4🏠) (2fb) ✠ in 2 bedrooms TV in 1 bedroom CTV in 2 bedrooms ✠ ®
✱B&b£8.50–£12.50 Bdi£13.50–£18 W£90–£120 ⅟ LDO6pm

📺 CTV ✤

Ⓥ

GH Beech Hotel 6–7 Longfield Ter, Bootham ☎(0904) 34581
Closed Xmas & New Year

A pair of Victorian terraced houses converted into very smart and comfortable accommodation.

7hc (3fb) CTV in all bedrooms ✠
✱B&b£7.50–£11 W£52.50–£77 ⋈
📺 5P nc5yrs

Ⓥ

GH Bootham Bar Hotel 4 High Petergate ☎(0904) 58516
Closed Xmas Eve–Boxing Day

Delightfully restored 18th-century town house adjacent to the old city walls.

8🏠 (2fb) CTV in all bedrooms ✠ ®
B&b£15–£20

lift 📺 CTV ✤

Ⓥ

GH Brontë House 22 Grosvenor Ter, Bootham ☎(0904) 21066
Closed 5 days Xmas

Bay-windowed Victorian terraced house near the Minster, with good facilities and smart bedrooms.

7hc (4🏠) (1fb) ✠ ® LDO4pm

📺 CTV 3P

GH Cavalier 39 Monkgate ☎(0904) 36615
Closed Xmas & New Year

Stylish town house near the walls of Monks Bar with restful lounge and good restaurant.

10hc (2⇨ 4🏠) (4fb) CTV in 9 bedrooms ®
✱B&b£11–£14 Bdi£17–£20 LDO4pm

Lic 📺 CTV 4P sauna bath

GH Clifton Bridge Hotel Water End ☎(0904) 53609
Closed Xmas week

Comfortable hotel with spacious lounge and oak-lined bar and dining room. 1 mile from city centre.

14hc (4⇨ 2🏠) (2fb) CTV in all bedrooms ® ✱B&b£15–£25 Bdi£21.50–£31.50 W£135.50–£198.50 ⅟ LDO8pm

Lic 📺 CTV 9P 4🛆
Credit cards ①③Ⓥ

See advertisement on page 432

GH Coach House Hotel Marygate ☎(0904) 52780

Tastefully furnished old building with beams and exposed brickwork situated a short way from city centre.

13hc (6⇨ 5🏠) ✠ ✱B&b£14–£16.50 Bdi£21–£23.50 W£140–£154 ⅟ LDO9.30pm

Lic 📺 CTV 13P
Credit card ③

GH Coppers Lodge 15 Alma Ter, Fulford Rd ☎(0904) 39871

Simple, good value accommodation in a former police HQ (and jail house) 1m from town centre.

8hc (4fb) CTV in all bedrooms ✱B&b£8–£9 Bdi£13–£15 LDO4pm

📺 CTV P
Credit card ③Ⓥ

GH Craig-y-Don 3 Grosvenor Ter, Bootham ☎(0904) 37186

A town house of Victorian vintage, neat, tidy accommodation and hospitable welcome.
→

6hc (1⇄) CTV in all bedrooms ®
✱B&b£8–£14
⬛ 4P
Ⓥ

GH Crescent 77 Bootham ☎(0904)
23216
9hc (5fb) CTV in all bedrooms ✕ ®
✱B&b£10–£12 Wfr£70 Ⓜ
⬛ CTV 3P 1🛏
Ⓥ

GH Croft Hotel 103 Mount Rd ☎(0904)
22747

*Tall Victorian end-of-terrace house with
friendly lounge and caring hosts.*

10hc (1fb) CTV in all bedrooms ®
✱B&b£10–£14 Bdi£16–£18.50 W£105 ⎍
LDOnoon
Lic ⬛ CTV 1🛏
Credit card ③

GH Dairy 3 Scarcroft Rd ☎(0904) 39367
Feb–Nov

*Restored Victorian house with stylish
décor and many pleasing features.*

4hc (1⇄) Annexe: 2hc (1⇄ 1�🚿) (2fb) TV
in all bedrooms ✕ ® B&b£9.50–£11.50
W£66.50–£80.50 Ⓜ
⬛ CTV 🅿 ♨

York

Recommended

GH Field House Hotel 2 St George's
Pl ☎(0904) 39572

*An impressive building standing in its
own attractive gardens near the
famous racecourse. Built in 1897 as a
gentleman's residence, it was
completely renovated and
refurbished in 1979 and now offers a
tastefully decorated lounge with
separate lounge bar, lower ground
floor dining room and well-fitted
modern bedrooms.*

17hc (1⇄ 10🚿) CTV in all bedrooms
✕ ® ✱B&b£16.50–£24 Bdi£24.50–
£32 W£108.50–£161 Ⓜ LDO7pm
Lic ⬛ 20P
Credit cards ① ② ③ Ⓥ

GH Gables 50 Bootham Cres ☎(0904)
24381

*Clean, compact and friendly
accommodation.*

6hc (2fb) CTV in all bedrooms ✕ ®
✱B&b£8.50–£16 Bdi£17–£19
⬛ CTV

GH Georgian 35 Bootham ☎(0904)
22874
Closed Xmas

12hc (2⇄ 1🚿) (1fb) CTV in 3 bedrooms ®
B&b£10.50–£13.50
⬛ CTV 16P

Recommended

GH Grasmead House Hotel 1
Scarcroft Hill, The Mount ☎(0904)
29996

*A small family-owned and run hotel
near the city centre. The special
attractions here are the bedrooms –
all luxuriously appointed and every
one boasting a traditional four-poster
bed (most are genuine antiques) and
an en-suite bathroom. The corner bar
in the lounge is operated by the
proprietor who dispenses expert
tourist advice along with the drinks.*

6⇄ (2fb) ✕ in 1 bedroom CTV in all
bedrooms ✕ ® ✱B&b£16.50–£19
W£106–£120 Ⓜ
Lic ⬛ CTV 1P
Credit cards ① ③ Ⓥ

GH Greenside 124 Clifton ☎(0904)
23631
Closed Xmas

*Charming detached house in centre of
Clifton Hamlet, about a mile from city
centre.*

6hc (2⥾) (2fb) CTV in 1 bedroom TV in 1 bedroom ✱B&b£9.50–£12

䷀ CTV 4P 1🚗

Ⓥ

GH Hazelwood 24–25 Portland St, Gillygate ☎(0904) 26548
Closed 16 Dec–Jan

15hc (2⇨ 6⥾) (1fb) CTV in all bedrooms ✗ Ⓡ B&b£11.50–£14 W£76.50–£94 M

䷀ 10P

Credit card ③

GH Heworth 126 East Pde ☎(0904) 426384

York

Neat and tidy guesthouse convenient for town facilities.

7hc (1fb) ✱B&b£8.50–£10.50 Bdi£13.50–£15.50 W£77–£98 Ⱡ LDO2pm

Lic ䷀ CTV 1P 1🚗

Ⓥ

GH Inglewood 7 Clifton Gn ☎(0904) 53523

Commendable hotel with delightful fittings and furnishings in bustling suburb of Clifton.

7hc (3⥾) (2fb) CTV in all bedrooms ✗ B&bfr£10

䷀ CTV 1🚗

Ⓥ

GH Linden Lodge Nunthorpe Av, Scarcroft Rd ☎(0904) 20107
Closed Dec

9hc (3fb) Ⓡ ✱B&b£9.50–£11 Bdi£15–£16.50 LDOnoon

Lic ䷀ CTV Ᵽ

Ⓥ

The Priory Hotel, York

The Priory offers comfortable accommodation with full English breakfast, and is situated 600 yards south of York's medieval city walls, within easy direct reach of the nearby inner and outer ring roads. The city centre can be reached by a pleasant riverside walk.

The 20 bedrooms, all equipped with colour TV and tea/coffee making facilities, include single, double and family accommodation, all with en suite shower and toilet facilities.

The Hotel is AA listed, and has full central heating, a licensed bar and restaurant. The pleasant garden leads to the large private car-park.

Reductions are available for children sharing accommodation with their parents. Please send for brochure and tariff.

Proprietors:
George and Barbara Jackson
The Priory Hotel
Fulford Road
York YO1 4BE
Telephone York (0904) 25280

GH *Mayfield Hotel* 75 Scarcroft Rd ☎(0904) 54834

A small family-run hotel close to city centre and racecourse

7hc (2🛁 4🚿) (3fb) CTV in all bedrooms 🐕 Ⓡ LDO7.15pm

Lic 🍽 🚭

Credit cards [1] [2] [3]

See advertisement on page 434

GH Minster View 2 Grosvenor Ter ☎(0904) 55034

8hc (3🛁 1🚿) (4fb) CTV in all bedrooms Ⓡ ✱B&b£12–£19 Bdi£18.50–£25.50 W£129.50–£178.50 Ł LDO5.30pm

Lic 🍽 CTV 6P

ⓥ

GH *Moat Hotel* Nunnery Ln ☎(0904) 52926

Interesting Victorian-style house beneath medieval walls, with comfortable, suitably furnished accommodation.

9hc (6🚿) (1fb) 🐕

CTV 10P

Credit cards [2] [3] [5]

See advertisement on page 434

GH *Orchard Court Hotel* 4 St Peters Gv ☎(0904) 53964

An elegant Victorian house in quiet cul-de-sac, close to city centre. The lofty public rooms are tastefully decorated.

11hc (1🛁 6🚿) (4fb) CTV in 7 bedrooms Ⓡ LDO7.30pm

Lic CTV 11P

Credit cards [1] [3]

GH Priory Hotel 126 Fulford Rd ☎(0904) 25280

Closed Xmas week

A pair of large double-fronted Victorian town houses with rear gardens, near city centre.

20hc (2🛁 18🚿) (5fb) CTV in all bedrooms 🐕 Ⓡ ✱B&b£14.50–£16 LDO9.30pm

Lic 🍽 CTV 24P

Credit cards [1] [2] [3] [5] ⓥ

See advertisement on page 435

GH St Denys Hotel St Denys Rd ☎(0904) 22207

Closed Xmas

Former vicarage offers comfortable spacious accommodation and cosy lounge.

11hc (7🛁 4🚿) (4fb) CTV in all bedrooms Ⓡ ✱B&b£18–£28 Bdi£24–£30 LDOnoon

Lic 🍽 CTV 9P

ⓥ

GH *St Raphael* 44 Queen Anne's Rd, Bootham ☎(0904) 645028

Comfortable and friendly guesthouse near Minster.

7hc (1fb) CTV in all bedrooms 🐕

🍽 CTV nc8yrs

See advertisement on page 434

GH *Sycamore Hotel* 19 Sycamore Pl ☎(0904) 24712

Compact terraced property with well-fitted bedrooms.

6hc (2fb) CTV in all bedrooms 🐕 Ⓡ LDO9.30am

Lic 🍽 3P nc5yrs

GH Town House Lodge 112–114 Holgate Rd ☎(0904) 34577

Closed 24 Dec–1 Jan

Very comfortable bedrooms and a feature top floor lounge with views of the city are the attractions here.

12hc (3🛁 6🚿) (7fb) CTV in all bedrooms Ⓡ ✱B&b£12.50–£15

🍽 18P

Credit cards [1] [2] [3] [5] ⓥ

YOULGREAVE

Derbyshire
Map **8** SK26

INN Bulls Head Church St ☎(062986) 307

4hc (2fb) CTV in all bedrooms 🐕 Ⓡ ✱B&b£8–£10 Bdi£10–£16 W£70–£112 Ł LDO9pm

P nc5yrs snooker

YSBYTY IFAN

Gwynedd
Map **6** SH84

FH Mrs F G Roberts ***Ochr Cefn Isa*** *(SH845495)* ☎Pentrefoelas (06905) 602

Etr–Oct

Farm set in elevated position with good views high above A5.

2rm (1hc) (1fb) 🐕 LDO5pm

2P nc5yrs 123acres mixed

Index of Recommended Guesthouses, Farmhouses and Inns

ENGLAND

AVON
Bath — Orchard House Hotel
Bristol — Glenroy Hotel

BEDFORDSHIRE
Swineshead — Manor Farm

BUCKINGHAMSHIRE
Kingsey — Foxhill Farm

CHANNEL ISLANDS, GUERNSEY
St Peter Port — Midhurst House

CORNWALL
Newquay — Pendeen Hotel
Priory Lodge Hotel
St Ives — Dean Court
St Just in Roseland — Rose da Mar
Tintagel — Trebrea Lodge

CUMBRIA
Ambleside — Grey Friar Lodge Country House Hotel
Rydal Lodge
Catlowdy — Bessiestown Farm
Keswick — Rickerby Grange
Kirkoswald — Prospect Hill
Troutbeck — Lane Head Farm

DERBYSHIRE
Bakewell — Merlin House
Glossop — Wind in the Willows

DEVON
Bampton — Holwell Farm
Bovey Tracey — Willmead Farm
Colyford — Swallows Eaves
Holne — Wellpritton Farm
Mortehoe — Sunnycliffe Hotel
Plymouth — Georgian House Hotel
Sidmouth — Mount Pleasant Hotel
Torquay — Glenorleigh Hotel
Totnes — Ridgemark Hotel
Yealmpton — Broadmoor

DORSET
Beaminster — Hams Plot
Bournemouth — Cliff House Hotel
Naseby Nye Hotel
Halstock — Old Mill
Lulworth — Lulworth Hotel
Wareham — Redcliffe Hotel

CO. DURHAM
Sedgefield — Dun Cow Inn

ESSEX
Chelmsford — Boswell House
Dedham — Dedham Hall
Frinton on Sea — Montpellier

GLOUCESTERSHIRE
Willersey — Old Rectory

HAMPSHIRE
Milford on Sea — Sea Spray
Warsash — Solent View Private Hotel

HEREFORD & WORCESTER
Hanley Castle — Old Parsonage Farm

KENT
Boughton Monchelsea — The Tanyard

LANCASHIRE
Harrop Fold — Harrop Fold Farm
Slaidburn — Parrock Head Farm

LINCOLNSHIRE
Skegness — Crawford Hotel

LONDON
London SE3 — Bardon Lodge
London SE9 — Yardley Court
London W2 — Pembridge Court Hotel
London W14 — Avonmore Hotel

NORTHUMBERLAND
Allendale — Bishopfield Farm
Eglingham — West Ditchburn Farm
Haltwhistle — Broomshaw Hill
Longframlington — Granby Inn

OXFORDSHIRE
Kidlington — Bowood House
Lew — University Farm
Oxford — Westwood Country Hotel

SCILLY, ISLES OF
St Mary's — Carnwethers Country House

SHROPSHIRE
Church Stretton — The Rectory
Clun — Sun Inn
Diddlebury — Glebe Farm

SOMERSET
Beercrocombe — Whittles Farm
Glastonbury — Berewell Farm
Wells — Coach House

437

SUFFOLK
Gislingham   Old Guildhall
Higham   Old Vicarage

SURREY
Redhill   Ashleigh House Hotel
Reigate   Cranleigh Hotel

SUSSEX (East)
Alfriston   Pleasant Rise Farm
Brighton   Adelaide
   Corner Ways Private Hotel
   Marina House Hotel
   Regency Hotel
   Twenty-One
Eastbourne   Chalk Farm
   Little Crookham Private Hotel
   Park View Hotel
Saltdean   Linbrook Lodge

WARWICKSHIRE
Atherstone   Chapel House
Bidford on Avon   Bidford Grange
Hatton   Northleigh Farm

WILTSHIRE
Melksham   Shaw Farm

YORKSHIRE (North)
Giggleswick   Close House Farm
   Woodlands
Hutton le Hole   The Barn
Pateley Bridge   Grassfields Country House Hotel
   Roslyn
Raskelf   Old Farmhouse
Richmond   Whashton Springs Farm
Scotch Corner   Vintage Inn
West Layton   West Layton Manor
York   Field House Hotel
   Grasmead House Hotel

WALES

DYFED
Llanfair Clydogau   Pentre Farm
Llangynog   Plas Farm

GLAMORGAN (West)
Reynoldston   Fairy Hill Country House

GWENT
Llandogo   Sloop Inn

GWYNEDD
Beaumaris   Liverpool Arms
Llandudno   Buile Hill Private Hotel
Llandeiniolen   Ty'n Rhos

POWYS
Llanwrtyd Wells   Lasswade House

SCOTLAND

BORDERS
Tweedsmuir   Menzion Farm

CENTRAL
Bo'ness   Kinglass Farm
Callander   Highland House Hotel

DUMFRIES & GALLOWAY
Moffat   Well View

GRAMPIAN
Ballater   Moorside
Fordoun   Ringwood Farm

HIGHLAND
Beauly   Tomich House
Gairloch   Horisdale House
Golspie   Stag's Head Inn
Inverness   Craigside House
Kingussie   Homewood Lodge
Nairn   Sunny Brae
Rogart   Rovie Farm

LOTHIAN
Dunbar   St Beys

STRATHCLYDE
Abington   Netherton Farm
Machrihanish   Ardell House
Prestwick   Fernbank

TAYSIDE
Aberfeldy   Guinach House
Brechin   Blibberhill Farm
   Wood of Auldbar Farm
Forfar   Queen's Hotel Inn
Pitlochry   Balrobin Private Hotel
   Dundarave House

ORDNANCE SURVEY
LEISURE GUIDES

LAKE DISTRICT

Voted the best new publication about the area in 1984, this superb guide describes the topography and traditions of the area and offers scenic drives, walks, and masses of information about what to see and where to stay, linked to large-scale Ordnance Survey maps, and illustrated throughout in colour.

NEW FOREST

Walks, drives, places to see, things to do, where to stay, all linked to large-scale Ordnance Survey mapping, with useful background information to the area. Illustrated throughout with superb colour photography.

YORKSHIRE DALES

Descriptions of scenery, history, customs and 'a day in the life of a dalesman' evoke the atmosphere of this remote and beautiful region and introduce the walks, drives and directory of places of interest. Large-scale Ordnance Survey maps and a wealth of colour photography make this guide a must for tourist and walker alike.

COTSWOLDS

Pretty villages of native limestone, impressive churches built on the wealth of the wool trade, ancient hillforts and Roman roads, rolling upland and gentle river valleys – these and much more are described and colourfully illustrated in this guide. Walks, drives and Ordnance Survey maps complete this ideal companion to the area.

SCOTTISH HIGHLANDS

Scottish Highlands – a treasure house of nature, packed with breathtaking scenery and fascinating traditions. The book captures the flavour, the scents and the grandeur of Europe's foremost 'wilderness' area. Walks, drives, things to do, places to stay are listed, with maps to show the way.

All available in hardback or paperback

The National Grid

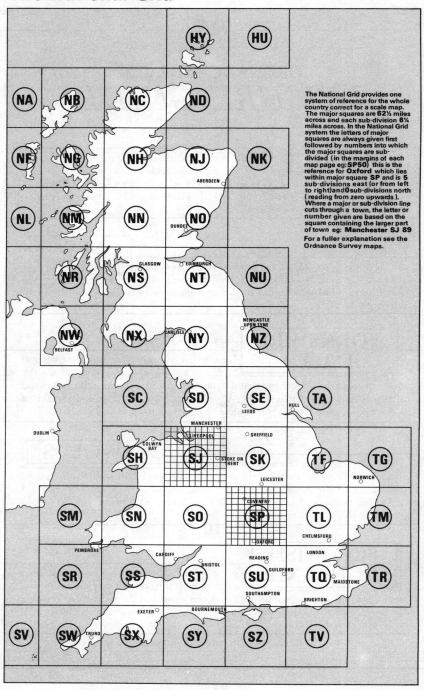

The National Grid provides one system of reference for the whole country correct for a scale map. The major squares are 62½ miles across and each sub-division 6¼ miles across. In the National Grid system the letters of major squares are always given first followed by numbers into which the major squares are sub-divided (in the margins of each map page eg: **SP50**) this is the reference for **Oxford** which lies within major square **SP** and is **5** sub-divisions east (or from left to right) and **0** sub-divisions north (reading from zero upwards). Where a major or sub-division line cuts through a town, the letter or number given are based on the square containing the larger part of town eg: **Manchester SJ 89**

For a fuller explanation see the Ordnance Survey maps.

Key to Atlas

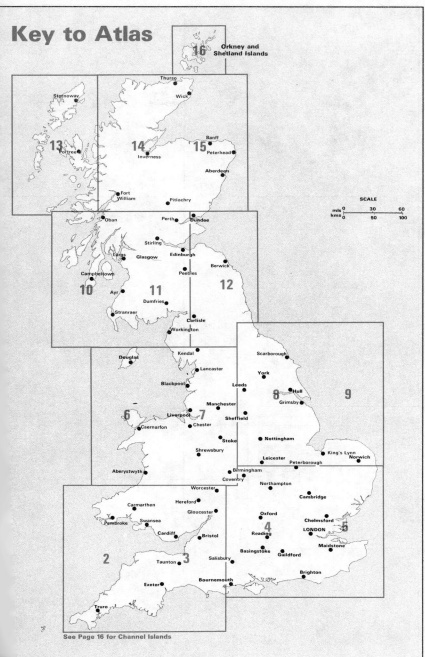

16 Orkney and Shetland Islands

Thurso
Stornoway
Wick

13 Portree
14 Inverness
15 Banff
Peterhead

Fort William
Pitlochry
Aberdeen

Oban
Perth
Dundee

Stirling
Largs
Glasgow
Edinburgh

Campbeltown
Peebles
Berwick

10
Ayr
11 Dumfries
12

Stranraer
Carlisle
Workington

Douglas
Kendal

Blackpool
Lancaster
Leeds
Scarborough
York

Manchester
8 Hull
Grimsby
9

Liverpool
7
Sheffield

6 Caernarfon
Chester

Stoke
Nottingham

Shrewsbury
Leicester
King's Lynn
Norwich

Aberystwyth
Birmingham
Peterborough

Worcester
Coventry
Northampton

Carmarthen
Hereford
Cambridge

Pembroke
Swansea
Gloucester
Oxford
Chelmsford

Cardiff
Bristol
4
Reading
LONDON
5
Maidstone

2
Taunton
3
Salisbury
Basingstoke
Guildford

Exeter
Bournemouth
Brighton

Truro

SCALE
mls 0   30   60
kms 0   50   100

See Page 16 for Channel Islands

Maps produced by
The AA Cartographic Department
(Publications Division), Fanum House,
Basingstoke, Hampshire RG21 2EA

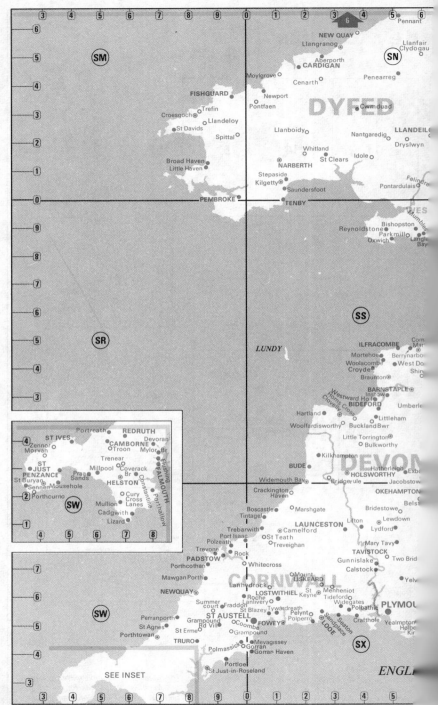

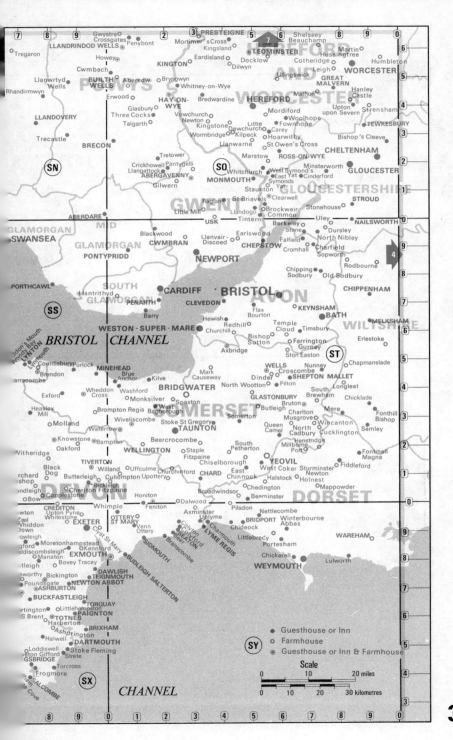

Scale

0   10   20 miles

0   10   20   30 kilometres

● Guesthouse or Inn
○ Farmhouse
◑ Guesthouse or Inn & Farmhouse

3

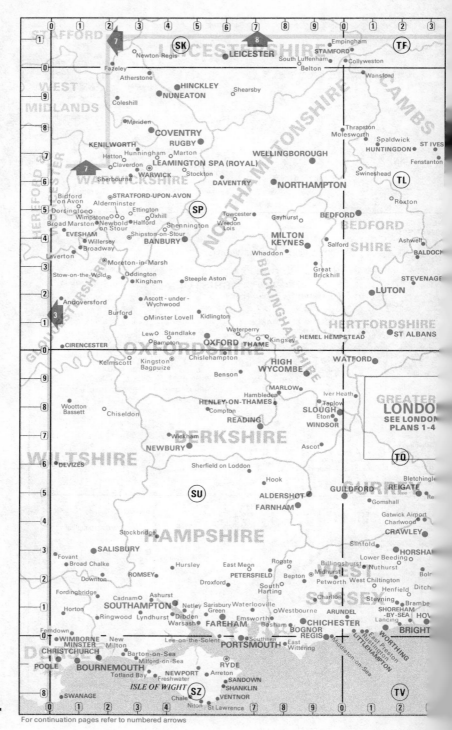

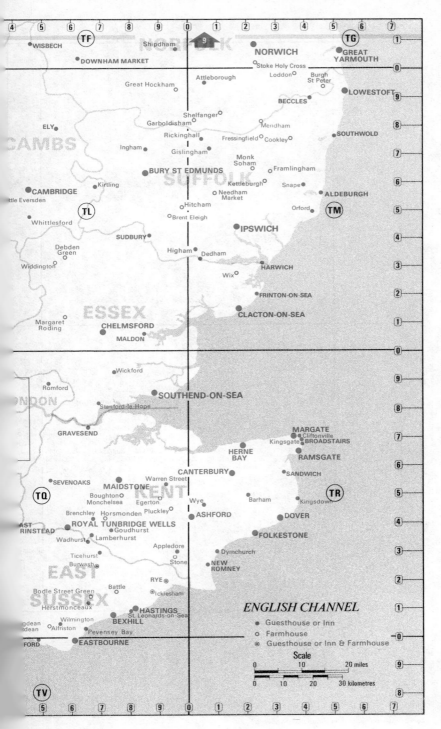

ENGLISH CHANNEL

- ● Guesthouse or Inn
- ○ Farmhouse
- ◉ Guesthouse or Inn & Farmhouse

Scale

0 .... 10 .... 20 miles

0 .... 10 .... 20 .... 30 kilometres

5

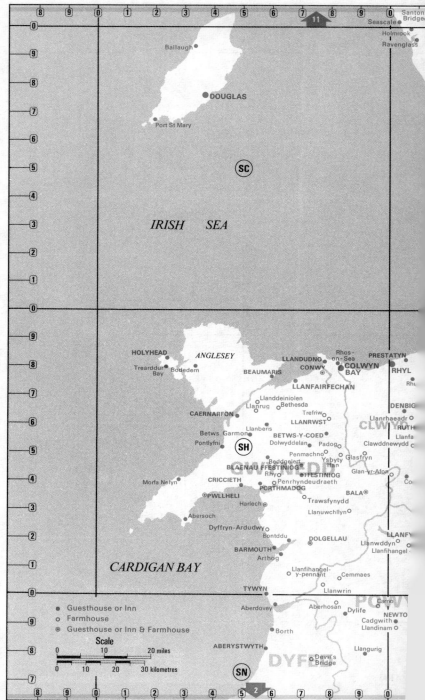

IRISH   SEA

Ballaugh

DOUGLAS

Port St Mary

Santon
Bridge
Seascale
Holmrook
Ravenglass

SC

11

HOLYHEAD   ANGLESEY   Rhos-   PRESTATYN
                               LLANDUDNO on-Sea
Trearddur Bodedern   CONWY   COLWYN
Bay   BEAUMARIS   BAY   RHYL
                                                   Rhu
                          LLANFAIRFECHAN
                                                   DENBIG
                        Llanddeiniolen
                   Llanrug   Bethesda   Trefriw   Llanrhaeadr
CAERNARFON   Llanfa
            Betws Garmon Llanberis LLANRWST   CLW   RUTH
Pontllyfni   BETWS-Y-COED   Llanfa
                   SH   Dolwyddelan Padog   Clawddnewydd
                            Penmachno   Glasfryn
                         Beddgelert   Ysbyty
          BLAENAU FFESTINIOG Rhyo   Ifan   Glan-yr-Afon
Morfa Nefyn   CRICCIETH FFESTINIOG   Co
                         Penrhyndeudraeth
                  PORTHMADOG
              PWLLHELI   Trawsfynydd BALA
                   Harlech   Llanuwchllyn
Abersoch
            Dyffryn-Ardudwy   LLANF
                      Bontddu   Llanwddyn
              BARMOUTH   DOLGELLAU   Llanfihangel
                   Arthog
CARDIGAN BAY   Llanfihangel-   POW
                            y-pennant   Cemmaes
                     TYWYN   Llanwrin
                                            Carno
            Aberdovey   Aberhosan Dylife NEWTO
                                    Cadgwith
                  Borth   Llandinam

ABERYSTWYTH   DYF   Llangurig

                     Devil's
                     Bridge
          SN
                                2

● Guesthouse or Inn
○ Farmhouse
◎ Guesthouse or Inn & Farmhouse

Scale
0   10   20 miles
0   10   20   30 kilometres

6

For continuation pages refer to numbered arrows

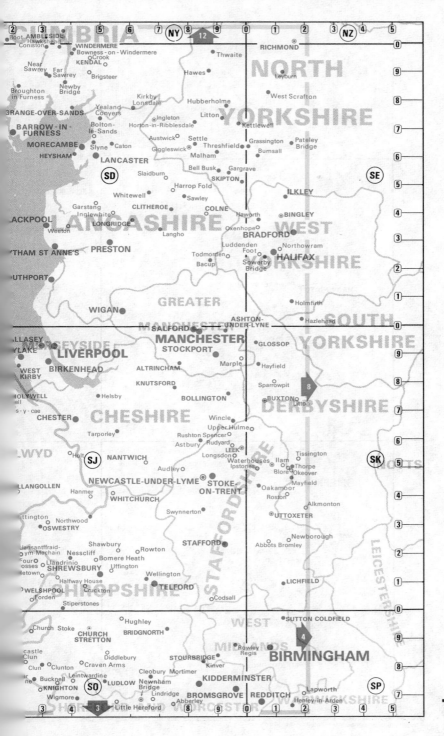

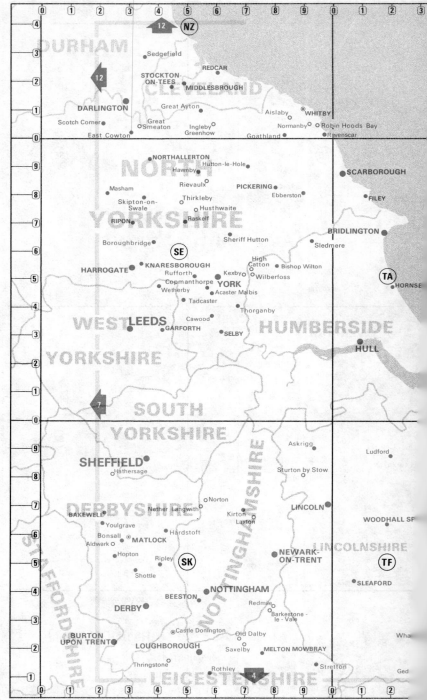

For continuation pages refer to numbered arrows

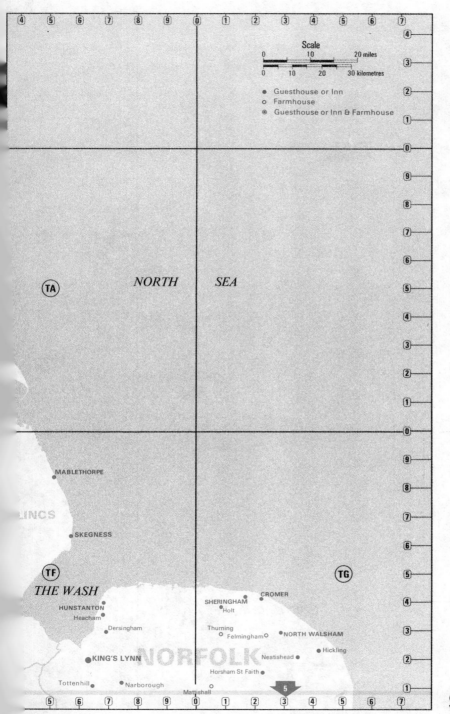

Scale

0   10   20 miles

0   10   20   30 kilometres

● Guesthouse or Inn
○ Farmhouse
◉ Guesthouse or Inn & Farmhouse

(TA)   *NORTH*   *SEA*

(TF)   (TG)

THE WASH

MABLETHORPE

LINCS

SKEGNESS

CROMER
SHERINGHAM
HUNSTANTON   ●Holt
Heacham
Thurning
Dersingham   ○ Felmingham○ ●NORTH WALSHAM
●Hickling
Neatishead ●
●KING'S LYNN   NORFOLK
Horsham St Faith ●
Tottenhill   ●Narborough
Mattishall   5

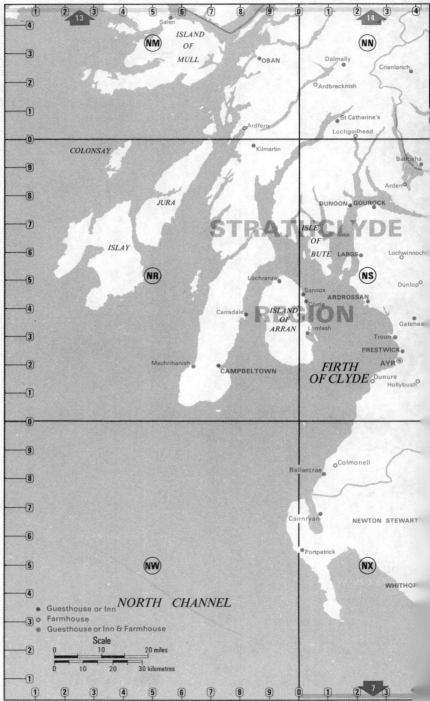

10

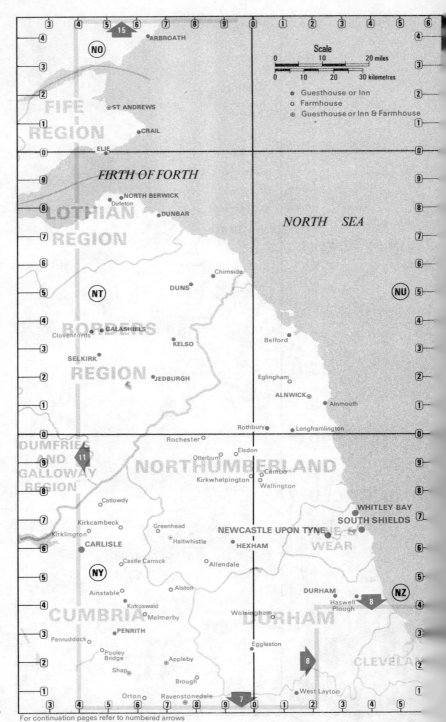

Scale

0   10   20 miles
0   10   20   30 kilometres

● Guesthouse or Inn
○ Farmhouse
◉ Guesthouse or Inn & Farmhouse

FIRTH OF FORTH

NORTH SEA

ARBROATH

NO

FIFE
REGION

● ST ANDREWS

● CRAIL

ELIE

● NORTH BERWICK
Dirleton
● DUNBAR

LOTHIAN

REGION

Chirnside ●

NT

DUNS ●

NU

BORDERS

● GALASHIELS
Clovenfords

Belford ●

● KELSO

SELKIRK ●

REGION

● JEDBURGH

Eglingham ○

ALNWICK ◉

● Alnmouth

Rothbury ● ● Longframlington

Rochester ○

DUMFRIES
AND
GALLOWAY
REGION

Elsdon
Otterburn ○ ● Cambo

NORTHUMBERLAND

Kirkwhelpington ○ Wellington

Catlowdy ○

Greenhead ○

WHITLEY BAY
SOUTH SHIELDS

Kirkcambeck ○

NEWCASTLE UPON TYNE

Kirklington ○
● Haltwhistle

CARLISLE

● HEXHAM

WEAR

NY

● Castle Carrock

○ Allendale

Ainstable ○

○ Alston

DURHAM

NZ

● Kirkoswald
● Melmerby

Wolsingham ○

Haswell
Plough

PENRITH

Penruddock ○

Eggleston ○

DURHAM

○ Pooley
Bridge

CLEVELAND

Shap ◉

○ Appleby

Brough ○

Orton ○ Ravenstonedale

● West Layton

12

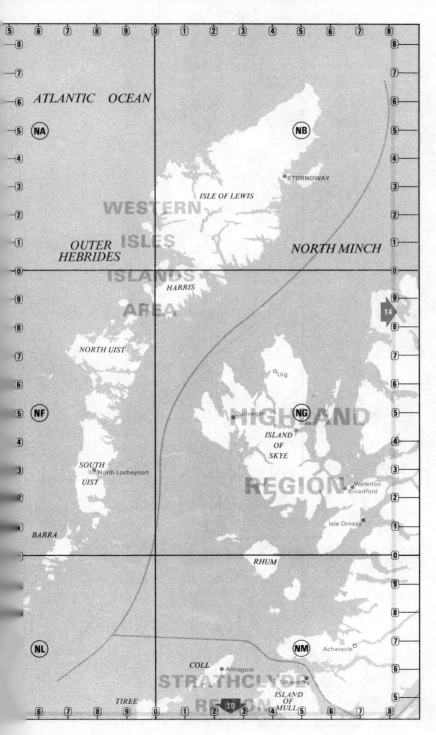

ATLANTIC OCEAN

NA

NB

WESTERN

OUTER
HEBRIDES

ISLES

ISLANDS

AREA

ISLE OF LEWIS

●STORNOWAY

NORTH MINCH

HARRIS

NORTH UIST

NF

SOUTH
UIST
● North Locheynort

BARRA

NL

○Uig

Dunvegan ●

HIGHLAND

NG

Portree ●
ISLAND
OF
SKYE

REGION

Waterloo ●
Broadford

Isle Ornsay ●

RHUM

14

NM
Acharacle ○

COLL
● Arinagour

STRATHCLYDE

TIREE

Tobermory ●

ISLAND
OF
MULL

10

13

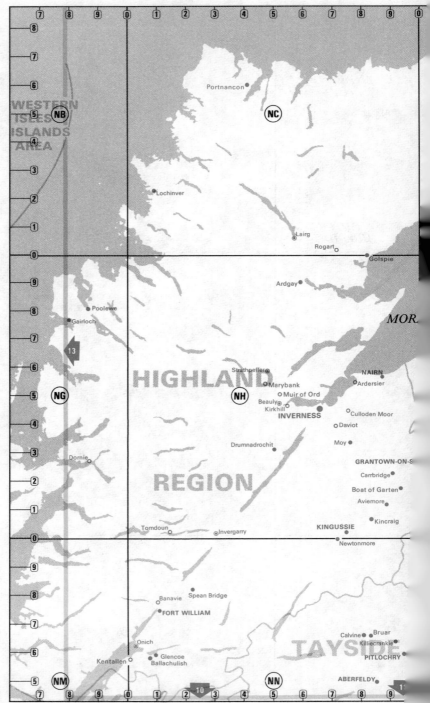

NB
NC
Portnancon
Lochinver
Lairg
Rogart
Golspie
Ardgay
MOR
Poolewe
Gairloch
13
NG
HIGHLAND
Strathpeffer
Marybank
NAIRN
Ardersier
Muir of Ord
NH
Beauly
Kirkhill
INVERNESS
Culloden Moor
Daviot
Moy
Drumnadrochit
GRANTOWN-ON-S
Dornie
Carrbridge
REGION
Boat of Garten
Aviemore
Kincraig
Tomdoun
Invergarry
KINGUSSIE
Newtonmore
Banavie
Spean Bridge
FORT WILLIAM
Calvine
Bruar
Killiecrankie
Onich
TAYSIDE
PITLOCHRY
Kentallen
Glencoe
Ballachulish
NM
10
NN
ABERFELDY

14

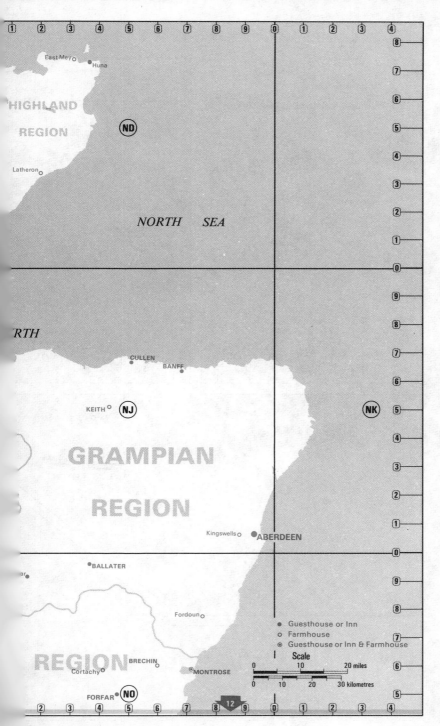

Scale

| 0 | 10 | 20 miles |

| 0 | 10 | 20 | 30 kilometres |

• Guesthouse or Inn
○ Farmhouse
◉ Guesthouse or Inn & Farmhouse

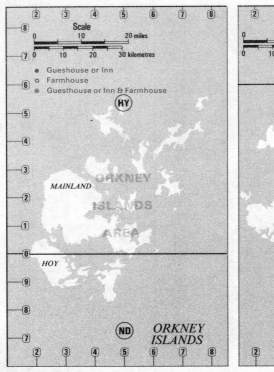

ORKNEY
ISLANDS

Scale
0 · 10 · 20 miles
0 · 10 · 20 · 30 kilometres

● Guesthouse or Inn
○ Farmhouse
◉ Guesthouse or Inn & Farmhouse

HY

ORKNEY
ISLANDS
AREA

MAINLAND

HOY

ND

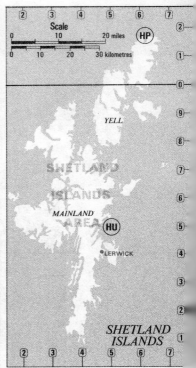

SHETLAND
ISLANDS

HP

Scale
0 · 10 · 20 miles
0 · 10 · 20 · 30 kilometres

YELL

SHETLAND
ISLANDS
AREA

MAINLAND

HU

LERWICK

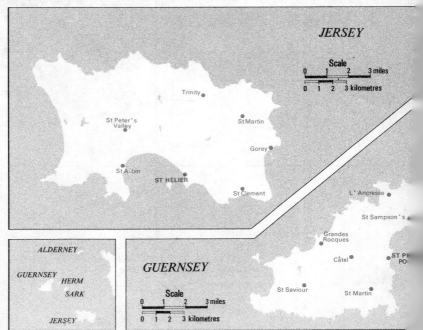

JERSEY

Scale
0 · 1 · 2 · 3 miles
0 · 1 · 2 · 3 kilometres

Trinity

St Peter's
Valley

St Martin

Gorey

St Aubin

ST HELIER

St Clement

ALDERNEY

GUERNSEY

HERM

SARK

JERSEY

GUERNSEY

Scale
0 · 1 · 2 · 3 miles
0 · 1 · 2 · 3 kilometres

L' Ancresse

St Sampson's

Grandes
Rocques

Câtel

ST P
PO

St Saviour

St Martin